THE INSTRUMENT FLIGHT MANUAL

The Instrument Rating & Beyond

Sixth Edition

William K. Kershner

THE INSTRUMENT FLIGHT MANUAL

The Instrument Rating & Beyond

Aviation Supplies & Academics, Inc.
Newcastle, Washington

To the memory of William Thomas Piper, Sr.

William K. Kershner, the 1992 FAA flight instructor of the year, a recipient of the 99's Award of Merit in 1994 and the National Aeronautics Association Elder Statesman of Aviation Award in 1997, and an inductee into the Flight Instructor Hall of Fame in 1998, has over five decades of experience in flying airplanes from light trainers to jets. In the early 1950s he was an all-weather/night carrier fighter pilot and was instrument training officer for the squadron that furnished all-weather/night fighter teams to carriers in the Pacific fleet. He currently operates a flight school in Sewanee, Tennessee, and is author of *The Student Pilot's Flight Manual, The Advanced Pilot's Flight Manual, The Flight Instructor's Manual,* and *The Basic Aerobatic Manual.*

ILLUSTRATED BY THE AUTHOR

First Edition published 1967, Iowa State University Press. Sixth Edition 2002. Third Printing (of Sixth Ed.) 2006 by Aviation Supplies & Academics, Inc.

Aviation Supplies & Academics, Inc.
7005 132nd Place SE
Newcastle, WA 98059
Email: asa@asa2fly.com
Internet: www.asa2fly.com

Printed in the United States of America

2009 2008 2007 2006   9 8 7 6 5 4 3

ASA-FM-INSTRMENT
ISBN   1-56027-619-3
        978-1-56027-619-7

Library of Congess Cataloging-in Publication Data:
Kershner, William K.
    The instrument flight manual: the instrument rating and beyond / William K. Kershner.—6th ed.
        p.   cm.
1. Instrument flying. I. Title.
TL711.K4 2002
629.132'5214—dc21   2001007112

CONTENTS

Preface, vi

1 AIRPLANE PERFORMANCE AND BASIC INSTRUMENT FLYING, 1

1. The Instrument Rating, 3
2. Flight and Engine Instruments, 6
3. Review of Airplane Performance, Stability, and Control, 29
4. Basic Instrument Flying, 45

2 NAVIGATION AND COMMUNICATIONS, 83

5. Navigational Aids and Instruments, 85
6. Communications and Control of Air Traffic, 126

3 PLANNING THE INSTRUMENT FLIGHT, 143

7. Weather Systems and Planning, 145
8. Charts and Other Printed Aids, 176
9. Planning the Navigation, 204

4 THE INSTRUMENT FLIGHT, 213

10. Before the Takeoff, 215
11. Takeoff and Departure, 219
12. En Route, 220
13. Instrument Approach and Landing, 232
14. Instrument Rating Knowledge Test, 249
15. Instrument Rating Practical Test, 252

5 SYLLABUS, 263

Instrument Flight Manual Syllabus, 265

Appendix 297

Airport/Facility Directory Legend, 298

Bibliography and Suggested Reading for Further Study, 303

Index, 305

En Route Low-Altitude Chart, follows 312

FIRST EDITION

This manual is aimed at the pilot interested in obtaining an instrument rating and the already rated pilot wanting to do refresher work.

Since it has been written for the general aviation pilot, airspeeds, expected clearances, and altitudes used are based on a high-performance, retractable-gear, four-place, general aviation airplane unless otherwise noted. Jet and other high-altitude (above 18,000 feet) IFR operations are best left for coverage in other texts.

An area most neglected by many current texts on instrument flying is that of air traffic control. This is the most complicated (it seems) part of flying IFR. One of the primary aims of *The Instrument Flight Manual* is to cover this subject in somewhat more detail than usual and yet keep it as uncomplicated as possible. Whether this is successful will, of course, be judged by the reader.

One concern that arose during the writing of this manual was that of repeating certain things already covered in *The Student Pilot's Flight Manual* and *The Advanced Pilot's Flight Manual,* such as flight instrument operation, airplane performance, and other areas. In each case the attempt was made to add to the previous material information that would directly apply to instrument flying. It was felt that repeating the basics was necessary to have the book complete in itself. The question was whether the reader of this book would have immediate access to that basic material (or had forgotten, for instance, how a vertical speed instrument operates), so the information was inserted. In most such cases, new illustrations were drawn to show a different view of the situation, even though the ones used in the first two books would have worked as well.

Needless to say, the charts in this book are *not* to be used for navigation purposes. The Air Traffic Control System is changing fast. Many changes had to be made to the manuscript during the process of writing because of this, and finally a cutoff date for changes had to be set. If by the time this gets to the reader's hands some of the particular example airport approaches no longer exist, please consider them as general examples. As far as frequencies are concerned (FSS, Center, and tower), even the government publications are hard put to keep up with changes, and it takes at least six months for a big revision of a book, so use the *Aeronautical Information Manual* or *Airport/Facility Directory* for such existing numbers. The same goes for weather information.

In researching this book, I came away from the Center, towers, Flight Service Stations, and Weather Bureau Airport Stations with even more respect, if possible, for their personnel. Many of them are active pilots themselves and know how it is to be "on the other end."

I was fortunate in having knowledgeable people help me on this book; however, any errors are mine. I would like to thank the following:

Appreciation is expressed to W. W. Parker, Chief of the Memphis Air Route Traffic Center, for allowing me to visit at my convenience; particular thanks must go to Roy G. Koeller, ATC Specialist at the Memphis Center, for answering numerous questions and furnishing information on the Center and air traffic control.

John Omohundro, Jr., Chief, Air Traffic Control Tower; Spencer Wise, Tower Watch Supervisor; Ramon Nelson, also Tower Watch Supervisor; and especially James Ayers, ATC Specialist, all of the Nashville tower, must be thanked for the time and effort they put into reviewing the chapters applying to air traffic control. Their suggestions were a great help.

Special recognition must go to Jack LeBarron, top aviation writer and pilot, for sending most useful information (most of which he personally evolved) not generally available to the instrument trainee. Herbert Price, Watch Supervisor, and E. D. De Shields, ATC Specialist, at the Chattanooga tower, who always had information when needed. John Lenti and George Bullis, of the Memphis tower, for furnishing information and answering questions. Willis Singletory, Chief of the Memphis Flight Service Station; and John Edwards, George Roe, and George Rhodes of that facility for their help in discussing the functions of the FSS in filing an instrument flight plan. Berl Henry, M. H. Smith, H. E. Pritchard, and Delbert Robertson of the Chattanooga Weather Bureau Airport Station for sending actual (past date) weather sequences and forecasts for use in illustrations.

John Hornaday and Bill Whitmore, of the FAA General Aviation District Office at Nashville, for reviewing the manuscript and offering both practical help and encouragement for its completion. Elmour D. Meriwether, veteran pilot of Nashville, who reviewed the manuscript and made valuable suggestions. Fred C. Stashak, Chief Stress Engineer of Piper Aircraft Corp., for sending Information on aircraft stress.

W. D. Thompson, Chief of Flight Test and Aerodynamics of Cessna Aircraft Co., who kindly furnished needed performance data on Cessna airplanes for use in writing this manual. John Kruk, Electrical Design Engineer of Piper Aircraft Corp., for providing much needed electrical background knowledge aimed at the needs of the instrument pilot. Allen W. Hayes, pilot, instructor, and engineer, of Ithaca, New York, who cut through manuscript verbosity, corrected errors and misprints and made valuable suggestions. Norbert A. Weisand, Senior Product Engineer, Deicing Systems Engineering, B. F. Goodrich Co., for furnishing data on that equipment.

Appreciation is expressed to personnel of the Coast and Geodetic Survey of the Environmental Science Services Administration, especially Frank McClung, for ensuring that I received the latest charts available at the time the manuscript was in preparation.

I want to thank the avionics and other manufacturers who furnished information on their products. They are listed in the Bibliography.

Col. Leslie McLaurin, manager of the Sewanee Airport, who reviewed the manuscript and used it as an instrument refresher and made suggestions valuable for that area of the manual. Mr. and Mrs. Phillip Werlein, of Sewanee, who helped at a critical stage of the manuscript by giving needed extra working room. Mary Lou Chapman, of St. Andrews School in Sewanee, for furnishing working space at the school. The College Entrance Examination Board (Southern Region) at Sewanee aided the effort to a large degree by allowing me to use their facilities.

SECOND EDITION

The revisions in this edition complete the transition from the old-type approach procedures and minimums to the current TERPS (Terminal Instrument Procedures). TERPS are the only procedures the new instrument trainee will be concerned with. For the refresher pilot, the "old" approach procedures are mentioned only when necessary to provide some measure of comparison with TERPS. This edition takes an overall look at the requirements for obtaining the instrument rating and the following flights in the ATC environment without going into details that might confuse the instrument trainee. As the reader gains experience in IFR work, understanding of the more complex situations will follow naturally.

I would like to thank the following people for their assistance in preparing the second edition: James Ayers, ATC Specialist, John Omohundro, Chief, Air Traffic Control Tower, both at Nashville; Herbert Price, Watch Supervisor, Chattanooga tower; Hugh Pritchard and W. R. Wright of the Chattanooga Weather Service Airport Station; Frank McClung of the U.S. Coast and Geodetic Survey for furnishing the latest charts; Roy T. Koeller, ATC Specialist at the Memphis Center; and D. G. Peavyhouse of the Crossville, Tenn., Flight Service Station.

THIRD EDITION

This edition covers in more detail the Center and terminal area radar computer systems and updates terms, ATC procedures, and available COM/NAV equipment.

As for the first two editions, I had advice and suggestions from knowledgeable people, but, again, any errors are mine.

At the Memphis Center, I particularly owe thanks to Carl Graves, who patiently explained the computer system and answered my many questions over a two-day period there. Roy Koeller sent me much needed information from the center before my visit so that I could be prepared to ask reasonable questions.

At the Nashville tower facility, Don Wells devoted much time to showing me the operations and bringing me up-to-date on the latest procedures from the terminal controller's standpoint, under both radar and nonradar conditions.

Others at the Nashville tower who let me "sit in" at the radar consoles and answered questions were Galyon Northcutt, David Pyrdum, Bill Duke, and Bill Allen. Ed Stoddart sent information to me before the visit.

The weather chapter of this book was the result of the help of the late Ray McAbee, former FSS specialist who helped me in every way possible. Tennessee aviation will miss him.

The specialists at the Chattanooga Weather Service Office should have gotten tired of my calls and questions but never indicated it; Hugh Pritchard, Ed Higdon, and others were more than generous with information.

C. S. (Chuck) Davis of Narco Avionics sent many photos and data with permission to use them. I would also like to thank Dave Speer of King Radio for use of photos and information he sent. Appreciation is also in order for Nat Toulon of Sewanee and Fred Gardner of the FAA at Oklahoma City for their help. I owe much thanks to William C. Lewis, Jr., CFI-I of Madison, Wis., who reviewed the second edition and made a great number of good suggestions, which were incorporated here.

FOURTH EDITION

This edition is intended to update the information on the ATC System and procedures as well as cover the more recent improvements in aircraft instrumentation and avionics. The performance, stability, and control, and basic instrument flying chapters have been expanded with more partial-panel recoveries and added information on spin recoveries under the hood (or in actual weather).

It is the intent of this book to give an overview of IFR operational requirements and to help establish patterns of aeronautical decision making pertaining to instrument flight. Parts One, Two, and Three give background on the airplane instruments, systems, navigation, communications with ATC, and weather. The weather information was obtained from actual charts, hourly reports, and forecasts so that the reader might compare the accuracy of forecast information with the weather that later occurred during the forecast period.

Part Four uses the background given in the first three parts, tieing it together in a "trip" from Memphis to Nashville in the weather conditions cited earlier, with attendant minor incidents and clearances, to emphasize points. This shows the reader how isolated items of information might fit into overall IFR operations.

Since this is a textbook, the routes and approaches have been selected to give the best examples, and a particular approach or route segment may have been changed or deleted before this reaches the reader's hands.

I would like to thank the following people and organizations for aid in writing this edition:

Particular thanks to Allen Henninger, Operations Supervisor, Memphis Center, who reviewed the chapters dealing with Center operations and who made many valuable suggestions and comments on the current operations and plans for equipment there.

At the Nashville tower, Galyon Northcutt, Plans and Procedures Specialist, patiently answered many questions and sketched the approach control flight patterns that a pilot might expect for the various instrument approaches on the sample IFR trip from Memphis to Nashville used in the book.

Jim Gregory of the Nashville Automated FSS, who furnished a full day's weather information for the United States, which formed the basis for Chapter 7. Robert N. Turner, of the Crossville FSS, who furnished other material and answered questions over the past couple of years. Ken King, Area Supervisor, Huntsville, Ala., tower, gave information on what a pilot could expect at HSV and also reviewed the last chapters of the book, bringing me up-to-date on procedures.

David Preble, of the Nashville FSS for furnishing information on location identifiers. Ed Higdon, U.S. Weather Service, Chattanooga. John Blackwell, Memphis tower. Bill Scott, Chattanooga tower, who described the frequencies and transponder codes used in the VFR trip from Knoxville to Chattanooga described in Chapter 6. Karol Abrahms, Southern Illinois University Weather Department, for furnishing actual reports and forecasts. Norbert Weisand, B. F. Goodrich Co., for the latest information on anti- and deicing equipment. H. H. Gulberg, for deicing data.

Kay Roam, Air Traffic Training Specialist at the Prescott, Ariz., FSS, alerted me to the impending changes in aviation area forecasts.

Doug Mathews, Supervisor, National Aviation Weather Advisory Unit (NAWAU), Kansas City, Mo., and John Ferree, Forecaster at NAWAU, for the latest area forecast/AIRMET information.

Lee Harrison, NWS Coordinator at the FAA Academy at OKC, and Robert Hamilton, Meteorologist at the FAA Academy, answered many of my questions pertaining to the new area forecast/AIRMET format.

Jim Murphy, long-time pilot and instructor, made me aware of some information about altimeters that most pilots do not know.

Jim Oliver, Training Specialist at the Nashville FSS, gave me up-to-date information on NOTAMs and other functions of that facility.

My son Bill, a pilot for American Airlines who worked with me on this book, particularly in the last chapters, for help on finding references for the answers in the written test. William C. Lewis, Jr., CFI-I of Madison, Wis., whose review of the earlier chapters for this edition and valuable and cogent comments and suggestions on the third edition and its printings helped make the book much better than it otherwise would have been. Mary Katherine MacKinnon, for help in editing and arranging parts of this edition. Eleanor Ulton, Sewanee, whose typing and editing talents helped clear up some murky areas.

I would like to thank Gene Demaray and Nick Cook at Iowa State University Press for their skills in composition, layout, and makeup, particularly because of the number of illustrations that had to be fitted in to match the copy.

Special thanks to Kathleen Schlachter, meteorology instructor at the FAA Academy at OKC, for translating weather presentations to the METAR/TAF format.

And, of course, most thanks must go to my wife, who encouraged, typed, and retyped as this edition progressed and whose patience was outstanding throughout.

I would appreciate suggestions from readers for improving subsequent printings.

FIFTH EDITION

This edition is an update of current FAR 61.65 requirements for the instrument rating, the conversion to the METAR/TAF weather reporting/forecasting system, and information on the global positioning system.

I would like to thank again Allen Henninger, Operations Supervisor, Air Route Traffic Control Center at Memphis, for his review of the material concerning Center operations.

Again, thanks to Katherine Schlachter, Meteorologist, for her further help with the transition to the METAR/TAF system.

Lynne Bishop, editor at Iowa State University Press, for her humor and quick grasp of my editorial errors on several occasions. It is a pleasure to work with her on this book and others.

Thanks to my wife, Betty, who patiently typed and corrected spelling errors before the manuscript was submitted.

SIXTH EDITION

This edition is revised and updated. Because the actual questions for the Knowledge Test are available from other, more timely, sources, the questions, answers, and explanations for a sample test have been omitted. The *Aeronautical Information Manual Glossary* has been left out for the same reason. *Charts, approaches, equipment, and procedures may change or be eliminated while this edition is in print. Charts and approaches that appear in this edition are for example purposes only.*

A syllabus for a course on training for the instrument rating (airplane—single engine land) has been added to act as a checklist for the reader pursuing such a rating.

I am again indebted to people who helped with this edition, particularly Lynne Bishop, editor at Iowa State Press, whose patience and good humor make the effort of writing a pleasure.

Thanks to Lara Zook, Flight Instructor, for suggestions for improving this printing.

To my wife of 48 years, I give thanks again for her patience when asked to type my handwritten original or corrected manuscripts and who was always my support in the early lean times of my aviation writing.

Bill Kershner

1 AIRPLANE PERFORMANCE AND BASIC INSTRUMENT FLYING

THE INSTRUMENT RATING

For a long time now, you've sat on the ground and watched other pilots take off into weather that kept you haunting the Weather Service Office at Podunk Greater International Airport or other such well-known places. You squeaked in by the skin of your teeth (the airport went well below VFR minimums shortly after you got in and has been that way for days), and the bitter part about it is that the tops are running only 3000 or 4000 ft. It's *CAVU* (Ceiling *And* Visibility *Unlimited*) above, and the weather at your destination is very fine VFR—and there you sit. That one over at the Flight Service station counter is filing IFR and is going and doesn't appear to have any more on the ball than you have. After a few occasions of this nature, you've decided to get that instrument rating. Or maybe your decision came about because one time you were a "gray-faced, pinheaded holeseeker" (Fig. 1-1). Looking back at it, you'll have to confess that you were pinheaded to get in such a predicament, and while you couldn't see your face, it sure felt gray from your

side of it. If that hole hadn't showed up when it did, well, that could have put you between a rock and a hard place.

The instrument-rated pilot is still held in some awe by the nonrated people at the airport. The pilots with this rating don't always try to dispel the awe, but that's only human. Generally speaking, the two *extreme* schools of thought by those considering the instrument rating are: (1) It is a license to fly anywhere, anytime, and weather will no longer be an important consideration; or (2) it will be used only as an emergency method of getting down and may never be needed.

If you belong to the first group, give up any idea of getting an instrument rating. You'll be a menace to the rest of us clear thinkers and very likely have an exciting but extremely brief career.

If you are in group 2, you could be wasting your time and money by getting an instrument rating for use only in an emergency—you may never use it. However, it is good training and would help the other areas of your flying.

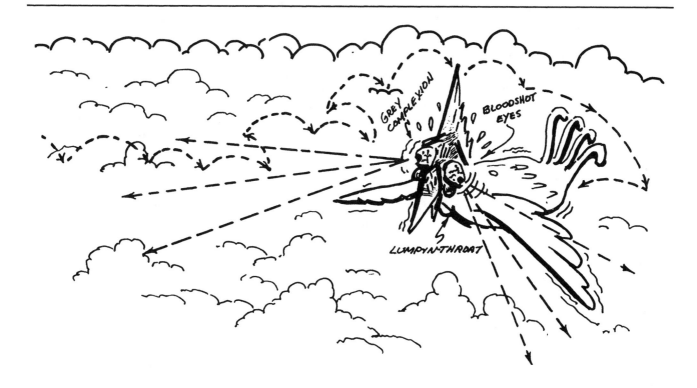

Fig. 1-1. The gray-faced pinheaded holeseeker has an exciting but often brief career.

Of course, *you* don't fall into either of the extremes. You know that there will be times after getting the rating that you'll still be sitting on the ground because of the weather. But you will be able to get out more often than is the case now.

One thing you'll notice as you work on the rating is that all your flying will become more precise. You'll be much more aware of altitude and heading and how power and airspeed combinations affect performance.

FAR 61.65: THE REQUIREMENTS FOR THE INSTRUMENT RATING — AIRPLANE

(a) *General.* A person who applies for an instrument rating must:

(1) Hold at least a current private pilot certificate with an airplane, helicopter, or powered-lift rating appropriate to the instrument rating sought:

(2) Be able to read, speak, write, and understand the English language. If the applicant is unable to meet any of these requirements due to a medical condition, the Administrator may place such operating limitations on the applicant's pilot certificate as are necessary for the safe operation of the aircraft;

(3) Receive and log ground training from an authorized instructor or accomplish a home-study course of training on the aeronautical knowledge areas of paragraph (b) of this section that apply to the instrument rating sought;

(4) Receive a logbook or training record endorsement from an authorized instructor certifying that the person is prepared to take the required knowledge test;

(5) Receive and log training on the areas of operation of paragraph (c) of this section from an authorized instructor in an aircraft, approved flight simulator, or approved training device that represents an airplane, helicopter, or powered-lift appropriate to the instrument rating sought;

(6) Receive a logbook or training record endorsement from an authorized instructor certifying that the person is prepared to take the required practical test;

(7) Pass the required knowledge test on the aeronautical knowledge areas of paragraph (b) of this section; however, an applicant is not required to take another knowledge test when that person already holds an instrument rating; and

(8) Pass the required practical test on the areas of operation in paragraph (c) of this section in—

(i) The aircraft category, class, and type, if applicable, appropriate to the rating sought; or

(ii) A flight simulator or a flight training device appropriate to the rating sought and approved for the specific maneuver or procedure performed. If an approved flight training device is used for the practical test, the procedures conducted in that flight training device are limited to one precision and one nonprecision approach, provided the flight training device is approved for the procedure performed.

(b) *Aeronautical knowledge.* A person who applies for an instrument rating must have received and logged ground training from an authorized instructor or accomplished a home-study course on the following aeronautical knowledge areas that apply to the instrument rating sought:

(1) Federal Aviation Regulations of this chapter that apply to flight operations under IFR;

(2) Appropriate information that applies to flight operations under IFR in the "Aeronautical Information Manual";

(3) Air traffic control system and procedures for instrument flight operations;

(4) IFR navigation and approaches by use of navigation systems;

(5) Use of IFR en route and instrument approach procedure charts;

(6) Procurement and use of aviation weather reports and forecasts and the elements of forecasting weather trends based on that information and personal observation of weather conditions;

(7) Safe and efficient operation of aircraft under instrument flight rules and conditions;

(8) Recognition of critical weather situations and wind-shear avoidance;

(9) Aeronautical decision making and judgment; and

(10) Crew resource management, including crew communication and coordination.

(c) *Flight proficiency:* A person who applies for an instrument rating must receive and log training from an authorized instructor in an aircraft, or in an approved flight simulator or approved

flight training device, in accordance with paragraph (e) of this section, that includes the following areas of operation:

(1) Preflight preparation;

(2) Preflight procedures;

(3) Air traffic control clearances and procedures;

(4) Flight by reference to instruments;

(5) Navigation systems;

(6) Instrument approach procedures;

(7) Emergency operations; and

(8) Postflight procedures.

(d) *Aeronautical experience.* A person who applies for an instrument rating must have logged the following:

(1) At least 50 hours of cross-country flight time as pilot in command, of which at least 10 hours must be in airplanes for an instrument-airplane rating; and

(2) A total of 40 hours of actual or simulated instrument time on the areas of operation of this section. to include—

(i) At least 15 hours of instrument flight training from an authorized instructor in the aircraft category for which the instrument rating is sought;

(ii) At least 3 hours of instrument training that is appropriate to the instrument rating sought from an authorized instructor in preparation for the practical test within the 60 days preceding the date of the test;

(iii) For an instrument-airplane rating. Instrument training on cross-country flight procedures specific to airplanes that include at least one cross-country flight in an airplane that is performed under IFR, and consists of—

(A) A distance of at least 250 nautical miles along airways or ATC-directed routing;

(B) An instrument approach at each airport; and

(C) Three different kinds of approaches with the use of navigation systems.

(e) *Use of flight simulators* or *flight training devices.* If the instrument training was provided by an authorized instructor in a flight simulator or flight training device—

(1) A maximum of 30 hours may be performed in that flight simulator or flight training device if the training was accomplished in accordance with part 142 of this chapter; or

(2) A maximum of 20 hours may be performed in that flight simulator or flight training device if the training was not accomplished in accordance with part 142 of this chapter.

If you are getting the instrument rating "on your own" and not going through a formal program, you'll have to think about a means of simulating instrument conditions in the airplane. One method is the hooded visor, which, when worn, cuts the vision to that of straight ahead only. It is the most simple and inexpensive arrangement, being worn like a cap, but it restricts side vision to the extent of requiring a great deal of head turning to adjust power, set radios, and check engine instruments. Such quick head turning tends to invite vertigo, a condition in which you *know* (well, you *think* you know) that the airplane is not doing what the instruments indicate.

While we're on the subject, some think that they can grab a hood and go out and practice instruments solo. Not only would that be a bad situation, it's in violation of FAR 91, which says, "No person may operate a civil aircraft in simulated instrument flight unless (1) an appropriately rated pilot occupies the other control seat as safety pilot, (2) the safety pilot has adequate vision forward and to each side of the aircraft or (3) a competent observer in the aircraft adequately supplements the vision of the safety pilot."

If you are using a single-engine airplane for your instrument instruction and the instructor or safety pilot determines that the flight can be conducted safely (and you have a private certificate with appropriate category and class ratings), a single throwover control wheel may be used. In earlier times, dual control wheels were required for all types of instruction.

Try to work it so that once you start on the rating you can go on with it. Don't stretch the program over too long a period. Stretching it out may make it necessary to use a part of each flight as a review. It's also best to be flying as you study for the written—one area helps the other. But get the written out of the way before you have those last few hours of brush-up time prior to the flight test.

During the training period, when you are flying cross-country VFR, fly airways as much as feasible. Borrow a low-altitude en route chart (or you may want to start subscribing to one of the chart services available) and fly as if you were on an IFR flight plan. Of course, if you are flying VFR, you actually will be flying some altitude plus 500 and will be looking out for other airplanes all the time. Also, you'll do no hooded work unless you have an "appropriately rated pilot" in the right seat. but you can smooth out your estimates even while flying VFR.

Get as much as possible of your dual instruction in the later stages on actual instruments, filing a flight plan, and flying in the clouds (with an appropriately rated instructor, of course). It's a more realistic situation than practicing with the hood, and your confidence will be increased. This doesn't mean that you and the instructor will go out and crack through the worst squall line you can find or fly into the worst icing conditions seen in your area for 29 yr, but that you will choose the type of weather to "practice" in. The regulations are such that you don't have to have any actual instrument experience in that 40 hr required for the rating; but if you do have some, you'll enjoy that first flight on actual instruments more.

You might talk to some of the approved schools in your area. (They are certificated under FAR 141 and require less time.) Also, if you plan on getting a commercial certificate, not having an instrument rating can limit you severely, so that's another reason to get cracking.

After you get the rating, don't go busting into IFR with a vengeance. Take it easy and set yourself comparatively high minimum weather conditions. As your experience increases and you get better equipment, you can gradually lower your minimums to those as published on the approach charts. You always have to keep up your proficiency to a safe level; if you get rusty, you have to ease back into it again.

This is a general look at the requirements as of this printing; get the latest issuances of FAR 61.65 to be sure.

Last but not at all least, the same things that apply to any flying apply to instrument flying. So in order of importance:

1. AVIATE (FLY THE AIRPLANE FIRST).
2. NAVIGATE.
3. COMMUNICATE.

FLIGHT AND ENGINE INSTRUMENTS

2

The flight instruments will naturally now be of even greater interest and value than before, and it is extremely important that you understand how they work. Not only must you know how to fly by reference to them, but you will have to be aware of what you as a pilot must do to keep them operating properly and be able to recognize signs of impending instrument or system trouble. This chapter will cover the flight and other instruments of utmost importance to the instrument pilot. For instance, you know that the gyro horizon (or attitude indicator, as it is also termed) is one of the most important flight instruments, but to date you have probably paid very little attention to the suction gauge, which can give warning of possible problems with the vacuum-driven instruments. The ammeter will also be of added importance; an electrical failure while flying under instrument conditions would pose many more problems than if you lost the electrically driven flight instruments and radios during VFR operations. An electrical failure, for instance, *could* cause you to lose the airspeed indicator in icing conditions.

REQUIRED INSTRUMENTS AND EQUIPMENT (PARAPHRASED)

■ **Visual Flight Rules (Day)** For flying VFR (day) the airplane is required to have the following instruments and equipment (FAR 91):

1. Airspeed indicator.
2. Altimeter.
3. Magnetic direction indicator.
4. Tachometer for each engine.
5. Oil pressure gauge for each engine using pressure system.
6. Temperature gauge for each liquid-cooled engine.
7. Oil temperature gauge for each air-cooled engine.
8. Manifold pressure gauge for each altitude engine.
9. Fuel gauge indicating the quantity of fuel in each tank.
10. Landing gear position indicator if the aircraft has retractable landing gear.
11. For small airplanes certificated after March 11, 1996 in accordance with Part 23 of this chapter, an approved aviation red or aviation white anticollision light system. (If any parts fail, you continue to a location where repairs or replacments can be made.)

12. If the aircraft is operated for hire over water and beyond power-off gliding distance from shore, approved flotation gear should be readily available to each occupant, and at least one pyrotechnic signaling device should be on board.
13. Approved safety belt for each occupant who has reached his or her second birthday (each safety belt must be equipped with an approved metal-to-metal latching device).
14. For small civil airplanes manufactured after July 18, 1978, an approved shoulder harness for each front seat.

■ **Visual Flight Rules (Night)** For VFR flight at night, the following instruments and equipment are required in addition to those specified for VFR day flying:

1. Approved position lights.
2. An approved aviation red or aviation white anticollision light system on all large aircraft, on all small aircraft when required by the airworthiness certificate, and on all small aircraft manufactured after August 11, 1971. In the event of the failure of any light in the anticollision light system, operations with the aircraft may be continued to a stop where repairs or replacement may be made.
3. If the aircraft is operated for hire, one electric landing light.
4. An adequate source of electrical energy for all installed electrical and radio equipment.
5. One spare set of fuses or three spare fuses of each kind required.

■ **Instrument Flight Rules**

1. For IFR flight the following instruments and equipment are required in addition to those specified for VFR day and VFR night flying:
2. Two-way radio communications system and navigational equipment appropriate for the ground facilities to be used.
3. Gyroscopic rate of turn indicator except on large airplanes with a third attitude instrument system usable through flight attitudes of 360° of pitch and roll and installed in accordance with FAR 121.305(j).
4. Slip-skid indicator.
5. Sensitive altimeter adjustable for barometric pressure.

6. A clock displaying hours, minutes, and seconds with a sweep-second pointer or digital presentation. The clock will be very important, even at the early stage of your training. Time is a factor that you coped with in your previous flying, but now it will assume major importance in your IFR planning and flying. As you read the description of the instruments, think how each is affected by time (altitude, heading changes, and distances covered)—the clock and the selected instruments are tied together).

7. Generator or alternator of adequate capacity.

8. Gyroscopic bank and pitch indicator (attitude indicator).

9. Gyroscopic direction indicator (heading indicator or its equivalent).

If the aircraft is operated above 24,000 ft mean sea level (MSL), distance measuring equipment (DME) is required. (If it fails in flight at or above this altitude, you as pilot in command must notify ATC immediately but then operate at or above 24,000 ft MSL to the next airport of intended landing where repairs or replacement of the equipment can be made.)

Again, be sure to have the latest FARs available in your aviation library.

PITOT-STATIC INSTRUMENTS

These are the flight instruments that indicate air pressure or changes in pressure and include the airspeed indicator, altimeter, and rate of climb (or vertical speed) indicator. All three require static pressure, but only the airspeed indicator requires pitot (dynamic) pressure as well.

■ **Airspeed Indicator** The airspeed indicator is an air pressure gauge calibrated to read in miles per hour or knots rather than pounds per square foot (psf). The airspeed system is made up of the pitot and static tubes and the airspeed indicator itself. As the airplane moves through the air, the relative wind exerts an impact pressure (or dynamic pressure) in the pitot tube, which expands a diaphragm linked to an indicating hand (Fig. 2-1).

In addition to the dynamic pressure, static air pressure also exists in the pitot tube. As shown in Figure 2-1, the diaphragm contains both dynamic *and* static pressures. The static tube allows the static pressure to enter the instrument *case* so that these two static pressures cancel each other as far as the diaphragm is concerned; it expands only as a function of the dynamic pressure.

Dynamic pressure, sometimes called "q," has the equation $(\varrho/2)(V^2)$ where ϱ (pronounced rho) is the air density in slugs per cubic foot, and V is the *true* velocity of the air in feet per second (fps). A slug is a unit of mass and may be found by dividing the weight of an object by the acceleration of gravity (32.2 fps/sec). Hence, a 161-lb man would have a mass of 5 slugs; $161 \div 32.2 = 5$. A beauty queen weighing 128.8 lb would have a mass of 4 slugs, which is certainly an unromantic way to think of her.

Realizing that the dynamic pressure is made up of the combination of one-half the density *times* the true speed (squared) of the air particles, you can see that a calibrated airspeed (CAS) of 150 knots could result either from high density and comparatively low speed of the air or a lower density and higher true airspeed. The density of the air at sea level is 0.002378 slugs/ft³, and at a calibrated airspeed of 150 knots CAS would also be the true airspeed at *sea level standard conditions* (29.92 in. of mercury pressure at 59°F, or 15°C). The airspeed indicator cannot compensate for density change; it can only indicate the combination of density *and* velocity of the air.

At 10,000 ft the air density is only about ¾ of that at sea level; hence, if the plane has a CAS of 150 knots at that altitude, it is meeting the fewer air particles at a higher speed than was done at sea level in order to get the same dynamic pressure (CAS). If you are interested in the mathematics of the problem, the following is presented:

$$\text{Dynamic pressure (psf)} = \frac{\varrho}{2}(V^2)$$

$$\text{At sea level V} = 150 \text{ knots} = 254 \text{ fps}$$

$$\text{Dynamic pressure} = \frac{0.002378}{2} \times (254)^2$$

$$= 76.3 \text{ psf}$$

A rule of thumb for finding dynamic pressure in pounds for various airspeeds is

$$\text{psf} = \frac{V^2 \text{ (knots)}}{295}$$

Using the earlier example of 150 knots, the answer would be

$$\frac{(150)^2}{295} = \frac{22,500}{295} = 76.27 \text{ psf (call it 76.3)}$$

At 10,000 ft the standard air density is 0.001756 slugs/ft³. Since the airplane has a CAS of 150 knots at 10,000 ft, the dynamic pressure is also 76.3 psf, and the true airspeed or true relative speed of the air can be found by solving for V as follows:

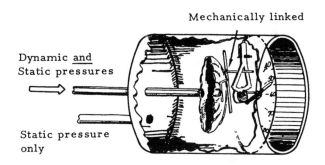

Mechanically linked

Dynamic *and* Static pressures

Static pressure only

Fig. 2-1. Airspeed indicator.

$$76.3 = \frac{0.001756}{2} \times V^2$$

$$V^2 = \frac{152.6}{0.001756} \, ; \, V = \sqrt{\frac{152.6}{0.001756}}$$

V = 295 fps, or 175 knots

You do this type of calculation with your computer (whether you know it or not). You can check the above with your computer (the standard temperature at 10,000 ft is –5°C). You don't work with feet per second, however. You'll note that an indicated (or rather calibrated) airspeed of 150 knots at 10,000 ft density-altitude gives a true airspeed of 175 knots (174+).

In the illustration, it was assumed that the airspeed indicator was giving you the exact, straight story; this is not always the case. On your computer you are working with calibrated airspeed (CAS), which is the indicated airspeed (IAS) corrected for errors in the airspeed system (includes errors in the instrument plus errors in the pitot-static system, normally called position and/or installation errors). Your airplane may have an airspeed correction table that allows the correcting of IAS to CAS. In the majority of cases in practical application for smaller airplanes, airspeed system error is ignored and IAS is assumed to equal CAS in the cruise range. At low speeds near the stall, however, the difference between IAS and CAS can be 10 knots or more.

Figure 2-2 is a typical airspeed calibration chart for the normal static source. More about the alternate static source later.

AIRSPEED CALIBRATION
NORMAL STATIC SOURCE

CONDITION:
Power required for level flight or maximum rated RPM dive.

FLAPS UP												
KIAS	50	60	70	80	90	100	110	120	130	140	150	160
KCAS	56	62	70	79	89	98	107	117	126	135	145	154
FLAPS 10°												
KIAS	40	50	60	70	80	90	100	110	---	---	---	---
KCAS	49	55	62	70	79	89	98	108	---	---	---	---
FLAPS 30°												
KIAS	40	50	60	70	80	85	---	---	---	---	---	---
KCAS	47	53	61	70	80	84	---	---	---	---	---	---

Fig. 2-2. Airspeed calibration chart (normal static source).

Another term used is *equivalent airspeed* (EAS), and this is CAS corrected for compressibility effects. This is not of consequence below 250 knots and 10,000 ft, so it's not likely that you would need a compressibility correction table for your present work. Normally, your corrective steps will be IAS to CAS to TAS (true airspeed). If you have no

correction card for instrument error, it will be IAS to TAS. If you are operating at altitudes and speeds where compressibility effects exist, note that the full number of steps would be IAS to CAS to EAS to TAS. The problem is that the static air in the pitot tube is being packed (compressed) and gives a high reading (remember that the pitot tube is measuring *both* dynamic *and* static pressures), so the effect is, as far as the airspeed indication is concerned, that of a higher dynamic pressure than actually exists. In other words, the CAS is higher than it should be, and computing for EAS gives the true picture.

AIRSPEED INDICATOR MARKINGS. The FAA requires that the airspeed indicator be marked for various important speeds and speed ranges (Fig. 2-3 shows the required markings):

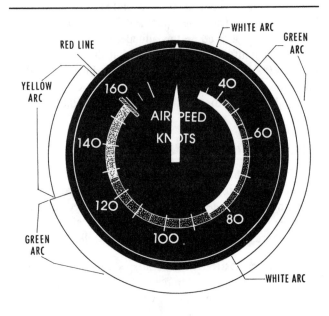

Fig. 2-3. Airspeed indicator markings.

Red line—*Never* exceed speed (V_{NE}). This speed should not be exceeded at any time.

Yellow arc—Caution range. Strong vertical gusts could damage the airplane in this speed range; therefore, it is best to refrain from flying in this range when encountering turbulence of any intensity. The caution range starts at the maximum structural cruising speed (V_{NO}) and ends at V_{NE}.

Green arc—Normal operating range. The airspeed at the lower end of this arc is the flaps-up, gear-up, power-off (wings-level, 1 g) stall speed at gross weight, V_{S1}. For most airplanes the landing gear position (full up or full down) has little or no effect on stall speed. The upper end of the green arc is the maximum indicated airspeed (V_{NO}) where no structural damage would occur in moderate vertical gust conditions (30 fps).

White arc—The flap operating range. The lower limit is the power-off stall speed with recommended landing flaps

(V_{SO}) at gross weight (gear extended and cowl flaps closed), and the upper limit is the maximum flap extended speed (full flaps).

Older airplanes have the airspeed indicator markings as *calibrated* airspeed in miles per hour or knots. Newer airplanes will have the airspeed markings as *indicated* airspeed in knots. As a general rule, 1976 model (and later) airspeed indicators will be marked in knots of IAS, but you should confirm this in the *Pilot's Operating Handbook (POH)* or *Airplane Flight Manual*. (More about the *POH* at the end of this chapter.)

■ **Altimeter** The altimeter (Fig. 2-4) is the most important of the three instruments of the pitot-static group as far as instrument flying is concerned. It is an aneroid barometer calibrated to read in feet instead of inches of mercury. Its job is to measure the static pressure (or ambient pressure as it is sometimes called) and register this fact in terms of feet or thousands of feet.

Fig. 2-4. Altimeter. The 10,000-ft indicator (small triangle) and the hatched low-altitude warning flag won't be shown in the exercises that follow in this book.

The altimeter has an opening that allows static (outside) pressure to enter the otherwise sealed case. A series of sealed diaphragms or "aneroid wafers" within the case are mechanically linked to the three indicating hands. Since the wafers are sealed, they retain a constant internal "pressure" and expand or contract in response to the changing atmospheric pressure surrounding them in the case. As the aircraft climbs, the atmospheric pressure decreases and the sealed wafers expand; this is duly noted by the indicating hands as an increase in altitude.

Standard sea level pressure is 29.92 in. of mercury, and the standard sea level temperature is 15°C, or 59°F. The altimeter is calibrated for this condition, and any change in local pressure must be corrected by the pilot. This is done

by using the setting knob to set the proper barometric pressure (corrected to sea level) in the setting window. For instance, a station at an elevation of 670 ft above sea level has an *actual* barometric pressure reading of 29.45 in. of mercury according to its barometer. Since the pressure drop is 1.06 in. of mercury for the first 1000 ft above sea level, an addition of 0.71 in. to the actual reading of 29.45 will correct the pressure to the sea level value of 30.16 in. of mercury. This, of course, assumes that the pressure drop is standard. This is the normal assumption and is accurate enough for *indicated* altitude.

There are several altitudes that will be of interest to you:

Indicated altitude is the altitude read when the altimeter is set to the local barometric pressure corrected to sea level as just mentioned.

True altitude is the height above sea level (MSL).

Absolute altitude is the height above the terrain (AGL).

Pressure altitude is the altitude read when the altimeter is set to 29.92. This indication shows what your altitude would be if the altimeter setting was 29.92, if it was a standard-pressure day at sea level.

Density-altitude is the pressure altitude computed with temperature; it is used in performance. If you know your density-altitude, air density can be found using tables and the airplane performance can be calculated. You go through this step every time you use a computer to find the true airspeed. You use the pressure altitude and the outside air temperature (OAT) at that altitude to get the true airspeed. Usually, there's not enough difference in pressure altitude and indicated altitude to make it worthwhile to set up 29.92 in the setting window, so the usual procedure is to use the *indicated* altitude and OAT.

The fact that the computer used pressure altitude and temperature to obtain density-altitude in finding true airspeed didn't mean much, since you were only interested in the final result. You may not even have been aware that you were working with density-altitude during the process. Most computers also allow you to read the density-altitude directly by setting up pressure altitude and temperature. This is handy in figuring the performance of your airplane for a high-altitude and/or high-temperature takeoff or landing. The *POH* gives graphs or figures for takeoff and landing performance at the various density-altitudes. After finding your density-altitude, you can find your predicted performance in the *POH*. Computers are not always available, and the manufacturer sometimes furnishes conversion charts with the *POH* (Fig. 2-5).

Suppose you are at a pressure altitude of 5000 ft, and the outside air temperature is 90°F. Using the conversion chart, you see that your density-altitude is 8000 ft (Fig. 2-5). Looking at the takeoff curves for your airplane, you can find your expected performance at that altitude.

You and other pilots fly *indicated altitude*. When you're flying cross-country, you will have no idea of your exact altitude above the terrain (although over level country you can check airport elevations in your area, subtract this from

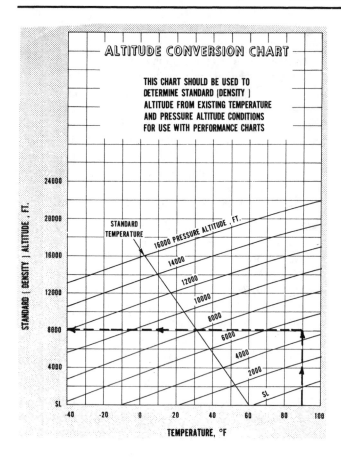

Fig. 2-5. Altitude conversion chart. Move up the 90° line until the 5000-ft pressure altitude is reached; directly across from this point is the standard (density) altitude for that combination (8000 ft). (*Piper Aircraft*).

your indicated altitude, and have a barnyard figure). Over mountainous terrain, this won't work, since the contours change too abruptly for you to keep up with them. As you fly, you'll get altimeter settings from various ground stations; keep up-to-date on pressure changes so your indicated altitude will be correct.

The use of indicated altitude for all planes makes good sense in that all pilots are using sea level as a base point, and proper assigned altitude separation results.

ALTIMETER ERRORS

Instrument or *system error*—If you set the current barometric pressure (corrected to sea level) for your airport, the altimeter should indicate the field elevation when you're on the ground. FAR 91 specifies that airplanes operating in controlled airspace (IFR) must have had each static pressure system and altimeter instrument tested by the manufacturer or an FAA-approved repair station within the past 24 calendar months.

Pressure changes—When you fly from a high-pressure area into a low-pressure area, the altimeter "thinks" you have climbed and will register accordingly—even if you haven't changed altitude. You will see this and fly the plane down to the "correct altitude" and will actually be

low. (This is a gradual process, and you will be easing down over a period of time to maintain what is the "correct altitude.") When you fly from a low- to a high-pressure area, the altimeter thinks you've let down to a lower altitude and registers too low. A good way to remember (although you can certainly reason it out each time) is: HLH—High to Low, altimeter reads High. LHL—Low to High, altimeter reads Low. (High to Low—look out below!)

You can see that it is worse to fly from a high-pressure to a low-pressure area as far as terrain clearance is concerned. Double-check altimeter settings as you fly IFR en route.

Temperature errors—The equation of state, which shows the relationship between pressure, density, and temperature of the atmosphere, notes that atmospheric pressure is proportional to the temperature. If the temperature is above normal, the pressure will be higher than normal (constant density). Therefore, if you are flying at a certain indicated altitude and the temperature is higher than normal, the pressure at your altitude is higher than normal. The altimeter registers *lower* than your *true* altitude. If the temperature is lower, the pressure is lower and the altimeter will register accordingly—*low temperature, altimeter reads high.*

You might remember it this way, using the letters H and L as in pressure change: Temperature High, altimeter reads Low—HL. Temperature Low, altimeter reads High—LH. Or maybe it's easier to remember HALT (*H*igh *A*ltimeter because of *L*ow *T*emperature).

For both temperature *and* pressure, remember "from High to Low, look out below." The best thing, however, is to know that higher temperature means higher pressure (and vice versa) at altitude and reason it out from there.

The temperature error is zero at sea level (or at the elevation of the station at which the setting is obtained) and increases with altitude so that the error could easily be 500–600 ft at the 10,000-ft level. In other words, you can have this error at altitude even if the altimeter reads correctly at sea level. Temperature error can be found with a computer, as shown in Figure 2-6. For indicated altitude this error is neglected; but it makes a good question for an instrument rating written exam or practical test, so keep it in mind.

These errors (particularly temperature errors, which are normally ignored) affect everybody in that area (though slightly differently for different altitudes), so that the altitude separation is still no problem. Temperature errors could cause problems as far as terrain clearance is concerned, however.

A final altimeter note: For computer work you are told to use the *pressure altitude* to find the true airspeed. For practical work, use *indicated altitude* (current sea level setting) for true airspeed computations. Remember that the TAS increases about 2%/1000 ft, so the most you will be off will be 2%. That is, your sea level altimeter setting could possibly be 28.92 or 30.92, but this is extremely unlikely. So...*assume*

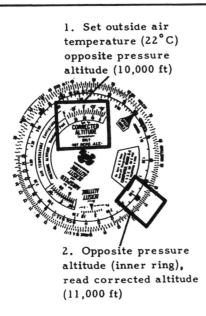

1. Set outside air temperature (22°C) opposite pressure altitude (10,000 ft)

2. Opposite pressure altitude (inner ring), read corrected altitude (11,000 ft)

Fig. 2-6. Correcting the altimeter for temperature errors.

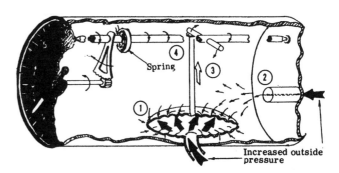

Increased outside pressure

Fig. 2-7. Vertical speed indicator and how it reacts to a descent.

that a total error of no more than 1% *will* be *introduced by using indicated altitude.* For a 200-knot airplane, this means you could be 2 knots off true airspeed. But the instrument error or your error in reading the instrument could be this much.

As you progress in your instrument flying to heavier and more complex equipment, you'll use altitude indicators such as encoding altimeters (used with the transponder) and radar altimeters (which give absolute altitude readings). These will be covered in more detail in later chapters as their use is introduced.

■ Rate of Climb or Vertical Speed Indicator (VSI) Like the altimeter the VSI has a diaphragm. But unlike the altimeter, it measures the *rate of change* of pressure rather than the pressure itself.

The diaphragm has a tube connecting it to the static tube of the airspeed indicator and altimeter (or the tube may just have access to the cabin air pressure in the case of cheaper or lighter installations). This means that the inside of the diaphragm has the same pressure as the static pressure of the air surrounding the airplane. Opening into the otherwise sealed instrument case is a capillary tube, which also is connected to the static system of the airplane.

Figure 2-7 is a schematic diagram of a typical VSI. As an example, suppose the airplane is flying at a constant altitude. The pressure within the diaphragm is the same as that of the air surrounding it in the instrument case. The rate of climb is indicated as zero.

The plane is put into a glide or dive. Air pressure inside the diaphragm increases at the same rate as that of the surrounding air (1). However, because of the small size of the capillary tube, the pressure in the instrument case does not change at the same rate (2). In a glide or dive, the diaphragm

expands; the amount of expansion depends on the difference between the pressures. Since the diaphragm is mechanically linked to a hand (3), the appropriate rate of descent in hundreds (or thousands) of feet per minute is read on the instrument face (4).

In a climb the pressure in the diaphragm decreases faster than that within the instrument case, and the needle will indicate an appropriate rate of climb.

In a climb or dive the pressure in the case is always "behind" the diaphragm pressure in this instrument, thus a certain amount of lag results. The instrument will still indicate a vertical speed for 6–9 sec after the plane has been leveled off. That's why the VSI is not used to maintain altitude. On days when the air is bumpy, this lag is particularly noticeable. The VSI is used, therefore, either when a constant rate of ascent or descent is needed or as a check of the plane's climb, dive, or glide rate. The sensitive altimeter is used to maintain a constant altitude, although the VSI can show the trend away from a desired altitude—if you realize that the lag is present. On the other hand, the VSI will also give a slight early indication of the direction of the altitude change before it is detectable on the altimeter, but it takes time to establish an accurate rate,

The pointer should read zero while the airplane is on the ground, and any deviation from this can be corrected by turning the adjustment screw on the instrument. You may also use the deviation (say, *plus* 100 ft) as the zero point. A 500-fpm climb would be performed at an indication of 600 fpm; a 500-fpm descent would call for the needle to be at a 400-fpm down-indication. It's better, though, to have the instrument set properly.

There is an IVSI (instantaneous vertical speed indicator) in some airplanes that does not have lag and is very accurate even in bumpy air. It contains a piston-cylinder arrangement whereby the airplane's vertical acceleration is immediately noted. The pistons are balanced by their own weights and springs. When a change in vertical speed is effected, the pistons are displaced and an immediate change of pressure in the cylinders is created. This pressure is transmitted to the diaphragm, producing an almost instantaneous change in indication. After the acceleration-induced pressure fades, the pistons are no longer displaced, and the diaphragm and capillary tube act as on the old type of indicator (as long as there is no acceleration). The actions of the acceleration elements and the diaphragm-capillary system overlap for smooth action.

It's possible to fly this type of instrument as accurately as an altimeter, but its price is understandably higher than that of the standard vertical speed indicator.

■ **The Pitot-Static System** The three instruments just discussed must have a dependable source of static (outside) air pressure in order to operate accurately. Figure 2-8 shows a schematic diagram of the pitot-static system and the instruments.

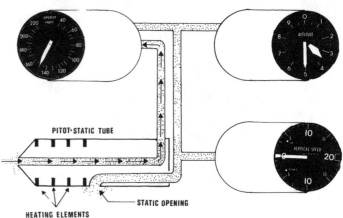

Fig. 2-9. System with static opening in the pitot-static tube.

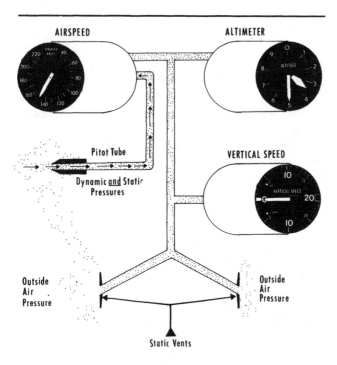

Fig. 2-8. Pitot-static system using flush type Y static vents in the fuselage.

The static system shown in Figure 2-8 uses a Y-type vent system to decrease static errors in yaw. The locations of the static vents are carefully chosen to obtain the most accurate static (outside) pressure. The usual location is on each side of the fuselage between the wing and the stabilizer. (You've seen the signs, "Keep this vent clean.") This is usually the most accurate system of those used.

Another pitot-static system is shown in Figure 2-9. The static vent is located in the pitot-static tube.

The system shown in Figure 2-9 is not usually as accurate as the Y system, and in addition, the static opening at this location may be more susceptible to icing over if the airplane does *not* have pitot heat. (An airplane that expects to fly in icing had better have pitot heat!) This could mean loss of *all three* of the pitot-static instruments—not just the airspeed, as would be the case of the pitot tube–Y vent system. (You'd still have static pressure to the airspeed indicator in

the Y vent system but no impact pressure, so it would be out of the running if the pilot tube iced over. This will be covered in more detail at the end of this section.)

The instruments in older light trainers get the static pressure from the cabin. Because of the effect of the air passing by the cabin, a venturi effect may result, and the static pressure will be lower than the actual outside pressure, which would mean a slightly high airspeed and altimeter indication. Once the airspeed is stabilized, the VSI will not be affected because it is a "rate" instrument and would measure *change* of pressure as mentioned earlier.

FAR 23 (Airworthiness Standards for Normal, Utility, and Aerobatic Category Airplanes) notes that the static air vent system must be such that the opening and closing of windows, airflow variation, and moisture or other foreign matter do not seriously affect its accuracy.

PITOT-STATIC SYSTEM PROBLEMS

Pitot system—The big problem you can expect to encounter as far as the *pitot* system is concerned is that of ice closing the pitot tube (pressure inlet). The airspeed will be the only instrument affected in this case. The application of pitot heat, if available, is the move to make. It is best, however, to apply pitot heat before you enter an area of suspected icing and leave it on until clear. However, the pitot heat is a great current drain, and under some conditions you may want to use it intermittently.

Here is a little more detail about a blocked pitot tube. If the pressure is trapped in the pitot tube by ice or other debris, the airspeed will tend to increase erroneously as the airplane climbs. The static pressure in the case will decrease as the outside pressure decreases with altitude while the static pressure in the diaphragm stays the same, resulting in the diaphragm expanding and showing an "increase" in airspeed. The pilot raises the nose to correct for this (instead of also monitoring the attitude indicator), and there have been cases of stalls occurring in this situation. If the ram inlet is blocked and the water drainhole on the bottom of the pitot tube is not, the pitot tube pressure may escape and the airspeed will go to zero.

Static system—The more complex airplanes have an alternate static source that can be used if the primary system should get stopped up. This normally consists of a selector that the pilot turns to the "alternate" setting, which opens the system to cabin air (nonpressurized cabin). This then may have the same inaccuracies discussed earlier for the older system. (But it's a lot better than no static source at all.) Opening windows and vents and using the heater will affect the airspeed indicator readings on the alternate static source selections for many airplanes. With some airplanes the alternate static selection may cause the altimeter to read *lower* than normal at some indicated airspeeds, which would be the opposite you'd expect from "theory." Check the *Pilot's Operating Handbook* for the airplane you are flying. Have at least a general figure for corrections for the airspeed and altimeter, using the alternate static source at cruise and expected approach speeds. For larger airplanes, a separate copilot alternate air source is available.

Figure 2-10 shows the indications of the instruments just as the alternate static air system is selected. (The alternate system uses the cabin static air.) The airspeed and altitude have increased in this example, and the VSI is temporarily showing a climb (it will return to zero when the pressure stabilizes).

Figure 2-11 is an airspeed calibration and altimeter correction table for a particular airplane. Note that corrections have been made for heater and vents, opened or closed. Pressurized airplanes would naturally *not* have the alternate static source vented into the cabin, but it may be vented into the baggage compartment and other unpressurized areas.

For airplanes without an alternate static source, one means of getting static pressure to the three instruments is to break the glass on the face of the rate of climb (VSI) instrument, since it is considered the least important of the three; *but stop a minute:* Figure 2-12 is another picture of the rate of climb instrument, showing the effects of using it (vertical speed) as a source of static pressure for the system.

Note that the only source of static pressure is through the face of the instrument and thence through the capillary tube into the static system. Because the capillary tube is specifically designed to create a lag in pressure changes, the airspeed and altimeter will lag in response as compared to the "true" static pressure changes. The rate of climb will indicate in reverse as can be seen by analyzing Figure 2-12. Compare what would be happening with that discussed in the normal action of the rate of climb. In Figure 2-12, if the airplane climbs, the static pressure in the case surrounding the diaphragm would drop immediately while the pressure in the diaphragm would still be holding up, since the change must "work its way" through the capillary tube. The *diaphragm would expand*, which would give an indication that the plane was *descending!* It might be added that the *rate* would be accurate; the *direction* of vertical speed would be wrong. Of

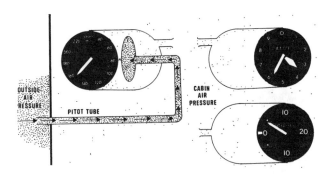

Fig. 2-10. Instrument indications just as the alternate system (cabin air pressure) is selected. The vertical speed indicator will return to zero shortly and react normally thereafter, since it measures *rate of change* of pressure rather than the pressure itself. Compare the instrument indications with those in Figure 2-8.

course, if you broke the glass and punched on through to leave a good-sized hole in the diaphragm, the other two instruments wouldn't have any lag (just the errors mentioned previously), but your VSI would be kaput.

By breaking the glass in the airspeed or altimeter (easy does it!), all three instruments will be about as accurate as they would be with a cabin alternate source.

The *theoretical* results of a suddenly and completely *plugged static system* in flight would be:

Airspeed—The airspeed would still be accurate as long as the static pressure trapped in the system was the same as the actual "outside" static pressure. If the airplane descended, the actual static pressure would be greater than that trapped in the system, so the airspeed would read *high*. If the airplane climbed, the airspeed would read *low*. You can see this by looking back at Figure 2-1. At the lower altitude, the diaphragm would expand farther than normal for a particular dynamic pressure because only a part of the static pressure entering the pitot tube would be canceled by the now comparatively low static pressure trapped in the case. Naturally, the degree of error would depend on the altitude change. If the trapped static pressure has a pressure of that found at 10,000 ft, the airplane has descended, and the pitot tube is taking in the true dynamic or impact pressure *plus* the static pressure of *sea level,* the result would be an airspeed of awesome values indeed!

Altimeter—The altimeter would read the altitude at which the complete stoppage occurred—and that's all. This would be a hairy IFR situation in that you might be easing up (or down) into the next guy's assigned altitude— or you might be easing down to connect with a cloud full of rocks.

Vertical speed indicator—The same thing will happen to this as happened to the altimeter—nothing. Easing the nose up or down in cruise by watching the attitude gyro does not result in an indication of rate of climb or

AIRSPEED CALIBRATION
ALTERNATE STATIC SOURCE

NOTES:
1 Indicated airspeed assumes zero instrument error
2 The following calibrations are not valid in the pre-stall buffet

VENTS AND HEATER CLOSED

FLAPS UP								
NORMAL KIAS	80	100	120	140	160	180	200	210
ALTERNATE KIAS	87	112	133	154	175	195	215	225
FLAPS 10°								
NORMAL KIAS	70	80	90	100	120	140	160	175
ALTERNATE KIAS	74	85	97	108	130	151	172	186
FLAPS 30°								
NORMAL KIAS	60	70	80	90	100	110	125	- - -
ALTERNATE KIAS	66	75	85	96	106	117	133	- - -

VENTS AND/OR HEATER OPEN

FLAPS UP								
NORMAL KIAS	80	100	120	140	160	180	200	210
ALTERNATE KIAS	85	108	130	151	171	192	211	221
FLAPS 10°								
NORMAL KIAS	70	90	90	100	120	140	160	175
ALTERNATE KIAS	73	84	95	106	127	147	167	182
FLAPS 30°								
NORMAL KIAS	60	70	80	90	100	110	125	- - -
ALTERNATE KIAS	62	72	81	93	102	113	129	- - -

ALTIMETER CORRECTION
ALTERNATE STATIC SOURCE

NOTE:
Add correction to desired altitude to obtain indicated altitude to fly

VENTS AND HEATER CLOSED

CONDITION	CORRECTION TO BE ADDED - FEET							
	KIAS							
	80	90	100	120	140	160	180	200
FLAPS UP								
Sea Level	40	60	90	150	200	240	290	330
10,000 Ft	50	80	120	180	250	310	370	430
20,000 Ft	60	110	160	250	340	430	510	590
FLAPS 10°								
Sea Level	30	40	60	110	150	200	250	- - -
10,000 Ft.	40	60	90	140	200	260	330	- - -
20,000 Ft	60	90	130	210	290	375	460	- - -
FLAPS 30°								
Sea Level	30	50	70	100	- - -	- - -	- - -	- - -
10,000 Ft	40	60	80	130	- - -	- - -	- - -	- - -
20,000 Ft	- - -	- - -	- - -	- - -	- - -	- - -	- - -	- - -

VENTS AND/OR HEATER OPEN

CONDITION	CORRECTION TO BE ADDED - FEET							
	KIAS							
	80	90	100	120	140	160	180	200
FLAPS UP								
Sea Level	20	30	50	90	130	190	240	300
10,000 Ft.	30	50	70	120	180	250	310	380
20,000 Ft	50	80	110	180	260	350	440	530
FLAPS 10°								
Sea Level	10	30	40	80	110	150	190	- - -
10,000 Ft	20	40	60	100	140	190	240	- - -
20,000 Ft	30	60	90	150	210	270	340	- - -
FLAPS 30°								
Sea Level	10	20	30	50	- - -	- - -	- - -	- - -
10,000 Ft	10	30	50	70	- - -	- - -	- - -	- - -
20,000 Ft	- - -	- - -	- - -	- - -	- - -	- - -	- - -	- - -

Fig. 2-11. Airspeed and altimeter corrections for the alternate static source for a particular airplane. (*Advanced Pilot's Flight Manual*)

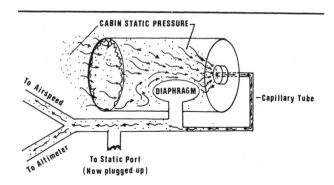

Fig. 2-12. Using the vertical speed indicator as a method of obtaining a static source.

descent on the VSI. What will be more likely to happen is that all instruments will lag considerably with altitude change because the system itself will not be perfectly sealed throughout.

If you have reason to believe that the normal static system is plugged, you'd better switch to the alternate or *carefully* break the glass of the airspeed indicator. It might be

better to *wreck* the rate of climb as mentioned rather than to risk damaging the other two instruments. (Leave the altimeter alone.)

FAR 91.411 states that no person may operate an airplane in controlled airspace under IFR (1) unless (within the preceding 24 calendar months) each static system, altimeter instrument, and automatic pressure-altitude reporting system has been tested and inspected and found to comply with certain requirements of FAR 43 and (2) unless (except for the use of system drain and alternate static pressure valves), following any opening and closing of the static pressure system, that system has been tested and inspected and found to comply with the requirements of FAR 43. (This has been paraphrased; check the actual detailed requirements in FAR 91.)

MAGNETIC INDICATORS

■ **Magnetic Float Compass** The magnetic compass is basically a magnet that aligns itself with the lines of the earth's magnetic field—the airplane turns around it.

The magnets in the compass also tend to align themselves parallel to the earth's lines of magnetic force. This tendency is more noticeable as the Magnetic North Pole is approached. The compass would theoretically point straight down when directly over the pole. The compass card magnet assembly is mounted so that a low center of gravity fights this dipping tendency. This mounting to fight dip causes errors to be introduced into the compass readings as discussed below.

NORTHERLY TURNING ERROR. In a shallow turn the compass leads by about 30° when passing through South and lags about 30° when passing through North. On passing East and West headings in the turn, the compass is approximately correct. (The value of 30° is a round figure for U.S. use; it's actually considered equal to the latitude of the area in which the compass is being used.)

For instance, you are headed South and decide to make a right turn and fly due North. As soon as the right bank is entered, the compass will indicate about 30° of right turn, when actually the nose has hardly started to move. So, *when a turn is started from a heading of South, the compass will indicate an extra fast turn in the direction of bank.* It will then hesitate and move slowly again, so that as the heading of West is passed, it will be approximately correct. The compass will lag as North is approached, so that you will rollout when the magnetic compass indicates 330° (or "33"). To be more accurate, you should start the roll-out early—the number of degrees of your latitude *plus* the number of degrees you would allow for the roll-out. Thus at a latitude of 35° N, using 5° for roll-out, you would start the roll-out 40° early or, in this case, when 320° is indicated.

Figure 2-13 shows the reactions of the compass to the 180° right turn from a heading of South.

If you had made a left turn from a South heading, the same effects would have been noticed: an immediate indication of turn in the direction of bank, a correct reading at the heading of East, and a compass lag of 30° when headed North.

If you start a turn from a heading of North, the compass will initially register a turn in the opposite direction but will soon race back and be approximately correct as an East or West heading is passed. It will then lead by about 30° as the airplane's nose points to Magnetic South. The initial errors in the turn are not too important. Set up your turn and know what to expect after the turn is started.

Here is a simple rule to cover the effects of bank (assuming a shallow bank of 20° or less; if the bank is too steep, the rule won't work).

Northerly turning errors (Northern Hemisphere):

North heading—Compass *lags* 30° at the start of the turn or in the turn.
South heading—Compass *leads* 30° at start of the turn or in the turn.
East or *West heading*—Compass correct at start of the turn or in the turn.

Just remember that North *lags* 30° and South *leads* 30°, and this covers the problem. Actually 30° is a round figure; the lead or lag for rolling out of a turn depends on the latitude and angle of bank being used, but 30° is close enough

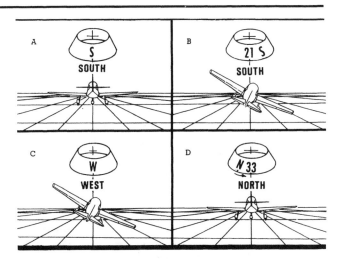

Fig. 2-13. (A) When the airplane is flying straight and level, headed Magnetic South, the compass is correct (disregarding deviation).
(B) As soon as the bank is entered, the compass indicates 210° ("21").
(C) As the nose passes West, the compass is reasonably accurate.
(D) In this example the airplane has been quickly rolled out when the compass indicated "33." The compass will immediately start to roll to indicate North. For accuracy, turns using the compass as a reference should be held below 20° bank.

for the work you'll be doing with the magnetic compass and is easy to remember.

ACCELERATION ERROR. Because of its correction for dip, the compass will react to acceleration and deceleration of the airplane. This is most apparent on East or West headings where *acceleration results in a more northerly reading. Deceleration gives a more southerly heading.* Remember the term ANDS (Accelerate and the compass "turns" North; Decelerate and the compass "turns" South).

The magnetic compass reads correctly *only* when the airplane is in straight and level unaccelerated flight (and sometimes not even then). In bumpy air the compass oscillates so that readings are difficult to take and more difficult to hold. The fluid in the case (acid-free white kerosene) is designed to keep the oscillations at a minimum, but the problem is still there.

VARIATION. The magnetic compass naturally points to the Magnetic North Pole, and this leads to the necessity of correcting for the angle between the Magnetic and Geographic North Poles.

In your earlier VFR flying days, you measured the course from a midpoint meridian; this was the "True Course" or the course referred to as the True or Geographic North Pole. To get the magnetic course, the following applied (and still does). Going from True to Magnetic:

East is least—Subtract the East variation as shown on the sectional or world aeronautical chart (WAC).

West is best—*Add* the West variation as shown on the sectional or WAC chart.

The variation (15° E or 10° W, etc.) given by the isogonic lines means that the Magnetic North Pole is 15° East or 10° West of the True North Pole—from your position. Naturally, if you happen to be at a point where the two poles are "in line," the variation will be zero. Courses on IFR en route charts and approach charts are oriented with respect to Magnetic North, so variation is already taken care of for that type of flying.

DEVIATION. The compass has an instrument error due to electrical equipment and the ferrous (iron) metal parts of the plane. This error varies between headings, and a correction card is placed near the compass, showing these errors for each 30°.

The compass is "swung" or corrected, on a compass rose—a large calibrated circle painted on the concrete ramp or taxiway away from metal interference such as hangars. The airplane is taxied onto the rose, and corrections are made in the compass with a nonmagnetic screwdriver. The engine should be running and normal radio and electrical equipment should be on, with the airplane in a level-flight attitude. Attempts are made to balance out the errors; it is better to have all headings off a small amount than some correct and others badly in error. The corrections are noted on the compass card, which is posted at a prominent spot near the compass.

As a review for navigation purposes (and for use on the written if necessary) the following steps would apply:

Remember TVMDC or *True Virgins Make Dull Company*, or The *Very Mean Department of Commerce* (left over from the days when aviation was under the jurisdiction of the Department of Commerce).

1. *True* course (or heading) plus or minus *Variation* gives *Magnetic* course (or heading).

2. *Magnetic* course (or heading) plus or minus *Deviation* gives *Compass* course (or heading).

The chances are that in your normal flying you've paid little attention to deviation and have been doing fine. But remember, now that you plan on getting that instrument rating, there'll be some pretty good questions on the subject, so it might be a good idea to start thinking about it again.

If you lost all gyro instruments and had no other method of keeping the wings level during a descent to get out of clouds, the magnetic compass could be used. Set up a heading of South on the mag compass. A deviation from this heading would mean that the wings weren't level and the airplane was turning. You would make corrections as necessary to stay on the South heading. Why South? One reason is that acceleration errors are smallest on North or South headings. Another is that the compass deviations on a South heading are in the *proper direction* and exaggerated. (On a heading of North, any bank will cause the compass to swing in the

opposite direction. This could be confusing for wing leveling purposes.)

The magnetic float compass has many quirks, but once you understand them, it can be a valuable aid. One thing to remember—the mag compass "runs" on its own power and doesn't need electricity or suction to operate. This feature may be important to you some day when your other more expensive direction indicators have failed.

■ **Remote Indicating Compass** A more sophisticated and expensive type of directional indicator is the remote indicating compass. The transmitter or magnetic "brain" of the assembly is usually located at a position well away from disturbing elements of iron or electrical leaks—often in or near one of the wing tips.

The transmitter is electrically connected through an amplifier to the indicator on the instrument panel. Figure 2-14 shows some components. This one is connected or synchronized to a gyro for damping the oscillations, in which case they are called magnetic slaved gyro compasses. The magnetic compass is continually correcting the precession of the gyro automatically instead of the pilot manually resetting the heading indicator by reference to the float compass during the flight.

Note that the system in Figure 2-14 has a selector by which the system can either be a slaved or a free gyro. (Near the magnetic poles the magnetic compass has large errors, so the free gyro selection is best in those areas.) The slaving rate (when a slaved compass is selected) may be in the order of 2°/min, and a synchronizing knob can be used to reset the indicating hand for large deviations such as might exist when the equipment is turned on for the flight (Fig. 2-14).

There are several different designs of this type of compass gyro, and the basic characteristics were covered in a general manner here. You should make it a point to become familiar with the advantages and limitations of this instrument if your plane is, or becomes, so equipped.

You could get in trouble if you rely too much on the slaved compass and don't check it against the wet compass often. If the checks show that the slaved compass has failed, you'll have to use normal nonslaved techniques.

GYRO FLIGHT INSTRUMENTS

■ **Principles of Operation** The gyro instruments depend on two main properties of the gyroscope for operation: "rigidity in space" and "precession." Once spinning, the gyroscope resists any effort to tilt its axis (or plane of rotation). The attitude indicator and heading indicator operate on this principle. If a force is exerted to try to change the plane of rotation of a rotating gyro wheel, the gyro resists. If the force is insistent, the gyro reacts as if the force had been exerted at a point 90° around the wheel (in the direction of rotation). Precession is the property used in the operation of the needle of the turn and slip indicator (or needle and ball as you may call it) (Fig. 2-15).

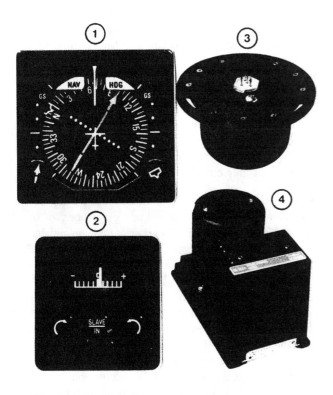

Fig. 2-14. Slaved compass system.

(1) The pictorial navigation indicator here is the panel display for the slaved system (which only affects the heading indicator function). The contrasting colors of the indicators aren't seen here.

(2) The slaving control and compensator is panel mounted and the pilot can select either the slaved or free gyro modes. The meter indicates when the system is being slaved.

(3) The magnetic slaving transmitter (remote mounted).

(4) The gyro stabilization unit containing the slaving circuitry (remote mounted). (*Bendix-King*)

■ **Vacuum-Driven Instruments** For the less expensive airplanes, the gyro instruments are usually vacuum-driven, either by an engine-driven pump or a venturi system. A disadvantage of the venturi system is that its efficiency depends on airspeed, and the venturi tube itself causes slight aerodynamic drag. Although a venturi system can be installed on nearly any airplane in a short while, the engine-driven vacuum or pressure pump is best for actual instrument operations, since it starts operating as soon as the engine(s) start. Multiengine airplanes have a vacuum pump on each engine so that the vacuum- or pressure-driven instruments will still operate in the event of an engine failure. Each pump has the capacity to carry the system. The multiengine airplane will have either a manual or automatic means to select each power source and a means to indicate the power being supplied by each source. The failure of an instrument or energy supply from one source will not interfere with the operations of the other instruments or source (FAR 23.1331).

The vacuum- or pressure-driven gyro instruments usually operate at a suction of 4.5–5.2 in. of mercury (29.92 in. of mercury is standard sea level pressure). The 4.5–5.2 in. of mercury shows a *relative* difference between the outside air pressure and the air in the vacuum system. The operating limits for the attitude and heading indicators are normally from a suction of 3.8–4.2 in. of mercury, whereas the vacuum-driven turn and slip uses a suction of 1.8–2.1 or 4.6–5.2 in. of mercury. The automatic pilot may use one or more of the panel gyros as its "brain" and the usual requirement is for a higher suction. Although the earlier suction figures probably will apply, check for the normal values for your particular airplane and equipment.

Errors in the instruments may arise as they age and bearings become worn or as the air filters get clogged with dirt. Low suction means low rpm and a loss in efficiency of operation. One of the greatest enemies of the vacuum-driven gyro instruments is tobacco smoke. The gum resulting from

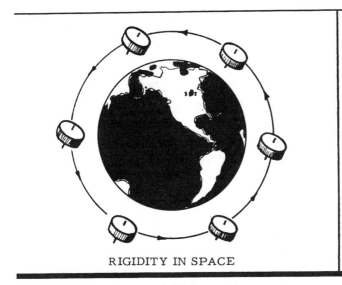

RIGIDITY IN SPACE

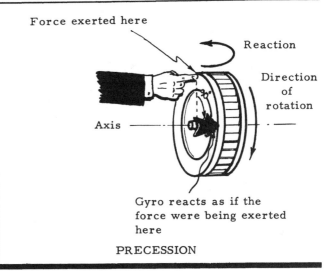

Force exerted here

Reaction

Direction of rotation

Axis

Gyro reacts as if the force were being exerted here

PRECESSION

Fig. 2-15. Rigidity in space and precession are the two principles used in operation of gyro instruments.

smoking in the cabin over a period of time can cause filter(s) and operational problems.

Figure 2-16 shows a normal (A) and a standby (B) vacuum system installation for a particular airplane. The standby system should be checked during the preflight inspection of the first flight of the day and/or when IFR flight is anticipated. Note that the standby pump is electrically driven. It's checked by turning the master switch ON, turning the standby switch ON, checking the suction gauge for 4.5–5.2 in. of mercury, and noting that the low-vacuum warning light is OFF. (Secure the master and pump switches after this check.) There may be a small compass deviation existing anytime the standby vacuum pump is operating.

Figure 2-17 shows some electrically operated gyro instruments. Note that each has a warning flag to indicate loss of power (arrows).

■ **Electrically Driven Instruments** The electrically driven gyro instruments got their start when high-performance aircraft such as jets began to operate at very high altitudes. The vacuum-driven instruments lost much of their efficiency in the thin air, and a different source of power was needed.

Below 30,000 ft, either type of gyro performs equally well. It is common practice to use a combination of electrically and vacuum-driven instruments for safety's sake if one

type of power source should fail. A typical gyro instrument group for a single-pilot airplane would probably include a vacuum-driven attitude indicator and heading indicator and an electric turn and slip or turn coordinator. Large airplanes have two complete sets of flight instruments, one set of vacuum-driven gyros and the other set electrically driven.

Many of the newer attitude indicators will not tumble, and aerobatics such as loops, rolls, etc., may be done by reference to the instrument. (Also see Fig. 2-19.) This writer teaches rolls and loops using the attitude indicator (and airspeed) and spin recoveries using the turn and slip.

■ **Attitude Indicator** The attitude indicator or gyro horizon (or artificial horizon or attitude gyro) operates on the "rigidity in space" principle and is an attitude instrument. The plane of rotation of the gyro wheel is horizontal and maintains this position, with the airplane (and instrument case) being moved about it (Fig. 2-18).

Attached to the gyro is a face with a contrasting horizon line on it. When the instrument is operating correctly, this line will always represent the actual horizon. A miniature airplane attached to the case moves with respect to this artificial horizon precisely as the real airplane moves with respect to the real horizon. A knob allows you to move the miniature airplane up or down to compensate for small deviations in the horizontal line position.

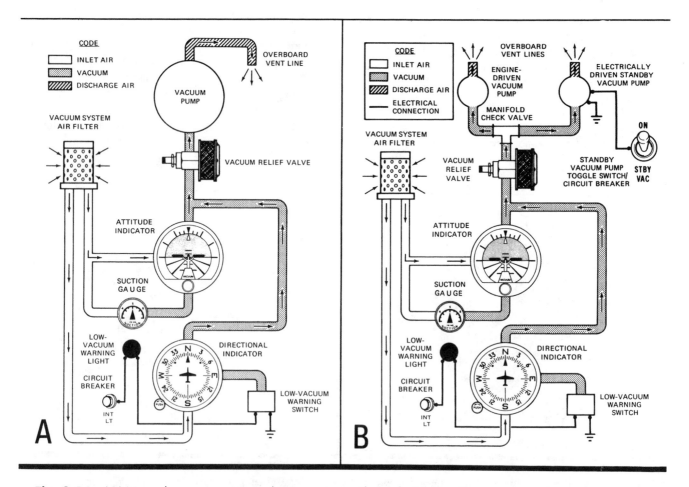

Fig. 2-16. **(A)** Normal vacuum system and **(B)** a system with an electric standby vacuum pump.

ATTITUDE GYRO
510 Series

ATTITUDE GYRO
500E(ECF)

DIRECTIONAL GYRO
200DC

ATTITUDE GYRO
500DCF

Fig. 2-17. Electrically operated attitude and directional gyros. Note warning flags (arrows). (*Castleberry Instruments and Avionics*)

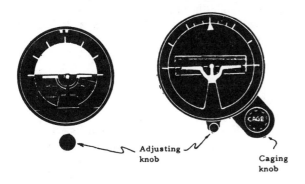

Fig. 2-18. Two types of attitude indicators. The one on the right is an older type of instrument.

Fig. 2-19. Air-operated attitude gyro with roll and 360° pitch capabilities. Note the warning flag, unusual for air-driven attitude indicators. (*Sigma-Tek*).

Figure 2-19 is an air-operated attitude indicator (4.5–5.2 in. of mercury differential pressure).

There are limits of operation on the less expensive vacuum-driven attitude indicators, and these are, in most cases, 70° of pitch (nose up or down) and 100° of bank. The gyro will "tumble" above these limit stops and will give false information when forced from its rotational plane. The instrument also will give false information during the several minutes required for it to return to the normal position after resuming straight and level flight.

"Caging" is done with a knob located on the front of the instrument. Because it is possible to damage the instrument through repeated tumbling, this caging is a must before you do deliberate aerobatics. The caging knob is useful also for quickly resetting the attitude indicator if it has tumbled. Some attitude indicators have caging knobs, some don't. The caging knobs are often removed by the aircraft manufacturer for various reasons, and if the instrument has tumbled, several minutes of straight and level flight may be required to let it erect itself again. While the chances are slim of getting into an attitude resulting in tumbling of the instrument,

you would be wise to do at least one of the following: (1) install a nontumbling attitude indicator in your airplane, (2) install a caging knob in the old type of attitude indicator if it doesn't have one, or (3) maintain proficiency in flying the turn and slip indicator or turn coordinator.

This instrument allows the pilot to get an immediate picture of the plane's attitude. It can be used to establish a standard-rate turn if necessary, as can be shown.

A good rule of thumb to find the amount of bank needed for a standard-rate turn at various airspeeds is to divide airspeed in knots by 10 and add one-half of the answer. For 130 knots (150 mph), the angle of bank required is:

$$\frac{130}{10} = 13 + (\text{one-half of } 13) = 13 + 6.5 = 19.5°$$

of bank required (call it 20°).

Keep an eye on the actions of your attitude gyro day by day as you fly it. If it's wobbling, slow to erect itself, or has excessive errors, don't use it for IFR work.

■ **Heading Indicator** The heading indicator functions because of the principle of "rigidity in space" as did the gyro horizon. In this case, however, the plane of rotation is vertical. The heading indicator has a compass card or azimuth scale that is attached to the gyro gimbal and wheel. The wheel and card are "fixed" by the gyro action, and as in the case of the magnetic compass, the airplane turns around them (Fig. 2-20).

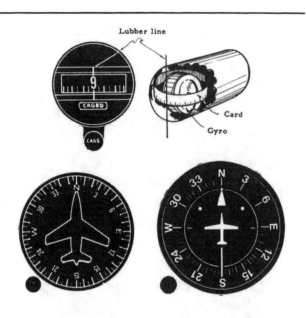

Fig. 2-20. Types of heading indicator presentations. The older type is at the top of the illustration.

The heading indicator has no magnet that causes it to "point" to the Magnetic North Pole and must be set to the heading indicated by the magnetic compass. The heading indicator should be set when the magnetic compass is reading correctly. This is generally done in straight and level flight when the magnetic compass has "settled down."

It's *very* important that you set the heading indicator (or directional gyro) with the magnetic compass before taking off on an IFR flight. Figure 2-21 shows how a heading indicator might be set during the pretakeoff check at the end of the runway. *Take a good look at it.*

The advantage of the heading indicator is that it does not oscillate in rough weather and gives a true reading during turns when the magnetic compass is erratic. A setting

Fig. 2-21. Set the heading indicator to the magnetic compass before takeoff (and during the flight too). There's a problem here; sometimes you'll subconsciously tend to "match" the relative positions of the compass lubber line and the heading indicator pointer and get a wrong setting (the compass indicates 100° and the heading indicator shows 080°). The 20° error here could cause significant confusion after lift-off. The best procedure is to state to yourself the compass indication and state it again as you set the heading indicator.

knob is used to cage the instrument for aerobatics and to get the proper heading.

A disadvantage of the older types of heading indicators is that they tumble when the limits of 55° nose up or down or 55° bank are exceeded. Although, if you happen to be maneuvering (pitching or rolling) parallel to the plane of rotation of the gyro wheel, this limitation does not apply. For instance, on some heading indicators, the plane of rotation of the gyro is in the 090°–270° line through the card. The airplane could be looped starting at a heading of 090° or 270° without tumbling. Other makes have the plane of rotation on the 180°–360° line through the instrument card, and the rule just cited would be in reverse. You shouldn't be doing such actions, but it's an interesting note.

The heading indicator creeps and must be reset with the magnetic compass about every 15 min. (Maximum allowable creep is 3° in 15 min.)

More expensive gyros are connected with a magnetic compass in such a way that this creep is automatically compensated for as noted earlier (slaved gyros).

The greatest advantage of the "plain" heading indicator is that it allows you to turn directly to a heading without the allowance for lead or lag necessary with a magnetic float compass, but it doesn't have a brain and you must set it by that compass.

Figure 2-22 shows examples of air-driven heading indicators.

■ **Turn and Slip Indicator** The turn and slip indicator is actually two instruments. The slip indicator is merely a

A   B   C

Fig. 2-22. Different types of heading indicators (directional gyros).

  (A) Heading indicator with an airline-style face (4.5–5.2 in. of mercury).

  (B) Popular general aviation presentation (4.5–5.2 in. of mercury).

  (C) Horizontal situation indicator, which combines a heading indicator with VOR and/or ILS information. More about this in Chapter 5. (*Castleberry Instruments and Avionics*)

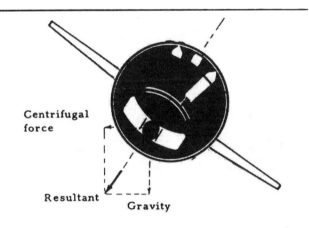

Fig. 2-23. The ball in the turn and slip is kept centered in a balanced turn by the forces acting upon it.

liquid-filled, curved glass tube containing an agate or steel ball. The liquid acts as a shock damper. In a balanced turn, the ball will remain in the center as centrifugal force offsets the pull of gravity (Fig. 2-23).

In a slip there is not enough rate of turn for the amount of bank. The centrifugal force will be weak, and this imbalance will be shown by the ball's falling down toward the inside of the turn.

The skid is a condition in which there is too high a rate of turn for the amount of bank. The centrifugal force is too strong, and this is indicated by the ball sliding toward the outside of the turn. Usually, a turn in an airplane is considered to be balanced if more than one-half the ball is within the indicator marks.

The turn part of the turn and slip indicator, or "needle" as it is called, uses precession to indicate the direction and approximate rate of turn of the airplane.

Older turn and slip indicators are calibrated so that a "standard-rate turn," of 3°/sec will be indicated by the needle being off center by one needle width. This means that, by setting up a standard-rate turn, it is possible to roll out on a predetermined heading by the use of a watch or clock. It requires 120 sec or 2 min to complete a 360° turn. The latest types of turn and slip indicators are calibrated so that a double needle-width indication indicates a standard-rate turn.

If your heading is 030° and you want to roll out on a heading of 180°, first decide which way you should turn (to the right in this case). The amount to be turned is 180° – 030° = 150°. The number of seconds required at standard rate is 150 ÷ 3 = 50. If you set up a standard-rate turn and hold it for 50 sec and roll out until the needle and ball are centered, the heading should be very close to 180°.

One thing often brought up in the written test for the instrument rating (and missed) is that the needle deflection tells whether the turn is standard rate or not and the ball has nothing to do with it. If the needle is deflected the proper amount for a standard-rate turn, the nose of the airplane is moving around at a rate of 3°/sec. The turn may be slipping, skidding, or balanced. The ball indicates the *quality* of the turn. Figure 2-24 shows three variations of an airplane making a standard-rate turn to the right. The airspeeds are the same (130 knots) in each case, requiring a 20° bank for a *balanced* standard-rate turn.

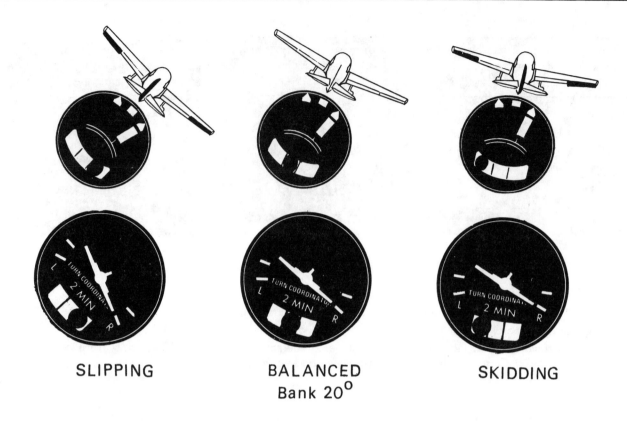

SLIPPING   BALANCED   SKIDDING
                  Bank 20°

Fig. 2-24. The needle in the turn and slip or the small airplane in the turn coordinator indicates the rate at which the nose is moving; the ball indicates the quality of the turn.

The advantage of the turn and slip over other gyro instruments is that it does not "tumble" or become erratic as certain bank and pitch limits are exceeded.

A disadvantage of the turn and slip is that it is a rate instrument, and a certain amount of training is required before the pilot is able to quickly transfer the indications of the instrument into a visual picture of the airplane's attitudes and actions.

The gyro of the turn and slip, like the other gyro instruments, may be driven electrically or by air, using an engine-driven vacuum pump or an outside-mounted venturi.

An interesting note is that the turn and slip becomes less accurate as the bank increases. For instance, in a level turn at a 90° bank (if you could hold it), the needle should *theoretically* come back to the center after the turn is established, indicating that the airplane is not turning at all. (You are doing a loop in a horizontal plane.)

TURN COORDINATOR. The turn coordinator is used in some airplanes to replace the turn and slip. The wheel reacts to precession around an axis that is tilted 30° upward compared to the turn and slip. Once the roll is stopped (the bank is established), the yaw rate is indicated. Figure 2-25 compares the face presentations and theory of operations of the turn and slip indicator and the turn coordinator.

■ **Outside Air Temperature Gauge (OAT)** The OAT falls into a category of its own, but it is very important for instrument flying and should be covered as such.

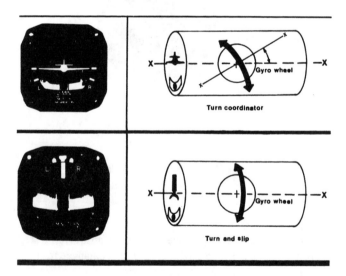

Fig. 2-25. Electric turn coordinator and turn and slip showing gyro wheel arrangements.

The OAT (or free-air thermometer) will assume much greater importance now that you'll be flying IFR. Whereas previously the OAT has been mostly a matter of curiosity, it will now be a matter of vital interest in the temperature range where icing may occur. The usual type of thermometer used is that of the bimetal direct reading type. The fact that two dissimilar metals have different expansion (or contraction) rates with temperature change makes possible a comparatively simple method of registering this change.

The two strips of metal are welded together in the form of a coil spring. One end is anchored, and the other is attached to an indicating hand. The thermometer may read in Celsius or Fahrenheit and is marked in both scales for most instruments. The probe or pickup is in the free airstream, and the dial faces into the cockpit for ready reference. (The instrument is normally at a corner or at the top of the windshield.)

Because of errors in the individual instrument and effects in location (it *should* register the exact ambient or true temperature of the air), you should look for the possibilities of structural icing when in visible moisture and the temperature is down to within a few degrees of freezing.

Figure 2-26 is a correction chart for the outside air temperature gauge for a particular airplane.

ENGINE INSTRUMENTS

■ **Tachometer** The centrifugal tachometer operates on the same principle as a car speedometer. One end of a flexible shaft is connected to the engine crankshaft and the other is connected to a shaft with counterweights within the instrument. The rate of turning of the crankshaft (and cable) causes expansion of the counterweight system. The instrument hand is mechanically linked to the counterweight assembly so that the engine speed is indicated in rpm.

For direct-drive engines, the engine and propeller rpm are the same (Lycoming 0–320, 0–540, 0–360). The geared engine (Lycoming GO–480, etc.) has different engine and propeller speeds, and this is noted in the *Airplane Flight Manual* (the propeller rpm is less than the engine rpm). The tachometer measures *engine* rpm, and this is the basis for your power setting.

Another type of tachometer is the magnetic, which utilizes a flexible shaft that turns a magnet within a special collar in the instrument. The balance between the magnetic force and a hairspring is indicated as rpm by a hand on the instrument face. This type of tachometer does not oscillate as sometimes happens with the less expensive centrifugal type.

A third type is the electric tachometer, which depends on a generator unit driven by a tachometer drive shaft. The generator is wired to an electric motor unit of the indicator, which rotates at the same rpm and transmits this through a magnetic tachometer unit that registers the speed in rpm. This type of tachometer is also smoother than the centrifugal type. (It doesn't depend on the electrical system of the airplane.)

■ **Manifold Pressure Gauge** For airplanes with controllable pitch propellers (which includes constant-speed propellers), this instrument is used in combination with the tachometer to set up desired power from the engine. The

TEMPERATURE RISE DUE TO RAM RECOVERY

NOTE:
1. Subtract temperature rise from indicated outside air temperature to obtain true outside air temperature

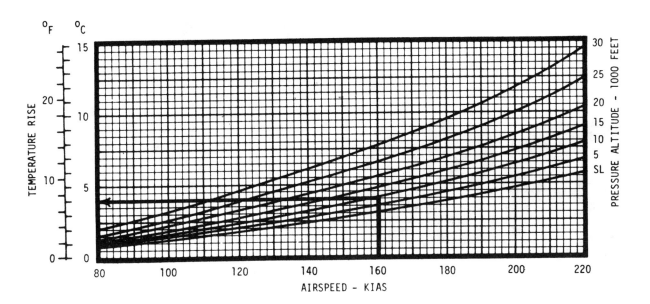

Fig. 2-26. Ram recovery temperature rise chart for a particular airplane. At 160K and 10,000 feet, you would subtract 4°C or 7°F from the indicated OAT. *(Advanced Pilot's Flight Manual)*

manifold pressure gauge measures absolute pressure of the fuel-air mixture going to the cylinders and indicates this in inches of mercury.

The manifold pressure gauge is an aneroid barometer like the altimeter, but instead of measuring the outside air pressure, it measures the air or fuel and air pressure in the intake manifold. When the engine is not running, the outside air pressure and the pressure in the intake manifold are the same, so that the manifold pressure gauge will indicate the outside air pressure as a barometer would. At sea level on a standard day, this would be 29.92 in. of mercury, but you can't read the manifold gauge this closely, and it would appear as approximately 30 in.

You start the engine with the throttle cracked or closed. This means that the throttle valve or butterfly valve is nearly shut. The engine is a strong air pump in that it takes in fuel and air and discharges residual gases and air. At closed or cracked throttle setting, the engine is pulling air (and fuel) past the nearly closed throttle valve at such a rate that a decided drop in pressure is found in the intake manifold and is duly registered by the manifold pressure gauge. As the engine starts, the indication of 30 in. drops rapidly to 10 in. or less at idle. It will never reach an actual zero, since this would mean a complete vacuum in the manifold (most manifold pressure gauges don't even have indications of less than 10 in. of mercury). Besides, if you tried to shut off all air (and fuel) completely, the engine would quit running.

As you open the throttle, you are allowing more and more fuel and air to enter the engine, and the manifold pressure increases accordingly.

The unsupercharged engine will never indicate the full outside pressure on the manifold gauge in the static condition. The usual difference is 1–2 in. of mercury. The maximum indication on the manifold pressure gauge you could expect to get would be 28–29 in. Ram effect may raise the manifold pressure because of "packing" of the air in the intake at higher speeds.

Figure 2-27 shows manifold pressure gauges for a single-engine (A) and a twin-engine (B) airplane.

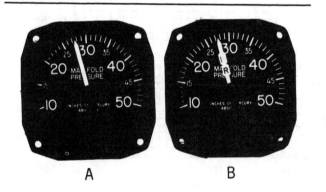

Fig. 2-27. Manifold pressure gauges. *(Sigma-Tek)*

■ **Oil Pressure Gauge** The oil pressure gauge consists of a curved Bourdon tube with a mechanical linkage to the indicating hand, which registers the pressure in pounds per square inch (Fig. 2-28). As shown, oil pressure tends to straighten the tube, and the appropriate oil pressure indication is registered. This is the direct pressure type of gauge.

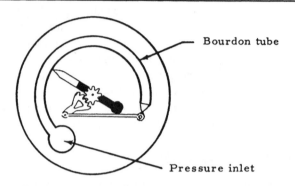

Fig. 2-28. The oil pressure gauge.

Another type of oil pressure gauge uses a unit containing a flexible diaphragm, which separates the engine oil from a nonflammable fluid that fills the line from the unit into the Bourdon tube. The oil pressure is transmitted through the diaphragm and to the Bourdon tube by this liquid because liquids are incompressible.

■ **Oil Temperature Gauge** The vapor type of oil temperature gauge is the most common in use. This instrument, like the oil pressure gauge, contains a Bourdon tube connected by a fine tube to a metal bulb containing a volatile liquid. Vapor expansion due to increased temperature exerts pressure, which is indicated as temperature on the instrument face.

Other types of oil temperature gauges may use a thermocouple rather than a Bourdon tube.

■ **Cylinder Head Temperature Gauge** The cylinder head temperature gauge is an important instrument for engines of higher compression and/or power. Engine cooling is a major problem in the design of a new airplane. Much flight testing and cowl modification may be required before satisfactory cooling is found for all airspeeds and power settings. The engineers are faced with the problem of keeping the engine within efficient operating limits for all air temperatures.

The cylinder head temperature gauge usually warns of any possible damage to the engine long before the oil temperature gauge gives any such indication.

The "hottest" cylinder, which is usually (though not always) one of the rear ones in the horizontally opposed engine, is chosen during the flight testing of the airplane. A thermocouple lead replaces one of the spark plug washers on this cylinder.

The cylinder head temperature gauge uses the principle of the galvanometer. Two metals of different electrical potentials are in contact at the lead. Since the electric currents of these two metals vary with temperature, a means is established for indicating the temperature at the cylinder through electric cables to a galvanometer (cylinder head temperature gauge), which indicates temperature rather than electrical units.

Exhaust gas temperature gauges have been designed to monitor engine performance and fuel-air ratio. The usual procedure for the operation of these instruments is to use a probe in the exhaust to measure the temperature of the exhaust gases. When the mixture is leaned from full rich, the exhaust temperature will increase peak, and then decrease with further leaning. The idea is to get the mixture to the fuel-air ratio for continuous operation and also have an indication for the best mixture for takeoff and climb under different situations, such as taking off at a high density-altitude, climb, etc.

Read the *EGT Manual* or the *Pilot's Operating Handbook* for your airplane, since procedures may vary between engine and/or airframe manufacturers.

■ **Fuel Gauge** The electric transmitter type of fuel gauge may be considered to have the following components: (1) the float and arm; (2) the rheostat type of control; and (3) the indicator, a voltmeter indicating fuel either in fractions or in gallons. The float and arm are attached to the rheostat, which is connected by wires to the fuel gauge. As the float level in the tank (or tanks) varies, the rheostat is rotated, changing the electrical resistance in the circuit, which changes the fuel gauge indication accordingly. This is the most popular type of fuel measuring system for airplanes with electrical systems.

Fuel gauges of any type are not always accurate, and it is best not to depend on them completely (if at all). A good visual check before the flight and keeping up with the time on each tank (knowing your fuel consumption) are the best policies. Making frequent checks on the fuel gauge as a cross-reference is a good idea; the sudden dropping of the fuel-level indication may be caused by a serious fuel leak, and you'd like to know about this (particularly when IFR).

■ **Clock** The clock is a required instrument for IFR work and will be used on every flight. As simple as it seems, you should know whether it's electrical or windup, for instance. The clock will gain great significance for you during your instrument flight training.

A clock with a sweep-second hand and a digital timer are shown in Figure 2-29. (They were stuck in here to see if you're really reading this.) Again, the clock is more important to instrument flying than first supposed. It's a fuel gauge (time versus consumption), a navigation instrument (time versus estimated groundspeed), and a must for nonprecision approaches (and lost communications procedures). It's as important as any other flight instrument. On all flights be sure that the clock works and is set to the

Fig. 2-29. Two handy items for IFR work. There's the story of a VIP (nonpilot) who, on an airline flight, was invited up to the cockpit as a gesture of good will. Seeing (to him) thousands of dials, he knew he should express interest and ask a question about one or more of the instruments. Pointing to one dial at random, he asked its function. The captain replied that that item was the clock, causing several people a great deal of embarrassment. (The VIP gambled and lost.) There can be times, you'll find, when the clock is about the most important instrument in the cockpit.

proper time before takeoff. (Have a good watch as a backup, also.)

A LOOK AT SOME AIRPLANE SYSTEMS

This section is intended to be a checklist to bring to your mind some items of interest not only for the instrument rating flight test but also in regard to your actual instrument flying later. To cover the theory and operation of each system in detail is impossible—and the *Pilot's Operating Handbook* or operating instructions on the particular type or make of equipment will cover the operations procedures in detail.

■ **Electrical System** The system discussed here is the battery-generator (older airplanes) or battery-alternator combination, which is important even in VFR conditions (for instance, loss of cockpit and instrument lighting at night can be extremely serious), but when you are flying in actual instrument conditions, electrical failure could result in a fatal accident. It's your job to know just what equipment depends on this system and what your actions should be in case of trouble. Look at Figure 2-30.

The battery stores electrical energy, and the alternator creates current and replenishes the battery as necessary,

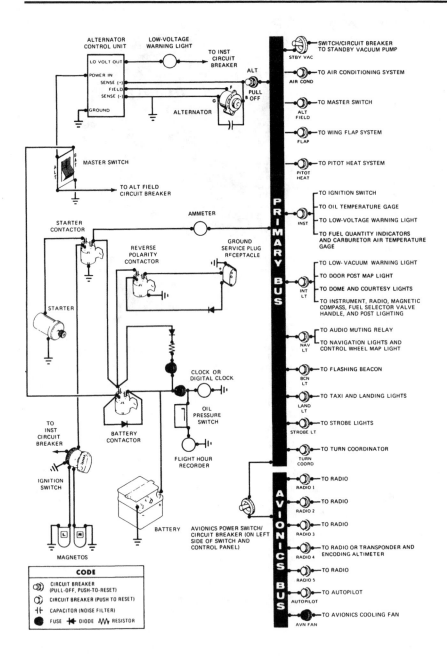

Fig. 2-30. A 28-volt electrical system. The system is powered by a belt-driven, 60-amp alternator and a 24-volt battery.

item causing the problem. These may be pushed back in the panel to reestablish current flow. It's best to allow a couple of minutes for cooling before doing this. Continual popping of a circuit breaker means a problem; and corrective action (electrical equipment check by an expert) should be taken in this case. Some pilots figure that the third time in a row that a circuit breaker pops out is just cause for leaving it out. To *hold* a circuit breaker in is to ask for strange smells, a smoky cabin, and increased adrenalin flow in the occupants of the airplane.

It would be well for you to know what equipment is protected by circuit breakers and where all of them are located. (Generally, they'll be in one area on the instrument panel or side panel, but there may be one or two scattered at random spots in the cabin.) Some pilots memorize the exact location of each circuit breaker for quick reference, but the main thing to know is that such and such an item has a circuit breaker and check (by looking at the circuit breaker panel) for a popped breaker if this equipment should suddenly fall down on the job. Some circuit breakers can be pulled out to shut off a circuit if an overload is suspected or the pilot wants that item out of operation *for* some reason. Very few VFR pilots stop to consider that they could overload some systems by turning everything electrical on at the same time.

Talk to some of the local electronic and electrical system pros to get some pointers on your particular equipment. It's better to know the system *now* and to know where a circuit breaker is located than to have to learn the hard facts when smoke starts easing out from under the instrument panel—and you're on solid IFR.

Figure 2-31 shows the two major types of ammeters in use by general aviation aircraft with normal and abnormal indications.

The ammeter on the left is the type found in some Cessnas and other airplanes. The normal indication is (A) and you should check for this throughout any flight, but it's infinitely more important during IFR operations. When the engine is operating and the master switch is ON, the ammeter indicates the charging rate applied to the battery.

Point (B) indicates that the alternator is *not* functioning or that the electrical load is exceeding the output of the alternator and the ammeter is indicating the battery discharge rate. This will be attended by a low-voltage light indication.

Point (C) shows that overcharging is occurring. This is acceptable during the initial part of the flight (particularly after starting or a long session of low engine speeds such as

directed by the voltage regulator (or alternator control unit), which is the "automatic valve" to ensure proper current flow to the battery. A master switch is provided to close the circuit or "energize" the electrical system. For older light twins, a paralleling relay is installed so that the two generators are carrying an equal share of the load. The generators may each have a switch to take them out of the system and for checking purposes before takeoff. Light twins using alternators (the vast majority) do not require a paralleling relay.

Circuit breakers or fuses are installed to ensure that the various circuits are not overloaded, with a resulting overheating and possible electrical fire. The circuit breakers "pop" out when an overload occurs and break the connection between the battery-alternator/generator system and the

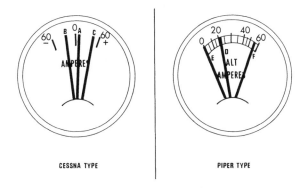

Fig. 2-31. Two types of ammeters (or loadmeter). (A) and (D) are normal indications. The others are explained in the text.

extended taxiing), but after 30 min of flight, the ammeter should be indicating less than two needle widths of charging current. If the charging rate continued at this value on a long flight, the battery would overheat and evaporate the electrolyte at an excessive rate.

The right half of Figure 2-31 shows a type of ammeter found in some Pipers and other aircraft.

Point (D) would be an expected normal value for most electrical loads. (Find out what you can expect of different loads for *your* instrument flying requirements.) This ammeter shows in amperes the load placed on the alternator. (It doesn't indicate battery discharge.) With all electrical equipment off (except the master switch) the ammeter will be indicating the amount of charging current demanded by the battery. As each item of electrical equipment is turned on, the current will increase to a total indicated on the ammeter. (This total includes the battery.) For one particular airplane, the average continuous load for night flight, with radios on, is about 30 amps. This value, plus approximately 2 amps for a fully charged battery, will appear continuously under these conditions.

The indication at (E) shows a zero reading, indicating that the alternator has failed. You would check that the reading is really zero and not merely low by actuating electrical equipment such as a landing light. If there is no increase in the ammeter reading, you can assume that the alternator has failed. (Don't leave the landing light or other equipment on long, or the battery will be drained. See Fig. 2-32 for some ampere requirements for various equipment.)

An indication like (F) shows that there is an electrical overload existing. For one airplane, an ammeter reading of more than 20 amps above the known electrical load indicates an overload, and the procedures in the *Pilot's Operating Handbook* for such a condition should be followed.

Figure 2-32 is an electrical load analysis chart for a current four-place instrument trainer. The chart is included here to give some indication of the requirements of various electrical items.

■ **Deicing and Anti-Icing Equipment** You should be familiar with the operation of the deicing and anti-icing

ELECTRICAL LOAD ANALYSIS CHART

	AMPS
STANDARD EQUIPMENT (Running Load)	REQUIRED
Battery Contactor	0.5
Fuel Indicators	0.1
Flashing Beacon Light	6.0
Instrument Lights	0.7
Position Lights	2.5
Turn Coordinator	0.3

OPTIONAL EQUIPMENT (Running Load)	
Altitude Blind Encoder	0.1
Strobe Lights	3.0
ADF	1.0
Nav/Com	1.0*
	2.25**
Transponder	2.0
Glide Slope	0.5
Marker Beacon	0.1
Autopilot	2.5
Encoding Altimeter	0.1
Nav/Com (720 Channel)	2.9
DME	1.2
Pitot Heat	2.9
Post Lights	0.6
RNAV	0.65
Interphone System	†
Avionics Fan	1.0

ITEMS NOT CONSIDERED AS PART OF RUNNING LOAD	
Cigarette Lighter	7.0
Clock	†
Control Wheel Map Light	0.1
Courtesy & Dome Lights	1.2
Flap Motor	8.5
Landing and Taxi Lights	9.0 ea
Map Light (Door Post)	0.2
Air Conditioner (High Blower)	6.7
Ventilation System Blower	5.0
(High Speed)	

† Negligible
* 1.0 Receiving
** 2.25 Transmitting

Fig. 2-32. Electrical load analysis chart. The values given were picked for typical equipment in a four-place airplane. The equivalent items for *your* airplane may have slightly different electrical power requirements, but the main idea is to compare the various demands of different components. (For instance, compare the landing/taxi lights with the turn coordinator or ADF.)

equipment of any airplane you plan to use for actual instrument flight.

ELECTRIC PROP DEICERS. If the airplane has an electrical prop deicer(s), you should know the current drain while it is in use.

The *Airplane Flight Manual* or *Pilot's Operating Handbook* will have a Supplement attached to it explaining the operations and limitations of the equipment and will probably include such items as:

Description and operating principles—How the system operates and the order of the cycle of heat. Prop deicer systems are cycled, but the order of heating may differ.

On some aircraft the deicers on the blade of the propeller are heated simultaneously throughout the length of each deicer. On other systems the outboard section of the deicer on each blade of a propeller is heated in the same sequence, followed by heating of the inboard portion of the deicer on each blade.

Operating procedures—Normal procedures, such as how to turn the system on, what to watch for on the deicing system ammeter, and expected current requirements (for one light twin, operation of both prop deicers requires 22–26 amps, as noted in its Supplement). Some aircraft may have a timer/current monitor unit that eliminates the system ammeter.

Emergency procedures can include the steps to follow in the event of abnormal deicer ammeter indications and precautions such as turning off noncritical equipment in the event of excessive power requirements that might occur after the loss of one generator (or engine).

PNEUMATIC DEICING SYSTEMS. The light twin normally uses pneumatic "boots" for wing and tail leading edges (larger airplanes sometimes pipe hot air inside the leading edge of the wing). There is a great deal of discussion going on about the deicing of single-engine airplanes but not too much has been done, so the light twin is the airplane being discussed here.

This equipment will also have a Supplement to the *Pilot's Operating Handbook,* which will list such things as:

Preflight check—Physical examination of the boots and the check for normal operation. There may be such notes as, "Limit the preflight check to two cycles to reduce wear and premature failure of the vacuum pumps."

Normal operations—Included here will be such things as suggestions for operation in the various icing conditions and limits of operation.

Placards—A list of the placards or control panel markings for the equipment. Your airplane may have a placard such as "Deicers to be off during takeoff or landing." Others have no such limitation but note in the Supplement that an increase in stall speed may be expected when the deicers are in operation. This item will be discussed further in Chapter 7.

Emergency operations—The procedures to take if the timer (which controls the timing of the cycles or inflating of the various portions of the tubes) should fail. There probably will be tips for operation. (The newer lightweight systems, which operate off the engine-driven *pressure* pumps, are able to operate with only one pump; that is, the capacity of *each* pressure pump is such that it can carry the pressure-driven instruments and the pneumatic deicer system, if necessary.)

FLUID ANTI-ICING SYSTEMS. Some airplanes use fluid as a means of combating propeller ice. The fluid usually has an alcohol base with an additive to thicken it to prevent quick evaporation and excessive runoff.

The fluid is piped from a reservoir to the prop where it is distributed along the blades by centrifugal force. The pilot is able to regulate the rate of flow by a control in the cabin. If your airplane has such a system, your job will be to have a good idea of the capacity (and flow rate) of the fluid. You should also know how to replenish it and what type of fluid is to be used. (Part of your preflight check for actual IFR work will be to check the fluid level.)

Note that this is an anti-icing system, meaning that it's to be used more to prevent ice than to get rid of it after it has become well formed.

Read and know the instructions concerning the use of your particular equipment.

In Chapter 7 the anti-icing and deicing systems will be covered as they pertain to actual situations.

■ **Summary** To cover all the different makes and models of airplane equipment and systems is impossible. It is recommended that you write to the various airframe, engine, or equipment manufacturers listed at the end of this book for information. You should know the operation of the particular type of electrical system, radio, deicing, and other so-called auxiliary equipment in your airplane. For instance, in addition to the systems just covered, you probably will have to be able to operate an autopilot or oxygen system as you progress in your instrument flying.

To repeat, the time to learn the systems is while you are on the ground and before something happens in flight. Read the Supplements to the *Airplane Flight Manual* or *Pilot's Operating Handbook* and other material available from the manufacturer.

AIRPLANE PAPERS

This might seem a strange place to cover the airplane papers—in a chapter on instruments and systems—but the *Airplane Flight Manual* is closely tied in with flight limitations, instrument markings, and placards and should be covered with the rest of that type of information.

There are three documents that must be in the airplane at all times:

1. The *Airplane Flight Manual* (or equivalent information).
2. The Airworthiness Certificate.
3. The Certificate of Registration.

■ ***Pilot's Operating Handbook (POH)*** Starting with 1976 models, manufacturers are publishing a *POH* for their airplanes, which could be considered a combination *Owner's Handbook* and *Airplane Flight Manual.* One manufacturer is printing *POHs* for its older models as well.

The idea is to "put it all together" arranging day-to-day, normal operating procedures so that the material required in an *Airplane Flight Manual* makes for easier pilot use. Also, the *POHs* for all airplanes (12,500-lb maximum certificated weight is the top limit for now) are arranged in the same order for quick reference as needed, for instance:

Section 1—General information (weights, fuel and oil capacity, dimensions, etc.).

Section 2—Limitations (airspeed, powerplant, weight and center of gravity limits, maneuvering and flight load and other limits, and a listing of placards).

Section 3—Emergency procedures, with amplified procedures at the end of the section (engine failures, fire, icing, electrical problems, and landing with a flat main tire).

Section 4—Normal procedures (checklists for preflight, start, taxiing, and all other aspects of normal flight plus amplified procedures at the end of the section).

Section 5—Performance (takeoff, landing, and cruise plus stall speeds and other information).

Section 6—Weight and balance and equipment list.

Section 7—Airplane and systems descriptions.

Section 8—Handling, service, and maintenance.

Section 9—Supplements (optional systems description and operating procedures, such as for oxygen, radio, anti-icing or deicing, and autopilot systems).

Some of the models do not require that the *POH* be carried in the airplane at all times, but furnish separate information as required in an *Airplane Flight Manual* (this information must be in the airplane at all times). Other models require that the *POH* be carried in the airplane because it contains the information required for an *Airplane Flight Manual* by the FARs under which the airplane was certificated.

■ **Airworthiness Certificate** This document must be *displayed* so that it can be seen readily by the pilot and/or passengers. The airworthiness certificate will be valid indefinitely as long as the airplane is maintained in accordance with the FARs. This means that each aircraft must have had an annual inspection within the preceding 12 calendar months. If an aircraft is to be operated for hire, it must also have had an inspection within the last 100 hr of flight time—the inspection being in accordance with the FARs (and either done by or supervised by a certificated mechanic). One of the 100-hr inspections may be used as an annual inspection by following certain procedures and noting the fact in the aircraft and engine logs.

Some airplanes may use the *progressive inspection* in which the airplane is continuously inspected after the owner shows that he or she can provide proper personnel, procedures, and facilities for it. The purpose is to permit greater utilization of the aircraft. This type of inspection eliminates the need for annual and 100-hr inspections during the period this procedure is followed.

■ **Certificate of Registration** This document must be in the airplane and has such information as the owner's name and address, manufacturer, model, registration number, and manufacturer's serial number. When the airplane changes hands or the registration number is changed, a new certificate of registration must be obtained.

■ **Aircraft Radio Station License** This is not required by the Federal Communications Commission for any transmitting equipment on board for domestic flights.

■ **Logbooks** There must be a logbook for the airframe, each engine, and each propeller or rotor. Entries are made for maintenance, alterations, repair, and required inspections. The logbooks are required to be available for inspection by authorized persons and are usually kept in the the most logical place for this. Make sure the logs for your airplane are kept up-to-date.

REVIEW OF AIRPLANE PERFORMANCE, STABILITY, AND CONTROL

3

The airplane has four forces acting on it in flight: *weight, thrust, lift,* and *drag* (Fig. 3-1). As a neophyte instrument pilot, your job will be to see that these forces are balanced (or not balanced) to obtain the required performance. This will be done by your reference to the various instrument indications.

WEIGHT

The person who develops a device that can turn off the force of gravity as desired will soon be a multibillionaire and also put a lot of aerodynamicists out of work. The problem of keeping airplane weight down has probably caused

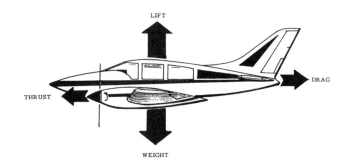

Fig. 3-1. The four forces.

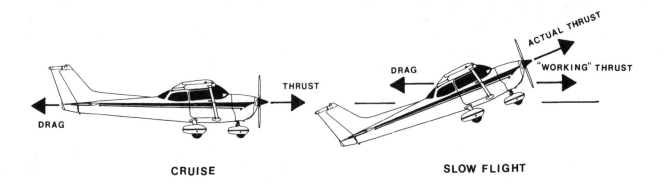

CRUISE   **SLOW FLIGHT**

Fig. 3-2. Thrust vectors at two flight regimes. The slow-flight attitude has been exaggerated. The "working" thrust component is that acting along the flight path. The vertical component of thrust makes the airplane "weigh" less and lowers the stall speed.

more grief in the aircraft industry than any other single factor. Suffice it to say that weight exists and is considered always to act downward toward the center of the earth—which means that, while the other three forces (lift, thrust, and drag) may operate in various directions as the plane is maneuvered, the direction of the weight vector remains constant.

Weight is considered to work through one point of the airplane—the center of gravity.

THRUST

Thrust is one of the four forces that acts on an airplane in flight and may be produced by a propeller, jet, or rocket. One of the statements often made in introducing the concept of the four forces is that thrust equals drag in straight and level, unaccelerated flight, but this actually depends on the attitude (speed) of the airplane. At slow speed near the stall in level flight and in climbs, thrust is greater than drag, as can be seen by analysis. Only under conditions where the thrust line is parallel to the line of flight is thrust actually equal to drag in straight and level flight.

Figure 3-2 shows the thrust vectors at high- and low-speed flight.

■ **Torque** The propeller airplane has the problem of "torque," which is a misnomer as far as the majority of the actual forces working on the airplane are concerned, but the term will be used here to cover the several forces or moments that tend to cause the nose to yaw left at high power settings and low speeds.

In instrument flying during the climb and at low speeds with power, beginners usually forget about this factor. They watch the airspeed, their white knuckles, or the wing attitudes and forget that such a thing as torque ever existed. They suddenly wake up to realize that the airplane has slipped about 60° off heading.

Torque is the result of several factors. The fact that the propeller is a rotating airfoil means that it is subject to stalls, induced drag (to be covered later), and the other problems associated with airfoils.

Slipstream effect—For the single-engine airplane the most important factor is that of the rotating slipstream.

In producing thrust, the propeller takes a comparatively large mass of air and accelerates it rearward, which results in the equal and opposite reaction of the airplane moving forward. This law was discovered by Isaac Newton (1642–1727) a couple of hundred years before the first airplane flew successfully. Because of the rotation of the propeller and its drag forces, a rotating motion is imparted to the air mass as it moves rearward from the prop. The rotating airstream exerts a force on the left side of the fin and rudder, which results in a left-yawing tendency. (If the airplane had a fin and rudder of equal size and position on the bottom, the *yawing* forces would tend to be balanced but would tend to roll, as shown in Figure 3-3.)

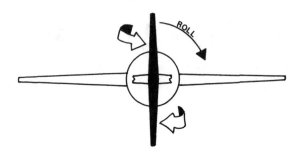

Fig. 3-3. Effects of a vertical fin on the *bottom* of the tail cone.

Of course, it's not all that simple; the varying shape of the fuselage and interference of the wings can affect the rotational path of the slipstream.

For the multiengine airplane with a single fin and rudder, the slipstream effect is not as critical a factor as found for the single-engine type. (You may have flown some of the tricycle-gear, light twins and noted that torque or left-turning tendency was not as strong on take-off as for some single-engine planes.) For twins with counterrotating propellers, the slipstream effect (and P factor) is totally balanced out.

The manufacturer may correct for this slipstream effect on the single-engine plane by one of two ways so that at cruise (the regime in which the airplane operates the majority of its flight time) the airplane does not tend to yaw to the left.

One method is to offset the fin so that at cruise it has a zero angle of attack in reference to the combination of slipstream and free-stream velocity; therefore, no yawing tendency will be present.

Some manufacturers "cant" the engine or offset the thrust line a few degrees, which results in the same effect of no yawing tendency at cruise. The airplanes you'll be using for instrument training will most likely have rudder trim, and it will assume added importance with speed changes while flying on the gauges.

Precession—Back in the discussion of the gyro instruments, precession was mentioned as the factor in operation of the turn and slip and turn coordinator instruments. Precession will affect the airplane only during a change of attitude and is not a factor in steady-state flight. Part of your training may include an ITO (instrument take-off), and precession could give you a little trouble in the tailwheel airplane if you try to raise the tail too quickly. The propeller arc acts like a gyro wheel and resists any tendency to change its plane of rotation.

As seen from the cockpit, the propeller is rotating clockwise. When the tail is raised, it is as if a force was exerted on the top of the propeller arc from behind. Because precession acts at a point 90° around the wheel (or propeller), the airplane acts as if a strong force was acting *from behind on the right side of the prop arc* (check Fig. 2-15 again). The result is a pronounced left-turning tendency; the more abruptly the tail is raised, the worse the effect. Precession in this case is additive to the other left-turning factors of torque, and control could be marginal for a few seconds. Because of its attitude, the tricycle-gear airplane doesn't normally have precession problems on takeoff.

Asymmetric disk loading or *P factor*—This is a situation usually encountered in the climb or during slow flight and results from the fact that the relative wind is not striking the propeller disk at exactly a 90° angle. This results in a difference in angle of attack between the two (or three) blades. The down-moving blade, which is on the right side as seen from the cockpit, has a higher angle of attack than "normal" and consequently higher thrust (A); whereas the opposite is the case for the up-moving (left side) blade. The result is a left-turning moment (B) (Fig. 3-4).

This effect can also be encountered in yaws (a left yaw would give a nose-down tendency, a right yaw, the opposite). P factor also is credited for the fact that the left engine of light twins is the worst engine to lose (or

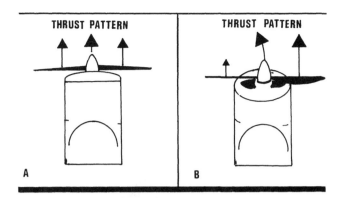

Fig. 3-4. Asymmetric disk loading (P factor) effects.

it is the *critical* engine). Perhaps it should be said, rather, that the left engine is the critical one for twins with both propellers turning clockwise (as seen from the cockpit), as Figure 3-5 shows. Many engineers and pilots think the role of P factor is overrated in establishing the critical engine and believe that slipstream effects are a major factor here also.

You may encounter the effects of asymmetric thrust when the airplane is sitting 90° to a relatively strong crosswind on the ground at a certain rpm. A roughness will be noted. (If you have a rough-running engine on the ground, you might check for the conditions just cited and turn the airplane.)

Equal and *opposite reaction*—This is the effect that comes closest to the term "torque" and is a factor in Newton's law, "For every action there is an equal and opposite reaction." However, the strength of this effect is overrated for airplanes of higher power loadings (or lower horsepower per pound of airplane weight). The airplane tends to rotate opposite to the propeller. This can be corrected by "wash-in" (higher angle of incidence) and higher drag on the left wing. For light, fabric-covered airplanes, this is normally a part of the rigging procedures before the airplane leaves the manufacturer. (Airplanes have bendable tabs on the aileron(s) or aileron trim tabs to do the job.) This rigging also can contribute *slightly* to a left-turning tendency.

These factors make up what pilots call torque. As an instrument trainee, you'll be surprised how smoothly it can sneak into the picture when everything else is going so well.

LIFT

Lift is made up of the following factors and has the equation:

$$\text{Lift} = C_L \frac{\varrho}{2} V^2 S \text{ or } L = C_L \times \frac{\varrho}{2} \times V^2 \times S$$

C_L = *coefficient of lift,* a dimensionless factor (not measured as pounds, feet, etc.) that increases in direct proportion to the angle of attack (which you will remember is the angle between the chord line of the airfoil and the relative wind) until the stall angle is reached. Check Figure 3-6.

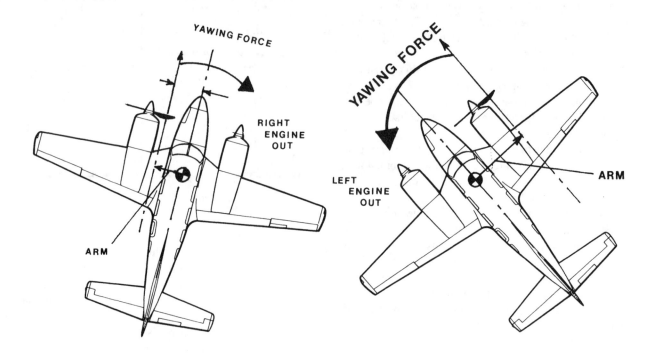

Fig. 3-5. The critical engine. Slipstream effect, as well as P factor, has an effect in establishing the critical engine.

Since lift is a combination of C_L and airspeed (plus the other factor of S, or wing area), the airplane with the airfoil and flap combination that has the greatest possible coefficient of lift (or C_{Lmax}) will be able to fly (or land) at a slower airspeed than another airplane of equal weight and wing area. Figure 3-6 shows the effect of flaps on coefficient of lift for a particular airfoil-flap combination.

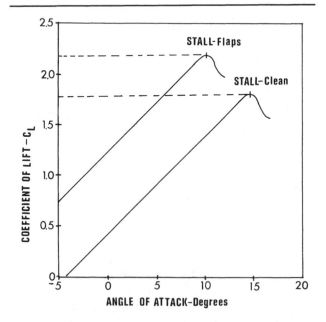

Fig. 3-6. Coefficient of lift versus angle of attack.

An expression often used concerning flaps is that they are designed to increase lift. The purpose and normal use of flaps is to *maintain the required lift at a lower airspeed,* or put more technically, it allows a greater C_{Lmax}, which means that the airplane can fly at a lower minimum speed. On the approach and landing, for instance, the forces acting perpendicular to the flight path are balanced as in the climb. With the flaps down on approach and landing, the "up" and "down" forces remain in equilibrium, which means a steeper approach path and slower landing speed. Only if positive g's are being exerted would lift be expected to be greater than weight.

$$\frac{\varrho}{2}V^2 = \text{the equation for } \textit{dyamic pressure}$$

which is called q by the engineers and is discussed in Chapter 2 in the section on the airspeed indicator. Dynamic pressure is measured by the airspeed indicator, but instead of being expressed in pounds per square foot, it is indicated as miles per hour or knots. The symbol ϱ is the air density in slugs per cubic foot. The slug is a unit of mass and is found by dividing the weight of an object (in pounds) by the acceleration of gravity, 32.2 fps/sec. At sea level the standard air density is 0.002378 slugs/ft^3.

The V^2 in the equation, you remember, is the *true* velocity of the air particles (squared), so that the dynamic pressure is a combination of one-half the air density times the true air velocity in feet per second (squared).

S = the *wing area* of the airplane in square feet. Lift is the least understood of the four forces acting on the airplane.

Contrary to popular belief, the pilot in normal unaccelerated flight (not pulling any g's) has little control over lift because, when the power and airspeed are set to obtain the required performance, lift automatically assumes the correct value.

The biggest fallacy is the belief that lift is greater than weight in a steady-state (normal) climb, and "excess lift is what makes the airplane go up." This is not the case at all. On the contrary, if we assume that lift is equal to weight in straight and level, unaccelerated flight, then lift must be *less* than weight in the climb.

Figure 3-7 shows the forces acting on an airplane in a steady-state climb; that is, the airplane is moving along a constant climb path at a constant speed. This means that the airplane and pilot are subjected to the normal 1 g. For such a condition to exist, the forces as measured perpendicular, or 90°, to the flight path must be in equilibrium. Since true weight, or gravity, always acts "downward" or toward the center of the earth, its direction never changes with changes in the airplane's attitude. Lift always acts perpendicular, or 90°, to the relative wind or flight path, and Figure 3-7 shows what must be happening to maintain the steady-state climb. The angle of attack required to provide the flight path shown is omitted here to avoid complication.

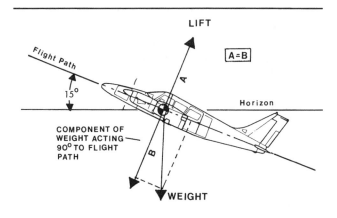

Fig. 3-7. A simplified look at the lift and weight forces acting on the airplane in a steady-state climb (attitude exaggerated).

As you can see, the lift force must *equal* the component of weight acting at 90° to the flight path and therefore must be less than total weight. The weight can be broken down into two vectors, one acting perpendicular and the other parallel and backward along the flight path. The thrust required to maintain the steady-state condition is equal to the "rearward" component of weight *plus* the aerodynamic drag developed at the climb speed. While thrust is not of prime importance in this discussion, it should be noted that for equilibrium to exist, the forces acting *parallel* to the flight path (which is the reference axis) must be in equilibrium as well as those acting perpendicular to it (lift and weight component).

If you are interested in the mathematics of the problem: Lift = weight × cos γ of the climb angle, or L = W cos γ.

Assuming (again) that lift equals weight in straight and level flight, an airplane weighing 3000 lb would require 2898 lb of lift to maintain a steady-state climb at a 15° angle to the horizon. (The cosine of 15° is 0.966.) Lift is 102 lb less than weight in such a condition. If lift isn't what makes the airplane climb, what does? *Power* does, and this is one of the things that must be remembered in instrument *flying—power plus attitude equals performance.* In wings-level flight it can also be said that power plus airspeed equals performance, but the first statement covers all possibilities better.

Suppose you are flying straight and level at cruise and decide to climb. At the point you *ease* the nose up, the angle of attack is increased without an instantaneous decrease in airspeed, and temporarily, lift *is* greater than weight; but only a very sensitive accelerometer, or g meter, would show that more than the normal 1 g is being pulled. If you made a very abrupt transition to the climb attitude, this would be quite evident. Your normal transition to the climb is slow enough so that the very small amount of added g is not noticeable.

As you increase the angle of attack and obtain this "excess" lift, drag increases also and the airplane starts slowing immediately, which has the effect of "decreasing" lift again. As you are maintaining a steady climb speed and attitude, lift must settle down to the proper value to balance the component of weight as shown in Figure 3-7. You are then back in 1-g flight.

A measure of g forces is the ratio of lift to weight. If the forces acting in the direction of lift are greater than weight, then positive g's are being pulled; if the forces acting in the direction of lift are less than weight and other forces acting "downward," negative g's result. The reason the phrase "forces acting in the direction of lift" was used is that other factors may be introduced (such as down forces on the tail, etc.).

DRAG

The total drag of an airplane is made up of a combination of two main types of drag—parasite and induced. Drag acts in an opposite direction to the direction of flight (Fig. 3-8).

■ **Parasite Drag** Parasite drag is not caused by just one factor but three:

Form drag—This is a result of the fact that a form (the airplane) is being moved through a fluid (air). A blunt object will naturally have more form drag than a streamlined one. Examples of added form drag are extended landing gear, antennas, etc. These objects will also have interference drag at their junctions with the airplane and skin friction drag.

Skin friction drag—This is a result of the air moving over the aircraft skin and is one argument for a waxed and clean airplane.

Interference drag—This is caused by aerodynamic interference and burbling between components and is found, for instance, at the junction of the wing and fuselage, stabilizer and fuselage, etc.

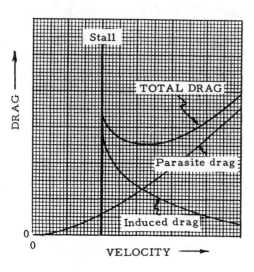

Fig. 3-8. Drag versus velocity curve.

Parasite drag increases with the square of the airspeed; double the airspeed, and parasite drag increases four times. Triple the airspeed, and parasite drag increases nine times. Naturally, parasite drag is greater for the gear-down configuration, and a lot of antennas sticking out can cost a few knots at cruise. (You have a choice between no radios or a few less knots, which isn't a choice at all for instrument flying.)

■ **Induced Drag** Induced drag is caused by the fact that the wing is creating lift. In creating lift, the relative air is deflected downward, and wing-tip vortices are formed that result in a drag force. As you can see in Figure 3-8, induced drag *increases* as the airplane flies slower and is greatest just at or above the stall. It's directly proportional to the square of the coefficient of lift, so that when flying at lower airspeeds induced drag may increase several times its original value. By decreasing the airspeed, the C_L required to

maintain a constant value of lift is increased, hence induced drag has increased. Slow flight with a high coefficient of lift with no flaps being used creates the worst wake turbulence, so keep this in mind when following a heavy airplane on an approach. The vortex strength also depends on the "span loading" or weight per foot of wingspan (Fig. 3-9).

POWER CURVE

■ **Force, Work, Power, Horsepower** Maybe it's been a few years since you had physics, so a quick and dirty review of the above terms might be in order.

A *force* is considered to be a pressure, tension, or weight. The fact that a force is being exerted doesn't mean that *work* is being done. You can press against a brick wall with great force all day and, from the viewpoint of physics, haven't done any work at all. (Tell this to those aching muscles.) *Work* is done when something moves. If you lift a 1100-lb weight to a height of 10 ft, you've done 11,000 foot-pounds (ft-lb) of *work*. Or you can raise an 11-lb weight 1000 ft and will also have done 11,000 ft-lb of *work*. Notice that nothing is said about time. You can do the job in 1 sec or 24 hr; the work done is the same. *Power* is a different matter; that's where *work per unit of time* comes in. If the 11,000 ft-lb of *work* is done in 1 sec, a great deal more *power* is used than if a full day was taken. The most familiar measurement of power is *horsepower* (hp), and this is established as 550 ft-lb of work being done in 1 sec, or 33,000 ft-lb of work/min. Then, to do 11,000 ft-lb of work in *1 sec* requires the developing of 20 hp for that period.

The type of horsepower most familiar to the pilot is that of *shaft* or *brake horsepower* (BHP)—that horsepower being developed as measured at the crankshaft by means of various devices such as a torque meter, dynamometer, or prony brake. (Wags have suggested that it should be called a "pony brake" as, after all, it's measuring *horsepower*.) BHP is used to set up power on the power chart because it is considered to be constant for all speed ranges. It is comparatively easy to measure as a combination of manifold

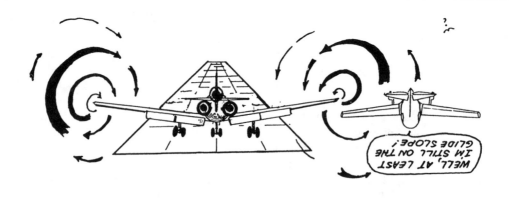

Fig. 3-9. Wing-tip vortices effects are most critical at low altitudes.

pressure and rpm. *Thrust horsepower* (THP) is a term of more interest to aeronautical engineers. THP is the horsepower being developed by a force (thrust) moving an object through the air at some rate (velocity).

$$THP = \frac{thrust\ (lb) \times velocity\ (fps)}{550}$$

If the propeller is exerting 1000 lb of thrust to move an airplane through the air at a constant 275 fps, the THP being developed is

$$\frac{1000 \times 275}{550} = 500\ THP$$

If you prefer to think in terms of miles per hour:

THP = TV ÷ 375. (This is because 550 fps = 375 mph.) To convert miles per hour to feet per second, multiply by 1.467, or 1.467 × 375 mph = 550 fps. Roughly, any value in feet per second is one and a half times its value in miles per hour. For knots use THP = TV ÷ 325.

As a prop pilot you have no direct way of measuring the thrust, so power is used as a measure of what the engine is contributing to the process of flight. Figure 3-10 is a graph of THP required versus indicated (calibrated) airspeed for a particular airplane at sea level.

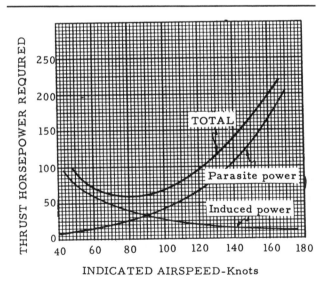

Fig. 3-10. Thrust horsepower required versus velocity.

Notice that the power-required curve has more than a passing resemblance to the drag curve. Instead of being expressed in terms of parasite drag and induced drag, Figure 3-10 is shown as parasite power required and induced power required, which are combined to make up the curve of total power required. Let's take another look at THP, or the

horsepower actually being developed by the propeller in moving the airplane through the air. The propeller is only up to 85% efficient in utilizing the brake or shaft horsepower, so that for a specific airspeed the following might apply in finding how much THP is being developed:

$$0.85 \times BHP = \frac{TV\ (knots)}{325},\ \text{or}\ 0.85 \times BHP = \frac{T \times V}{325}$$

Assuming that thrust equals drag in unaccelerated straight and level flight, the THP equation could be written:

$$THP_{required} = \frac{DV\ (knots)}{325}$$

Since drag in the cruise area is *roughly* proportional to the square of the velocity, the horsepower required is multiplied by another V so that horsepower required is a function of V^3, the cube of the velocity. Boiled down, this means that to double the speed in cruise or top speed area, approximately *eight* times the horsepower is required for a particular airplane. This goes for *brake* or *thrust* horsepower, but again, since you are only really interested in BHP, this would be the item of interest.

Figure 3-11 shows BHP required and available versus indicated airspeed (IAS) for a fictitious airplane at sea level and gross weight. Brake horsepower and indicated (calibrated) airspeed are used here because these are the two items used by the pilot to obtain the desired performance in climbs, cruise, and descents.

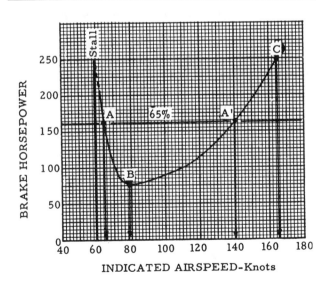

Fig. 3-11. Brake horsepower versus velocity.

Notice that the airplane can fly at two speeds for most power setting percentages. For instance, at 65% power, the airplane can fly straight and level at 65 knots and also at 140 knots, as shown by A and A'. This works for all power settings down to that of minimum power required, which will run at about 35–40% normal rated power (BHP) at gross weight for most airplanes of the type you'll be flying on instruments. It would take the least horsepower to maintain altitude at the airspeed under Point B.

The airspeed at Point B in theory would be the one to use at gross weight in the instrument holding pattern. The term "in theory" was inserted because other factors may enter. Your airplane may have poor handling characteristics at fairly low speeds. The propeller low-rpm characteristics may not be of the best plus the fact that turbulence could cause additional handling problems, so that a slight increase in airspeed to slightly above that given for Point B might be better. Another factor is that the brake-specific fuel consumption, or pounds of fuel burned per BHP per hour, normally increases at both ends of the power setting range. By adding some power, you may decrease the fuel consumption per horsepower to such an extent that the efficiency of the engine is increased.

Looking back to Figure 3-11. Point C shows the top speed (level flight) of the airplane at the particular altitude. Since Figure 3-11 was drawn for sea level, this would be the *absolute maximum level flight speed* for the airplane with an unsupercharged engine (or engines). While Figure 3-11 hints that in theory there is also a corresponding low speed for 100% power, it is highly unlikely that the stall characteristics of the normally configured airplane would allow it to fly at such a low speed that 100% power would be necessary to maintain level flight; the stall break would occur first.

■ Setting Power

UNSUPERCHARGED ENGINE. Along with the theory should come some practical application, and Figure 3-12 is a true airspeed (TAS} versus standard (density) altitude chart for a four-place retractable gear airplane at maximum certificated (gross) weight. The airplane is powered by a 260-hp unsupercharged engine (Fig. 3-13).

Point 1 in Figure 3-12 shows that for the unsupercharged engine the maximum level-flight airspeed is found at sea level, and the level-flight speed at maximum power decreases with altitude. This is because the amount of horsepower available is dropping faster than the gain of TAS effects.

It's a different story with power settings of less than maximum; take a look at the line for 75% power. The TAS increases with altitude until at about 7000 ft (point 2) the airspeed starts dropping again. This is because 7000 ft is the highest altitude at which 75% power can be maintained at the recommended max cruise rpm of 2400. Point 2 (7000 ft) would be the full-throttle altitude (or critical altitude) for 75% power at 2400 rpm. If, for instance, you prefer 65% power for cruise on an instrument flight (and this is certainly more economical and easier on the engine), then l0,000 ft (point 3) would be the full-throttle altitude and would be the altitude to fly for the most airspeed and range for that power setting. (For 75% power, 7000 ft would be the magic altitude to pick.) This, naturally, doesn't take into

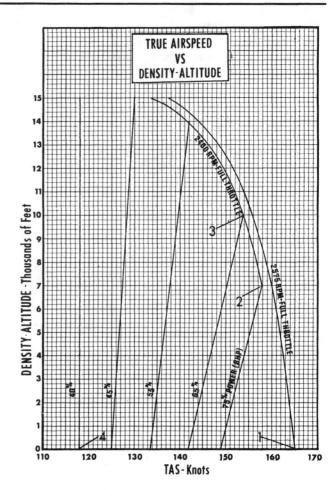

Fig. 3-12. Performance chart. *(Advanced Pilot's Flight Manual)*

account such things as wind at that altitude or assigned altitudes on IFR, but it would still be best as far as getting the max *true airspeed* is concerned.

You'll find that full-throttle operation will probably produce a maximum manifold pressure of 28–29 in. of mercury in standard sea level conditions (unsupercharged engine). Since the barometric pressure drops about 1 in. of mercury per 1000 ft, you would at some altitude run out of the manifold pressure necessary to maintain the desired percentage of power. You've reached the full-throttle or critical altitude for that power setting.

Figure 3-13 is the power setting table for the Lycoming IO-540-D engine (260 hp) using a constant-speed prop. For a given rpm, less manifold pressure is required for a specific percentage of power as altitude increases. Note that at 65% power, using 2300 rpm, 23.2 in. of manifold pressure is required at sea level. At 7000 ft only 21.5 in. of manifold pressure is required to maintain 65% power. There are mainly two reasons for this:

1. The air is cooler at higher altitudes, and if you used the same manifold pressure as you carried at sea level, the mixture density and the horsepower developed would be greater because a lower temperature

means a greater density if the mixture pressure (manifold pressure) remains the same.

2. The exhaust gases have less back pressure (outside pressure) to fight at higher altitudes. The "explosion" in the cylinder is sealed, and some power is required to expel the waste gases. The less back pressure existing, the less power is wasted, and more can be used to "drive" the airplane.

Most pilots prefer a particular rpm for cruise at either 65 or 75%, and looking at Figure 3-13, an interesting fact comes to light concerning the manifold pressure drop. For 2300 rpm at sea level (again), 23.2 in. is needed for 65% power, and 25.8 in. is necessary to obtain 75% power. Another look shows that the required manifold pressure to maintain the chosen power at 2300 rpm drops about ¼ in./1000 ft. You can subtract ¼ in./1000 ft from the sea level manifold pressure and get the power setting table figure. If you want the manifold pressure required for 65% at 5000 ft, you would subtract (5 ¼), or 1¼ (1.25) in. from the sea level figure of 23.2, for an answer of 21.95. (The table says 22.0.) For 5000 ft at 75% it would be 25.8 – (5 × 0.25) or 25.8 – 1.25 = 24.55 in. (table figure is 24.4 in.). For cruise information, if you use 2300 rpm, you could remember 23.2, 25.8, and ¼-inch drop/1000 ft and not have to refer to the power setting table every time when using 65 or 75% power respectively.

Power Setting Table - Lycoming Model IO-540-D, 260 HP Engine

Press. Alt. 1000 Feet	Std. Alt Temp. °F	143 HP - 55% Rated Approx. Fuel 11.4 GPH RPM AND MAN. PRESS.				169 HP - 65% Rated Approx. Fuel 12.7 GPH RPM AND MAN. PRESS.				195 HP - 75% Rated Approx. Fuel 14.1 GPH RPM AND MAN. PRESS.			
		2100	2200	2300	2400	2100	2200	2300	2400	2200	2300	2400	2500
SL	59	22.3	21.5	20.7	19.8	25.3	24.1	23.2	22.2	26.9	25.8	24.8	24.0
1	55	22.1	21.3	20.5	19.6	25.1	23.9	22.9	22.0	26.6	25.5	24.5	23.7
2	52	21.9	21.0	20.3	19.4	24.8	23.6	22.7	21.8	26.3	25.3	24.3	23.5
3	48	21.7	20.8	20.0	19.2	24.5	23.4	22.5	21.6	26.0	25.0	24.0	23.2
4	45	21.4	20.6	19.8	19.0	24.2	23.1	22.2	21.4	25.7	24.7	23.8	22.9
5	41	21.2	20.3	19.6	18.8	24.0	22.9	22.0	21.1	25.4	24.4	23.5	22.7
6	38	21.0	20.1	19.4	18.6	23.7	22.6	21.7	20.9	-	24.1	23.3	22.4
7	34	20.7	19.9	19.1	18.4	23.5	22.4	21.5	20.7	-	-	23.0	22.2
8	31	20.5	19.6	18.9	18.2	-	22.1	21.2	20.5	-	-	-	21.9
9	27	20.3	19.4	18.7	18.0	-	21.9	21.0	20.3				
10	23	20.0	19.2	18.5	17.7	-	-	20.7	20.0				
11	19	19.8	18.9	18.2	17.5	-	-	-	19.8				
12	16	19.6	18.7	18.0	17.3								
13	12	-	18.5	17.8	17.1								
14	9	-	-	17.5	16.9								
15	5	-	-	17.3	16.7								

To maintain constant power, correct manifold pressure approximately 0.17" Hg. for each 10° F variation in induction air temperature from standard altitude temperature. Add manifold pressure for air temperature above standard; subtract for temperatures below standard.

Fig. 3-13. Power setting table. *(Lycoming Division of AVGO)*

Another tip for setting power for cruise after level-off (VFR or IFR) is to leave the power at the climb value until the expected cruise IAS is approached. This expedites the transition. In addition, if the cruise power was set just as the plane leveled off at a comparatively low speed right out of the climb, it would mean resetting the manifold pressure as cruise speed is approached (you'll have to throttle back slightly). Why? Because ram effect will be packing in more air at the higher speed, the manifold pressure will increase, and you've just given yourself another little chore.

Figure 3-13 shows that corrections for variations from standard temperatures must be taken into account. This follows the same principle mentioned concerning the lower manifold pressure required to maintain the same power at higher altitudes. This is because of the fact that one of the real measures of horsepower developed is the mixture *density*. The temperature being higher or lower would vary the density if the manifold pressure was held the same. Since there is no simple way to measure mixture density, the manifold pressure must be varied to take care of temperature variations. In general, the *equation of state* (gases) puts the relationship of pressure, temperature, and density this way:

Pressure constant—Temperature increase means a density *decrease* and vice versa. (At a constant pressure, density is inversely proportional to temperature.)

Temperature constant—Pressure increase means a density increase, or density is directly proportional to pressure.

Density constant—Temperature increase means a pressure increase, or pressure is directly proportional to temperature.

AIRPLANE STABILITY AND WEIGHT AND BALANCE

It's very important that the airplane be in a stable condition on any flight but even more so when flying IFR. The unstable airplane can require constant pilot attention, which means that a lapse of attention, such as chart checking or clearance copying, can spell trouble for the single-pilot aircraft without an autopilot. Even if you have an autopilot, it will work harder and in correcting may cause the flight to be rougher than it would be if the airplane was stable. Your knowledge of weight and balance procedures will become even more important.

Figure 3-14 shows the three axes around which the airplane maneuvers. FARs 23 and 25 require that an airplane certificated in the normal, utility, and transport categories must meet certain minimum requirements of stability about each axis.

But before getting into the specifics of the airplane, take a look at the basic idea of stability.

■ **Static Stability** The term "static" might well express the idea of "at rest." When you are flaked out on the couch

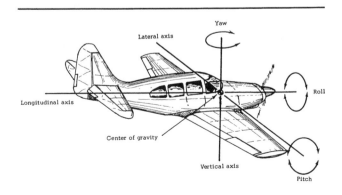

Fig. 3-14. The three axes.

for a nap, you could be said to be "static." An object or system that has an initial tendency to return to its original position and resists being offset in the first place may be termed *statically stable*. Figure 3-15 shows three possible static stability situations involving a "system"—a perfectly smooth bowl or hubcap, a flat surface, and a steel ball.

Figure 3-15A shows a *positive static stability* or a system that is *statically* stable. If you tried to displace the ball from its center position, it would resist displacement and tend to return to its original position. For example, the equivalent condition for an airplane would be for it to tend to return to its trim speed if displaced.

System B is *neutrally stable,* or has neutral static stability; it's a steel ball on a flat plate. If a force acts on it, it moves and stops at some new position when the force or the effects of that force are gone. The ball has no tendency to return to the original position (nor for the airplane to return to the trim speed).

System C is *negatively stable.* If it is displaced from its balanced position, as shown, it will get farther and farther, at an increasingly faster rate, from the original position.

As a pilot, *you* control the static stability of the airplane with your weight and balance control. Notice that only in the statically stable system does the ball have any tendency to return to its original position, and this brings up the following point.

■ **Dynamic Stability** The actions a body takes in response to its static stability properties show its dynamic stability (dynamic = active). Dynamic stability is considered to be the time history of a body's responses to its static stability condition. In System A in Figure 3-15, the ball would resist any tendency to be moved from its center position and is *statically stable.* When released, it would return toward the center, overshooting and returning in decreasing oscillations until it would again come to rest in its original position. In such a case it would also be *dynamically stable,* or it would have *positive dynamic stability* (because the actions of the ball returned it to the original position). If you had added an outside force by rocking the hubcap, you might cause the oscillations to continue with the same magnitude *(neutral dynamic stability),* or you could rock it enough so that the oscillations get more violent until the ball shoots over the side *(negative dynamic stability).*

The experiment just accomplished will work only if the system is statically stable to begin with—the ball would

hardly oscillate on the flat plate (Fig. 3-15B) and certainly not if it was on the outside of the hubcap as shown in Figure 3-15C. This leads to the brilliant conclusion that in order for a system to have any oscillatory properties at all it must be *statically stable* or have *positive static stability.*

LONGITUDINAL (PITCH) STABILITY

The rather complicated title of this section basically means taking a look at how the airplane wants to hold its trim airspeed or its actions in returning to that airspeed.

Longitudinal stability, or stability around the lateral axis (check Fig. 3-14 again), is the most important of the three types of stability because the pilot can affect it more with placement of weight. Sure, burning more fuel out of one wing tank can affect lateral stability, and moving weight rearward *can* affect directional (yaw) stability (it's doubtful that you could notice it, though), *but* longitudinal stability problems have pranged more airplanes by far than the other two combined.

As a review, an airplane in steady-state flight (such as straight and level, steady climb, or steady glide, etc.) must be in "equilibrium." This means that the summing up of forces and moments must equal zero; the idea of equilibrium of forces was touched on briefly in Chapter 2.

You recall that a force can be considered as a pressure, tension, or weight. A "moment" usually is the result of a force or weight acting at some distance from a fulcrum, or pivot point, at a 90° angle to its "arm." A seesaw is a good example of a system of moments, as shown in Figure 3-16.

The two moments are equal, but the distances (arms) and weights are different. Moments may be expressed as pound-feet or pound-inches to keep from confusing a "moment" with "work," which, you remember, was expressed as "foot-pounds," using the distance factor first.

You are trying to balance a 200-lb rock with a mechanical lever system, as shown in Figure 3-17. If you are holding the lever at 40 in. from the fulcrum, how much force do you have to exert to "assure equilibrium of the system" (balance the rock)? It's assumed that the bar is rigid, and its weight will be neglected.

Since the system is in equilibrium (you're balancing the rock), the two moments are equal. The moment on the rock side of the fulcrum can be found as 200 lb × 10 in. = 2000 lb-in. The moment on your side must also be 2000 lb-in., so you will have to exert *50 lb* at a 90° angle to the lever at the

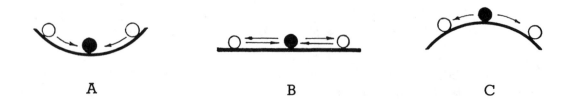

A   B   C

Fig. 3-15. (A) Positive, **(B)** neutral, and **(C)** negative static stability.

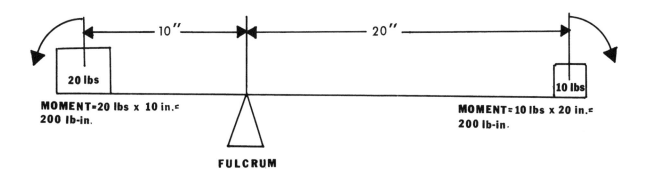

Fig. 3-16. System of moments in equilibrium.

distance of 40 in. to balance the rock (50 lb × 40 in. = 2000 lb-in.). (*Why* you're wasting your time standing around balancing a rock is not a subject for this book.)

Take a look at Figure 3-18 to see some of the forces and moments acting on a typical high-performance, four-place, general aviation airplane flying in straight and level cruising flight.

In Figure 3-18, rather than establish the vertical acting forces (lift, weight, and tail force) with respect to the center of gravity (CG) as is the usual case, they will be measured fore and aft from the center of lift. Assume at this point that lift is a string holding the airplane "up" and its value will be found later. The airplane in Figure 3-18 weighs 3000 lb, is flying at 150 knots IAS (CAS), and at this particular loading the CG is 5 in. ahead of the "lift line."

Summing up the major moments acting on *the airplane* (check Fig. 3-18 for each):

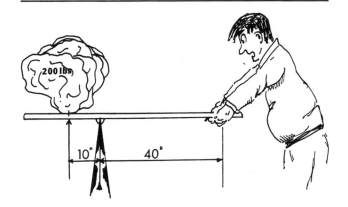

Fig. 3-17. Simple lever system.

1. **Lift—weight moment – 15,000 lb-in.**

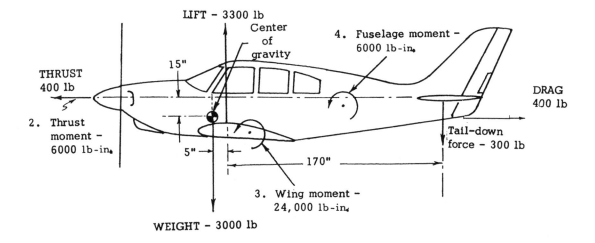

Fig. 3-18. Forces and moments acting on an airplane in straight and level cruising flight.

1. *Lift-weight moment*—The weight (3000 lb) is acting 5 in. ahead of the center of lift, and this results in a 15,000 lb-in. *nose-down* moment (5 in. × 3000 lb = 15,000 lb-in.).

2. *Thrust moment*—Thrust is acting 15 in. above the CG and has a value of 400 lb. The *nose-down* moment resulting is 15 in. × 400 lb = *6000 lb-in.* (The moment created by thrust will be measured with respect to the CG. For simplicity, it will be assumed that the drag is operating back through the CG. Although this is not usually the case, it saves working with another moment.

3. *Wing moment*—The wing, in producing lift, creates a nose-down moment that is the result of the forces working on the wing itself. Figure 3-19 shows force patterns acting on a wing at two airspeeds (angles of attack). These moments are acting with respect to the aerodynamic center, a point considered to be located at about 25% of the chord for all airfoils.

Notice that as the speed increases (the angle of attack decreases), the moment becomes greater as the force pattern varies. The nose-down moment created by the wing increases as the *square* of the airspeed if the airfoil is not a symmetrical type. (There is no wing moment if the airfoil is symmetrical because all the forces are acting through the aerodynamic center of the airfoil.)

For an airplane of the type, airspeed, and weight used here a nose-down moment created by the wing itself of 24,000 lb-in. would be a good round figure. Remember that this would vary with IAS. *Nose-down moment created by the wing = 24,000 lb-in.*

4. *Fuselage*—This may also be expected to have a moment about its CG because it too has a flow pattern and, for this example, airplane type and airspeed would be about *6000 lb-in. nose-down.* (This is not always the case.)

Summing up the nose-down moments:

Lift-weight moment	= 15,000
Thrust moment	= 6,000
Wing moment (at 150 knots)	= 24,000
Fuselage moment (at 150 knots)	= 6,000
Total nose-down moment	= 51,000 lb-in.

For equilibrium to exist, there must be a *tail-down* moment of 51,000 lb-in., and this is furnished by the tail-down force. Figure 3-18 shows that the "arm," or the distance from the lift line to the center of the tail-down force, is 170 in. So the moment (51,000 lb-in.) and the arm (170 in.) are known, and the force acting at the end of that arm (the tail-down force) can be found as 51,000 lb-in. ÷ 170 in. = 300 lb. The airplane nose does not tend to pitch either way.

Since the forces acting perpendicular and parallel to the flight path must also be in equilibrium, a couple of other steps could be taken to complete the problem. Figure 3-18 shows that the forces acting parallel to the flight path are

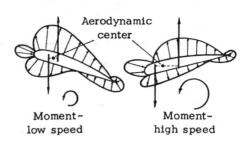

Fig. 3-19. Moments created by an unsymmetrical airfoil at two different airspeeds. The angles of attack and pressure patterns have been exaggerated.

equal (thrust and drag are each 400 lb), and a summation of the vertical forces, or forces acting perpendicular to the flight path, is checked next. The "downward" acting forces are weight (3000 lb) and the tail-down force (300 lb), for a total of 3300 lb. The only opposing force is lift, and for equilibrium to exist, this must be 3300 lb.

Looking back at the idea of the wing moment, you'll notice that it tends to keep the nose down and the airspeed up, and for the unsymmetrical airfoil, this tendency increases with the square of the airspeed. Suppose, as an example, that you moved weight back in the airplane at cruise so that the lift-weight moment is a minus factor—you've moved the CG so far back that lift is acting *ahead* of weight. Say, for example, that lift is acting 10 in. ahead of weight at the cruise airspeed of 150 knots; the lift-weight moment is now a *minus* factor (minus means a nose-up moment).

Lift-weight moment	= −30,000
Thrust moment	= 6,000
Wing moment (at 150 knots)	= 24,000
Fuselage moment (at 150 knots)	= 6,000
Total nose-down moment	= 6,000 lb-in.

Summing the nose-up and nose-down moments, the result is a 6000 lb-in. nose-down moment, which is to be balanced by the tail-down force. The arm is 170 in. so that the required tail-down force is 6000 lb-in. ÷ 170 in. = 35 lb. You can see that the tail-down force is rapidly disappearing and the airplane is becoming less statically stable.

The wing moment is a function of the *square* of the airspeed, so if the plane is slowed up to one-half its cruise speed, the wing and fuselage moments would be one-fourth of their values at cruise. As the airplane was slowed to holding speed, you just might find yourself running out of the forward wheel (down elevator) necessary to furnish the nose-down moment. The nose could rise abruptly and a stall could occur, followed by a loss of control (on instruments!).

The treatment given here is that the weight (CG) was moved aft *in flight,* and you were able to control it until you slowed down and lost your "helpful" wing and fuselage moments. The realistic view would be that the airplane would have problems on takeoff and probably never get to the cruise condition. Your job as a pilot is to make sure that the airplane is loaded properly so that problems don't arise. Remember that even though the airplane is controllable at cruise and at holding speeds, *in turbulence* control might be marginal when your attention is directed to other things such as taking clearances, checking engine instruments, etc. Sometimes, it seems that ATC has a TV camera in the cabin and knows the exact time that you least want a clearance. ("Okay, boys, he's in turbulence, is picking up ice, and his pencil just rolled all the way back under the back seat; let's give him Clearance 332, that always leaves them climbing the walls.") That's when prior checking of weight and balance could have helped.

WEIGHT AND BALANCE

The *basic* empty weight of the airplane is initially established by the manufacturer and, for a particular airplane, *includes unusable fuel, full oil, hydraulic fluid, and all equipment necessary for flight (and optional equipment).* In other words, the airplane is mechanically ready to fly but lacks usable fuel, occupants, and baggage.

To obtain the empty weight, the airplane is weighed as shown in Figure 3-20.

One thing to consider is whether the airplane was weighed at the factory *before* or *after* being painted. The weight of the paint of a four-place, single-engine, general aviation airplane can be from 10 to 30 lb (or more) depending on the area covered. If the airplane is unpainted at the time of weighing, the paint weight is added to it on the Weight and Balance Form.

The newly manufactured airplane is placed on scales as shown in Figure 3-20. The total empty weight for this airplane is the sum of the three scale figures and is 1697 lb. The resulting figure is called the "empty weight as weighed," and the unusable fuel and full oil (and the weight of the paint, if necessary) are added to this to get the "basic empty weight." The airplane in this example is painted, and all radios and optional equipment are installed.

To find the empty weight CG, the "datum" is used. This is an imaginary point located at or some distance ahead of a well-defined spot on the airplane, such as the front side of the firewall, wing leading edge, etc. In this case, the datum is located 79 in. ahead of the straight leading edge of the wing. On airplanes with tapered wings the datum may be established a certain distance ahead of the junction of the wing leading edge and the fuselage. When the datum is ahead of the airplane, as is the case here, all the arms are positive; when the datum is located at the leading edge of the wing or front side of the firewall, the arm is in a positive direction when aft of the datum and negative when forward.

The empty weight (or "as weighed") CG is located by using the principle of moments and using the datum point as the fulcrum or pivot point.

The weight concentrated on the nosewheel is 575 lb, and it is 31 in. from the datum; hence, its moment would be 575 lb × 31 in. = 17,825 lb-in.

The moment created by the weights on the main gear would be (560 + 562)lb × 109 in. = 1122 lb × 109 in. = 122,298 lb-in. The two weights on the main wheels are combined, since the two wheels are the same distance from the datum (or should be if the airplane hasn't been taxied into something).

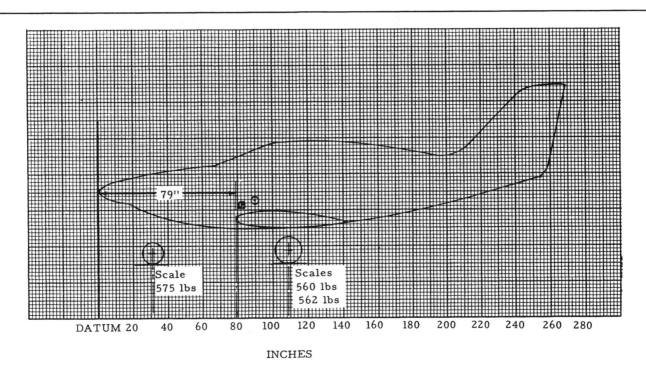

Fig. 3-20. Determining the empty weight and empty weight center of gravity.

Rearranged, the problem would look like this:

	Weight	Arm (in.)		Moment
	575	× 31	=	17,825
	1122	× 109	=	122,298
Total	1697 lb			140,123 lb-in.

Dividing the total moment by the weight, the empty CG is found to be located at: 140,123 ÷ 1697 = 82.6 in. aft of the datum.

This particular airplane is considered to have 4 gal of unusable fuel and was weighed with no oil, so the step to get the basic empty weight is:

Item	Weight	Arm (in.)	Moment
Empty weight as weighed	1697	82.6	140,123
Oil (3 gal)	23	28.0	644
Unusable fuel (4 gal)	24	90.0*	2,160
Total	1744 lb		142,927 lb-in.

The *basic* empty weight for this particular airplane is 1744 lb, and the empty CG is found by dividing the total moment (142,927 lb-in.) by the total weight (1744 lb). The answer is 81.9 in., as shown by the small square in Figure 3-20. The answers were rounded off to the nearest 0.1 of an inch. What about that mysterious 90.0* that showed up in the last calculation? That's the distance of the CG of the fuel load from the datum, that is, 90 in. This information is given in the Weight and Balance Form for the airplane. Incidentally, fuel (gasoline) is considered to weigh 6 lb/gal; oil weighs 7.5 lb/gal. It's best to use the actual passenger weights.

You could then find out the effects of adding usable fuel, passengers, and baggage as shown below (the maximum certificated, or gross, weight is 2900 lb for this airplane):

Item	Weight	Arm	Moment
Basic empty weight	1744		142,927
Fuel (56 gal)	336	90.0*	30,240
Pilot	170	84.8*	14,416
Passenger (front)	170	84.8*	14,416
Passenger (rear)(l)	170	118.5*	20,145
Baggage	200	142.0*	28,400
Total	2,790 lb		250,544 lb-in.

The total moment is divided by the weight to find the CG with that loading to get an answer of 89.8 in. aft of the datum. This is shown by the small circle in Figure 3-20. Those arms marked with an asterisk are the same for each airplane of this model and are given on the Weight and Balance Form.

Figure 3-21 is from the Weight and Balance section of a *Pilot's Operating Handbook* showing loading arrangements for a four-place airplane. Note that the two front seats are

adjustable from 34 to 46 in. aft of datum, but the "average" person's CG is at 37 in. Some people's CGs are *lower* than others, but remember that this is an average here and only concerns fore and aft CGs.

LOADING ARRANGEMENTS

*Pilot or passenger center of gravity on adjustable seats positioned for average occupant. Numbers in parentheses indicate forward and aft limits of occupant center of gravity range.

**Arm measured to the center of the areas shown.

1. The usable fuel C.G. arm for standard, long range and integral tanks is located at station 48.0.

2. The rear cabin wall (approximate station 108) or aft baggage wall (approximate station 142) can be used as convenient interior reference points for determining the location of baggage area fuselage stations.

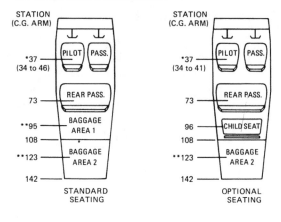

Fig. 3-21. Loading arrangements for a four-place airplane.

Pilot's Operating Handbooks for 1976 models (and later) use the term "basic empty weight" rather than "licensed empty weight" the older term, in case this is a review. Again, the airplane basic empty weight includes unusable fuel *and full oil,* the latter not being considered as part of the empty weight on the earlier models. The *POH* will have a Weight and Balance Form with blanks for the specific airplane.

WEIGHT AND BALANCE ENVELOPE

You know that the airplane is legal from a weight standpoint; but is the CG in the proper range?

Figure 3-22 is a weight and balance envelope for the four-place, high-performance airplane used in the example.

The range is from 80.5 to 93 in. aft of the datum, and it can be found that the loading checked earlier is within safe limits. In the problem no fourth passenger was taken, but the full allowable 200 lb of baggage was included. You could work out various combinations of items and check for safe operation by referring to the weight and balance envelope.

The forward CG limit is set by control in ground effect rather than stalls at altitude.

Notice that Figure 3-22 has a remark that the moment due to retracting the landing gear is 1266 lb-in. The empty weight CG was checked with the landing gear down, so that when it is retracted (the nosewheel swings back and maybe

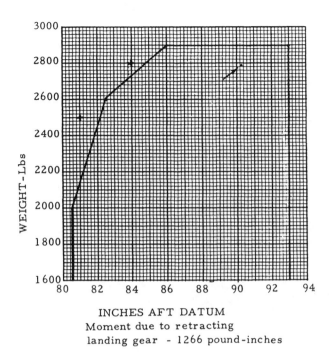

Fig. 3-22. Weight and balance envelope.

the main gear also moves back slightly with respect to the datum), the value cited must be added to the total moment of the airplane, people, fuel, etc., to get the true CG position *in flight*.

The final CG would be found by adding the moment of 1266 lb-in. to the total moment to find the CG with the gear retracted (which is what you are really interested in). Notice that the total weight would be the same; it's just been moved back, thus increasing the moment. The new CG is

$$\frac{(250{,}544 + 1266)}{2790} = \frac{251{,}810}{2790} = 90.3 \text{ in. aft of the datum}$$
$$\text{(rounded off).}$$

While it's not a critical factor for this problem, it could nudge you over the line if the CG was right at the rearward limits to begin with. The dot in Figure 3-22 shows that the final CG is within safe limits. This is mentioned to cover a factor you might not have considered.

The baggage placard is to be respected; not only could the CG be moved too far aft but also the baggage compartment floor could be overstressed. The baggage compartment floor area is designed to withstand a certain number of g's with 200 lb (or whatever the placard limit indicates), and if you pull that same number of g's with, say, 400 lb in it, what used to be the baggage compartment may be just a memory. The allowable positive and negative load factors and airplane categories are given in the *Pilot's Operating Handbook*.

■ **Forward CG Considerations** The envelope in Figure 3-22 is not square but has cutoff areas in the upper

left-hand corner. For instance, you would not be legal flying at 2800 lb with the CG located at 84 in. or at 2500 lb with a CG at 81 in. aft of the datum (as shown by the crosses).

Everybody worries so much about the rear limit of the envelope that the idea of a forward limit is forgotten. For simplification, the rear limit is basically established to ensure stability, and the forward limit is to ensure proper controllability.

Suppose you kept moving weight forward while in flight; it would require more and more up-elevator (or trim) to maintain "longitudinal equilibrium" (keep the nose up). You could reach a situation where *full* up-elevator would be necessary in the cruise regime. When power was chopped, the nose would drop again and the airspeed would pick up. You'd be in trouble trying to land the airplane in this exaggerated situation. Actually, the *allowed* forward limit of the airplane would be even farther forward if it was not for ground effect.

At altitude, the elevators may still be effective near the stall with a well-forward CG but may lose effectiveness because of ground effect as shown by Figure 3-23.

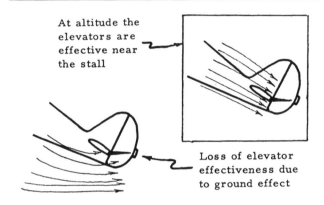

Fig. 3-23. Ground effect and elevator effectiveness.

Figures 3-24 and 3-25 show an approach to the weight and balance computations for another airplane. Instead of thinking in terms of pounds and inches aft of the datum as in the case for the envelope of Figure 3-22, these use the graph form of pounds versus moment (pound-inches) as the criterion. If a certain airplane weight comes up with a moment (which is distance times pounds) that falls within the envelope, it really doesn't matter whether you know the exact position of the CG (in inches) or not; it is in a safe range.

Figure 3-24 shows a simplified loading graph. The slope of the lines represents the effects of distance on the moment. Notice that a pilot and passenger weighing a total of 340 lb in the front seat created a moment of 12,200 lb-in., as compared to about 24,000 lb-in. created by rear passengers totaling 340 lb. (Notice that 120 lb of baggage, because of its location, makes a moment nearly as great as the 340 lb worth of people in the front seat.)

This sample airplane is a four-place, single-engine type and has a gross weight of 2800 lb. It's given that the airplane

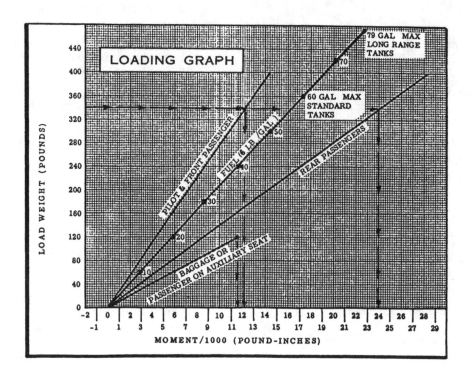

Fig. 3-24. Loading graph for a particular airplane.

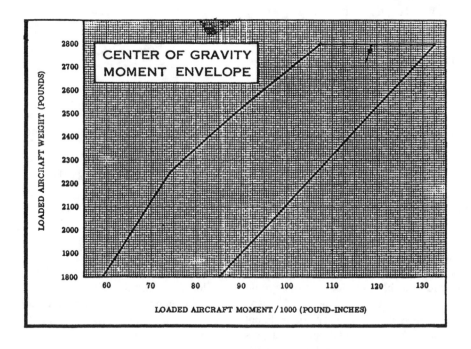

Fig. 3-25. Center of gravity moment envelope for the airplane of Figure 3-24.

has a basic empty weight of 1682 lb with an empty-weight moment of 57,600 (or 57.6 × 1000) lb-in. The datum is located on the front face of the firewall, and the oil has a

negative moment because it is *ahead* of that point. You could make up a table. Refer to Figure 3-24 for the moments resulting for the various items.

Item	Weight	Moment (thousands)
Basic empty weight (given)	1682	57.6
Pilot and passenger (front)	340	12.2
Fuel—60 gal (at 6 lb/gal)	360	17.3
Rear passengers	340	24.1
Baggage	78	7.6
Total	2800 lb	118.8 lb-in.

(More properly, this is 118,800 lb-in.)

Figure 3-25 is the CG moment envelope for this airplane. You can see by the arrow that the airplane is legal both from a weight standpoint and CG, or total moment consideration. Notice how the envelope "leans" to the right as the weight increases. At 1800 lb, a large moment (say, 90,000 lb-in.) would mean that the CG was quite far back from the datum (50 in. to be exact), whereas at a higher weight of 2250 lb a moment of 90,000 lb-in. is quite acceptable because the arm is shorter (40 in. aft of the datum) and the CG is not in a rearward critical condition. If, out of curiosity, you wanted to find the exact location of the CG of the airplane just discussed, you could divide the total moment (118,800 lb-in.) by the total weight (2800 lb) and find that the CG is located at approximately 42.4 in. aft of the datum. Notice that if you wanted to take the time and trouble, you could convert either type of envelope (Figs. 3-22, 3-25) to the other form.

SUMMARY

There's plenty more to be said about stability, weight, and balance. This chapter covered only longitudinal stability because it is the one area that the pilot can affect most easily. Directional and lateral stability are pretty much built in at the factory, and the airplane must meet certain minimum requirements in that regard. As far as longitudinal stability is concerned, the airplane will meet the requirements for safe operation as required by the FAA *only* if the weight and CG are kept within the envelope. Be sure that you can work out the weight and balance for the airplane you are using.

Don't load the airplane so that it's right on the rear limits of the envelope. It could be acceptable in smooth air, but turbulence and icing could cause the handling to become marginal or cause additional fatigue over the duration of the flight, and an approach in conditions of a 200-ft ceiling and ½-mi visibility needs all the attention and alertness you can give it.

BASIC INSTRUMENT FLYING

It's quite possible that you can fly an airplane both VFR or on instruments without knowing the theory of performance. But if you are going to the trouble of learning a new area of flying, you might as well get the background. A lot of pilots have reacted wrongly to an unusual situation in flying—and paid for it because they didn't know what the airplane could or could not do. Even experienced pilots have gotten into a bind, for instance, by unconsciously trying to stretch a glide or descent by pulling the nose up farther instead of adding power in a situation where outside distractions have become almost intolerable. You are making an ILS approach and have picked up a lot of ice, the ceiling and visibility are right on minimums, it's turbulent, and there's a lot of communication between you and the tower. You might end up close to a stall by trying to stay up on the glide slope by using the elevators and not enough power.

It's funny, but pilots pay lip service to the statement, "Power controls altitude, and the elevators control airspeed," and can (and will) rattle it off as a schoolchild recites the Preamble to the Constitution. Unfortunately, too often neither stops to think about what the words really mean.

Of course, when you are at cruise and pull back on the wheel the airplane climbs, so "obviously" the elevators make it climb. Not so; you are moving to a different (slower) airspeed using the same power setting, so excess horsepower—and energy altitude—are working to gain altitude. In practicality, at *high* speeds, you move the nose up to climb. Don't do this near the stall.

There are several ideas concerning instrument flying that are often presented to the pilot at the start of training for the rating. One is that somehow, as soon as the pilot is unable to fly by outside references, the airplane is subjected to a new set of "laws."

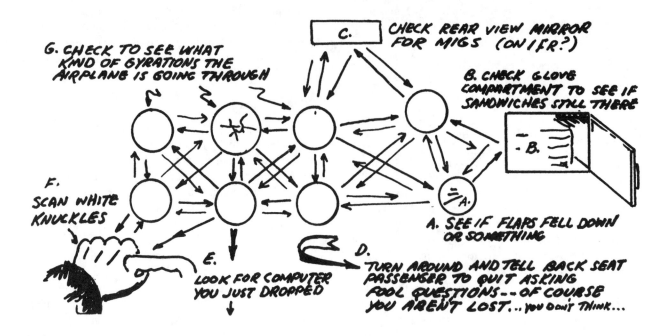

Fig. 4-1. A constant instrument scan is important for safe IFR flight.

It is the job of the instruments to provide a picture so that you can "see" and control the actions of the airplane, and the theory and manner of control are exactly the same as those used with visual references.

Assume for this chapter that in discussion of performance IAS = CAS.

INSTRUMENT SCAN (THE BIG PICTURE)

Shown in Figure 4-2 is one established arrangement of flight instruments in which the attitude gyro is the nucleus. This is a good logical arrangement and makes for a reasonably simple scan.

Fig. 4-2. "Basic T" arrangement for flight instruments. Note that the turn coordinator (or a turn and slip) and vertical speed indicator "fill in the gaps."

Notice that the airspeed is in the upper left-hand corner of the instrument panel. This is a good spot for that instrument because during takeoff or on final approach you don't have to move your scan so far in checking the runway and airspeed. Some older model airplanes had the airspeed indicator at the position of the rate of climb shown in Figure 4-2.

Maybe you don't like to use somebody else's idea for the order of looking at the gauges, so develop and use your own. You can work this out during your basic instrument flying. The main thing is to cover all of the flight instruments (and later you'll have to monitor the navigation instruments also) and *not* let your attention stick on one instrument. (This problem of fixation, or staring at one instrument, is quite common in the beginning for instrument trainees.)

The guess is that you'll have less trouble maintaining altitude than with keeping up with the heading. Why? Because you've been flying many hours keeping an eye on the altimeter, which is the only instrument for checking altitude, whereas quite a bit of your directional references have been outside the airplane. As for airspeed in the cruise regime, if the power is set and the altitude kept constant, the airspeed is usually ignored, but the altimeter is a prime instrument. It's funny, but heading can sneak off more insidiously than altitude. You know that you can sense altitude change with your eyes shut. (The change in sound is most often a clue in this regard.) Also, the heading can slip off even when the wings are level as indicated by the attitude gyro, particularly in a climb where torque is a factor.

In keeping with the idea that maintaining a constant altitude probably will be less of a problem than heading, the diving spiral (and altitude loss) is the final result of neglecting the heading (letting the airplane get into a wing-down attitude with heading change).

Don't think that speed of scan does the trick; this is as bad as staring at one instrument too long. You don't try for a speed record when, say, you start playing the banjo. Sometimes in training you'll have to slow down because you may be looking but not seeing. If you get excited or scared you may be looking from one instrument to another too fast, so slow down.

The scan can be summed up by stating that the necessary instruments should be checked at the right time. Don't try to set up and memorize the primary bank or pitch instrument for a particular maneuver, but fly the airplane by "seeing" its actions through the instruments; flying the airplane comes ahead of *all* other considerations (voice reports, etc.).

For instance, if you've been flying under the hood at *cruise* power at a constant altitude and suddenly notice that the airspeed is low and decreasing, you don't have to be told that the airspeed is a pitch reference. Without looking (assuming no power reduction), you could say that the altitude is increasing (if things haven't gone too far, but the airspeed will tell you this), and the attitude indicator will show a nose-up attitude. The wing attitude is another matter; wings may be level or banked, and you could check this by the attitude indicator or turn and slip or the turn coordinator. (If the needle or small airplane is deflected and the ball is in the center, the wings are banked. A needle or small airplane deflection with a skid indication may or may not indicate a bank; it would certainly indicate some degree of nose movement.) The heading indicator will also show a change in heading, which could be the result of either a "flat" or a banked turn.

■ **Primary and Supporting** The system of "primary" and "supporting" instruments as has been advocated requires that you memorize the various instruments/flight conditions. In that system a particular flight instrument may be primary for pitch at the initiation of a maneuver then be replaced by another after the maneuver has started. For instance, in a constant-airspeed climb (talking about pitch instruments only):

Initiating the climb—The attitude indicator is primary for pitch. The tachometer or manifold pressure gauge is primary for power.

Stabilized climb at a constant airspeed—Airspeed is now primary for pitch; the attitude indicator is supporting pitch, as is the vertical speed indicator.

In a stabilized climb at a constant rate, the vertical speed indicator is now the primary pitch instrument, with the airspeed indicator being primary for power and the attitude indicator supporting for pitch. (In some cases, at least for a short while, the airplane can be climbing at a constant airspeed and constant rate; which instruments do what, now?)

Leveling off to cruise—The altimeter is primary for pitch; the vertical speed is supporting pitch, as is the attitude indicator. The airspeed indicator is now considered primary for power as it approaches the desired value.

Looking back through the sequence of entering a climb, climbing, and then leveling off, the primary and supporting

instruments vary, *which complicates* a *simple procedure*. So this book is an advocate of control (attitude indicator and manifold pressure/tachometer) and performance instruments (airspeed, altimeter, vertical speed indicator, heading indicator, and turn coordinator or turn and slip).

■ **Back to Basics** The *control instruments* (attitude indicator and manifold pressure/tachometer gauges) are those used to *control* the airplane. You set the attitude and the power and the airplane performs. How well it's *performing* is indicated by the *performance instruments* just mentioned. What's the rate of climb, rate of descent, or rate of turn? Are you holding a constant altitude and heading (if that's what you want)?

Your job is to get the "big picture," as the advertising people would probably put it, through several sources (the various instruments). The present method of instrumentation is crude and unhandy; the pilot should be able to focus attention on one area, as if viewing the ground through a television screen with data such as altitude, heading, and airspeed superimposed on the attitude—and ground presentation.

Now you have to cross-check one instrument against the other; the attitude indicator, while the center of attention, only tells attitude (which actually is only what it was designed to do), not performance. Show most pilots who've not had instrument training a picture of an attitude indicator with the small reference airplane (wings level) above the horizon, and they'll say flatly that the airplane is in a straight climb. Not you as instrument pilot; you're suspicious. What does the airspeed show? Is it to the point of stall or holding steady at the proper climb speed? Is the altitude increasing, or is the airplane in slow-flight condition (nose up and low airspeed in level flight)? How much power is being used? The attitude indicator is very valuable in setting up initial positions for required climb or descent attitudes. You'll find, after practice, that you can approximate the required airspeeds by flying the airplane so that the small reference airplane is a certain number (or fraction) of horizon bar widths above (or below) the horizon. The airspeed is to be used as a more precise measure, however.

After some time practicing basic instrument flying, you'll figure that you have the situation well in hand. Then comes the introduction to radio navigation. Your "new scan" will have to include copying clearances, changing frequencies, and monitoring the navigation, engine, and aircraft systems instruments plus the clock. The advent of the horizontal situation indicator (HSI), which combines radio navigation indications with the heading indicator, and flight control systems (with autopilots), has done a great deal to simplify pilots' scanning chores. (See Chapter 5.)

One thing you can do is spend some time on the ground, sitting in the cockpit and pinning down the instrument arrangement and position of switches, circuit breakers, and other controls so that there is no fumbling in flight. Work out the probable scan for *your* airplane's instrument and radio arrangement and modify it in flight as necessary.

Probably the first thing your instructor will do before you fly that first flight will be to pick certain working airspeeds for your airplane, such as best speeds for approach, climb, holding, and turbulence penetration. Then the instructor will find the general power settings required for performance at these speeds, and you will use these numbers for a starting point. (When you start working on the instrument rating in earnest. you should have an instructor so that you get started out right.) After picking the working speeds, the instructor will introduce you to the pitch and bank instruments.

PITCH INSTRUMENTS

Figure 4-3 shows the pitch instruments, and the instructor will "introduce" them to you. Most pilots who haven't worked on the instrument rating before haven't really looked at each instrument in detail in flight.

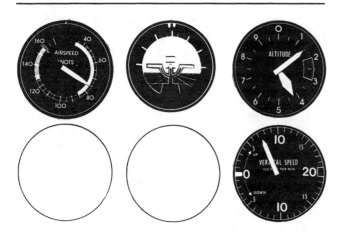

Fig. 4-3. Pitch instruments.

The instructor will very likely have you fly the pitch instruments one at a time so that you can check the response of, say, the airspeed, altimeter, or vertical speed indicator to various pitch changes of the attitude indicator. He or she may discuss the instruments in the following order:

Attitude indicator—You'll probably fly this instrument noting the effects of a one-half or one bar-width or pitch reference mark pitch change. Most noninstrument trained pilots haven't noticed the effects of very small pitch changes as referenced by the attitude indicator. (Most have used the attitude indicator for bank references and noted that in a climb it might indicate two or more bar widths up from level flight position—and that's about the extent of it.)

Bank won't be a major factor in your introduction to the pitch use of the attitude indicator, but you should keep the wings reasonably level. As a suggestion, once the airplane is established in straight and level cruising flight, with the setting knob, line up the *top* of the wings of the miniature airplane with the top of the horizon line and use this as the level-flight reference. The instructor may cover the other flight instruments and have you fly

a couple of minutes (or longer) using the attitude indicator for pitch and altitude information.

When the altimeter is uncovered, you can see how well you handled the pitch problem.

Altimeter—The instructor may have you check the altimeter's response to various rates of pitch change; but because you are more familiar with this one, you may not spend as much time with it as the other pitch instruments.

Because the altimeter is simple, it is a basic pitch instrument. When you stop to think about it, the altimeter and heading indicator are the major flight instruments for IFR; you need to know the altitude (so that you won't fly into the terrain or hit other airplanes) and the heading (for flying the proper course). You can estimate rates of climb or descent or the rate of turn by these two instruments alone (but the nav and power instruments are needed too). With practice you can come pretty close to setting up a prechosen rate of climb or descent by checking the altimeter's change rate. (See Fig. 4-8.)

Airspeed indicator—You'll find that the airspeed indicator has more to offer as a pitch indicator than you'd thought. Sure, you've been using the airspeed for climbs and descents, but you may have been thinking in terms of keeping the indications within 5 knots of what you wanted. Now you'll start thinking in terms of 1-knot variations (or maybe even less) as you see how the airspeed not only acts as a pitch reference for straight and level but can also help keep the proper pitch for maintaining a constant altitude in a standard rate turn.

Vertical speed indicator—You'll probably be really looking at this instrument for the first time and will get a chance to fly various rates of descent and climb as well as "flying it" in straight and level hooded flight with the other pitch instruments covered. You can see that controlling the vertical speed indicator can keep altitude within limits. You'll learn how to correct your rates of descent or climb to get a required rate.

Your instructor later may cover the altimeter, attitude indicator, and vertical speed indicator, using only the airspeed indicator for pitch information. The usual introduction is in smooth air with a constant power setting and altitude. After the airspeed has stabilized, you may be required to fly straight and level at cruise, using the elevator as the airspeed control. You'll fly the airplane for 2 or 3 min and your instructor will uncover the altimeter to let you see how you did or may have you set up a 360° standard-rate turn at a particular altitude, then cover the altimeter. The procedure is, as you roll into the turn, to ease in enough back pressure to decrease the established cruise airspeed by about 3% during the turn. As the roll-out is started, relax the back pressure to return to the cruise airspeed. (Uncover the altimeter to check.) This exercise is good for improving the accuracy of your pitch control. Most new instrument trainees tend to chase the airspeed because they want an instant correction. (This is a problem, particularly in the climb.)

Following are some numbers derived from a Cessna 172 at a light weight and medium altitude (5000–6000 ft MSL). The figures on the left represent the wings-level flight airspeeds, and the minus numbers on the right are the decreases in airspeed (pitch-up) required to maintain a constant altitude in a standard-rate turn (no power change):

Straight and Level	Level Standard Rate Turn
60 knots	−2 knots = 58 knots
70 knots	−2 knots = 68 knots
90 knots	−3 knots = 87 knots
105 knots	−3 knots = 102 knots

BANK INSTRUMENTS

Figure 4-4 shows the instruments used for bank control.

Note that the attitude indicator is the only instrument that gives both pitch and bank information. That's the reason for its location in the "basic T."

The turn and slip indicator is being replaced in many airplanes by the turn coordinator (Chapter 2). You'll get a chance to practice plenty of timed turns during the basic portion of your instrument training with whichever instrument your airplane has.

The heading indicator, like the altimeter for the pitch instruments, tells you the result of your bank control. The instructor will probably have you practice timed turns using either the turn and slip or turn coordinator with the heading indicator covered. Then you'll look at it to check your accuracy. (The attitude indicator may be used to check the validity of the bank thumb rule for a standard-rate turn with the heading indicator covered.)

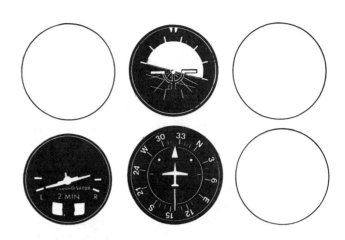

Fig. 4-4. Bank instruments.

STRAIGHT AND LEVEL FLYING

On instruments as in VFR flying, the majority of your time will be spent flying straight and level. If you wander all over the sky, ATC—particularly the en route radar controllers—will be wondering what is going on up there.

The ability to make transitions from cruise to holding speeds and back, while maintaining altitude and heading, is of particular importance. In actual instrument flying, you *may* have to talk and listen on the radio, compute ETAs, and absorb other information *at the same time* that you are making a transition.

Figure 4-5 shows the airplane's position on the power curve and the instrument indications for normal cruise at 65% at a density-altitude of 5000 ft.

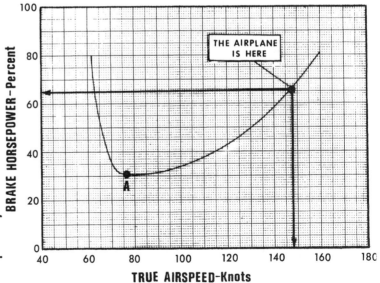

POWER CHART - LYCOMING MODEL O-540-A, 250 HP ENGINE

Press. Alt. 1000 Feet	Std. Alt. Temp. °F	138 HP—55% Rated Approx. Fuel 10.3 Gal./Hr. RPM & MAN. PRESS.				163 HP—65% Rated Approx. Fuel 12.3 Gal./Hr. RPM & MAN. PRESS.				188 HP—75% Rated Approx. Fuel 14.0 Gal./Hr. RPM & MAN. PRESS.		
		2100	2200	2300	2400	2100	2200	2300	2400	2200	2300	2400
SL	59	21.6	20.8	20.2	19.6	24.2	23.3	22.6	22.0	25.8	25.1	24.3
1	55	21.4	20.6	20.0	19.3	23.9	23.0	22.4	21.8	25.5	24.8	24.1
2	52	21.1	20.4	19.7	19.1	23.7	22.8	22.2	21.5	25.3	24.6	23.8
3	48	20.9	20.1	19.5	18.9	23.4	22.5	21.9	21.3	25.0	24.3	23.6
4	45	20.6	19.9	19.3	18.7	23.1	22.3	21.7	21.0	24.8	24.1	23.3
5	41	20.4	19.7	19.1	18.5	22.9	22.0	21.4	20.8	FT	23.8	23.0

Fig. 4-5. Normal cruise—straight and level at 5000 ft. The instrument indications and the power settings are shown. Note that the IAS is 137 knots for the TAS of 148 knots at 5000 ft (standard) altitude. (The altimeter setting here is 29.92 and the outside air temperature is +5°C.)

Remember that the attitude indicator, if set properly, can be a valuable aid in establishing the nose attitude for straight and level.

After you have pretty well gotten the idea about straight and level in the cruise area, check the power setting required to maintain a constant altitude at a speed of 30% above the power-off stall speed (gross weight), given as calibrated airspeed. (This is for single-engine, retractable one-gear types and light twins.) For single-engine planes with fixed gear, a speed of 20% above the stall is recommended. Find out how much power is required to maintain a constant altitude at this speed. It will be at *approximately* the minimum power point as indicated by (A) in Figure 4-5.

In making level-flight transitions, lead the power setting by 3 in. of manifold pressure, if possible. Say it takes 22 in. for cruise and 13 in. for the holding speed at a particular weight and altitude. When making the transition from cruise to holding, throttle back to 10 in. Then as the airspeed approaches the proper value, set up the required 13 in. For going back to cruise, set up 25 in. (if you can get it at your altitude), and as the airspeed reaches cruise, set the power to 22 in. again.

The manifold pressure and tachometer settings given throughout this book are arbitrary. Your airplane will have its own requirements, and the basic figures will vary with weight and density-altitude.

■ **Trim** Instrument trainees often have trouble with straight and level flight under the hood (or on actual instruments) because they don't trim the airplane properly. It's usually a throwback to their VFR flying—they never learned how to do it. Too many students and private pilots, when leveling off for cruise from a climb, take their *hands off* the controls and try to "catch" the proper nose position by juggling the trim control. This takes a lot of time and effort that could be used more wisely in checking the instruments. Needless to say, these people use the same crude technique in making the transition from cruise back to slow flight. Instructors have been known to fall asleep waiting for a transition to be completed by the student. The proper method for level-off is to hold the nose where it belongs with reference to straight and level flight, get the cruise power and airspeed established, and *use the trim* to *take care of the pressure you are exerting on the wheel* or *stick*. The same applies in slowing up—establish the nose position and let the trim take off the control pressure during and after the transition.

Practice straight and level flight at minimum controllable airspeeds also.

THE CLIMB

The flight instrument for initially establishing the proper straight-climb pitch attitude is the attitude indicator. You'll set climb power and will have the wings level in order to get the best prolonged climb.

The airspeed indicator is used as a finer reference. (You should soon be able to control the climb airspeed to within 1 knot in smooth air.) The main thing is, *don't* chase the airspeed; if you look over and see that it's well off the climb value, use the attitude indicator to set the proper attitude and *wait*. *Don't* try to get the proper airspeed back all at once because you'll end up chasing it.

The climb on instruments is what causes a lot of VFR pilots to get confused again about what makes the airplane go up. There have been cases of pilots who swore under oath that power was the factor that made the airplane climb and that the elevator was only used to control the proper airspeed. *But,* when the instructor told them that the airplane would climb better at a slower airspeed, they *throttled back!* Apparently, no matter how much was said about power controlling altitude, etc., they really didn't believe it.

Going back to the power-required curve, Figure 4-6 shows the power required and power available versus airspeed for a fictitious, single-engine, retractable-gear airplane at sea level and at 10,000 ft.

Thrust horsepower is used because this is the actual horsepower working to fly the airplane. The airplane's climb rate depends on the excess thrust horsepower working to "pull it up." Looking at Figure 4-6, you can see that at one point the excess horsepower is greatest, and this is the airspeed recommended for best climb at the conditions of weight and altitude shown in Figure 4-6. Sea level was used as one altitude for simplicity. The power available is that available at the recommended climb power.

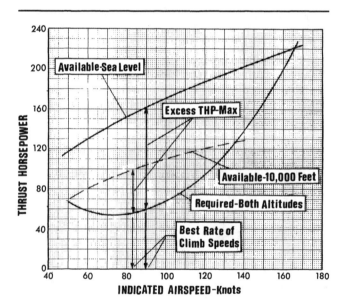

Fig. 4-6. Power-required and power-available (thrust horsepower) curves for a four-place general aviation airplane at sea level and 10,000 ft density-altitude.

Note that at the extreme ends of the curve the excess horsepower decreases pretty rapidly, which means that the airplane has a zero rate of climb at the top speed and near the stall where all the horsepower is being used to maintain altitude. This is not to say the airplane will not climb at all speeds between the two extremes (assuming climb horsepower is being used as shown), but as you approach the limits, the rate of climb will decrease rapidly.

The equation for rate of climb is:

$$\text{Rate of climb (fpm)} = \frac{\text{excess thrust horsepower} \times 33{,}000}{\text{airplane weight}}$$

This is nothing more than a variation of the basic facts of horsepower discussed in Chapter 3.

For instance, remembering that power is a force or weight moving a certain distance in a certain length of time and that 1 hp is equal to 550 ft-lb of work/sec, or 33,000 ft-lb/min., the 33,000 in the equation begins to make sense, since we are interested in the rate of climb of the airplane in *feet per minute.* The excess horsepower is that available to move the airplane's weight upward in a certain period of time. The greater the excess horsepower, the faster that same weight can be moved upward; hence, the greater the rate of climb. The greater the weight to be moved upward for a certain amount of horsepower available, the less the rate of climb. So the equation says that the rate of climb (in feet per minute) is directly proportional to the excess horsepower available above that required just to maintain altitude (more excess horsepower, more rate of climb), and the rate of climb is inversely proportional to the weight (less weight, more climb, and vice versa).

Suppose you are climbing at the recommended airspeed and power setting but are getting impatient. Believing that the elevators make the airplane climb, you exert back pressure to get a little more climb. The airspeed decreases, and as you can see in Figure 4-6, the excess horsepower (and rate of climb) decreases, and you do the same thing again; so the cycle begins. It ends when the airplane stalls. You've had enough experience by this time to avoid this sort of foolishness.

The dashed line in Figure 4-6 shows the power available for the airplane at 10,000 ft standard altitude. (Assume the THP required is the same for both altitudes.) The unsupercharged engine loses (roughly) 3–4% of its original (sea level) power per 1000 ft of additional altitude, and so goes the excess horsepower—and rate of climb. Rate of climb decreases in a straight line with density-altitude to the absolute ceiling, where rate of climb is zero. The service ceiling, you recall, for single-engine airplanes or multi's with all engines in operation, is the standard (density) altitude at which rate of climb is 100 fpm.

The maximum rate of climb V_Y is found at the airspeed where the maximum amount of excess thrust horsepower is available (about 60% above the flaps-up, power-off stall speed at gross). The maximum angle of climb V_X is found at a lower airspeed where the maximum excess *thrust* is available.

The thrust available to the propeller airplane decreases with increased airspeed for a given power. The best angle of climb is found at the airspeed where the maximum excess *thrust* exists. A plot of *thrust* available and drag versus airspeed for the airplane used in Figure 4-6 would show this speed to be lower than that required for max *rate.*

The maximum angle climb is normally found between 10 and 30% above the flaps-up power-off stall speed at gross weight, depending on the airplane. As the name implies, this is the situation where more feet of altitude are gained per foot of forward travel. (The maximum angle climb, however, has a lesser rate of climb than the maximum rate of climb, but you will be more likely to clear obstructions with it.)

When you are cleared to *another higher altitude, ATC will expect you* to *climb at the maximum rate until reaching 1000 ft below the new assigned altitude; then a rate of 500–1500 fpm will* be *used.* So, if you are at 6000 ft and are cleared to 9000, you would climb at your max rate until reaching 8000 and then set up a 500–1500 fpm climb to 9000. Knowing that rate of climb is a function of excess horsepower, should you throttle back at reaching 8000 but still hold the max rate of climb *speed?* (The max rate of climb speed would still give the best rate of climb for any particular power setting or power available, although the absolute maximum rate of climb would only be found at full power.) Figure 4-7 shows two possible procedures in such a case. You could make a cruise-type climb the last 1000 ft and would be making better time along your route. Or, you could maintain the max rate of climb speed all the way up and vary the power to get the required 500–1500 fpm the last 1000 ft of climb as shown by the dashed lines. (Assume a 500 fpm climb here.)

So, as you can see, the 500-fpm climb can be obtained by increasing speed or decreasing power to get the same rate. (This could lead to the assumption by some pilots that the elevator controlled the change in rate of climb, but you know differently; the elevator merely acted as a control to slide you along the power-required and power-available curves until the proper excess horsepower is available to give the required rate of climb.) You don't know how much excess power is needed to obtain 500 fpm, and it wouldn't make any difference if you did. One method is to establish the particular rate of climb at the climb speed and vary the power as needed to maintain that rate. In an actual situation you would make a constant-rate climb (500 fpm) as shown by (B) in Figure 4-7 using the VSI. You want to get on with the flight, which leads to the following procedure.

Start determining power settings and airspeeds for your airplane in various maneuvers—a 500-fpm climb is one to keep in mind. Others will be covered as they come up. There are a lot of maneuvers available to get you in the habit of a good scan for your airplane.

It would be good to have the power settings required to get climbs of 250, 500, and 1000 fpm (the last climb rate, of course, is probably available only at low altitudes). But, practically speaking, 500 fpm is the only one to really have fixed in your mind. The purpose of this book is not to give you data on power settings of various airplanes (it's readily available). This is included to have you understand the principles, so that you could go out to a Curtiss Robin or Bleriot and establish the various power settings and airspeeds that would be necessary (after a little experimenting) to obtain the desired performance. You will choose the airspeed that

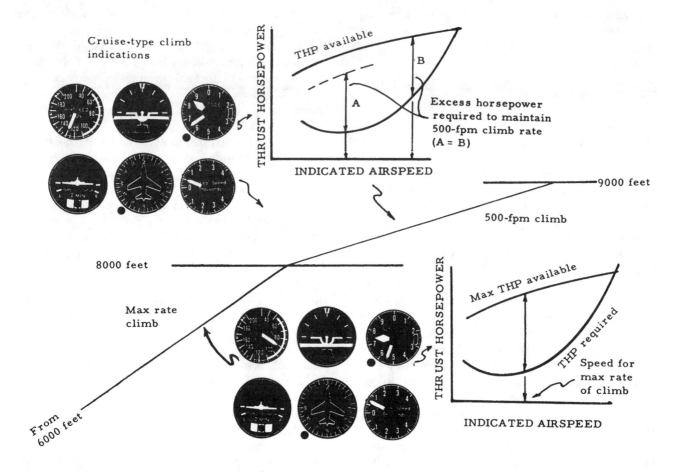

Fig. 4-7. Two possible procedures for setting up a 500-fpm climb (constant power and increase airspeed or constant climb airspeed and decrease power). The maximum rate of climb airspeed for this example airplane is 90 knots.

you need for a maneuver and then find out what power is required. For simplicity you might, for instance, want to use the same prop control setting for climbs and descents, so that the only variable would be manifold pressure—if you have a constant-speed prop. That is, if an rpm of 2400 is used for a climb, don't go to the trouble of moving the prop control for descents.

The vertical speed indicator is a valuable instrument. However, if you had a choice of which flight instrument to lose, this probably would be your choice. It's a fine reference for smooth air and a smooth pilot but may not be so useful if it is "chased" in turbulent air.

Under some conditions, it would be valuable as an aid to finding the power setting required to get a particular rate of climb or descent, but you'll be introduced to the timed climb later. This maneuver is good for your scan development and as a method for finding out the amount of power needed to get a specific rate of climb; it will give a rough figure for remembering.

Figure 4-8 shows an example of the first 500 ft of the 500-fpm climb from 8000 to 9000 ft (see Fig. 4-7). The speed for max rate of climb varies with altitude. For airplanes using max rate of climb speeds in the vicinity of 100 knots (IAS), subtract ½ knot/1000 ft for best climb. For

max angle climb add ½ knot/1000 ft. (It's not quite that much usually, but it's easy to remember.)

Suppose you find that at a certain weight at sea level at 2400 rpm you can get a 500-fpm rate of climb in your airplane by using 20 in. of manifold pressure at the max rate of climb speed of, say, 90 knots. At 5000 ft (same weight), the speed you should hold would be about 87 knots (IAS) for max climb; but check it in the *Pilot's Operating Handbook*. How much power should you use? If you use 20 in. of pressure, that will be too much because you remember back in Chapter 3 that the manifold pressure must be decreased by roughly 0.25 in. of manifold pressure per 1000 ft of density-altitude. Assuming that you're using the same IAS, the aerodynamics, or power required, will be the same (in other words you'll be flying at the same angle of attack, or C_L (and same weight), so the lift and drag and power-required equations will have the same requirements as before). In order to maintain the same margin of excess horsepower and the same 500-fpm rate of climb, at altitude you will vary the manifold pressure as just given. You might check your own airplane's power setting chart to get the amount of manifold pressure drop/1000 ft of density-altitude. You'll find it to be from 0.25 to 0.30 in. of mercury/1000 ft.

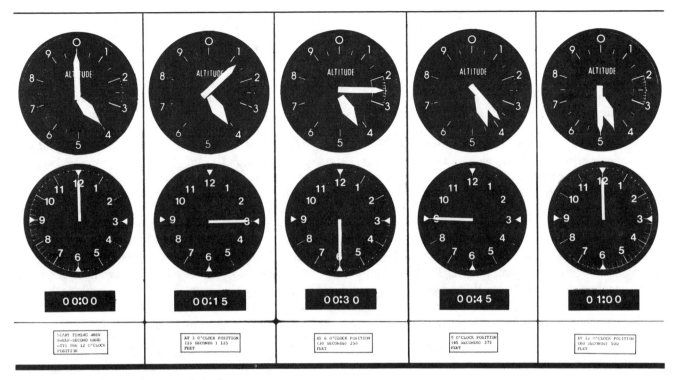

Fig. 4-8. The 500-fpm timed climb.

As far as weight is concerned, it's already known that more weight requires more power to get the same rate of climb. At 5000 ft, the manifold pressure required at the same weight for a 500-fpm climb for the example would be 20 – (5 × 0.25) or 18.75 in. It would be tough to read any manifold pressure gauge that closely. Suppose, now, that you are 10% over the weight used to find the original required manifold pressure of 20 in. This would require an additional 10% (or more) of excess horsepower to have the same rate of climb (referring back to the equation). While you could figure out exactly the power required for every flyable weight at 500 fpm, it's not worth the effort. If the rate of climb is too low, add power. If it is too high, reduce power. The idea is to have some power setting from which to start.

■ **Climbs—Turn and Slip or Turn Coordinator, Airspeed, and Altimeter** During the practical test you'll be expected to do turns, climbs, and descents plus straight and level flight using only the turn and slip or turn coordinator, airspeed, and altimeter for flight instruments. As before, the two climbs of most interest will be the max rate and the 500-fpm climb. It will be most important to have the approximate power setting for the 500-fpm climb in mind.

Figure 4-9 shows a 500-fpm "partial-panel" climb at the best rate of climb speed.

The straight climb is a tough maneuver at first. You will have to keep a close eye on the turn and slip or turn coordinator because this is now your primary direction indicator. The magnetic compass is not much help in the climb, particularly in choppy air. The mag compass can be used to check

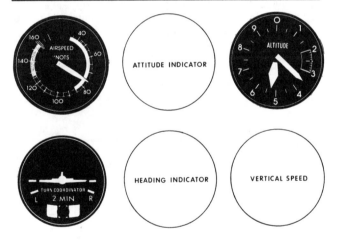

Fig. 4-9. Straight climb (partial-panel). This is also referred to as the "emergency panel."

for large variations in heading, but you remember that on East or West headings acceleration will result in a more northerly reading. This can be used as a check, *but* the needle or small airplane is still the primary heading indicator. If the needle or small airplane is deflected to one side a certain amount, deflect it an equal amount to the other side for what you think is an equal amount of time.

Torque will be a particular nuisance in the partial-panel climb. In full-panel climbs where the heading indicator can be used, you'll have a good heading check and can see immediately if torque is giving you trouble. You may think that you're correcting very well for torque, but the needle or small airplane has to be off only a little to cause problems.

Most instructors do not cage the attitude indicator and heading indicator but cover them so that the instruments can be uncovered at any time to check progress or to make a point in training. In such a situation try climbing partial panel for 1 min, starting out on a particular heading. Then uncover the heading indicator to check your heading. Climb another minute and uncover. You can have a good idea from this that careful supervision of the needle can result in a straight path. (It's a good feeling, after several minutes of turn and slip or turn coordinator and airspeed work, to check the heading indicator and find that you are still very close to your original heading.)

It's particularly important that you be smooth in partial-panel climbs. In general, the same thing applies for leveling off and entering the climb as for VFR work except that you'll have a little more problem with rudder use, altitude, and heading during the transitions.

THE DESCENT

In VFR flying, the descent has been only a method of getting down to a new altitude. Sometimes you let down fast (sounds of passengers' eardrums popping) and sometimes slow, and you never really worried about keeping a particular rate of descent. In instrument flying a controlled rate of descent is one of the most important (if not *the* most important) factors in successful completion of an instrument flight. To make a perfect takeoff and climb, to hit every estimate en route, and to hold altitude within 20 ft all the way on an IFR flight are all fine. However, if you aren't able to

make a precise, controlled descent, it's all wasted—unless you want to hold until it gets VFR again (this is assuming you have a tanker plane following you around the holding pattern so that endurance is no problem).

The descent is covered right after the climb because there is a tie-in between the two. The climb is the result of excess horsepower, the descent a result of deficit horsepower.

First, look at the descent as a *power-off condition.* Figure 4-10 shows a rate of sink versus velocity curve for our fictitious airplane at maximum certificated weight at sea level and at a higher altitude (dashed line). Basically, the curve is derived by gliding the airplane at various airspeeds at a particular weight and altitude and noting the rate of descent for each speed. Obviously, it would be impractical to glide through sea level in most areas, so other density-altitudes are used and the data extrapolated to sea level. True airspeed is used in Figure 4-10 to give a better look at altitude effects on rate of sink.

This curve looks like the power curve turned upside down. Basically, that's what it is. Point A shows the airspeed for the minimum rate of descent under the conditions stated, or weight and sea level altitude. Incidentally, it might as well be noted at this time that the absolute minimum rate of sink is found at sea level (standard altitude) if all other conditions of weight, airplane configuration, etc., are equal. Then, following this and looking again at Figure 4-10, it can be said that for any *indicated* airspeed the lower the altitude, the lower the rate of sink in the power-off condition (and partial power condition as well, which will be covered later with further explanation). Point B is the maximum distance glide airspeed and is found by extending a line from the origin, tangent to the curve. No other speed will give the shallowest

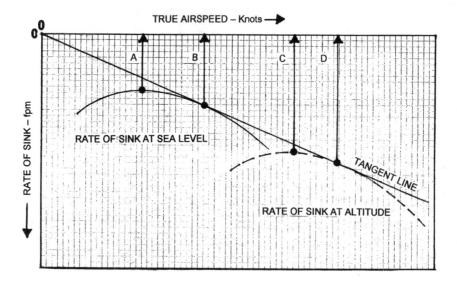

Fig. 4-10. Rate of sink versus velocity curves for a particular airplane at sea level and at altitude. Points A and B are for minimum sink and max distance glides at sea level. Points C and D represent the two types of glides at some higher altitude.

glide angle for the conditions as set up in Figure 4-10. Points C and D are the true airspeeds at altitude for minimum sink and max distance glides respectively. It's interesting to see that the line extended through B also goes through Point D, which leads to the conclusion that the *maximum distance glide ratio is the same for all altitudes.* While at altitude at the speed of Point C. the airplane is sinking faster. It is also moving through the air faster because of a greater true airspeed, and the angle of glide remains the same. The glide ratio is a function of the lift-to-drag ratio (L/D) of the airplane. L/D varies with angle of attack. At one particular angle it is the greatest value. If the L/D of an airplane is 9/1 at some angle of attack, this is also its glide ratio. Since L/D is a function of angle of attack or, more properly, C_L (coefficient of lift), it is often expressed as the C_L/C_D ratio because the other factors that affect both lift and drag—dynamic pressure, $(\varrho/2)V^2$, and wing area, S—are the same for any particular situation and cancel out, leaving only the C_L and C_D as

$$\frac{L}{D} = \frac{C_L \frac{\varrho}{2} V^2 S}{C_D \frac{\varrho}{2} V^2 S} = \frac{C_L}{C_D} \quad .$$

The maximum distance glide is always found at the same C_L.

As far as altitude is concerned, you would see the same indicated airspeed for all altitudes to get the C_L/C_D max, or maximum, glide distance. But as far as weight is concerned, the indicated airspeed (or more technically correct, *calibrated* airspeed, but, again, we are assuming for this chapter that they are the same) for max distance glide must be decreased with decreased weight to maintain the magic

coefficient of lift. This is understandable if the lift equation is examined again:

$$\text{Lift} = C_L \frac{\varrho}{2} V^2 S$$

If weight is decreased, lift must be decreased in order to maintain the same balance of forces. Since only one C_L provides the max C_L/C_D, it will be fixed. The wing area (S) is fixed so that the expression $(\varrho/2)V^2$, or dynamic pressure (or indicated/calibrated airspeed), must be decreased to maintain the same C_L at the required lower lift.

Following the reasoning given for the climb, the rate of sink might be expressed as

$$\text{Rate of sink} = \frac{\text{deficit thp} \times 33,000}{\text{airplane weight}}$$

By controlling the amount of deficit horsepower, you can readily control the rate of descent at a chosen airspeed. In making an ILS approach, the rate of descent must be carefully controlled in order to stay on the glide path.

Figure 4-11 shows part of an ILS approach chart for Nashville Metropolitan Airport.

The glide slope is set up at 2.5–3° above the horizon, depending on the terrain and obstructions on the final course at a particular airport. The full details on the ILS will come later, but the idea of descending on the glide slope should be covered here. Chapter 5 has information on rates of descent required to follow various glide slopes (2½°, 2¾°, and 3°) at different approach speeds. Incidentally, you can get a *rough* idea of the rate of descent required for a 3° slope by adding a "zero" to the speed and dividing by 2 (110 knots + 0 = 1100 ÷ 2 = 550 fpm).

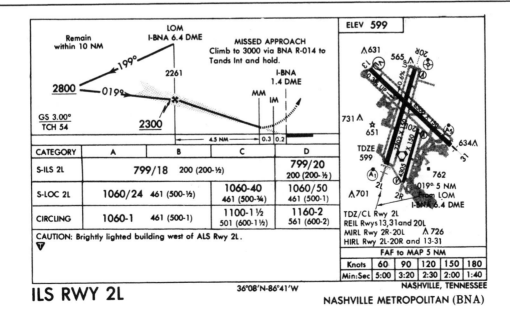

Fig. 4-11. Part of an ILS approach chart for Nashville Metropolitan Airport.

Speeds given are for *no-wind* conditions or, more accurately, are groundspeeds. If you are indicating 110 knots and are only moving down the glide slope at 90 knots but are using the descent as required for the 110-knot speed, you'd run below the glide slope and run out of altitude well before getting to the field. If, on the other hand, you are indicating 90 knots on the approach and have a tailwind (and, say, a groundspeed of 110 knots), you'd better descend at the rate required for 110 knots, or you'll be above the glide slope and won't get down to make the field. Of course, the problem is that you don't always know the groundspeed, and it may be constantly changing in gusty wind conditions. Your job will be to maintain a constant indicated airspeed and set the power required to maintain the proper rate of descent. In smooth air and no-wind conditions, it seems that you should be able to set the power at a particular manifold pressure and maintain a constant airspeed and fly right down the glide slope—but that's not always the way it works. Looking at Figure 4-11, you see that the airplane descends 1500 ft on the glide slope during the approach. (The "decision height" (or "decision altitude") is 799 ft MSL and the descent starts at 2300 ft MSL at the outer marker, a descent of 1500 ft on the glide slope, but the full discussion of decision height and other terms will be reserved for Chapter 8.) If you set the manifold pressure at 13 in. at the start of the approach and then left the throttle alone, you'd have roughly another 1.5 in. of manifold pressure before you got to the minimum altitude; the manifold pressure will pick up this amount in descending the 1500 ft. True, in order to maintain a constant power in descending, you would have needed to add about 0.35–0.40 in. to compensate for the decrease of 1500 ft. In Chapter 3 it was noted that you had to *decrease* the manifold pressure about 0.25 in. for the sample airplane for each 1000 ft of altitude *increase* in order to maintain the same power at a constant rpm. But the manifold pressure

has increased about 1.5 in., so you'll have a little over an inch more of manifold pressure than is correct for the rate of descent. You'll find that leaving the throttle completely alone on the ILS approach (or any similar approach) will result in trouble in maintaining the rate of descent required to stay down on the glide slope. If the power change is ignored, the airplane must be nosed down and ends up crossing the boundary at a *higher speed* than desired. Figure 4-12 shows what happens to the power-required and power-available curve in such an instance.

You subconsciously lower the nose to pick up the speed at which the required power deficit (rate of sink) is again obtained. You don't know what this speed is, but nose over until the rate of sink is proper. You may have to overdo it slightly for a while to get back down on the glide slope, this is, of course, assuming that you haven't touched the throttle since the beginning of the descent.

An airplane of the type you'll be flying (for a while at least) will be likely to make its best ILS approach at an indicated airspeed of from 90 to 120 knots. What is meant is that you are not allowed this variation, but that you're not likely to pick less than 90 nor more than 120 knots for the approach airspeed. A too slow approach speed delays other traffic and in turbulent air can result in marginal control. A too fast airspeed may result in excessive floating on landing or maybe an overshoot with an unnecessary missed approach. This may not be too much of a problem for a combination of your type of airplane and airports with ILS approaches. But this is a poor habit to get into for someone who may be flying jet airliners later.

For instance, for a Piper Aztec, a speed of 125 mph is often used for an ILS approach for several reasons:

1. This is 110 knots, a figure easily interpolated on approach charts (actually, it's 109 knots, but this is close enough for practical purposes).

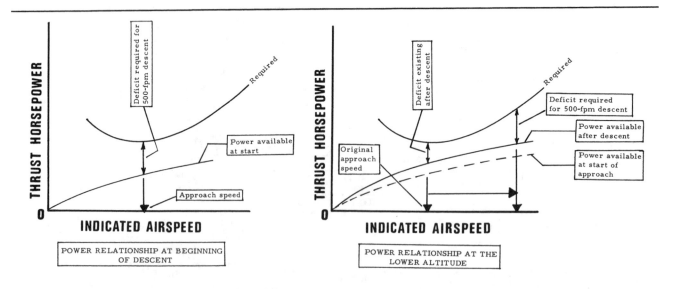

Fig. 4-12. Power-required and power-available curves for an airplane during an ILS approach. The throttle was set at the beginning and not changed. It's a vicious cycle, because if the pilot shoves over to a speed to pick up a 500-fpm rate of descent, the new airspeed will require a greater rate of descent in order to stay on the glide slope.

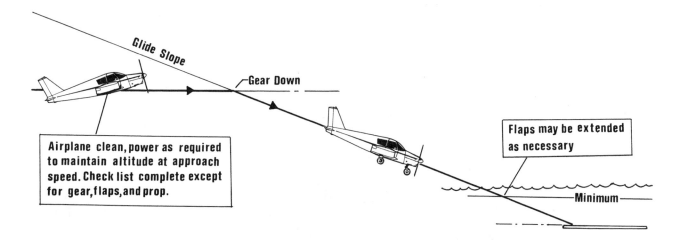

Fig. 4-13. As the airplane comes up on the glide slope, extend the gear and set the prop. The glide slope angle is exaggerated.

2. It is a speed that allows for a good margin of control in turbulent air.

3. It is fast enough to help expedite traffic flow and yet not so fast that upon reaching ILS minimums of 200 ft and ½ mi (with the landing surface in sight, naturally) the power can be reduced to idle and the airplane landed without excessive floating.

4. 125 mph is the maximum full-flaps speed so that when visual contact is made with the field the flaps can be extended without structural problems.

5. Because it is the max speed for full flaps, it is the top of the white arc on the airspeed indicator (Fig. 2-3) that makes a quick reference, or "how goes it," for an aid in your scan on the glide slope.

Figure 4-13 shows one technique, and you'll note that there is a period of level flight as you fly to intercept the glide slope. (Actually, you may have about a couple of minutes to lose 100 ft or so on some approaches, but for practical purposes it would be level flight.) One procedure would be to fly this part at the final approach speed, using enough power to maintain a constant altitude at this speed in the clean condition. Then, as you approach the glide slope, extend the gear and set the prop, maintaining the approach airspeed. For some airplanes of the type you'll be flying, extension of the gear is exactly what is needed to get the desired rate of descent of around 500 fpm.

Of course, the throttle must be retarded slightly as the plane descends, for the reasons cited earlier. The theory of Figure 4-13 is shown in Figure 4-14.

Other airplanes may require slight changes in power as the glide slope is approached, or it might be better to use partial flaps as well as gear, all during the approach. For airplanes with fixed gear, the power will have to be decreased because on the level part of the approach it will already be in the "down and dirty" condition as far as the gear is concerned. Instead of increasing the horsepower required, you'll throttle back and *decrease* the horsepower available

and get your horsepower deficit that way. Starting at the end of the level portion of the approach, you can set up a deficit horsepower for the required rate of sink.

Too many new instrument trainees try to fly only the glide slope indications on the approach. This makes for a considerable amount of overcontrolling. They have no idea of the combination of power and airspeed required to get the right rate of sink and try to outguess the glide slope needle by throttle jockeying and elevator flapping. The final result is a power variation from idle to full power and back to idle, with the glide slope needle going up and down like a bandleader's baton. Figure 4-15 shows the instrument indications on an ILS approach.

The glide slope is only 1.4° thick. That is, from full-up to full-down, deflection of the needle on the instrument

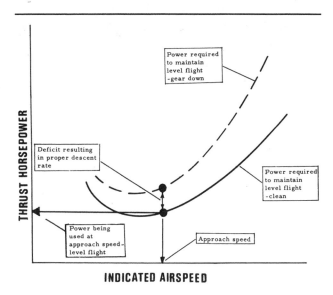

Fig. 4-14. Power-available and power-required curves for the two conditions shown in Figure 4-13.

Fig. 4-15. Instrument indications on an ILS approach. The attitude indicator shows a more nose-down indication than might be seen in an actual situation. The airplane is on course, slightly above the glide slope, and has the landing gear down.

means only 1.4° of travel through the glide slope. At ½ mi out, the 0.7° up or down means that you'd have a margin of about 32 ft up or down to keep the glide slope needle in the instrument.

Select your procedure, find a reference power setting for the descent, and use that as a quick and dirty figure. Obviously, that power setting will vary with conditions, such as variations in weight and density-altitude, but you'll have something with which to start. Your instructor probably will have available all of the power settings for the various rates of climbs and descents that you'll be working with.

If you are flying a twin, practice some 500-fpm descents with one engine throttled back to zero thrust, so that you'll have a good idea of the power setting required with gear up or down. You might also shoot a few ILS approaches with a simulated engine failure.

Figure 4-16 shows an exaggerated condition for a typical four-place, general aviation airplane on the glide slope (or on any controlled descent). In this example the pilot has gotten (or a strong downdraft has done it) well on the backside of the power curve. The pilot has pulled the nose up to "get back up on the glide slope" and applied full power but is still sinking and not moving back up on the proper glide path.

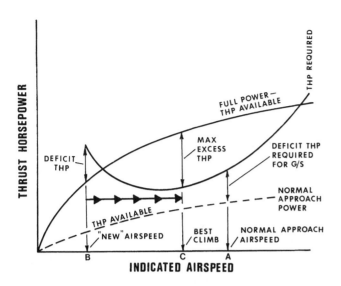

Fig. 4-16. A fictitious four-place general aviation airplane in approach configuration well on the back side of the power curve. The position (airspeed and deficit horsepower) at (A) shows conditions for a normal approach. The airplane has ended up below the glide path because of a strong downdraft or the pilot's shortcomings, and the situation is that as shown at (B). The pilot has raised the nose and added full power in an attempt to climb. The illustration has been "stretched" horizontally for clarity.

The airplane should be at Point A on the glide path with the deficit horsepower existing for the proper rate of descent.

Instead, here the airplane is at Point B, with full power on, below the glide path and still sinking. If the nose is pulled up any more, the rate of sink will increase. With full power already being used, the situation is critical, so the pilot must move the stick or wheel forward to climb (moving to Point C for the maximum rate of climb if that's what is needed). With the glide slope above the airplane, the nose must be moved away from it (or lowered) in order to move *up* to the slope. Had you "pitched to the glide slope" here, you would have been in (more) trouble. On the *front side* of the power curve (A), which is a normal state of affairs, pitching to the glide slope works.

In this exaggerated example the move would be to lower the nose to increase the airspeed, as shown by the heavy arrows. The power could be adjusted to stay on the glide slope after it's reached again, or perhaps in this case the best climb speed (and full power) could be maintained, the airplane cleaned up, and a missed approach initiated.

■ Descents—Turn and Slip or Turn Coordinator, Airspeed, and Altimeter

You should practice straight descents using the "partial-panel" instruments. The straight descent probably will be easier to handle than the climb because of the lack of torque. But if the heading gets out of control, it can still end up as a diving spiral.

The same general requirements of the partial-panel straight climb apply here. The needle or small airplane (and ball) is the primary directional and wing attitude indicator. If the indicator deviates to one side, deflect it (with coordinated controls) an equal amount to the other side for what you think is equal time. To try to chase what you think is the proper rate of descent with the throttle is a surefire way for everything to get out of hand. If you forget everything else in this chapter, remember that even a barnyard power setting and airspeed to shoot for will keep the airplane from getting away if your attention is momentarily diverted—such as may happen on the glide slope when you have to report the outer marker or when the tower calls and gives information. If you are *only* flying the glide slope needle and using all kinds of power settings and airspeed to do it, any distraction from the glide slope needle would mean losing it—and the possibility of having to go around for another try. With the right power and airspeed, you still might be off if distracted but not enough that you can't get things back on course.

The term "turn indicator" will be used in *the rest of the book to describe either the turn and slip needle* or *the turn coordinator's small airplane, whichever applies to the instrumentation in the airplane you're using.*

■ Practice Maneuvers for Climbs and Descents

There are several good practice maneuvers that will help your transitions to and from climbs and descents.

Don't make the mistake of some pilots in overemphasizing the importance of the maneuvers. They are only intended to show the fundamentals of instrument flying and are not an end in themselves. You can do beautiful practice patterns all day and wouldn't be a foot closer to your destination. Don't fly the maneuvers mechanically. *Remember what power settings it takes to get the 500-fpm (or 250 or 1000) rate of climb or descent—and then use this knowledge.* Too many pilots have the numbers for power settings and airspeeds for all kinds of flight configurations and maneuvers but forget this information under actual conditions. Keep a copy in the airplane for easy access if needed.

There are all kinds of patterns, and you can make up your own. Figure 4-17 shows one that might be used to smooth out straight-ahead climbs and descents.

The pattern in Figure 4-17 can be varied to fit your airplane. The descents can be made clean at first and then in approach configuration, or at least in the configuration you plan to use for the ILS or other types of letdowns. You may not get a 500-fpm climb from your airplane at higher altitudes and so could use 400 fpm or even 300 fpm for the practice climbs and descents.

Look at the power effects throughout the airspeed range, but don't waste time practicing oddball and impractical combinations over and over. After you are proficient at full-panel patterns, practice the same patterns using turn indicator, airspeed, and altimeter. You might practice Figure 4-17 without any straight and level flight, going directly from climb to descent and vice versa. This will help to pin down exact power settings—and also give a look at what could happen in a missed approach situation.

Fig. 4-17. A maneuver for smoothing out climbs, descents, and transitions thereto. Pick your own speed if you don't like that one.

Other good exercises under the hood would be to set up simulated traffic patterns at a safe altitude, using gear and flaps (changing flap settings as might be done on approach) and maintaining constant altitudes or rates of descent as applicable. Practice missed approaches (go-arounds) adding climb power, pulling the gear up and flaps up in increments. This will help your scan. Also practice this with the turn indicator, airspeed, and altimeter to smooth out your procedures.

THE TURN

When under positive (radar) control, you'll be expected to make all turns standard rate, unless otherwise requested. This way the controller will know, for instance, when to start you turning onto final to intercept the ILS. If you rack the airplane around one turn and sneak around on the other, the poor controller will always be trying to outguess you.

A standard-rate turn is 3°/sec, or 180°/min for the airplane you'll be training in. That's one thing you'll learn about instrument flying, particularly flying partial panel; the steeper the bank, the easier it is to lose control of the airplane. A good exercise in some of the clean, retractable-gear airplanes in current use is to do some turns on partial panel at double or triple standard rate at about cruise airspeed. You'll find that at first it requires a great deal of concentration to maintain altitude and avoid a spiral at steep banks.

The thumb rule for angles of bank for a standard-rate turn given back in Chapter 2 still stands; that is,

$$\text{Bank} = \frac{\text{airspeed (knots)}}{10} + \text{½ of the first answer}$$

The airspeed used for the thumb rules is true airspeed rather than indicated or calibrated. But for practical use, you can use indicated—for lower altitudes anyway.

Knowing the angle of bank required will give another check of the turn indicator. Before practicing basic instruments, check the calibration of the needle or small airplane by setting up a standard-rate turn and checking as follows:

Set up the indication for a standard-rate turn in either direction on the turn indicator as required for your particular instrument. Turn for 1 min and then roll out. Find out the number of degrees turned in that time. If, say, 150° instead of 180°—and you had held the proper turn indicator deflection all the way—then you should hold about 1⅕ times the

indicated deflection in order to get the required 180° in one minute, that is, 180 ÷ 150 = 1⅕. If you had turned 210° in the minute, you should then use 6/7 of the earlier turn indicator deflection to get the proper rate of turn. To double check, turn in the other direction and time it again.

The reason for practicing timed turns is to be able to do them almost unconsciously and to be able to do them without actually having to use the clock. It's a good maneuver for ensuring that the clock is included in your scan. In practical use, you'll have a specific heading to turn to and won't waste your time checking to see if the turn is exactly 3° or 3.001°/sec. There'll be clearances to acknowledge, navigational aids to check, and other things that will be of more vital interest. You must be precise, but don't get so involved in one aspect of instrument flying that others are neglected. You could get so engrossed in making a perfectly timed turn that you'd turn past the heading needed to get on the localizer, or the heading given by the radar controller.

Suppose you were directed by the radar controller to make a 180° turn to the right. It's likely that you *won't* make a perfect timed turn and will roll out off heading if you follow the clock blindly. In an actual situation, you would set up a standard-rate turn and roll out on the proper heading. You would roll out on the required heading, whether a few seconds late or early. After all, that's the purpose of the turn—to get to a specific heading—and a few seconds either way won't make any difference, whereas a few degrees would. A thumb rule for rolling out on a specific heading is to start rolling out at a point one-third the degree of bank. In other words, if you're in a 30° banked turn, start the roll-out about 10° before the desired heading is reached. It is unlikely that your standard-rate turns will be quite this steeply banked at this point of your training, since that would require a true airspeed of about 200 knots. As a round figure, 10° wouldn't be bad for a lead in rolling out for *all* standard-rate turns at cruise for airplanes of the type in which you'll be training.

As a little review of theory, Figure 4-18 shows the power required for a particular airplane to fly at a constant altitude (sea level), straight and level, and in a 60° banked turn.

Point A in Figure 4-18 shows that in straight and level flight at 65% power a certain speed (150 knots) results. In the 60° banked turn (B), in order to fly at a constant altitude. a lower speed must result. Remember, a constant altitude

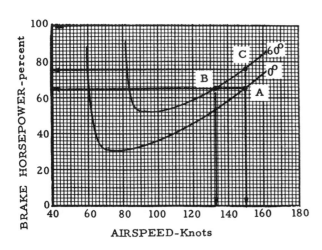

Fig. 4-18. Brake horsepower required to maintain a constant altitude for straight and level and a 60° banked turn. Brake horsepower is used here because the pilot would be thinking of this in setting power.

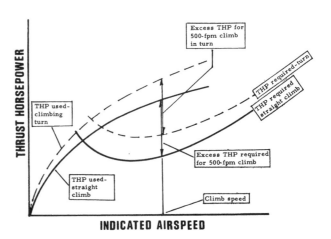

Fig. 4-19. Excess horsepower for the wings-level climb and the climbing turn. (Must be the same value for the same rates of climb.)

results when the power available equals the power required. Of course, the power-required curves for banks of 1–59° would fall between those shown.

If for some reason you also *had* to maintain exactly the same airspeed in the turn as in straight and level flight, this could be done only by increasing the power available to the value shown by the higher line, which intersects the power-required curve top (Point C). Now you will be able to maintain a constant altitude at the greater airspeed. Did adding power increase your airspeed? Not at all. You could have increased the airspeed merely by relaxing back pressure and letting the nose drop. The added power let the airplane fly at the higher airspeed *and still maintain a constant altitude.*

For the shallower banks used for standard-rate turns, the airspeed loss is negligible. For steep turns it is a good idea to add power. This not only allows you to maintain altitude at a higher airspeed but also lowers the stall speed slightly. This spreads the two areas (stall and your flight speed) a little more than would be so otherwise and may help avert an unexpected stall in a tight situation.

Climbing turns are another matter. If turning while executing a maximum-rate climb, the climb rate will decrease slightly, and there's nothing you can do about it, since you are already using all of the legal power. For 500-fpm climbs, the decrease in climb rate due to the turn can be offset by slightly increased power (unless your plane is so underpowered that 500 fpm *is* the max rate of climb with climb power and wings level so that there's no reserve). Where, for instance, 20 in. and 2400 rpm give a 500-fpm wings-level climb, in a climbing turn perhaps 20.5 in. might be necessary to maintain that rate. In Figure 4-19 look at the maximum excess horsepower point as shown for a wings-level at 500 fpm and a climbing turn at the same rate. Since thrust horsepower is the criterion for climb performance, Figure 4-19 uses thrust horsepower and indicated airspeed.

At any rate, you should normally not exceed a standard-rate turn at any time in the climbing turn. The steeper the bank, the less the rate of climb for any given power setting. The same basic idea applies to the descending turn. If you've picked your speed and have a power setting for a wings-level descent of so many feet per minute, the turn should require more power to maintain that same descent. Where it took 12 in. for a 500-fpm descent in the wings-level clean condition (probably another 2 in. would be required with the gear down), the turn would require perhaps 12.5 in. for the same rate of clean descent. You will practice straight climbs and descents, plus climbing and descending turns, as a part of your introduction to basic instrument flying. Practically speaking, it won't make that much difference to worry about changing power in *shallow* climbing or descending turns.

■ Turns—Turn Indicator, Airspeed, and Altimeter

The timed turn will be of value when you have no heading indicator or equivalent. Again, a steeply banked turn—particularly using turn indicator, airspeed, and altimeter only—will radically increase chances of loss of control, so at no time make turns steeper than standard rate.

In using the turn indicator, some pilots say to lead with the rudder, deflecting the indicator and then following with the ailerons. If this is the way you make all your turns—VFR and full panel—then go ahead. If not, then don't throw in a new technique here. It is recommended that you use simultaneously coordinated controls so that the turn indicator is deflected the proper amount and the ball is centered. If the ball is centered, the turn indicator will give an approximate picture of the wings' attitude. If the ball is centered and the indicator is deflected, the wings will be down in that direction. In instrument flying, in theory at least, the ball should *always* be centered; there are no maneuvers in normal or predictable IFR that would require slipping or skidding.

As you know by now, adverse yaw at the beginning of the roll-in may cause the turn indicator temporarily to indicate a turn in the opposite direction. This is one of the reasons given for leading slightly with the rudder when using the turn and slip as a turn reference as opposed to a turn coordinator. Since such indicator action is expected, it shouldn't cause any confusion if you are slightly late in rudder action. In rough air you have to average the indicator swings to maintain a standard rate of turn and will be likely to overdo your roll-ins, roll-outs, and "averaging" of the indicator swings at the beginning of your instrument training.

As a possible crutch in an emergency, another method of turning to an approximate heading is the use of the turn indicator and magnetic compass, using the "Four Main Directions" method.

In a shallow banked turn, the compass is fairly accurate on the headings of East or West, lags by about 30° as the plane passes the heading of North, and leads by about 30° as the plane passes the heading of South. The exact lag and lead will have to be checked for your situation, which will include latitude and other variables. For illustration purposes here, it is assumed to be 30°. This "northerly turning error" affects the compass while the plane is turning.

Assume that you are flying on a heading of 060° and want to make a 180° turn. The desired new heading will be 240°. By turning to the left, there is a cardinal heading (West) reasonably close to the new heading. A standard-rate turn is made to the left, but no timing is attempted. You will be watching for West on the compass, and as the plane reaches that heading, you will start timing. The desired heading is 30° (270 – 240°) past this, and the 30° will require 10 sec at the standard rate. The timing can be done by counting "one thousand and one, one thousand and two," and so forth, up to 10, at which time the turn indicator and ball are centered (Fig. 4-20).

A turn to the right could have been made, realizing that the nearest major compass heading (South) will be 60°, or 20 sec, short of the desired heading of 240°. In that case, you will set up a standard-rate turn to the right and will not start timing until the compass indicates 210°. Remember that the compass will lead on a turn through South and will be ahead of the actual heading by about 30°, as a round figure (Fig. 4-21).

When the 210° indication on the magnetic compass is given, the 20-second timing begins, either by the sweep-second hand of the aircraft clock, by your watch, or by counting.

There are several disadvantages to this system, the major one being that it requires a visual picture of the airplane's present and proposed heading and mental calculations. You may not have time or may be too excited for a mental exercise at this point. Also, in bumpy weather the compass may not give accurate readings on the four main headings.

The main advantage is that reasonably accurate turns may be made without a timepiece, since any selected heading will never be more than 45°, or 15 sec, away from a major heading.

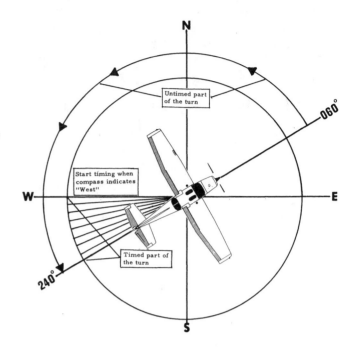

Fig. 4-20. A turn to the left using the four main directions method.

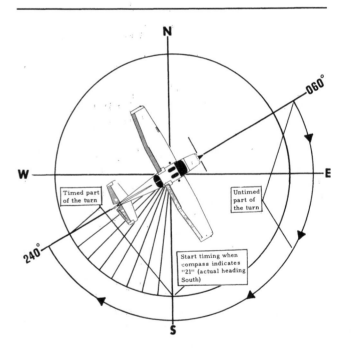

Fig. 4-21. A turn to the right using the four main directions method.

You should also practice steep turns—both full and emergency or partial panel. You'll see in such turns, with the turn indicator pegged, that your scan will have to be well developed or you'll end up in a spiral. It's also a graphic display of why you want to keep turns standard-rate (and maybe even less) when using the turn indicator, airspeed, and altimeter.

The equation for *rate* of turn is:

$$\text{Rate of turn (degrees/sec)} = \frac{1091 \tan \phi}{V \text{ (knots)}}$$

The term ϕ is the bank, in degrees. The tangent of the angle may be found on many pocket calculators but is given here for several banks (rounded off):

Angle	Tangent
15°	0.27
30°	0.58
45°	1.0
60°	1.73

So for a bank of 15° at 100 knots:

$$\text{Rate of turn} = \frac{1091 \times 0.27}{100 \text{ (knots)}} = 2.95° / \sec$$

The thumb rule cited earlier gives an answer of 3°/*sec,* or a standard-rate turn.

The *radius* of turn may be found by the equation:

$$\text{Radius} = \frac{V^2 \text{ (knots)}}{11.3 \tan \phi}$$

Assuming a bank of 30° and a true airspeed of 150 knots, the radius is:

$$\frac{(150)^2}{(11.3)(0.58)} = 3433 \text{ ft}$$

PRACTICE MANEUVERS FOR THE FOUR FUNDAMENTALS

One maneuver that combines all the expected flight patterns is shown in Figure 4-22. You can make up others to suit your requirements. Do these using the full panel at first and, of course, under the hood with a safety pilot on board.

After problems on timed turns and descents are pretty well ironed out, a realistic practice procedure is to simulate a holding pattern, as shown in Figure 4-23. At first, you'll do this without using a holding fix or electronic aids. Later, you'll practice holding over a VOR, radio beacon, or intersection. Make sure the wind doesn't drift you over into the next county when practicing without electronic aids. The safety pilot can keep an eye out for this.

For realism you might make two level circuits and then descend 1000 ft (at 500 fpm) sometime during the next one. Make two more circuits and then descend another 1000 ft at 500 fpm. You'll note that the holding pattern in Figure 4-23 takes 4 min for a complete circuit. Descending at 500 fpm would mean that part of the descent would be in the straightaway and part in the turn. In an actual situation of

being shuttled down from a holding pattern, such as would be the case for airplanes being stacked over the approach fix, you will commence the descent immediately upon clearance from ATC. You would not wait for the sweep-second hand to conveniently reach the 12-o'clock position—you descend *immediately.* This means that a knowledge of the power setting required for a 500-fpm clean descent is important. You'll be holding in the clean condition (don't require extra power by having the gear or flaps down—if the gear is retractable, that is). You might also practice setting up the conditions of manifold pressure, rpm, and mixture that would be used to conserve fuel during holding.

Practice holding patterns, using 1-min legs for both straightaways. You'll find that an actual holding pattern may require extending or shortening the time for the outbound leg to take care of wind for a 1-min inbound leg. Figure 4-24 shows what might be the case.

Holding patterns as applied to an actual IFR situation will be covered in Chapter 12. You should *practice* them using only the turn indicator, airspeed, altimeter, and magnetic compass after becoming proficient in using the full panel of instruments. You may ease into simple holding patterns, using a fix (VOR, etc.), at the end of these sessions.

While being required to set up a holding pattern in real conditions is becoming rarer and rarer, knowledge of the procedure is necessary, and practice here will also help develop your scan.

Here are some maneuvers that can help build your confidence (in every case the manifold pressure gauge and/or tachometer will be part of your scan).

■ Straight and Level

1. Cover the turn indicator, heading indicator, and airspeed. Fly for 2 min, keeping the wings level with the attitude gyro and maintaining a constant altitude. Uncover the heading indicator and check your heading change (if any) after the 2-min period (normal cruise at 65% power).
2. Use only the heading indicator and altimeter to fly straight and level. You will find that the heading indicator is a very important aid in keeping the wings level. If the direction changes, a wing is down. You'll soon find you can use the heading indicator for wing attitude information almost as well as the attitude gyro (normal cruise).
3. Set up a cruise at a constant altitude, noting the airspeed after things are stabilized, then fly straight and level for 3 min, using only the airspeed for pitch and the heading indicator for bank information. (Cover the other four flight instruments.) You'll be surprised how closely you can fly the airspeed and how little altitude variation there is after the altimeter is uncovered at the end of 3 min.

TRANSITIONS (CONSTANT ALTITUDE AND HEADING). You should be able to make smooth constant-altitude and heading transitions from cruise airspeed down to holding and approach speeds.

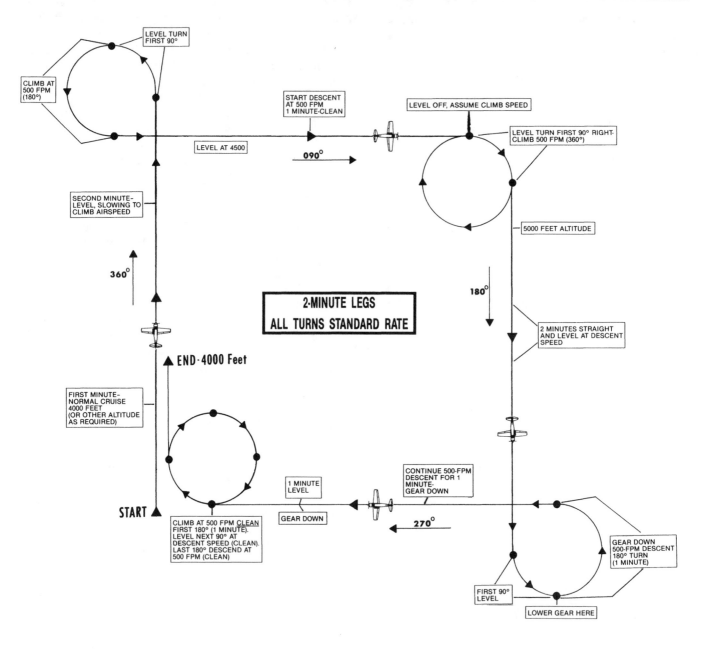

Fig. 4-22. A simple (?) practice pattern. There will be times it will keep you as busy as someone scratching chiggers but will help establish a good scan for your particular airplane.

You can use the following exercise (hooded, with a safety pilot) to check on your scan and control of the airplane (full panel at first):

1. Trim the airplane and fly straight and level at normal cruise for 2 min.
2. Slow to 10 knots below cruise, adjust power, and trim. Fly for 2 min.
3. Continue to reduce the airspeed by 10 knots (your instructor may want to use 5 knots) until down to 10 knots above a stall, or the approach/holding speed, whichever is lowest. Fly for 2 min, level and with a constant heading. Here's where you'll learn the importance of trimming the airplane.

4. Work back up to cruise in 10-knot intervals. If you're taking instrument training in a clean retractable, you will see the need for planning ahead when slowing from cruise—it seems that altitude is gained and you'll tend to still be trying to lose airspeed while passing the holding fix.

Your instructor may require some less radical airspeed/altitude changes in the approach configuration (if it's different from the en route configuration).

Some **common errors** in transitions are:

Poor altitude control—You will at first tend to gain altitude as you slow up and lose altitude when increasing the

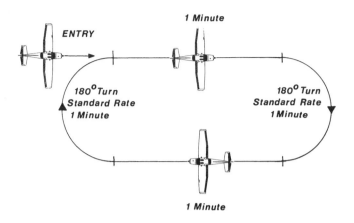

Fig. 4-23. A practice holding pattern.

airspeed. This is normally the result of pitch changes that are too rapid.

Heading control problems—You'll tend to get fixated on altitude and may discover that the airplane has moved well off the prechosen heading.

Poor trim use—You may feel that you can "hold it" and trimming is too much trouble for the short periods. Get in the habit of automatically trimming for airspeed, power, and configuration changes. Again, good trim habits can keep the airplane under control if you're distracted. Use the rudder trim at low speeds if it's available.

Power control problems—Don't try to get the rpm or manifold pressure *exactly* right with your first power change. Get back to the flight instruments and then readjust power more closely as needed. If you stay concentrated on power adjustment (or, in other cases, nav instruments) for too long at a time, altitude *and* heading control will suffer.

The vertical speed indicator will be a good indicator of trends, but don't "chase" it.

■ **Turns**

1. Make a constant-altitude standard-rate turn, using the attitude indicator, airspeed, and altimeter only—setting up the bank as required to get a 3°/sec turn for a particular airspeed (normal cruise at 65% power). Start out on a prechosen heading and make timed turns of 90°, 135°, 180°, etc. Uncover the heading indicator and check your accuracy after each turn.

2. Turn to predetermined headings using the heading indicator, airspeed, and altimeter only. You can approximate the correct rate of turn by the rate of direction-change. With a little practice you can set up a rate of turn that's close to standard rate. The main thing is to keep your scan going and not let the rate of direction-change be too great (bank too steep). If this is the case, shallow the bank and get the turn back to a more reasonable rate. In actual flight, if you have lost the attitude indicator and turn indicator (an unlikely loss combination to be sure), a serious situation exists. The main idea is to keep the

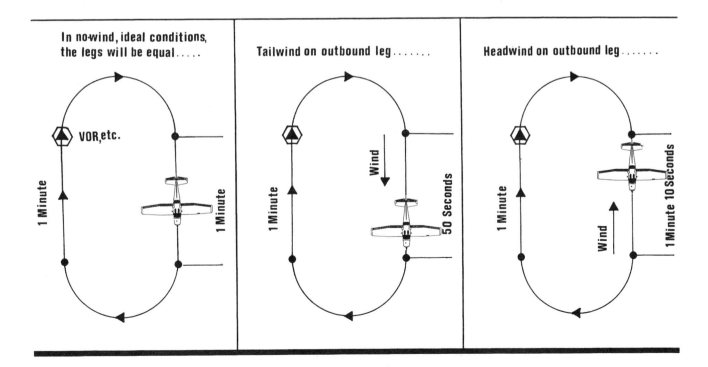

Fig. 4-24. Some possible variations of time for the outbound legs in the holding pattern for different wind conditions.

airplane under control and roll out on predetermined headings. An exact standard turn rate is less important than those two requirements.

Practice the above at slow-flight speed and expected holding speed. Use the airspeed and turn indicator only for some turns.

■ Descents

1. Make straight descents at 500 fpm using the heading indicator, airspeed, altimeter, and vertical speed indicator. Use the power setting worked out earlier to get the 500-fpm descent at the chosen approach speed. Notice that the proper combination of power and airspeed gives the required rate of sink. In smooth air you can easily check the relationship of power, airspeed, and descent by covering up the airspeed indicator. By setting power and carefully keeping the 500-fpm descent (with the elevators), you can uncover the airspeed indicator to find that the approach speed is being held. (The elevators had controlled the proper airspeed while that instrument was covered.) You'll see that by using the heading indicator, altimeter, vertical speed, and power instruments you can make pretty accurate descents in smooth air without airspeed, attitude gyro, or turn indicator.

2. Do the same as above, using the attitude gyro and then the turn indicator to replace the heading indicator. Check your heading (uncover the heading indicator) after a couple of minutes of straight descent.

You might cover the altimeter also during one of your descents and see what can be done with the heading indicator, power setting, vertical speed indicator, and timing. (After a 500-fpm descent at a prechosen number of minutes—don't fly into the ground—uncover the altimeter and see how close you are to the correct altitude.)

Practice descending turns using the flight combinations just discussed.

The instructor will have you practice missed approaches by having you descend at, say, 500 fpm in approach configuration to a predetermined "DH/DA" or "MDA" and have you execute a missed approach, noting the altitude required to add climb power and stop the descent; then you will clean up and climb. This is one of the most critical phases of instrument flying and you'll be very busy the first few times. You must be able to *stop the descent* and get a climb rate started. The distraction of raising gear and flaps (if used) can cause a problem with heading and altitude that could be fatal in an actual situation. *So practice.*

■ Climbs

1. Make climbs at recommended climb power and airspeed. Check the approximate rate of climb at a "medium" altitude (4000–6000 ft MSL for most of the United States). Say it's 700 ft/min at the chosen altitude, power setting, and airspeed. Using the heading indicator, altimeter, and vertical speed indicator plus proper power, set up a straight climb (turn

indicator, airspeed, and attitude gyro covered). By carefully (easy!) maintaining the expected rate of climb, the airspeed can be held reasonably close to the recommended value.

2. Make climbs and climbing turns using the airspeed and altimeter plus turn indicator or attitude gyro. Use power required for a 500-fpm climb rate.

Figures 4-25, 4-26, 4-27, and 4-28 show flight instrument combinations you can use in smoothing out the Four Fundamentals and basic instrument flying.

These maneuvers will show the relationships between the various flight instruments and power settings. Confidence in your ability to fly the airplane with some flight instruments out of action will increase radically.

RECOVERIES FROM UNUSUAL ATTITUDES

Turbulence or other outside factors could result in the airplane getting into such an attitude that control could be temporarily lost as well as tumbling the attitude indicator and heading indicator. If this happens, you are left with the job of using the turn indicator, airspeed, and altimeter for immediate recovery.

Remember, for the average, less expensive heading indicators, the tumbling (or spilling) limits are 55° of pitch or roll; the attitude indicator will tumble at 70° of pitch and 100° of bank.

After these two instruments have tumbled, you'll recover with the turn indicator, etc., and reset the two that failed you. Naturally, all airplanes have caging and setting knobs on the heading indicator, but some airplane makes and models do not have a resetting knob for the attitude indicator. If it has tumbled, you'll have to fly *straight and level* for several minutes before it will reerect itself. This is a decided disadvantage in turbulent air, and you may have to use the turn indicator for some time. However, getting the *heading indicator* back in action can be a great help.

The two most common results of loss of control are the power-on spiral and/or the climbing stall. The climbing stall may turn into a power-on spiral, and sometimes vice versa, but you should catch it before this happens.

Because the attitude indicator could be tumbled in more radical attitudes, its information may not always be trustworthy. If you are the kind of person who stares rigidly at the attitude indicator without cross-checking the other instruments—if the attitude indicator is the *only* instrument as far as you are concerned—then you're in for a harsh awakening when you try to fly a tumbled one. Some beginning instrument pilots are so wrapped up in the attitude indicator that, if through mechanical failure it shows the airplane as rolling over on its back, the student would roll the airplane over on its back to "turn right side up" again, without bothering to cross-check other instruments.

■ Power-On Spiral
Figure 4-29 shows what the partial-panel instruments would be showing in a power-on spiral, after the attitude indicator and heading indicator have tumbled.

Fig. 4-25. (*below left*) Instrument combinations for practice of straight and level flying. Uncover the other instruments after several minutes of using the various combinations.

(A) Airspeed, attitude indicator, and altimeter to show relationships between three of the four pitch instruments.

(B) The two flight instruments absolutely necessary for flying IFR. All other flight instruments are aids to these.

(C) The turn indicator is used for turn indications (what else?), and the attitude indicator and altimeter are used for pitch control here.

(D) Flying straight and level with airspeed for pitch (after equilibrium has been established) and the turn coordinator for heading control. Uncover the altimeter and heading indicator to check progress after 3–4 min of flying by these two instruments.

(E) Heading indicator and vertical speed indicator.

(F) Airspeed for pitch and heading indicator.

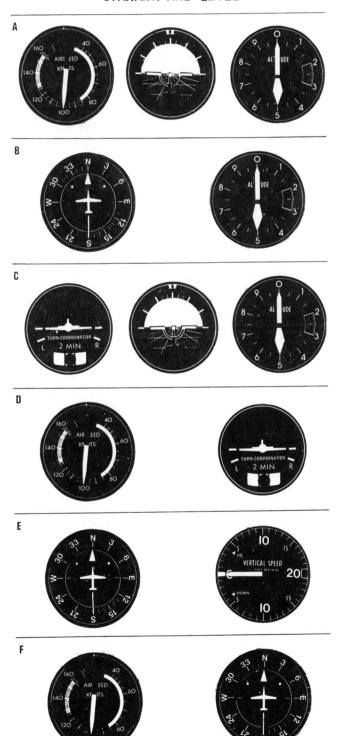

STRAIGHT AND LEVEL

TURNS

A — **TIMED TURN TO A PREDETERMINED HEADING** — **UNCOVER WHEN TIME IS COMPLETE.....**

B — (UNCOVER)

Fig. 4-26. (*above*) Instrument combinations for practice of turns.

(A) Attitude indicator and altimeter. Set up the proper bank to maintain a standard-rate turn at the chosen airspeed. Start at a particular heading, then cover the heading indicator. Roll out at the time required to turn to a predetermined heading and uncover the heading indicator.

(B) Do the same exercise using the turn coordinator or turn and slip and altimeter.

(C) Airspeed and heading indicator combination. Note that the airspeed has been decreased by 3% for the pitch required to maintain altitude in a standard-rate turn, as mentioned earlier in the chapter. Here you are using the rate of direction change to maintain a standard rate of turn (or as close to it as possible).

DESCENTS

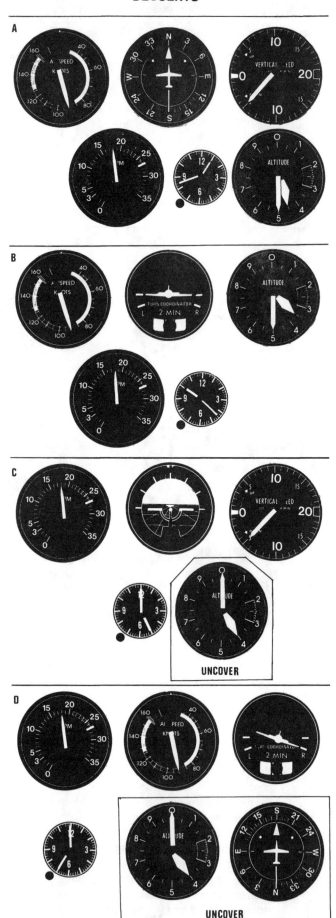

Actually, it would take some doing to tumble the attitude indicator in the spiral—you'd have to be banked past vertical to do it—but perhaps the gyro tumbled earlier when you first flew into that thunderstorm and did the barrel roll.

Look at the indications of the instruments that are still functioning (Fig. 4-29).

A. *Airspeed*—High and/or increasing.
B. *Turn indicator*—The needle or small airplane will show a great rate of turn. The ball may or may not be centered.
C. *Altimeter*—Showing a loss of altitude, probably rapid loss.
D. *Vertical speed indicator*—A high rate of descent.

It won't be any help for you to try to pull the nose up without leveling the wings. You can impose very high load factors at high airspeeds and could cause structural failure *without* helping the recovery. The following steps (in the order cited here) are recommended (Fig. 4-30):

1. *Reduce power*—This is particularly important for the fixed-pitch prop, which may be turning up over the red line in the spiral. For the constant-speed prop, it will cause the blades to flatten and increase drag.
2. *Center the turn indicator through coordinated and simultaneous use of the aileron and rudder*—As indicated by Figure 4-29, you would use right aileron and right rudder. Don't use any gimmicks; the instruments tell you the airplane is in a spiral dive. Under visual conditions, you would use coordinated controls in such a maneuver, so do it here.

Fig. 4-27. (*left*) Descents.

(A) Straight descent without the attitude indicator or turn indicator. The power is set to get 500 fpm at the chosen descent speed.

(B) A timed straight descent without the attitude indicator or heading indicator. Check (uncover) the heading indicator after leveling off. Use an altitude "lead" of 10% of the rate of descent; for a descent of 500 fpm, start to level off 50 ft above the chosen altitude. (For 1000 fpm, use 100 ft, etc.)

(C) A timed straight descent using the attitude indicator, vertical speed indicator (VSI), and clock (plus power for 500-fpm descent). You'll find that by using the proper power setting and maintaining a 500-fpm rate of descent on the VSI, if the airspeed indicator is uncovered during the descent, the airspeed will be very close to 90 knots for this example airplane. After the proper lapsed time and leveling, uncover the altimeter to check your descent accuracy. Also check the heading indicator to see how you fared on heading. Theoretically, if you kept the wings level, the heading should be close on, but check it anyway.

(D) A timed descending turn to a predetermined altitude and heading. After rolling out and leveling off, uncover the altimeter and heading indicator.

CLIMBS

Fig. 4-28. (*left*) Climbs. This airplane uses 75 knots as the best climb airspeed.

(A) Straight climb, using all flight instruments (plus power).

(B) Straight timed climb without the attitude indicator, heading indicator, or altimeter. Uncover the heading indicator and altimeter at the end of the prechosen time period to check your accuracy.

(C) Timed climbing turn to a predetermined heading and altitude (airspeed, attitude indicator, and altimeter covered). At the end of the time period uncover those instruments and check your altitude. The heading should be good, since you have use of the heading indicator during the climbing turn.

(D) A climb (500 fpm) and turn to a prechosen altitude and heading using all flight instruments. Stop the climb and turn as the prechosen indications are reached.

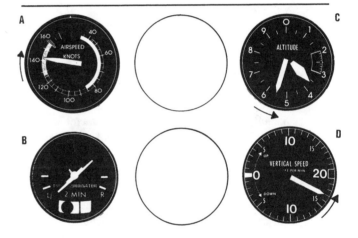

Fig. 4-29. A power-on spiral to the left. The heading indicator and attitude indicator are not in business.

Misuse of the aileron or rudder at high airspeeds can impose large twisting moments on the wings and/or can cause failure of the vertical fin by excess yaw.

As the wings are leveled, it is most likely that the nose will start to rise sharply because of your original trim condition and/or because of back pressure you've added unconsciously. *Do not allow too quick a pull-up.* True, you have been, and are, going downhill at a prodigious rate and your every instinct is to get back *up*, but this can be as fatal as if you flew into a hill. Take it easy.

Don't make a *rolling* pull-out. A rolling pull-out imposes greater stress on the wings than the straight one (all other factors equal). A g meter, or accelerometer, would show the same number of g's being pulled, but one wing will have more stress imposed on it than the "average," as shown on the g meter. If you are already pulling the limit as an "average," that wing could decide to go out on its

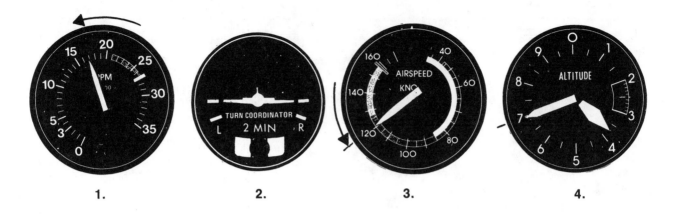

Fig. 4-30. Recovery from a power-on spiral using the partial or emergency panel (Steps 1-4 in the text).

own. For speeds *well* below the red line and for a nonviolent pull-up on your part, the rolling pull-out will expedite the recovery.

In an actual situation you'll tend to be jerky in your responses during the recovery, and overcontrolling may be a factor. One problem students have in using the turn indicator in a spiral recovery is rolling the wings past level, particularly if adverse yaw is present. Okay, the answer is to be coordinated. Adverse yaw will be less a factor at high speeds than low and will be more of a problem on the recovery from an approach to a stall.

3. *Check the airspeed—As* the wings are being leveled, the nose will start to come up of its own accord. In fact, it's unlikely that any measurable amount of back pressure will be needed. You'll have to judge this for yourself, however.

In the recovery an approximation of level nose attitude is reached when the airspeed makes its first perceptible change. In the spiral dive, the airspeed will either be increasing or will be steady at some high speed. As the nose moves up in recovery, the airspeed at some point will stop increasing or start to decrease if it was steady. This hesitation or decrease occurs when the nose is approximately level. So at this first sign of airspeed change, relax back pressure, or *apply forward pressure* as necessary, to keep the nose from moving farther upward.

Don't pull the nose up until cruise (or climb airspeed) is reached in the third major step of recovery. The nose will be so high that control will be lost (again). It's not inconceivable that you might end up on your back at the top of a loop.

Don't try to rush the airspeed back to cruise. It will soon settle down of its own accord if you stop the altimeter and have the power back at cruise. Read on!

4. *Immediately after the "rough" leveling is done by reference to the airspeed change, you will "stop the altimeter"—* You'll be at some particular altitude

when you make the rough recovery to level flight using the airspeed. *Try to keep it,* or at least don't go below it (it's more likely that you will tend to climb above it because of excess airspeed). Use the turn indicator to keep the wings level during this stage. Here you have two choices: (a) You can "pin down" that altitude and hold it as the airspeed eases back to cruise (assuming you have cruise power back on), or (b) you immediately can start a climb back to the original altitude as you recover. The second alternative is usually considered when the loss of altitude may have been such that obstructions, such as mountains, television towers, etc., could be a hazard. Also, if you lost control while en route on an IFR flight, you just might be down in somebody else's assigned altitude, and that's no place to be for any length of time. *Ease up to the airspeed and altitude; don't overdo it and lose control again.*

After the compass has settled down somewhat, set the heading indicator; even a quick and dirty setting will be better than nothing. You can make fine adjustments later. If the attitude indicator has a caging knob, cage it and uncage it again when the airplane is in straight and level flight as shown by the basic instruments. If the attitude indicator does not have a caging knob, the heading indicator will come in handy as an aid to the basic instruments in flying straight and level for the required period of time for it to reerect itself.

Figure 4-31 shows two techniques of recovery from a power-on spiral using the attitude indicator (assuming that it's still in action).

Once having regained control, you can make a climbing turn back to the original altitude and heading. Perhaps you'd better revise your estimate to the next IFR reporting point. You *have* been dawdling, you know.

Figure 4-32 presents an idea on climbing to a predetermined altitude and heading after recovery from a "real" power-on spiral. (The numbers usually won't work out evenly in a real situation.) The point is that a certain heading

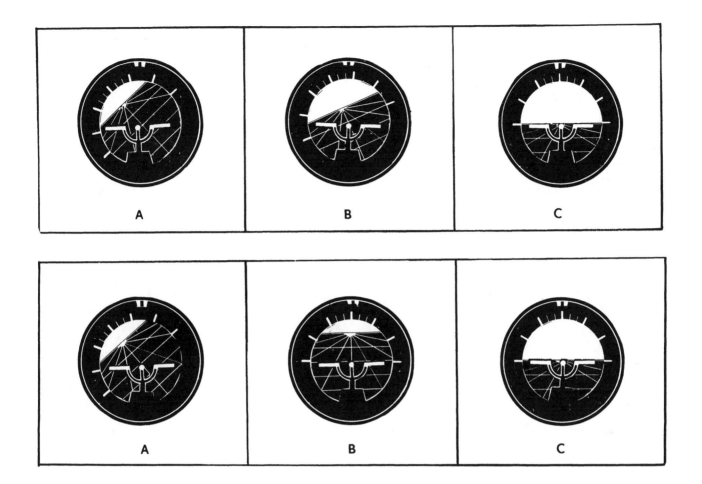

Fig. 4-31. *(Top)* If the attitude indicator is still in action, it could be used to recover from the power-on spiral. A simultaneous roll-out and pull-up will expedite the recovery, but as noted earlier, at higher speeds a rolling pull-out can put high stress on the airplane.

(Bottom) A technique using the attitude indicator; this is close to the partial-panel recovery procedure. The wings are leveled in the dive and then the nose is eased up to the level flight attitude. *(The Flight Instructor's Manual)*

and altitude are to be attained, and the goals aren't often reached at the same time. As the example in Figure 4-32 shows, the heading is reached before the altitude, so that the wings are leveled and a straight climb is continued. (The altitude could be reached *first* in another situation, so that the airplane is leveled off and the turn continued.)

■ Recovery from the Approach to a Climbing Stall and from the Stall Itself

The climbing stall often happens because you were too eager to gain back altitude lost in the power-on spiral. Or maybe you neglected to catch that airspeed change when the nose was level and just kept pulling back until....

Being pessimistic (again), it will be assumed that you have lost the heading and attitude indicators. Figure 4-33 shows what you would probably be seeing in such a case.

It's assumed that you'll enter this condition at cruise power. Reviewing the instrument indications:

1. *Airspeed*—Decreasing, and probably doing so rapidly.

2. *Turn indicator*—May or may not be centered. However, it is likely that the needle or airplane will be deflected to the left, and the ball will show a left skidding turn because of torque effects. You could, however, be in the climbing *right* turn.

3. *Altimeter*—Altitude increasing or steady in the last part of the stall.

4. *Vertical speed indicator*—A high rate of climb. Because of the lag of the instrument, it is likely that it will still be showing a good rate of ascent even as the stall break is occurring.

The recovery technique will be as follows:

1. *Relax the back pressure (or use forward pressure if necessary) until the airspeed stops decreasing; or if it has been holding fairly constant, until it starts to increase*—Try to stop the nose at the instant of the airspeed change. This works very well if the stall break hasn't occurred. If you've just reached the stall break, let the nose move down slightly past the

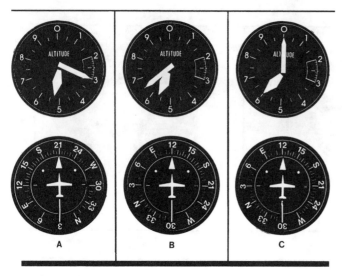

Fig. 4-32.

(A) Control of the airplane is recovered on a heading of 210° and altitude of 5300 ft. The desired heading and altitude are 120° and 6000 ft respectively. A climb and a standard-rate turn is started.

(B) The heading of 120° is reached, the turn is stopped, and a straight climb is continued to the required altitude.

(C) The requirement is complete when the airplane is on both the desired heading and altitude.

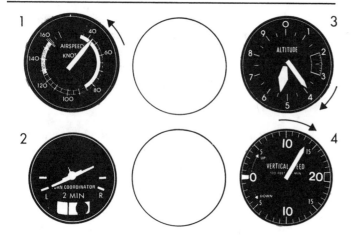

Fig. 4-33. Approach to a climbing stall. Attitude indicator and heading indicator are inoperative.

point of this indication to ensure enough of a nose-down attitude to avoid a secondary stall.

2. In both situations, *apply full power as the nose is lowered*—This lowers the stall speed, hastens the recovery, and decreases altitude loss.

3. *Center the turn indicator*—If the stall has broken, make sure that the *ball* is kept centered if possible. It doesn't matter too much whether you are turning

slightly (as shown by an offset needle or small airplane) during the recovery, but avoid yawing or skidding flight (as shown by the offset ball). A skid or slip can result in one wing stalling before the other, which could possibly lead to a spin. Try the unusual attitude maneuvers in VFR conditions without a hood. Notice that for most airplanes, as long as the ball remains centered at the break, problems of one wing or the other paying off first, with rolling tendencies, are minimized. *However, you should check the reactions of your particular airplane in this regard.* The problem is having enough rudder power at low speeds to keep the ball centered. In your VFR stalls, you'll notice in most cases that the airplane tends to roll away from the ball at the break. If the ball is to the right, roll, if present, will most likely be to the left (and vice versa). Notice that here the centering of the turn indicator is secondary to keeping the airspeed up. You can (and will) probably do Steps 1 and 2 simultaneously as you progress.

4. *Use the altimeter to level off*—It's unlikely that the altitude loss will be the problem in this situation because you've been climbing at a goodly rate as the stall was approached. After you've checked airspeed, look at the altimeter. Then, rather than trying to stop the altimeter exactly there, perform as described in the first phase of the recovery; allow about 100 ft of altitude loss during recovery to ensure that you'll stay out of a secondary stall that would cost even more altitude. Of course it's always best to recover without further loss of altitude. Perhaps you can do this in the trainer you're using, particularly if the break has not occurred. It depends on the particular airplane whether this can be done or not.

After the airspeed and altitude are under control, make the turn to the required heading and get back to the proper altitude. Get the heading and attitude indicators back in action as soon as possible to help in this. Adjust the power as necessary.

The primary objective is to get that airspeed back in a safe range, and you can make heading corrections later.

Figure 4-34 sums up the steps in recovering from an approach to a climbing stall (partial panel).

Figure 4-35 shows two methods of recovery from an approach to a climbing stall if the attitude indicator is still in action. The technique (top) is a simultaneous lowering of the nose as the wings are leveled; this works well if the airplane hasn't stalled. The nose is lowered first (bottom), and the wings are leveled after the nose is below the horizon; this method is best if a stall has occurred. There will be considerable feelings of slipping during this technique.

SPIN RECOVERIES

It's extremely unlikely that you will have problems with a spin. The modern certificated (normal and utility category) airplane is highly resistant to spins and, even if forced into one, will usually sneak into a diving spiral unless held in the

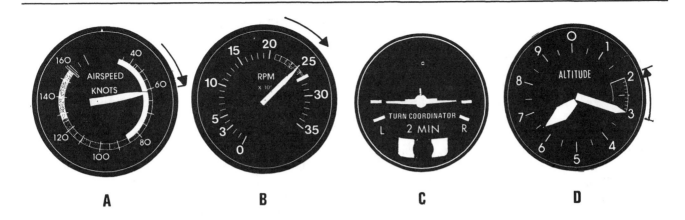

Fig. 4-34. Steps in recovering from an *approach* to a climbing stall (partial panel).

(A) Use forward pressure until the airspeed starts to increase.

(B) Add full power as the nose is lowered.

(C) Level the wings with the turn coordinator or turn and slip.

(D) If the altimeter hesitates at an altitude indicating level flight, "fly down" another 100 ft to ensure getting farther from the stall.

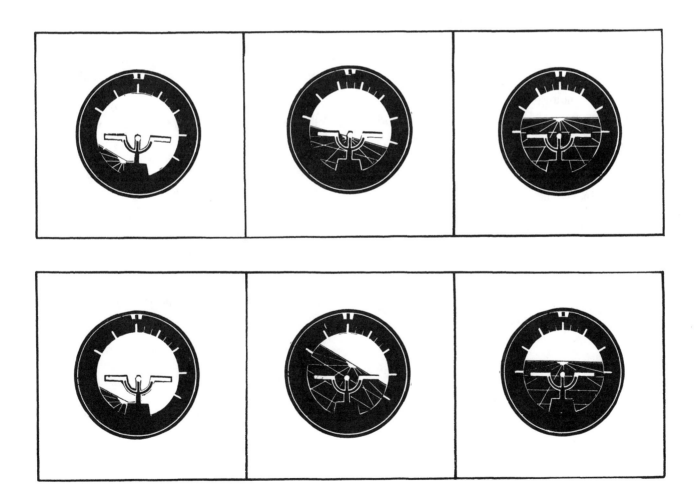

Fig. 4-35. *(Top)* Simultaneously dropping the nose and leveling the wings, using the attitude indicator (if it's available). *(Bottom)* The nose is lowered, *then* the wings are leveled, using the attitude indicator. Expect some slipping feelings in this type of recovery. In both cases the nose is brought down well below the horizon to avoid a secondary stall. *(The Flight Instructor's Manual)*

spin. However, being under stress and/or flying an illegally loaded plane could be different matters.

The spin is an aggravated stall with autorotation. It's called autorotation because one wing is more deeply stalled and has less lift than the other. A rolling moment is produced, which tends to maintain that stall condition and imbalance of lift.

The spin is usually the result of one wing being stalled before the other. This is why it's important to keep that ball centered during the stall approach and break when you're on instruments. The normal procedure in practicing spins under VFR conditions *(don't,* unless you are in a utility—approved for spins—or an aerobatic category airplane) is usually described as follows.

You would be sure that you had plenty of altitude and the area was clear of other airplanes. Regulations require that the recovery be completed no lower than 1500 ft above the surface (3000 ft is better). Make sure that you are operating in accordance with FAR 91.303. (Take a qualified instructor with you.)

You would "clear the area" by making a 90° turn in each direction, looking to all sides and particularly below you. Swallow that lump and wipe your sweaty palms one more time, then pull the carburetor heat (if recommended for your airplane) and ease the nose up to do a straight-ahead, power-off stall. (Some airplanes require use of power to get the spin started.)

Just before the break occurs, use full rudder in the direction in which you want to spin (as an example, to the left). This will yaw the nose to the left, slowing down the relative speed of the left wing and speeding up the right. A rolling motion is produced to move the left wing down, suddenly increasing its angle of attack past the critical point, and it stalls while the right wing is still flying. A definite rolling motion is produced, and the nose moves over and down to the left. If you relax back pressure, the maneuver would become a spiral, but you have the stick or wheel full back and are holding it.

In Figure 4-36 the spin is developing, and the indications show that the attitude indicator and heading indicator have vacated the premises, so to speak.

The basic instruments (plus the vertical speed instrument) will indicate that the plane is in the spin by the following indications (Fig. 4-37):

Turn indicator—The needle or small airplane will indicate the direction of rotation, but the ball in many airplanes will *always* go to the left side of the instrument (if the instrument is on the left side of the panel as shown in Fig. 4-36). Look at Figure 4-39. The ball will be to the left for a left panel instrument, no matter what the direction of spinning is. However, the ball in a right-side instrument position will always go to the right, whether in a left or right spin.

Airspeed—Although you are descending at a good rate in the spin (5500–7500 fpm in some general aviation airplanes), the airspeed will remain low and fairly constant, but the value may oscillate to some extent.

Altimeter—This instrument will be showing a rapid loss of altitude.

Vertical speed indicator—This also shows that the airplane has a high rate of descent.

The clues that indicate that the airplane is spinning must be judged together. There is rotation, as shown by the needle or small airplane. It could be that the needle and ball would indicate a *skidding turn;* don't use the ball, but note what the other indications (needle or small airplane, airspeed, altimeter, vertical speed indicator) indicate. The facts that (1) the airspeed is low, (2) a high rate of turn is indicated, and (3) a high rate of descent is occurring lead to the conclusion that the airplane is spinning. The turn indicator shows that the spin is to the left, so the following recovery technique should be used:

Close the throttle. For many airplanes power tends to flatten the spin and delay recovery, so get it off (Fig. 4-38).

Opposite rudder (right rudder here) to needle or small airplane. This is not to imply that the needle is flown with the rudder and the ball with the ailerons, as has been sometimes advocated. It's just that you've been told by the instruments that you're in a spin and are using the VFR mechanical technique (Fig. 4-39).

Relax back pressure or use brisk forward pressure as recommended by the manufacturer as soon as the rudder reaches its stop. (Some airplanes may require a *brisk* forward movement of the stick or wheel right after opposite rudder is used.) *Check the airspeed.* As soon as it starts picking up, you are out of the spin and should get off the recovery rudder. You are now in a straight dive. The spin itself puts practically no stresses on the airplane, but a sloppy or delayed pull-out from the dive following the recovery does (Fig. 4-40).

The first thought would be that you should perhaps keep the nose down until cruise speed is indicated before starting the pull-out to be sure to avoid another stall and possible spin. *However,* you would readily see in a VFR spin that, as soon as the back pressure is relaxed, or forward pressure applied, the airspeed will pick up very rapidly (the nose of the airplane is practically straight down) so that any delay in the pull-out could cause you to exceed the red line speed, *plus* causing an excessive loss of altitude. So as soon as the airspeed starts increasing, get off the rudder and start applying back pressure *smoothly.* The airspeed will continue to increase during this process. Watch for the airspeed to stop increasing. That point, as discussed in the pull-out of the power-on spiral, shows that the nose is approximately level, and you should relax back pressure or use forward pressure to stop the nose in the level position.

Check the altimeter as soon as the forward pressure has been exerted (or back pressure has been relaxed). Use this instrument to level off (Fig. 4-41).

Figures 4-38 through 4-41 summarize the steps during the spin recovery and back to cruising flight.

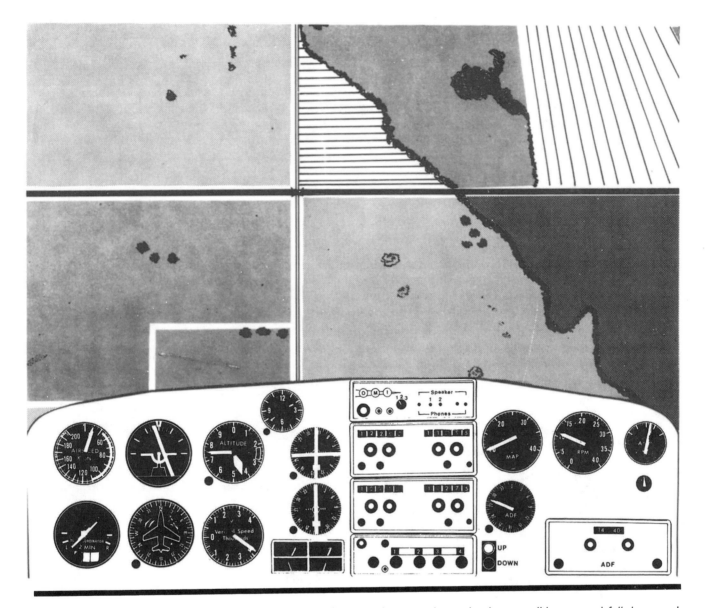

Fig. 4-36. The instrument indications in the onset of a spin. The vertical speed indicator will be pegged *full down* as the spin develops. The heading indicator and attitude indicator have tumbled here. Figures 4-38–4-41 show the steps for recovery.

Adjust power, heading, and altitude as necessary to get back to where you were when this fiasco started. Reset the attitude and heading indicators as soon as possible.

Again, it is *extremely* unlikely that you will ever get into a spin accidentally, either VFR or on instruments. Of course, it wouldn't be much help to you if people said, "Isn't it amazing; Ol' Joe spun in all the way from 9000 feet on IFR—first time I've heard of *that* in years."

INSTRUMENT TAKEOFF (ITO)

You've been making takeoffs for some time and probably rightly feel that there's not much to be shown to you as far as this maneuver is concerned. However, during your instrument training, you'll be introduced to the ITO.

Actually, except as a training maneuver confidence builder, the ITO is not of too much value. If the weather is so bad that you must use the instruments to stay on the runway, you should think of an extremely good reason for not going. If the conditions are that lousy, how would you get back to the runway if trouble developed right after takeoff? Possibly the ITO can be of practical use when the bad weather is strictly a local situation, such as early morning fog at a river bottom airport (and is CAVU everywhere else around). It could save you from waiting for a fog only 100–200 ft thick to lift and burn off. But it's still a calculated risk, and you'd be banking on the fact that in case of trouble you could make it into another airport close by. For most cases it's smart *not* to take off when ceiling and visibility are below approach minimums for that field, particularly

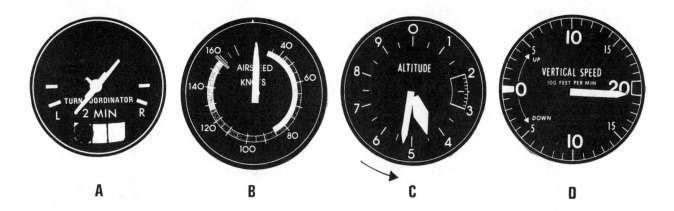

Fig. 4-37. Indications of a developed left spin.

(A) The turn and slip needle or turn coordinator (small airplane) will probably be deflected to the stop. In this side-by-side seating example, the ball is pegged to the left (and will be so for left *or* right spins) because of the instrument's position on the left side of the instrument panel.

(B) The airspeed is very low, and in some spin modes may indicate *zero*.

(C) The altimeter will show a rapid loss of altitude.

(D) The vertical speed indicator will probably be pegged, since rates of descent (depending on the airplane type and spin mode) may be in the 6000- to 10,000-fpm range.

Fig. 4-38. Close the throttle.

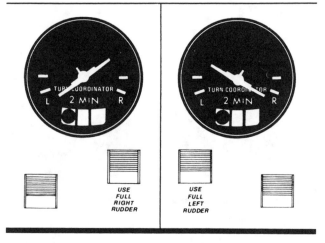

Fig. 4-39. Both instruments are on left panels. Check the turn indicator. Apply full opposite rudder to the needle or small airplane indication. *(Basic Aerobatic Manual)*

if there are no fields with lower minimums immediately nearby.

You may hear a number of "gimmicks" on setting the reference airplane on the attitude indicator before making an instrument takeoff (or a takeoff that will put you into instrument conditions right away). *Ignore them. Before takeoff, set the small airplane as closely as you can to the actual attitude of the airplane at that time.* That way you will have a true picture of your airplane for takeoff, climb, and cruise without having to change it later.

Setting the attitude indicator for the tricycle-gear airplane is simple, in that the attitude of the airplane is generally considered to be level.

The tailwheel type is a different matter. If you are the scientific type, you could use a protractor and measure the

angle the longitudinal axis makes with the ground, or better yet, some *Pilot's Operating Handbook*s contain this information. (For instance, the Beech Super 18 gives this figure as *11.5°*, assuming proper tire and oleo inflation.) During VFR or simulated instrument flight you could, at a fairly low altitude (say, 2000 or 3000 ft), establish a high cruise. Maintain a constant altitude, and after a constant airspeed is established, set the small reference airplane (or the "pip" of the reference airplane—it depends on the type of instrument you have) on the horizon bar. If you don't rack the airplane around a lot before you land and don't hit the ground too hard, the small airplane should be at the right position when the airplane is sitting in the three-point position on the

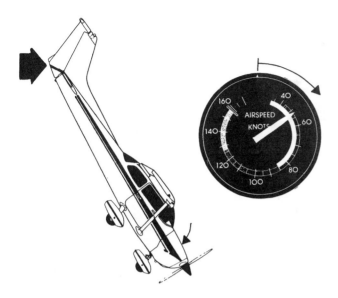

Fig. 4-40. After applying full opposite rudder and moving the wheel briskly forward, the airspeed moving from zero (or from a very low airspeed) shows that the recovery has started. Neutralize the rudder and start applying (centered) back pressure on the wheel. During the recovery the increasing airspeed tells you that the airplane is out of the spin. Don't fixate on the turn and slip or the turn coordinator after checking the direction of rotation or during the forward motion of the wheel *or* during the pull-out; the turn indicator(s) could, in some cases, be jammed to one side or the other, even as a wings-level pull-up is being accomplished.

ground. You can note the number of horizon bar widths that the reference is above the horizon bar and use that in setting the instrument on the ground. The chances are that you could be accurate enough by setting the wings of the small airplane in line with some of the reference marks on the sides of the instrument face. Your instructor probably will already have the setting.

■ **Instrument Takeoff—Tailwheel Type** After you've completed the pretakeoff check (covered in Chapter 10) and have received takeoff clearance, taxi to the center of the runway and line up with the center line. Taxi forward slightly to straighten the tailwheel and lock it if the airplane has such a control. Set the heading indicator on the runway heading and *make sure that it is uncaged.* Wake up the safety pilot.

Hold the brakes and run up the engine(s) to a setting that will aid in rudder control, then release the brakes as you apply full power.

Don't shove the power on abruptly but open it smoothly all the way. Your copilot may "back you up on the throttle" by putting a hand behind them to make sure they don't creep back and will also be the lucky one to look out at the runway and offer such helpful hints as "Dagnabit! Left! No, not

so much," etc., until you are ready to commit mayhem—if you could spare the time from the gauges. Here's the place during your training where you'll discover that even after quite a bit of experience with the old-fashioned type of heading indicator, you can still manage somehow to correct the wrong way for any heading deviations on the ITO. You and the safety pilot may have a brief scuffle as to who can exert the most pressure on the rudder pedals.

Here's where heading will be a most important factor. Maybe you've been a sloppy pilot and 5° of heading means nothing in the air. *But* if you are in the center of a 100-ft wide runway, a 5° error can put you off the edge before you go 600 ft.

In addition to the fact that you may want to correct the wrong way at first, there will be the problem of overcorrecting. The heading sneaks off, and you, thinking of that deep rich mud alongside the runway, decide that there'll be none of *that,* and enthusiastically apply too much opposite rudder; and the takeoff will resemble some of the first ones you ever made.

On some of the older tailwheel twins, it is sometimes necessary to use asymmetric power to help keep them straight on the takeoff run before the rudder becomes effective (this is why you should add power before releasing brakes). This contributes to overcontrolling, gives the pilot much more to think about, and is definitely *not* recommended as a technique unless everything else fails. As far as using brakes to keep straight is concerned—*don't.* If your airplane is so tricky that brakes are required to keep it straight on the takeoff run, well, you'd be better off to forget about instrument takeoffs in it.

We've mentioned the precession effects resulting if the tail is raised abruptly, so don't shove it up. Allow the tail to come up, or assist slightly, so that the attitude of the airplane is that of a shallow climb.

It is assumed that your airplane will have a static system that has an outlet on the fuselage or at the pitot-static head. For some of the older and lighter trainers, the airspeed and altimeter (and vertical speed indicator, if available) had no static tubes but were open to the cabin. As speed picks up, the result is a drop in normal cabin (and instrument) static pressure. The airspeed will very likely read high, and the altimeter may show an altitude "jump," even though you can still feel and hear the tires rolling on the runway. Fortunately, this type of setup is going the way of the helmet and goggles.

Ground effect can induce instrument error by changing the airflow about the airplane. (This is speaking for the airplanes with static ports on the fuselage or a pitot-static tube.) The result is that the airspeed and altimeter will tend to read *low.* This is, of course, a factor on the safe side. You may have noticed on VFR takeoffs that as the airplane lifted there seemed to be a sharp jump in airspeed and altitude.

Some larger general aviation aircraft have a calibration graph for airspeed correction during the takeoff ground roll. An example: A rotation at 91 knots indicated airspeed is actually at 94.5 knots calibrated airspeed for one airplane.

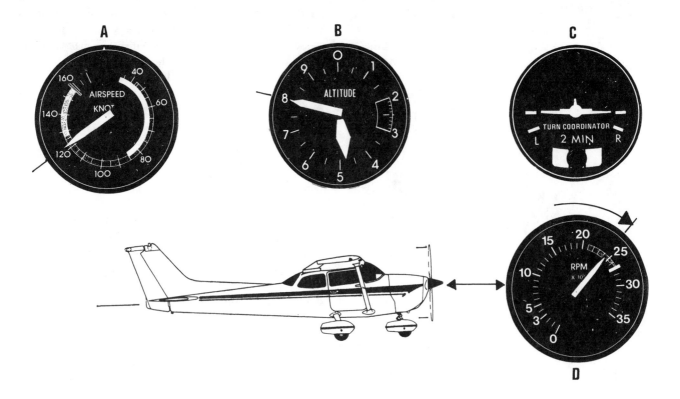

Fig. 4-41. After the pull-out is started, the following steps are recommended to complete the spin recovery:

(A) Continue the back pressure (or allow the nose to rise), watching the airspeed. When the airspeed hesitates or stops increasing, the pitch attitude is approximately level.

(B) Look at the altimeter immediately and pick the closest altitude to "fly." (Don't let the altitude increase or decrease—"fly" the altimeter with the elevators as the airspeed bleeds back to the cruise regime.) Significant forward pressure may be needed initially to keep the nose from continuing to pitch up.

(C) The turn coordinator or turn and slip is again dependable once the airplane is in the straight and level condition. Keep the wings level. "Fly" the altimeter.

(D) As the cruise airspeed is approached, add power to cruise value.

Ground effect may fool you into thinking the airplane is all set to climb out when that's not the case. Remember that the airplane performs better in ground effect, and things might not be so great when you get a few feet of altitude.

This is one time that you should assure yourself that you have sufficient flying speed before lift-off. In fact, it would be better to let the airplane lift itself off if you have established the proper attitude on the tail-up part of the run.

As the airplane lifts off, establish a rate of climb. Do not ease the nose over to try to pick up the best rate of climb speed right away—you could overdo it and settle back in. One problem at this point is that the forces of acceleration (you're picking up speed) work on some attitude indicators to give a slightly more nose-high reading than actually exists. You may lower the nose to get the "proper reading" and settle in. Of course, the attitude gyro can be used for wing attitude, but you would be better off to use the airspeed and altimeter (and heading indicator) for proper climb *immediately* after lift-off.

Along this same line, you should allow 5 min (or more) after engine start for the vacuum/pressure gyros to build up

to full efficiency. There have been fatal accidents because pilots started up and then took off almost immediately into zero-zero conditions with gyros that hadn't gotten up to speed. (Whatever happened to using a checklist?) Taxiing and using a careful IFR checklist should take at least 5 min.

Attain a safe altitude (at least 500 ft) before reducing power. You don't need the distraction of changing power when you're still getting used to the idea of being in the soup. Don't retract the gear under 100 ft above the surface. Establish the proper climb speed and follow your instrument clearance.

■ Instrument Takeoff — Tricycle Gear As in VFR takeoffs, the nosewheel makes for more positive control and simplifies matters considerably. Naturally, you'll taxi out and line up with the center line and move forward a few feet to straighten the nosewheel.

As the airplane picks up airspeed, ease the nosewheel off and assume the normal takeoff attitude. (Be prepared for the need for more right rudder as the nosewheel lifts.) For the light twin it is recommended that the airplane not be lifted before V_{MC} (minimum control speed—single engine) is attained. Don't rush *any* airplane.

The attitude of the airplane should be practically the same as that for the tailwheel type. As an example, consider the Cessna 180 and 182 models; they have the same maximum weight, wing areas, airfoils, and stall and takeoff speeds. In short, they are exactly alike except for the landing gear configuration, and as you know, the 180 is a tailwheel type and the 182 has a nosewheel. The attitudes at lift-off should be the same because for all practical purposes the airplanes *are* the same. You are interested during the latter part of the run in having the attitude that will allow the airplane to become airborne at the optimum time. If you keep the nosewheel on the ground or, in the tailwheel type, have the tail too high, you'll waste runway. On the other hand, the takeoff will suffer if the tail is held too low on this part of the run. Start paying attention to the attitude indicator during VFR takeoffs. What is best for a clear day is also the best for a day when clouds are overhead—assuming that runway conditions, airplane weight, and other variables are the same.

Figure 4-42 shows the steps (A, B, C) for an instrument takeoff in a popular two-place trainer.

THE WELL-BALANCED PILOT

During the basic instrument part of your training you may first encounter the effects of spatial disorientation. (Turning or moving your head quickly while flying under the hood or on actual instruments is a good way to discover just what it is.) If you've always associated this with little old ladies who are a bit tiddly from sampling the cooking sherry, take a look at it from an instrument flying standpoint.

Under normal situations, most of your balance depends on sight (sure, the other senses help too). The feel of gravity, for instance, helps you know which way is "up" or "down" *under normal conditions*. But what about the artificial gravity created by turns, pull-ups, and vertical gusts? Your body doesn't know the difference unless sight helps to separate the "natural" from the "artificial" gravity. The fun houses in amusement parks are examples of how much the eyes have to do with equilibrium. The crazily angled walls make people forget the natural gravity force that all the "seat of the pants" pilots say they use.

So your eyes can fool you too. Take autokinetic illusions, for instance. These five-dollar words mean that your eyes are telling you something that isn't true. The military used to have night fighter pilot trainees move into a darkened room where only one very small bright light was visible. Various pilots would be asked to describe the various motions ("up, now it's moving right," etc.). The lights were turned on and they then saw a permanently attached, stationary light on the opposite wall. Without other references, the involuntary movements of the eyes gave the illusion of movement of the light.

Statements have been made by noninstrument pilots that they could fly in solid clouds without any flight instruments at all (or blindfolded—the choice of condition usually depended on how far the evening's festivities had progressed). There's no argument about that. They *can* fly in clouds without flight instruments—for quite a number of seconds sometimes (the length of time depends on how high the airplane was above the ground when the experiment started). Birds don't fly in solid instrument conditions. (ATC records have no known case of a bird filing IFR, so this proves it.)

At any rate, the inner ear is the place where most of the *nonvisual* balance sensations originate. They (nearly everybody has two) react to forces and couldn't really care less about which way is "up" or "down" and are about as believable as the guest speaker at a Liar's Convention.

What does spatial disorientation in flight feel like? It's a feeling that all is not well. The instruments appear to be lying because your sensations tell you that you *couldn't* be doing what they indicate. There may be a struggle in your mind, but *always* believe the instruments over your own sensations when outside visual references aren't available. One instrument instructor noticed an instrument trainee leaning over to one side while flying under the hood. The student was doing a great job, the instructor remarked—but why the Tower of Pisa bit? The student answered that he knew the blank blank instruments were right so was flying by reference to them, but *he* felt more comfortable about the whole thing if he listed to starboard a little.

You should be prepared for a different sensation when flying actual instruments compared to flying under the hood. First, flying actual instruments is easier in that you don't have to twist your head as much as when under the hood—you have a much wider field of vision. On the other hand, there is the psychological effect of being "committed." You're in the soup and in the system and have to go on with it; there's no taking off the hood and saying, "Well, I goofed on that last approach, didn't I?"

Sometimes the grayness (or blackness) outside creates the effect of the airplane rushing at greater than normal speeds, and at other times it seems you are hanging suspended and only the instruments' indications show that you are moving at such and such an airspeed and altitude. These effects can be disquieting if you encounter them on one of your first actual IFR flights with a load of passengers and you are the only pilot on board. This is a good reason for getting as much flying in actual conditions as possible during your training for the rating.

Something else to consider is that turbulence could be bad enough so that you could have trouble reading the instruments—you'll be moving up and down so fast that they will be blurred, and this could also tend to induce spatial disorientation. It could also tend to induce hyperventilation, a condition caused by too deep and/or rapid breathing resulting in an imbalance between the carbon dioxide and oxygen. When people are scared, they tend to hyperventilate.

Spatial disorientation can last a short while or an hour or more, depending on the situation and physical condition of the pilot. It's a rather weird sensation when first encountered, but take a deep breath and settle down to doing a good

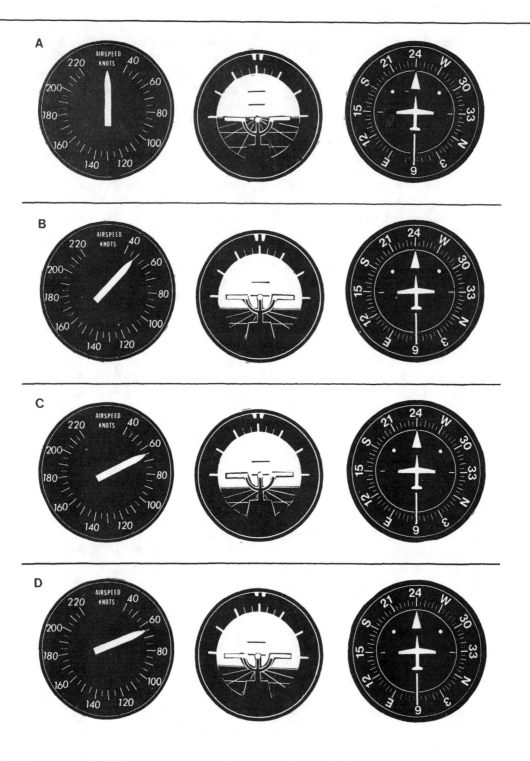

Fig. 4-42. Instrument takeoff for a particular two-place trainer (nosewheel).

    (A) Set the heading indicator when the airplane is taxied forward a few feet and lined up with the runway and apply full power smoothly, watching for heading deviations.

    (B) At 50 knots, the nose is raised to the first reference line (10°) and held there. Maintain the exact runway heading with the rudder.

    (C) At 65 knots the airplane will lift off. Maintain heading and watch for a tendency for the nose to pitch up as the airplane leaves ground effect.

    (D) Continue the climb-out at 65 knots (best rate of climb airspeed for this example airplane).

job with the instruments. The cockpits of some airplanes, it seems, are designed to induce spatial disorientation, with widely separated radio equipment requiring twisting and/or quick head movements. Your instructor may try to induce it on one of your training flights to let you recognize it. Some pilots say they've never had it and probably haven't.

The Medical Handbook for Pilots (DOT/FAA 1974) is a must for any pilot's library, instrument rated or not. It discusses in an interesting and easily understood way how such things as hypoxia, hyperventilation, alcohol, carbon monoxide, spatial disorientation, fatigue, aging, and other factors affect pilots. The *Aeronautical Information Manual* has a good medical section and you should read it carefully.

It goes without saying that drinking alcohol just before flying is stupid, but doubly so when flying instruments. *The Medical Handbook* also brings out some points on drugs that should be of interest to you.

Fatigue has caused fatal accidents, particularly at night. The problem is that maybe after a full day's work before flying and after fighting a long siege of weather en route, you are usually at your physical worst when the most alertness is needed for the approach. Your senses may lie to you more easily because of this fatigue.

In short, when flying instruments, don't trust your own sensations at all; take the indications of one instrument with a grain of salt; confirm what all the operating instruments combine to show.

■ **The Glass Cockpit** Many of the new airplanes being manufactured now have an arrangement of instruments called the "glass cockpit" wherein the images of various flight and other instruments are projected on a flat panel. In addition, an older type airspeed indicator, attitude indicator and altimeter are installed (on the lower instrument panel in most cases). Figure 4-43 shows the Primary Flight Display from the Garmin G1000 cockpit Reference Guide for Cessna Nav 111.

SUMMARY

You should be able to have the airplane under complete control in any normal condition before attempting to add navigational and letdown work to the basic instrument flying. Control of the airplane through the instruments must become practically second nature. To be a completely qualified instrument pilot, you have to be proficient in doing other things, such as calculations for a revised ETA, flying the VOR or other navaids, taking and acknowledging clearance, making voice reports, and getting weather information—and the airplane won't be waiting for you while you do so.

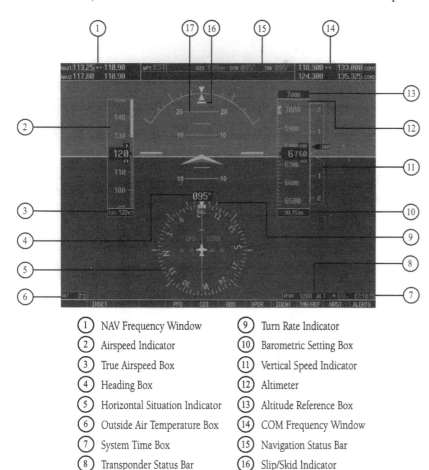

① NAV Frequency Window	⑨ Turn Rate Indicator		
② Airspeed Indicator	⑩ Barometric Setting Box		
③ True Airspeed Box	⑪ Vertical Speed Indicator		
④ Heading Box	⑫ Altimeter		
⑤ Horizontal Situation Indicator	⑬ Altitude Reference Box		
⑥ Outside Air Temperature Box	⑭ COM Frequency Window		
⑦ System Time Box	⑮ Navigation Status Bar		
⑧ Transponder Status Bar	⑯ Slip/Skid Indicator		
	⑰ Attitude Indicator		

Garmin G1000 Cockpit Reference Guide for Cessna Nav III

Fig. 4-43.
Courtesy of Garmin USA, Inc. The panel is in contrasting colors. (Image reproduced with the permission of Garmin. ©2006 Garmin Ltd or its subsidiaries, all rights reserved.)

2 NAVIGATION AND COMMUNICATIONS

NAVIGATIONAL AIDS AND INSTRUMENTS

It's likely that in your VFR flying you've been relying on radio navigation and have been keeping the sectional and WAC charts under the seat. However, you could always haul out a sectional or WAC chart and go on about your business should the VOR receiver quit on you.

The following chapters are intended to tie in the gray areas of en route IFR navigation and the ATC system.

Too many neophyte instrument pilots get submerged in details of the flight and neglect to look at the overall picture, which, believe it or not, is comparatively simple.

You want to go from A to B. Under VFR conditions, you would plan your flight and go; you may or may not file a VFR flight plan—it's up to you. Okay, so the weather is below VFR minimums, but the purpose of the flight is the same. You are still trying to get from A to B. Because of the weather, you'll have to fly the airplane by reference to instruments. If you were the only person flying that day, you could, in theory anyway, hop in the plane and go—without worrying about other people—and could leave when you got ready and go the way you wanted to after picking an altitude to clear all obstacles en route. However, there are fatheads who have the audacity to want to fly on the same day and even in the same area that *you* do. It's those other guys who make IFR a little more complicated.

Because separation between airplanes becomes a problem now that you can no longer "see and be seen," you'll have to follow predetermined paths, and the ground coordinators (ATC) will be interested in knowing your altitude (and may assign you a different one than you requested). ATC may even send you to B by a different route than the one you prefer—all because of those other people who want to fly at the same time you do.

Victor (VOR) airways were established to allow the pilot to follow known routes with information available for safe altitude, using navigational aids within certain reception distances. Nowadays, many IFR flights are direct, either through radar vectoring or, as will be the case more and more, LORAN C operations.

Before going on, it might be a good idea to review the radio frequency bands (Note: "Hertz" is used for "cycles per second"—kilohertz [kHz], megahertz [MHz], etc.; 1 kHz = 1000 cycles per second, 1 MHz = 1000 kHz):

Very low frequency (VLF)	10–30 kHz
Low frequency (LF)	30–300 kHz
Medium frequency (MF)	300–3000 kHz
High frequency (HF)	3–30 MHz
Very high frequency (VHF)	30–300 MHz
Ultrahigh Frequency (UHF)	300–3000 MHz

REVIEW OF THE VHF OMNIRANGE (VOR)

The VOR operates in the frequency range of 108.00–117.95 MHz, which puts it close to the middle of the VHF band (30–300 MHz).

It uses even-tenths frequencies (108.2, 108.4, 109.0, 109.2, etc.). The odd tenths in that area (108.1, 108.3, 111.1, etc.) are ILS localizer frequencies and will be covered later in this chapter.

The frequencies in the 112.00–117.95 MHz range use all of the tenths, both odd and even (112.0, 112.1, 112.2 MHz, etc.). Some pilots have trouble at their first introduction to the radio in separating VHF and UHF from LF/MF, as far as reading the number in the *Airport/Facility Directory* is concerned. The LF/MF frequencies are whole numbers (212, 332, etc.), while the VHF and UHF frequencies are always "point something" (112.3, 243.0). You would read the 112.3 as "one one two *point* three." You'll find that there won't be any confusion between the frequency bands after you start using them. The kilohertz is the lowest whole-frequency measurement, so that 112.3 could not be LF/MF because this would be working with a part of a kilohertz. You won't be using any frequencies as low as 112 kilohertz, since none of the LF/MF air frequencies are that low. So if it has a "point something," it's VHF or UHF.

Following are the VOR class designations and expected ranges of each, as given by the *AIM:*

Class of VOR, VOR/DME, or VORTAC	Altitude Range and Boundaries
T (terminal)	Up to and including 12,000 ft at radial distances out to 25 NM
L (low altitude)	Up to 18,000 ft and including radial distances out to 40 NM
H (high altitude)	Up to and including 14,500 ft AGL at radial distances out to 40 NM. From 14,500 ft AGL up to and including 60,000 ft at radial distances out to 100 NM. From 18,000 ft AGL up to and including 45,000 ft AGL at radial distances out to 130 NM

■ **VOR Theory** The VOR receiver in your airplane uses the principles of electronically measuring an angle. The VOR (ground equipment) puts out two signals; one is all-directional, and the other is a rotating signal. The all-directional signal contracts and expands 30 times a second, and the rotating signal turns clockwise at 30 revolutions/sec. The rotating signal has a positive and a negative side.

The all-directional or reference signal is timed to transmit at the same instant the rotating beam passes Magnetic North. These rotating beams and the reference signal result in radial measurements.

Your VOR receiver picks up the all-directional signal. Some time later it picks up the maximum point of the positive rotating signal. The receiver electronically measures the time difference, and this is indicated in degrees as your *magnetic* bearing in relation to the station (Fig. 5-1). For instance, assume it takes a minute (it actually takes 1/30 of a second) for the rotating signal to make one revolution. You

receive the all-directional signal, and 45 sec later you receive the rotating signal. This means that your position is $^{45}/_{60}$ or $^{3}/_{4}$ of the way around. (Three-fourths of 360° is 270°, and you are on the 270 radial.) The VOR receiver does this in a quicker, more accurate way.

Since the VOR operates to give you the airplane's relative position to (or from) the station, based on Magnetic North, all directions on en route and letdown charts and the directions given relative to various navigation aids on charts are *magnetic*. This saves extra figuring at a time when you might have your hands full.

The aircraft VOR receiver presentation is made up of four main parts: (1) frequency selector; (2) omnibearing selector (OBS) calibrated from 0 to 360; (3) course deviation indicator (CDI), a vertical needle that moves left or right and indicates the relative position of the airplane to the selected omni radial; and (4) TO-FROM indicator (Fig. 5-2).

Figure 5-2 shows a combination communications and navigation arrangement:

1. ON/OFF/VOL control switch. Pull out for TEST; push in for automatic squelch. This ON/OFF switch is for both COMM and NAV but does not control the NAV volume.
2. COMM frequency transfer button. You are now talking on 118.90 MHz and have set up 126.00 (the next expected COMM frequency) on the right. When the time comes to switch to that new frequency, you'd push the transfer button and the standby frequency is now the use frequency. Now 118.90 would be the standby frequency. (If you had needed to go *back* to the original 118.90 from 126.00 MHz, pressing the transfer button would have done that.) You would then set up the *next* expected COMM frequency on the standby and be ready for a quick switch as necessary. This saves a lot of time in last-minute frequency

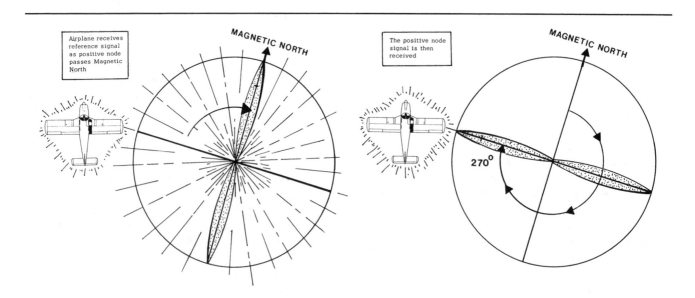

Fig. 5-1. VOR theory.

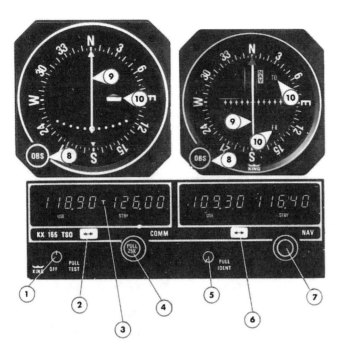

Fig. 5-2. COMM/NAV "one and a half" set consisting of a two-way communications receiver on the left (the "one") and a navigation and voice receiver on the right (the "half"). Two examples of VOR indicators are shown. Items (1)-(4) concern the transceiver (COMM) and (5)-(10) the VOR(NAV). (*Bendix-King*)

changing or having another COMM/NAV set standing by.

3. "T," when lighted, indicates that the mike button is depressed. (How do you cheer up a depressed mike button?)
4. COMM frequency selector knobs.
5. VOL/IDENT switch. Pull for VOR identification; turn for NAV volume control.
6. NAV frequency transfer button. By pushing this, the VOR on 116.40 MHz becomes the station being used.
7. NAV frequency selector knobs.
8. Omni bearing selector (OBS). In both indicators the chosen bearing is North, but there are 360 radials to choose.
9. Course deviation indicator (CDI). The indicator on the left is a "windshield wiper" type, swinging left or right from the top attachment. The VOR receiver face on the right has rectilinear needle action; that is, the needle remains vertical as it moves left or right. Each dot or pip on the indicator represents deviation from the selected VOR radial, or center line of the ILS localizer, of 2° and ½° respectively. (More about the ILS later.)
10. TO-FROM indicators. On the presentation on the left TO-FROM would be indicated as applicable; on

the right a white triangle would point to the applicable TO-FROM condition. (The faces shown are with the electrical power OFF.)

Since the "radials" (there are 360 of them, or one for every degree) are fixed in reference to the ground, the airplane's heading has no bearing on what radial it is on. However, in tracking to or from a VOR, it is best for the omni bearing selector of the simpler VOR receivers to be selected to the *course* to be followed, so that the left-right needle reads correctly. Figure 5-3 shows the radial idea.

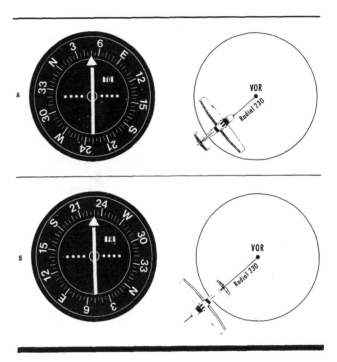

Fig. 5-3. Both airplanes are on the 230 radial, but (A) is inbound (course 050°) and (B) is outbound (course 230°).

Airplane A doesn't have to select 050 on the OBS, but it's a lot more reasonable to do this; otherwise, the needle would sense incorrectly. The needle is sensing correctly when it is pointing in the proper direction to get you on the selected radial. Turn and fly "toward the needle." If the OBS of Airplane A was set at 230 and it drifted to the right of the course, the needle would be deflected to the right, implying that a right turn would be needed to get back on the original course—which is incorrect.

To show that the heading of the airplane has nothing to do with the indications in the cockpit, take a look at Figure 5-4. The combination of needle, TO-FROM, and OBS merely gives you the airplane's position relative to the station.

You will get the indications shown in Figure 5-4A if you tune in the VOR and set the OBS to 050. Of course, the needle would soon leave the center in the cases where you are flying *across* the 230 radial, but at the particular instant of tuning, the indications would be as shown. The VOR and the cockpit indications are straightforward. They merely combine

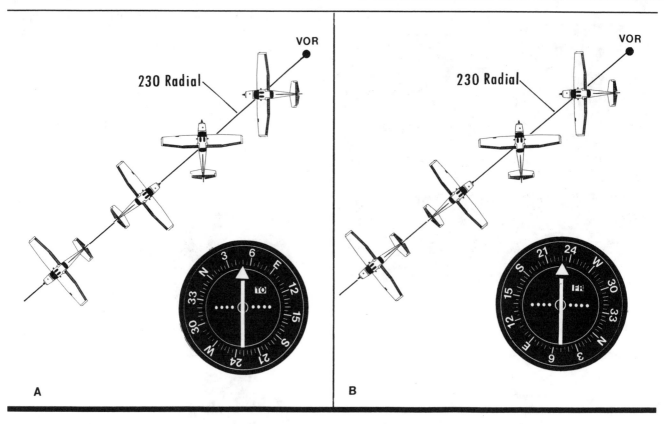

Fig. 5-4. The heading of the airplane has nothing to do with the cockpit indications. In (A) the OBS has been set to 050 and the TO-FROM indicator says TO. In (B) the OBS has been set to 230 and the TO-FROM indicator says FROM.

to state that the airplane is to fly a magnetic course of 050° to get TO the station. The VOR and your cockpit equipment couldn't care less what your particular heading is at that instant. Although as soon as the airplane leaves the selected course, the needle will let you know about it.

In Figure 5-4B the VOR and cockpit equipment are also doing their jobs. The airplane is on a bearing of 230° from the station, and that's all the equipment is supposed to tell. If you're just passing by, then it's only a matter of interest that your airplane is at that instant on a bearing of 230° magnetic from VOR "X."

Figure 5-5 shows what happens to an airplane that has the set tuned into a certain VOR and is trying to track inbound on the 230 radial (050° course). It has drifted to the right because of a northerly wind, and the indications are as shown. The needle is indicating that the selected radial is to the left.

In Figure 5-6 the airplane is in the same situation, except that for some reason the pilot set in 230 on the OBS but plans to track into the station on a course of 050°. The needle seems to be giving you a bum steer.

The VOR equipment in the airplane is still doing what it was designed to do—the pilot was the one who was out to lunch. If the pilot suddenly rotated the airplane to the heading set up on the OBS (230°), the selected radial or course *would* be to the right (Fig. 5-7).

The cockpit indicators tell you that you are south of the selected line of flight to the VOR.

■ **Using the VOR for Cross Bearings** The idea covered in the last section can be used to check whether you've passed a VOR intersection (there is another method also, which will be covered shortly). Look at Figure 5-8.

You are flying along V-116, minding your own business, feeling satisfied that you've done your duty as an instrument pilot, having earlier given ATC an ETA for WIN, and everything is OK. (Use a lot of initials in your talk around the hangar; it'll drive VFR pilots crazy PDQ.)

Assume here that you aren't in radar contact and so have to keep up with and report your positions—a rare instance in today's radar coverage, but this is an example that *could* happen.

Anyway, ATC asks, in a tone of voice that implies you have been extremely remiss, if you have passed HECTO intersection. Looking at the chart, you see HECTO and figure that you are somewhere in that area but can't be sure whether you've passed it yet. (Your mind is going like a squirrel in a cage, trying to remember if previous clearances had mentioned anything about reporting at HECTO. Forget it; at this point you'd better find out whether you've passed it or not—and as soon as possible.)

You tune in PAL (Palmyra VOR) on the other VOR receiver—and *identify it.* Notice that the 300 radial of PAL intersects your airway, forming the intersection in question. You set up the OBS to 120; the bearing TO the station (from HECTO) and the cockpit indications look like those shown in Figure 5-9.

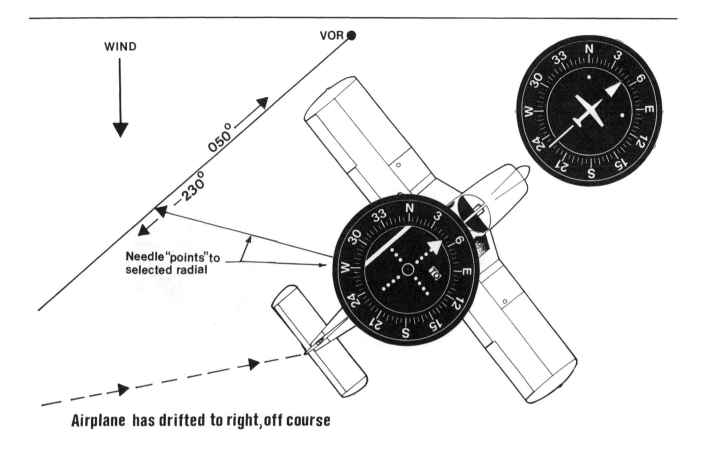

Fig. 5-5. The airplane has drifted to the right of course, and the needle points toward the selected bearing.

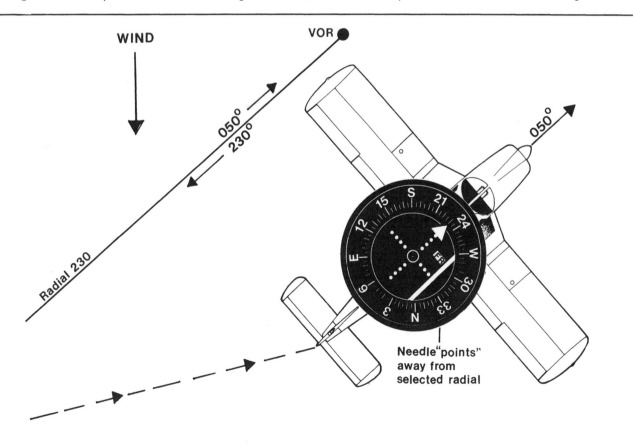

Fig. 5-6. The indications of the cockpit equipment for the same airplane position and heading as in Figure 5-5 but with the OBS set on 230, or reverse to the course to be flown.

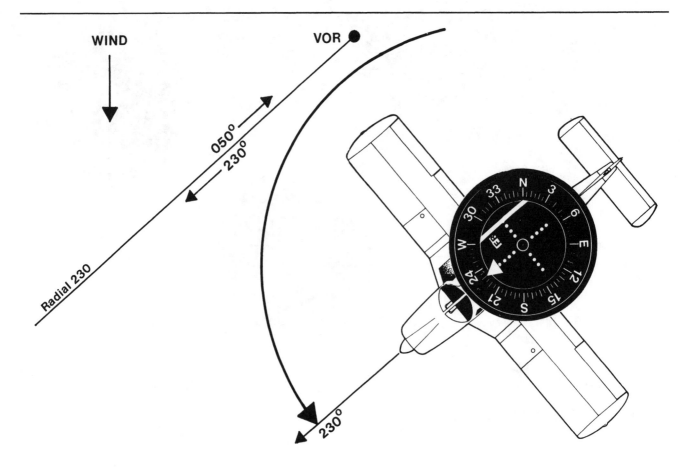

Fig. 5-7. The selected radial is to the right. Note that the needle did not move within the instrument, or it still has the same relative position to the pilot.

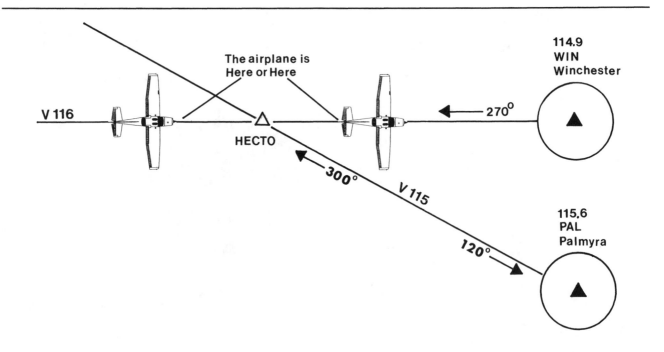

Fig. 5-8. Have you passed the VOR intersection in question?

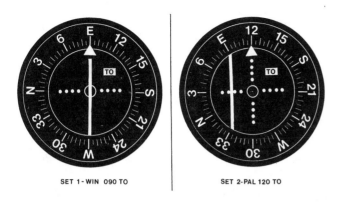

SET 1 - WIN 090 TO   SET 2-PAL 120 TO

Fig. 5-9. Cockpit indications when checking for HECTO intersection.

Set 1 shows that you are right on course to Winchester, as you are supposed to be, but what about HECTO intersection?

In your *mind's eye,* turn the airplane (at your present position) to a heading of 120°, and look at the needle on Set 2. It's to the left, so the radial making up the intersection is to the left—and you *have not passed it* (Fig. 5-10).

The needle is "pointing" to the radial in question. If you had set in 300, the same answer would be given (you haven't reached the intersection yet), but the presentation would be a little different, as shown in Figure 5-11.

In Figure 5-11 the needle is still "pointing" to the reference line (radial).

One tip for this technique: If the station being used for the cross bearing is "ahead of the wing tips" of the airplane, use the TO indication (turn the OBS to the bearing that would give a TO) and then look at the needle and "turn" the

airplane in your mind. If it's behind the wing tip (dashed VOR and radial), use the cross bearing that would give the "FROM" indication. This would mean that you would not have to "turn" the airplane so far in your mind.

If you had passed the intersection, the needle would show the opposite indications (to the right in Figure 5-10 and left in Figure 5-11).

Perhaps you don't like the idea of "turning" the airplane in your mind, so a quicker way would be to always set the actual radial for the cross-bearing VOR or for the bearing to the intersection FROM the station. If the VOR's relative position to your heading and the needle indication jibe, then you haven't reached the intersection (the cross-bearing VOR station is to your *right* as you fly the course line—whether ahead or behind—and if the needle is to the *right,* you haven't reached the intersection). Naturally, if the VOR is to the left and the needle is to the left, you haven't reached the intersection either.

So *tune the cross-bearing VOR and rotate the OBS to the outbound bearing from the VOR* to *the intersection as given on the chart.* If the relative position of the VOR to your course line and the needle position match, then you haven't reached the intersection. If they don't match, you've passed it (Fig. 5-12).

Of course, it's easiest to have distance measuring equipment (DME) in the airplane and just read whether you have reached the intersection. (If the intersection is 17 mi on this side of the VORTAC ahead and the DME is indicating 20 mi, you still have 3 mi to go.) DME will be covered shortly.

■ **Time-to-Station Work** One problem used in getting familiar with VOR operations is the estimation of the required time to fly to a VOR off a wing tip. You'll find that,

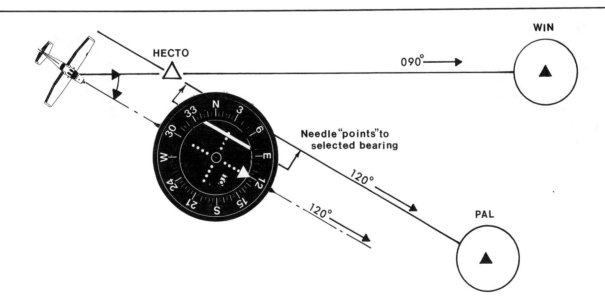

Fig. 5-10. The needle indicates that the radial is to the left on the imaginary heading of 120°, hence ahead of the airplane on the real heading.

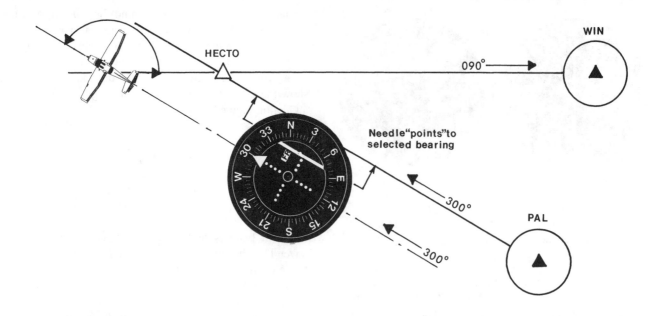

Fig. 5-11. The OBS has been set at 300 (Palmyra) and the TO-FROM indicator says FROM. The airplane is "turned" to a 300° heading.

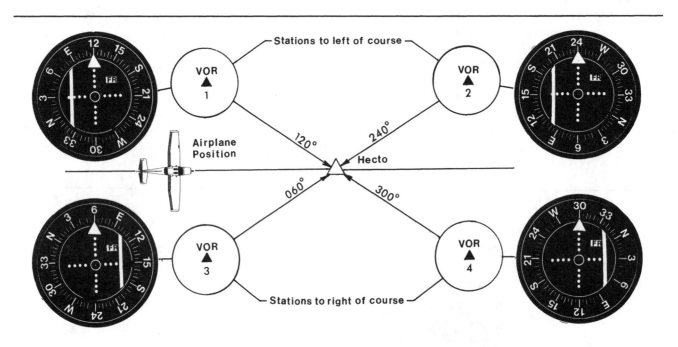

Fig. 5-12. After setting up *outbound* bearings from the cross-bearing VORs, if the relative position of the needle and station match, the intersection has not been reached.

for a certain period of time, flying "perpendicular" to the course to the VOR, a certain time longer is required to reach the station after turning inbound to it. (You recall from your trigonometry that the ratio of two legs of a right triangle can be found readily if the angle is known.) You will fly through an angle of either 10° or 20° and will have a fixed multiple of the time required in either case (6 and 3 respectively). Figure 5-13 shows the principle involved.

Suppose you want to find your distance (time) to the station in Figure 5-13. You would tune the VOR and center the needle with the TO-FROM indicator showing TO. Figure 5-13A shows your relative position to the station. You would then turn the airplane to the nearest heading that would put that bearing 10° ahead of the wing tip. In the example, your original heading is 045°, so a right turn is in order. You would turn right to a heading of 090°. (You would see that

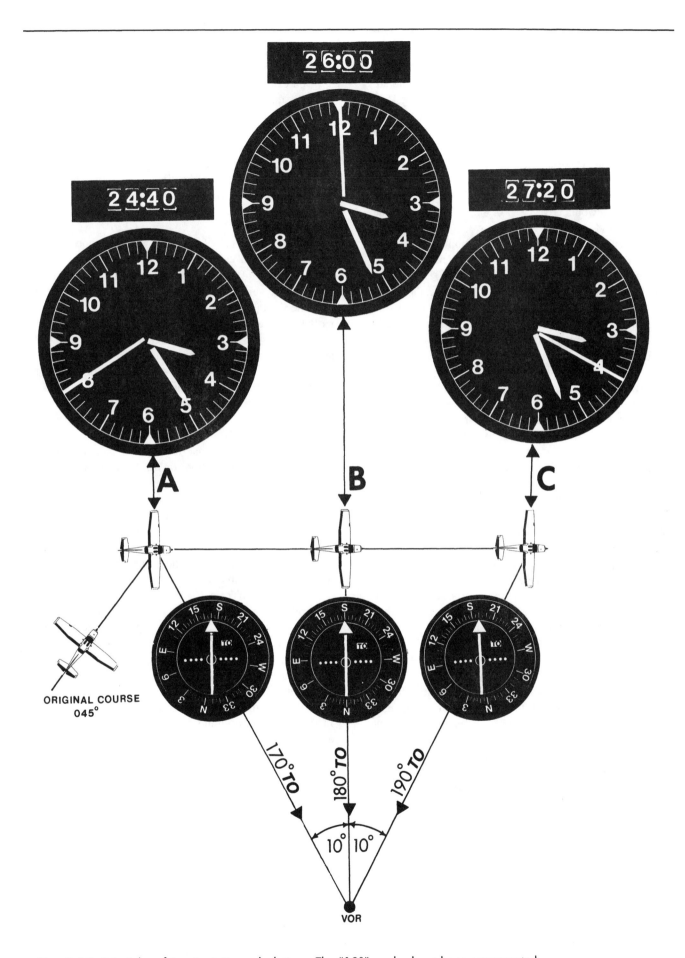

Fig. 5-13. Principles of time-to-station calculations. The "10°" angles have been exaggerated.

this would put the station at a *relative* bearing of 080°, or 10° ahead of the right wing tip.) You would fly the 090° heading and make a note of the time that the needle was centered. Then you would rotate the OBS to get a new bearing 180° TO. (The needle is no longer centered because you aren't at the newly selected radial yet.) You would hold the heading of 090° until the needle is centered again (point B) and make a note of the time. The elapsed time multiplied by 6 would give the time required to fly to the VOR from point B. If it took 1 min and 20 sec to fly from A to B, the time required to fly to the station would be 6 × 1 ⅓ or 8 min. If you timed the flight from A to C (20°), the multiplier would be 3. (It should take 2 min and 40 sec. and 3 × 2 ⅔ = 8 min to the station.) Note that the multiplier and the number of degrees flown are a function of the number 60. If you fly only 10° of arc, the multiplier is 6 (6 × 10 = 60). If you fly 20° of arc, the multiplier is 3 (3 × 20 = 60). In theory, if you flew 30° of arc, the multiplier would be 2 (2 × 30 = 60); but 20° is plenty, and 10° works closely enough and saves time in actual practice. Or you may prefer to remember: "For each 10 sec it takes to make a 10° change, you are 1 min from the station." (If at a great distance out, you may use "each 5 sec for 5° equals 1 min from the station.")

In no-wind conditions the estimate of time to the VOR should be reasonably accurate, but with a wind, the inbound leg could be affected. Wind from any direction or velocity at your altitude will affect the accuracy of the estimate.

You can actually track around a VOR and approach the station from any given direction. Under no-wind conditions the airplane (in theory) would remain a constant distance from the VOR—this is assuming that you made perfect corrections for the different compass deviation errors for different headings and that you flew those headings right on the button. There are VOR/DME approaches that use this basic principle of tracking around the station, and the DME is a great aid in assuring that the proper radius is maintained. (This will be discussed shortly.)

In this day of radar and GPS, the idea of tracking around a station using only VOR (no DME) is academic. But as a training maneuver, it can serve in keeping you alert while flying the airplane and doing calculations at the same time. Looking back at Figure 5-13, at point C the heading would be changed 20° to the right and the OBS set to 210. When the needle centers, another 20° right turn is made and 20° is added to the OBS selection. This is done until the airplane is on the desired radial for turning in. (It may work out that you'll have to cut one of the segments short when the radial is reached.)

The amount of needle lead for a turn into the station depends on your distance from it. Normally 5°, or when the needle is deflected about ½ to one side (to the left in this case), is used as a lead. However, it really depends on the rate of needle movement, which is a function of your distance from the VOR. If you were 60 mi out, 5° would mean

a 5-mi lead for a 90° standard-rate turn. For the airplanes you'll be flying, this will be too much.

You can check groundspeed en route by cross bearings and probably have been doing so in your VFR flying. The drawback to this is a lack of accuracy in the airplane and/or ground equipment. As will be covered later, you could have up to 6° error in your airplane equipment, as checked, and still be OK for instrument flying.

You may also check the time to a station by turning either way 90° to your course and finding the time required to fly through 5°, 10°, or 20° of arc. (If using 5°, the multiplier is 12.)

The disadvantages of this are obvious. Supposedly, you are on an assigned Victor airway. This requires that you leave the center line of the assigned airway and mosey off into other people's airspace, particularly if you are some distance from the VOR (Victor airways extend 4 NM out from the center line or are 8 NM wide). This technique could cause a great deal of interest down at the ARTCC radar console. For Victor airway navigation in the United States, you'll be a lot better off to take a cross bearing, get an approximate distance to the station, and (if you haven't had a groundspeed check) use your true airspeed and estimated wind to make a time estimate to the station. (VOR radial errors should be just about the same for only a 10° difference in selection.)

Another time check that may be used, though not particularly practical for operations on assigned airways, is called "double the angle off the bow," a term more descriptive when applied to the automatic direction finder than to the VOR—but the principle is the same in both cases. Basically. you will fly two legs of an isosceles (two equal sides) triangle.

Assume you are flying to a VOR on an inbound bearing of 080°. Figure 5-14 shows the procedure. You may make the turn in either direction.

You would make a 10° turn to either the left or right (left in this case) and reset the OBS 10° to the *right* (or 10° greater, that is, 090°). You were originally tracking on an inbound bearing of 080°, as shown by Figure 5-14. With a crosswind you were holding some heading other than the inbound bearing. At any rate, change the *heading* 10° (to the left in this case). Fly that heading until the needle centers on the OBS selection of 090°; that is the completion of Leg 1. In theory and in no-wind conditions, Leg 1 should be the exact length (and time) as Leg 2. When the needle centers, the time into the station is the same as that required to fly the first leg. You can see, for instance, that a wind perpendicular to your original course could make a slight difference in the times on the two legs.

These two procedures are good training aids for improving the instrument scan and VOR use but are all but gone in practical use today.

FAR 91.171(a–d) covers the tolerances of the airborne omni equipment as follows:

VOR equipment check for IFR operations:

(a) No person may operate a civil aircraft under IFR using the VOR system of radio navigation unless the VOR equipment of that aircraft—

(1) Is maintained, checked, and inspected under an approved procedure; or

(2) Has been operationally checked within the preceding 30 days, and was found to be within the limits of the permissible indicated bearing error set forth in paragraph (b) or (c) of this section.

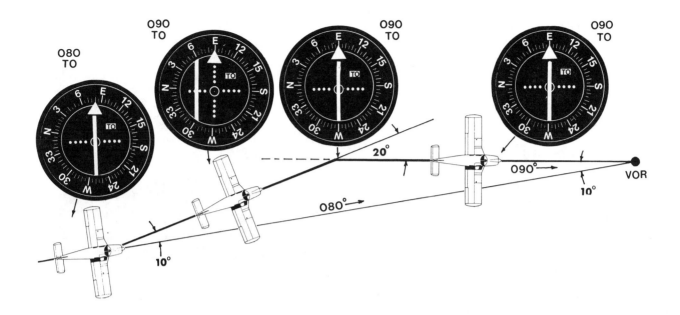

Fig. 5-14. The "double the angle off the bow" method of estimating time to the station.

b) Except as provided in paragraph (c) of this section, each person conducting a VOR check under subparagraph (a)(2) of this section shall—

(1) Use, at the airport of intended departure, an FAA operated or approved test signal or, outside the United States, a test signal operated or approved by appropriate authority, to check the VOR equipment (the maximum permissible indicated bearing error is plus or minus 4 degrees);

(2) Use at the airport of intended departure a point on an airport surface designated as a VOR system checkpoint by the Administrator or, outside the United States, by appropriate authority (the maximum permissible bearing error is plus or minus 4 degrees);

(3) If neither a test signal nor a designated checkpoint on the surface is available; use an airborne checkpoint designated by the Administrator or, out-side the United States, by appropriate authority (the maximum permissible bearing error is plus or minus 6 degrees); or

(4) If no check signal or point is available, while in flight—

(i) Select a VOR radial that lies along the centerline of an established VOR airway;

(ii) Select a prominent ground point along the selected radial preferably more than 20 miles from the VOR ground facility and maneuver the aircraft directly over the point at a reasonably low altitude; and

(iii) Note the VOR bearing indicated by the receiver when over the ground point (the maximum permissible variation between the published radial and the indicated bearing is 6 degrees).

(c) If dual system VOR (units independent of each other except for the antenna) is installed in the aircraft, the

person checking the equipment may check one system against the other in place of the check procedures specified in paragraph (b) of this section. He shall tune both systems to the same VOR ground facility and note the indicated bearings to that station. The maximum permissible variation between the two indicated bearings is 4 degrees.

(d) Each person making the VOR operational check as specified in paragraph (b) or (c) of this section shall enter the date, place, bearing error, and his signature in the aircraft log or other record.

In addition, if a test signal radiated by a repair station, as specified in paragraph (b)(1) of this section, is used, an entry must be made in the aircraft log or other record by the repair station certificate holder or his representative certifying to the bearing transmitted by the repair station for the check and the date of transmission.

Note that the tolerance for ground checking is ±4° and that for an airborne check is ±6°. The *Airport/Facility Directory* lists VOR receiver airborne and ground checkpoints for various facilities.

The VOR test facility (VOT) transmits a test signal that gives the VOR user an accurate method of testing a receiver(s) on the ground. The airports with a VOT have the frequency listed in the *A/FD* with the other information pertaining to VOR checkpoints.

When the receiver is tuned to the proper frequency and the needle centered by use of the OBS, it should indicate 0° when the TO-FROM needle indicates FROM or 180° when

the TO-FROM indicator says TO. (A good way to remember is "Cessna 182" or 180-TO.)

The deviation from these figures is the error of the aircraft equipment. Some VOTs are identified by a continuous series of dots, while others use a continuous tone.

An RMI/VOR receiver (covered later in the chapter) will indicate 180° on any OBS setting when you use a VOT.

The ground station accuracy is generally ±1°, but roughness is sometimes present, particularly in mountainous terrain. You may observe a brief left-right needle oscillation, such as would be expected as an indication of approaching the station. Always use the TO-FROM indicator as an assurance of passing the station, rather than assuming you're there when the needle suddenly pegs to one side.

A problem that sometimes occurs with the airborne equipment is that at certain prop rpm settings, the left-right needle (or, more technically, the course deviation indicator) may fluctuate as much as ±6°. A slight change in rpm will straighten out this problem (which, incidentally, can occur in helicopters as well). If you are having this sort of trouble, try the rpm change before casting aspersions on the veracity of your set (don't wreck it until you check it) or the ground station.

The *A/FD* contains the latest information on possible VOR problems. For instance, you could find that the VOR portion of the Pulaski (Va.) VORTAC is unusable in the area 206–216° beyond 5 NM below 5000 ft, and the 268–288° azimuth is unusable beyond 8 NM at all altitudes.

■ **VOR Identification** *Always* identify the station either by its Morse code identifier or by the code *and* automatic voice identifier. *Don't* identify, for instance. the Palmyra VOR just by hearing (on a VOR frequency) somebody in an FSS saying something about "Palmyra radio, etc." Remember that many FSSs operate several remote VORs, and none may carry the name of the controlling facility.

If the VOR is down for maintenance, the code, or code and voice, is removed. The VOR receiver may indicate periodically, but if you don't hear the continuous identifier, don't trust it. Some facilities may radiate a T-E-S-T code (— • ••• —), or the identification code may be removed during the periods of maintenance.

Remember, too, that being VHF, the VOR only operates line of sight. If you are too low, it will have a warning flag showing.

It's suggested you get copies of the *AIM* and carefully read the section that goes into detail on use of the VOR. In fact, if you plan on flying IFR, you should subscribe to that publication. It will be discussed in more detail in Chapter 8.

■ **Horizontal Situation Indicator (HSI)** The HSI is an improvement over the straight VOR/ILS indicator in that the heading indicator and VOR and ILS (including glide slope) are combined in one display. Figure 5-15 is a sample display with a description of the various functions:

1. The lubber line has the same function as that of heading indicators.
2. The NAV warning flag shows whenever an unusable VOR or localizer signal is being received.
3. The heading select bug set by the knob (10) as a *reference* for heading or as a part of the coupling to an autopilot or flight director.
4. The glide slope pointers drop into view when a usable glide slope signal is being received.
5. The symbolic aircraft is a fixed representation of the actual aircraft and always points to the top of the display and lubber line.
6. The deviation bar, like the needle in an older VOR display, is displaced to indicate the relative position of the selected course.

Fig. 5-15. Horizontal situation indicator (HSI) and display functions. The heading indicator portion may be free or slaved to a remote magnetic compass system. (*Bendix-King*)

7. The course select knob.
8. The deviation scale. When on VOR frequencies each dot represents 2° deviation; on localizer frequencies each is ½° deviation. In RNAV approach mode the scale is ¼ NM per dot; in RNAV "en route," the scale is 1 NM per dot.
9. Compass card with the same function as a slaved or free heading indicator.
10. Heading select knob (or OBS).
11. Glide slope deviation scale. References for the relative position of the glide slope.
12. The TO-FROM indicator. (The arrowhead is adjacent to the lubber line for TO and away from it for FROM.)
13. The selected course pointer.
14. Compass warning flag. This is indicated whenever the electrical power is inadequate or the heading indicator is not up to speed.

Figure 5-16 shows the indications of an HSI during a flight from Kansas City to St. Louis:

1. After takeoff from Kansas City, the heading bug is set at 060° to intercept the 110° course to Napoleon (ANX).
2. The VOR deviation bar is starting to center, and the airplane is in the process of turning to 110°.
3. The TO swings to FROM as the airplane flies over Napoleon VOR and the course pointer is set to 088°.
4. On course from Napoleon to Tiger (Columbia 111.2) with a heading of 080° to correct for wind drift (course 088°).

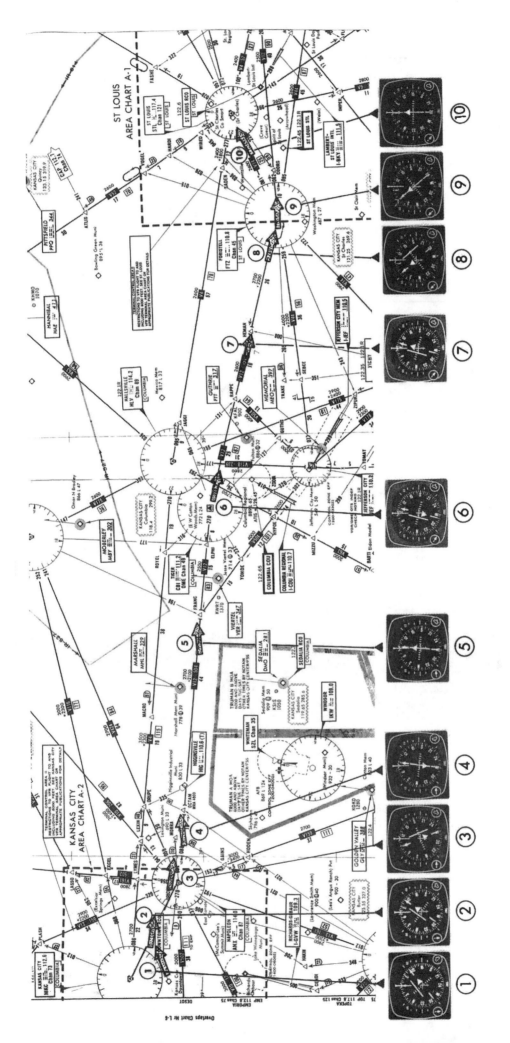

Fig. 5-16. Use of the HSI during a flight from Kansas City (MKC) to St. Louis (STL). The display information (1-10) matches the positions as shown by the arrows (1-10). The arrows show the approximate position and heading at each point discussed. (*Bendix-King*)

5. About halfway to Columbia (CBI) the set is switched to that frequency (111.2) and the TO-FROM switches to TO. (The course arrow is now changed from 088° to 090°.)

6. Over Columbia (Tiger) VOR the TO-FROM goes to FROM; since the course on V12 to Foristell VOR-TAC (FTZ) is 098°, the course pointer is set to this, and the heading to keep the deviation bar centered is flown.

7. Near the Heman intersection, the set is switched to Foristell (110.8), and the course arrow is set to 100°. The TO-FROM indicator is now TO.

8. The clearance is V12 to Foristell, then V14 to the St. Louis (STL) VORTAC, direct to Lambert Field. The St. Louis VORTAC is selected and the course pointer is set on 062.

9. As Foristell VORTAC is crossed, the deviation bar aligns with the course arrow. The heading bug is set to 062; turn left to follow V14 to the St. Louis VOR-TAC.

10. Tracking to the St. Louis VORTAC, correcting for any wind drift to keep the deviation bar centered.

Figure 5-17 is a holding pattern with HSI indications at four points in the process.

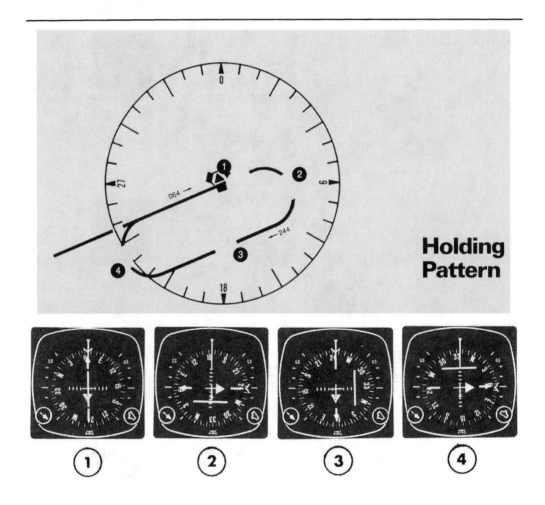

Fig. 5-17. A holding pattern at St. Louis VORTAC with the HSI indications shown at four positions.

(1) You're cleared to hold southwest of the VORTAC on the 244 radial, right turns. You're now over the station with a 064° course selected (the TO-FROM indicator has just flipped to FROM). Set the heading bug to 244 for reference and start the right turn.

(2) Halfway through the outbound turn the deviation bar is behind the symbolic airplane, indicating that you will eventually have to fly *back* to that radial in order to be on course during the inbound leg.

(3) Outbound. The heading bug is still set at 244° as a reference. That radial is off the wing and parallel to the outbound course. (More about wind drift correction in the holding pattern in Chapter 12.)

(4) Halfway through the turn to the inbound 064° course the symbolic airplane "approaching" the deviation bar at a right angle. (The reference heading bug has been reset to 064). By keeping the top of the deviation bar on the lubber line as you continue to turn, you can complete the turn and roll out on course. (*Bendix-King*)

■ **VOR Receiver Antennas** In order to know some of the characteristics of your VOR receiver (and other radio equipment), you should know the locations of the antennas and which item of electronic gear uses which antenna. For instance, for airplanes with two transceivers, one of the *communications* antennas may be on top of the fuselage and the other on the bottom. When the airplane is sitting on the ground, the set with the bottom antenna may be blanketed out and unusable as far as contacting ground control is concerned. The top antenna may be in a bad spot for communications directly over a facility. Rocking your wings may help or hinder.

Figure 5-18 shows some VOR receiver antenna types and probable locations on an airplane.

DISTANCE MEASURING EQUIPMENT (DME)

DME is a UHF facility operating in the range from 962 to 1213 MHz. While the ground equipment is normally located at the VOR site (this is not the case for certain military installations), it's a separate piece of gear.

Basically, it works this way: When you select the station on your DME, the airborne equipment sends out paired pulses at a specific spacing (interrogation). The ground station equipment wakes up and transmits paired pulses back to the aircraft on a different frequency and pulse spacing. The time required for the round trip is read as distance (nautical miles) from the aircraft to the station. (Since the pulses are moving at the speed of light—161,000 NM/sec—you can imagine about how little time it takes to make a round trip of, say, 20 NM.)

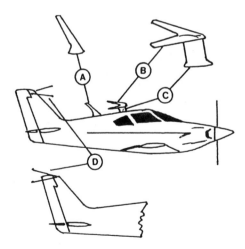

Fig. 5-18. Types of VOR and communications antennas. (A) Broad-band communications antenna (118–136 MHz). (B) VOR/LOC antenna is combined with a (C) broad-band communications antenna. (D) VOR/LOC antennas. There are too many different models and types to show them here, but you should know which of the antennas on your airplane go to what radio and discuss with your instructor the possible weaknesses of each.

VORTAC is a combination of two facilities, VOR and TACAN (Tactical Air Navigation). TACAN, used by the military, provides both distance and azimuth information on UHF frequencies for the aircraft with the proper equipment installed.

Your equipment is able to pick up the distance information part of TACAN, but you'll use the VOR for azimuth information.

For each VOR frequency at VORTAC facilities, there is an associated TACAN channel for distance information. For instance, all VORTACs with the VOR portion having a frequency of 112.2 MHz have TACAN channel 59 (and that UHF frequency) associated with them. Current DME equipment uses this idea, and the DME frequency selector is set up as 112.2 rather than having a separate channel selector operating in the 962–1213 MHz (UHF) range. When you select 112.2 on the DME, you are actually selecting the proper UHF frequency and don't need to know what it is (Fig. 5-19).

On the en route low-altitude chart, the facilities having VORTAC are indicated as shown in Figure 5-19.

Basically speaking, on the National Aeronautical Charting Office Service (NACO) low-altitude en route chart, if a channel number is given with the VOR frequency box, you can use DME equipment with that VOR facility (it's a VORTAC). Of course, you can also learn this by looking at the symbol in the center of the VOR rose as shown in Figure 5-19. The quickest way is just to see if a channel is given. Each NOS chart has a legend that explains the symbols. This will be covered later.

The DME equipment in the airplane measures the distance *direct* to the station or gives the *slant range*. If you are flying at an altitude of 6080 ft above the VORTAC, your distance indicator will never show less than a mile, even though you pass directly over the station, because you never get closer than 1 NM (6080 ft) to it. Figure 5-20 shows this idea.

You will note in Figure 5-20 that at a distance of 5 mi. the lateral (or ground) distance is 4.9 mi. At a 2-mi indication, the lateral distance to the station is about 1.72 mi. Okay, so an error exists, but *you and the controller will always base reports and clearances on what the distance indicator says*. The error becomes very small at distances greater than 10 mi and is ignored. (The error also depends on altitude above the station as well as the distance out.) *Don't* depend on the DME for station passage information; use your VOR TO-FROM indicator.

DME equipment has the capability of reading off the distance from the selected VORTAC (in nautical miles), minutes to the station, and groundspeed. Figure 5-21 shows a DME receiver with these capabilities. This equipment can be used with area navigation (RNAV), to be discussed later in the chapter.

The DME uses a small antenna that weighs about one-fourth of a pound. It's located underneath the fuselage, usually in the center section area (Fig. 5-22). The identification is a single-coded one approximately every 30 sec, showing that the DME (only) is working. No ID, no working.

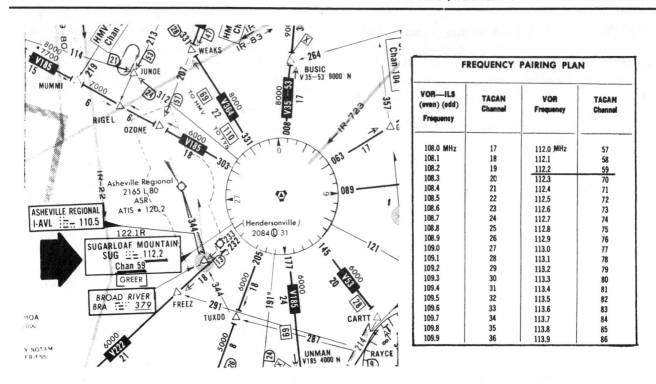

Fig. 5-19. Sample of a VORTAC frequency pairing plan. As more "in-between" frequencies are used, you may see TACAN channels split—59X (112.20 MHz) and 59Y (112.25 MHz) for example.

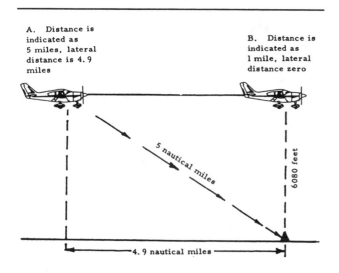

A. Distance is indicated as 5 miles, lateral distance is 4.9 miles

B. Distance is indicated as 1 mile, lateral distance zero

Fig. 5-20. The DME measures the distance direct to the VORTAC (slant range). The airplane at Point A would report its position as 5 mi (even if exact ground distance was calculated).

DME ARCS. Figure 5-23 is an approach chart for Muscle Shoals (MSL) VOR 29 approach showing a DME arc, instead of a procedure turn, when approaching from the southeast on V7 (R-153 of the Muscle Shoals VOR).

Assuming at first a no-wind condition, you would start the procedure by tracking inbound on the R-153 (inbound bearing 333°), and as the DME (set on MSL) approaches 7

mi (the lead would depend on the groundspeed), a turn is made to a heading of 063°. The VOR is set to 323° TO (the needle is deflected to the right) and the airplane flown until the needle is again centered. A 10° turn to the left is made to 053° and the OBS reset to 313°. The airplane flies two more 10° segments after this until the needle centers at 293° (or the last segment may be 2° to get lined up on the 291° inbound track). You would lead the turn based on the VOR needle movement rate.

You would constantly monitor the DME as you tracked around and would turn a few degrees toward the station if the DME started to indicate more than 7 mi and would turn away on a segment or segments if the distance started to decrease from 7 mi.

Figure 5-24 shows in more detail the steps in moving from V7 to the 7 NM DME arc and the turn inbound.

Some approach charts to localizer or ILS approaches have "lead radials" to be used as a reference for turning into the facility; this is particularly useful for an airplane with only one VOR/LOC receiver. A turn lead of 5° might be considered a reasonable figure to start with for the type of airplanes you'll initially be flying. (More about this later.)

Figure 5-25 is a VOR/DME approach chart for Centerville, Tenn.

LF/MF NAVIGATION AIDS

The nondirectional radio beacon (NDB) is a ground facility that operates in the LF (30–300 kHz) and MF (300–3000 kHz) bands. (The old LF/MF ranges had four fixed legs—the radio beacon transmits in *all* directions.)

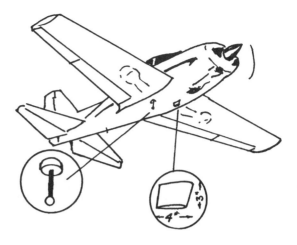

Fig. 5-22. DME antenna types. Check with your instructor for the type and location of DME antennas on your airplane.

Fig. 5-21. Distance measuring equipment (DME) showing distance to the station, groundspeed, and minutes to the station. The top indicator shows that it is set to the NAV 1 (N1) set. (The bottom indicator is a slaved set that may be used for indications on the copilot's side.) The "hold" setting keeps the DME on the last selected frequency even though the *NAV* frequency selectors are subsequently changed. (*Bendix-King*)

The majority of the NDBs are assigned a frequency in the 190–535 kHz range, Unlike the VOR, which gives geographic information, the NDB and airborne equipment give the station's position *relative* to the aircraft. You'll be using an automatic direction finder (ADF) in the airplane to work with the NDB.

■ Types of Ground Transmitters

COMPASS LOCATOR. The compass locators are a part of the ILS, and a particular ILS may have a compass locator at either or both of the two (middle and outer) markers.

Figure 5-26 is an approach chart for the Owensboro–Daviess County Airport (OWB) showing the outer compass locator (Locator at Outer Marker—LOM) for the localizer approach. The frequency is 341 kHz and the identifier is "OW" In earlier days, a compass locator was established at a middle fan marker (LMM) and in this case would have an identification of "WB" or the second two letters of the ILS identifier.

The LMM is being phased out at most locations except where it might be necessary for safety due to a local condition. Because the compass locators are used as a part of the ILS approach, they don't need to have a great range. They normally have a power output of less than 25 watts. Don't expect to receive one accurately at a distance over 15 mi. (The compass locator is considered to be a special class of radio beacon.) At some locations higher power radio beacons,

up to 400 watts, are used as outer marker compass locators. These generally carry transcribed weather broadcast information. (Weather planning is covered in Chapter 7.) The complete ILS will be covered later in this chapter.

NONDIRECTIONAL BEACON (NDB). The term "beacon" is used for those LF/MF navigational or approach facilities *other* than compass locators—even though the LOM and LMM are radio beacons also.

The NDB comes in three classes:

MH facility—Power output less than 50 watts. Expect up to about 25 NM of accurate reception under normal atmospheric and terrain conditions.

H facility—Power output greater than 50 watts but less than 2000 watts. Expect about a 50-NM range at all altitudes.

HH facility—Power greater than 2000 watts (75 NM) and continuous identification in three-letter code as is the case for MH and H facilities. The NDBs with voice facilities cut out the code during voice transmissions. You can get voice transmissions, except on those having the letter "W" (without voice), included in the class designation in *A/FD*. On the en route chart or approach chart, the frequency is underlined if no voice is available.

COMMERCIAL BROADCAST STATIONS. Commercial broadcast (AM) stations may be used for en route ADF work, and a few nonofficial letdowns at uncontrolled airports may use them. The commercial station is more powerful but has the disadvantage of not giving continuous identification. At your home airport you would recognize the announcers' voices and also get information from local advertising, such as when the announcer mentions "Schwartz's Livery Stable on Gitchygoomy Street." Basically, the commercial broadcasting station is a fine VFR homing aid and is good for picking up music or news, but it's not to be considered an IFR navigation aid.

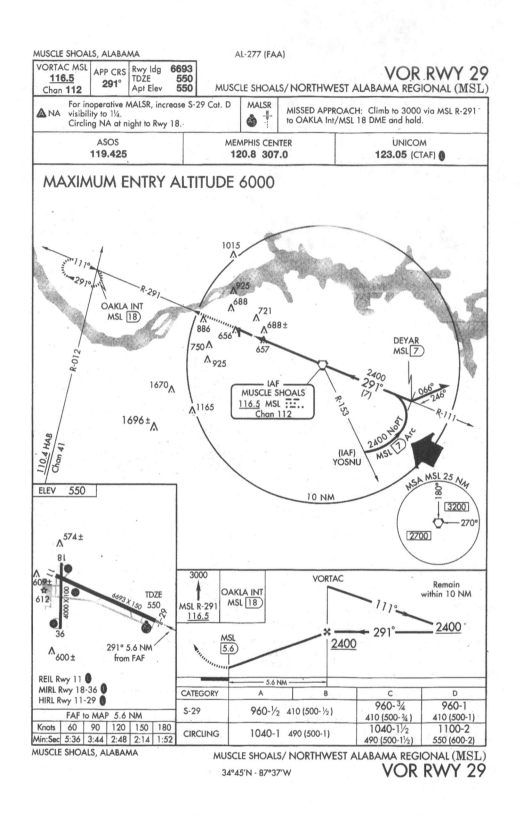

Fig. 5-23. Using the DME (and VOR receiver) to fly an arc from V7 around to the final approach course for a VOR approach to Runway 29 at Muscle Shoals (arrow). Without this convenience, the airplane would have to be flown to the VOR and back out on Radial 111 to make a procedure turn, then inbound, taking up much more time to do the approach. Note that you are protected for obstacle clearance at 2600 ft MSL throughout the segment.

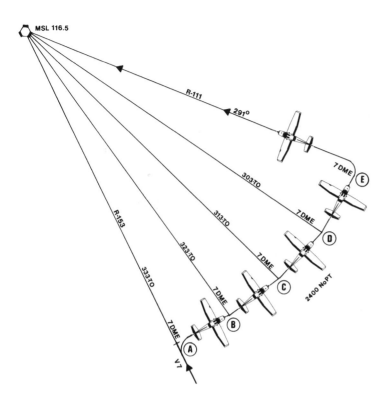

Fig. 5-24. Steps in flying a (no-wind) DME arc from V7 to make a straight-in instrument approach to the Muscle Shoals Airport Runway 29.

(A) As the airplane approaches the 7-NM DME point on R-153 (V7), the airplane is turned to a heading of 063° and the OBS set to 323 TO.

(B) As the needle centers, the airplane is turned 10° left (to 053°) and the OBS is set to 313 TO.

(C) As the needle centers, a 10° left turn is made to 043°, and the OBS is set to 303 TO.

(D) When the needle centers on the 303 setting, set in 291 TO to make a 10° left turn.

(E) Use enough lead so that the airplane completes the turn to 291° on R-111. Note that this last segment was 12°, rather than 10° like the first three. Usually, 10° is the angle used in tracking around the station, although smaller angles would give more accuracy (and take more time and effort than is practicable).

■ **The Loop Principle** You know that most portable AM radios (550–1650 kHz), such as you carry (or used to carry) on picnics with that good-looking member of the opposite sex, have directional properties. The reception was better (on the radio, that is) if it was turned in a certain direction.

The loop operates on the principle that the minimum reception is found when the plane of the loop is set perpendicular to the station. The maximum reception is obtained when the plane of the loop is in line with the station. Figure 5-27 shows a loop in the two positions.

Notice that the null or *minimum* reception area is much narrower (and hence would give more directional accuracy)

than the *maximum* reception position. The null position of the loop is the one used in radio navigation. One way of remembering which position of the loop is null is to think in terms of most of the signal "slipping through the hole"—giving the minimum reception.

In earlier times, airplanes had a fixed-loop antenna (the null running fore and aft) that allowed them to "home" into a station or fly to the station by pointing the nose at it. In a crosswind a curved path always resulted (Fig. 5-28).

The loop could be accurately used on an LF/MF range only if the particular range had a continuous carrier wave or special extra antenna at the station.

There was the problem of 180° ambiguity with the old fixed loop and with the MDF (the old manual direction finder). This impressive term means simply that, even though you had a null setup, you still didn't know in which direction the station was located.

The ADF solves this problem and the head of the needle "always" points to the station except for problems like thunderstorms, which can act as a "station." The airplane can also *home* to a station with an ADF, but for IFR and other precision flying, *tracking* is the way to go (Fig. 5-28).

■ **Automatic Direction Finder (ADF)** The ADF was a big step in the development of airborne direction finding equipment. The problem of 180° ambiguity was solved—the needle always points to the station. (Of course, this depends on whether you have the set tuned properly or whether a big lusty thunderstorm happens to be closer to the station than you are. The latter consideration, however, has been somewhat less of a factor with later equipment.) Always tune for maximum signal when tuning in a station, either by ear or by using the max signal indicator (older type equipment). Newer ADF equipment has decreased the pointing-to-the-thunderstorm tendency, but it is still present in varying degrees.

The ADF can be used for tracking around a station to approach from a certain direction, as discussed for the VOR.

It would be a good idea to cover the basics and use of the ADF equipment, including some terms that may be new to you. Figure 5-29 shows a representative (simple) ADF receiver and indicator.

RELATIVE BEARING. The airplane's heading plus its relative bearing equals the bearing TO the station. Unlike VOR, which has fixed radials, the ADF indicator shows changes in relative bearing as the airplane changes its geographic direction or *heading*. Assume that the head of the needle is connected to the station (NDB or other facility) by a taut wire.

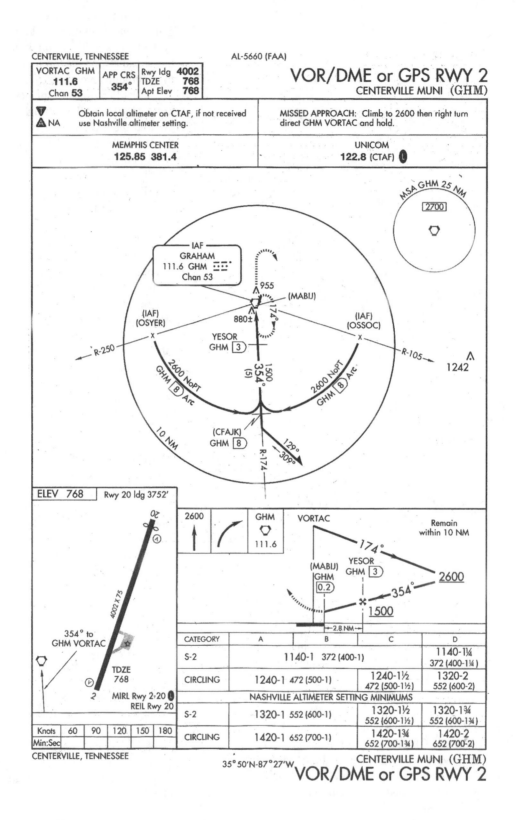

Fig. 5-25. VOR/DME or GPS Runway 2 approach for Centerville, Tenn. More details on NOS approach charts and approaches will be covered in Chapters 8 and 13.

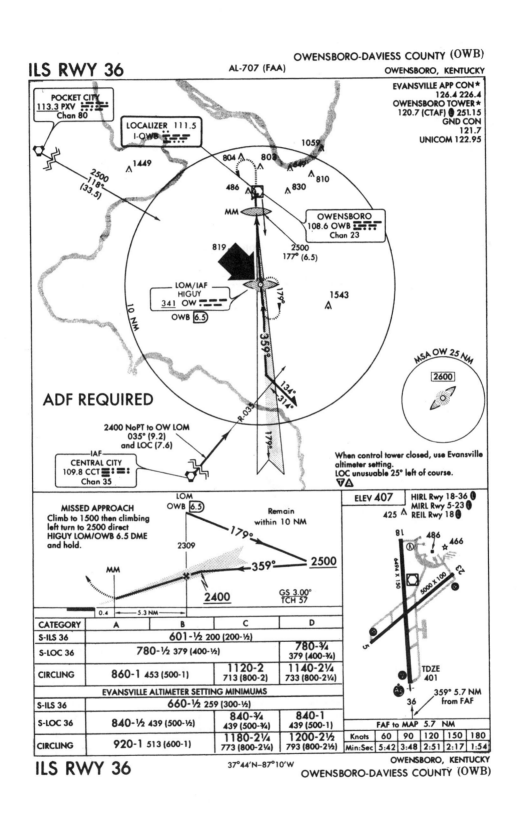

Fig. 5-26. A compass locator, a special type of nondirectional beacon (NDB), as depicted on an ILS approach chart.

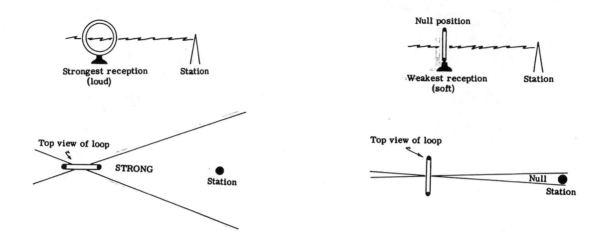

Fig. 5-27. The maximum and minimum reception loop positions.

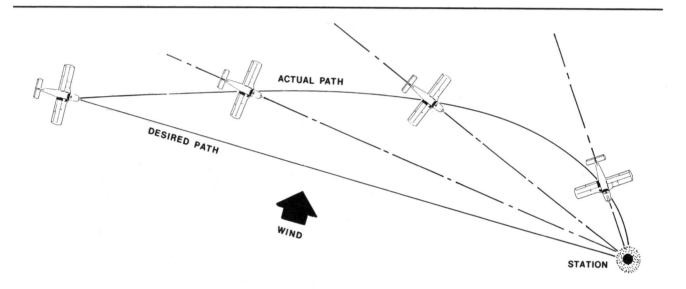

Fig. 5-28. Back in the olden days of the fixed loop and radio ranges, the airplane could only "home on the range." (Sorry.)

You can see that by either moving or turning the airplane the relative bearing TO (or FROM) the station changes. Figure 5-30 shows the idea.

Looking at Figure 5-29 again, the relative bearing is 305° (or preferably, the station is 55° to the left of the nose). With the relative bearing alone, without a compass (or heading indicator), you couldn't tell the bearing in degrees to or from the station but could home into it by turning the airplane left 55°, putting the needle there, and keeping it on 0° relative bearing until the NDB is reached. A simple form of tracking without a heading indicator might be done for, say, a cross-wind from the left by estimating the connection needed. A 10° (or other) turn could be made to put the needle on the 010° relative bearing and then you could fly to the station.

The present system of marking the ADF indicator from 0° to 359° is ponderous and sometimes confusing. For instance, the airplane is headed 325° with the ADF needle pointed at 280° relative. Adding 325 and 280 results in an answer of 605. Subtracting 360 from 605 gives a bearing to the station: 605 − 360 = 245°. Another, and the most commonly used, method is to note that the relative bearing is 80° to the left, so that this value is *subtracted* from the heading of 325°, giving the answer of 245° to the station. You'll work out your own method (which will probably be to think in terms of degrees left or right of the nose or tail or degrees ahead of or behind the wing). Figure 5-31 shows some possible presentations for the fixed-face ADF indicator.

The point is that the ADF work requires that you visualize your position in reference TO or FROM the station. Remember that with the heading indicator set to the magnetic compass (as it should be), the relative bearing plus heading will give the *compass course* to the station (at that

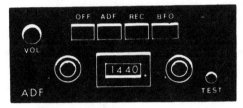

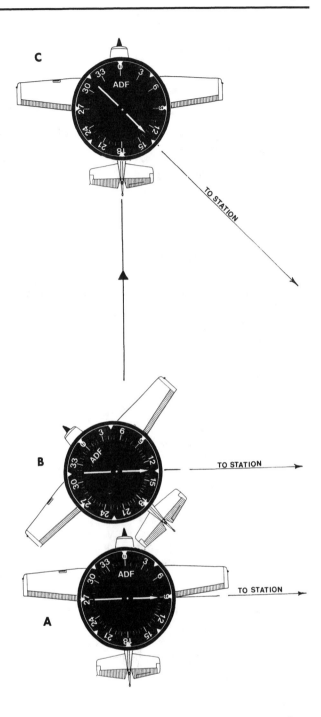

Fig. 5-29. An ADF console and indicator. The REC (antenna) position is used for clearer AM reception. The BFO (beat frequency oscillator) is used for stations outside the United States. The ADF selection gets the needle in action. The ADF receiver normally has a range of reception of from 200 to 1799 kHz.

instant), but a crosswind may require a different *compass heading* to track to it. Note also that the distance required to make the turn to the station and a different deviation value for that heading might mean that the final *compass* bearing to the station could be different after the turn is completed.

Note that earlier, in discussing Figure 5-31, the term "fixed-face" ADF indicator was used. More than likely the ADF in your initial training airplane has a fixed-face indicator; that is, the needle moves but the face does not rotate. Figure 5-32 shows a sample problem of tracing TO the station using the heading indicator and a fixed ADF face. Assume that you have worked out the *exact* required drift correction of 30° and are tracking into and out of the NDB at a course of 000°. (That's a pretty good crosswind component.)

As is the case in real life, very seldom is the wind, and hence the required correction angle, either known or constant, so during your training you'll get practice in correcting back to a prechosen track or bearing. Figure 5-33 gives an example of correcting back to a prechosen 000° track into the station. In the example, the airplane starts out on a heading of 000° (the pilot assumed a no-wind condition) but has now drifted so that the ADF needle has a relative bearing of 345°, or 15° left. The most common procedure is to turn into the wind or to make a correction angle twice that of the drift angle (15°), or to turn 30° to the left in this case.

The airplane is flown on this heading until the angle of deflection (or angle of relative bearing) equals the angle turned to intercept the chosen bearing (a 30° cut to the left

Fig. 5-30. The relative bearing is affected by changing the heading and/or the geographic position,

(A) The relative bearing is 090°.

(B) By immediately turning the airplane 45° to the left, the relative bearing is changed to 135°.

(C) The relative bearing is the same as (B) because the airplane has flown on using the initial heading.

was taken). The airplane is then turned to the estimated heading for wind drift correction, or 15° left in this example. How *fast* this works in getting you back to the course

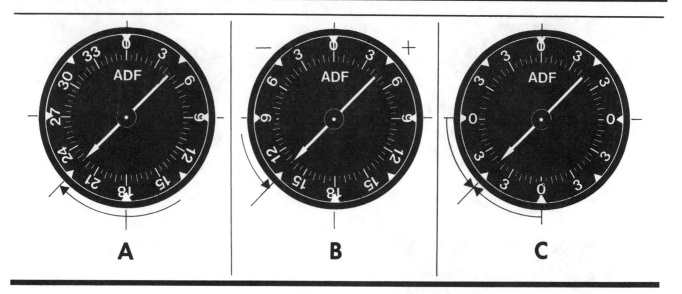

A   **B**   **C**

Fig. 5-31. (above) Three possible presentations for fixed-face ADF indicators with the needles pointing in the same relative position *(assume that the airplane's heading is 270°).*

(A) The relative bearing is 225°; 270° + 225° = 495° – 360° = 135° to the station.

(B) The relative bearing is 135° left; 270° – 135° = 135° to the station.

(C) The relative bearing is 45° behind the left wing; 180° – 45° = 135° to the station. Or the needle is 45° to the left of the tail; 090° (tail heading) + 45° = 135° to the station.

will depend on how far you are from the station. A cut of *more* than double the drift angle might be used if you're well out and want to get back into your own territory sooner; on the other hand, if you are close in, a very minor correction would be made (or you'd make no correction if you are coming right up on the station). One of the biggest problems with low-time instrument pilots and trainees is that they tend to want to keep the VOR or ADF needle on a prechosen position and when close in may literally "box" the station by turning around it. Most instrument instructors show their trainees the fallacy of this by having them come out from under the hood and then rolling the airplane up on a wing to show that the station is *right there* and maybe the airplane was a couple of hundred feet to the side as it passed, but that's close enough. In other words, if you've been holding a

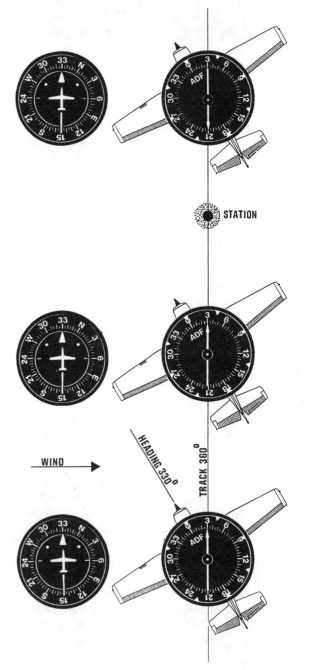

Fig. 5-32. (right) A look at tracking TO and FROM an NDB. In this case the wind and required drift correction are known exactly and are constant. If you turn the airplane *left* 30° into the wind, the relative position of the needle will be 30° to the *right;* as long as these two angles agree, the track is being made good. (A 30° drift correction means a crosswind vector of monumental proportions, but it makes an easy-to-see example, anyway.)

Fig. 5-33. (right) Returning to the desired track (000° here). The problem starts at the bottom of the illustration.

(A) You've been assuming that there's no wind and so have been holding 000° (or north) as you fly toward the station. You suddenly realize that the station, which initially was on the nose, now has a relative bearing of 345° or 15° to the left. You have been holding the exact heading of 000°, so the airplane has drifted to the right.

(B) You make a cut to the left of 15° (the new heading is 345°) and fly awhile. You finally decide that the 15° left correction is apparently keeping you parallel to the desired track. (At least you don't seem to be getting any closer to it after a reasonable amount of time.)

(C) You turn the airplane to the left another 15° so that the heading is now 330° (the "cut" is 30°) and the ADF needle is deflected 15° to the right. As you fly, the ADF needle starts moving from 015° slowly to the right.

(D) When the needle reaches a *deflection of 30°*, equaling your 30° *angle of interception* of the 000° (or 360°) bearing, the airplane is on that bearing to the station. (*Angle of deflection equals angle of interception when the desired bearing is intercepted.*) Your heading is 330°, or 30° to the *left* of the 360° bearing; the needle is 30° to the *right,* and if at that instant you turned the airplane right to a 000° (360°) heading, the ADF needle would be at the 000° relative position.

(E) A heading of 345° (or a 15° left correction) results in a relative bearing of 15° to the right. As long as these two angles are equal, you're maintaining the desired track.

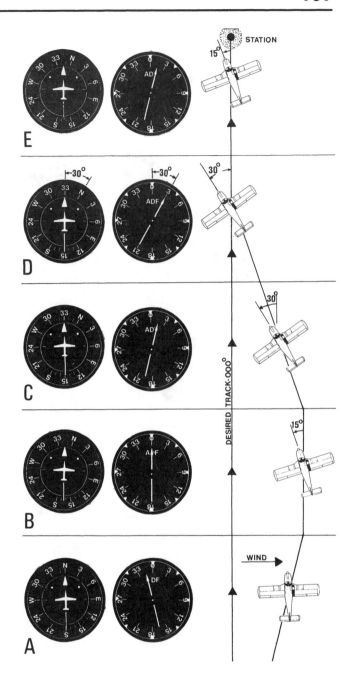

good track for the last 5 min and the needle (VOR or ADF) starts to move at a fairly rapid rate as the station is approached, this is no time to make radical corrections.

Figure 5-34 shows the idea of intercepting a prechosen course FROM a station. Some pilots prefer to use the "tail" of the ADF needle for reference when they are flying FROM the station, but use the procedure that works best for you. The same principle as shown in Figure 5-34 would apply if you had been tracking out (or *trying* to track out) on a prechosen bearing and found that the airplane had drifted from the course. The problem in Figure 5-34 has been slightly exaggerated to show the concept.

Figure 5-35 shows a closer view of a drift problem when tracking outbound on a prechosen bearing of 330°.

Figures 5-33 and 5-35 deliberately did not superimpose the ADF indicator on the airplane as has been done for other drawings on ADF procedures in this and other books. You need to get the information on the airplane's position from the heading indicator and ADF face. You'll have to develop a "picture" of what the airplane is doing from the separate instruments. ADF work is harder than using the VOR for most instrument trainees, but with practice you'll start orienting yourself with respect to the station.

■ **Timing to the Station** There are two ways to get an estimate of the NDB station passage: (1) the "double the

angle off the bow" method, where the airplane is deliberately turned off course at a small angle (usually 10°) as done with the VOR (Fig. 5-14) and (2) turning 90° to the original course and flying a timed leg of 5°, 10°, or 20° and then turning to track directly to the station from the new position. As with the VOR (Fig. 5-13) the time multiplier is 12 for 5°, 6 for 10°, and 3 for 20° angle changes. (To review: If it takes 2 min to fly a segment of 5°, 12 × 2 = 24 min to the station. If a 10° segment is used and 3½ min is the time required to fly that segment, the time to the station is 6 × 3½ = 21 min, etc.) As noted in the section on the VOR, these procedures are more for training purposes than for practical application.

DOUBLE THE BOW ANGLE. Figure 5-36 is a sample problem of "double the angle off the bow." Using segments of 20° seems to work better than the 10° cuts used for the VOR/DME example (Fig. 5-24).

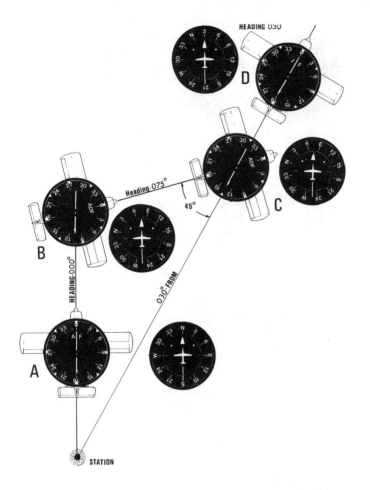

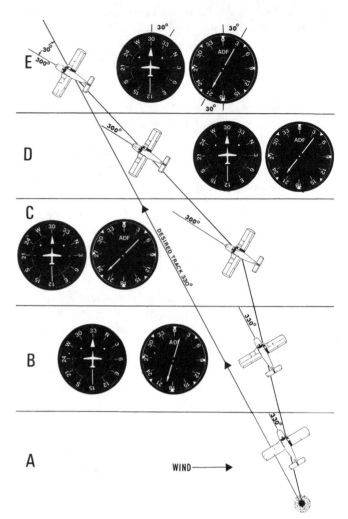

Fig. 5-34.

(A) The airplane is flying from the station on a heading of 000° with the ADF at the 180° relative position.

(B) The pilot decides to track outbound on a 030° bearing from the station. (Or maybe had started by tracking out on the 030° bearing and was careless or drifted to the position at (B). The airplane is turned to intercept the 030° bearing at a 45° angle, so the airplane is turned to 075° (030° + 45° = 075°). As the turn is complete, the relative bearing is 105°. (Assume that little or no distance was taken by the turning process.)

(C) As the airplane flies on the heading of 075°, the head of the needle moves aft until, as (C) is reached, the head of the needle indicates that the relative bearing is 135° or 45° off the left tail. *The relative bearing and interception angle are equal,* and the airplane is then turned to *track* out the 030° bearing from the station.

(D) Here the airplane has been turned to a heading of 030° and at this instant is on the 030° bearing. A heading for an estimated drift correction might then be set up to track on 030°.

Fig. 5-35.

(A) The airplane departs outbound from the station. The pilot holds a heading of 330°, the no-wind heading. Already drift is apparent.

(B) Checking the heading indicator and ADF, the pilot realizes that the airplane is to the right of the course.

(C) A 30° cut is made. The relative bearing is 225° (or 45° off the left tail).

(D) As the airplane continues the 300° heading, the head of the needle is moving toward the tail (relative bearing is 217°).

(E) When the relative bearing of the needle (30° off the tail) equals the 30° heading correction, the airplane is back on the desired track. The airplane is then turned to a heading that will correct for wind drift.

to the actual compass heading, the needle indicates that actual bearing TO or FROM the station. The only problem with this is that anytime the airplane's heading is changed, the "heading" on the ADF indicator must be reset (Fig. 5-37).

RADIO MAGNETIC INDICATOR (RMI). The RMI goes one step further in that the heading indicator and ADF head are

A handy aid for cutting down confusion is an ADF indicator that can be turned by hand to match the reading of the heading indicator. When the ADF indicator is turned by hand

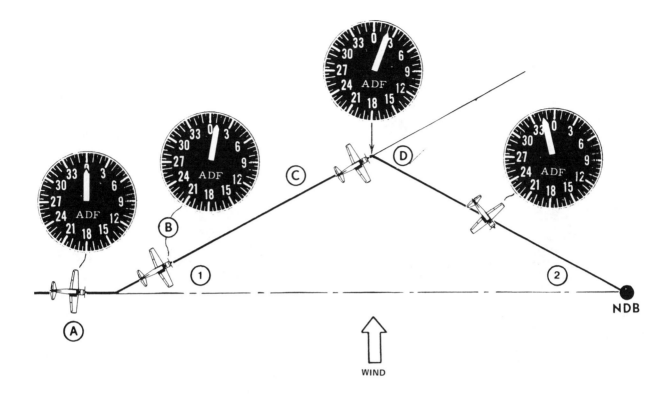

Fig. 5-36. (above) The "double the angle off the bow" method of getting an ETA to the station.

(A) Tune in and identify the station. Turn the airplane to get a course to the station (relative bearing 000°).

(B) Turn 10° (left in this example), which will put the ADF needle in the 010° position. You may want to use 20° cuts for the first few practices. Start timing.

(C) Fly this heading until the relative bearing has doubled (20°). Get the time and turn to *track* into the station. The time for the second leg should be close to that used to fly the first but will be longer in the wind situation indicated. You might set up a couple of problems on your computer using specific true airspeeds and winds to see this effect. (*Flight Instructor's Manual*)

Fig. 5-37. (right) An ADF with an adjustable compass rose. The adjusting knob is used to set the "heading" (matched to the heading indicator) to get a quick look at the geographic bearing TO or FROM the station. The heading indicator (*left*) indicates a heading of 120°; the ADF heading indicator (*right*) is set to this and the relative bearing of the needle (045° to the right) is pointing to the actual bearing TO the station, (120° + 45° = 165° TO).

one presentation. In addition, the heading indicator is *continually* showing the heading, so the ADF needle (if the set is properly tuned) will continually indicate the actual bearing TO or FROM the station. Visualize the right half of Figure 5-37 without the heading knob but with the heading indication being automatically changed as the airplane turns, and you will have an RMI with an ADF function. Some RMIs have slaved gyro compasses so that the pilot doesn't even have to adjust the heading indicator for precession every few minutes. Figure 5-39 shows a type of RMI indicator.

Some RMIs may be set up to have an ADF and a VOR needle or two ADF needles (or two VOR needles). The pilot may select any combination on the particular equipment needed at the moment (Fig. 5-40).

AUTOMATIC DIRECTION FINDER/MANUAL DIRECTION FINDER (ADF/MDF) ANTENNAS. Shown in Figure 5-41 are several types of ADF/MDF antennas.

LET'S SEE. MY HEADING IS 067°, THE
RELATIVE BEARING IS 323° I WANT
TO TRACK OUTBOUND ON 176°.....

Fig. 5-38. ADF work can be extremely interesting at times.

INSTRUMENT LANDING SYSTEM (ILS)

The ILS is the backbone of the approach aids and allows the pilot not only to fly a precise course to the runway but also to fly a precise descent, which allows for lower landing minimums than for VOR or ADF approaches. Figure 5-42 shows the ILS components:

Localizer—Course information.

Glide slope (glide path)—Descent information.

Marker beacon—Range or distance information.

In addition, the compass locators mentioned earlier and special approach lighting are parts of the system.

■ **Localizer** The localizer transmitter is located at the far end of the ILS runway and operates on the *odd* VHF frequencies between 108.0 and 112.0 (or, more properly, from 108.10 through 111.95 MHz). You remember that the *even* frequencies in that frequency range are used by VORs.

The localizer signal emitted is adjusted to produce an angular width of between 3° and 6° as necessary to provide a linear width of approximately 700 ft at the runway threshold. Five degrees is considered "standard."

The transmitter sends two signal patterns, one modulated at 90 Hz and the other at 150 Hz. When the airplane is at a position where these patterns have an equal signal strength, it is on an extension of the center line of the runway, and the localizer needle (the same needle used for VOR work) is centered. If the pilot is on the proper heading to keep the needle centered, the airplane will remain on the line down the center of the runway.

Older VOR heads (indicators) were divided into blue (150 Hz) and yellow (90 Hz), and the localizers on approach charts are marked with shaded (150 Hz) and clear (90 Hz) sectors. Later VOR heads don't show the colors (Fig. 5-43).

The 150-Hz (blue) area is to the right of the center line for the airplane approaching on the "front" or normal course. (Obviously, this leaves the 90-Hz, or yellow, sector on the left.) The localizer course extends on in the opposite

Fig. 5-39. Radio magnetic indicator (RMI). (*Bendix-King*)

Fig. 5-40. An RMI with selections for VOR or ADF for each needle. (*AAR Aeronetics*)

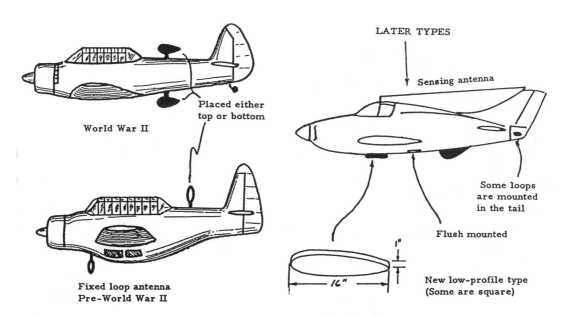

Fig. 5-41. A cross section of fixed and ADF/MDF (manual direction finder) antenna types. Some of the new low-profile antennas have "fixed loops" (the loop is "turned" electronically). The sensing antenna is a fixed "reference" antenna. The latest systems have combined sense and loop antennas (no wire-sensing antenna). Manual direction finders are rare these days.

direction, and this portion may be used for a "back course approach" (Fig. 5-44).

For the airplane approaching on the back course, the 150-Hz (blue) sector will be on the left. You'll note on your omni head that the blue is on the *left* side of the face and the yellow is on the right. *The needle always indicates the color of the sector the airplane is in. If the airplane is on the front course, you correct toward the needle,* as *would be expected.* Look at Airplane A in Figure 5-44. It's over in the 150-Hz (blue) sector, and the needle shows this. The needle also indicates that the center line is to the left. Airplane B is in the 90-Hz (yellow) sector, and the needle gives this news (and indicates that a correction to the right is needed). Airplane C is right on the center line (at least temporarily).

Looking at the back course, Airplane D is to the left of the center line and in the 150-Hz (blue) sector. The needle is to the left. But *on a back* course *inbound you correct opposite* to *the needle.* Airplane E is to the right of the center line and would have to correct *left,* away from the needle. Airplane F is, of course, right down the center.

If the airplanes on the front course (A, B, and C), chose to fly on past the runway down the localizer, they would still correct *into* the needle. If the airplanes on the back course flew on past the airport, they would still have to correct *against* the needle. The needle gives the straight story on the color sector, whether front or back course, but you only correct *into* it if you are flying the airplane on the localizer using the front course magnetic bearing. Some airplanes have avionics equipment to set it otherwise. It's doubtful that your trainer will be so equipped, but check on it.

Figure 5-45 shows the planviews for front and back courses of McKellar Field (Jackson, Tenn.). The localizer

identification consists of a three-letter code preceded by the letter I transmitted on the localizer frequency (I-MKL for McKellar). Note that the LOM (compass locator) is 394 kHz, identification MK. Back course approaches are being eliminated at larger airports and replaced by additional front course approaches.

The localizer is only 5° wide, or 2.5° on each side of the center line. The needle, when deflected completely to the side of the deviation indicator, indicates that the airplane is 2.5° (or more) from the center line. You remember that for most omni heads a full deflection of the needle to either side meant that you were 10° (or more) from the selected radial. One of your biggest problems in starting work with the ILS is this sensitivity of the needles on both the localizer and glide slope (particularly the glide slope). You can consider the needle to be approximately four times as sensitive on the localizer as it was for the VOR, so watch those corrections—don't overdo it!

The localizer antenna on the airplane is the same one used for the VOR.

■ **Glide Slope (or Glide Path)** The glide slope transmitter is UHF (329.15–335.00 MHz), and 40 channels are available for use. Each glide slope channel is associated with a particular localizer frequency, as shown by Figure 5-46. Older airborne equipment had a separate selector for the glide slope. On newer crystal-controlled equipment, it's just a matter of turning the glide slope power switch on and selecting the proper localizer frequency, and the glide slope is automatically tuned in.

The glide slope transmitter is situated 750–1250 ft in from the approach end of the runway and 250–650 ft from

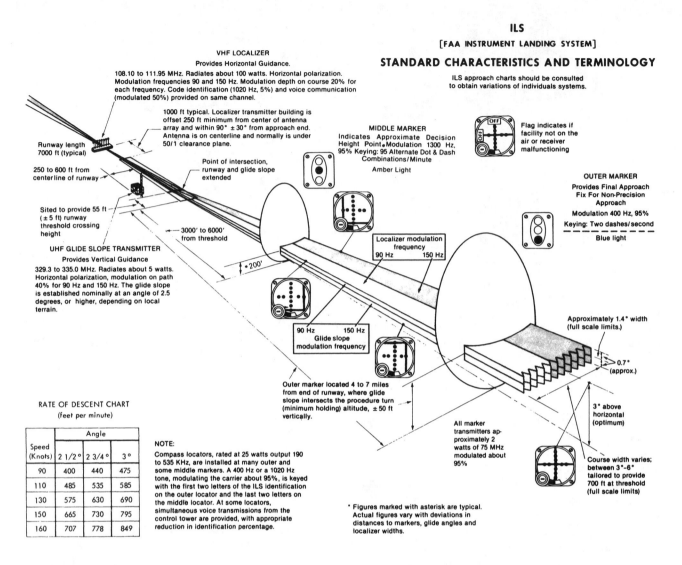

Fig. 5-42. The instrument landing system components. (*Aeronautical Information Manual*)

RATE OF DESCENT CHART
(feet per minute)

Speed (Knots)	Angle		
	2 1/2°	2 3/4°	3°
90	400	440	475
110	485	535	585
130	575	630	690
150	665	730	795
160	707	778	849

NOTE:
Compass locators, rated at 25 watts output 190 to 535 KHz, are installed at many outer and some middle markers. A 400 Hz or a 1020 Hz tone, modulating the carrier about 95%, is keyed with the first two letters of the ILS identification on the outer locator and the last two letters on the middle locator. At some locators, simultaneous voice transmissions from the control tower are provided, with appropriate reduction in identification percentage.

* Figures marked with asterisk are typical. Actual figures vary with deviations in distances to markers, glide angles and localizer widths.

the center line. Whereas the localizer can be used from both directions (at some airports, obstructions make a back course approach unfeasible), the glide slope is a one-directional item at present. The glide slope works on basically the same idea as the localizer (except that it is oriented differently) in that the center of the glide slope is found at the area of equal signal strength between 90 and 150 cycles/sec patterns.

The glide slope extends about 0.7° (7/10°) above and below its center. On the VOR/ILS instrument, a full deflection of the glide slope needle represents this amount (0.7°). (If you think the localizer is going to be sensitive as compared to the VOR, wait until the first time you get in close on the glide slope!)

The glide slope normally is between 2.5° and 3° above the horizontal, so that it intersects the middle marker at about 200 ft and the outer marker at about 1400 ft above the runway elevation. (Don't get the idea that a particular ILS glide slope varies from 2.5° to 3°—it stays the same, but

that represents the extremes of the various installations in the country.)

Nulls occur above the glide slope, which result in the flag on the omni head showing (as well as the centering of the glide slope needle). You'll notice this particularly when flying over the airport with the glide slope tuned in.

If you are making a back course approach, don't expect to get glide slope information. If the glide slope needle is acting like it knows what it's doing in such a situation, *ignore it.* You'll have to depend on VOR cross bearings or other aids for knowing when to descend.

Figure 5-47 shows the ILS RWY 32 chart with the lead radial (LR—146) for the approach at FWA.

GLIDE SLOPE ANTENNAS. Figure 5-48 shows typical glide slope antenna installations. Most older types are exposed, while newer ones may be installed behind a fiberglass nose cone. More than one greenhorn has tried to tow a twin by the older type glide slope antenna.

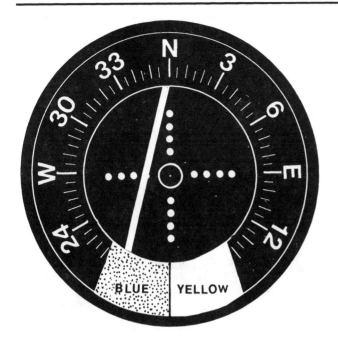

Fig. 5-43. An older-type VOR presentation. Approaching on the *front course* of the localizer, the indication is that the airplane is in the blue (150-Hz) "right-hand" sector and a correction to the left is needed to get back on the center line. On a back course, on final approach, the needle is indicating that the airplane is in the 150-Hz sector but the pilot would have to correct *against* the needle to get to the center line. In both cases the airplane is on the same geographic side of the center line (in the 150-Hz or blue sector).

■ **Marker Beacon** The airborne equipment consists of a three-light aural and visual system, as shown in Figure 5-49.

The outer and middle markers are low-powered and elliptical (up to 3 watts power output). The outer marker, located at from 4 to 7 mi from the approach end of the runway, is keyed at two dashes per second and is modulated at 400 Hz. A blue light and aural tone are indicated. The middle marker is modulated at 1300 Hz and triggers an amber light and an alternating dots and dashes aural signal. It's located 3500 ft, plus or minus 250 ft, from the end of the runway.

Several selected, larger airports have installed DME facilities to be used with the ILS localizer so that distance information will be available throughout the approach. Possibly, the OM and MM will be phased out in the future.

MARKER BEACON ANTENNAS. Figure 5-50 shows three types of marker beacon antennas.

ILS COURSE DISTORTION. Disturbances to localizer and glide slope courses may occur when surface vehicles or aircraft are operated near the localizer or glide slope antennas. You may see signs that denote an ILS CRITICAL AREA, and you'll particularly have to avoid these when CAT II approach minimums apply. (Category II minimums are decision height, 100 ft, and runway visual range, 1200 ft, or a visibility of ¼ mi. There will be more about this in Chapter 8.) On clear days taxi on ahead to the usual runway hold line, but you might confirm with ground control.

■ **Simplified Directional Facility (SDF)** The SDF provides a final approach similar to the ILS localizer (but no

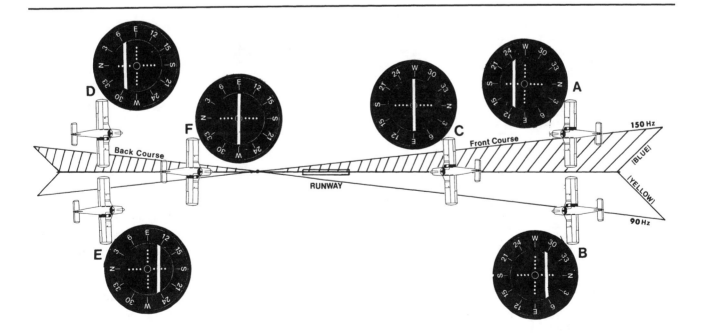

Fig. 5-44. The ILS localizer. The setting of the omnibearing selector has no effect on the needle indications when the set is tuned to a localizer frequency. However, many pilots set up the published inbound course on the OBS as a quick reminder of the base course when on approach.

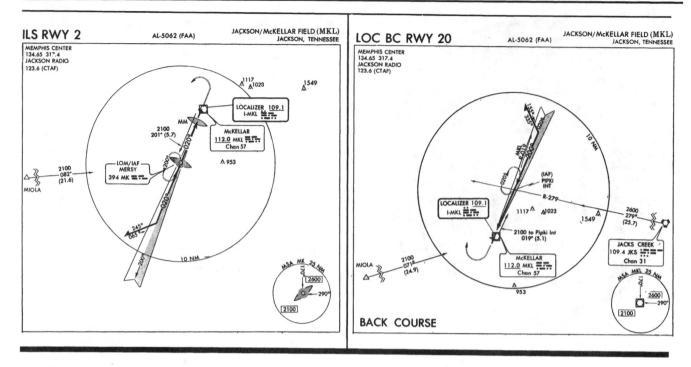

Fig. 5-45. Planviews of front and back course ILS approaches for McKellar Field, Jackson, Tenn.

glide slope information). The SDF transmits signals in the 108.10–111.95 range. The approach procedure is generally the same as that for a localizer approach except that the SDF course may not be lined up with the runway (it could be off up to 3°). The SDF antenna may be offset from the runway center line, and since the approach course originates at the antenna site, an approach continued beyond the runway threshold will lead you to the SDF offset position rather than along the runway center line.

Usable off-course indications are limited to 35° either side of the course center line. Any instrument indications beyond this should be disregarded.

The identification is a three-letter identifier in Morse code on the SDF frequency.

Figure 5-51 is the SDF approach chart for Runway 18 at Tullahoma, Tenn. (Note the SDF antenna at the south end of the runway.) The details of approach charts (or plates) will be covered in Chapter 8. After reading that chapter you may want to come back to the approach plates in this one to get a look with more detail.

TRANSPONDER

Basically, a transponder is an airborne "radar transceiver." It picks up the interrogations of the ATCRBS (Air Traffic Control Radar Beacon System) and transmits or "replies."

Mode A is a transponder without altitude information. ATC can detect where you are but doesn't have a means of automatically registering the altitude. (Mode B is not in use in the United States at this time.) Mode C is used for automatic altitude information by ATC.

Mode C will be discussed in Chapter 6 from the controllers' standpoint, but *you* should have an idea of what aircraft equipment is required. Basically, altitude reporters speak to ground radar stations through the aircraft's transponder, letting the ATC computer know your altitude relative to standard pressure at 29.92 in. of mercury. The computer converts this to known local pressure and displays the precise altitude on the scope. (There will be some sample Mode C displays in Chapter 6.) FAR 91.215 details the airspace where Mode C transponders are required. There are two basic types: (1) the encoding altimeters that combine a normal barometric altimeter with a built-in altitude digitizer

ILS

Localizer mHz	Glide Slope mHz	Localizer mHz	Glide Slope mHz
108.10	334.70	110.1	334.40
108.15	334.55	110.15	334.25
108.3	334.10	110.3	335.00
108.35	333.95	110.35	334.85
108.5	329.90	110.5	329.60
108.55	329.75	110.55	329.45
108.7	330.50	110.70	330.20
108.75	330.35	110.75	330.05
108.9	329.30	110.90	330.80
108.95	329.15	110.95	330.65
109.1	331.40	111.10	331.70
109.15	331.25	111.15	331.55
109.3	332.00	111.30	332.30
109.35	331.85	111.35	332.15
109.50	332.60	111.50	332.9
109.55	332.45	111.55	332.75
109.70	333.20	111.70	333.5
109.75	333.05	111.75	333.35
109.90	333.80	111.90	331.1
109.95	333.65	111.95	330.95

Fig. 5-46. Localizer/glide slope frequency pairings.

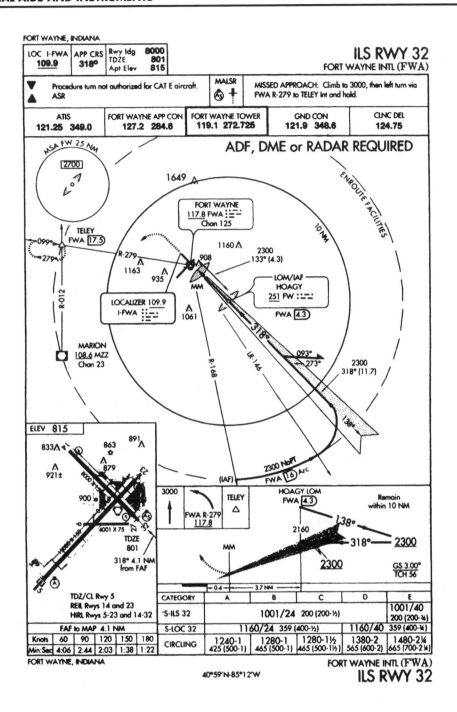

Fig. 5-47. The ILS RWY 32 approach at Fort Wayne, Indiana. Note the lead radial (LR—146) for assistance for turning in on the localizer final course. The new layout of the approach chart is shown here, and as each is updated, the new format will be used.

and (2) "blind" encoders that operate independently of the aircraft's altimeter, as Figure 5-52 shows.

A transponder will accept only the interrogator signals of its mode. After it accepts the interrogation, the transponder will transmit a coded reply. The ground station is "tuned" in to receive this reply (after all, the controller told you to reply on this code), and you no longer are wandering in the wilderness.

When you file an IFR flight plan, you would write in after the aircraft type, for instance, a slant and the letter "B." This tells ATC that you have DME and a transponder with

no altitude encoding. Some flight plan designators are as follows (see the complete list of designators in AIM Chapter 5, Section 1):

/X — no transponder.

/T — transponder, no altitude encoding capability.

/U — transponder with altitude encoding capability.

/D — DME, no transponder.

/B — DME, transponder with no altitude encoding.

/A — DME, transponder with altitude encoding capability.

/M — TACAN only, no transponder.

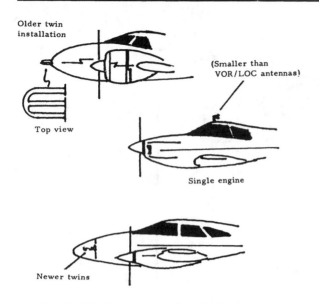

Fig. 5-48. Some types of glide slope antennas.

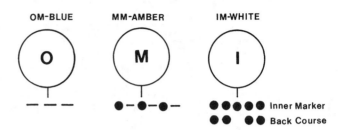

Fig. 5-49. Marker beacon indicators and audio signals as would be seen and heard in the airplane. OM—the outer marker indicates a blue light on the panel and is heard as a series of dashes. MM—the middle marker triggers off an amber indicator and is heard as alternating dots and dashes. IM—the inner marker is a white light and a series of dots. The back course marker (a white light and series of double dots) normally indicates the back course final approach fix where approach descent is commenced.

/N — TACAN only, transponder with no altitude encoding.

/P — TACAN only, transponder with altitude encoding.

/G — Global Positioning System (GPS).

The suffix is only to be used on the *flight plan* and with the *aircraft type*. When you've done this, you've passed the word to ATC. There's no need to mention it further, either on the rest of the flight plan or over the radio.

If there is a question as to your identification, the controller may have you "Ident," which means that you will press the "Ident" button on your transponder and your pip will stand out from all the rest.

In earlier times, separate radar equipment was necessary for the use of the IFF (identification—friend or foe). But now the primary radar (which picks up reflected signals) and secondary surveillance radar (which receives transmitted airborne transponder or IFF signals) are presented on the same screen.

Figure 5-53 shows the basic idea of the synchronized primary and secondary radars. Note that the interrogator transmits on a frequency of 1030 MHz and your transponder replies on 1090 MHz *for all codes.*

The VFR code = 1200 for any altitude.
Loss of communications = 7600.
Emergency = 7700.

Notice that each number is the basic code. With the increase in traffic, the Center may have several airplanes climbing (for instance) at low altitudes, and with the greater number of codes available, several codes in the 1000 range may be used (1010, 1020, etc.).

The emergency code is 7700, and all secondary surveillance radar sites are ready to receive this one at all times. (You remember that the other codes are chosen by the controller at will but this one is kept standing by.) Code 7700

practically lights up the entire radar screen (and fires off red lights), and you definitely won't be overlooked.

The hijack code is 7500, and this is guaranteed to get the attention of ATC. Code 7500 will never be assigned by ATC without prior notification of the pilot that his or her aircraft is subject to unlawful interference.

The transponder must have been tested and inspected by an FAA-approved station within the past 24 calendar months, and this must be noted in the Airframe Logbook (FAR 91.413).

Figure 5-54 shows the control panel of a transponder. The transponder antenna is similar in appearance (and location on the aircraft) to the DME antenna.

OTHER INSTRUMENT FLYING FACILITIES AND INSTRUMENTS

■ **Radar Altimeter** Figure 5-55 is a radar altimeter presentation (and a caution) with this particular installation providing AGL altitude information from 20 ft to 2500 ft. You

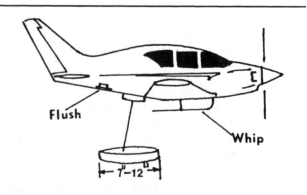

Fig. 5-50. Marker beacon antennas.

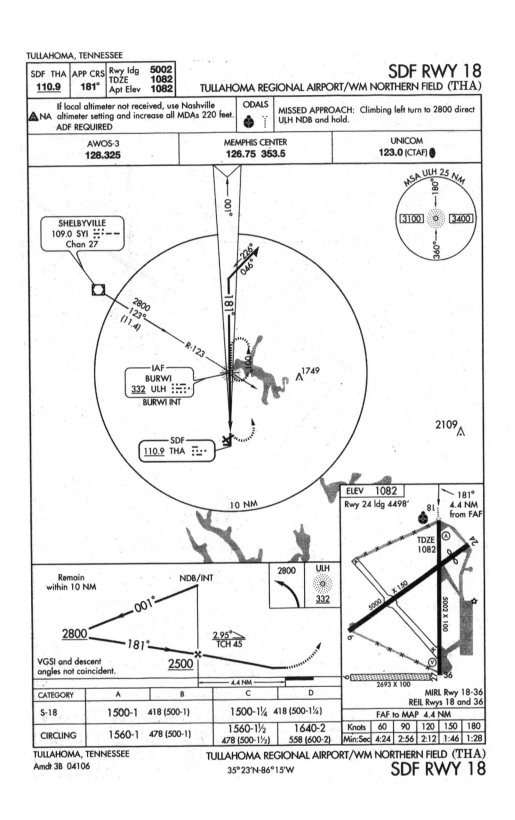

Fig. 5-51. A simplified directional facility (SDF) approach chart for Tullahoma, Tenn.

119

Fig. 5-52. Encoding altimeters and blind encoders. The system is linked to the transponder to send altitude information to the Air Traffic Control Radar Beacon System (ATCRBS). Later versions include the KEA 129 (20,000 ft) and KEA 130 (35,000 ft) encoding altimeters. There will be more detail on this in Chapter 6. (*Bendix-King*)

can preset the decision height with the "bug" and get the DH lamp warning light and 2-sec audio tone if (or as) the airplane descends below the decision height. The radar altimeter (or radio altimeter as it was called in earlier days) may show rapidly varying values over mountainous terrain (note the warning), but this writer found it to be a valuable aid in making night approaches to the old straight-deck carriers.

■ **Global Positioning System (GPS) (Ref: Aeronautical Information Manual)** *Author's Note:* The following information is derived from the *AIM* and is paraphrased and condensed to give a simplified view of the system; for the full discussion the reader is referred to that publication, which goes into much more detail.

■ **Background** The Global Positioning System (GPS) is a U.S. satellite–based radio navigational, positioning, and

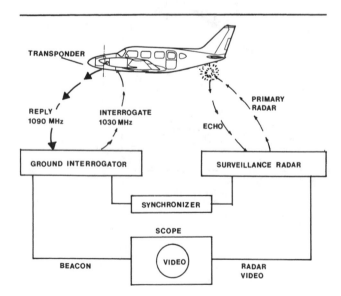

Fig. 5-53. Basic primary (echo return) and secondary (transponder reply) radar system.

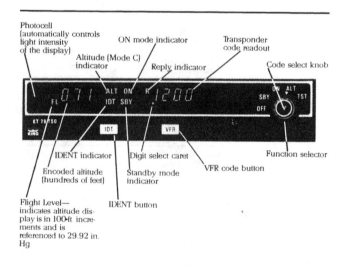

Fig. 5-54. A transponder control panel. (*Bendix-King*)

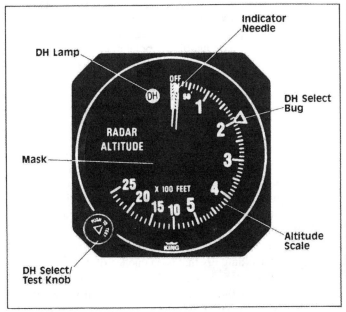

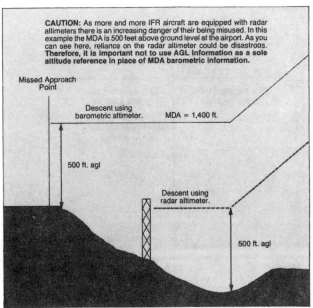

Fig. 5-55. A radar altimeter presentation with a useful warning. (*Bendix King*)

time transfer system operated by the Department of Defense.

The advantage of the system is that it may be used by an unlimited number of properly-equipped users. Unlike some other navigational aids, it is not affected by weather and can be used worldwide.

Civilian use is limited to a system that has a horizontal positioning accuracy of 100 meters or less (probability of 95 percent); the military equipment is more accurate.

The system consists of 24 satellites in orbits designed so that a minimum of five are always observed by a user anywhere on earth. The receiver (hand-held or attached to the airplane) uses data from a minimum of four satellites available above the horizon at its position.

The operation depends on measuring the time of signals from the various satellites available for use and is based on the speed of light (approximately 186,000 miles per second, give or take a little). Each satellite transmits a specific code, and the receiver checks the time required for the signal from each satellite in use to reach it; the result is a triangulation, and the position of the receiver is established. (Each satellite is continuously transmitting information on its exact orbital location.)

The GPS receiver verifies the usability of the signals received from the satellite "constellation" through receiver autonomous integrity monitoring (RAIM) to check if a satellite is sending incorrect information. The RAIM function needs another satellite for a minimum of five to check the integrity of the information. RAIM can also work with four satellites and a barometric altimeter to check for problems of system integrity. *Without RAIM capability, the pilot has no assurance of the accuracy of the GPS position.*

Authorization to conduct any operation under IFR requires that:

1. The GPS navigation must be approved and installed in the aircraft in accordance with required specification (see *AIM*).
2. Aircraft using GPS nav equipment under IFR must be equipped with an approved and operational alternate means of navigation appropriate to the flight. Active monitoring of alternate navigation equipment is not required if the GPS receiver uses RAIM for integrity monitoring. Procedures must be established for use in the event RAIM is not available (or expected to be lost). Use other approved equipment, delay departure, or cancel the flight.
3. The GPS operation must be conducted in accordance with FAA-approved aircraft flight manual (AFM) or flight manual supplement. Know the particular GPS equipment (there are many different brands available), and it's a good idea to use it in VFR conditions first.
4. Aircraft navigating by IFR-approved GPS are considered to be RNAV aircraft. If the GPS avionics become inoperative, advise ATC and change the equipment suffix. (See Chapter 5, *Transponder*, in this book for equipment suffixes.)
5. Prior to the GPS IFR operation, the pilot must review appropriate NOTAMs and aeronautical information.
6. Air carrier and commercial operators must meet the appropriate provisions of their approved operations specifications.

The authorization to use GPS to fly instrument approaches is limited to U.S. airspace.

The GPS equipment may be used in lieu of ADF and/or DME. The required integrity of such operations is provided by at least en route RAIM or an equivalent method; i.e., Wide Area Augmentation System (WAAS).

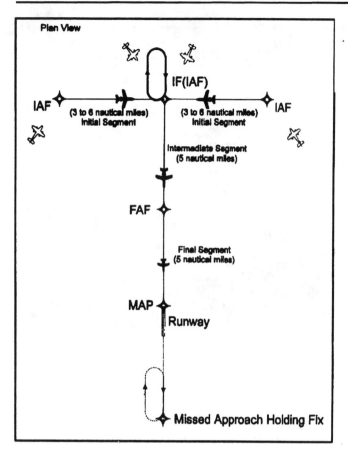

Fig. 5-56. The Basic "T" design of the terminal arrival area. An important advantage is that ground geographic references or ground navigation equipment are not needed. The IAF could be an imaginary point in the middle of a bay or swamp. IF or IAF—Initial Approach Fix. FAF—Final Approach Fix. MAP—Missed Approach Point. (*Aeronautical Information Manual*)

■ **GPS Standard Instrument Approach Procedure (SIAP)** The *Terminal Arrival Area* (TAA) procedure is designed to provide a new transition method

for arriving aircraft equipped with GPS or FMS (Flight Management System). The TAA contains within it a "T" structure that provides a NoPT (no procedure turn) for aircraft using the approach. This gives a very efficient method of routing traffic from en route to the terminal structure (Figure 5-56).

Figure 5-57 shows the Basic "T" with a Missed Approach Holding Fix that is on one leg of the "T."

The Basic "T" contained in the TAA normally aligns the procedure on the runway centerline with the missed approach point (MAP) located at the runway threshold, the final approach fix (FAF) 5 nautical miles from the threshold, and the intermediate fix (IF) 5 nautical miles from the final approach fix (FAF). Two initial approach fixes (IAFs) are located 3 to 6 nautical miles from the center IF (IAF). All of these way point fixes will be named with a five character pronounceable name. The length of the initial approach varies with the category of aircraft using the procedure or descent gradient requirements. For Category A aircraft, the minimum length is 3 NM and for Category E the minimum is 6 NM, hence the 3- to 6-NM item mentioned earlier in the

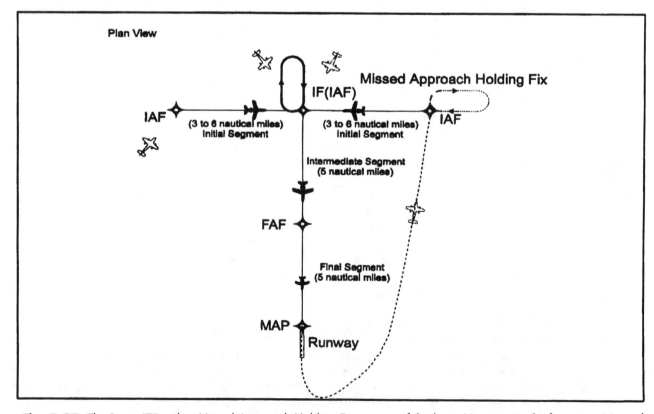

Fig. 5-57. The Basic "T" with a Missed Approach Holding Fix on one of the legs. (*Aeronautical Information Manual*)

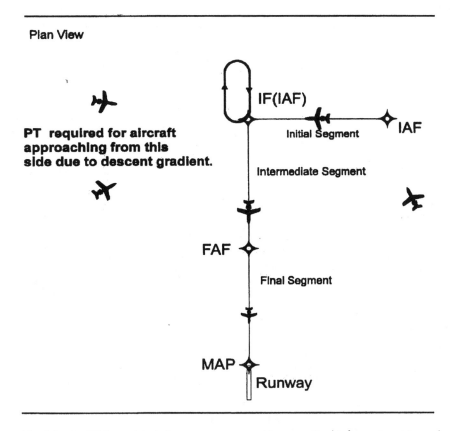

Fig. 5-58. A modified Basic "T" for added descent purposes. (*Aeronautical Information Manual*)

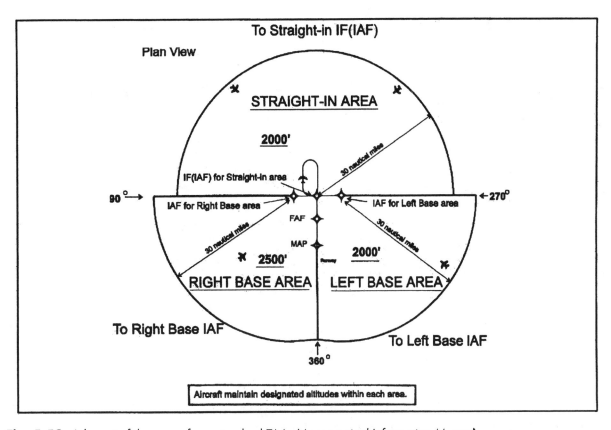

Fig. 5-59. A layout of the areas for a standard TAA. (*Aeronautical Information Manual*)

paragraph. (For a review of aircraft categories, see Figure 8-8, *Aircraft Approach Categories* in Chapter 8 of this book.)

These initial segments are normally constructed perpendicular to the intermediate segment. Note in Figures 5-56 and 5-57 there are holding patterns at the IF (IAF) for course reversal requirements. For example, some pilots may want to make a procedure turn (PT) to meet a descent gradient requirement. The missed approach is aligned with the final approach course and normally terminates in a direct entry into a holding pattern. Conditions may require a different routing, however.

Another modification for the Basic "T" is set up to accommodate descent from a high en-route altitude to the initial segment altitude. A procedure turn holding pattern provides an extended distance for the necessary descent gradient. The holding pattern for this purpose is always established on the IF (IAF) way point (Figure 5-58).

Another modification may be required for parallel runways. The normal "T" IAFs serve all parallel runways, but only one initial intermediate and final segment combination will be depicted on the approach chart for the landing runway.

The standard TAA consists of three areas that are established by the extension of the legs of the Basic "T." These are straight-in, left base, and right base. The 30 NM arc

**TAA with Left and Right
Base Areas Eliminated**

Plan View

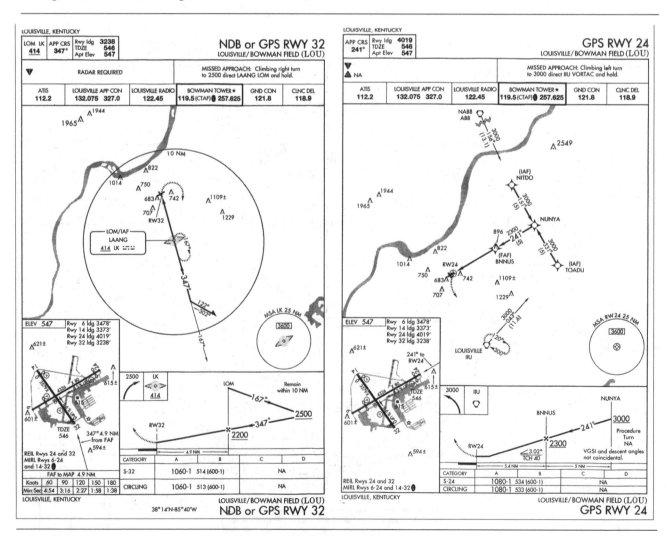

Fig. 5-60. TAA showing 120° approach sectors when the base areas are eliminated. (*Aeronautical Information Manual*)

Fig. 5-61. GPS approach charts for Bowman Field, Kentucky.

boundary of each area is equivalent to a feeder fix. The procedure turn (PT) holding pattern at the IF (IAF) is standard. Area boundaries are *magnetic course* lines to the IF (IAF). (See Figure 5-59.)

There may be modifications to the area of the standard TAA because of operation requirements, and the right or left base areas may be modified or eliminated. Pilots approaching the IF (IAF) within 120° of the final approach course (this is the maximum angle; a smaller angle could be required) are expected to fly a NoPT straight-in approach. Pilots approaching the IF (IAF) on a course greater than 120° (or a specified smaller angle) from the final approach course are required to execute a procedure turn (Fig. 5-60).

There are other modifications to the approach patterns to the IF (IAF), and the pilot should use the particular GPS approach chart as a guide.

A few points (receiver autonomous integrity monitoring):

1. If a RAIM failure/status annunciation occurs prior to the final approach way point (FAWP), the approach should be broken off because the GPS may not be providing the required accuracy.

2. If the RAIM failure occurs after the FAWP, the missed approach should be executed immediately.

Here is a summary of some abbreviations for GPS approach operations (some have been covered earlier):

1. MAHWP—Missed Approach Holding Way Point

2. MAWP—Missed Approach Way Point. The runway threshold way point, which is normally the MAWP, may have a five-letter identifier (SNARF) or be coded RW ## (RW 36, RW 36L)

3. FAF—Final Approach Fix

4. FAWP—Final Approach Way Point

5. IAWP—Initial Approach Way Point

6. IAF—Initial Approach Fix

7. IF—Intermediate Fix

Figure 5-61 shows approach chart examples. (Phase I has been completed.)

Phase II can be used without actively monitoring the ground-based NAVAID(s), which defines the approach. However, the ground-based NAVAID(s) must be operational. The aircraft must have the related avionics installed, but they don't have to be turned on during the approach. Approaches must be required and approved using the published title of the existing approach procedure such as "VOR RWY 24."

In phase III, ground-based NAVAIDs are not required nor do receivers have to be installed or operational. GPS approaches are required to use or are approved using a GPS title, such as "NDB or GPS RWY 32" or "GPS RWY 24." The "NDB or GPS RWY 32" is called an "overlay" in which the GPS approach can be flown following the same path as the original NDB approach. (Figure 5-61).

In each case, any required alternate airport must have an approved instrument procedure other than GPS; such a procedure is anticipated to be operational and available at *the estimated time of arrival and by which the aircraft is equipped to fly.*

As indicated earlier, the best thing for the instrument rated pilot new to the GPS system is to fly routes and approaches using the equipment in VMC. Get the services of an instrument instructor who is familiar with the system and your particular airborne equipment before venturing out on your own in actual IMC.

It may be some years before GPS totally replaces the ground-based equipment because there are still problems with the system to be ironed out.

■ **Visual Descent Point (VDP)** The VDP is a defined point on the final approach of a nonprecision approach to which the pilot should proceed at or above the minimum descent altitude. It also identifies the point in the approach from which a normal descent can be made to the touchdown point on the runway *if* the pilot has visual contact with the runway, light, etc. A visual approach slope indicator system is normally associated with the VDP. If the VDP is reached and the ground isn't seen, a missed approach is likely. The VDP will normally be identified by DME on VOR and LOC procedures and is indicated on the profile view of the approach chart by the symbol V.

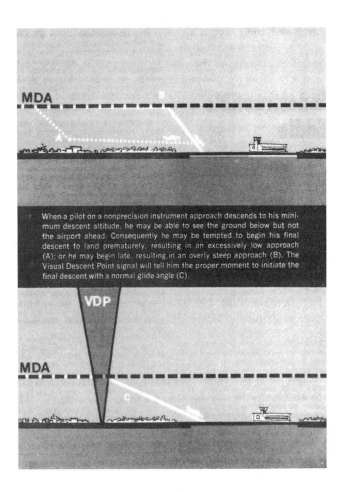

Fig. 5-62. Visual descent point. (*FAA General Aviation News*)

Figure 5-62 is a description of a VDP, with its advantages.

SUMMARY

Throughout this book various new aids will be mentioned; but the primary purpose here is to cover the fundamentals of VOR, ADF, etc., so that you may, with only a short period of instruction on their use, go on about your business. The aim is not to copy the avionics manufacturers' operating manuals. Look at the equipment in one of the bigger airplanes on the field, and fly the plane if you have a chance. For further information, check the listing at the end of the book for avionics (and other) manufacturers' addresses.

6

COMMUNICATIONS AND CONTROL OF AIR TRAFFIC

When you were first flying out of that uncontrolled field, you were on your own and kept separated from other aircraft by the eyeball method. This worked fine because there was very little transient traffic, and you could keep up with everybody anyway. Things were so quiet that everyone would quit hangar flying and rush out of the airport office to watch a transient airplane land. There would be much discussion as the plane approached as to where it could be from. (You would know as soon as it landed, but it was part of the program to throw out conjectures.) Later, as transient traffic began to pick up and radio equipment was available for the airplanes, a Unicom, or aeronautical advisory station, was set up in the office. It was just that—an advisory station—and woe betide anyone who started acting like a controller in the tower at Atlanta Hartsfield Airport and issued takeoff or landing clearances to all and sundry within range. Unicom was a further step; you could communicate with approaching and departing airplanes, and it helped you keep up with the increased traffic in and near the field. Unicom got to be no big deal, and you'd been using the radio like a professional—around your home airport.

Then came the day when you had to fly some parts over to the field at Whitesville for the operator where there was a TOWER. Well, you kind of sweated that one on the way over and practiced your lines until you had them cold and, of course, got mike fright and called "ZEPHYR ONE TWO THREE FOUR PAPA, THIS IS WHITESVILLE TOWER, OVER"—instead of the other way around—and wound up drenched with sweat by the time you had landed and taxied in. (And, if you recall, there was a little problem contacting ground control, so there was a period of limbo when you weren't talking—or listening—to anybody.) Well, they didn't arrest you, and they even let you taxi back and take off when you got ready to go home. Going into controlled airports is routine now. You even know the controllers personally and visit the tower and

drink coffee with them in the airport restaurant. In fact, after you'd done it a few times, you felt more comfortable going into a controlled airport than landing at an uncontrolled airport unfamiliar to you. You figured that at the controlled field somebody was helping you keep up with other traffic, even if the responsibility for safety was still yours.

Then you used approach control for the first time to get traffic information. You also later used VFR traffic advisory (radar), both for approaching and departing from big airports. For en route service you've been using the FSSs for some time, so that's no problem.

Probably at this stage of your career, you've used all of the facilities available to you except the Air Route Traffic Control Center (ARTCC), but it would be a good idea to review a little to tie it all together. The purpose of this chapter is to cover the communications areas generally; the specifics will come later.

FLIGHT SERVICE STATION (FSS)

FSSs have the prime responsibility for preflight pilot briefing, en route communications with VFR flights (and IFR flights too, if necessary), assisting lost VFR aircraft, originating NOTAMs, broadcasting aviation weather, accepting and closing flight plans, monitoring radio NAVAID, and participating with search and rescue units in locating missing aircraft. At some locations FSSs take weather observations, issue airport advisories, and advise Customs and Immigration of transborder flights.

Selected FSSs will provide En Route Flight Advisory Service (EFAS) on a frequency of 122.0 MHz. This service covers the 48 contiguous states and Puerto Rico from 6 A.M. to 10 P.M. (See Fig. 6-1).

The majority of Flight Service Stations have been converted to Automated Flight Service Stations (AFSSs), a consolation that results in more-efficient operations.

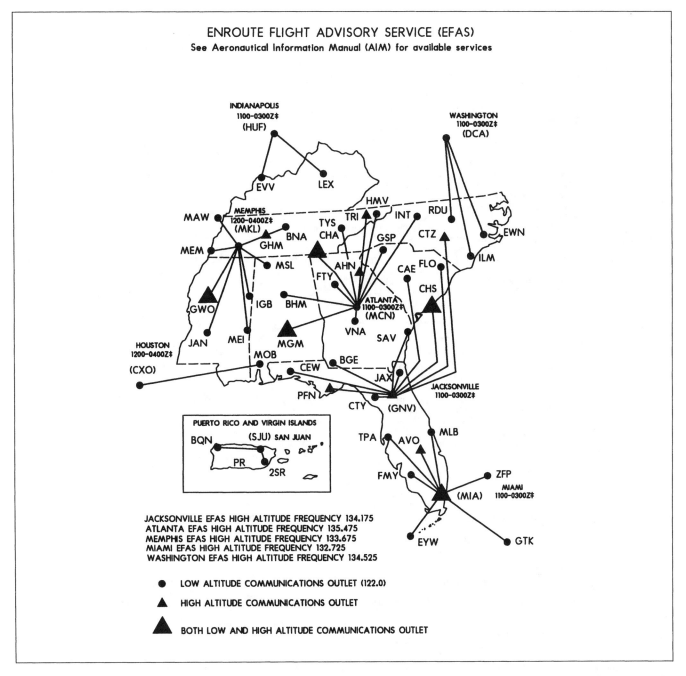

ENROUTE FLIGHT ADVISORY SERVICE (EFAS)
See Aeronautical Information Manual (AIM) for available services

JACKSONVILLE EFAS HIGH ALTITUDE FREQUENCY 134.175
ATLANTA EFAS HIGH ALTITUDE FREQUENCY 135.475
MEMPHIS EFAS HIGH ALTITUDE FREQUENCY 133.675
MIAMI EFAS HIGH ALTITUDE FREQUENCY 132.725
WASHINGTON EFAS HIGH ALTITUDE FREQUENCY 134.525

● LOW ALTITUDE COMMUNICATIONS OUTLET (122.0)

▲ HIGH ALTITUDE COMMUNICATIONS OUTLET

▲ BOTH LOW AND HIGH ALTITUDE COMMUNICATIONS OUTLET

Fig. 6-1. En Route Flight Advisory Service locations in the southeastern United States and Puerto Rico. *(Airport/Facility Directory)*

THE TOWER

Everybody talks of "the tower" (including nonpilots who've seen too many aerial disaster movies for their own, and aviation's, good), and you've used the facility a few times yourself, but a review might be in order.

Assume that you flew by airline into McGhee-Tyson Airport at Knoxville, Tenn., to ferry an airplane to Chattanooga. You've checked it over carefully and are ready to start up and go. The weather is great VFR, but you still will go through the same general procedures as for an IFR departure, so take a look at the steps involved. Check Figure 6-2.

■ Automatic Terminal Information Service (ATIS)

ATIS is the continuous broadcast of recorded *non-control* information in selected terminal areas. The purpose is to improve control effectiveness and cut the chatter by both sides by having the repetitive transmission of essential but routine information such as:

"McGHEE-TYSON INFORMATION DELTA. ONE FOUR ZERO ZERO ZULU. MEASURED CEILING FOUR THOUSAND FIVE HUNDRED BROKEN. VISIBILITY ONE ZERO. TEMPERATURE FOUR THREE. DEWPOINT THREE TWO. WIND ZERO

A

TENNESSEE

McGHEE TYSON (TYS)   10 S   UTC–5(–4DT)   N35°48.75' W83°59.57'   **ATLANTA**
 981   B   S4   **FUEL** 100LL, JET A OX 1 LRA   ARFF Index C   **H–4H, L–20E, 22E**
  RWY 05L–23R: H9008X150 (CONC–GRVD)   S–90, D–200, DT–350, DDT–540   HIRL   CL   **IAP**
   RWY 05L: VASI(V4L)—GA 2.7°TCH 75'. TDZL. Tree. 0.6% up.
   RWY 23R: ALSF2. TDZL. VASI(V4L)—GA 3.0°TCH 55' . Rgt tfc.
  RWY 05R–23L: H9000X150 (ASPH—GRVD)   S–75, D–150, DT–250   HIRL
   RWY 05R: REIL. VASI(V4L)—GA 3.0°TCH 54'. Rgt tfc.   **RWY 23L:** REIL. VASI(V4L)—GA 3.0°TCH 55'. Tree.
  AIRPORT REMARKS: Attended continuously. CAUTION: Birds on and invof arpt. 205' lgtd and flagged crane located
    on air carrier ramp Mon–Fri 1230–2230Z‡. Twy G1 clsd indef. PPR from Air National Guard for civil acft to use Twys
    G1, G2, G3, G4, and G South of twy G5. Flight Notification Service (ADCUS) avbl.
  WEATHER DATA SOURCES: ASOS (865) 981–4053. LLWAS.
  COMMUNICATIONS: ATIS 128.35 (1200–0400Z‡)   **UNICOM** 122.95
   NASHVILLE FSS (BNA) TF 1–800–WX–BRIEF. NOTAM FILE TYS.
   RCO 122.3 122.2 (NASHVILLE FSS)
  ® **KNOXVILLE APP/DEP CON** 118.0 (051°–229°) 123.9 (230°–050°) 120.65 132.8
   KNOXVILLE TOWER 121.2   **GND CON** 121.9   **CLNC DEL** 121.65
  AIRSPACE: CLASS C svc continuous ctc APP CON
  RADIO AIDS TO NAVIGATION: NOTAM FILE TYS.
   VOLUNTEER (H) VORTAC 116.4   VXV   Chan 111   N35°54.29' W83°53.68'   224° 7.3 NM to fld. 1290/03W.
    HIWAS.
   BENFI NDB (LOM) 353   TY   N35°44.53' W84°04.88'   049° 6 NM to fld.
   ILS 110.3   I–TYS   Rwy 05L.   LOM BENFI NDB. BC unusable.
   ILS 111.7   I–BUI   Rwy 23R.   LOC unusable byd 15 NM blo 3,000'.
   ASR

B

LOVELL FLD (CHA)   5 E   UTC–5(–4DT)   N35°02.12' W85°12.23'   **ATLANTA**
 682   B   S4   **FUEL** 100LL, JET A LRA   ARFF Index C   **H–4H, L–14H**
  RWY 02–20: H7401X150 (ASPH–GRVD)   S–120, D–160, DT–265   HIRL   CL   **IAP**
   RWY 02: MALSR. VASI(V4R)—GA 3.0°TCH 56'. Antenna.   **RWY 20:** ALSF1. TDZL. Railroad.
  RWY 15–33: H5000X150 (ASPH)   S–120, D–160, DT–265   MIRL
   RWY 15: VASI(V4L)—GA 3.16°TCH 58'. Dike.   **RWY 33:** VASI(V4L)—GA 3.25°TCH 59'. Trees.
  AIRPORT REMARKS: Attended continuously. Flocks of birds on and invof arpt. Sections of ramp between Twy G and
    Twy F clsd indef. Transient acft avoid security zone within 300 ft of terminal building. MIRL Rwy 15–33 unavailable
    when tower clsd. ACTIVATE HIRL and CL Rwy 02–20; MALSR Rwy 02 and ALSF1 Rwy 20 and TDZL Rwy
    20—CTAF. Flight Notification Service (ADCUS) available.
  WEATHER DATA SOURCES: ASOS (423) 499–5973. LLWAS.
  COMMUNICATIONS: CTAF 118.3   **ATIS** 119.85   **UNICOM** 122.95
   NASHVILLE FSS (BNA) TF 1–800–WX–BRIEF. NOTAM FILE CHA.
   CHATTANOOGA RCO 123.65 122.2 (NASHVILLE FSS)
  ® **CHATTANOOGA APP CON** 125.1 (021°–199°) 119.2 (200°–020°) 126.5 (1100–0450Z‡)
   CHATTANOOGA TOWER 118.3 (1100–0450Z‡)   **GRND CON** 121.7   **CLNC DEL** 120.95
  ® **CHATTANOOGA DEP CON** 125.1 (021°–199°) 119.2 (200°–020°) (1100–0450Z‡)
   ATLANTA CENTER APP/DEP CON 132.05 (0450–1100Z‡)
  AIRSPACE: CLASS C svc 1100–0450Z‡ ctc **APP CON** other times CLASS E.
  RADIO AIDS TO NAVIGATION: NOTAM FILE CHA.
   CHOO CHOO (H) VORTAC 115.8   GQO   Chan 105 N34°57.68' W85°09.20'   330° 5.1 NM to fld. 1030/01E.
    HIWAS.
   DAISY NDB (HW) 341   CQN   N35°09.99' W85°09.44'   198° 8.2 NM to fld. (Unmonitored when twr clsd).
   ILS 109.5   I–CHA   Rwy 20.   (ILS umonitored when twr clsd).
   ILS 108.3   I–CGW   Rwy 02.   BC unusable. (ILS unmonitored when twr clsd).
   ASR (1100–0450Z‡)

Fig. 6-2. Airport and frequency information for **(A)** Knoxville (TYS) and **(B)** Chattanooga (CHA) airports. *(Airport/Facility Directory)*

FOUR ZERO AT ONE ZERO. ALTIMETER THREE ZERO ZERO FOUR. RUNWAYS FIVE LEFT AND FIVE RIGHT IN USE. ADVISE ON INITIAL CONTACT YOU HAVE DELTA"

The ATIS provides current departure information as appropriate. (It also provides arrival information, but that will be covered later.) Departure information in the ATIS broadcast may be omitted by clearance delivery (or the tower) if the pilot states the appropriate ATIS code.

This is your first contact with ATC for your trip, and you'd do it by listening at your parking spot. It gives you an overall look at the weather and runway situation before

contacting clearance delivery for clearance and then ground control for taxi instructions.

In the ATIS the alphabet will be used sequentially from Alfa to Zulu and be repeated without regard to the beginning of a new day. In the event of a broadcast interruption of more than 2 hr, the first resumed broadcast will be an Alfa.

There will be a new recording (Alfa changes to Bravo, etc.):

1. Upon receipt of new official weather whether or not there is a change in values.

2. When runway braking reports are received indicating braking is worse than that included in the current ATIS ("braking advisories in effect").

3. When there is a change in any other pertinent data, such as runway change, instrument approach in use, new or canceled NOTAM/SIGMET, PIREP, etc.

Some pilots turn the master switch and transceiver ON and listen to ATIS before starting the engine. Your choice would probably depend on the condition of the airplane's battery, outside temperatures, and the number of people and vehicles close to the propeller. From an ideal standpoint it would be good to listen to ATIS, get your clearance from clearance delivery, start the engine, get ground control information, and then taxi out of the parking place. The McGhee-Tyson ATIS frequency is 128.35 MHz (Fig. 6-2). You might want to write down the salient information.

■ **Clearance Delivery** At the less busy airports, you'll be given an instrument clearance on the ground control frequency, usually after you reach the warm-up area. (You'll be notified that the clearance is forthcoming.) However, at airports with heavy IFR traffic, this could cause a great deal of clutter on that frequency, so a special frequency called "clearance delivery" is set up. It's just as the name implies, a frequency used strictly for pretaxi IFR (or VFR) clearances. *Don't* be taxiing out on clearance delivery and taking a clearance when you should be listening to ground control and minding the store. If you have a trustworthy copilot, he or she might put on a set of earphones and be dealing with clearance problems to save time, while you and ground control are working to get you to the active runway in one piece. (Taxiing into a large, expensive, immovable object while copying a clearance is hardly an ideal way to start a flight.) The clearance delivery frequency is given with the other airport data in the *Airport/Facility Directory (A/FD)*. Clearance delivery has nothing to do with the direct control of air or ground traffic.

As some tower-controlled airports become busier, VFR as well as IFR traffic must get clearance for departing the area, as in this example. It may seem rather strange getting what is apparently a full IFR departure clearance at 0600 on a clear morning with no other traffic, but you'll soon get used to the idea.

You'll contact clearance delivery on 121.65 MHz at Knoxville (Fig. 6-2) and in this case, after initial contact (including your full airplane number), you'd indicate that you are going VFR to Chattanooga, are a Zephyr Six, and have Delta. You would also tell clearance delivery your route (if other than direct) and altitude. (Be ready to copy the clearance.) For instance, you might get, "NOVEMBER 7557 LIMA, AFTER DEPARTURE TURN TO AND MAINTAIN A HEADING OF 350, MAINTAIN AT OR BELOW 2000 FEET. SQUAWK ZERO THREE ONE ONE. DEPARTURE CONTROL ONE TWO THREE POINT NINE." You would read it back and especially note the departure control frequency.

■ **Ground Control** Ground control regulates traffic moving on the taxiways and those runways not being used for takeoffs and landings. Ground control will coordinate with the tower if you have to cross a "hot," or active, runway.

Ground control is naturally on a different frequency than that of the tower. You can imagine the radio clutter that would result if some pilots were asking for taxi directions while others were calling in for landing instructions.

For simplification and comparison of local (tower) and ground control duties: (1) Local control has jurisdiction over aircraft in the process of landing and taking off. (This includes aircraft while in the pattern and *on* the active runway.) (2) Ground control is used for ground traffic at the airport *other than on the active runway during the takeoff or landing process.* The ground controller will be in the tower beside the local controller. (In some cases, the same person may talk to you in both capacities, but on a different frequency, of course.)

You may get your IFR clearances on the ground control frequencies, but this was covered earlier.

You would contact McGhee-Tyson ground control for taxi on 121.9 MHz (Fig. 6-2) and tell them where you are. In this case you'll be told to taxi to Runway 5 right. (Ground control frequencies are in the range from 121.6 to 121.9 MHz.)

When ATC (ground control) tells you to "taxi to" an assigned takeoff runway, the absence of holding instructions (such as "Hold clear of Runway X") authorizes the airplane to "cross" all intercepted runways *except the assigned takeoff runway.* It does not give you authorization to taxi onto or to cross the assigned runway at any point.

You should acknowledge all runway crossings, hold short, or takeoff clearances unless there is some misunderstanding, at which time you should question the controller until the clearance is understood. *If you are not sure, don't do anything until the situation is understood.* (This writer was taking off from a tower-controlled airport and was cleared by the tower for takeoff "Four Four Tango, cleared for takeoff." There was another airplane ready for takeoff on a cross runway and something jogged my memory. I asked if "Six Five Four Four Tango is cleared?" The answer was that another Four Four Tango with different first two numbers was cleared for takeoff on the *other* runway. The two airplanes might have had an interesting encounter at the intersection.) Normally, in the case of a possible conflict like this, the controllers will use the airplane's full numbers. (Keep in mind that controllers, like pilots, can err sometimes.)

When you're taxiing, *you have the final responsibility* for avoiding that herd of buffalo or the Shriners' parade moving across the taxiway.

Ground control will be helpful on where to turn if you are new to the airport and the taxiway layout is complicated. Don't hesitate to ask for help.

An important point: Stay on a particular assigned frequency; don't leave it without checking with ATC. Sure, you're taxiing out and need to give a quick call back to Unicom to see if you left the fuel receipt there, so what's a few seconds? Well, maybe during those few seconds ground control (or local control, etc.) needs to talk to you very urgently. (The runway that you were cleared to cross in the initial instruction now has unauthorized traffic on short final.)

When *landing,* don't switch to ground control until told to do so by the tower.

■ **Local Control** Local control is the function that pilots think of as "the tower" and has jurisdiction over air traffic within the airport traffic control service area. This service is provided by the control tower for aircraft operating on the movement area and in the vicinity of an airport.

The tower is considered to control the traffic pattern entry and the pattern itself, including takeoffs and landings. The local controllers are in the glassed-in part of the tower, since their control is dependent on visual identification of aircraft for takeoffs and landings. The local control (tower) frequencies are in the *A/FD,* and as you can see in Figure 6-2, the tower frequency at McGhee-Tyson is 121.2 MHz.

After you've made the pretakeoff check behind the taxiway hold lines, switch to tower frequency (121.2 MHz) and give the word that you're ready to go. You'll probably get one of the three following immediate replies:

1. "ZEPHYR SEVEN FIVE FIVE SEVEN LIMA, HOLD SHORT."
2. "ZEPHYR SEVEN FIVE FIVE SEVEN LIMA, TAXI INTO POSITION AND HOLD."
3. "ZEPHYR SEVEN FIVE FIVE SEVEN LIMA, WIND ZERO FOUR ZERO AT EIGHT KNOTS, MAINTAIN RUNWAY HEADING, CLEARED FOR TAKEOFF."

You would already have the transponder on 0311 and STANDBY and would activate as you started the takeoff roll.

■ **Departure Control** Shortly after takeoff (usually within a half-mile of the runway end) the tower will say, "ZEPHYR SEVEN FIVE FIVE SEVEN LIMA, CONTACT DEPARTURE CONTROL."

The departure control frequency is not given, since you got it from clearance delivery, although you can ask for it if you forgot or lost the paper with the clearance on it. You should repeat, for instance, "DEPARTURE, ONE TWO THREE POINT NINE." (Wait a couple of seconds and if you don't get a correction, change to that frequency: "KNOXVILLE DEPARTURE, ZEPHYR SEVEN FIVE FIVE SEVEN LIMA, OUT OF FIVE HUNDRED FOR TWO THOUSAND." Departure control will say, "RADAR CONTACT," and might turn you to a heading of 350°. *Don't* break your altitude restriction of 2000 ft (as given in this particular clearance) unless cleared to do so by departure control. If you have a Mode A transponder (no altitude reporting), you are expected to report reaching any assigned altitude. With Mode C, altitude reporting by the pilot is cut down sharply. You can expect that shortly departure control will clear you on course and to climb to your assigned altitude.

Departure control will release you ("RADAR SERVICE TERMINATED, RESUME NORMAL NAVIGATION, FREQUENCY CHANGE APPROVED, SQUAWK ONE TWO ZERO ZERO"), and in VFR conditions you are free to change altitudes and headings as you desire. For safety and as a matter of courtesy do *not change altitude (Mode* A) or *headings unless you notify departure control.* If you are

about to fly into another airplane, you may do whatever is necessary to avoid it, but otherwise they'll expect you to maintain the altitude you initially stated for cruise. If you decide that 6500 ft is better than 4500 (because of clouds or other reasons), then let departure control know of your plans. In an IFR environment you would be switched to a Center frequency for control en route. (Figure 6-2A shows the information just discussed as presented in the *A/FD.* (That publication will be covered more fully in Chapter 8.)

■ **Approaching Chattanooga (VFR)**
AUTOMATIC TERMINAL INFORMATION SERVICE (ATIS). Well before entering the Class C airspace listen to Chattanooga (Lovell Field) ATIS (119.85 MHz) (see Fig. 6-2B) so that you'll have the needed information to save some talking. Assume that you get information Foxtrot:

You: "CHATTANOOGA APPROACH, ZEPHYR SEVEN FIVE FIVE SEVEN LIMA, OVER."
Chattanooga approach: "ZEPHYR SEVEN FIVE FIVE SEVEN LIMA, GO AHEAD, OVER."
You: "ZEPHYR SEVEN FIVE FIVE SEVEN LIMA, ZEPHYR SIX, TWO ZERO MILES NORTHEAST, FOUR THOUSAND FIVE HUNDRED, INFORMATION FOXTROT, LANDING LOVELL FIELD."
Chattanooga approach: "SEVEN FIVE FIVE SEVEN LIMA SQUAWK ZERO TWO ZERO FIVE..." (you would comply).
Chattanooga approach: "ZEPHYR FIVE SEVEN LIMA RADAR CONTACT, ONE NINE MILES NORTH-EAST OF THE AIRPORT"

You would continue straight in or be vectored as necessary to fall into the traffic flow and then would be switched to the tower frequency (118.3 MHz) for landing.

After landing, don't take it upon yourself to switch to ground control (121.7 MHz) (Fig. 6-2B) while on the runway, without authorization of the tower. You'd continue rolling (taxiing) in the landing direction, proceed to the nearest suitable taxiway, and exit the runway without delay, *then* contact ground control. *Don't* (unless instructed to do so by the tower) turn onto another runway or make a 180° turn to taxi back.

Again, if you need taxi directions at a strange (to you) airport, don't hesitate to ask.

The VFR procedures cited are different from IFR procedures primarily because clearance delivery would give assigned altitude, routing, and other information. Also, instead of being on your own for most of the trip from Knoxville to Chattanooga, you'd be communicating with Atlanta Center on the straight and level portions. Okay, take a look at the functions of the Air Route Traffic Control Center.

AIR ROUTE TRAFFIC CONTROL CENTER (ARTCC)

When you filed your IFR flight plan at the FSS, you set off a beehive of activity. Your plans, hopes, and dreams (and flight plan) for the next few hours go into the hands of the ARTCC for your area.

The United States (the 48-state portion) is divided into 20 areas, each with the responsibility of a particular ARTCC (Atlanta, Memphis, Los Angeles, etc.). Figure 6-3 shows the location and relative size of the Memphis Low-Altitude (surface to FL230) Center area.

The job of each Center is to coordinate IFR traffic within its area and alert the next Center of your approach to *its* area. In nearly all areas, if you're not flying at too low an altitude, they will be able to monitor your flight by radar all the way. In fact, your flight is so well monitored that you may be quietly chided at being "4 miles south of course," or may hear other ego-shattering statements that blare out over the cabin speaker for your passengers to hear. (That's *one* reason why it's better to wear earphones.) Figure 6-4 shows the boundary between two Centers as depicted on an en route chart.

As the United States is broken down into Center areas, so are the Centers divided into Sectors.

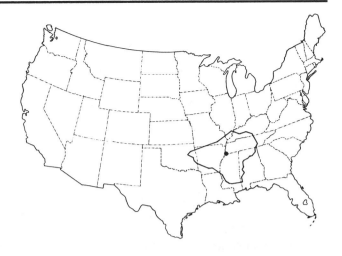

Fig. 6-3. The approximate size and location of the Memphis Air Route Traffic Control Center.

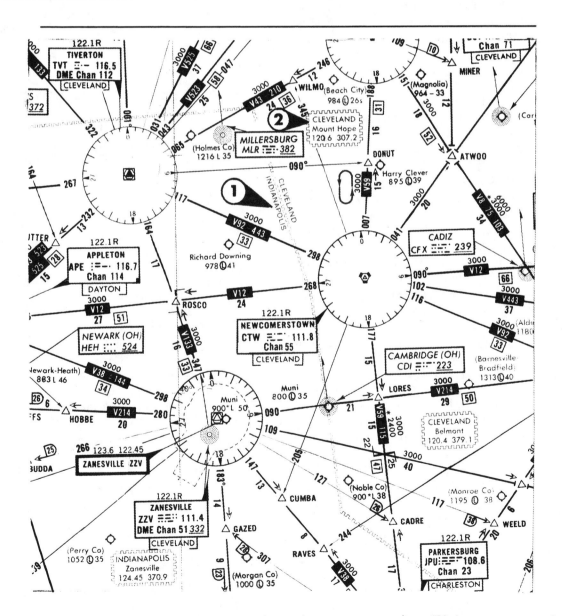

Fig. 6-4. (1) The boundary between two Centers as depicted on an en route chart. **(2)** A remote communications position for Cleveland Center.

Figure 6-5 gives a simplified look at the Memphis Center boundary and the Sectors within this area.

The heavy black line (arrow) is the route of an example instrument flight to be discussed in this and later chapters.

Figure 6-6 is the Low-Altitude Center area, showing more details, such as airway structures and frequencies. Each Sector has its own controllers and assigned VHF and UHF frequencies. For instance, Sector 67 (GLH) is the Greenville, Miss., Sector; the frequency (VHF) is 135.8 MHz (269.3 MHz-UHF). That particular Sector has two remote communications air/ground (RCAG) sites as indicated by the arrows. Both sites transmit and receive on 135.8 MHz because that's the Sector frequency. The sites are located to give the best coverage; most Sectors need only one, while others, the example here, may need two (or more).

You, as a pilot, don't have access to the drawing of the Center area, but the *A/FD* that most IFR pilots carry has the frequencies for the various Sectors. The insert in Figure 6-6 is from the *A/FD* and gives the frequency for a particular Sector. Note that the Greenville low-altitude frequency is 135.8 MHz. (The *high*-altitude Sectors' frequencies are in bold type.)

As you can see in Figure 6-6, each Sector has its own frequencies, UHF and VHF, and the airways have been marked in (but not identified there).

Figure 6-7 has the same information on the GLH RCAG sites as Figure 6-6 but is shown as presented on the en route low-altitude chart.

You'd file your IFR flight plan with the FSS by phone or in person. It's sent to the host computer system at the Center by Teletype. A master copy is kept by the computer. The computer assigns a discrete beacon code for the full trip (departure, en route, *and* arrival) if the computers, that is, ARTCC and the Automatic Radar Terminal System (ARTS), can coordinate. It may be that you'll have to use a new code for the departure or destination airport if they aren't tied in with the Center computer.

When the IFR flight plan gets to the computer system, the computer analyzes it for route and departure area and will buy any altitude you put on the flight. It will reject erroneous routes, so if you say in your flight plan that you're going from Memphis to Nashville via some airway that runs north and south along the West Coast, the computer will sneer and spit it out. It will reject all "errors" except those controller prerogatives such as cruise and climb rates.

If you don't want a DP (standard instrument departure), which will be covered in more detail in Chapter 8, you will so indicate on the remarks portion of the flight plan. You'll be given verbal details of the procedure for getting away from the airport and on your way. Figure 6-8 shows that you would *read* the altitude information on the DP. Clearance delivery would (and must) give you that information verbally if a DP is not used.

Assuming you have DP information, your conversation with Memphis clearance delivery would probably go like this:

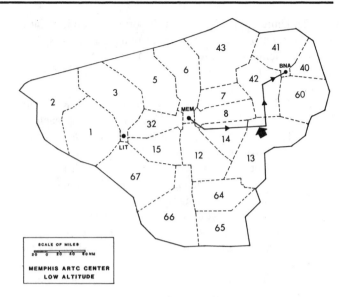

Fig. 6-5. A simplified look at the Sectors in the Memphis Center area. The black line (arrow) is the sample route to be filed to Nashville later.

You: "CLEARANCE DELIVERY, THIS IS ZEPHYR THREE FOUR FIVE SIX JULIET. INFORMATION DELTA. IFR NASHVILLE, OVER."

Memphis clearance delivery: "ZEPHYR THREE FOUR FIVE SIX JULIET, (THIS IS) CLEARANCE DELIVERY. CLEARED TO THE NASHVILLE AIRPORT VIA MEMPHIS FOUR DEPARTURE, THEN AS FILED. MAINTAIN THREE THOUSAND. DEPARTURE (CONTROL) FREQUENCY ONE TWO FOUR POINT ONE FIVE (124.15 MHz), SQUAWK FIVE FIVE ONE TWO (5512)."

Figure 6-8 is the DP-Memphis Four, which gives the departure route description.

If, after you've filed but haven't gone to the airplane yet, you decide on a different route to Nashville (or maybe even changed your destination), contact the FSS and they will pass the word to the Center. Your clearance, in order to avoid confusing it with the earlier flight plan, would contain the full route structure (not "cleared as filed").

Figure 6-9 shows that through coordination with the Center, departure control may tell you to climb before reaching the departure control boundary.

If radars fail, the controllers will require that you go to the old-fashioned "pilot estimates and position reporting" operation. It could be that as a further move you'd have to give your position report to the nearest FSS for direct line relay to the Center. This is the way IFR flying was done for many years before the good coverage of radar and direct contact with Sector controllers was available. (Also the navigation was done by the old four-leg low-frequency radio range, so things are better now even in the worst case.) If operating in the blind, the controller will keep any crossing

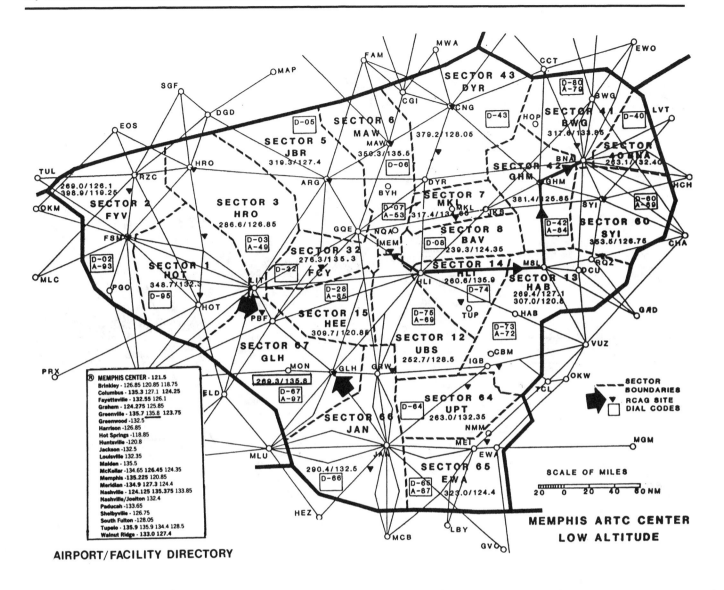

Fig. 6-6. The Memphis Low-Altitude Center area with the route to Nashville marked. The arrows point out the two RCAG (remote communications air to ground) in the Greenville, Miss., Sector. The insert is frequency data as found in the *Airport/Facility Director.*

traffic 10 min apart or will have 1000 ft altitude separation. A complete computer backup system (direct-access radar channel. or DARC) will later be available at all Centers.

Okay, suppose you have to work directly with FSSs. It's not as convenient as working directly with the Center, but there's no problem.

If you had to make a position report to a FSS, you'd use the PTA-TEN procedure. Suppose you're over Muscle Shoals VOR and your last verbal contact with the Center was when they told you that radar contact was lost. Let's say you can't talk on the Sector frequency because your comm set doesn't go that high.

You could call Muscle Shoals radio on the proper frequency, and after establishing initial contact you'd give the following information:

P—Position (Muscle Shoals VOR).

T—Time over.

A—Altitude.

T—Type of flight plan. (The Center knows full well that you are blundering toward Nashville, but Muscle Shoals doesn't have this knowledge, so you'd tell them that you are IFR.)

E—ETA at the next compulsory reporting point (Graham VOR).

N—Next succeeding required reporting point (Graham VOR). You'd say, "NASHVILLE," which is the next reporting point after Graham, but wouldn't give an ETA for Nashville. Or, putting it together: "MUSCLE SHOALS RADIO THIS IS ZEPHYR THREE FOUR FIVE SIX JULIET, OVER." (And, after contact):

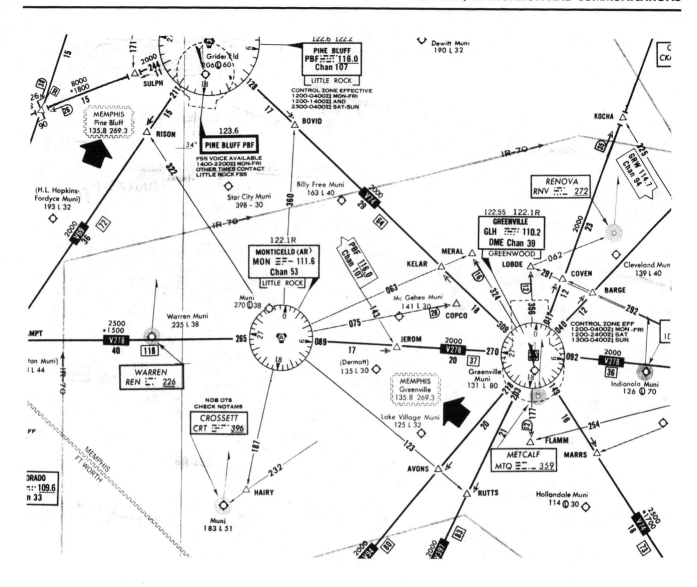

Fig. 6-7. RCAG locations of Figure 6-6 (arrows) for the Greenville Sector as depicted on the en route chart.

"MUSCLE SHOALS AT THREE ONE, 5000 FEET, INSTRUMENT FLIGHT RULES, GRAHAM AT FIVE FIVE, NASHVILLE, OVER." (Muscle Shoals would confirm and probably give you an altimeter setting. Your time over MSL, altitude, and estimate to Graham would be called into the Center by phone.)

■ **Back to Radar** After takeoff, you'll be vectored to a point on the 089 radial, 39 NM from Holly Springs VOR (HLI). (This could change, but that's the planned move.) Then you fly via V54 to Muscle Shoals VOR, V7 to Graham VOR, and V16 to Nashville. Figure 6-10 shows the expected path from Memphis airport to intercept V54 past Holly Springs VOR.

The reason for the deviation from the "expected" routing from Memphis direct to Holly Springs VOR is that that path is an Approach Gate and is set up for *inbound* flights to Memphis. As you'll see in Figure 6-11, the Holly 4 STAR

(standard terminal arrival) funnels *inbound traffic* from the south and east over the Holly Springs VOR. You'd be swimming upstream if you flew outbound to Holly Springs.

SCOPE SYMBOLS

Figure 6-12, taken from the *AIM,* shows an ARTS III radarscope with various alphanumeric data. A number of radars don't have this equipment. The ARTCC and ARTS computer facilities can "talk" to each other.

Figure 6-13, also taken from the *AIM,* shows the information available at a National Airspace System (NAS) Stage A controller's PVD when operating in the full automation RDP (radar data processing) mode. When not in the automation mode, the display is similar to that shown in Figure 6-12.

It's too much for you to be able to take in all of the information given in Figures 6-12 and 6-13 at once. But you

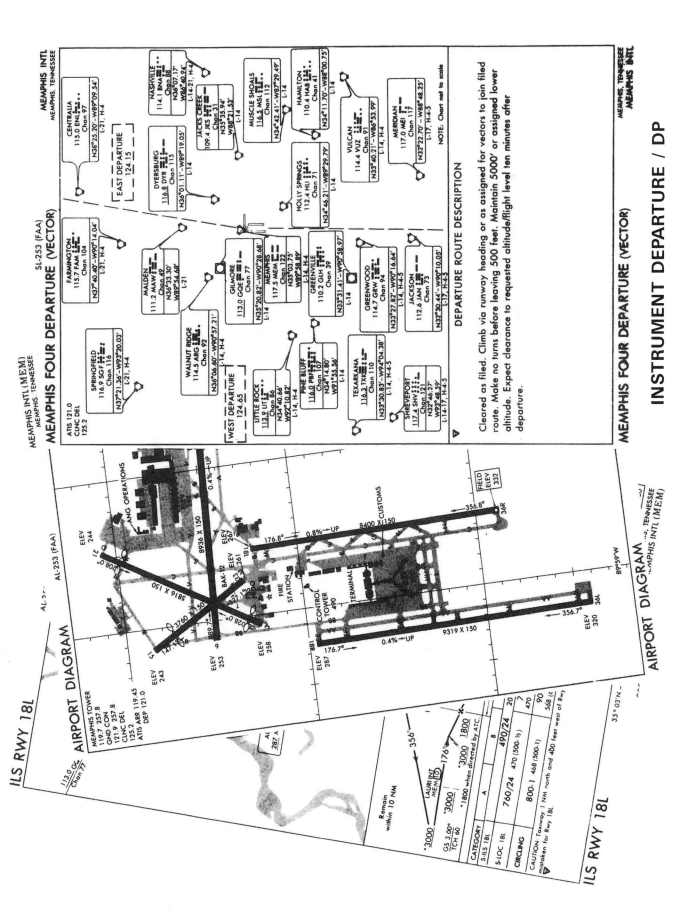

Fig. 6-8. Instrument departure (DP). The MEMPHIS FOUR DEPARTURE (vector). DPs for a particular airport are found in the NOAA *U.S. Terminal Procedures* book with the approach procedures charts and airport diagram for that facility.

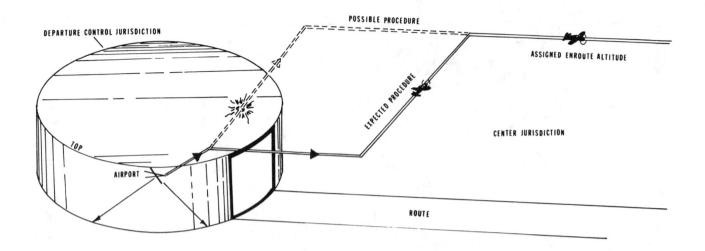

Fig. 6-9. Departure control will usually hold you below a certain altitude until you are out of its area of jurisdiction. If traffic permits, departure will coordinate with the Center and you may be climbed to the final assigned altitude sooner. The approach (or departure) control area probably won't be a smooth round cylinder as shown but may have corridors and projections.

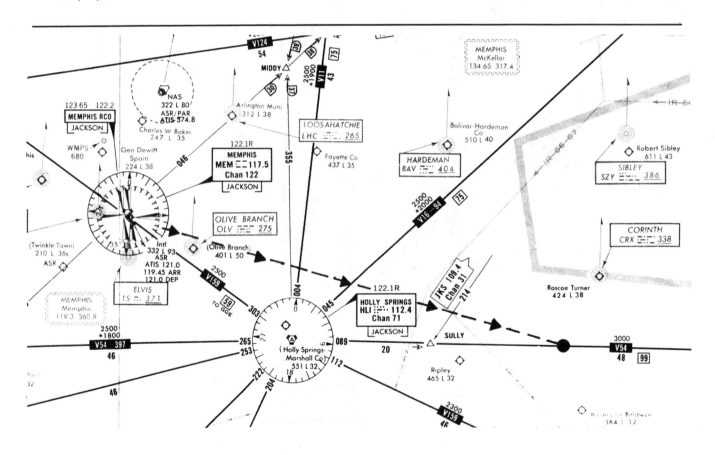

Fig. 6-10. The dashed line with arrows shows a direct line from the Memphis Airport to the 39-NM point on the 089 radial of the Holly Springs VOR. The final result may *not* be such a direct line, since you may be vectored to avoid traffic or get onto the filed route closer or farther than shown.

may want to use them as references to get a better picture of the controllers' displays and the radar information available to ATC and to the pilot through communications with ATC.

■ **Notes** Memphis Center and tower will have a letter of agreement concerning specific departure routes and arrival gates for the Memphis terminal area. You may be instructed

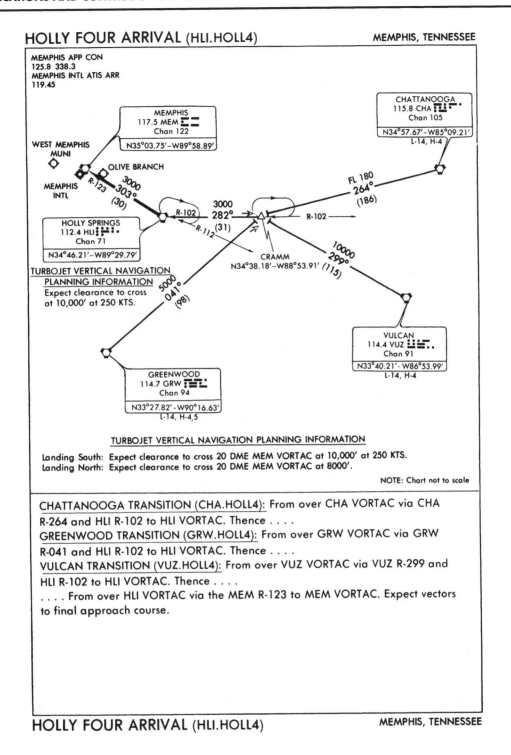

HOLLY FOUR ARRIVAL (HLI.HOLL4)   MEMPHIS, TENNESSEE

MEMPHIS APP CON
125.8 338.3
MEMPHIS INTL ATIS ARR
119.45

CHATTANOOGA
115.8 CHA
Chan 105
N34°57.67'-W85°09.21'
L-14, H-4

MEMPHIS
117.5 MEM
Chan 122
N35°03.75'-W89°58.89'

WEST MEMPHIS
MUNI

OLIVE BRANCH

MEMPHIS
INTL

R-123
3000
303°
(30)

FL 180
264°
(186)

R-102

3000
282°
(31)

R-102

HOLLY SPRINGS
112.4 HLI
Chan 71
N34°46.21'-W89°29.79'

R-112

CRAMM
N34°38.18'-W88°53.91'

10000
299°
(115)

TURBOJET VERTICAL NAVIGATION
PLANNING INFORMATION
Expect clearance to cross
at 10,000' at 250 KTS.

5000
041°
(98)

VULCAN
114.4 VUZ
Chan 91
N33°40.21'-W86°53.99'
L-14, H-4

GREENWOOD
114.7 GRW
Chan 94
N33°27.82'-W90°16.63'
L-14, H-4,5

TURBOJET VERTICAL NAVIGATION PLANNING INFORMATION

Landing South: Expect clearance to cross 20 DME MEM VORTAC at 10,000' at 250 KTS.
Landing North: Expect clearance to cross 20 DME MEM VORTAC at 8000'.

NOTE: Chart not to scale

CHATTANOOGA TRANSITION (CHA.HOLL4): From over CHA VORTAC via CHA
R-264 and HLI R-102 to HLI VORTAC. Thence . . . .
GREENWOOD TRANSITION (GRW.HOLL4): From over GRW VORTAC via GRW
R-041 and HLI R-102 to HLI VORTAC. Thence . . . .
VULCAN TRANSITION (VUZ.HOLL4): From over VUZ VORTAC via VUZ R-299 and
HLI R-102 to HLI VORTAC. Thence . . . .
. . . . From over HLI VORTAC via the MEM R-123 to MEM VORTAC. Expect vectors
to final approach course.

HOLLY FOUR ARRIVAL (HLI.HOLL4)   MEMPHIS, TENNESSEE

Fig. 6-11. The HOLLY 4 ARRIVAL at Memphis.

to depart from the airport in a direction that's not precisely direct to your route. The letter of agreement sets out the best coordination between the facilities for best traffic sequencing in or out.

If you have a general idea of what the Center does with a flight plan and what the Sector layout looks like, you'll feel more at ease with the system. Just when you are having good communication with a controller, you are asked to switch to another Sector controller on another frequency. A short study of Sectors and Sector controllers' duties will clear things up. It's strongly suggested that you visit and get a good look at the Center operations.

Figures 6-5 and 6-6 are examples of Sector numbers, boundaries, and frequencies used. Those factors may change, but the principle is valid as far as showing what happens to your flight plan at the Center.

Figure 6-14 takes a look at communications used during an IFR flight.

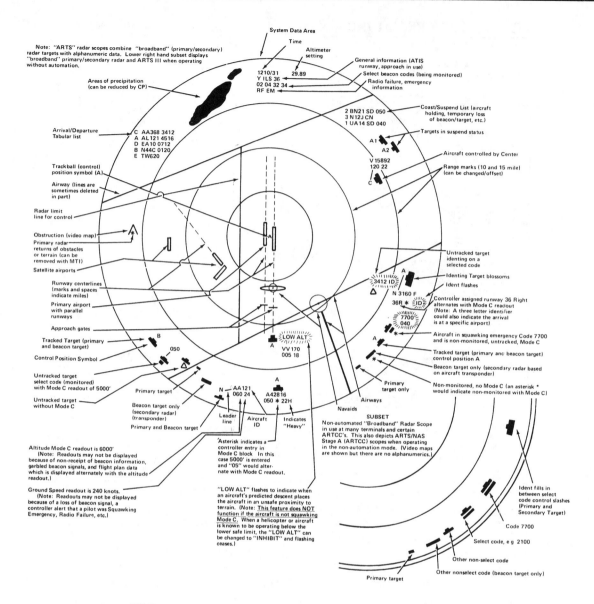

Fig. 6-12. ARTS III radar scope alphanumeric data. Check the latest *AIM* for changes for Figures 6-12 and 6-13. *(Aeronautical Information Manual)*

Figure 6-15 is the Atlanta Center Sector chart (surface to FL 23,000 except as indicated). This illustration, like that of the Memphis Low-Altitude Sector chart (Fig. 6-3), will no doubt become obsolete with time due to changed frequencies and Sector boundaries, but it is inserted here to show that Centers all have basically the same setup. (For *Pete's sake, don't use any of the charts* or *approach plates in this book for navigation purposes!*)

■ **Tower En Route Control (TEC)** Tower en route control is an ATC program for aircraft flying between metropolitan areas. It links designated approach control areas by a network of identified routes of the existing airway structure. The expanded TEC program is applied generally for non-turbojet aircraft operating at or below 10,000 ft. (There are exceptions; for instance, turbojets between certain city pairs such as Milwaukee and Chicago get special dispensation.)

In other words, you're passed from one approach control area to the next, and the system is aimed at being used for relatively short flights of 2 hr or less. You are subject to the same delay factor at the destination airport as other aircraft in the ATC system. (Departure and en route delays can be a problem too.) If the major metropolitan airport is having significant delays, you might want to use an alternate.

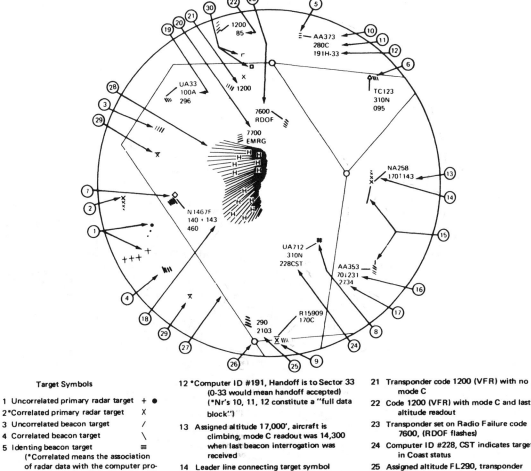

Target Symbols

1 Uncorrelated primary radar target   + ●

2 *Correlated primary radar target   X

3 Uncorrelated beacon target   /

4 Correlated beacon target   \

5 Identing beacon target   ≡
(*Correlated means the association of radar data with the computer projected track of an identified aircraft)

Position Symbols

6 Free track (No flight plan tracking) △

7 Flat track (flight plan tracking) ◊

8 Coast (Beacon target lost) #

9 Present Position Hold X̄

Data Block Information

10 *Aircraft Identification

11 *Assigned Altitude FL280, mode C altitude same or within ±200' of asgnd altitude

12 *Computer ID #191, Handoff is to Sector 33 (0-33 would mean handoff accepted) (*Nr's 10, 11, 12 constitute a "full data block")

13 Assigned altitude 17,000', aircraft is climbing, mode C readout was 14,300 when last beacon interrogation was received

14 Leader line connecting target symbol and data block

15 Track velocity and direction vector line (Projected ahead of target)

16 Assigned altitude 7000, aircraft is descending, last mode C readout (or last reported altitude was 100' above FL230

17 Transponder code shows in full data block only when different than assigned code

18 Aircraft is 300' above assigned altitude

19 Reported altitude (No mode C readout) same as assigned. An "N" would indicate no reported altitude)

20 Transponder set on emergency code 7700 (EMRG flashes to attract attention)

21 Transponder code 1200 (VFR) with no mode C

22 Code 1200 (VFR) with mode C and last altitude readout

23 Transponder set on Radio Failure code 7600, (RDOF flashes)

24 Computer ID #228, CST indicates target is in Coast status

25 Assigned altitude FL290, transponder code (These two items constitute a "limited data block")

Other symbols

26 Navigational Aid

27 Airway or jet route

28 Outline of weather returns based on primary radar (See Chapter 4, ARTCC Radar Weather Display. H's represent areas of high density precipitation which might be thunderstorms. Radial lines indicate lower density precipitation)

29 Obstruction

30 Airports Major: □ , Small: ⌐

NAS Stage A Controllers View Plan Display. This figure illustrates the controller's radar scope (PVD) when operating in the full automation (RDP) mode, which is normally 20 hours per day. (Note: When not in automation mode, the display is similar to the broadband mode shown in the ARTS III Radar Scope figure. Certain ARTCC's outside the contiguous U.S. also operate in "broadband" mode.)

Fig. 6-13. National Airspace System Stage A controller's planview display. *(Aeronautical Information Manual)*

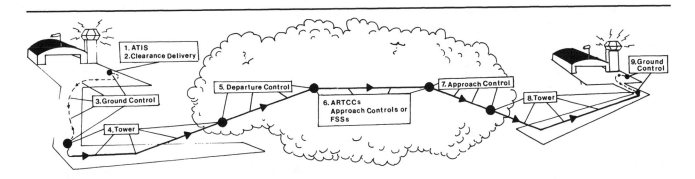

Fig. 6-14. A simplified view of facilities used on a "typical" IFR flight. The Center may be climbing or descending you in parts of the areas shown for departure control or approach control.

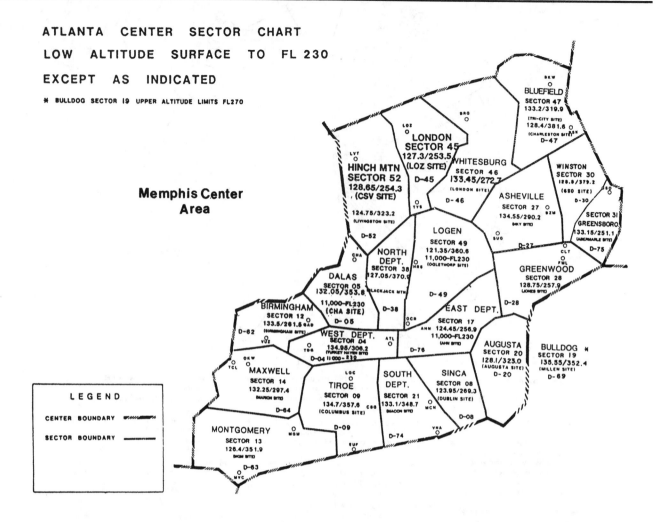

ATLANTA CENTER SECTOR CHART

LOW ALTITUDE SURFACE TO FL 230

EXCEPT AS INDICATED

✕ BULLDOG SECTOR 19 UPPER ALTITUDE LIMITS FL270

Fig. 6-15. (above) The Atlanta Center Sector chart. Note that it joins Memphis Center to the west.

You don't have to meet any unique requirements as far as flight plan filing is concerned, but you should put "TEC" in the remarks section of the flight plan if you want it.

COMMUNICATIONS TECHNIQUES

The example flight in Part 4 of this book will cover the Center/approach control actions more from a pilot's standpoint.

As far as communications techniques are concerned, here are some tips:

1. *Listen* before you transmit. Many times you can get the information you want through ATIS or by monitoring the frequency. Except for a few situations where some frequency overlap occurs, if you hear someone else talking, the keying of your transmitter will be futile and you will probably jam their

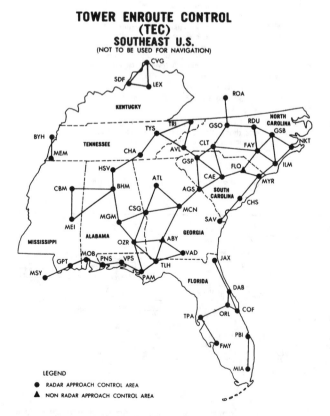

Fig. 6-16. (left) Tower en route control as published earlier for the southeastern United States. *(Airport/Facility Directory)*

receivers, causing them to repeat their call. If you have just changed frequencies, pause for your receiver to tune, listen, and make sure the frequency is clear.

2. *Think* before keying your transmitter. Know what you want to say and if it is lengthy (for example, a flight plan or IFR position report) jot it down. (But do not lock your head in the cockpit.)

3. The microphone should be very close to your lips and after pressing the mike button, a slight pause may be necessary to be sure the first word is transmitted. Speak in a normal conversational tone.

4. When you release the button, wait a few seconds before calling again. The controller or FSS specialist may be jotting down your number, looking for your flight plan, transmitting on a different frequency, or be in the process of selecting your frequency.

5. Be alert to the *sounds* or *lack of sounds* in your receiver. Check your volume, recheck your frequency, and *make sure that your microphone is not stuck* in the transmit position.

6. Be sure that you are within the performance range of your radio equipment and the ground station equipment. Remote radio sites do not always transmit and receive on all of a facility's available frequencies, particularly with regard to VOR sites where you can hear from a ground station but not reach its receiver. Remember that a higher altitude increases the range of VHF line-of-sight communications.

3 PLANNING THE INSTRUMENT FLIGHT

WEATHER SYSTEMS AND PLANNING

Before working out the navigation, you'd better check the weather to see whether you can go or not and to get some wind information for estimating groundspeeds. In order to do this, review the weather systems and hazards and weather services available.

This book is not going into detail on meteorological theory. There are complete books—and good ones—dedicated to weather (see bibliography at the end of the book). While it might be nice to know that the low ceilings at your destination airport were created by a Maritime Tropical or Maritime Polar air mass, it still doesn't alter the fact that certain conditions exist, and you'll have to cope with them or cancel the flight. In fact, you may not have access to information as to the type of air mass involved, but you *will* have ceilings, visibilities, temperatures, and other information that will tell you what to expect.

PRESSURE AREAS

You've been watching TV weather reports long enough to have gained a good idea of how pressure areas affect the weather (and studied it in getting your private certificate).

High-pressure areas, you've learned, *usually* mean good weather. Low-pressure areas *usually* mean less than good weather. Sometimes, the circulation around a high-pressure area (clockwise and outward in the Northern Hemisphere) can pull warm moist air into an area, where it is cooled and condensed to such an extent that fog and/or low clouds are formed (Fig. 7-1).

The circulation around a Low in the Northern Hemisphere is counterclockwise and inward, caused by a combination of low pressure and the earth's rotation, just as the clockwise (and outward) circulation around a High is caused by the high pressure and the earth's rotation. The effect of the earth's rotation is called the "Coriolis effect" and is a good conversational gambit if nothing else is available.

Buys-Ballot's law states that, in the Northern Hemisphere if you stand with your back to the wind and stick out your left hand, you will be pointing to the low-pressure area. However, local effects could be such (obstructions, etc.) that you are merely pointing to the left at some object of dubious interest. You'll do better to check weather information.

Lines connecting points of equal pressure are called *isobars* (Fig. 7-1).

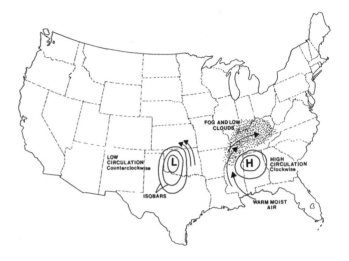

Fig. 7-1. Pressure areas and isobars.

Elongated high-pressure systems are called *ridges*. The equivalent low-pressure shapes are called *troughs*. A *col* is a neutral area between two Lows and two Highs.

FRONTAL SYSTEMS

■ **Fronts in General** A front is a boundary between two air masses of different character. Although a front is considered to be a sharply defined line, it may be many miles in width. The more different the characteristics of the two air masses, the more defined the frontal zone.

Figure 7-2 shows a sample weather system with pressure patterns and frontal systems existing at a particular time.

Some weather is the result of circulation or local conditions, but most problems are caused by frontal systems. Let's examine the weather associated with the various types of fronts.

■ **Cold Front** Figure 7-3 is the cross section of a cold front as indicated by A–A in Figure 7-2.

The cold front normally contains more violent weather than the warm front, and the band of clouds and precipitation is narrower. The faster the front moves, the more violent the weather ahead of it. Cold fronts normally move at

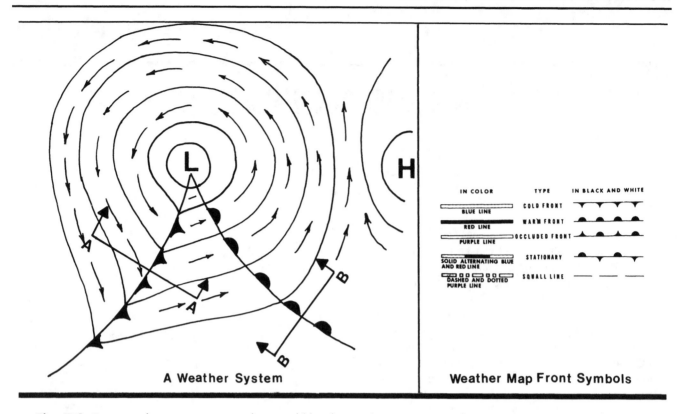

A Weather System

Weather Map Front Symbols

Fig. 7-2. Fronts and pressure areas as they would be depicted on a current surface weather map.

about 20–25 knots, but some (called "fast-moving cold fronts" for obvious reasons) move as fast as 60 knots.

The slope of the front, as indicated in Figure 7-3, is exaggerated. Slopes of cold fronts vary from 1:50 to 1:150 and average about 1:80. The "top" of the cold air mass would be at 1 mi altitude at a position 80 mi behind the surface position of the front.

In the Northern Hemisphere, strong cold fronts are usually oriented in a northeast-southwest direction and move east or southeast.

As a typical cold front approaches, the southerly winds in the warm air ahead pick up in velocity. Altocumulus clouds move in from the direction from which the front is approaching. The barometric pressure decreases rapidly (Fig. 7-4).

The ceiling will lower rapidly as the cumulonimbus clouds move in. Rain will occur and will intensify as the front approaches. After frontal passage, the wind will shift to westerly or northerly, and the pressure rises in short order. Rapid clearing (with lower temperatures and dew points) is the usual rule after the cold front passage. The surface winds are likely to be strong and gusty.

A slow-moving cold front may have a wider band of weather with lesser buildups and may have many of the characteristics of a warm front if the warm air is stable.

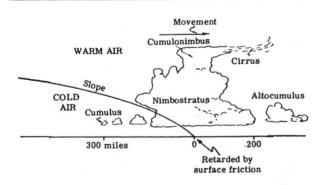

Fig. 7-3. Cross section of a cold front.

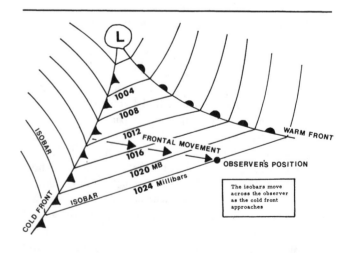

Fig. 7-4. As the cold front approaches, there is a drop in pressure.

SQUALL LINES. Sometimes a solid line of thunderstorms develops in front of a rapidly moving cold front. Such "squall lines" may extend up to 40,000 ft with isolated buildups to 60,000–70,000 ft. The squall line sometimes is found 50–300 mi ahead of the front and is aligned generally parallel to it.

■ **Warm Front** The warm front normally has a wider band of less violent weather (it says here), and ceilings and visibilities are low. The warm front may hang around for days. More than one pilot (instrument-rated) has had to sit staring at the four walls of a hotel room because practically half the country (his half) was below IFR minimums.

Figure 7-5 shows the cross section of a "typical" warm front, as shown by the B–B in Figure 7-2. (You are looking the way the arrows are pointing in Fig. 7-2.)

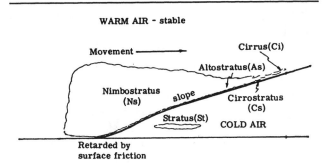

Fig. 7-5. Cross section of a warm front (warm air stable). Rain falls out of the warm air (clouds); if the cold air is below 32°F, freezing rain results.

The slope of the warm front is about 1:100 as an average, but slopes may vary from 1:50 to 1:200. The warm front moves about one-half as fast as the cold front, and since the band of weather is much broader, the result is that it can be in the area a longer time.

In Figure 7-5 the warm air is stable, which means that stratus-type clouds would be expected to predominate. If the warm air is unstable, clouds of vertical development may be found.

In the winter, freezing rain may be encountered if the cold air ahead of the front is below freezing.

If freezing rain is encountered, climb if possible. The air above the front line is warm, and the rain will be in its usual liquid form. (ATC would be interested in your altitude or heading changes if you are IFR or plan on getting into the clouds.) You can expect to have to let down through it, and you should make the transition as expeditiously as possible without overdoing it. (Another option is to make a *180°* turn.) Incidentally, you are required by the FAR to report encountering *any* icing, and freezing rain qualifies very well in this regard.

■ **Occluded Front** The fact that the cold front moves faster than the warm front can result in a situation such as the occluded front. Figure 7-6 shows the cross section of "typical" cold- and warm-front occlusions as shown at C–C.

Notice that by sliding under the cool and warm air, the cold air has created an upper warm-front condition. As the occlusion develops, the warm-front cloud system disappears, and the weather and clouds are similar to conditions associated with a cold front. The warm-front occlusion is less common than the cold-front occlusion.

In this case the air ahead of the warm front is colder than that behind the cold front. The cool air moves up over the denser cold air. The surface weather would be similar to that of a warm front; but in flying through the occlusion during its initial stages, you might expect to encounter weather of both types of fronts, with thunderstorms within stratus cloud areas. As the development progresses, the severity of the associated weather decreases.

■ **Stationary Front** Sometimes the pressures and circulation on each side of a front act in such a way as to stop the frontal movement. Such a front is naturally called a stationary front, which is as good a name as any. The weather associated with a stationary front is a milder form of warm-front clouds and precipitation. The problem is that if the front

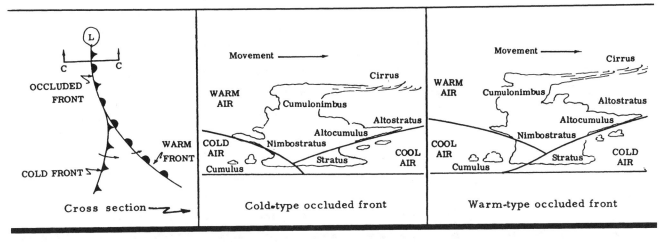

Fig. 7-6. Warm- and cold-type occluded fronts.

bogs down, the weather can be from below average to unsatisfactory for several days until things get moving again.

CLOUDS

Before now your interest in clouds has been academic. You were mostly interested in (1) the heights of the bases, (2) the amount of cloud cover, and (3) whether various forms of precipitation could fall out on you. Now their internal characteristics will be of prime importance.

Clouds are broken down into families according to their heights:

Low clouds—The bases are found from the surface to 6500 ft in middle latitudes.

Middle clouds—The bases are found from 6500 to 23,000 ft.

High clouds—The bases are found at heights from 16,500 up to 45,000 ft.

Clouds with extensive vertical development—The height of the cloud bases may be from 1000 to 10,000 ft. The cloud can, in extreme cases, extend up to 60,000–70,000 ft.

The clouds are further described by their form and appearance. The puffy or billowy type formed by local vertical currents are called "cumulus," and those formed of widespread (or fairly widespread) layers have the term "stratus" or "strata" somewhere in the name. Figure 7-7 shows some representative clouds of the various families.

A cloud with the term "nimbo" or "nimbus" in the name is expected to produce precipitation.

Flying near clouds of stratus formation, you would expect fairly smooth air. Cumulus clouds, by their very nature, are the product of air conditions that indicate the presence of vertical currents.

Clouds are composed of minute ice crystals or water droplets and are the result of moist air being cooled to the point of condensation. The high clouds (cirrus, cirrostratus, and cirrocumulus) are composed of extremely fine ice crystals. When the water droplets become a certain size, rain results (or snow or sleet, depending on the conditions). Hail is a form of precipitation associated with cumulonimbus clouds and is the result of rain being lifted by vertical currents until it reaches an altitude where it freezes and is carried downward again. The cycle may be repeated several times, giving the larger hailstones their characteristic "layers," or strata.

Turbulence can be found near these clouds, and hail can fall from the "anvil head" into what could appear to be a clear area.

Clouds may be composed of supercooled moisture. The impact of your airplane on these particles causes them to freeze immediately on the airplane.

Since clouds are formed by moist air being cooled to the point of condensation, this leads to the subject of lapse rates.

For dry air, the adiabatic lapse rate is 5.5°F/1000 ft. (Adiabatic refers to a process during which no heat is withdrawn or added to the system or body concerned.) The normal lapse rate for "average" air is 3.5°F, or 2°C. The moist adiabatic lapse rate is produced by convection in a saturated atmosphere, such as within a cumulus cloud. At high

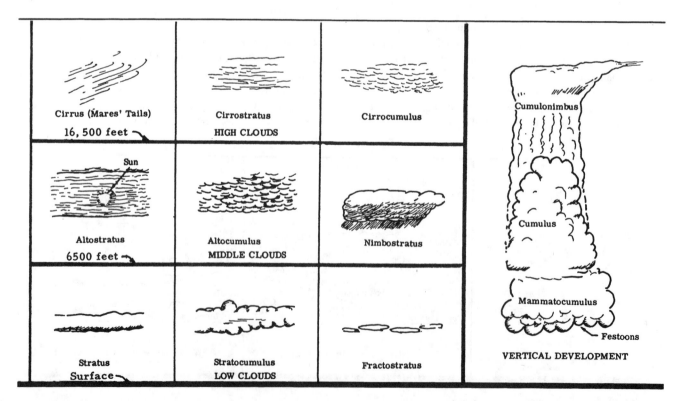

Fig. 7-7. Some cloud types.

temperatures, it will be 2–3°F/1000 ft, and at low temperatures, it will be in the vicinity of 4–5°F. The dew point lapse rate is about 1°F/1000 ft.

For cumulus clouds that are formed by surface heating, the base of the clouds may be estimated by the rate at which the dry lapse rate "catches" the dew point. (The dry lapse rate is 5.5°F and the dew point drop is 1°F/1000 ft, so the temperature is dropping 4.5°F faster than the dew point, per thousand feet.) Assume the surface temperature is 76°F and the dew point 58°F, a difference of 18°F. Dividing this number by 4.5, it is found that the temperature and dew point make connections at 4000 ft—the approximate base of the clouds. This works only for the type of cloud formed by surface heating and is not suitable for locations in mountainous or hilly terrain.

When clouds have a temperature of between 0° and –15°C, they consist mostly of supercooled water droplets with some ice crystals. There's an old physics experiment in which distilled water is cooled very slowly and remains liquid below 32°F until the container is jostled or other outside factors are introduced; then it freezes instantly. In the case of the supercooled water droplets in the cloud, *your airplane* is the outside factor. The shock of the airplane flying into the particles can cause them to freeze on the surface, but in-flight icing will be covered in more detail later.

When the temperature within the cloud is lower than –15°C, the cloud is usually composed entirely of ice crystals.

As you have noted in your flying, the addition of nuclei to moist air can result in the formation of clouds or fog. Specks of dust or smoke form the center of the particles, and airports located in river bottoms near industrial plants are notorious for being socked in when everything else is good VFR.

When moist air is orographically lifted (moved up a slope), it may be cooled and condensed to the point where clouds are formed. If the warm moist air is unstable to begin with, the result may be well-developed cumuliform clouds.

HAZARDS TO FLIGHT

■ **Thunderstorms** Thunderstorms constitute a real menace to the instrument pilot because it is possible to fly into one with little or no warning. Airborne radar has been of great value in finding "soft spots" (or *comparatively* soft spots). ATC radar can help too.

Figure 7-8 shows a display of airborne radar on the weather display mode. The set displays weather in four colors, but since this illustration is in black and white, numbers have been inserted to give the relative weather (rain) intensities.

Weather radar can give a clue to the presence of turbulence. Areas of the display where the colors change rapidly over a short distance represent steep rainfall gradients, which are usually associated with severe turbulence. It's suggested that you always maintain at least 10 NM separation between any weather display and your aircraft.

A big problem (*one* of your big problems) will be turbulence within the cell. Updrafts and downdrafts may cause structural failure of the airplane or loss of control.

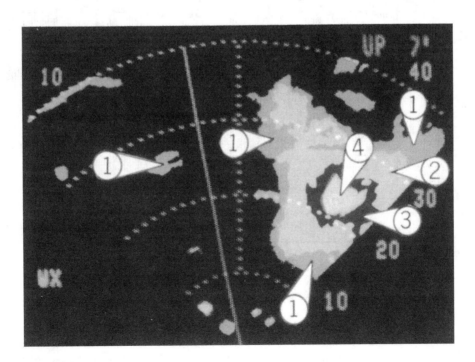

Fig. 7-8. Digital weather radar indications. The actual scope would show colors indicating the intensity of the precipitation (and can warn of possible turbulence). Check the numbers in this black and white presentation. **(1)** Green—very light rain, 1–4 mm/hr. **(2)** Yellow—light to medium rain, 4–12 mm/hr. **(3)** Red—heavy rain, 12–50 mm/hr. **(4)** Magenta—very heavy rain, over 50 mm or 2 in./hr. *(Bendix-King)*

If you know you're about to penetrate a thunderstorm, you'll want to slow the airplane below the maneuvering speed or speed recommended by the manufacturer for such a situation. Secure all loose gear. Set your power to maintain level altitude at the recommended speed *before* penetration and *leave the power alone.* Fly a straight-and-level attitude. Don't, repeat, *don't* try to maintain a constant altitude (height). In attempting to keep at the same altitude, you may put extreme stresses on the airplane. You fly into an updraft and shove the nose over—just as you hit a violent downdraft. Remember that even *near* the cells the air can be extremely violent, and many a VFR pilot has found out about "sucker holes" when trying to fly between cells.

MANEUVERING AND GUST ENVELOPES. Turbulence and strong vertical gusts are associated with thunderstorms.

Figure 7-9 shows the *gust envelope* of a four-place general aviation airplane at a gross weight of 2650 lb, using 15 and 30 fps *instantaneous* vertical gusts up (+) and down (−) as indicated.

As the airspeed increases, the effects of a particular gust value also increase; for instance, in Figure 7-9, at 86 knots (3) a 30-fps up-gust results in about 2.6 positive g's being imposed on the airframe just as it stalls. So in this example if the airplane was flying at a calibrated airspeed of *less* than 86 knots and encountered a 30-fps up-gust, it would stall (a transient condition; the airplane would soon be flying again—at least away from the effects of *that* particular gust). At 148 knots (4) the same 30-fps gust intercepts the 3.8 positive g limit line of the maneuvering envelope. If the airplane was flying at an airspeed of about 68 knots (5) and encountered a 15-fps up-gust, approximately 1.6 g's would result just as it stalled (Fig. 7-9).

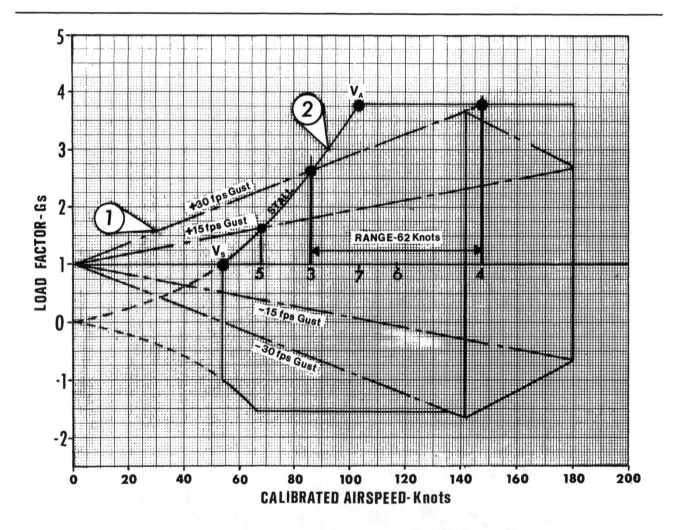

Fig. 7-9. Gust envelope **(1)** superimposed on a maneuvering envelope **(2)** of an airplane at its maximum weight of 2650 lb. Gust values of 15 and 30 fps *instantaneous* gust effects are used here to show the idea of the airplane's reaction to vertical gusts. Some later envelopes use 25- and 50-fps gusts but add a gust alleviation factor that brings the effects close to the instantaneous values shown. V$_S$ is the stall speed at 1 g at 2650 lb, and V$_A$ is the maneuvering speed at that weight. Note that the "allowed gust value" decreases to less than +30 fps above 141 knots. This is a manmade limitation and the actual, physical gust effects continue to increase with increased airspeed. (If you extend the +30 fps gust line to 180 knots, about 4.3 +g's would result.) Always use the *Pilot's Operating Handbook* references for best turbulence penetration airspeeds for *your* airplane.

The stall relieves the stress imposed on the airplane by either a gust or the pilot's yanking back on the stick or wheel.

If you were thinking in terms of neither stalling nor exceeding the 3.8 g positive load factor when flying in turbulence with 30-fps positive gusts, the airspeed range to stay within at the 2650-lb weight is to fly no slower than 86 knots and no faster than 148 knots, a range shown in Figure 7-9 to be 62 knots. The ideal airspeed would then seem to be at a midpoint in this range, or 117 knots (6).

The maneuvering speed (V_A) is shown in Figure 7-9 as being 104 knots (7), and this is within the range of 86–148 knots discussed and is slightly toward the stall or lower portion of the "safe" range for 30-fps gust penetration. This leads to the assumption that V_A would be a reasonable airspeed to assume in the event that 30-fps vertical gusts are being encountered. The problem is that V_A is not known at a particular time of flight because it decreases as airplane weight decreases. (Actually, it decreases as the *square root* of the weight decrease, but more about that later.)

Figure 7-10 shows the maneuver and gust envelopes for the airplane in Figure 7-9 at the manufacturer's minimum flying weight of 1665 lb, which by definition is the basic empty weight plus the minimum crew required at 170 pounds each and the fuel necessary for ½ hr of operation at max continuous power. You aren't likely to be flying IFR at that weight, but Figures 7-9 and 7-10 are included to show the extremes.

Note in Figure 7-10 that the stall induced by the 30-fps gust would occur (at 1665 lb) at about 71 knots (4), and the speed exceeding the 3.8 positive load factor is at about 109 knots (5), giving a "safe range" of about 38 knots. The midrange speed for avoiding either the stall or exceeding 3.8 positive g's is 90 knots (6).

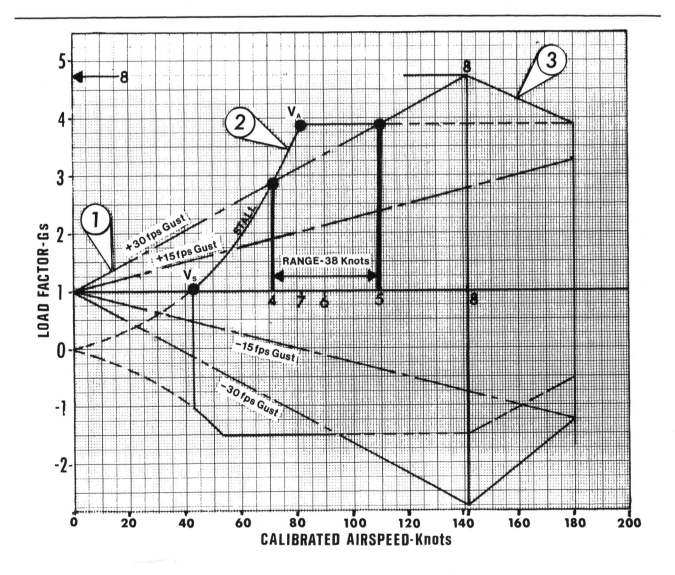

Fig. 7-10. The gust **(1)**, maneuvering **(2)**, and combined envelope **(3)** for the airplane of Figure 7-9 at the minimum flying weight of 1665 lb. The combined envelope is the maneuvering envelope with extensions as developed by the manufacturer to meet gust effects at lower weights as required by FAR 23 and might be considered the "maneuver envelope with lumps."

A rule of thumb might be used to find the maneuvering and safe midpoint airspeeds at lower weights: Decrease V_A or the midpoint safe airspeed by one-half the percentage of the weight change. If the weight decreases 20%, decrease the original airspeed by one-half that amount, or 10%. As an example, using the maneuvering speeds at the two weights of the airplane (2650 and 1665 lb), it can be seen that the weight has decreased by 985 lb, or 37%. The V_A should decrease by one-half, or 18.5% (call it 19%), or by about 21 knots, to 83 knots. This is close enough to the computed value (82 knots in Fig. 7-10) to be useful (7).

Looking at the midrange safety airspeeds for 30-fps gusts, the same idea could be used. The airspeed for 2650 lb was 117 knots, and at 1665 lb it was 90 knots. Following the rule of thumb used earlier for the maneuvering speed, the weight has decreased by 37%, so the safe speed of 117 knots should also be decreased by one-half of the weight decrease (19%, or approximately 22 knots) to 95 knots. This is slightly higher than the 90 knots calculated for the minimum weight but will be safe at that weight and higher intermediate weights.

The discussion on safe airspeed ranges assumed in Figure 7-10 that it was unsafe to penetrate an area of 30-fps gusts at any airspeed greater than 109 knots (5) where the result puts the load factor outside the maneuvering envelope maximum of 3.8 positive g's. After calculating that the 30-fps gust would put the airplane outside the envelope at lower weights, the manufacturer must design the structure and components to sustain those g values. The result of these calculations is the *limit combined envelope* (item 3 in Fig. 7-10). In Figure 7-10 at the design cruise speed (V_c) of 142 knots (8), the airplane would sustain approximately 4.75 g's in hitting a 30-fps instantaneous up-gust. The limitation of 3.8 g's was used to show the increasing effects of particular gust values as weight decreased.

In short, as the airplane gets lighter, you can expect a rougher ride in turbulence; *a particular gust velocity can cause higher acceleration on the airplane for a given airspeed.*

Fig. 7-11. Flying through thunderstorms can be a "rending" experience.

OTHER POINTS ON TURBULENCE. The "altitude hold" portion of the autopilot should be off, or the airplane can be overstressed as the equipment tries to do an impossible job of maintaining a constant altitude.

Maybe you haven't flown into severe or extreme turbulence and don't realize that you may be bouncing around so much that the instruments are very hard to read, and since you are IFR, this can be an interesting situation.

Figure 7-12 is a turbulence criteria table for your and the airplane's reaction to various intensities of turbulence.

Precipitation static will be a problem for the LF/MF equipment in heavy rain or snow, so you might as well turn the volume down. Attempting ADF tracking in a thunderstorm or thunderstorm area can be one of the biggest wastes of time in your flying career. You'll be busy enough trying to keep the airplane under control.

Try to maintain as near a constant heading as possible. Pick a heading that should get you out in the shortest time—you wouldn't want to go through a squall line the *long way.*

Because of lightning flashes, it would be best to have the cockpit lights full bright during night penetrations. You'll lose your night vision anyway and shouldn't be looking out at this stage. Lightning has damaged airplanes on occasion, but this relatively rare possibility will be of secondary importance compared with what turbulence and hail can do to you.

The *AIM* sums up thunderstorm flying techniques:

A. Above all, remember this: Never regard any thunderstorm "lightly" even when radar observers report the echoes are of light intensity. Avoiding thunderstorms is the best policy. Following are some Do's and Don'ts of thunderstorm avoidance:

(1) Don't land or take off in the face of an approaching thunderstorm. A sudden gust front of low-level turbulence could cause loss of control.

(2) Don't attempt to fly under a thunderstorm even if you can see through to the other side. Turbulence and wind shear under the storm could be disastrous.

(3) Don't fly without airborne radar into a cloud mass containing scattered embedded thunderstorms. Scattered thunderstorms not embedded usually can be visually circumnavigated.

(4) Don't trust the visual appearance to be a reliable indicator of the turbulence inside a thunderstorm.

(5) Do avoid by at least 20 miles any thunderstorm identified as severe or giving an intense radar echo. This is especially true under the anvil of a large cumulonimbus.

(6) Do clear the top of a known or suspected severe thunderstorm by at least 1,000 feet altitude for each 10 knots of wind speed at the cloud top. This should exceed the altitude capability of most aircraft.

(7) Do circumnavigate the entire area if the area has six-tenths thunderstorm coverage.

TURBULENCE REPORTING CRITERIA TABLE

INTENSITY	AIRCRAFT REACTION	REACTION INSIDE AIRCRAFT	REPORTING TERM-DEFINITION
Light	Turbulence that momentarily causes slight, erratic changes in altitude and/or attitude (pitch, roll, yaw). Report as **Light Turbulence**;* or Turbulence that causes slight, rapid and some- what rhythmic bumpiness without appreciable changes in altitude or attitude. Report as **Light Chop**.	Occupants may feel a slight strain against seat belts or shoulder straps. Unsecured objects may be displaced slightly. Food service may be conducted and little or no difficulty is encountered in walking.	Occasional – Less than 1/3 of the time. Intermittent – 1/3 to 2/3. Continuous – More than 2/3.
Moderate	Turbulence that is similar to Light Turbulence but of greater intensity. Changes in altitude and/or attitude occur but the aircraft remains in positive control at all times. It usually causes variations in indicated airspeed. Report as **Moderate Turbulence**;* or Turbulence that is similar to Light Chop but of greater intensity. It causes rapid bumps or jolts without appreciable changes in aircraft altitude or attitude. Report as **Moderate Chop**.	Occupants feel definite strains against seat belts or shoulder straps. Unsecured objects are dislodged. Food service and walking are difficult.	**NOTE** 1. Pilots should report loca- tion(s), time (UTC) , in- tensity, whether in or near clouds, altitude, type of aircraft and, when appli- cable, duration of turbu- lence. 2. Duration may be based on time between two locations or over a single location. All locations should be readily identifi- able. EXAMPLES: a. Over Omaha, 1232Z, Moderate Turbulence, in cloud, Flight Level 310, B707.
Severe	Turbulence that causes large, abrupt changes in altitude and/or attitude. It usually causes large variations in indicated airspeed. Aircraft may be momentarily out of control. Report as **Severe Turbulence**. *	Occupants are forced vio- lently against seat belts or shoulder straps. Unsecured objects are tossed about. Food service and walking are impossible.	b. From 50 miles south of Albuquerque to 30 miles north of Phoenix, 1210Z to 1250Z, occasional Moderate Chop, Flight Level 330, DC8.
Extreme	Turbulence in which the aircraft is violently tossed about and is practically impossible to control. It may cause structural damage. Report as **Extreme Turbulence**.*		

* High level turbulence (normally above 15,000 feet ASL) not associated with cumuliform cloudiness, including thunderstorms, should be reported as CAT (clear air turbulence) preceded by the appropriate intensity, or light or moderate chop

Fig. 7-12. Intensities of turbulence. *(Aeronautical Information Manual)*

(8) Do remember that vivid and frequent lightning indicates the probability of a severe thunder-storm.

(9) Do regard as extremely hazardous any thunder-storm with tops 35,000 feet or higher whether the top is visually sighted or determined by radar.

B. If you cannot avoid penetrating a thunderstorm, fol-lowing are some Do's *before* entering the storm:

(1) Tighten your safety belt, put on your shoulder harness if you have one, and secure all loose objects.

(2) Plan and hold your course to take you through the storm in a minimum time.

(3) To avoid the most critical icing, establish a pene-tration altitude below the freezing level or above the level of –15°C.

(4) Verify that pitot heat is on and turn on carburetor heat or jet engine anti-ice. Icing can be rapid at any altitude and cause almost instantaneous power failure and/or loss of airspeed indication.

(5) Establish power settings for turbulence penetra-tion airspeed recommended in your aircraft manual.

(6) Turn up cockpit lights to highest intensity to lessen temporary blindness from lightning.

(7) If using automatic pilot, disengage altitude hold mode and speed hold mode. The automatic altitude and speed controls will increase maneu-vers of the aircraft thus increasing structural stress.

(8) If using airborne radar, tilt the antenna up and down occasionally. This will permit you to detect other thunderstorm activity at altitudes other than the one being flown.

C. Following are some Do's and Don'ts for action *dur-ing* the thunderstorm penetration:

(1) Do keep your eyes on your instruments. Looking outside the cockpit can increase danger of tem-porary blindness from lightning.

(2) Don't change power settings; maintain settings for the recommended turbulence penetration air-speed.

(3) Do maintain constant attitude, let the aircraft "ride the waves." Maneuvers in trying to maintain con-stant altitude increases stress on the aircraft.

(4) Don't turn back once you are in the thunder-storm. A straight course through the storm most likely will get you out of the hazards most quickly. In addition, turning maneuvers increase stress on the aircraft.

Never jeopardize control for voice transmissions. If ATC calls when you are hard put to just fly the airplane, tell them to wait; or if necessary, hang on to the controls and forget the mike and let *them* worry also.

■ **Icing** Area forecasts are a good source to check for possible structural icing along your route.

CARBURETOR ICE. You've probably had experience with carburetor ice and know that it is "not the heat (or lack of it) but the humidity" that is the big factor concerned. Carburetor icing can occur on warm days without a cloud in the sky.

The warm moist air enters the carburetor, where it is cooled by the combination of two factors: (1) the vaporization of the fuel and (2) the venturi effect of pressure change through the carburetor. The temperature drop will vary but may be up to 72°F. If the resulting temperature is below freezing, ice forms in the venturi and downstream in the intake system. As a review of the indications of carburetor ice: For the airplane with a fixed-pitch propeller, the rpm creeps off with no change in throttle position. Pulling the carburetor heat results in a still further drop in rpm—and that's where many pilots make a mistake; they don't leave the heat ON long enough but push it off with a feeling of well-being (no ice). Leave the heat on for at least 10 sec. If there is ice, the rpm will pick up from its even lower setting. When you push the heat OFF, the rpm will pick up sharply, particularly if you have been unconsciously easing the throttle forward to take care of the ice-caused power loss. If there is a lot of ice, it may cause a temporary roughness as the deluge goes through the engine.

A manifold pressure loss is the big indicator of ice for the airplane with a constant-speed propeller. The governor will mask the power drop (the blades flatten out to maintain the preset rpm). When heat is applied, the manifold pressure will drop further and will pick up *past* the manifold pressure at which the heat is finally pulled after the ice is cleared out and the heat is pushed off. Carburetor air temperature gauges or inlet air temperature gauges can be a great aid in preventing carb ice problems.

The use of full or partial heat depends on the airplane. Usually, for light trainers, it's all or nothing. For bigger airplanes, particularly those with carburetor air temperature gauges, partial heat is fine. Some of the bigger systems can cut down power by nearly 20% when on full heat.

Use of heat while taxiing can be bad. In most cases the carburetor heat system is taking in unfiltered air; and dust, sand, and other foreign material can be sent through the engine.

If the air scoop becomes iced over, the alternate air system can save the day (Fig. 7-13).

The warm air, being less dense than the outside air, causes some loss in power, but that is much better than a total power loss. Carburetor heat tends to richen the mixture, so further leaning may be required during its use. Naturally, the *Pilot's Operating Handbook* or equivalent information will take precedent for a particular airplane.

STRUCTURAL ICING. The air scoop icing situation just mentioned occurs when structural icing is the big problem. The windshield, wings, empennage, props, antennas, etc. will also be gaining weight and adding drag.

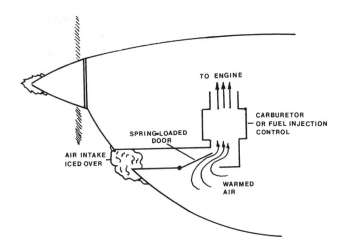

Fig. 7-13. Engine suction opens the spring-loaded door and allows the warm air from the engine compartment to enter the carburetor. Alternate air (or its equivalent) may be manually selected also. For some airplanes, this may result in a 10% loss of power at full throttle.

In most cases the weight of the added ice will be a comparatively minor factor—the drag increase, thrust decrease (for prop icing), and lift decrease are the factors that cause the big problems.

Structural icing is broken down into two main types (but they may be mixed at any particular time):

Rime ice—This is a milky granular deposit of ice with a rough surface. It's formed by instantaneous freezing of *small* supercooled water droplets as the airplane encounters them. Rime ice contains trapped air that contributes to its appearance and brittleness. Rime ice forms on leading edges and protrudes forward as a sharp nose. It is more easily removed than clear ice but spoils the airflow more because of its roughness. Rime ice is most often found in stratus clouds but may also be present in cumulus buildups at temperatures below −10°C. Rime ice is somewhat similar in appearance to the thick frost in the ice compartment of an older type of home refrigerator but is rougher.

Clear ice—You've seen this type of ice in "ice storms" (freezing rain). It's clear, solid, and very hard to remove. Clear ice is the result of large droplets and comparatively slow freezing. It is normally smoother than rime ice, unless solid precipitation (snow, sleet, or small hail) is trapped in it—this results in an airflow spoiling, hard-to-remove combination.

The accretion rate of structural ice depends primarily on (1) the amount of liquid water, (2) the drop size, (3) the airspeed, and (4) the size and shape of the airfoil. If you fly into an area of icing, it would be well to remember that, up to about 400 knots, ice collection increases with speed. Above this, frictional heating of the skin tends to lessen the chances of the ice sticking.

The effects of icing on the airplane are all bad. Lift (for a given angle of attack) decreases, thrust falls off, drag and weight increase. The stall speed rises sharply.

If your airplane has a stabilator, you should be aware of the possibility that the airflow disturbance and effects of the weight of ice on the leading edge could cause you to over-control at low speeds (it depends on how closely balanced the flying tail is in the clean condition). This should be something to consider if you still have ice on the airplane during the approach.

For more and up-to-date information, refer to the book *In-Flight Icing, Second Edition* by Porter J. Perkins and William J. Rieke of the NASA Glenn Research Center at Cleveland, Ohio. This book is based on a number of actual tests of icing clouds and aircraft performance (Sporty's $9.95).

There are videos from the same NASA source also available from Sporty's:

Tailplane Icing—This shoots down some previous theories about this phenomenon ($5.00).

Icing for Regional & Corporate Pilots—If you plan to fly for fun or profit in hard IFR, this video is a great help ($5.00). (The prices may change.)

The tail may be the more critical structure in heavy icing conditions.

DEICING AND ANTI-ICING SYSTEMS. Ice on the wings and tail can be removed by pneumatic deicer "boots," heat, or chemical fluid being continually "oozed out" through orifices in the leading edge. The deicer boot is the most popular. It expands in sections, and the ice is broken up to be blown away in the airstream. In heavy icing conditions, they may have to be operated continuously. The pneumatic boot system normally operates through the vacuum or pressure pump system, and "all-weather" twins usually have a pump on each engine, each capable of carrying the deicer load *plus* that required for the pressure- or vacuum-driven instruments. The term "all-weather" is not a good one, since some weather is too severe to be safely penetrated.

The boot system usually has a timer that inflates and deflates the boot sections when the pilot actuates the sequence. The deicer boots come in spanwise tube installations, as shown by Figure 7-14.

During your training, or later when you are flying that deicer-equipped airplane, climb to altitude VFR and test the stall characteristics of the airplane with the *deicers working* to check the possibility of landing in that condition if necessary. Your airplane may have a placard or warning against landing with the deicer boots working, and you must follow this. Other airplanes note that the stall speed is increased. It's also likely that ice remaining on the wing during the landing will be much more disturbing to the flight characteristics than the operating boots, but check any limitations for your airplane.

The other method of clearing ice from the wings is to circulate hot air from the exhaust inside the wing structure so that it is warm enough to prevent freezing on the leading

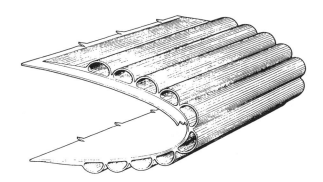

Fig. 7-14. Cross section of an inflated deicer boot. (B.F. Goodrich)

edge. The disadvantages of this system are that a considerable amount of power is used for the heat, and the thawing ice may slide rearward and refreeze on the unheated part of the structure. The heating of the boundary layer (the layer of air next to the wing surface) causes it to become more unstable, with possible slight changes in stall characteristics, but this is considered to be a very minor problem.

There are commercial products available that are designed to decrease the holding power of ice. Some are used on the bare (or painted) wing, and others are used on the boots to decrease ice adhesion and aid in the breakaway process.

For fighting propeller icing, there are two main methods: (1) fluid anti-icing and (2) electric deicing. The fluid (an alcohol mixture) is thrown out along the blades by centrifugal force and is most effective if the procedure is initiated *before* ice starts accumulating. The propeller blades may have rubber "feed shoes" to direct the fluid in the most effective direction. Fluid is used as necessary to keep the blades "wet."

If the other parts of the airplane are beginning to pick up ice, you can expect that the prop(s) is also getting its share. The anti-icing (fluid) systems have recommendations as to the procedure to be used. The amount of fluid available is limited but will last long enough to cover most icing situations if conserved.

Because of the propeller's faster speed and higher ice-collection efficiency (due to the small leading-edge radius of the blade), icing may occur on the propeller before it becomes apparent on other aircraft surfaces. That being the case, you should consider turning on the prop deicer before entering icing conditions or as soon as icing is evident. Turning on the deicers early will avoid shedding large ice particles that can impact on the fuselage of most twin-engine airplanes. (Such impacting will never fail to get your attention, and the results may be seen in the form of dents on the side of the fuselage in line with the prop blades.)

Icing can cause problems on antennas and in extreme conditions may cause them to be carried away. This is somewhat disconcerting particularly if, for instance, both VOR receivers are using that one antenna.

Windshield icing can sometimes be more of a menace than ice on other parts of the plane. The small storm pane in the side window has been a great aid for more than one pilot in landing the airplane with a load of windshield ice. Freezing rain is particularly bad in this regard because the ice film may be forming fast and thick and can get well ahead of the windshield defroster. Do whatever your *Pilot's Operating Handbook* says to get the maximum defrosting effect. You may have to deflect some of the cabin heat to get added defrost heat. It's better to be uncomfortable and be able to see out than vice versa.

Icing of the pitot tube and static vent can be a problem. If you expect icing or if it's starting, use the pitot heat. Pitot heat is a severe drain on the electrical system, so its use should be tempered with judgment if communications and navigation equipment are already using large electrical loads. Check the volt-ammeter when the heat is turned on—its effect will be indicated. See Figure 2-32.

Check back in Chapter 2 now for a review of alternate static system effects on the airspeed and altimeter indications and be prepared to use that system as necessary in icing conditions.

The *AIM* has some good advice on icing and particularly on reporting icing conditions (PIREPs) in flight:

1. *Trace*—Ice becomes perceptible. The rate of accumulation is slightly higher than the rate of sublimation. It is not hazardous even though deicing/anti-icing equipment is not utilized unless encountered for an extended period of time (over 1 hr).

2. *Light*—The rate of accumulation may create a problem if flight is prolonged in this environment (over 1 hr). Occasional use of deicing/anti-icing equipment removes/prevents accumulation. It does not present a problem if the deicing/anti-icing equipment is used.

3. *Moderate*—The rate of accumulation is such that short encounters become potentially hazardous and use of deicing/anti-icing equipment or flight diversion is necessary.

4. *Severe*—The rate of accumulation is such that deicing/anti-icing equipment fails to reduce or control the hazard. Immediate flight diversion is necessary.

There will be more about PIREPs later in the chapter.

The windshield may frost over on high-performance airplanes when a fast letdown is made from subfreezing temperatures to warm moist air. The surface of the windshield and airframe is still cold enough so that the moist air freezes on contact.

You may go to your airplane after it has been tied out for some time and find that it's covered with ice. Obviously, hot water will soon freeze, and you'd be back where you started, or worse, if you poured it on the plane. One thing sometimes forgotten by pilots who move an icy plane into a heated hangar is that the water from the melting ice can collect in control surface hinges, landing gear assemblies, and other vital spots. When the plane is moved back out into the freezing temperature, the water refreezes, and problems can result. Wipe the water out of such places and make sure they are dry before moving the plane out of the hangar. Along this same line, if you take off through puddles or slush and the temperature is near freezing, leave the gear down longer after takeoff to allow the airflow to blow off most of the moisture. Otherwise, if a large amount of water is collected on the gear and this freezes, it might cause extension problems later. In some cases, you may want to cycle the gear a time or two before leaving it up. Your actions in this case will depend on whether other factors (ceiling, visibility, and obstructions) will allow cycling without risking possible loss of control.

It was mentioned that accretion of ice on a stabilator in flight could cause problems. There have been incidents of control flutter and crashes immediately after takeoff caused by ice that accumulated inside or on the surfaces while the airplane was sitting on the ramp (maybe in freezing rain) or had been moved out of a heated hangar with water on (or in) the surfaces. Flutter occurred and the control surfaces were destroyed with a resulting loss of control on *climb-out*.

Frost—This phenomenon was mentioned earlier as occurring on the windshield in flight, but an airplane left out overnight will sometimes be covered with frost. For some reason, pilots tend to ignore the effects of frost on takeoff performance, and more than one accident has been caused by an almost paper-thin coating of frost on the airplane. Frost of this type forms during clear cold nights, so you're most likely to encounter it before early morning VFR flights; nevertheless, it's always something to consider. As the weather books say, frost sublimates (changes directly from a solid to a gas) quickly in warmer air and in motion, but you may have flown through the airport fence before this occurs. Don't underrate the effects of even a thin layer of frost on the airplane.

■ Hazards on Approach and/or Landing

MICROBURSTS *(Aeronautical Information Manual)*. Relatively recent meteorological studies have confirmed the existence of microburst phenomena. Microbursts are small-scale intense downdrafts that, on reaching the surface, spread outward in all directions from the downdraft center. This causes the presence of both vertical and horizontal wind shears that can be extremely hazardous to all types and categories of aircraft, especially at low altitudes. Due to their small size, short life span, and the fact that they can occur over areas without surface precipitation, microbursts are not easily detectable when using conventional weather radar or wind shear alert systems.

Parent clouds producing microburst activity can be any of the low- or middle-layer convective cloud types. Note, however, that microbursts commonly occur within the heavy-rain portion of thunderstorms and in much weaker, benign-appearing convective cells that have little or no precipitation reaching the ground. Figure 7-15 shows a microburst evolution and an encounter during takeoff.

The life cycle of a microburst as it descends in a convective rain shaft is seen in Figure 7-15A. An important consideration for pilots is the fact that the microburst intensifies for about 5 min after it strikes the ground.

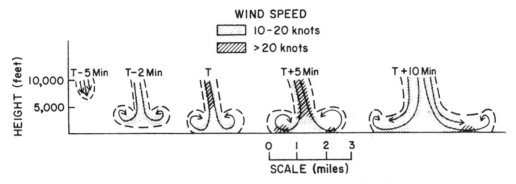

A Vertical cross section of the evolution of a microburst wind field. T is the time of initial divergence at the surface. The shading refers to the vector wind speeds. Figure adapted from Wilson et al., 1984, Microburst Wind Structure and Evaluation of Doppler Radar for Wind Shear Detection, DOT/FAA Report No. DOT/FAA/PM-84/29, National Technical Information Service, Springfield, VA 37 pp.

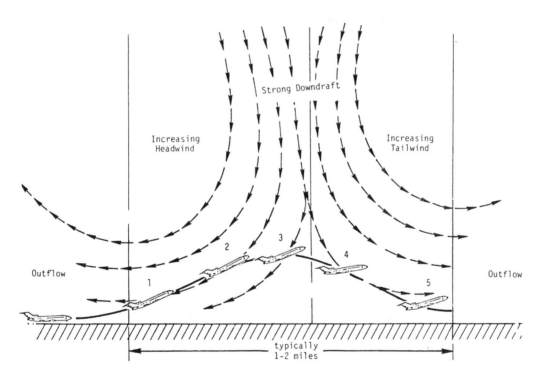

B A microburst encounter during takeoff. The airplane first encounters a headwind and experiences increasing performance (1), this is followed in short succession by a decreasing headwind component (2), a downdraft (3), and finally a strong tailwind (4), where 2 through 5 all result in decreasing performance of the airplane. Position (5) represents an extreme situation just prior to impact. Figure courtesy of Walter Frost, FWG Associates, Inc., Tullahoma, Tennessee.

Fig. 7-15. Microburst history **(A)** and takeoff flight profile **(B)** in an extreme situation. *(Aeronautical Information Manual and FWG Associates, Tullahoma, Tenn.)*

Characteristics of microbursts include:

Size—The microburst downdraft is typically less than 1 mi in diameter as it descends from the cloud base to about 1000–3000 ft above the ground. In the transition zone near the ground, the downdraft changes to a horizontal outflow that can extend to approximately 2½ mi in diameter.

Intensity—The downdrafts can be as strong as 6000 fpm. Horizontal winds near the surface can be as strong as 45 knots, resulting in a 90-knot shear (headwind to tailwind change for a traversing aircraft) across the microburst. These strong horizontal winds occur within a few hundred feet of the ground.

Visual signs—Microbursts can be found almost anywhere that there is convective activity. They may be embedded in heavy rain associated with a thunderstorm or in light rain in benign-appearing virga. When there is little or no precipitation at the surface accompanying the microburst, a ring of blowing dust may be the only visual clue of its existence.

Duration—An individual microburst will seldom last longer than 15 min from the time it strikes the ground until dissipation. The horizontal winds continue to increase during the first 5 min, with the maximum-intensity winds lasting approximately 2–4 min. Sometimes microbursts are concentrated into a line structure, and under these conditions activity may continue for as long as an hour. Once microburst activity starts, multiple microbursts in the same general area are not uncommon and should be expected.

Microburst wind shear may create a severe hazard for aircraft within 1000 ft of the ground, particularly during the approach to landing and landing and takeoff phases. The impact of a microburst on aircraft that have the unfortunate experience of penetrating one is characterized in Figure 7-15B. The aircraft may encounter a headwind (performance-increasing), followed by a downdraft and tailwind (both performance-decreasing), possibly resulting in terrain impact.

Pilots should heed wind shear PIREPs, since a previous pilot's encounter with a microburst may be the only indication received. However, since the wind shear intensifies rapidly in its early stages, a PIREP may not indicate the current severity of a microburst. Flight in the vicinity of suspected or reported microburst activity should always be avoided. If a pilot encounters one, a wind shear PIREP should be made at once.

LOW-LEVEL WIND SHEAR. This phenomenon has caused fatal crashes over the years and is particularly hazardous on approach because the airplane is in (usually) its dirtiest configuration, on low power, and descending. Low-level wind shear alert systems (LLWAS) have been established at selected airports around the United States. The system compares winds measured by sensors around the periphery of the airport, with the wind measured at a center field location. If the difference becomes excessive, a thunderstorm or thunderstorm gust front is probable. In this situation the tower controller will provide an advisory of the situation to arriving and departing aircraft, including the center field plus the remote site location and wind. The sensors are not always associated with specific runways, so descriptions of the remote sites are based on the eight-point compass system.

An airport equipped with LLWAS has this information in the *Airport/Facility Directory* under "Weather Data Sources" (Fig. 7-16).

BRAKING ACTION. It goes without saying that, if you are on an IFR flight plan, it's likely that you will be flying in

---

HUNTSVILLE
HUNTSVILLE INTL–CARL T JONES FLD   (HSV)   9 SW   UTC–6(–5DT)   **ATLANTA**
        Ń34°38.42′ W86°46.39′   **H–4H, L–14H**
        630   B   S4   **FUEL** 100LL, JET A   OX 1, 2, 3, 4   LRA   ARFF Index C   **IAP**
        RWY 18L–36R: H10000X150 (ASPH–GRVD)   S–90, D–200, DT–350, DDT–850   HIRL
            RWY 18L: MALSR. PAPI(P4R)—GA 3.0° TCH 70′. Pole.
            RWY 36R: REIL. VASI(V4L)—GA 3.0° TCH 55′. Thld dsplcd 200′. Trees. Rgt tfc.
        RWY 18R–36L: H8000X150 (ASPH–GRVD)   S–90, D–200, DT–350, DDT–850   HIRL   CL
            RWY 18R: ALSF2. TDZL. Rgt tfc.   **RWY 36L:** MALSR
        RUNWAY DECLARED DISTANCE INFORMATION
            RWY 18L: TORA–10000   TODA–10000   ASDA–9800   LDA–9800
            RWY 36R: TORA–10000   TODA–10000   ASDA–9800   LDA–9800
        AIRPORT REMARKS: Attended continuously. Migratory birds wild life refuge S and W of arpt. Twy X and Twy 'ONAN'
            CLOSED indefinitely. Approximately 300 ft of Twy J south of the terminal; southeast portion of Twy G where it
            enters the air carrier apron; and approximately 75 ft of Twy E between Twys E5 and E6 are not visible from the
            twr. Intersection of Twy J and svc road is uncontrolled. When twr clsd ACTIVATE MALSR Rwys 18L and 36L; REIL
            Rwy 36R and PAPI Rwy 18L—CTAF. VASI Rwy 36R opr continuously. 24 hr PPR for unscheduled air carrier ops
            with more than 30 passenger seats call arpt manager 205–772–9395 extension 265. Flight Notification Service
            (ADCUS) available.
———   **WEATHER DATA SOURCES:** ASOS (205) 772–8074. LLWAS.
        COMMUNICATIONS: CTAF 127.6   **ATIS** 121.25   **UNICOM** 122.95
            ANNISTON FSS (ANB) TF 1–800–WX–BRIEF. NOTAM FILE HSV.
            RCO 122.2 (ANNISTON FSS)
    Ⓡ **APP CON** 125.6 (360°–179°) 118.05 (180°–359°)118.75 Opr 1200–0559Z‡ Mon–Fri; 1200Z‡ Sat thru 0559Z‡
            Sun: other times ctc   **MEMPHIS CENTER APP CON** 120.8
            TOWER 127.6 (1200–0559Z‡ Tue–Fri; 1200Z‡ Sat thru 0559Z‡ Mon)   **GND CON** 121.9   **CLNC DEL** 120.35
    Ⓡ **DEP CON** 125.6 (359°–179°) 118.05 (180°–358°) 120.35 Opr 1200–0559Z‡ Mon–Fri; 1200Z‡ Sat thru 0559Z‡
            Sun: other times ctc   **MEMPHIS CENTER DEP CON** 120.8
        AIRSPACE: CLASS C svc Mon–Fri 1200–0559Z‡; Sat 1200Z‡ thru Sun 0559Z‡ ctc **APP CON** other times CLASS E.
        RADIO AIDS TO NAVIGATION: NOTAM FILE ANB
            DECATUR (L) VORW/DME 112.8   DCU   Chan 75   N34°38.90′ W86°56.37′   094° 8.3 NM to fld. 590/01W.
            CAPSHAW NDB (MHW) 350   CWH   N34°46.42′ W86°46.74′   179° 8 NM to fld. NOTAM FILE HSV.
            ILS 109.3   I–HSV   Rwy 18R.   (Unmonitored when twr clsd).
            ILS 108.5   I–ELL   Rwy 36L.   (Unmonitored when twr clsd).
            ILS 111.9   I–TVN   Rwy 18L.   (Unmonitored when twr clsd).
            ASR (Mon–Fri 1200–0559Z‡, Sat 1200Z‡ thru Sun 0559Z‡)

Fig. 7-16. Huntsville-Madison County (Alabama) Airport data showing the availability of a low-level wind shear alert system. *(Airport/Facility Directory)*

precipitation and that it is likely to be present at either the departure or arrival airports or both.

You will be concerned about braking action at the departure airport because of the possibility of an abort, and braking action certainly will affect the accelerate and stop distance (also snow and slush can be major factors in the takeoff run distance required). If you've filed IFR from a shorter strip, such factors could be decisive for a safe take-off. Slush on the landing gear could freeze after retraction and en route, as noted earlier, causing a possible problem of extension on the instrument approach. *(That's* what you need all right; the destination is at minimums, you barely have enough fuel to make the alternate legally, and you find that the gear won't extend.)

One suggestion for VFR flying after taking off through slush is to cycle the gear a couple of times or leave it down long enough to let the airstream clear it. Either one of these actions could be interesting in single-pilot conditions where the airplane climbs into IFR conditions at a low altitude. There could be a chance of loss of control if you're distracted too long.

Your problem may be that of braking effectiveness after breaking out and landing and also if you are making an approach and landing at an airport with shorter runways (and no tower) and, hence, have no information on braking action unless Unicom can give it. In this case, aerodynamic braking (drag) will be a greater factor in slowing up than it would be on dry concrete runways. Use it (hold up the nose as long as safely feasible after touchdown) and avoid getting on the brakes immediately after the wheels touch (assuming a direct headwind).

ATC will furnish the quality of braking action received from pilots or the airport management when available. The braking action is described as *good, fair, poor, nil,* or a combination of those terms. If you give a braking action report, talk in terms of portions of the runway (first third, last half, etc.).

When tower controllers have received runway braking action reports citing *poor* or *nil* or whenever weather conditions are conducive to deteriorating or rapidly changing braking conditions, the Automatic Terminal Information Service will broadcast the statement, "Braking action advisories are in effect."

When these advisories are in effect. ATC will issue the latest braking action report to each arriving and departing aircraft. If you suspect that braking action might be bad or worsening, you should request such information if the controllers don't mention it. You should be prepared to give a report of braking effectiveness or runway condition to the controllers after landing.

HYDROPLANING. You coped with icing, turbulence, a couple of holding delays and are tired and glad that the flight is over now that you're landing. You can relax at last. *Not at all.* There was heavy rain just before your landing, and there's water standing on the runway, which might cause hydroplaning. *Hydroplaning* is broken down into three basic types:

Dynamic—In total dynamic hydroplaning, water standing on the runway exerts pressure between the tires and the runway. The tires are not in contact with the runway surface itself. Braking is *nil,* and a crosswind can make directional control nonexistent. So, braking *and* control are a problem. The thumb rule for predicting the minimum dynamic hydroplaning speed (knots) is $8.6\sqrt{\text{tire pressure (psi)}}$. At a tire pressure of 36 psi, the expected minimum dynamic hydroplaning speed is 52 knots (rounded off, or $8.6 \times 6 = 51.6$ knots). In other words, *above* this speed you may encounter dynamic hydroplaning if conditions are right. Figure 7-17 shows a graphical representation.

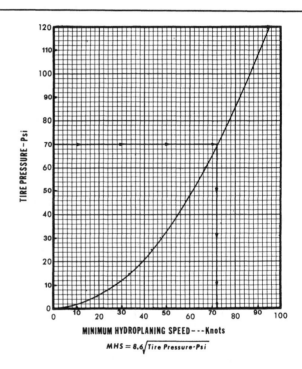

Fig. 7-17. Tire pressure versus minimum hydroplaning speed (72 K at 70 psi). *(Advanced Pilot's Flight Manual)*

Viscous hydroplaning—Painted runway areas or rubber deposits may set up this type of hydroplaning because the tire can't fully displace the moisture *film.* This effect can be felt in a car when your car slips momentarily as you cross an extra thickly painted highway center line covered with rain or dew. *This can occur at a much lower speed than dynamic hydroplaning.*

Reverted rubber hydroplaning—Applying brakes *immediately* after touchdown can cause this problem. (Remember that brakes are not effective immediately after touchdown even on dry concrete.) The airplane starts dynamic hydroplaning because the brakes are locked, and as it slows, the locked tires heat up because of added friction. A layer of steam occurs between the tires and the runway, and the rubber melts. This prevents water dispersal because the braking wheel tires are riding on a layer of steam and molten rubber. This is the worst of the hydroplane variations because it can happen down to zero speed. *(Don't* lock the brakes.)

Grooved runways can cut down the hydroplaning effect, but you should be ready for it anytime when taking off or landing on a wet runway. Think of braking and/or directional control problems and avoid excessive use of rudder or brakes. Reversing thrust under hydroplaning conditions in a crosswind can be an added hazard. For further reading see: (1) *ATP: Airline Transport Pilot,* third edition, K.T. Boyd. Iowa State University Press. 1988. (2) "You vs. Hydroplaning" (article), *Aerospace Safety,* Norton AFB, Calif.

WEATHER SERVICES

The final decision whether to go is up to you, but there is a lot of information available to help you make up your mind. Some pilots, when checking the weather, prefer to look at the weather maps first and *then* the sequence reports and forecasts. Others may reverse the order of checking. You can set up the order that's best for you, but check the different types of information against each other. Although flipping a coin or the twinges of rheumatism and corns may work pretty well for some endeavors, it's best to be more scientific in your approach to weather for instrument flying.

The following look at weather service information sources is based on what a pilot would check in planning an IFR flight from Memphis to Nashville with an estimated departure time of 2040Z. The charts, forecasts, and weather reports, except as indicated, are actual data as issued by the National Weather Service on the 18th of the month (January) for the time range indicated. Some of the charts *(which were used in an FSS)* had some wear and tear plus added notes and markings, so they have been recopied for clarity. Look at the actual weather reports as given and compare them with *what the various forecasts said would be happening at that time.*

■ Weather Charts

SURFACE ANALYSIS CHART. The surface analysis chart is also called a surface weather map and is transmitted every 3 hr in the 48-state portion of the United States.

The valid time indicated on the map is that of the plotted observations. The date-time group—Coordinated Universal Time (UTC) or Zulu time—tells when conditions plotted on the map were occurring.

The solid-line isobars are spaced at 4-millibar (mb) intervals; but if the pressure gradient is weak, dashed isobars are put at 2-mb intervals to better define the system. A "20" is 1020.0 mb, and a "96" stands for 996.0 mb. The Highs and Lows have a two-digit underlined number ("32" means that the pressure at the center is 1032 mb, etc.). In color presentations, Highs are blue and Lows are red. Figure 7-2 shows the frontal presentation symbols for black and white and color.

The Weather Service has a three-digit number on the map by the frontal systems to show type, intensities, and character of the front. Look in Figure 7-18 at the cold front running southward through Texas with the designation "450." It's a cold front at the surface (4), with moderate, little, or no change (5), and the character of the front has no specification (0). The warm front lying across the southeastern states has a notation "220," indicating that it is a warm front at the surface (2), it is weak, with little or no change (2), and the character of the front has no specification (0). The codes are available in the *Aviation Weather Service* (AC 00-45E), so don't try to memorize them.

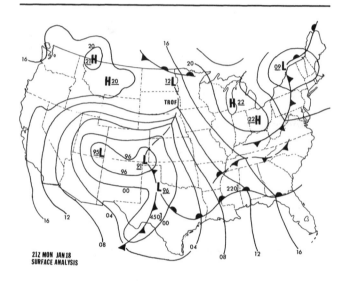

Fig. 7-18. A redrawn surface analysis for 2100Z on the 18th of the month for the same time period as the other data in this chapter.

As a pilot, you're more interested in using the surface analysis chart as a pictorial representation of the weather rather than in reading the detailed information at each station (although the temperature, dewpoint, and sky coverage would be of interest for a pattern). Since the map only comes out every 3 hr, the latest hourly sequence report would give more up-to- date information on various stations.

Figure 7-18 is a redrawn surface analysis chart of 2100Z on the 18th of the month. The actual map had too much detail for useful reduction to page size for this book, so the station models were deleted. (The station model is a group of figures at the various reporting stations showing wind, sky cover, temperatures, and other information of more value to meteorologists than pilots, so it won't be covered.)

The surface analysis chart gives a quick overall look at the systems you'll be coping with, and they're located at the positions where they were at the valid time (2100Z here).

Looking again at Figure 7-18, you can see that this surface analysis chart has numerous frontal systems, including a trough running down from eastern North Dakota to the panhandle of Oklahoma. The pressure values are indicated by the

Highs and Lows and are underlined. For instance, the Low just north of New York State has a pressure of 1009 mb.

WEATHER DEPICTION CHART. Figure 7-19 is an example of a weather depiction chart. Because the weather (ceilings, visibilities, and other factors) as given for each station may be well out of date (or time), you should check the hourly reports for that information. The best use of this chart is to give you a *general* look at the areas of low ceilings and visibilities. This is an important factor if conditions go below minimums at the destination and alternate or if you lose total electric power and have to fly to an area to let down in MVFR or VFR conditions. Admittedly, the odds are long against such problems, particularly the last one, but still you should know that, if you are flying in the IFR area of Figure 7-19, turning north or south in the conditions shown here would *not* be the quickest way to better weather.

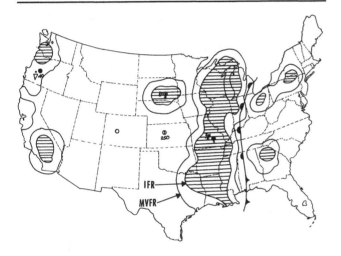

Fig. 7-19. A weather depiction chart. Note that the areas of less than 1000 ft *and/or* 3 SM (IFR) are cross-hatched. Areas of marginal VFR (MVFR-ceiling 1000–3000 ft and/or visibility 3–5 SM) are contoured without shading. VFR areas have ceilings greater than 3000 ft and visibilities greater than 5 mi and are not contoured.

RADAR SUMMARY CHART. Figure 7-20 is part of an actual radar summary chart. At the bottom of the full chart, the day of the week, time (Zulu), day of the month, and radar summary are indicated.

The shaded areas show radar echo areas, and the contours outline intensities. In north-central Alabama the intensities are shown building toward the center of the area with tops at 32,000 (320). Bases are noted by a bar *over* the height value in hundreds. Note also that there is a squall line in that area, as indicated by the solid line. The direction and velocities of movement of areas and lines are shown (that Alabama group is moving east-southeast at 20 knots). Solid areas are indicated by "SLD."

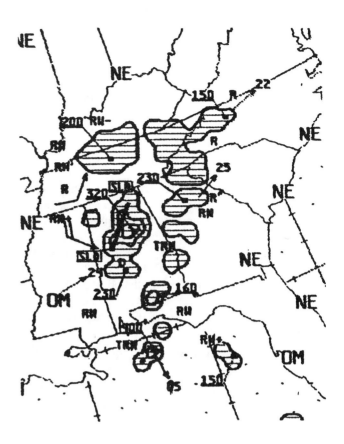

Fig. 7-20. A radar summary chart.

There is a rain shower area of increasing intensity (RW +) south of the Florida panhandle, with tops at 15,000 ft ASL. Rain showers of decreasing intensity are indicated. There is an area of thunderstorms and rain showers (TRW) south of Pensacola moving south (arrow) at 5 knots (05).

NE means "no echoes" and OM indicates that a station is out for maintenance.

There is an area with rain (R) and rain showers (RW) (tops at 23,000 ft) moving northeast at 25 knots (arrow) in the Atlanta area.

The radar summary chart is valuable to you as an instrument pilot for showing intensities, movements, and tops of areas of significant precipitation. Remember that these areas may have changed in size, position, and intensities by the time you get there.

Figure 7-21 contains sample radar reports (RAREPs) giving thunderstorms and precipitation areas in printed form. Looking at A, you see a report from Athens, Ga, that was observed at 1725Z; B is from Albany, N.Y. at 1630Z:

A. *Athens*—There is an area of four-tenths coverage of rain showers (RW) with no change in intensity located by the points *from* the station of 254° (True), 135 NM, 171°, 120 NM. It is on a line between those points and is an area 35 NM wide. Thunderstorm cells are moving from 250° at 35 knots. The maximum top is 17,000 ft at 238°, 107 NM from the station. All bearings are from True

A   AHN 1725 AREA 4RW/NC ·254/135 171/12Ø 35W C2535 MT 17Ø AT 238/1Ø7
   QI22111 RL122=

B   ALB 163Ø AREA RZR-/+ 37/11Ø 11Ø/1Ø5 18Ø/1Ø5 277/7Ø A2315 MT U15Ø
   IM1 JM111 KM121 LL112111 MK1111111 NK12221 OK11222 PO1=

Fig. 7-21. Radar reports.

North. The bottom line (QI22111 RL122 =) is the digital section used for preparing radar summaries.

B. *Albany*—This report indicates that there is an area of rain and light freezing rain (RZR−) of heavy intensity defined by the points from the radar station 037°, 110 NM, 110°, 105 NM, 180°, 105 NM, 277°, 70 NM, and back to the origin of 137°, 110 NM. The *area* (A) is moving from 230° at 15 knots. Maximum top is 15,000 ft and the top is uniform (U).

SIGNIFICANT WEATHER PROGNOSTICS. The low-level prognostic chart has four panels, as shown by Figure 7-22. The top panels (1 and 2) are 12- and 24-hr significant weather progs from the surface to 400 mb (24,000 ft). The lower charts (3 and 4) are 12- and 24-hr surface progs. The charts show the conditions as they are forecast to be at the valid time of the chart.

The dashed lines with accompanying numbers indicate the freezing levels (MSL) at 4000-ft intervals (40, 80, 120), and the surface freezing level is indicated by a dotted line.

Turbulence areas are outlined by dashed lines, and symbols indicate the intensity. There's a turbulent area extending into the central United States from Canada, as indicated by the dashed line (the Ts were added by the writer). The symbol ‿ indicates that it is moderate and from the surface to 18,000 MSL. Severe turbulence would be indicated by another inverted V over the center of the symbol ‿. The midwestern United States is almost covered by a moderately turbulent area that extends upward from 10,000 MSL (Panel 2).

When you first look at a significant weather prog, it will appear to be a jumble of solid and dashed lines and numbers; but as you spend a little more time with a particular chart, things begin to take shape. Look for each feature (ceiling and visibility or turbulence or freezing) alone to see its significance.

Figure 7-23 gives the symbols and meanings used on the significant weather progs.

On Panel 4 (Fig. 7-22) the shaded precipitation areas indicate the presence of continuous snow (A), continuous rain (B), and continuous drizzle (C); D indicates a rain shower area. (See Fig. 7-23 again.)

The two numbers with each High or Low are the pressure values. On Panel 3 of Figure 7-22 the High at the junction of Oklahoma, Kansas, Texas, Colorado, and New Mexico has a pressure of 1020 mb and is stationary. The

Low off the coast of South Carolina is 1012 mb and moving north at 10 knots (arrow).

OTHER CHARTS

High-level significant weather progs—Charts encompassing airspace from 400 to 70 mb (above 24,000–60,000 feet), including turbulence and cirriform and cumulonimbus clouds. (See Fig. 14-3.)

International flights—Significant weather prog charts are available for international operations if you think you might overshoot your U.S. destination.

Winds and temperatures aloft—Winds aloft charts, forecast and observed, are transmitted by facsimile. The forecast winds aloft charts also contain forecast temperatures for that altitude or flight level. Figure 7-24 shows a few sample stations and aids to deciphering the wind direction and velocity.

Other charts are available for freezing levels, stability, severe weather outlook (Fig. 14-5), constant pressure and constant pressure prognostics, and tropopause and wind shear charts. Satellite pictures of U.S. weather are available from the facsimile machine, but you may have to dig for them because they aren't always out on display.

Charts are the best way to get an overall look at the situation, but sequence reports, terminal forecasts, and other printed matter are the sources for detailed information.

■ **Hourly Reports.** The METAR (think of *MET*eorological *A*viation *R*eport) is a surface weather observation and, as such, gives the local conditions at the time of observation. Fig. 7-25 shows abbreviations used for METARs and TAFs (*T*erminal *A*viation *F*orecasts to be discussed later).

Fig. 7-26 (page 166) shows actual hourly reports for 5 hr before your departure at 2040Z from Memphis (KMEM) to Nashville (KBNA). Note that Chattanooga, TN (KCHA), the original alternate, is included and Huntsville, AL (KHSV), is put into your planning loop as the Chattanooga weather starts looking worse as an alternate. (All 3-letter identifiers for the contiguous states are preceded by "K.")

Actual weather reports start at 1600Z on the 18th of the month and in the following discussion, these reports will be compared to actual terminal forecasts (TAFs) for the same airports and time periods.

Reports for 1600Z weather (line by line):

Memphis (KMEM)—In each case, the hourly report will start with either METAR (routine report) or SPECI

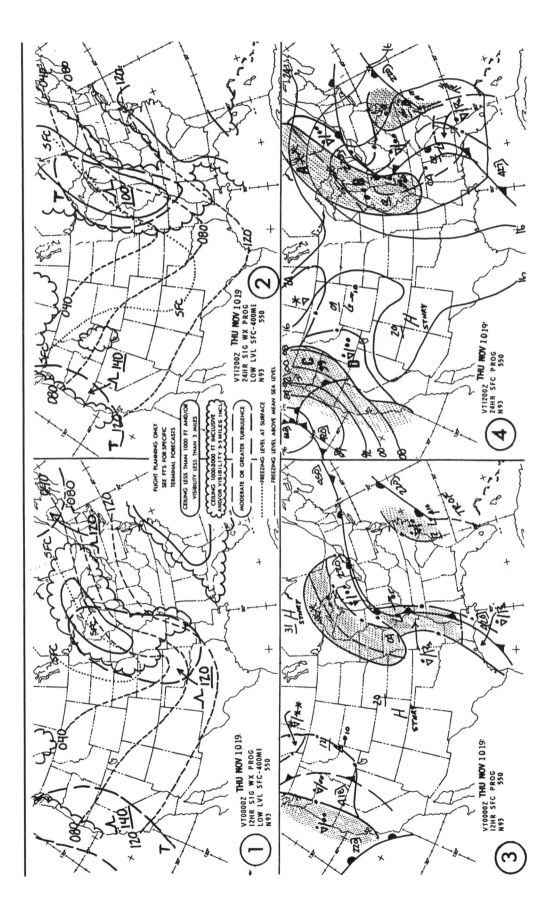

Fig. 7-22. Low-level significant weather prognostic charts. Note that these are examples only and are not valid at the time and date of the sample trip. (*Aviation Weather Services*)

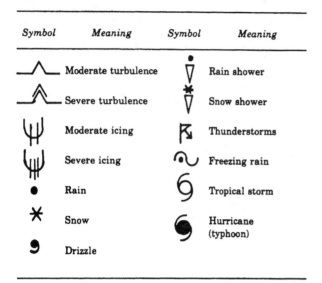

Symbol	Meaning	Symbol	Meaning
⌃ (line)	Moderate turbulence	▽ with dot	Rain shower
⌃⌃ (line)	Severe turbulence	▽ with star	Snow shower
⍦	Moderate icing	⏁	Thunderstorms
⍦⍦	Severe icing	∿	Freezing rain
●	Rain	⊙	Tropical storm
✱	Snow	🌀	Hurricane (typhoon)
9	Drizzle		

NOTE: Character of stable precipitation is the manner in which it occurs. It may be intermittent or continuous. A single symbol denotes intermittent and a pair of symbols denotes continuous.

Examples

Intermittent	Continuous	
●	● ●	Rain
9	9 9	Drizzle
✱	✱ ✱	Snow

Fig. 7-23. Symbols and meanings for the prog charts. *(Aviation Weather Services)*

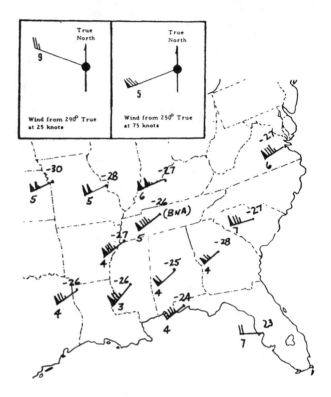

Fig. 7-24. Sample forecast winds aloft chart for a few stations at 28,000 ft. The temperature in °C is written in above each station. Each pennant is 50 knots, each full barb is 10 knots, and each half barb is 5 knots. The number by the barbs helps pin down the exact direction; for instance you see that the wind is from the west-southwest at Nashville and the "5" indicates that it is from 250° true. The wind is 85 knots and the temperature is –26° at Nashville.

(special report). This METAR is issued at 1550Z on the 18th of the month (181550Z).

The wind is from 060° true at 8 knots (06008KT). The visibility is 4 statute miles (4SM) in mist (BR). [BR is an abbreviation for *brouillard,* French for "mist"; see Fig. 7-25.] If the visibility is less than 5/8 SM, the abbreviation for fog (FG) is used; if greater than 5/8 but not more than 6 SM, mist (BR) is used. There's an overcast at 700 ft (OVC007), temperature is 12°C, dewpoint is 11°C (12/11), and the altimeter setting is 30.01 inches of mercury (A3001). Remarks (RMK)—sea level pressure is 1016.3 (SLP163) hectoPascals, or millibars.

Nashville (KBNA)—Wind is from 100° at 6 knots (10006KT). Visibility is 1/2 SM (1/2SM). Runway visual range for runway (R) 02 left (L) is better than 6000 ft (R02L/P6000FT) in fog (FG). There's a broken layer at 500 ft (BKN005) and overcast at 2000 ft (OVC020). Temperature and dewpoint are 11°C each

(11/11), and the altimeter setting is 30.12 (A3012). Remarks (RMK)—sea level pressure is 1020.0 (SLP200) hectoPascals.

Chattanooga (KCHA)—This METAR is released on the 18th at 1549Z. The wind is from 080° true at 5 knots (08005KT), the visibility is 3/4 SM (3/4SM) with runway 20 having a visual range of 5500 ft (R20/5500FT) in mist (BR). The SCT000 indicates that there is a partial obscuration at the surface. There is overcast at 200 ft (OVC002). Both temperature and dewpoint are 7°C (07/07). The altimeter setting is 30.11 (A3011). Remarks (RMK)—mist (BR) was the cause of the partial obscuration (SCT000); the sea level pressure is 1019.7 hectoPascals (SLP197).

Nashville Specials (SPECI KBNA)—At 1605Z a special was issued when the visibility improved to 4 SM in mist (BR). At 1629Z the visibility improved to 5 SM with the height of the lower cloud layer dropping slightly from 2000 ft overcast to 1800 ft broken. Note a couple of other insignificant changes in wind and altimeter settings.

Abbreviations

AO1   Automated Observation without
       precipitation discriminator (rain/snow)
AO2   Automated Observation with
       precipitation discriminator (rain/snow)
AMD   Amended Forecast (TAF)
BECMG Becoming (expected between 2 digit
       beginning hour and 2 digit ending hour)
BKN   Broken 5-7 octas (eighths) cloud
       coverage
CLR   Clear at or below 12,000 feet
       (ASOS/AWOS report)
COR   Correction to the observation
FEW   >0-2 octas (eighths) cloud coverage
FM   From (4 digit beginning time in hours
       and minutes)
LDG   Landing
M   In temperature field means "minus" or
       below zero
M   In RVR listing indicates visibility less than
       lowest reportable sensor value
       (e g M0600)
NO   Not available (e g SLPNO, RVRNO)
NSW   No Significant Weather
       Note: NSW only indicates obstruction
       to visibility or precipitation previously
       noted has ended Low ceilings, wind
       shear, and other weather conditions
       may still exist
OVC   Overcast 8 octas (eighths) cloud
       coverage
P   In RVR indicates visibility greater than
       highest reportable sensor value
       (e g P6000FT)
P6SM   Visibility greater than 6 SM (TAF only)
PK WND Peak wind
PROB40 Probability 40 percent
R   Runway (used in RVR measurement)
RMK   Remark
RY/RWY Runway
SCT   Scattered 3-4 octas (eighths) cloud
       coverage
SKC   Sky Clear
SLP   Sea Level Pressure
       (e g , 1001 3 reported as 013)
SM   Statute mile(s)
SPECI Special Report
TEMPO Temporary changes expected (between
       2 digit beginning hour and 2 digit
       ending hour)
TKOF   Takeoff
T01760158, 10142, 20012 and 401120084
In Remarks—examples of temperature information

V   Varies (wind direction and RVR)
VC   Vicinity
VRB   Variable wind direction when
       speed is less than or equal to
       6 knots
VV   Vertical Visibility
       (Indefinite Ceiling)
WS   Wind shear (In TAFs, low level
       and not associated with
       convective activity)

Descriptors

BC   Patches
BL   Blowing
DR   Low Drifting
FZ   Supercooled/freezing
MI   Shallow
PR   Partial
SH   Showers
TS   Thunderstorm

Weather Phenomena

BR   Mist
DS   Dust Storm
DU   Widespread Dust
DZ   Drizzle
FC   Funnel Cloud
+FC   Tornado/Water Spout
FG   Fog
FU   Smoke
GR   Hail
GS   Small Hail/Snow Pellets
HZ   Haze
IC   Ice Crystals
PL   Ice Pellets
PO   Dust/Sand Whirls
PY   Spray
RA   Rain
SA   Sand
SG   Snow Grains
SN   Snow
SQ   Squall
SS   Sandstorm
UP   Unknown Precipitation
       (Automated Observations)
VA   Volcanic Ash

Cloud Types

CB   Cumulonimbus
TCU   Towering Cumulus

Intensity Values

-      Light
no sign Moderate
+   Heavy

Fig. 7-25. METAR and TAF abbreviations.

At 1629Z, the weather was improving and the trend is for more improvement. But the weather can deteriorate just as fast (or sometimes faster, it seems). As you'll see in the following hourly reports, Nashville will come back down slightly after improving, but it will be VFR; in fact, a later illustration will show the weather for Memphis, Nashville, and Huntsville during and after the flight (2100Z and 2200Z), so that you can see what happened *after* you departed Memphis.

Reports for 1700Z weather:

Memphis—A slight improvement in ceiling and visibility and the temperature and dewpoint have spread another 1°C.

Nashville—The ceiling has gone from 500 broken at 1600Z to broken at 1800 (BKN018) at 1700Z [see the 1629Z SPECI also].

Chattanooga—Still not good as an alternate, even if the visibility has improved from 3/4 SM to 1 SM. Remarks—there's a partial obscuration because of mist (RMK BR SCT000).

Huntsville—This is inserted here because, after checking Chattanooga, KHSV is picked as a reasonable alternate with 3 SM in mist and overcast at 600 ft (3SM BR OVC006).

Nashville Special—At 1725Z, KBNA has improved radically to 12 SM visibility, with clouds at 1800 ft scattered, at 12,000 ft scattered, and at 25,000 ft broken (12SM SCT018 SCT120 BKN250). Note that the winds at KBNA have held fairly steady at about 6 knots from an easterly direction.

Reports for 1800Z weather:

Memphis—The visibility is still 5 SM in mist and the ceiling is 800 ft overcast (5SM BR OVC008). The temperature/dewpoint *spread* is holding at 2°C. The wind is not a factor for the flight.

Nashville—The weather is opening up well; visibility is 12 SM with clouds scattered at 1800 ft and 25,000 ft (12SM SCT018 SCT250).

Chattanooga—KCHA is still not a viable alternate with a visibility of 1 1/2 SM in mist and overcast at 300 ft (1 1/2SM BR OVC003), although conditions are improving from the west for the area.

Huntsville—With a gradual improvement, KHSV can be kept on tap as an alternate if KBNA has a change for the worse at arrival time. KHSV has a visibility of 4 SM in mist and is overcast at 800 ft (4SM BR OVC008) and a 1°C temperature/dewpoint spread. Note that the barometric pressure is higher at the eastern stations (KHSV and KCHA) as compared with KMEM.

Reports for 1900Z weather:

Memphis—A special report (SPECI) is issued for this hour meaning there has been a significant change in the weather (good or bad) since the last report. Memphis has improved to 6 SM in mist and overcast at 1100 ft. The surface temperature is 14°C, and at a normal lapse rate of 2°C/1000 ft, the freezing level would be at about 7000 ft MSL; a check of the chart shows that the KMEM elevation is only 335 ft.

Nashville—Also a special report with visibility and ceiling lowered from the last hour, but the visibility of 10 SM and the ceiling overcast at 2300 ft is still good (10SM OVC023).

Huntsville—Huntsville has been moved to take Chattanooga's place as an alternate for consideration. Visibility is improving, and the last hour's overcast at 800 ft has become 700 broken with an overcast layer at 2000 ft (BKN007 OVC020). The clouds vary from broken to overcast (RMK BKN V OVC). Sea level pressure is 1016.4 hectoPascals (SLP164).

Chattanooga—The regular KCHA report issued at 1851Z has a slight improvement to 2 1/2 SM in fog with 500-ft overcast. The ceiling is ragged (CIG RGD) [see RMK]. The Chattanooga airport is in a bowl surrounded by mountains, and this can be a consideration when determining it as an alternate.

Chattanooga Special—At 1909Z KCHA has improved with visibility at 4 SM in mist/fog, but the lower layer is still

<u>1600Z</u>   METAR KMEM 181550Z 06008KT 4SM BR OVC007 12/11 A3001 RMK SLP163

METAR KBNA 181551Z 10006KT 1/2SM R02L/P6000FT FG BKN005 OVC020 11/11 A3012 RMK

SLP200

METAR KCHA 181549Z 08005KT 3/4SM R20/5500FT BR SCT000 OVC002 07/07 A3011 RMK BR

SCT000 SLP197

SPECI KBNA 181605Z 10006KT 4SM BR BKN005 OVC020 11/11 A3011

SPECI KBNA 181629Z 10007KT 5SM BR BKN018 11/11 A3010

<u>1700Z</u>   METAR KMEM 181652Z 10009KT 5SM BR BKN008 OVC011 13/11 A2999 RMK SLP156

METAR KBNA 181647Z 12006KT 8SM BKN018 11/09 A3010 RMK SLP194

METAR KCHA 181650Z 34003KT 1SM R20/P6000FT BR SCT000 OVC002 08/08 A3010 RMK BR

SCT000 SLP192

METAR KHSV 181649Z 11008KT 3SM BR OVC006 12/11 A3004 RMK SLP174

SPECI KBNA 181725Z 09006KT 12SM SCT018 SCT120 BKN250 12/09 A3008 RMK SLP 193

<u>1800Z</u>   METAR KMEM 181755Z 10012KT 5SM BR OVC008 13/11 A2996 RMK SLP146

METAR KBNA 181750Z 08005KT 12SM SCT018 SCT250 13/12 A3007 RMK SLP183

METAR KCHA 181751Z 35004KT 1 1/2SM BR OVC003 09/08 A3008 RMK SLP185

METAR KHSV 181748Z 12012KT 4SM BR OVC008 12/11 A3004 RMK SLP174

<u>1900Z</u>   SPECI KMEM 181849Z 10009KT 6SM BR OVC011 14/12 A2992 RMK SLP133

SPECI KBNA 181849Z 03005KT 10SM OVC023 13/11 A3004 RMK SLP173

METAR KHSV 181846Z 12009KT 5SM BR BKN007 OVC020 12/11 A3001 RMK BKN V OVC SLP164

METAR KCHA 181851Z 07003KT 2 1/2SM BR OVC005 09/09 A3006 RMK SLP180 CIG RGD

SPECI KCHA 181909Z 06005KT 4SM BR BKN005 OVC009 09/09 A3005 RMK SLP 164 CIG RGD

<u>2000Z</u>   METAR KMEM 181950Z 11010KT 6SM BR OVC013 14/12 A2991 RMK SLP129

METAR KBNA 181947Z 09004KT 10SM BKN023 OVC250 14/10 A3002 RMK SLP165

METAR KHSV 181948Z 09010KT 5SM BR BKN009 OVC030 13/12 A2996 RMK SLP145 BINOVC N

SPECI KCHA 182016Z 07004KT 4SM BR BKN007 OVC010 11/09 A3004 RMK CIG RGD

Fig. 7-26. Hourly reports (METARs) for Memphis (KMEM), Nashville (KBNA), Chattanooga (KCHA), and Huntsville (KHSV) starting at 1600Z and ending at 2000Z, the last regular report available before the 2040Z departure.

at 500 ft but broken instead of overcast (BKN005) with a 900-ft overcast layer. Remarks—The sea level pressure is 1016.4 hectoPascals, and the ceiling is still ragged (RMK SLP 164 CIG RGD), meaning that you could be out of, then back into, clouds.

Reports for 2000Z weather:

This is the last hourly report you would see before departing at 2040Z.

Memphis—Still improving and holding a 2°C spread.

Nashville—Visibility is still 10 SM, and the last hour's overcast is now broken at 2300 ft and overcast at 25,000 ft (BKN023 OVC250). The temperature spread is now 4°C.

Huntsville—Visibility is 5 SM in mist, and the clouds are broken at 900 ft with a 3000-ft overcast (BKN009 OVC030). Remarks—there's a break in the overcast north of the station (BINOVC N).

Chattanooga—There's a special at 2016Z with a slight improvement in the broken and overcast heights to 700 ft and 1000 ft respectively, but Huntsville is the choice for an alternate.

Figure 7-27 has hourly reports on Memphis, Nashville, and Huntsville that include 2200Z, which would be issued just before your ETA of 2212Z at Nashville. You wouldn't see these before departing, but they show the weather at those stations during the flight.

Reports for 2100Z weather:

Memphis—No change in visibility, ceiling, and temperature/dewpoint spread since 2000Z.

Nashville—Visibility has dropped from 10 SM to 9 SM. The broken cloud layer at 2300 ft has gone to scattered at 2500 ft and overcast at 25,000 ft (SCT025 OVC250).

Huntsville—Visibility is 5 SM in mist with overcast at 1100 ft (OVC011). The temperature/dewpoint spread has increased from 1°C to 2°C.

Reports for 2200Z weather:

Memphis—Visibility has decreased to 5 SM in mist. The ceiling has dropped by 500 ft to 800 ft overcast (OVC008).

Nashville—Still very good. The wind is east-north-east at 6 knots, close to the earlier KBNA reports in general direction and speed. A 12,000-ft scattered layer has moved in. There's still a scattered layer at 2500 ft and a 25,000-ft overcast (SCT025 SCT120 OVC250).

Huntsville—The ceiling has raised to 1300 ft overcast. Very little change otherwise (OVC013).

Shortly after the 2200Z reports, Figure 7-27 shows a radar report [RAREP] from Nashville at 2225 [note there is no Z], which indicates returns of precipitation with three-tenths coverage, rain showers (3RW) established by a line from a point 157°, 80 NM to a point 184°, 75 NM from the station. The area is 15 NM wide (15W) centered along that line. The cells are moving from 230° at 20 knots (C2320).

The maximum top is 20,000 ft at 162°, 81 NM from the station (MT 200 AT 162/81).

When checking the weather—including hourly reports, forecasts, and charts—always pick the best weather (preferably good VFR) to fly to in the event of an electrical failure. Go to the nearest VFR-safe altitude, taking into consideration the terrain and avoiding climbing or descending through an IFR altitude. In other words, if you've been assigned 5000 ft (easterly heading) and all electricity has been lost, *climb* to 5500 ft, which is the VFR altitude. You won't cross an *even* altitude (4000 or 6000 by doing this), The main idea is to go to the nearest VFR altitude for your hemispheric rule (with safe terrain clearance) and to try not to climb or descend through an IFR altitude. In the actual weather analyzed for this example, the weather is VFR at the expected ETA to the north of Nashville in the vicinity of Bowling Green, KY (KBWG). You would land at an airport as soon as practicable after becoming VFR.

FORECASTS

■ **Terminal Forecast (TAF)** Terminal forecasts are for specific airports and cover an area within a radius of 5 miles of the runway complex. TAFs are issued four times daily in the United States at 00Z, 06Z, 12Z, and 18Z and are referenced to AGL heights.

Fig. 7-28 contains actual TAFs for the stations and periods covered by the hourly reports (METARs) for Memphis, Nashville, Huntsville, and Chattanooga. The TAFs cover a 24-hr period from 1800Z on the 18th to 1800Z on the 19th. Let's look at the various stations.

Memphis (KMEM)—The TAF is issued on the 18th at 1730Z and, as noted earlier, is good from the 18th at 1800Z to the 19th at 1800Z (181730Z 181818).

At the beginning of the period, the wind is forecast to be from 090° true at 8 knots. Visibility is greater [plus] than 6 statute miles (P6SM). Cloud cover will be scattered at 1000 ft with overcast at 2500 ft (SCT010 OVC025).

2100Z   METAR KMEM 182050Z 10008KT 6SM BR OVC013 14/12 A2990 RMK SLP125

METAR KBNA 182052Z 07009KT 9SM SCT025 OVC250 14/10 A3000 RMK SLP158

METAR KHSV 182047Z 12010KT 5SM BR OVC011 13/11 A2996 RMK SLP145

2200Z   METAR KMEM 182151Z 10008KT 5SM BR OVC008 14/12 A2990 RMK SLP125

METAR KBNA 182147Z 07006KT 9SM SCT025 SCT120 OVC250 14/09 A3000 RMK SLP 159

METAR KHSV 182148Z 10009KT 5SM BR OVC013 13/11 A2996 RMK SLP144

BNA 2225 AREA 3RW 157/80 184/75 15W C2320 MT 200 AT 162/81

Fig. 7-27. Hourly weather reports that follow up on the earlier flight conditions shown in Figure 7-26. A radar report (RAREP) at 2225Z is given at the bottom of the illustration.

```
TAF
    KMEM 181730Z 181818 09008KT P6SM SCT010 OVC025 TEMPO 0105 3SM BR BKN010
        FM0500 13012KT 3SM BR OVC010 TEMPO 0812 1SM TSRA
        FM1200 13006KT 3SM TSRA BR OVC010=


TAF
    KBNA 181730Z 181818 12008KT P6SM BKN025
        FM2300 14010KT 5SM BR OVC012
        FM0800 12012KT 3SM BR OVC010 TEMPO 0812 3SM TSRA=


TAF
    KHSV 181730Z 181818 11008KT 3SM BR OVC006 TEMPO 1803 2SM -RA BR VCTS OVC004
        FM0300 VRB03KT 1SM BR VV003 TEMPO 0306 1/2SM -DZ FG VV001 BECMG 0608 1/4 FG VV001 TEMPO
        0812 -DZ=


TAF
    KCHA 181730Z 181818 18006KT 5SM BR SCT003 OVC012 TEMPO 1823 2SM -SHRA BR BKN003
        FM2300 18006KT 3SM BR OVC010 PROB40 0106 3SM SHRA BECOMG 1218 1SM BR OVC008=


TAF AMD
    KCHA 181910Z 181918 18006KT 3SM BR OVC005 TEMPO 2001 5SM BR SCT005 OVC012 PROB30 0310
    SHRA
        FM1200 15010KT 1/2SM FG VV003=
```

Fig. 7-28. Actual terminal forecasts for Memphis, Nashville, Huntsville, and Chattanooga and times covered earlier in the METARs (Fig. 7-26).

TEMPO 0105 3SM BR BKN010 means that there will be temporary conditions (between 0100Z and 0500Z on the 19th) of 3 SM in mist with a broken layer at 1000 ft AGL. The TEMPO group is used for any conditions (wind, visibility, weather, or sky condition) that are expected to last for generally less than an hour at a time (occasional) and are expected to occur during less than half of the time period. The four digits following the TEMPO are the beginning hour and ending hour of the expected temporary conditions (in this case, 0100Z to 0500Z as indicated above).

After [from] 0500Z (FM0500), the winds are forecast to be from 130° true at 12 knots (13012KT). Visibility will be 3 SM in mist with overcast at 1000 ft (3SM BR OVC010). A temporary condition between 0800Z and 1200Z exists on the 19th, with a visibility of 1 SM in a thunderstorm and rain (TEMPO 0812 1SM TSRA).

From 1200Z, the wind is expected to be from 130° at 6 knots with conditions of 3 SM in thunderstorms, rain, and mist (3SM TSRA BR). The overcast will be at 1000 ft (OVC010).

Nashville (KBNA)—The time of issuance and validity is the same as the regular issuances for Memphis, Huntsville, and Chattanooga.

At the beginning of the period, the conditions are forecast for the wind to be from 120° at 8 knots (12008KT), visibility greater than 6 SM (P6SM), and a broken cloud layer at 2500 ft (BKN025).

From 2300Z, the wind will be from 140° at 10 knots, visibility 5 SM in mist (BR), with overcast at 1200 ft (OVC012).

From 0800Z, the forecast is for wind from 120° at 12 knots (FM0800 12012KT), 3 SM in mist with overcast at 1000 ft (3SM BR OVC010). Temporary conditions from 0800Z to 1200Z [19th] are for a visibility of 3SM in a thunderstorm and rain (TEMPO 0812 3SM TSRA).

Huntsville—At the beginning of the forecast period, the forecast is for wind from 110° at 8 knots, visibility 3 SM in mist, and overcast at 600 ft (181730Z 181818 11008KT 3SM BR OVC006). There are temporary conditions from 1800Z to 0300Z with visibility at 2 SM, in light rain (-RA) and mist, with vicinity thunderstorms (VCTS), and overcast of 400 ft (TEMPO 1803 2SM-RA BR VCTS OVC004).

From 0300, the forecast is for variable wind direction (VRB) at 3 knots, 1 SM, mist, with an indefinite ceiling, or vertical visibility, of 300 ft (VV003). Temporarily from

0300Z to 0600Z, conditions are forecast to be 1/2 SM, light drizzle (-DZ) and fog (FG) with a vertical visibility of 100 ft (TEMPO 0306 1/2SM -DZ FG VV00l), becoming from 0600Z to 0800Z, 1/4 SM and fog with an indefinite ceiling of 100 ft (BECMG 0608 1/4 FG VV001). There is also a temporary condition between 0800Z and 1200Z of light drizzle (TEMPO 0812 -DZ).

Chattanooga—For the first portion of the forecast, conditions are wind from 180° at 6 knots, visibility of 5 SM in mist, scattered clouds at 300 ft with overcast at 1200 ft (18006KT 5SM BR SCT003 OVC012). From 1800Z to 2300Z, temporary conditions will have a visibility of 2 SM in light rain showers (-SHRA) and mist, with broken clouds at 300 ft (TEMPO 1823 2SM -SHRA BR BKN003).

From 2300Z, wind will be from 180° at 6 knots, visibility 3 SM, mist, overcast at 1000 ft with a 40% probability, or chance (FM2300 18006KT 3SM BR OVC010 PROB40). Between 0100Z and 0600Z, conditions will be 3 SM, with rain showers (0106 3SM SHRA). The forecast between 1200Z and 1800Z is for conditions becoming 1 SM in mist, with overcast at 800 ft (1218 1SM BR OVC008).

Chattanooga has an amendment (TAF AMD) released at 1910Z on the 18th (181910Z). The new valid period is now from 1900Z *on the* 18th *to* 1800Z *on the* 19th (181918). [This is a fairly rare occurrence, an amendment this soon after issuance, but it *does* happen.] The amended forecast calls for wind 180° at 6 knots, visibility at 3 SM in mist, and overcast at 500 ft (18006KT 3SM BR OVC005). Temporarily between 2000Z and 0l00Z, conditions are forecast to be 5 SM in mist with scattered clouds at 500 ft and overcast at 1200 ft (TEMPO 2001 5SM BR SCT005 OVC012). There is a 30% probability of rain showers between 0300Z and 1000Z (PROB30 0310 SHRA). From 1200Z, the forecast is wind 150° at 10 knots, 1/2 SM in fog with a vertical visibility of 300 ft (FM 1200 15010KT 1/2SM FG VV003).

A reminder of when the symbols for mist (BR) and fog (FG) are used: BR (*brouillard*) is used when the obscuration or obstruction to visibility (mist) restricts visibility from 5/8 SM to 6 SM. FG is used when fog restricts visibility to less than 5/8 SM.

■ **Area Forecast (FA)** The FA covers states, parts of states, and coastal waters. Figure 7-29 shows the six areas of the contiguous states of the United States and the cities of issuance (San Francisco, Salt Lake City, etc.).

Figure 7-30 is a sample report from a different area than for the hourly reports (METARs) and terminal forecasts (TAFs).

Again, let's look at the report line by line.

1. The forecast was issued for Chicago on the 3rd of the month at 0945Z (CHIC FA 030945). The C after CHI indicates that this covers clouds and weather.
2. You'll be reading a synopsis of the system and getting the clouds and weather (SYNOPSIS AND VFR CLDS/WX) for the area covered.

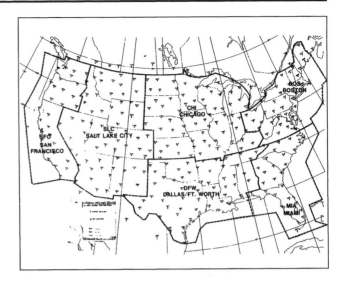

Fig. 7-29. The boundaries for the six forecast areas for the 48 contiguous states of the United States. FAs are issued three times a day by the National Weather Service. *(Aviation Weather Services)*

3. The synopsis is valid until the 4th of the month at 0400Z (040400). The clouds and weather forecast is valid until the 3rd at 2200Z (032200). The outlook (OTLK) is valid from the 3rd at 2200Z until the 4th at 0400Z.
4. The area forecast is for Minnesota (MN), North Dakota (ND), South Dakota (SD), Nebraska (NE), Iowa (IA), Wisconsin (WI), Missouri (MO), Lake Michigan (LM), Michigan (MI), Lake Superior (LS), Lake Huron (LH), Illinois (IL), Indiana (IN), and Kentucky (KY). (Whew!)
5. See AIRMET SIERRA for IFR conditions and mountain obscuration[s] (OBSCN). This alerts the pilot to check the weather advisory AIRMET SIERRA for these conditions in the area covered. Weather advisories win be covered next.

   Continuing to the next line in number 5, thunderstorms (TS) imply severe (SEV) or greater (GTR) turbulence (TURB), severe icing or ice, low-level wind shear (LLSW) and IFR conditions (CONDS).

   The next line indicates that nonmean sea level heights (NON MSL HGTS) are denoted by above ground level (AGL) or ceiling (CIG).

6. Synopsis—at 0900Z, there is a cold front (CDFNT) on a Beckley, WV (BKW), to Monroe, LA (MLU), line. There is a high pressure center in southwestern (SWRN) Minnesota. By 0400Z on the 4th of the month and at the end of the synopsis period, the high pressure will be over southern Lake Michigan (SRN LM). There will be a low pressure trough (LOW PRES TROF) from Minneapolis to the Lamar, CO, line (MLS-LAA LN).

   Now the forecast gets down to business.

7. North Dakota, South Dakota, and Nebraska. There will be scattered (SCT) cirrus (CI) with occasional

1. CHIC FA 030945

2. SYNOPSIS AND VFR CLDS/WX

3. SYNOPSIS VALID UNTIL 040400 CLDS/WX VALID UNTIL 032200...OTLK VALID 032200-040400

4. MN ND SD NE IA WI MO LM MI LS LH IL IN KY

5. SEE AIRMET SIERRA FOR IFR CONDS AND MTN OBSCN.

   TS IMPLY SEV OR GTR TURB SEV ICE LLWS AND IFR CONDS.

   NON MSL HGTS ARE DENOTED BY AGL OR CIG

6. SYNOPSIS...AT 09Z CDFNT BKW-MLU LN. HIGH PRES SWRN MN. BY 04Z HIGH PRES SRN LM. LOW

   PRES TROF MLS-LAA LN.

7. ND SD NE

   SCT CI. OCNL SCT100. TIL 12-14Z OCNL VIS 4-6SM BR. OTLK...VFR.

8. KS

   SW ICT-GLD LN...CIG OVC025 TOP 060. BY 14-16Z AGL SCT040. OTLK...VFR.

   NE ICT-GLD LN...SKC. TIL 15Z OCNL AGL SCT020. OTLK...VFR.

9. MN IA

   SCT CI. TIL 12-14Z OCNL VIS 4-6SM BR. OTLK...VFR.

10. MO

   S STL-SGF LN...AGL SCT030. TIL 14Z OCNL CIG BKN025 TOP 040 VIS 3-5SM BR. OTLK...VFR.

11. IL

   SRN 1/3 IL...AGL SCT030. TIL 14Z OCNL CIG BKN025 TOP 040 VIS 3-5SM BR. OTLK...VFR.

   NRN 2/3 IL...SKC. OCNL AGL SCT030. OTLK...VFR.

Fig. 7-30. An area forecast (FA) issued for the Chicago area (as shown in Figure 7-29).

scattered clouds at 10,000 ft (OCNL SCT100). Until 1200 to 1400Z, there will be occasional visibilities of 4–6 SM in mist (12-14Z VIS 4-6 SM BR). The outlook (check back to item 3) is for VFR conditions for the period of 032200Z to 040400Z.

Okay, let's take a look at the terms and weather limits used in the outlook:

VFR—Ceiling greater than 3000 ft with a visibility greater than 5 SM.

MVFR (marginal VFR)—Ceiling of 1000–3000 ft *and/or* visibility of 3–5 SM. Note the *and/or*. If there were no clouds at all but the visibility was 4 SM, it would still be cited as MVFR [as would a ceiling of 2000 ft with a visibility of 15 SM].

IFR—Ceiling 500 ft to less than 1000 ft and/or a visibility less than 3 SM.

LIFR (Low IFR)—Ceiling less than 500 ft and/or a visibility less than 1 SM.

8. Kansas (KS). Southwest of a Wichita-Goodland line (SW ICT-GLD LN), ceilings are forecast to be overcast at 2500 ft with tops at 6000 ft (CIG OVC025 TOP 060). The 2500-ft ceiling would be *above ground level*. The 6000-ft tops *have no AGL or CIG notation* so that value would be above mean sea level. By 1400–1600Z, there will be scattered clouds at 4000 ft above ground level (SCT040). The outlook is VFR.

Northeast of the Wichita-Goodland line (NE ICT-GLD LN), the sky will be clear (SKC). Until 1500Z, there will be occasional scattered clouds at 2000 ft above ground level (AGL SCT020). The outlook is VFR.

9. Minnesota (MN) and Iowa (IA). The forecast is for scattered cirrus. Until 1200 to 1400Z, the forecast is for occasional visibilities of 4–6 SM in mist (TIL 12- 14Z OCNL VIS 4-6SM BR). The outlook is VFR.

10. Missouri (MO). South of a St. Louis-Springfield line (S STL-SGF LN), the forecast is for scattered clouds at 3000 ft AGL. Until 1400Z, there will be occasional ceilings of broken clouds at 2500 ft with top[s] at 4000 ft, visibilities of 3-5 SM in mist (OCNL CIG BKN025 TOP 040 VIS 3-5SM BR). The outlook is VFR.

11. Illinois (IL). The southern (SRN) one-third of Illinois has scattered clouds at 3000 ft AGL. Until 1400Z, the forecast is for occasional ceilings of broken clouds at 2500 ft with tops at 4000 ft, visibilities 3–5 SM in mist. The outlook is VFR.

In the northern (NRN) two-thirds of Illinois, the sky is clear, but there will be an occasional ceiling of scattered clouds at 3000 ft AGL (SKC OCNL AGL SCT030). The outlook is VFR.

Amendments to area forecasts and AIRMETs are issued as necessary.

■ **Advisories** Following are some sample advisories for other areas of the conterminous United States.

The weather advisories will be of added value to you as an instrument pilot: they consist of AIRMETs (WA), SIGMETs (WS), convective SIGMETs (WST), center weather advisories (CWA), and severe weather forecast alerts (AWW).

AIRMETs (WA): AIRMETs within the conterminous United States are issued for phenomena that are potentially hazardous to aircraft:

1. Moderate icing.
2. Moderate turbulence.
3. Sustained winds of 30 knots or more at the surface.
4. Widespread ceilings of less than 1000 ft and/or visibility of less than 3 SM.
5. Extensive mountain obscurement.

AIRMETs have *fixed* alphanumeric designators:

SIERRA—IFR and mountain obscuration. (See item 5 in Figure 7-30.)
TANGO—Turbulence.
ZULU—Icing and freezing levels.

Figure 7-31 is a sample AIRMET SIERRA issued for the San Francisco area.

As we've been doing all along, let's look at the sample line by line.

1. This San Francisco SIERRA AIRMET (SFOS WA) was issued on the 1st of the month at 1550Z (011550). This AIRMET SIERRA is update (UPDT) number 4 for IFR and mountain obscuration (MTN OBSCN), and it is valid until the 1st of the month at 2000Z (012000).
2. This AIRMET is for mountain obscuration for California (CA) and is an update. From 50 SM north-northwest of Los Angeles (50NNW LAX) to 40 SM west-northwest of Palm Springs, CA (40WNW PSP), to 30 SM east-southeast of San Diego (30ESE SAN) to 20 SM south of San Diego (20S SAN) to Los Angeles (LAX) to 20 SM southeast of Santa Barbara (20SE SBA) to 50 SM north-northwest of Los Angeles (50NNW LAX). [This description should enclose the area affected.]

   The mountains will be occasionally obscured in clouds and mist (CLDS/BR). These conditions will be ending at 2000Z (ENDG 20Z) [on the 1st].
3. This AIRMET is for IFR conditions in Oregon (OR), California (CA), and coastal (CSTL) waters (WTRS). From 60 SM southwest of Eugene, Oregon (60SW EUG), to 30 SM east-southeast of Fortuna, CA (30ESE FOT), to 20 SM north of Ukiah, CA (20N UKI), to 100 SM west-southwest of Ukiah to 130 SM west of Fortuna to 90 SM west-northwest of Fortuna to 60 SM southwest of Eugene. Ceilings (CIG) will be below 1000 ft and visibilities below 3 SM in fog and mist (BLW 010/VIS BLW 3SM FG/BR). The conditions will be ending at 2000Z (ENDG 20Z).

SIGMETs (WS): SIGMETs warn of nonconvective weather that is potentially hazardous to all aircraft. In the conterminous United States, SIGMETs are issued when the following phenomena occur or are expected to occur:

1. Severe icing not associated with thunderstorms.
2. Severe or extreme turbulence or clear air turbulence (CAT) not associated with thunderstorms.
3. Duststorms, sandstorms, or volcanic ash that lowers surface or inflight visibilities to below 3 SM.
4. Volcanic eruptions.

SIGMETs are identified by alphabetic designators, which include NOVEMBER through YANKEE but exclude SIERRA and TANGO. (Remember that SIERRA, TANGO, and ZULU are used in AIRMETs for IFR, turbulence, and icing information.)

The first issuance of a SIGMET will be labeled UWS (urgent weather SIGMET). Issuances for the same

---

AIRMET
1. SFOS WA 011550
   AIRMET SIERRA UPDT 4 FOR IFR AND MTN OBSCN VALID UNTIL 012000
2. AIRMET MTN OBSCN...CA...UPDT
   FROM 50NNW LAX TO 40WNW PSP TO 30ESE SAN TO 20S SAN TO LAX TO 20SE SBA TO 50NNW LAX
   MTNS OCNL OBSC CLDS/BR. CONDS ENDG 20Z
3 AIRMET IFR ..OR CA AND CSTL WTRS
   FROM 60SW EUG TO 30ESE FOT TO 20N UKI TO 100WSW UKI TO 130W FOT TO 90WNW FOT TO 60SW
   EUG
   CIG BLW 010/VIS BLW 3SM FG/BR CONDS ENDG 20Z.

Fig. 7-31. An AIRMET SIERRA for the San Francisco area.

phenomenon will be sequentially numbered, using the original designator until the phenomenon ends. For instance, the first issuance in the Boston area is PAPA 1. Figure 7-32 is a sample SIGMET for the Boston area.

```
SIGMET
BOSP UWS 221820
SIGMET PAPA 1 VALID UNTIL 221920
PA NJ
FROM SLT TO EWR TO ACY TO JST TO SLT
OCNL SEV TURB BTWN FL270 AND FL350 EXP DUE TO WNDSHR.
CONS ENDG BY 1920Z.
```

Fig. 7-32. SIGMET PAPA 1 for the Boston forecast area.

Translating the figure line by line:

This is a Boston PAPA SIGMET (BOSP), the first one issued (UWS) at 1820Z on the 22nd of the month (221820), and is valid until 1920Z on the 22nd.

The states of Pennsylvania (PA) and New Jersey (NJ) are affected.

From Slate Run, PA (SLT), to Newark, NJ (EWR), to Atlantic City, NJ (ACY), to Johnstown, PA (JST), to Slate Run.

Occasional severe turbulence between flight level 27,000 ft (FL270) and flight level 35,000 ft (FL350) is expected (EXP) due to windshear (WNDSHR).

Conditions will be ending by 1920Z.

Convective SIGMETs (WST): Convective SIGMETs are issued for the eastern (E), central (C), and western (W) United States. At this printing, these bulletins are issued at 55 minutes past the hour (H+55) as special bulletins on an unscheduled basis. They are issued for the following phenomena:

1. Severe thunderstorms due to (a) surface winds greater than or equal to 50 knots; (b) hail at the surface, greater or equal to ¾ inch in diameter; (c) tornadoes.
2. Embedded thunderstorms.
3. A line of thunderstorms.
4. Thunderstorms greater than or equal to VIP level 4, affecting 40% or more of an area of at least 3000 square miles.

To understand the severity of the weather at level 4 (mentioned above), let's look at radar weather echo intensity levels:

Level 1, weak and *Level 2, moderate*—light to moderate turbulence is possible, with lightning.

Level 3, strong—severe turbulence possible, lightning.

Level 4, very strong—severe turbulence likely, lightning. (Comfort bags and prayers are broken out by the passengers.)

Level 5, intense—severe turbulence, lightning, organized wind gusts, hail likely. (Comfort bags and prayers *in use* by passengers.)

Level 6, extreme—severe turbulence, large hail, lightning, extensive wind gusts, probably structural failure. (Pilot plans ahead by wearing a parachute, *leaves* the airplane, and goes for help.)

Figure 7-33 is a sample convective SIGMET issued for Kansas City and the central United States.

```
1. MKCC WST 221855
   CONVECTIVE SIGMET 20C
   VALID UNTIL 2055Z

2. ND SD
   FROM 90W MOT-GFK-ABR-90W MOT
   INTSF AREA SEV TS MOV FROM 2445. TOPS ABV FL450. WIND GUSTS TO 60KT REP. TORNADOES...HAIL
   TO 2 IN...WIND GUSTS TO 65KT POSS ND PTN.

3. CONVECTIVE SIGMET 21C
   VALID UNTIL 2055Z

4. TX
   50SE CDS
   ISOL SEV TS D30 MOV FROM 2420. TOPS ABV FL450. HAIL TO 2 IN...WIND GUSTS TO 65KT POSS.

5. OUTLOOK VALID 222055-230055

6. AREA 1...FROM INL-MSP-ABR-MOT-INL
   SEV TS CONT TO DVLP IN AREA OVER ND. AREA IS EXP TO RMN SEV AND SPRD INTO MN.

7. AREA 2...FROM CDS-DFW-LRD-ELP-CDS
   ISOLD STG TS WILL DVLP OVR SWRN AND WRN TX THRUT FCST PD AS UPR LVL TROF MOV NE OVR
   VERY UNSTBL AIR.
```

Fig. 7-33. Convective SIGMETs 20C for North and South Dakota and 21C for Texas, respectively.

As we have been doing, the line-by-line interpretation is

1. Kansas City has issued a convective SIGMET (WST) on the 22nd of the month at 1855Z. Its designator is 20C, and it is valid until 2055Z.

2. North Dakota (ND) and South Dakota (SD) information.

   From 90 SM west of Minot, ND (MOT), to Grand Forks, ND (GFK), to Aberdeen, SD (ABR), to 90 SM west of Minot.

   There is an intensifying (INTSF) area of severe thunderstorms (TS) moving (MOV) from 240° at 45 knots (FROM 2445). Tops are above 45,000 ft MSL (ABV FL450). Wind gusts up to 60 knots have been reported (REP). Tornadoes, hail up to 2-in. diameter, and wind gusts up to 65 knots are possible (POSS) in the North Dakota portion (PTN).

3. Convective SIGMET 21C is valid until 2055Z.

4. Texas (TX).

   50 miles southeast of Childress, TX (50SE CDS). There is an isolated severe thunderstorm (ISOL SEV TS), diameter 30 miles (D30), moving from 240° at 20 knots (MOV FROM 2420). Tops above 45,000 MSL, hail up to 2-in. diameter, and wind gusts to 65 knots are possible.

5. The outlook is valid from 2055Z on the 22nd to 0055Z on the 23rd.

6. Area 1 from International Falls, MN (INL), to Minneapolis (MSP) to Aberdeen (ABD) to Minot (MOT) to International Falls (INL). Severe thunderstorms continue to develop in the area over North Dakota. The area is expected to remain severe and spread (SPRD) into Minnesota.

7. Area 2 from Childress to Dallas/Fort Worth (DFW) to Laredo (LRD) to El Paso (ELF) to Childress.

   Isolated strong thunderstorms (ISOLD STG TS) will develop over southwestern and western Texas (SWRN AND WRN TX) throughout the forecast period (THRUT FCST PD) as an upper level trough (UPR LVL TROF) moves northeastward over (MOV NE OVR) very unstable (UNSTBL) air.

Severe Weather Forecast Alerts (AWW) are preliminary messages issued in order to alert users that a Severe Weather Bulletin is being issued. These messages define areas of possible severe thunderstorms or tornado activity. These are unscheduled and issued as required by the National Severe Storm Forecast Center at Kansas City, MO.

The **Center Weather Advisory (CWA)** is an unscheduled inflight, flow control, air traffic, and air crew advisory. By nature of its short lead time, the CWA is not a flight planning product. It is a "nowcast" for conditions beginning within the next 2 hours. CWAs are issued as supplements to existing SIGMETs, convective SIGMETs, AIRMETs, or area forecasts (FAs). They may be based on pilot reports and other weather information if the observed weather conditions don't meet SIGMET, convective SIGMET, or AIRMET criteria.

```
PILOT REPORTS
UA/ OV KFSM 090040/ TM 1145/ FL130/ TP PA32/
1        2              3         4       5

SK BKN018-030/OVC045-120/ WX FV99SM RA000-100/ TA M06
            6                      7              8

WV 230045KT/ TB LGT-MOD CHOP BLW 100/ IC MOD CLR 110-120/
    9              10                        11

RM FRZLVL 110 RA INTMNT DURGC
            12

1.  TYPE OF REPORT - UUA IS URGENT  UA REGULAR
2.  LOCATION OF PILOT REPORT
3.  TIME OF REPORT
4.  FLIGHT LEVEL
5.  TYPE OF AIRCRAFT
6.  SKY COVERAGE, TOPS AND BASES
7.  WX AND FLIGHT VIS
8.  TEMPERATURE IN DEGREES C
9.  WINDS
10. TURB - INTENSITY, TYPE AND LOCATION
11. ICING - INTENSITY, TYPE AND LOCATION
12. RM - ANY REMARKS
```

Fig. 7-34. Pilot reports (PIREPs).

■ **Pilot Reports (PIREPs)** Figure 7-34 is a PIREP from a pilot in the vicinity of Fort Smith, AR (KFSM). Check the various underlined and numbered information segments.

1. UA is a regular PIREP.
2. The OV (over) is slightly misleading since the location is on the 090 radial, 40 NM from the Fort Smith VOR (KFSM 090040).
3. The time is 1145Z (TM 1145).
4. Flight level is 13,000 ft (FL130).
5. Type (TP) of aircraft is a PA-32.
6. The sky (SK) conditions are broken with the base at 1800 ft and the top of the first layer at 3000 ft. The second layer is an overcast with the base at 4500 ft and the top at 12,000 ft (BKN018-030/OVC045-120).
7. Weather (WX)—The flight visibility (FV) is unlimited (99SM). There was rain from the surface to 10,000 ft (RA000-100).
8. Temperature (TA) is minus 6°C (M06).
9. Wind velocity (WV) is from 230° at 45 knots (230045KT). [This might have been groundspeed and wind direction checked by DME, GPS, or other methods.]
10. Turbulence (TB) is light to moderate (LT-MOD) chop below 10,000 ft (BLW 100).
11. Icing (IC) is moderate and clear from 11,000 to 12,000 ft (MOD CLR 110-120).
12. Remarks (RM)—Freezing level is at 11,000 ft (FRZLVL 110), with rain (RA) intermittent (INTMNT) during climb (DURGC).

■ **Winds and Temperatures Aloft Forecasts** The winds are covered last because there's not much point in finding out the winds until you've looked at the weather and decided that you can go.

Figure 7-35 is an actual winds aloft forecast for several stations based on data on the 18th at 1200Z and is valid on the 19th at 0000Z and for use from 2100Z (18th) to 0600Z (19th). To save the space of putting minus signs on the temperatures at higher altitudes (where they are always "minus"), a note is made that all temperatures are negative above 24,000 ft. The altitudes are MSL.

Looking at some 3000-ft winds as an example:

3000—The wind at BNA (Nashville) is from 150° true at 18 knots. (Remember that *published* winds are true directions.) Note that none of the stations has a temperature listed for 3000 ft. Western stations of higher elevations may not publish a wind at 3000 ft MSL because it is too close to the surface. Note that AMA (Amarillo, TX) doesn't issue winds at 3000 ft. This is the case too with 6000-ft winds. Denver at 5000 ft (plus) would be an example.

Looking at FWA (Fort Wayne, IN), you note that the wind is from 990° at 00 knots. Obviously that can't be; 99ØØ is the symbol for light and variable winds (less than 5 knots, and the temperature is 0°C).

Looking at the wind at 24,000 ft at ABI (Abilene, TX), it can be noted that while the wind is given as 7316-29, it's actually from 230° at 116 knots (and the temperature is –29°C). When the wind is over 100 knots, which would require adding another digit to the speed, "50" is added to the direction and "100" subtracted from the wind speed by the weather folks. *You,* of course, would subtract 50 from the "73" to get 23 (230°) and add 100 to the "16" to get 116 knots. The temperature is straightforward.

BNA at 34,000 ft (762650) has a wind from 260° true, at 126 knots and the temperature is –50°C.

For winds over 200 knots, you might see "7799," which means that the wind is from 270° at 199 knots or higher.

Another example: 850552—Wind from 350° at 105 knots and the temperature is –52°C.

■ **Sources of Weather Information** Earlier in the chapter, the actual METARs and TAFs for the Memphis to Nashville flight were examined; however, the best source for getting all the information together before a trip is to contact the nearest Flight Service Station (FSS/AFSS) and get a standard briefing.

You should request a *standard briefing* if you're planning a flight and have not received a previous briefing or have not received preliminary information through TIBS, TWEB, HIWAS, PATWAS, etc.

TIBS (*Telephone Information Briefing Service*)—A continuous recording of meteorological and aeronautical information available by telephone. Information includes METAR observations, TAFs, winds/temperature aloft forecasts, etc. TIBS is *not* a substitute for specialist-provided preflight briefings. It can be used as a preliminary briefing for help in a "go/no go" decision. TIBS locations are found at the AFSS (Automated Flight Service Station), and the phone numbers, which require a touchtone phone, are in the *Airport/Facility Directory*.

```
DATA BASED ON 181200Z
VALID 190000Z    FOR USE 2100-0600Z. TEMPS NEG ABV 24000
```

FT	3000	6000	9000	12000	18000	24000	30000	34000	39000
ABI		2534+06	2534-03	2439-10	2477-20	7316-29	733241	733748	734558
ABQ			2419-07	2621-15	2628-28	2631-41	263450	253650	244449
ACY	2829	2736+01	2745-02	2751-08	2765-23	2776-35	279248	289150	288353
AGC	3020	3128-01	3037-04	2946-09	2964-22	2870-35	279049	729753	279255
ALB	2728	2629-03	2532-09	2537-13	2542-26	2650-37	265947	265950	265652
AMA		2323	2525-05	2428-13	2243-26	2248-38	226346	227747	227951
ATL	1515	2013+08	2419+03	2526-02	2750-15	2768-27	770441	772248	772857
AVP	2930	2833-03	2839-07	2847-12	2861-25	2871-36	288247	288050	287152
BDL	2728	2532-01	2439-06	2544-12	2551-25	2556-37	266347	266151	265853
BGR	2131	2233+00	2236-04	2235-10	2142-25	2 56-37	207551	217455	226456
BHM	1620	2020+09	2324+04	2426-01	2650-15	2673-26	760740	762148	762857
BNA	1518	1920+07	2222+02	2325-04	2653-17	2673-30	761042	762650	762959
FLO	2306	2410+08	2513+03	252 -04	2647-18	2760-28	288842	791751	783258
FSM	1530	1837+07	1937+01	2038-06	2162-19	2282-30	732044	743751	744659
FWA	9900	3005+00	2713-03	2725-09	2641-23	2648-35	267651	269155	279658
MEM	1623	1929+07	2028+03	2228-03	2454-17	2479-29	751142	752850	753959
MGM	1717	2221+10	2429+05	2529+00	2645-13	2670-25	760040	761148	761856

Fig. 7-35. Actual winds aloft/temperature forecasts.

TWEB (*Transcribed WEather Broadcast*)—Tapes of meteorological or aeronautical data are continually broadcast over selected low-frequency navigation aids and/or VORs. Generally, the broadcast contains route-oriented data with the specially prepared National Weather Service forecast, winds aloft and inflight advisories, plus preselected current information such as weather reports (METARs/SPECI), NOTAMs, and special notices.

HIWAS (*Hazardous Inflight Weather Advisory Service*)— This is a continuous broadcast of inflight weather advisories including summarized AWWs (severe Weather Alerts), CWAs (Center Weather Alerts), AIRMETs, SIGMETs, convective SIGMETs, and urgent PIREPs. When a HIWAS has been implemented, a HIWAS alert will be broadcast on all except emergency frequencies and will give frequency instruction, number, and type of advisory (SIGMET. etc.).

Remember that there are other sources for weather information including the Weather Channel, local TV, and the DUAT (*Direct User Access Terminal*) system, which is a toll-free personal computer access to weather information. Take advantage of every input available.

During your preflight briefing, ask for NOTAMs for your route, destination, and alternate.

■ En Route Flight Advisory Service (EFAS)

This is a weather service available to you from selected FSSs along heavily traveled airways at a service criterion of 5000 ft AGL at 80 mi from an EFAS outlet. All communications will be conducted on the designated frequency of 122.0 MHz, using the radio call (name of station) FLIGHT WATCH.

Routine weather information plus current reports on the location of thunderstorms and other hazardous weather as reported by ground observers or pilots (or radar) may be obtained from the nearest flight watch facility.

This service is not intended to be used for flight plan filing or routine position reporting or to obtain a complete preflight briefing in lieu of contacting an FSS or Weather Service office.

The EFAS was covered briefly in Chapter 6 and you might check back to Figure 6-1 to check the coverage for the southeastern United States and Puerto Rico.

SUMMARY

By the time you read this, some of the services covered may be changed or eliminated or new ones added. Check with FSS or NWS specialists for the latest presentations and information. The main point is to check the various inputs against each other. How have the earlier forecasts been comparing with the earlier weather? Look at PIREPs and other reports that may be more up to date than the last sequence or forecast. Remember that some of the charts may be several hours old, and winds and temperature aloft forecasts are just that—*forecasts.*

These METARs and TAFs are actual weather reports, and later chapters are based on a flight from Memphis to Nashville.

It's going to be up to you to ask the proper questions, because it's your neck. You may want to set up a weather checklist for your use in the Weather Service office or the FSS so that you don't forget a vital check.

Remember that the people in the FSS or Weather Service office are there to help you. If you have questions, ask them, because there may have been changes in weather presentation or release times since that last flight a few days ago.

Here are a couple of points you might consider when planning an IFR trip and checking the weather:

Don't just check the weather on the original route and to the alternate. Find out the nearest VFR weather area, but keep in mind that there may be days when there is no VFR weather within the range of your aircraft; however, these days are generally rare. If you have a total electrical failure and can't navigate or communicate, you may have to use the vacuum/pressure gyro instruments to fly the airplane to VFR conditions for a letdown and approach (and landing) visually. Go to a VFR altitude (odd + 500 or even + 500 as applicable for the direction). If terrain permits, you might want to *descend* to the safe VFR altitude in hopes of breaking out as the flight progresses. There will be more about inflight emergencies in Chapter 12, but the main point here is to locate the nearest VFR weather when you are checking en route IFR weather.

In many cases your briefing will be by phone, and sometimes it seems that the briefer talks pretty fast. The problem is that OVC (overcast) or BKN (broken) or SCT (scattered) takes a long time to write down and it's suggested that you use the "old" symbols for quick usage.

◑—Scattered.

◓—Broken.

⊕—Overcast.

With practice you can use these symbols and keep up with just about any briefer. You could, of course, ask him or her to slow down.

CHARTS AND OTHER PRINTED AIDS

8

■ **En Route Charts** The en route chart system is broken down into two main segments:

1. *En route high-altitude charts* cover the conterminous United States in six charts and concern airspace 18,000 ft MSL and above. These won't be covered in this book.

2. *En route low-altitude charts* cover altitudes up to but not including 18,000 MSL and the conterminous United States in 28 charts. There are also charts for Alaska and Hawaii and one for the Caribbean (Miami-Nassau-Puerto Rico.) The U.S. charts are printed back to back; for instance, L-13 and L-14 go together as shown by Figure 8-1.

In the back of this book there is part of an L-14 en route low-altitude chart with a legend block. The FAA occasionally changes the symbols. Be alert and check your latest charts for the current symbols in use. *All references to en route and approach charts used in this book are from the National Aeronautical Charting Office (NACO).*

Low-frequency facilities are, as on the sectional charts, in red or magenta on the actual chart (we had to stick to black and white here).

The tower (local, ground, departure, and approach controls) communications frequencies of each en route low-altitude chart are placed on the particular chart. In a box in the legend section of the sample chart are some pertinent airport tower frequencies that could be used in a later example trip. The towers are always listed alphabetically by city. (Those in the sample chart have been reshuffled a little.)

If you are a refresher pilot, note on the chart that the controlling FSS is now listed under the other VOR boxes. Review the legend for other presentations new to you.

■ **Area Charts** Certain congested terminal areas (Atlanta, Miami, etc.) have larger-scale charts for close-in work. Several of these are published on one sheet and are included with the en route chart subscription.

SOME INSTRUMENT FLIGHT RULES

Before discussing approach charts, it would be well to look at the basic FARs pertaining to IFR takeoffs and approaches.

■ Section 91.175 Takeoff and Landing under IFR: General

(a) *Instrument approaches to civil airports.* Unless otherwise authorized by the Administrator for paragraphs (a) through (k) of this section, when an instrument letdown to a civil airport is necessary, each person operating an aircraft, except a military aircraft of the United States, shall use a standard instrument approach procedure prescribed for the airport in Part 97 of this chapter.

(b) *Authorized DH or MDA.* For the purpose of this section, when the approach procedure being used provides for and requires use of a DH or MDA, the authorized decision height or authorized minimum descent altitude is the DH or MDA prescribed by the approach procedure, the DH or MDA prescribed for the pilot in command, or the DH or MDA for which the aircraft is equipped, whichever is higher.

(c) *Operation below DH or MDA.* Where a DH or MDA is applicable, no pilot may operate an aircraft, except a military aircraft of the United States, at any airport below the authorized MDA or continue an approach below the authorized DH unless—

(1) The aircraft is continuously in a position from which a descent to a landing on the intended runway can be made at a normal rate of descent using normal maneuvers, and for operations conducted under Part 121 or Part 135 unless that descent rate will allow touchdown to occur within the touchdown zone of the runway of intended landing;

(2) The flight visibility is not less than the visibility prescribed in the standard instrument approach procedure being used;

(3) Except for a Category II or Category III approach where any necessary visual reference requirements are specified by the Administrator, at least one of the following visual references for the intended runway is distinctly visible and identifiable to the pilot:

(i) The approach light system, except that the pilot may not descend below 100 feet above the touchdown zone elevation using the approach lights as a reference unless the red terminating bars or the red side row bars are also distinctly visible and identifiable.

(ii) The threshold.

(iii) The threshold markings.

(iv) The threshold lights.

(v) The runway end identifier lights.

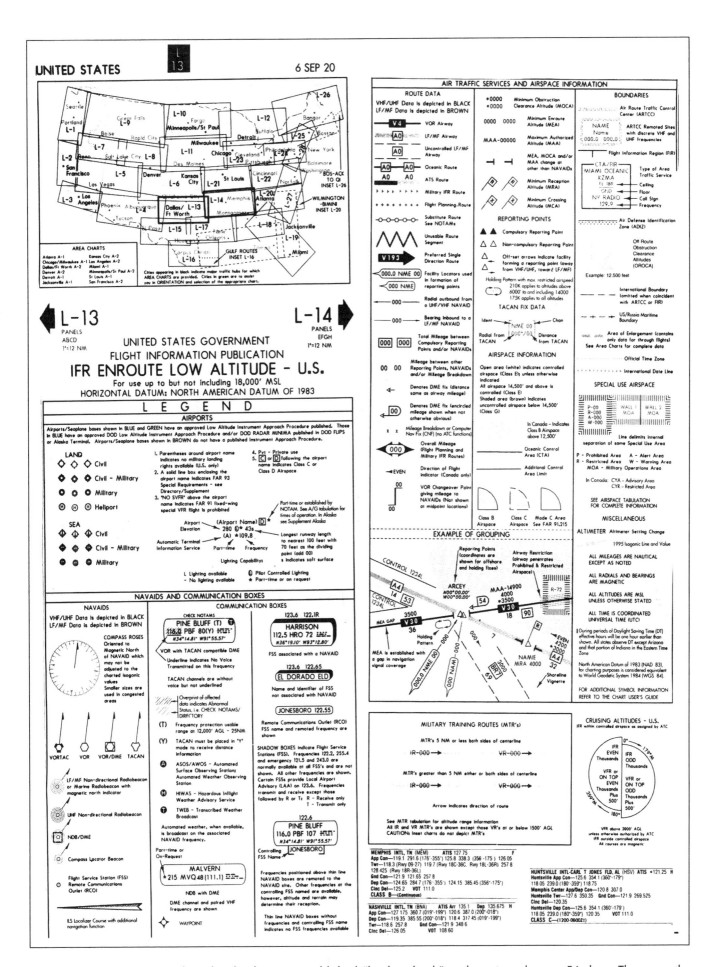

Fig. 8-1. The en route low-altitude charts are published "back to back" and are issued every 56 days. These are the latest symbols as of this printing, but they change periodically so check your latest chart.

(vi) The visual approach slope indicator.

(vii) The touchdown zone or touchdown zone markings.

(viii) The touchdown zone lights.

(ix) The runway or runway markings.

(x) The runway lights; and

(4) When the aircraft is on a straight-in nonprecision approach procedure that incorporates a visual descent point, the aircraft has reached the visual descent point, except where the aircraft is not equipped for or capable of establishing that point or a descent to the runway cannot be made using normal procedures or rates of descent if descent is delayed until reaching that point.

(d) *Landing.* No pilot operating an aircraft, except a military aircraft of the United States, may land that aircraft when the flight visibility is less than the visibility prescribed in the standard instrument approach procedure being used.

(e) *Missed approach procedures.* Each pilot operating an aircraft, except a military aircraft of the United States, shall immediately execute an appropriate missed approach procedure when either of the following conditions exist:

(1) Whenever the requirements of paragraph (c) of this section are not met at either of the following times:

(i) When the aircraft is being operated below MDA; or

(ii) Upon arrival at the missed approach point, including a DH where a DH is specified and its use is required, and at any time after that until touchdown.

(2) Whenever an identifiable part of the airport is not distinctly visible to the pilot during a circling maneuver at or above MDA, unless the inability to see an identifiable part of the airport results only from a normal bank of the aircraft during the circling approach.

(f) *Civil airport takeoff minimums.* Unless otherwise authorized by the Administrator, no person operating an aircraft under Part 121, 125, 127, 129, or 135 of this chapter may take off from a civil airport under IFR unless weather conditions are at or above the weather minimums for IFR takeoff prescribed for that airport under Part 97 of this chapter. If takeoff minimums are not prescribed under Part 97 of this chapter for a particular airport, the following minimums apply to takeoffs under IFR for aircraft operating under those parts:

(1) For aircraft, other than helicopters, having two engines or less—l statute mile visibility.

(2) For aircraft having more than two engines—½ statute mile visibility.

(3) For helicopters—½ statute mile visibility.

(g) *Military airports.* Unless otherwise prescribed by the Administrator, each person operating a civil aircraft under IFR into or out of a military airport shall comply with the instrument approach procedures and the takeoff and landing minimums prescribed by the military authority having jurisdiction of that airport.

(h) *Comparable values of RVR and ground visibility.*

(1) Except for Category II or Category III minimums, if RVR minimums for takeoff or landing are prescribed in an instrument approach procedure, but RVR is not reported for the runway of intended operation, the RVR minimum shall be converted to ground visibility in accordance with the table in paragraph (h)(2) of this section and shall be the visibility minimum for takeoff or landing on that runway.

(2)

RVR (feet)	Visibility (statute miles)
1,600	¼
2,400	½
3,200	⅝
4,000	¾
4,500	⅞
5,000	1
6,000	1¼

(i) *Operations on unpublished routes and use of radar in instrument approach procedures.* When radar is approved at certain locations for ATC purposes, it may be used not only for surveillance and precision radar approaches, as applicable, but also may be used in conjunction with instrument approach procedures predicated on other types of radio navigational aids. Radar vectors may be authorized to provide course guidance through the segments of an approach procedure to the final approach course or fix. When operating on an unpublished route or while being radar vectored, the pilot, when an approach clearance is received, shall, in addition to complying with 91.177, maintain the last altitude assigned to that pilot until the aircraft is established on a segment of a published route or instrument approach procedure unless a different altitude is assigned by ATC. After the aircraft is so established, published altitudes apply to descent within each succeeding route or approach segment unless a different altitude is assigned by ATC. Upon reaching the final approach course or fix, the pilot may either complete the instrument approach in accordance with a procedure approved for the facility or continue a surveillance or precision radar approach to a landing.

(j) *Limitation on procedure turns.* In the case of a radar vector to a final approach course fix, a timed approach from a holding fix, or an approach for which the procedure specifies "No PT," no pilot may make a procedure turn unless cleared to do so by ATC.

(k) *ILS components.* The basic ground components of an ILS are the localizer, glide slope, outer marker, middle marker, and, when installed for use with Category II or Category III instrument approach procedures, an inner marker. A compass locator or precision radar may be substituted for the outer or middle marker. DME, VOR, or nondirectional beacon fixes authorized in the standard instrument approach procedure or surveillance radar may be substituted for the outer marker. Applicability of, and substitution for, the inner marker for Category II or III approaches is determined by the appropriate Part 97 approach procedure, letter of authorization, or operations specification pertinent to the operations.

U.S. TERMINAL PROCEDURES

The Terminal Procedures, as the term implies, cover the operations in terminal areas and contain approach and departure routes plus the actual final approach procedures to various airports. (See Figure 8-3 for the areas covered by the various Terminal Procedures books, which are issued every 56 days.)

■ Instrument Approach Procedure (IAP) Charts

The IAP charts will be of the greatest importance for the successful completion of an instrument flight. If you're taking an instrument refresher, you may find the chart layouts have changed. The NOS charts will be discussed here.

■ Definitions

MDA—"Minimum descent altitude" means the lowest altitude, expressed in feet above MSL, to which descent is authorized on final approach, where no electronic glide slope is provided, or during circle-to-land maneuvering in execution of a standard instrument approach procedure.

DH—"Decision height," with respect to the operation of aircraft, means the height at which a decision must be made during an ILS or PAR (Precision Approach Radar) instrument approach to either continue the approach or to execute a missed approach. This height is expressed in feet above MSL, and for Category II ILS operation, the DH is additionally expressed as a radio altimeter setting. (Category II has special lower minimums and depends on equipment at the airport *and* in the airplane.) *The term Decision Height (DH) will be gradually changed to "Decision Altitude" (DA) for instrument approach procedures with vertical guidance.* DA will be MSL, DH is height above threshold.

HAA—"Height above airport" indicates the height of the MDA above the published airport elevation. The HAA is published in conjunction with circling minimums for all types of approaches.

HAT—"Height above touchdown" indicates the heights of the DH or MDA above the highest runway elevation in the touchdown zone (first 3000 ft of the runway). The HAT is published in conjunction with straight-in minimums.

NoPT—Means no procedure turn required.

"Precision approach procedure" means a standard instrument approach in which an electronic glide slope is provided (ILS or PAR).

"Nonprecision approach procedure" means a standard instrument approach in which no electronic glide slope is provided.

■ IFR Landing Minimums

Earlier, the ceiling at the airport and the visibility were used as landing limits. *This is no longer the case.* The published visibility is the required weather condition for landing as cited in FAR 91. FAR 91 now allows approach down to the MDA or DH as appropriate to the procedure being executed without regard to the reported ceiling.

The publication *Low-Altitude Approach Procedures* (Inter-Agency Air Cartographic Committee—IACC) goes into great detail on the making up of approach charts from the government's requirements; for instance, "When level flight is to be maintained from the primary facility or fix, prior to the beginning of the descent, the distance shall be shown by use of a 0.007" vertical line 0.10" in length extending downward from the procedure track at the point where the descent begins. The distance need not be shown to scale."

Well, as a pilot, you don't need that kind of information; but if you get a chance to look through that publication, you'll be gratified at the detailed work that goes into the charts. This chapter will stick to the information for actually using the charts for approaches (with an occasional aside).

Look at Figure 8-2 and note that the approach charts are issued for specified parts of the United States (16 volumes) and for an effective date of 56 days. Change notices (CNs) are published at the mid-28-day point and contain revisions, additions, and deletions to the last complete issue of the 16 volumes. The Index lists the approach procedures alphabetically *by city*. (If Aardvark Airport is located in the town of Zulu, Mont., it will be listed at or near the end, with the Zs.) You would replace the information (IFR takeoff minimums, departure procedures alternate minimums, civil radar instrument minimums, and the full approach charts listed in the CN Index).

Figure 8-3 shows the areas covered by the IAP chart volumes.

Figure 8-4 gives general information and abbreviations for the charts.

Each IAP chart is divided into the following sections:

1. Planview.
2. Profile.
3. Airport sketch.
4. Minimums data.

■ Planview

Here are a few points to consider about this part of the chart:

1. The chart pages are oriented to True North, but bearings and courses are magnetic.
2. The information in the solid line 10-NM inner ring is to scale. Base information is only shown within the 10-NM ring.
3. The radio aid to navigation for the final part of the instrument approach is positioned in the center of the inner ring.
4. The middle ring (labeled "feeder facilities") is made up of dashed lines concentric with the solid line 10-NM ring. Not all approach charts have feeder facilities. The line is broken as required to show facilities, fixes, and intersections as clearly as possible. Any feeder facilities shown on this middle ring are those used by the air traffic controller to direct you to intervening facilities/fixes between the en route structure and the initial approach fix (IAF).
5. The outer ring (labeled "en route facilities") is concentric with the inner and middle rings. These en route facilities are those radio aids to navigation, fixes, and intersections that are part of the en route low-altitude structure. From this point (or points, as the case may be), terminal routing is given to the IAF with bearings, distance, and altitude information, direct or via feeder facilities. When en route facilities are used in a dual capacity such as a transition facility and missed-approach facility, the pertinent information (name, frequency, etc.) is within a cartoon-type

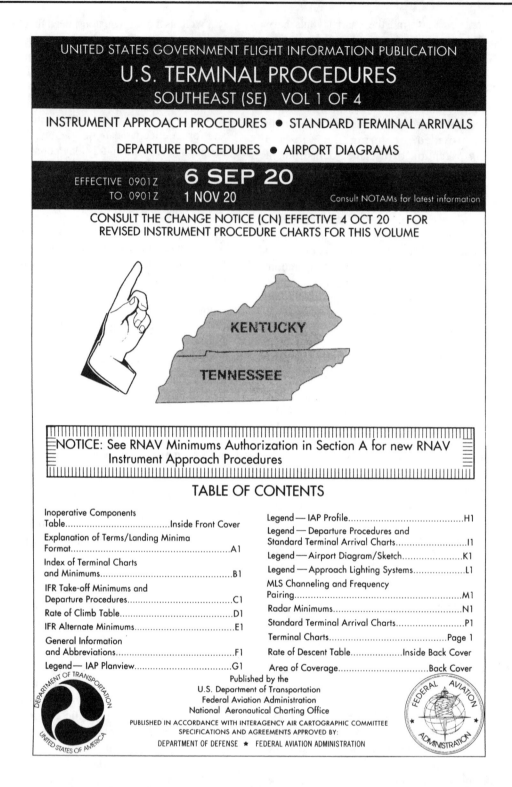

Fig. 8-2. U.S. Terminal Procedures. The books are issued for selected parts of the United States and have an effective period 56 days. The approach charts and accompanying information shown are for Volume 1 of 4 of the U.S. Southeast (SE-1). A booklet of change notices (CN) for the full 48-state part of the United States will be sent at the middle of each volume's valid period. The change notice here will be effective 6 Sep, giving an interim update (the pointing hand added by the writer). The user is advised to consult NOTAMs for the latest information. Check Figure 8-3 for the volumes available.

box. Many facilities with approach charts that do not have en route or feeder rings will have on the planview a large notation such as "RADAR OR

DME REQUIRED" (or RADAR REQUIRED"), but the main thing is to *read carefully* each approach chart for its requirements.

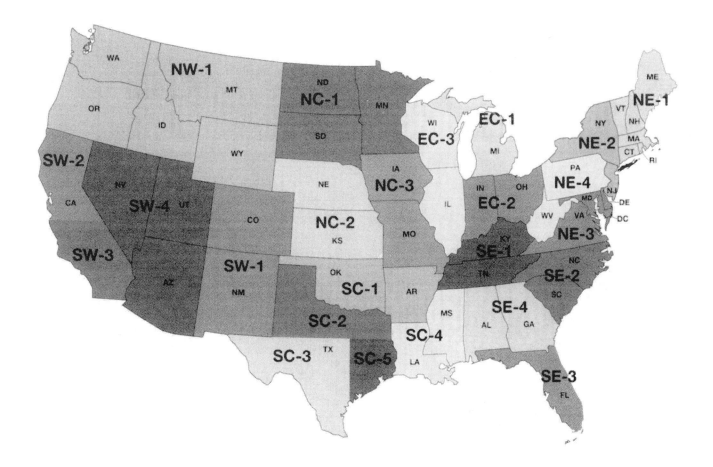

Fig. 8-3. U.S. Terminal Procedures charts coverage. As noted earlier, these books include information necessary for operating under IFR, such as approach and departure procedures, minimums for takeoff and landing, minimums for alternate airports, and airport diagrams. (See Figure 8-2 for the table of contents.)

6. Minimum safe altitudes (MSAs) are shown as *inbound magnetic* bearings. MSAs with the same altitude value for each of the four sectors have the information boxed and centered above the navaid symbol (Fig. 8-5A). Figure 8-5A is an IAP chart for ILS Runway 36L at Huntsville, Ala., showing the en route, feeder, and inner (10-NM) rings. Figure 8-5B shows the legend and the symbols for the planview part of the chart.

■ Profile View Looking at (2) in Figure 8-5A, you can see the profile view of the ILS Runway 36 approach at Huntsville.

Figure 8-6 is the legend for the minimum safe altitudes (MSA) and profile views that you'll see in the NACO charts.

■ Airport Diagram Figure 8-7 is the legend for the airport diagram airport sketch in the IAP charts. The airport sketch is *part* of the IAP chart and is located in the center; an airport diagram is a full-page detailed layout for a major airport accompanying the various pages of IAP charts. Figure 8-7 also shows a comparison of a sketch and diagram for the Huntsville-Madison County (Ala.) Airport. Take time to compare the data on the Huntsville airport information (Fig. 8-5A) with the legend.

■ Minimums Data The landing minimums data consists of the minimum descent altitude (MDA) or decision height (DH), runway visual range (RVR) or visibility, height above airport (HAA) or height above touchdown (HAT), and ceiling-visibility minimums in statute miles for the approach and approach-speed categories indicated in the Appendixes of the IAP chart volume.

The DH (DA) or MDA is MSL for the weather minimums for the type of approach. The RVR follows the DH or MDA, separated by a slash (/). Ceiling (remember that a ceiling is height above ground) and visibility values are shown in parentheses. RVR values are not shown at Huntsville (Fig. 8-5A).

The minimums data is applicable for both day and night unless specified on the procedure. If the night minimums are different, there will be an asterisk, and the data will be in the space below the minimums data.

Figure 8-8 is an explanation of terms (aircraft approach categories, RVR/meteorological visibility comparable values, landing minimums format, and radar minimums).

When the minimums for one type of approach are the same for two or more approach categories, the data is centered below the appropriate approach-speed categories. In

GENERAL INFORMATION

This publication includes Instrument Approach Procedures (IAPs), Departure Procedures (DPs), and Standard Terminal Arrivals (STARs) for use by both civil and military aviation and is issued every 56 days.

STANDARD TERMINAL ARRIVALS AND DEPARTURE PROCEDURES

The use of the associated codified STAR/DP and transition identifiers are requested of users when filing flight plans via teletype and are required for users filing flight plans via computer interface. It must be noted that when filing a STAR/DP with a transition, the first three coded characters of the STAR and the last three coded characters of the DP are replaced by the transition code. Examples: ACTON SIX ARRIVAL, file (AGN.AGN6); ACTON SIX ARRIVAL, EDNAS TRANSITION, file (EDNAS.AGN6). FREEHOLD THREE DEPARTURE, file (FREH3.RBV), FREEHOLD THREE DEPARTURE, ELWOOD CITY TRANSITION, file (FREH3.EWC).

PILOT CONTROLLED AIRPORT LIGHTING SYSTEMS

Available pilot controlled lighting (PCL) systems are indicated as follows:

1. Approach lighting systems that bear a system identification are symbolized using negative symbology, e.g. ⓐ, ⓑ, ⓒ.
2. Approach lighting systems that do not bear a system identification are indicated with a negative "●" beside the name.

A star (*) indicates non-standard PCL, consult Directory/Supplement, e.g. ●*

To activate lights use frequency indicated in the communication section of the chart with a ⓪ or the appropriate lighting system identification e.g., UNICOM 122.8 ⓪ ⓐ ⓑ

KEY MIKE   FUNCTION

7 times within 5 seconds   Highest intensity available

5 times within 5 seconds   Medium or lower intensity (Lower REIL or REIL-off)

3 times within 5 seconds   Lowest intensity available (Lower REIL or REIL-off)

CHART CURRENCY INFORMATION

```
               FAA procedure amendment number ──── Amdt 11A  99365 ──── Date of latest change
                                                ── Orig   00365
```

The Chart Date indentifies the Julian date the chart was added to the volume or last revised for any reason. The first two digits indicate the year, the last three digits indicate the day of the year (001 to 365/6) in which the latest addition or change was first published.

The Procedure Amendment Number precedes the Chart Date, and changes any time instrument information (e.g., DH, MDA, approach routing, etc.) changes. Procedure changes also cause the Chart Date to change.

MISCELLANEOUS

* Indicates a non-continuously operating facility, see A/FD or flight supplement.

# Indicates control tower temporarily closed UFN.

"Radar required" on the chart indicates that radar vectoring is required for the approach.

Distances in nautical miles (except visibility in statute miles and Runway Visual Range in hundreds of feet). Runway Dimensions in feet. Elevations in feet. Mean Sea Level (MSL). Ceilings in feet above airport elevation. Radials/bearings/headings/courses are magnetic. Horizontal Datum: Unless otherwise noted on the chart, all coordinates are referenced to North American Datum 1983 (NAD 83), which for charting purposes is considered equivalent to World Geodetic System 1984 (WGS 84).

ABBREVIATIONS

ADF.	Automatic Direction Finder
ALS.	Approach Light System
ALSF.	Approach Light System with Sequenced Flashing Lights
APP CON.	Approach Control
ARR.	Arrival
ASOS.	Automated Surface Observing System
ASR/PAR.	Published Radar Minimums at this Airport
ATIS.	Automatic Terminal Information Service
AWOS.	Automated Weather Observing System
AZ.	Azimuth
BC.	Back Course
C.	Circling
CAT.	Category
CCW.	Counter/Clockwise
Chan.	Channel
CLNC DEL.	Clearance Delivery
CNF.	Computer Navigation Fix
CTAF.	Common Traffic Advisory Frequency
CW.	Clockwise
DH.	Decision Height
DME.	Distance Measuring Equipment
DR.	Dead Reckoning
ELEV.	Elevation
FAF.	Final Approach Fix
FM.	Fan Marker
FMS.	Flight Management System
GCO.	Ground Communications Outlet
GPI.	Ground Point of Interception
GPS.	Global Positioning System
GS.	Glide Slope
HAA.	Height above Airport
HAL.	Height above Landing
HAT.	Height above Touchdown
HIRL.	High Intensity Runway Lights
IAF.	Initial Approach Fix
ICAO.	International Civil Aviation Organization
IM.	Inner Marker
Intcp.	Intercept
INT.	Intersection
LDA.	Localizer Type Directional Aid
Ldg.	Landing
LDIN.	Lead in Light System
LIRL.	Low Intensity Runway Lights
LOC.	Localizer
LR.	Lead Radial. Provides at least 2 NM (Copter 1 NM) of lead to assist in turning onto the intermediate/final course.
MALS.	Medium Intensity Approach Light System

MALSR.	Medium Intensity Approach Light System with RAIL
MAP.	Missed Approach Point
MDA.	Minimum Descent Altitude
MIRL.	Medium Intensity Runway Lights
MLS.	Microwave Landing System
MM.	Middle Marker
N/A.	Not Applicable
NA.	Not Authorized
NDB.	Non-directional Radio Beacon
NM.	Nautical Mile
NoPT.	No Procedure Turn Required (Procedure Turn shall not be executed without ATC clearance)
ODALS.	Omnidirectional Approach Light System
OM.	Outer Marker
R.	Radial
RA.	Radio Altimeter setting height
RAIL.	Runway Alignment Indicator Lights
RBn.	Radio Beacon
RCLS.	Runway Centerline Light System
REIL.	Runway End Identifier Lights
RNAV.	Area Navigation
RNP.	Required Navigation Performance
RPI.	Runway Point of Interception
RRL.	Runway Remaining Lights
Rwy.	Runway
RVR.	Runway Visual Range
S.	Straight-in
SALS.	Short Approach Light System
SSALR.	Simplified Short Approach Light System with RAIL
SDF.	Simplified Directional Facility
TA.	Transition Altitude
TAA.	Terminal Arrival Area
TAC.	TACAN
TCH.	Threshold Crossing Height (height in feet Above Ground level)
TDZ.	Touchdown Zone
TDZE.	Touchdown Zone Elevation
TDZ/CL.	Touchdown Zone and Runway Centerline Lighting
TDZL.	Touchdown Zone Lights
Tlv.	Transition Level
VASI.	Visual Approach Slope Indicator
VDP.	Visual Descent Point
VGSI.	Visual Glide Slope Indicator
WP/WPT.	Waypoint (RNAV)
X.	Radar Only Frequency

Fig. 8-4. General information and abbreviations for Terminal Procedures. You'll have to refer back to this from time to time as the chapter proceeds.

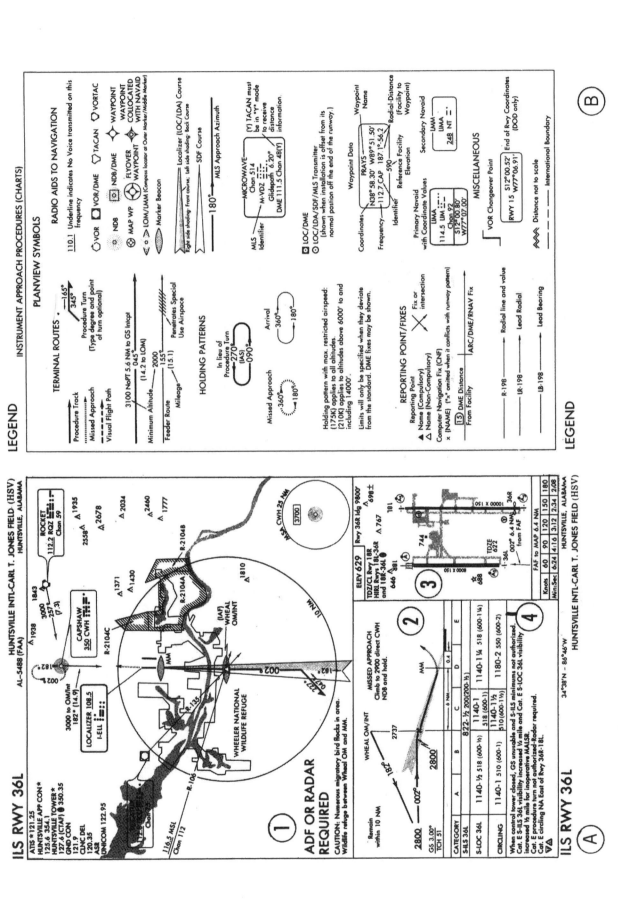

Fig 8-5. Approach chart for the Huntsville-Madison County (Alabama) Airport and legend for the planview portion of the chart. **A.** The chart, as mentioned earlier, has four major parts as numbered here: (1) planview, (2) profile view, (3) airport sketch, (4) minimums data. **B.** Planview legend and symbols.

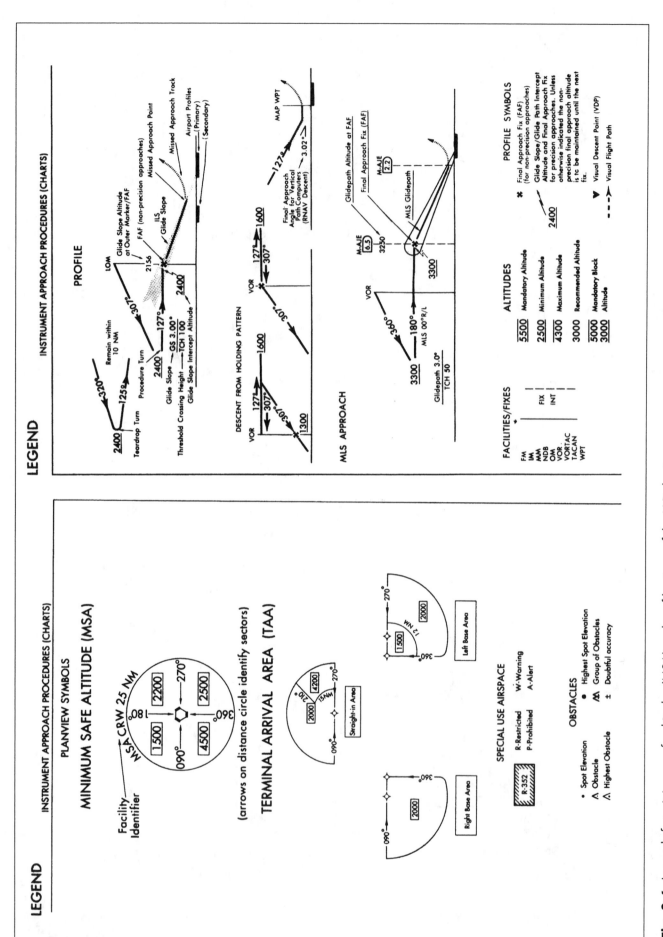

Fig. 8-6. Legends for minimum safe altitudes (MSA) and profile views of the IAP charts.

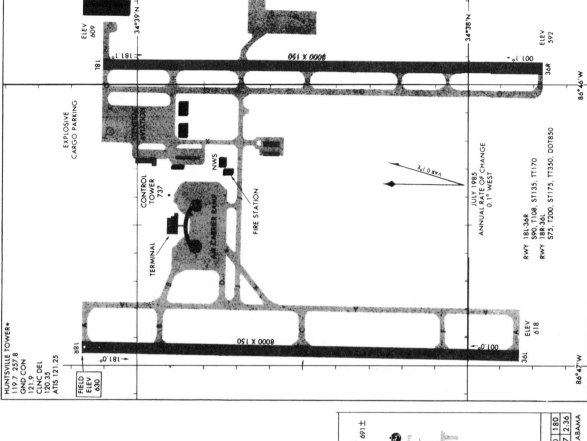

AIRPORT DIAGRAM

AL-5488 (FAA)

HUNTSVILLE INTL-CARL T. JONES FIELD (HSV)
HUNTSVILLE, ALABAMA

HUNTSVILLE TOWER*
119.7 257.8
GND CON
121.9
CLNC DEL
120.35
ATIS 121.25

FIELD
ELEV
630

EXPLOSIVE
CARGO PARKING

CONTROL
TOWER
737

TERMINAL

FIRE STATION

NWS

AIR CARRIER RAMP

ELEV
609

34°39'N

34°38'N

8000 X 150

9000 X 150

181

36R

18R

36L

ELEV
592

ELEV
618

86°46'W

86°47'W

JULY 1985
ANNUAL RATE OF CHANGE
0.1° WEST

VAR 0.1°E

RWY 18L-36R
S90, T108, ST135, TT170
RWY 18R-36L
S75, T200, ST175, TT350, DDT850

HUNTSVILLE, ALABAMA
HUNTSVILLE INTL-CARL T. JONES FIELD (HSV)

AIRPORT DIAGRAM

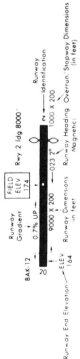

ELEV 629

094° 7.8 NM
from FAF

691 ±

767

181

657

737

36R

18R   36L

8000 X 150

8000 X 150

633   688

REIL Rwy 36R
TDZ/CL Rwy 18R
HIRL Rwys 18L-36R and 18R-36L

	FAF to MAP 7.8 NM				
Knots	60	90	120	150	180
Min:Sec	7:48	5:12	3:54	3:07	2:36

HUNTSVILLE, ALABAMA

Sketch

LEGEND
INSTRUMENT APPROACH PROCEDURES (CHARTS)

AIRPORT DIAGRAM/AIRPORT SKETCH

Runways

Hard
Surface

Closed   Other Than   Overruns, Stopways,   Parking
          Hard Surface Taxiways   Areas

Closed   X X X
Runway

Under   Metal
Construction Surface

ARRESTING GEAR: Specific arresting gear systems; e.g.
BAK-12, MA-1A etc. shown on airport diagrams, not
applicable to Civil Pilots. Military Pilots Refer to
Appropriate DOD Publications.

uni-directional   bi-directional

REFERENCE FEATURES

Buildings

Tanks

Obstruction

Airport Beacon #

Runway
Radar Reflectors

Control Tower #

Displaced
Threshold

Runway
Centerline
Lighting

Jet Barrier

When Control Tower and Rotating Beacon are
co-located Beacon symbol will be used and
further identified as TWR.

Runway length depicted is the physical length of
the runway end-to-end including displaced
thresholds if any but excluding areas designated
as overruns. Where a displaced threshold is shown,
an annotation is added to indicate the landing
length of the runway e.g. Rwy 13 ldg 5000'.

Runway Weight Bearing Capacity is
shown as a codified expression.
Refer to the appropriate Supplement Directory
for applicable codes. e.g. RWY 14-32
S75, T185, ST175, TT325

Helicopter Alighting Areas

Negative Symbols used to identify Copter Procedures
landing point

Runway TDZ elevation .... TDZE 123

Total Runway Gradient .... 0.8% UP
(shown when runway gradient exceeds 0.3%)

US Navy Optical Landing System (OLS). "OLS"
location is shown because of its height of
approximately 7 feet and proximity to edge of
runway may create an obstruction for some types
of aircraft.

Approach light symbols are shown in the
Flight Information Handbook.

Airport diagram scales are variable.

True magnetic North orientation may vary from diagram to diagram.

Coordinate values are shown in 1 or ½ minute increments. They are further broken down into 6 second ticks,
within each 1 minute increment.

Positional accuracy within ±600 feet unless otherwise
noted on the chart

NOTE
All new and revised airport diagrams are shown referenced to the World Geodetic System (W.G.S.) (noted on
appropriate diagram), and may not be compatible
with local coordinates published in FLIP. (Foreign Only)

SCOPE

Runway
Identification

1000 X 200

023.2°

9000 X 200

Runway
Gradient
0.7% UP

Rwy 2 ldg 8000'

FIELD
ELEV
174

Runway Heading Overrun/Stopway Dimensions
Magnetic   (in feet)

BAK-12   ELEV
          164

20

Runway End Elevation

Runway Dimensions
(in feet)

Airport diagrams are specifically designed to assist in the movement of ground traffic at locations with complex
runway taxiway configurations and provide information for updating Computer Based Navigation Systems (I.E., INS, GPS)
aboard aircraft. Airport diagrams are not intended to be used for approach and landing or departure operations. Requisitions
for the creation of airport diagrams must meet the above criteria and will be approved by the FAA or DOD on a case-by-case
basis.

Fig. 8-7. Airport sketch and diagram for the Huntsville- Madison County Airport. (IAP charts)

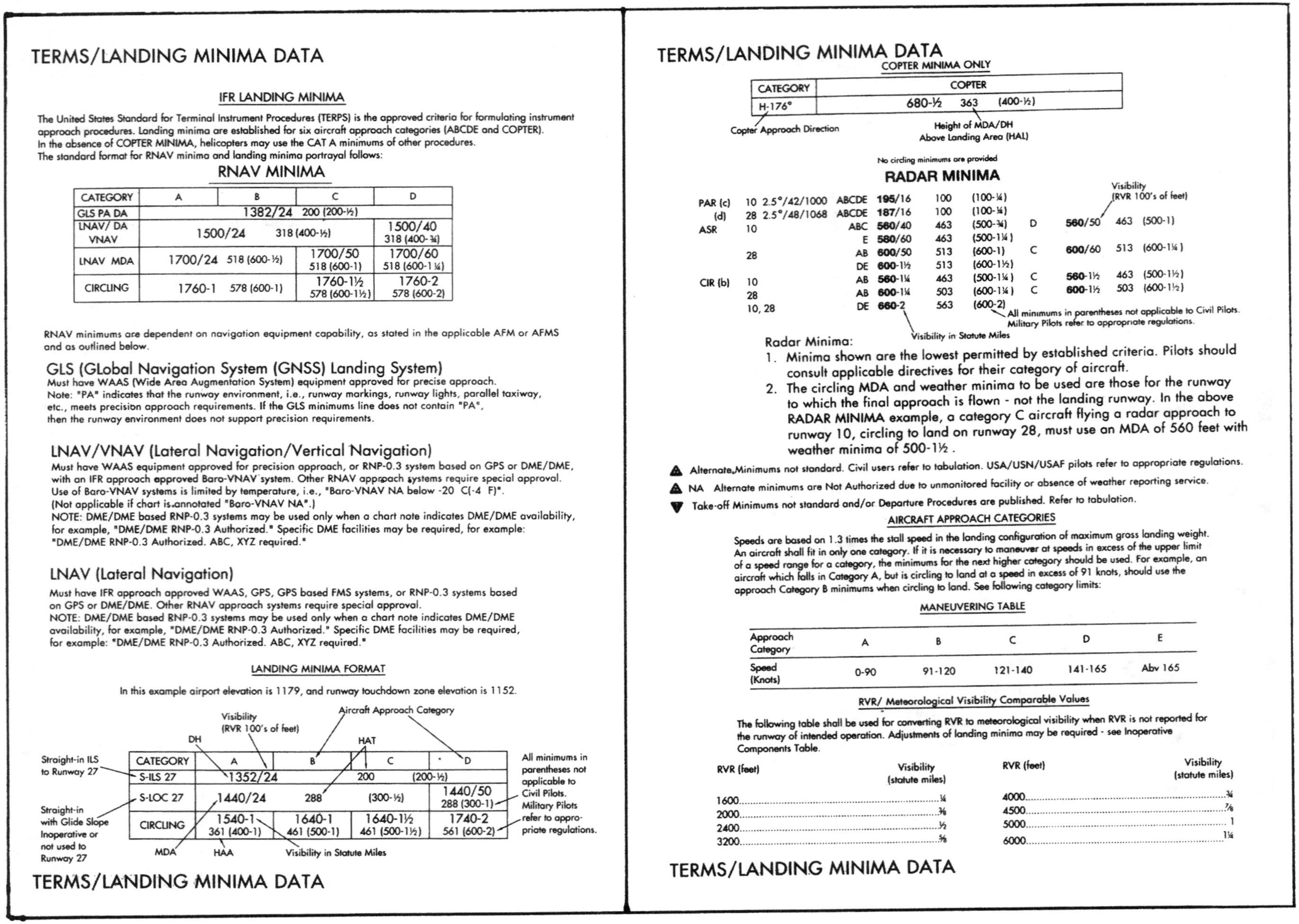

TERMS/LANDING MINIMA DATA

IFR LANDING MINIMA

The United States Standard for Terminal Instrument Procedures (TERPS) is the approved criteria for formulating instrument approach procedures. Landing minima are established for six aircraft approach categories (ABCDE and COPTER). In the absence of COPTER MINIMA, helicopters may use the CAT A minimums of other procedures. The standard format for RNAV minima and landing minima portrayal follows:

RNAV MINIMA

CATEGORY	A	B	C	D
GLS PA DA	1382/24 200 (200-½)			
LNAV/ DA VNAV	1500/24 318 (400-½)			1500/40 318 (400-¾)
LNAV MDA	1700/24 518 (600-½)		1700/50 518 (600-1)	1700/60 518 (600-1¼)
CIRCLING	1760-1 578 (600-1)		1760-1½ 578 (600-1½)	1760-2 578 (600-2)

RNAV minimums are dependent on navigation equipment capability, as stated in the applicable AFM or AFMS and as outlined below.

GLS (GLobal Navigation System (GNSS) Landing System)

Must have WAAS (Wide Area Augmentation System) equipment approved for precise approach.
Note: "PA" indicates that the runway environment, i.e., runway markings, runway lights, parallel taxiway, etc., meets precision approach requirements. If the GLS minimums line does not contain "PA", then the runway environment does not support precision requirements.

LNAV/VNAV (Lateral Navigation/Vertical Navigation)

Must have WAAS equipment approved for precision approach, or RNP-0.3 system based on GPS or DME/DME, with an IFR approach approved Baro-VNAV system. Other RNAV approach systems require special approval. Use of Baro-VNAV systems is limited by temperature, i.e., "Baro-VNAV NA below -20 C(-4 F)". (Not applicable if chart is annotated "Baro-VNAV NA".)
NOTE: DME/DME based RNP-0.3 systems may be used only when a chart note indicates DME/DME availability, for example, "DME/DME RNP-0.3 Authorized." Specific DME facilities may be required, for example: "DME/DME RNP-0.3 Authorized. ABC, XYZ required."

LNAV (Lateral Navigation)

Must have IFR approach approved WAAS, GPS, GPS based FMS systems, or RNP-0.3 systems based on GPS or DME/DME. Other RNAV approach systems require special approval.
NOTE: DME/DME based RNP-0.3 systems may be used only when a chart note indicates DME/DME availability, for example, "DME/DME RNP-0.3 Authorized." Specific DME facilities may be required, for example: "DME/DME RNP-0.3 Authorized. ABC, XYZ required."

LANDING MINIMA FORMAT

In this example airport elevation is 1179, and runway touchdown zone elevation is 1152.

Visibility (RVR 100's of feet) · Aircraft Approach Category · DH · HAT

CATEGORY	A	B	C	D
S-ILS 27	1352/24		200 (200-½)	
S-LOC 27	1440/24		288 (300-½)	1440/50 288 (300-1)
CIRCLING	1540-1 361 (400-1)	1640-1 461 (500-1)	1640-1½ 461 (500-1½)	1740-2 561 (600-2)

Straight-in ILS to Runway 27

Straight-in with Glide Slope Inoperative or not used to Runway 27

MDA · HAA · Visibility in Statute Miles

All minimums in parentheses not applicable to Civil Pilots. Military Pilots refer to appropriate regulations.

TERMS/LANDING MINIMA DATA

TERMS/LANDING MINIMA DATA

COPTER MINIMA ONLY

CATEGORY	COPTER
H-176°	680-½ 363 (400-½)

Copter Approach Direction · Height of MDA/DH Above Landing Area (HAL)

No circling minimums are provided

RADAR MINIMA

PAR (c)	10 2.5°/42/1000	ABCDE	195/16	100	(100-¼)				
(d)	28 2.5°/48/1068	ABCDE	187/16	100	(100-¼)				
ASR	10	ABC	560/40	463	(500-¾)	D	560/50	463	(500-1)
		E	580/60	463	(500-1¼)				
	28	AB	600/50	513	(600-1)	C	600/60	513	(600-1¼)
		DE	600-1½	513	(600-1½)				
CIR (b)	10	AB	560-1¼	463	(500-1¼)	C	560-1½	463	(500-1½)
	28	AB	600-1¼	503	(600-1¼)	C	600-1½	503	(600-1½)
	10, 28	DE	660-2	563	(600-2)				

Visibility (RVR 100's of feet) · Visibility in Statute Miles

All minimums in parentheses not applicable to Civil Pilots. Military Pilots refer to appropriate regulations.

Radar Minima:

1. Minima shown are the lowest permitted by established criteria. Pilots should consult applicable directives for their category of aircraft.
2. The circling MDA and weather minima to be used are those for the runway to which the final approach is flown - not the landing runway. In the above RADAR MINIMA example, a category C aircraft flying a radar approach to runway 10, circling to land on runway 28, must use an MDA of 560 feet with weather minima of 500-1½.

▲ Alternate Minimums not standard. Civil users refer to tabulation. USA/USN/USAF pilots refer to appropriate regulations.

▲ NA Alternate minimums are Not Authorized due to unmonitored facility or absence of weather reporting service.

▼ Take-off Minimums not standard and/or Departure Procedures are published. Refer to tabulation.

AIRCRAFT APPROACH CATEGORIES

Speeds are based on 1.3 times the stall speed in the landing configuration of maximum gross landing weight. An aircraft shall fit in only one category. If it is necessary to maneuver at speeds in excess of the upper limit of a speed range for a category, the minimums for the next higher category should be used. For example, an aircraft which falls in Category A, but is circling to land at a speed in excess of 91 knots, should use the approach Category B minimums when circling to land. See following category limits:

MANEUVERING TABLE

Approach Category	A	B	C	D	E
Speed (Knots)	0-90	91-120	121-140	141-165	Abv 165

RVR/ Meteorological Visibility Comparable Values

The following table shall be used for converting RVR to meteorological visibility when RVR is not reported for the runway of intended operation. Adjustments of landing minima may be required - see Inoperative Components Table.

RVR (feet)	Visibility (statute miles)	RVR (feet)	Visibility (statute miles)
1600	¼	4000	¾
2000	⅜	4500	⅞
2400	½	5000	1
3200	⅝	6000	1¼

TERMS/LANDING MINIMA DATA

Fig. 8-8. *IAP charts* explanation of terms, approach categories, RVR/meteorological visibility comparable values, and landing minimums format.

Figure 8-8 the straight-in localizer approach for Runway 27 has the same minimums for A, B, and C approach categories.

The A (IFR alternate) and T (IFR takeoff) minimums symbols in the minimums data box indicate that other than standard minimums apply.

■ **Alternate Requirements** The standard alternate airport minimums (if no alternate minimums are specified for that airport in the instrument approach procedure) are:

1. Precision approach procedure—Ceiling 600 ft and visibility 2 statute miles (SM).
2. Nonprecision approach procedure—Ceiling 800 ft and visibility 2 SM.

When you file an IFR flight plan (to be covered in detail in Chapter 9), listing of an alternate is not required if there is a standard instrument approach for the airport of first intended landing and, for at least 1 hr before and for 1 hr after the estimated time of arrival, the weather reports or forecasts or any combination of them indicate that (1) the ceiling will be at least 2000 ft above the airport elevation and (2) the visibility will be at least 3 SM.

■ **Takeoff Requirements** Note that Huntsville (Fig. 8-5A) has a symbol for nonstandard takeoff requirements in the minimums box. To check this out you would have to look in the IAP charts volume for further information. Figure 8-9 shows the nonstandard takeoff and alternate minimums for several airports, including Huntsville-Madison County.

■ **Inoperative Components** Figure 8-10 shows the effects of inoperative components for various types of approach aids. Note that runway lighting definitely has an effect on the minimums for the various aircraft approach categories (A, B, C, D).

■ **Lighting** Speaking of the importance of lighting, Figure 8-11 shows the approach lighting systems as given in the IAP chart volumes. There's also information in more detail in Chapter 2 of the *Aeronautical Information Manual (AIM)*. Most pilots take the lighting systems for granted, but each has a purpose. For example, the roll guidance bars (the lights *perpendicular* to the approach path lighting) are a great help in marginal visibility (particularly at night) to keep you from dropping a wing or getting into other lateral/directional problems.

Figure 8-12 shows runway markings as given in Chapter 2 of the *AIM*.

SOME SAMPLE APPROACH CHARTS

Following are different types of approaches as depicted in IAP charts. Study and "fly" each one in your mind, going through procedures step by step. The approach will be much clearer, and it will help your other approaches in the airplane.

■ **VOR Approaches**
VOR RWY 2. Figure 8-13 is a sample VOR Runway 2 approach to Centerville, Tenn., using the Graham VOR, which will be one of the navaids on the sample Memphis-Nashville IFR flight later. (Graham VOR was on the route shown in Chapter 6.)

To have a VOR approach for a specific runway (straight-in), the final approach course must be within 30° of the runway heading. The approach to Centerville is to Runway 2, which would have a lineup of close to 020° magnetic. It could be 016° or 024° magnetic, for instance (but assume that it's 020°), so that the final approach course is off about 26° or just within limits for a legal straight-in approach. The straight-in and circling approaches have the same minimums. This is an older approach chart.

Figure 8-14 is VOR-A and VOR/DME-B approaches for Mt. Sterling, Ky. If the final approach course is more than 30° from a runway, the designation is VOR-A, VOR-B, NDB-A, NDB-B, etc., rather than VOR RWY 2, NDB RWY 10, etc., discussed earlier. Note that radar (from Lexington approach control) is required for VOR-A and, of course, DME equipment in the airplane is required for VOR/DME-B. These approaches are no longer in existence, having been replaced by NDB, NDB or GPS RWY 3 and GPS RWY 21, but looking at them brings up a few points on those types of approaches that need to be covered.

The point is that only circling minimums are given, since an approach angle over 30° cannot be considered for a straight-in approach.

VOR-A. Note in the VOR-A approach in Figure 8-14 that the holding pattern associated with the missed approach procedure is shown by dashed lines to separate it from the en route or preapproach holding patterns (solid lines).

The minimum safe altitude is 3000 ft for 360° around the HYK (Lexington) VOR.

Note that the minimum altitude is 3000 ft until crossing the FILIE final approach fix (FAF). That would give you 8.8 NM to lose 1300 ft, which would certainly seem to give plenty of time; but one of the more common errors of trainees and low-time instrument pilots is that on nonprecision approaches they cruise along from the FAF, losing little or no altitude until they suddenly realize that, whoops, we're there!

Another common error on nonprecision approaches is to realize that you have passed the FAF but forgot to note the time. The instructor or check pilot may asks, "When will we be there?" and you are sitting under the hood with sweat rolling down. Most instructors or check pilots will keep you hooded until the time for the missed approach at which point you are to "come contact." If you haven't noted the time at the FAF, this can be a pretty tough problem indeed. Note that the time from the FAF to the missed approach point is 5 min and 52 sec at 90 knots *groundspeed*.

The idea of the 5 Ts is a good one here (and other times too):

*T*urn—(Not required at the FAF here but should always be considered.)
*T*ime—Utmost importance.
*T*wist—Do you need to change frequencies? (Not here.)
*T*hrottle—You'll probably want to reduce power at this point to set up a descent at the preselected approach speed.

⧍ ALTERNATE MINS

⧍ 00335

INSTRUMENT APPROACH PROCEDURE CHARTS
⧍ IFR ALTERNATE MINIMUMS
(NOT APPLICABLE TO USA/USN/USAF)

Standard alternate minimums for non precision approaches are 800-2 (NDB, VOR, LOC, TACAN, LDA, VORTAC, VOR/DME or ASR); for precision approaches 600-2 (ILS or PAR). Airports within this geographical area that require alternate minimums other than standard or alternate minimums with restrictions are listed below. NA - means alternate minimums are not authorized due to unmonitored facility or absence of weather reporting service. Civil pilots see FAR 91. USA/USN/USAF pilots refer to appropriate regulations.

NAME	ALTERNATE MINIMUMS
BRISTOL-JOHNSON-KINGSPORT, TN	
TRI-CITY	
REGIONAL TN/VA	ILS Rwy 5, 900-2¾
	ILS Rwy 23, 1000-3
	NDB or GPS Rwy 5, 900-2¾
	NDB or GPS Rwy 23, 1000-3

NA when control tower closed.

NAME	ALTERNATE MINIMUMS
CHATTANOOGA, TN	
LOVELL FIELD	ILS Rwy 2[1]
	ILS Rwy 20[1]
	NDB or GPS Rwy 20[2]
	RADAR-1[3]
	VOR or GPS Rwy 33[3]

NA when control tower closed.
[1]ILS, Categories A,B,C, 700-2; Category D, 900-2¾. LOC, Category D, 900-2¾.
[2]Categories A,B, 900-2; Categories C,D, 900-2¾.
[3]Category D, 900-2¾.

NAME	ALTERNATE MINIMUMS
COVINGTON, KY	
CINCINNATI/NORTHERN KENTUCKY	
INTL	ILS Rwy 9
	ILS Rwy 18L
	ILS Rwy 18R
	ILS Rwy 27
	ILS Rwy 36L
	ILS Rwy 36R

ILS, Category D, 700-2.

NAME	ALTERNATE MINIMUMS
HUNTSVILLE, AL	
HUNTSVILLE INTL-CARL T. JONES	
FIELD	ILS Rwy 18L
	ILS Rwy 18R
	ILS Rwy 36L
	NDB or GPS Rwy 18R
	RADAR-1

NA when control tower closed.

NAME	ALTERNATE MINIMUMS
LONDON, KY	
LONDON-CORBIN COUNTY-	
MAGEE FIELD	VOR/DME RNAV Rwy 5
	VOR Rwy 5

Category D, 800-2¼.

NAME	ALTERNATE MINIMUMS
LOUISVILLE, KY	
BOWMAN FIELD	VOR Rwy 24

Category C, 800-2¼; Category D, 800-2¾.

NAME	ALTERNATE MINIMUMS
LOUISVILLE INTL	
STANDIFORD FIELD	ILS Rwy 17L[1]
	ILS Rwy 17R[1]
	ILS Rwy 35L[1]
	ILS Rwy 35R[2]
	VOR or TACAN Rwy 29[3]

[1]Categories A,B, 900-2¼;Category C, 900-2½;
Category D, 900-2¾.
[2]Categories A,B, 900-2¼;Category C, 900-2¾;
Category D, 900-3.
[3]Category C, 800-2¼; Category D, 800-2¾.

NAME	ALTERNATE MINIMUMS
MEMPHIS, TN	
MEMPHIS INTL	ILS Rwy 9
	ILS Rwy 18C
	ILS Rwy 18L
	ILS Rwy 18R
	ILS Rwy 27
	ILS Rwy 36C
	ILS Rwy 36L
	ILS Rwy 36R
	VOR/DME Rwy 18R

Category E, 800-2¾.

⧍ TAKE-OFF MINIMUMS AND (OBSTACLE) DEPARTURE PROCEDURES

⧍ 99364

INSTRUMENT APPROACH PROCEDURE CHARTS
⧍ IFR TAKE-OFF MINIMUMS AND (OBSTACLE) DEPARTURE PROCEDURES
Civil Airports and Selected Military Airports

ALL USERS: Airports that have Departure Procedures (DPs) designed specifically to assist pilots in avoiding obstacles during the climb to the minimum enroute altitude, and/or airports that have civil IFR take-off minimums other than standard, are listed below. Take-off Minimums and Departure Procedures apply to all runways unless otherwise specified. Altitudes, unless otherwise indicated, are minimum altitudes in MSL.

DPs specifically designed for obstacle avoidance are described below in text, or published separately as a graphic procedure. If the (Obstacle) DP is published as a graphic procedure, its name will be listed below, and it can be found in either this volume (civil), or a separate Departure Procedure volume (military), as appropriate. Users will recognize (Obstacle) graphic DPs referenced below by the following note printed on the charted procedure: "If not assigned a Departure Procedure by ATC, this procedure may be flown to provide obstacle clearance." The term "(OBSTACLE)" will also be printed on the charted procedure. [Note: Graphic Departure Procedures that have been designed primarily to assist Air Traffic Control in providing air traffic separation (as well as providing obstacle clearance) are usually assigned by name in an ATC clearance and are not listed by name in this section.]

CIVIL USERS NOTE: FAR 91 prescribes standard take-off rules and establishes take-off minimums for certain operators as follows: (1) Aircraft having two engines or less - one statute mile. (2) Aircraft having more than two engines - one-half statute mile. These standard minima apply in the absence of any different minima listed below.

MILITARY USERS NOTE: Civil (nonstandard) take-off minima are published below. For military take-off minima, refer to appropriate service directives.

NAME	TAKE-OFF MINIMUMS
ADEL, GA	
COOK COUNTY	
DEPARTURE PROCEDURE: Rwy 5, turn left heading 360° to 1200 before turning on course.	
ALABASTER, AL	
SHELBY COUNTY	
TAKE-OFF MINIMUMS: Rwys 15, 33, 400-1.	
ALEXANDER CITY, AL	
THOMAS C. RUSSELL FIELD	
DEPARTURE PROCEDURE: Rwys 18, 36, climb runway heading to 1500 before turning on course.	
AMERICUS, GA	
SOUTHER FIELD	
DEPARTURE PROCEDURE: All runways, climb runway heading to 800 before turning.	

NAME	TAKE-OFF MINIMUMS
ANDALUSIA/OPP, AL	
ANDALUSIA-OPP	
TAKE-OFF MINIMUMS: Rwys 11, 29, 200-1 or std. with min. climb of 310' per NM to 500.	
DEPARTURE PROCEDURE: Rwys 11, 29, climb runway heading to 500 before turning.	
ANNISTON, AL	
ANNISTON METROPOLITAN	
TAKE-OFF MINIMUMS: Rwy 5, 900-1 or std. with a min. climb of 350' per NM to 1600.	
DEPARTURE PROCEDURE: Rwy 5, climbing right turn heading 090° to 3000 before proceeding on course. Rwy 23, climb runway heading to 3000 before turning on course.	

Fig. 8-9. IFR takeoff and alternate minimums. Check back to Figure 8-4 if some of the abbreviations aren't known to you. (IAP charts)

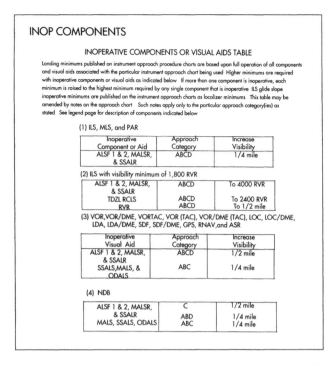

Fig. 8-10. Inoperative components or visual aids table—effects on minimums. *(IAP charts)*

*T*alk—You'd make any reports that would apply to Lexington approach control.

If you made a missed approach, you'd notify Lexington approach control *after* you've done whichever of the first four Ts are required. Too many pilots, once the FAF is passed, feel *committed to land.* Not so: Have the missed approach procedure in your mind before you start the approach.

The FLM (117.0 MHz) shown as part of the missed approach procedure is the Falmouth, Ky., VOR/DME.

Note that JESTR, the 14-NM radar fix, is 13.8 NM from the MAP and is the IAF. Two VOR receivers would be a great help holding at CODEL after the missed approach.

Your circling flight pattern would depend on several factors such as runway in use, other traffic, and ceiling and visibility.

The *AIM* covers circling this way:

Circling minimums—In some busy terminal areas, ATC may not allow circling and circling minimums will not be published. Published circling minimums provide obstacle clearance when pilots remain within the appropriate area of protection. Pilots should remain at or above the circling altitude until the aircraft is continuously in a position from which a descent to a landing on the intended runway can be made at a normal rate of descent using normal maneuvers. Circling may require maneuvers at low altitude, at low airspeed, and in marginal weather conditions. Pilots must use sound judgment, have an in-depth knowledge of their capabilities, and fully understand the aircraft performance to determine the exact circling maneuver since weather, unique airport design, and the aircraft position, altitude, and airspeed must all be considered. The following basic rules apply:

(1) Maneuver the shortest path to the base or downwind leg, as appropriate, considering existing weather conditions. There is no restriction from passing over the airport or other runways.

(2) It should be recognized that circling maneuvers may be made while VFR or other flying is in progress at the airport. Standard left turns or specific instruction from the controller for maneuvering must be considered when circling to land.

(3) At airports without a control tower, it may be desirable to fly over the airport to observe wind and turn indicators and other traffic which may be on the runway or flying in the vicinity of the airport.

VOR/DME-B. The Mt. Sterling VOR/DME-B is straightforward (Fig. 8-14). The Lexington VORTAC is the initial approach fix and, as indicated earlier, the aircraft must have DME equipment to use it. The airport is 23.8 mi from the VORTAC.

Notice that on the missed approach the "old" type of holding pattern for the missed approach procedure is depicted (see Fig. 8-5B).

Again, "fly" the approach in your mind, think of the power settings for each part of the approach for your airplane, and visualize the steps in the missed approach procedure.

Figure 8-15 is an NDB or GPS RWY 18 approach for Winchester, Tenn. Note that the minimum safe altitude is 3400 ft for all quadrants.

The SDF (simplified directional facility) was discussed in Chapter 5. Go back and study Figure 5-51, an SDF approach to Tullahoma, Tenn., in more detail.

Back course localizer approaches still exist but, as noted in Chapter 5, they are gradually being replaced at larger airports by additional front course approaches. You might go back and look at Figure 5-46 for the IAP chart presentation.

The IAP charts selected here and those referred to in Chapter 5 are fairly simple introductions to the presentation of approach information. Some can get pretty cluttered with information at bigger airports with complex equipment, and Chapter 13 will cover each of the Nashville approaches (there are 11 of them used in this printing) in more detail to show your choices at the end of the sample trip.

RADAR APPROACHES. Figure 8-16 shows civil radar instrument approach minimums for Nashville as presented in the IAP chart volume. (More about Nashville radar minimums in Chapter 13.)

Airport Surveillance Radar (ASR)—The ASR is designed to give relatively short-range coverage in the general vicinity of an airport and to be a quick and safe means of handling terminal area traffic precisely. The ASR can also be used as an instrument approach aid (Fig. 8-16).

The ASR scans 360° of azimuth and gives target information on the radar display in the approach control or center.

Precision Approach Radar (PAR)—The PAR is used as a *landing* aid rather than an aid for sequencing aircraft as is the case for the ASR. It may be used as a primary landing aid or to monitor other types of approaches. It displays *range, azimuth,* and *elevation* information.

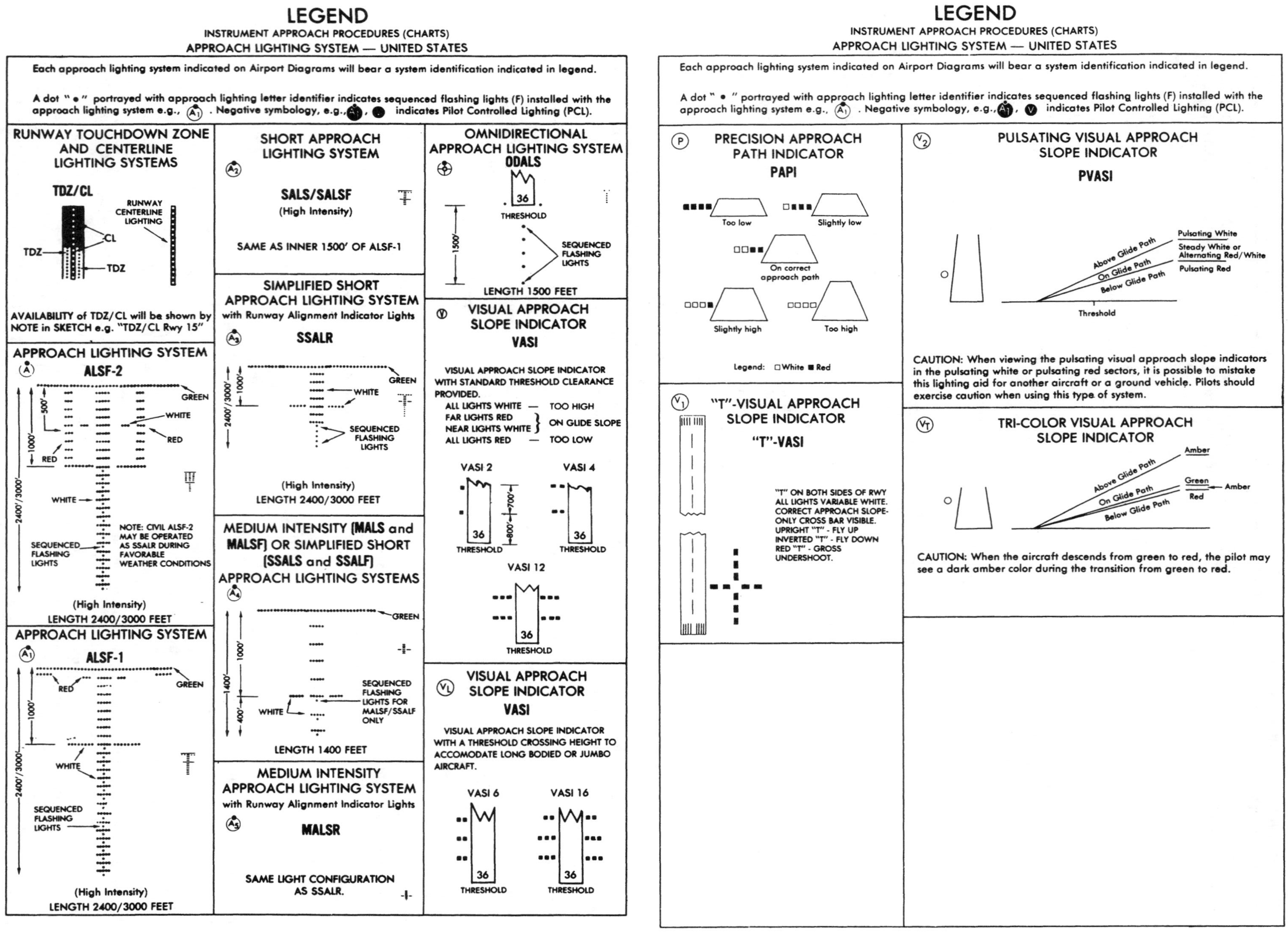

Each approach lighting system indicated on Airport Diagrams will bear a system identification indicated in legend.

A dot " • " portrayed with approach lighting letter identifier indicates sequenced flashing lights (F) installed with the approach lighting system e.g., (A₁) . Negative symbology, e.g., (A₁) . ● indicates Pilot Controlled Lighting (PCL).

PRECISION APPROACH PATH INDICATOR
PAPI
(P)

Too low

Slightly low

On correct approach path

Slightly high

Too high

Legend: ☐ White ■ Red

"T"-VISUAL APPROACH SLOPE INDICATOR
"T"-VASI
(V₁)

"T" ON BOTH SIDES OF RWY
ALL LIGHTS VARIABLE WHITE.
CORRECT APPROACH SLOPE-
ONLY CROSS BAR VISIBLE.
UPRIGHT "T" - FLY UP
INVERTED "T" - FLY DOWN
RED "T" - GROSS
UNDERSHOOT.

PULSATING VISUAL APPROACH SLOPE INDICATOR
PVASI
(V₂)

Pulsating White
Steady White or Alternating Red/White
Pulsating Red

Above Glide Path
On Glide Path
Below Glide Path
Threshold

CAUTION: When viewing the pulsating visual approach slope indicators in the pulsating white or pulsating red sectors, it is possible to mistake this lighting aid for another aircraft or a ground vehicle. Pilots should exercise caution when using this type of system.

TRI-COLOR VISUAL APPROACH SLOPE INDICATOR
(Vₜ)

Amber
Green
Red

Above Glide Path
On Glide Path
Below Glide Path

CAUTION: When the aircraft descends from green to red, the pilot may see a dark amber color during the transition from green to red.

LEGEND

INSTRUMENT APPROACH PROCEDURES (CHARTS)
APPROACH LIGHTING SYSTEM — UNITED STATES

Each approach lighting system indicated on Airport Diagrams will bear a system identification indicated in legend.

A dot " • " portrayed with approach lighting letter identifier indicates sequenced flashing lights (F) installed with the approach lighting system e.g., (A₁) . Negative symbology, e.g., (A₁) . ● indicates Pilot Controlled Lighting (PCL).

RUNWAY TOUCHDOWN ZONE AND CENTERLINE LIGHTING SYSTEMS
TDZ/CL

RUNWAY CENTERLINE LIGHTING
CL
TDZ
TDZ

AVAILABILITY OF TDZ/CL WILL BE SHOWN BY NOTE IN SKETCH e.g. "TDZ/CL Rwy 15"

SHORT APPROACH LIGHTING SYSTEM
SALS/SALSF
(A₂)
(High Intensity)

SAME AS INNER 1500' OF ALSF-1

OMNIDIRECTIONAL APPROACH LIGHTING SYSTEM
ODALS

36
THRESHOLD

SEQUENCED FLASHING LIGHTS

1500'

LENGTH 1500 FEET

APPROACH LIGHTING SYSTEM
ALSF-2
(A)

GREEN
WHITE
RED

500'
1000'
RED
WHITE
SEQUENCED FLASHING LIGHTS

NOTE: CIVIL ALSF-2 MAY BE OPERATED AS SSALR DURING FAVORABLE WEATHER CONDITIONS

2400'/3000'
(High Intensity)
LENGTH 2400/3000 FEET

SIMPLIFIED SHORT APPROACH LIGHTING SYSTEM
with Runway Alignment Indicator Lights
SSALR
(A₃)

GREEN
WHITE
SEQUENCED FLASHING LIGHTS

1000'
2400'/3000'

MEDIUM INTENSITY (MALS and MALSF) OR SIMPLIFIED SHORT (SSALS and SSALF) APPROACH LIGHTING SYSTEMS
(A₄)

GREEN
WHITE
SEQUENCED FLASHING LIGHTS FOR MALSF/SSALF ONLY

1000'
400'
1400'

(High Intensity)
LENGTH 2400/3000 FEET

LENGTH 1400 FEET

APPROACH LIGHTING SYSTEM
ALSF-1
(A)

GREEN
RED
WHITE

1000'
2400'/3000'

(High Intensity)
LENGTH 2400/3000 FEET

VISUAL APPROACH SLOPE INDICATOR
VASI
(V)

VISUAL APPROACH SLOPE INDICATOR WITH STANDARD THRESHOLD CLEARANCE PROVIDED.

ALL LIGHTS WHITE — TOO HIGH
FAR LIGHTS RED NEAR LIGHTS WHITE } ON GLIDE SLOPE
ALL LIGHTS RED — TOO LOW

VASI 2
36
THRESHOLD

800'
700'

VASI 12
36
THRESHOLD

VASI 4
36
THRESHOLD

VISUAL APPROACH SLOPE INDICATOR
VASI
(Vₗ)

VISUAL APPROACH SLOPE INDICATOR WITH A THRESHOLD CROSSING HEIGHT TO ACCOMODATE LONG BODIED OR JUMBO AIRCRAFT.

VASI 6
36
THRESHOLD

VASI 16
36
THRESHOLD

MEDIUM INTENSITY APPROACH LIGHTING SYSTEM
with Runway Alignment Indicator Lights
MALSR
(A₅)

SAME LIGHT CONFIGURATION AS SSALR.

Fig. 8-11. Approach lighting systems. (IAP charts)

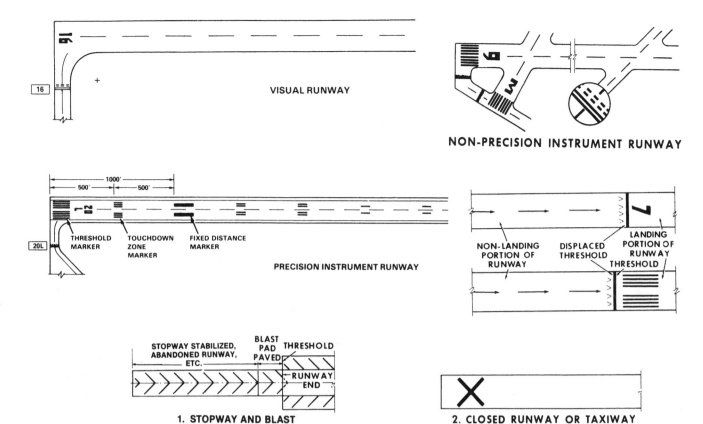

VISUAL RUNWAY

NON-PRECISION INSTRUMENT RUNWAY

1000'
500' | 500'

THRESHOLD MARKER TOUCHDOWN ZONE MARKER FIXED DISTANCE MARKER

PRECISION INSTRUMENT RUNWAY

NON-LANDING PORTION OF RUNWAY   DISPLACED THRESHOLD   LANDING PORTION OF RUNWAY THRESHOLD

STOPWAY STABILIZED, ABANDONED RUNWAY, ETC.   BLAST PAD PAVED   THRESHOLD

RUNWAY END

1. STOPWAY AND BLAST PAD AREA

2. CLOSED RUNWAY OR TAXIWAY

Section 3.   AIRPORT MARKING AIDS

60. AIRPORT MARKING AIDS

a. In the interest of safety, regularity, or efficiency of aircraft operations, the FAA has recommended, for the guidance of the public, the following airport marking.

NOTE.— Refer to ADVISORY CIRCULAR—150/5340-1 Marking of Paved Areas on Airports for detailed airport marking information.

b. Runway designators — Runway numbers and letters are determined from the approach direction. The runway number is the whole number nearest one-tenth the magnetic azimuth of the centerline of the runway, measured clockwise from the magnetic north. The letter, or letters, differentiate between left (L), right (R), or center (C) parallel runways, as applicable:

(1) For two parallel runways "L" "R"

(2) For three parallel runways "L" "C" "R"

c. Visual Runway Marking — Used for operations under Visual Flight Rules:

(1) Centerline marking.

(2) Designation marking.

(3) Threshold marking (on runways used or intended to be used by international commercial air transport.)

(4) Fixed distance marking (on runways 4,000 feet (1200 m) or longer used by jet aircraft.)

(5) Holding position markings (for taxiway/runway intersections.)

d. NonPrecision Instrument Runway Marking — Used on runways served by a nonvisual navigation aid and intended for landings under instrument weather conditions:

(1) Centerline marking.

(2) Designation marking.

(3) Threshold marking.

(4) Fixed distance marking (on runways 4,000 feet (1200 m) or longer used by jet aircraft.

(5) Holding position markings (for taxiway/runway intersections and instrument landing system (ILS) critical areas.)

e. Precision Instrument Runway Marking — Used on runways served by nonvisual precision approach aids and on runways having special operational requirements:

(1) Centerline marking.

(2) Designation marking.

(3) Threshold marking.

(4) Fixed distance marking.

(5) Touchdown zone marking.

(6) Side stripes.

(7) Holding position markings (for taxiway/runway intersections and ILS critical areas.)

f. Threshold —The designated beginning of the runway that is available and suitable for the landing of aircraft.

g. Displaced Threshold —A threshold that is not at the beginning of the full strength runway pavement. The paved area behind the displaced runway threshold is available for taxiing, the landing rollout, and the takeoff of aircraft.

Fig. 8-12. Runway markings. For complete details on runway and taxiway markings, see Figures 2-3-1 through 2-3-41 of the *AIM*.

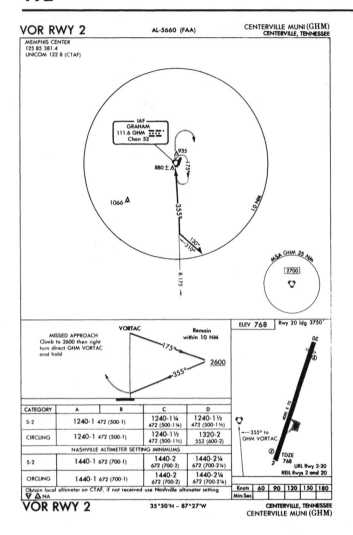

Fig. 8-13. VOR RWY 2 approach for Centerville, Tenn. Note that if you are unable to get the altimeter setting on the Common Traffic Advisory Frequency (CTAF—Unicom), using the Nashville altimeter setting raises the minimums, since BNA is 41 NM away.

Two antennas are used by the PAR, one scanning vertically, the other horizontally. The range is limited to 10 mi, the azimuth to 20°, and the elevation to 7°. Only the final approach area is covered. (The military used to refer to this system as GCA, or ground-controlled approach, but now it is also termed Radar Final Control.)

If your navaid receivers were all out but you still could communicate, the ASR or PAR approach might be the answer. For instance, if you lost all electrical equipment but had a battery-powered hand-held transceiver, you might have a safe IFR arrival by using the just-mentioned facilities. In addition to the pictured approach charts at Nashville for ILS, VOR, NDB, etc., there are also four ASR approaches available, plus circling minimums, as shown.

As noted, the IAP chart volumes also contain rates of climb and rates of descent tables for various groundspeeds, citing climb and descent angles required.

Chapter 13 will go into more detail on *using* the IAP charts but you should take plenty of time to study the IAP chart presentations now. During an approach is no place or time to realize that some of the symbols or notes are new to you.

■ **Instrument Departure (DP) Procedure** A DP is an ATC coded departure routing that has been established at certain airports to simplify clearance delivery procedures.

Pilots of civil aircraft operating from locations where DP procedures are effective may expect ATC clearances containing a DP. Use of a DP requires pilot possession of the textual description or graphic depiction of the approved effective DP. If you do not possess a preprinted DP description or for any other reason do not wish to use a DP, you are expected to advise ATC. Notification may be accomplished by filing "NO DP" in the remarks section of the filed flight plan or by the less desirable method of verbally advising ATC.

Controllers may omit the departure control frequency if a DP clearance is issued and the departure control frequency is published on the DP.

Pilot nav—These DPs are established where the pilot is primarily responsible for navigation on the DP route. They are established for airports when terrain and safety-related factors indicate the necessity. Some pilot nav DPs may contain vector instructions that pilots are expected to comply with until instructions are received to resume normal navigation on the filed/assigned route or DP procedure.

Vector DPs—These are established where ATC will provide radar navigational guidance to a filed/assigned route or to a fix depicted on the DP.

All effective DPs are published in textual or graphic forms and some contain climb information.

Figure 8-17 shows sample (and simple) DP information. These charts are published every 8 weeks and are included with that particular airport's approach charts.

■ **Standard Terminal Arrival Routes (STARs)** A STAR is an ATC coded IFR arrival route established for application to arriving IFR aircraft destined for certain airports. Its purpose is to simplify clearance delivery procedures.

Pilots of IFR civil aircraft headed to locations for which STARs have been published may be issued a clearance containing a STAR whenever ATC deems it appropriate. Until military STAR publications distribution is accomplished, STARs will be issued to military pilots only when requested in the flight plan or verbally by the pilot.

Use of STARs requires pilot possession of at least the approved textual description. As with any ATC clearance or portion thereof, it is the responsibility of each pilot to accept or refuse an issued STAR. You should notify ATC if you do not wish to use a STAR by placing "NO STAR" in the remarks section of the flight plan or by the less desirable method of verbally stating the same to ATC.

Figure 8-18 is a legend and sample STAR chart for Nashville Airport.

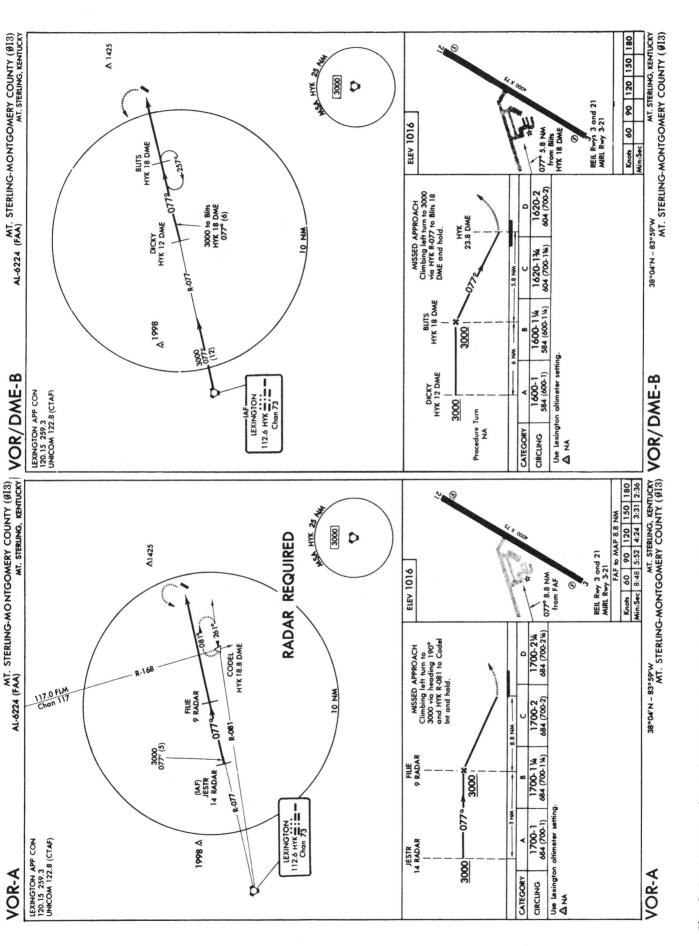

Fig. 8-14. VOR-A and VOR/DME-B IAP charts for Mt. Sterling, Ky. These have been replaced but are used as an example.

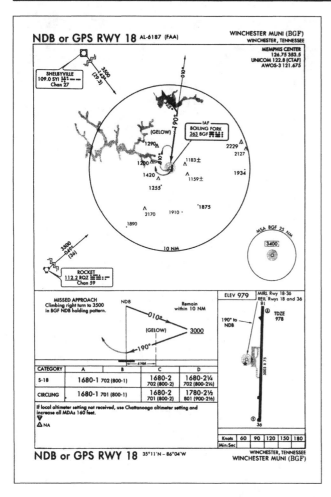

Fig. 8-15. NDB RWY 18 approach for Winchester, Tenn.

Pilots navigating on a STAR shall maintain the last assigned altitude until receiving authorization to descend so as to comply with all published/issued restrictions. This authorization will contain the phraseology "DESCEND VIA."

A "descend via" clearance authorizes pilots to navigate vertically and laterally, in accordance with the depicted procedure, to meet published restrictions. Vertical navigation is at the pilot's discretion; however, adherence to published altitude crossing restrictions and speeds is mandatory unless otherwise cleared. Minimum en route altitudes are not considered restrictions, but pilots are expected to remain at about MEAs.

Pilots cleared for vertical navigation using the terminology "descend via" shall inform ATC upon initial contact after changing to a new frequency. (For more details, check *AIM.*)

AERONAUTICAL INFORMATION MANUAL (AIM) (OFFICIAL GUIDE TO BASIC FLIGHT INFORMATION AND ATC PROCEDURES)

This publication (Fig. 8-19) contains instructional, training, and educational material that is basic and not often changed, such as the partial list discussed below.

■ Navigation Aids and Procedures

Radio aids—This section covers the basics of the air navigation aids such as VOR, TACAN, MLS (microwave landing system), ILS LORAN, and VHF/DF plus information on the Air Traffic Control Radar Beacon System (ATCRBS).

Aeronautical lighting and airport marking aids—Contains information on VASI and other airport lighting systems such as the rotating beacon, runway and approach lighting systems, obstruction lighting, and various types of runway markings (as shown in Figs. 8-11 and 8-12).

Airspace—Contains information on uncontrolled airspace and VFR and IFR requirements, minimum visibility and distance from clouds, altitudes, and flight levels.

"Controlled airspace" discusses control areas, transition areas, and Class A, B, C, D, E, and G airspace.

"Special-use airspace" is covered, particularly prohibited, restricted, warning areas plus military operations areas and alert and controlled firing areas.

The section on "Other Airspace Areas" includes information on airport traffic areas, airport advisory areas, and other airspace.

NASHVILLE INTL TN
RADAR—120.6 388.0   ELEV **599**

	RWY	GS/TCH/RPI	CAT	DH/ MDA-VIS	HAT/ HAA	CEIL-VIS	CAT	DH/ MDA-VIS	HAT/ HAA	CEIL-VIS
ASR	2L		ABC	980/40	381	(400—¾)	D	980/50	381	(400—1)
	20R		ABCD	980/60	402	(400—1¼)				
	31		ABC	1040—¾	464	(500—¾)	D	1040—1	464	(500—1)
	13		ABC	1060—1¼	488	(500—1¼)	D	1060—1½	488	(500—1½)
CIRCLING			AB	1060—1¼	461	(500—1¼)	C	1100—1½	501	(600—1½)
			D	1160—2	561	(600—2)				

Category D S—2L visibility increased to RVR 6000 for inoperative ALS.
Inoperative table does not apply to S—20R.

▼   SE-1

RADAR INSTRUMENT APPROACH MINIMUMS

Fig. 8-16. Civil radar instrument approach minimums for Nashville. You may want to refer to Figure 8-4 for some of the abbreviations.

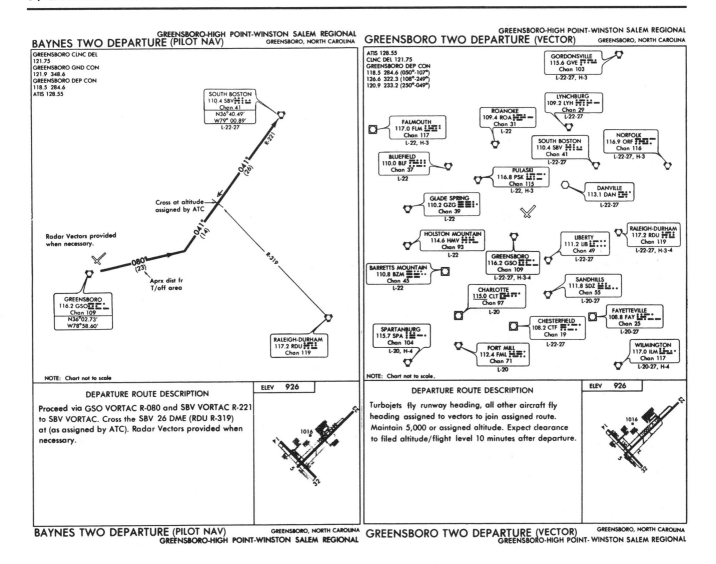

Fig. 8-17. Instrument Departure Procedures from Greensboro, N.C. The BAYNES TWO DEPARTURE is a pilot navigation DP. The GREENSBORO TWO DEPARTURE is a vector DP. Note that the pertinent information is listed on each type. These are examples of the general types.

Air traffic control—Contains detailed coverage of such subjects as Centers, FSSs, ATIS, designated Unisom and Multicom frequencies, use of radar for aid to VFR traffic, tower en route control, and transponder use.

A section on radio communications phraseology and techniques notes the procedures for contacting various facilities, including contacting the tower when either all transmitters or all receivers are inoperative.

Airport operations—Covers operations at tower-controlled airports, visual indicators, traffic patterns, braking action reports, intersection takeoffs, taxiing, use of aircraft lights, hand signals, and more.

ATC clearances—Includes the factors that govern the pilot and ATC in clearances including adherence to the clearance, IFR separation standards, and the use of visual clearing procedures.

Preflight—All about filing and closing VFR and IFR flight plans plus other good information on preflight preparation.

Departure—Gives clearances, departure control, and departure procedures, with particular attention to IFR departures.

En route procedures—Lots of information on airways and route systems, position reporting, and holding.

Arrival procedures—Standard terminal arrivals (STARs), which were covered earlier in this chapter and in Chapter 13, are cited here plus all you need to know about the various approaches, including approach and landing minimums and missed approach procedures.

Pilot/controller roles and responsibilities—More about clearances, approaches, missed approaches. Also there's information on visual separation, VFR on top operations, and minimum-fuel advisories (what *you* are supposed to do and how the controller is to respond).

■ **Emergency Procedures** *Your* responsibilities and authority are covered here plus radar service available for

GRAHAM FOUR ARRIVAL (GHM.GHM4)

NASHVILLE APP CON
120.6 387.0
NASHVILLE INTL ATIS
135.1

TURBOJET VERTICAL NAVIGATION PLANNING INFORMATION

Expect clearance to cross GHM VORTAC at 10,000'.
Expect clearance to cross GHM VORTAC at 250 KTS IAS
when landing RWYS 2L, 2C, 2R or 13.

NASHVILLE
114.1 BNA =:.::
Chan 88
N36°08.22' - W86°41.09'

NASHVILLE INTL
SMYRNA
MURFREESBORO MUNI

JOHN C. TUNE

VULCAN
114.4 VUZ :::.::
Chan 91
N33°40.21' - W86°53.99'
L-14, H-4

GRAHAM
111.6 GHM =:.::
Chan 53
N35°50.04' - W87°27.11'

7000
346°
(132)

BIGBEE
116.2 IGB :::.::
Chan 109
N33°29.13' - W88°30.82'
L-14, H-4

24000
016°
(150)

DYERSBURG
116.8 DYR =:.::
Chan 115

7000
066°
(62)

HELAM
N35°27.44'
W88°38.58'

R-132

R-275

R-246

7000
067°
(71)

24000
041°
(199)

SIDON
114.7 SQS :::.::
Chan 94
N33°27.83' - W90°16.64'
L-14, H-4

MEMPHIS
117.5 MEM :.::
Chan 122
N35°00.91' - W89°58.99'
L-14, H-4

Radar Required on the
SQS and IGB Transitions.

NOTE: Chart not to scale.

BIGBEE TRANSITION (IGB.GHM4): From over IGB R-016 to GHM VORTAC. Thence.

MEMPHIS TRANSITION (MEM.GHM4): From over MEM VORTAC via MEM R-067 and GHM R-246 to GHM VORTAC. Thence.

SIDON TRANSITION (SQS.GHM4): From over SQS VORTAC via SQS R-041 to GHM VORTAC. Thence.

VULCAN TRANSITION (VUZ.GHM4): From over VUZ VORTAC via VUZ R-346 to GHM VORTAC. Thence.

. . . . From over GHM VORTAC via BNA R-246 to BNA VORTAC. Expect radar vectors to final approach course.

GRAHAM FOUR ARRIVAL (GHM.GHM4)

LEGEND

STANDARD TERMINAL ARRIVAL (STAR) CHARTS
DEPARTURE PROCEDURE (DP) CHARTS

RADIO AIDS TO NAVIGATION

VOR
TACAN
VOR/DME
NDB/DME
VORTAC
LOC/DME
WAYPOINT
LOC
FLYOVER WAYPOINT
NDB (Non-directional Radio Beacon)
LMM, LOM (Compass locator)
Marker Beacon
Localizer Course
SDF Course

(T) indicates frequency protection range
Identifier
(Y) TACAN must be placed in "Y" mode to receive distance information
Geographic Position
Frequency
ORLANDO
112.25 (T) ORI :::.::
Chan 59 (Y)
N28°32.56' - W81°20.10'
L-19, H-5
DME or TACAN Channel
Underline indicates no voice transmitted on this frequency
Enroute Chart Reference
Waypoint Name
PRAYS
N38°58.30' - W89°51.50'
112.7 CAP 187.1°-56.2'
Coordinates
Identifier
590
Reference Facility Elevation
Radial-Distance (to Facility/Waypoint)

Reporting Points
N00° 00.00'
W00° 00.00'
▲ Name (Compulsory)
△ Name (Non-Compulsory)
—|— DME fix
x Mileage Breakdown/
Computer Navigation Fix (CNF)
N00° 00.00'
W00° 00.00'

75 DME Mileage (when not obvious)
∿∿∿ Distance not to scale

ROUTES

4500 MEA-Minimum Enroute Altitude
*3500 MOCA-Minimum Obstruction Clearance Altitude
270° Departure Route - Arrival Route
(65) Mileage between Radio Aids, Reporting Points, and Route Breaks
Transition Route
R-275 Radial line and value
Lost Communications Track
V12 Airway/Jet Route Identification
J80
Changeover Point
(IAS) Holding Pattern

Holding pattern with max. restricted airspeed (175K) applies to all altitudes above 6000' to and including 14000'. (210K) applies to all altitudes above 6000' to and including 14000'.

SPECIAL USE AIRSPACE

R-352
R - Restricted   W - Warning
P - Prohibited   A - Alert

ALTITUDES

5500 Mandatory Altitude
2300 Minimum Altitude
4800 Maximum Altitude
2200 Recommended Altitude
MCA (Minimum Crossing Altitude)
Altitude change at or other than Radio Aids

AIRPORTS

◇ Civil
● Military
Joint
Civil-Military

NOTES

All mileages are nautical.
# Indicates control tower temporarily closed UFN.
* Indicates a non-continuously operating facility, see A/FD or flight supplement.
All radials, bearings are magnetic.
All altitudes/elevations are in feet-MSL.
MRA- Minimum Reception Altitude.
MAA- Maximum Authorized Altitude.
(NAME2.NAME) - Example of DP flight plan Computer Code.
(NAME.NAME2) - Example of STAR flight plan Computer Code.
SL-0000 (FAA) - Example of a chart reference number.
▼ Take-Off Minimums not standard and/or Departure Procedures are published.

Fig. 8-18. Standard terminal arrival chart legend and sample for Nashville Airport.

U.S. Department
of Transportation
**Federal Aviation
Administration**

February 24, 20

Aeronautical
Information
Manual

Official Guide to
Basic Flight Information and ATC Procedures

Fig. 8-19. *Aeronautical Information Manual.*

VFR aircraft, transponder emergency operations, VHF/DF procedures, and search and rescue basics. Also there's the word on two-way communications failure.

■ Safety of Flight

Meteorology—FAA weather services, weather radar, PIREPs, wind shear, microbursts, and thunderstorms are covered here. (You might also review Chapter 7 in this book.)

Altimeter setting procedures—Includes setting procedures, altimeter errors, and other helpful hints.

Wake turbulence—Vortex generation, behavior and strength, avoidance procedures, and pilot responsibility.

Bird hazards—Bird strike risks, reporting bird and other wildlife activities, and flights over U.S. wildlife refuges and other natural areas.

Potential flight hazards—Cautions about midair collisions and flying under unmanned balloons; gives suggestions on mountain flying.

Safety, accident, and hazard reports—Aircraft accidents and incident reporting and a discussion of the reporting program.

■ Medical Facts for Pilots

This section discusses fitness for flight, hyperventilation, carbon monoxide, illusions and vision in flight, aerobatic flight, and judgment aspects of collision avoidance.

■ Aeronautical Charts and Related Publications

This section includes descriptions of charts and chart services available with additional information on auxiliary charts and related publications.

AIRPORT/FACILITY DIRECTORY (A/FD)

This publication is issued by the NACO every 56 days.

The publication, as the name implies, furnishes the latest information on airports and other aviation facilities. Figure 8-20 shows the coverage of the *A/FD* for the United States.

The *A/FD* for each region contains information on airports and facilities for that region. Figure 8-21 shows the cover information, directory legend, and information for Huntsville, Memphis, and Nashville airports and facilities.

Figure 8-22 is a sample collage of the types of information available in the *A/FD*. There may be additions or subtractions to the amount or type of information as time goes by, but you should have a general idea of what's available.

NOTICES TO AIRMEN (NOTAMS)

There are three categories of NOTAMs: NOTAM (D) or distant, NOTAM (L) or local, and Flight Data Center (FDC) NOTAMs:

The printed Notices to Airmen publication (Fig. 8-23) is divided into four parts (issued every 28 days):

Fig. 8-20. The *Airport/Facility Directory* has seven separate volumes for the conterminous United States.

UNITED STATES GOVERNMENT FLIGHT INFORMATION PUBLICATION

AIRPORT/FACILITY DIRECTORY

SOUTHEAST U.S.   SE

EFFECTIVE 0901Z **5 MAY 20**
TO 0901Z **30 JUN 20**

Consult NOTAMS for latest information

Published at Washington, D.C.
U.S. Department of Commerce
National Oceanic and Atmospheric Administration
National Ocean Service
Published in accordance with specifications and agreements approved by
the Federal Aviation Administration and the Department of Commerce

DIRECTORY LEGEND
TABLE OF CONTENTS

General Information .... Inside Front Cover
Abbreviations 1
Legend, Airport/Facility Directory 2
Airport/Facility Directory 11
Heliports 248
Seaplane Bases 250
Notices 251
FAA and National Weather Service Telephone Numbers 267
Air Route Traffic Control Centers 271
GADO and FSDO Addresses/Telephone Numbers 274
Preferred IFR Routes 275
VOR Receiver Check 280
Parachute Jumping Areas 285
Aeronautical Chart Bulletin 289
Tower Enroute Control (TEC) 296
National Weather Service (NWS) Upper Air Observing Stations ... 312
Enroute Flight Advisory Service (EFAS) .... Inside Back Cover

ALABAMA

HUNTSVILLE

§ **HUNTSVILLE-MADISON CO ARPT-CARL T. JONES FLD** (HSV) 9 SW   ATLANTA
  UTC–6(–5DT)   34°38′28″N 86°46′26″W   H-4H, L-14H
  630   B   S4   FUEL 100LL, JET A   OX 1, 2, 3, 4   LRA   ARFF Index C   IAP
  RWY 18R-36L: H8000X150 (ASPH-GRVD)   S-75, D-200, DT-350, DDT-850   CL HIRL
    RWY 18R: ALSF1. TDZ Rgt tfc.   RWY 36L: MALSR
  RWY 18L-36R: H8000X150 (ASPH)   S-90, D-108, DT-170   HIRL
    RWY 18L: MALSR.   RWY 36R: VASI(V4L)—GA 3.0° TCH 55′. Rgt tfc.
  AIRPORT REMARKS: Attended continuously. Migratory birds Oct 1–Mar 15, wildlife refuge South and West of arpt. Rwy
    18L-36R restricted to commuter and general aviation except by PPR ctc arpt manager 205–772–8728. Rwy
    18L-36R CLOSED to acft 75,000 lbs and over except emergency. When twr clsd ACTIVATE MALSR Rwy 18L and
    36L—CTAF. Flight Notification Service (ADCUS) available.
  WEATHER DATA SOURCES: LLWAS.
  COMMUNICATIONS: CTAF119.7   UNICOM 122.95   ATIS 121.25
    MUSCLE SHOALS FSS (MSL) TF 1-800-942-3162. NOTAM FILE MSL.
    DECATUR RCO 122.6 (MUSCLE SHOALS FSS)   ROCKET RCO 122.2 (MUSCLE SHOALS FSS)
  ® APP CON 125.6 (360°-179°) 118.05 (180°-359°) (1200-0800Z‡ Mon-Fri, 1200-0500Z‡ Sat-Sun), other times ctc
    ® MEMPHIS CENTER APP CON 120.8
    TOWER 119.7 (1200-0800Z‡ Mon-Fri, 1200-0500Z‡ Sat-Sun)   GND CON 121.9   CLNC DEL 120.35
  ® DEP CON 125.6 (359°-179°) 118.05 (180°-358°) 120.35 (1200-0800Z‡ Mon-Fri, 1200-0500Z‡ Sat-Sun), other
    times ctc ® MEMPHIS CENTER DEP CON 120.8
  ARSA ctc APP CON
  RADIO AIDS TO NAVIGATION: NOTAM FILE MSL.
    DECATUR (L) VORW/DME 112.8   DCU   Chan 75   34°38′54″N 86°56′22″W   094°7.8 NM to fld. 590/01W.
    CAPSHAW NDB (MHW) 350   CWH   34°46′25″N 86°46′44″W   182°7.3 NM to fld. NOTAM FILE HSV
    ILS 109.3 I-HSV Rwy 18R (Unmonitored when twr closed)
    ILS 108.5 I-ELL Rwy 36L (Unmonitored when twr closed).
    ILS 111.9 I-TVN Rwy 18L
    ASR (same as twr hours).

TENNESSEE

§ **MEMPHIS INTL** (MEM)   4 S   UTC–6(–5DT)   35°02′59″N 89°58′43″W   MEMPHIS
  332   B   S4   FUEL 100LL, JET A   OX 1, 2   LRA   ARFF Index C   H-4G, L-14F
  RWY 18R-36L: H9319X150 (CONC-GRVD)   S-100, D-173, DT-338   HIRL, CL   0.4% up S.   IAP
    RWY 18R: MALSR   Rgt tfc   RWY 36L: ALSF2. TDZ
  RWY 09-27: H8936X150 (ASPH-GRVD)   S-125, D-178, DT-300   HIRL   0.4% up E
    RWY 09: MALSR. Tree   RWY 27: MALSR. VASI(V4L)—GA 3.0° TCH 54′. Rgt tfc.
  RWY 18L-36R: H8400X150 (CONC-GRVD)   S-100, D-190, DT-337   HIRL CL,   0.8% up S.
    RWY 18L: MALSR.   RWY 36R: MALSR. TDZ. Rgt tfc
  RWY 03-21: H5816X150 (ASPH)   S-30 +   MIRL   Lgtd between dsplcd thld.
    RWY 03: REIL SAVASI(S2L)—GA 3 0° TCH 21′ Thld dsplcd 515′ Taxiway
    RWY 21: REIL. SAVASI(S2L)—GA 3 0° TCH 24′. Thld dsplcd 740′. Road
  RWY 15-33: H3760X150 (ASPH)   S-30
    RWY 15: Thld dsplcd 918′ Road
  AIRPORT REMARKS: Attended continuously. CAUTION—42′ highway embankment 100′ from departure end Rwy 33,
    obstruction could be a hazard if engine lost on departure from Rwy 33. N-S taxiway 1 mile N and 400′ to right of
    Rwy 18L has false appearance of runway when landing South Twy W S-30, D-60. General Aviation parking and
    service contact airport security UNICOM. Portions of rwy 09-27, 03-21, 15-33 intersection not visible from twr
    Taxiway Y restricted to acft with 108′ or less wing span Flight Notification Service (ADCUS) available
  WEATHER DATA SOURCES: LLWAS.
  COMMUNICATIONS: ATIS ARR 119.45   DEP 121 0   UNICOM 122.95
    JACKSON FSS (MKL) TF 1–800–WX–BRIEF. NOTAM FILE MEM.
    MEMPHIS RCO 123.65 122.2 (JACKSON FSS)   MEMPHIS RCO 122.1R 117.5T (JACKSON FSS)
  ® APP CON 119.1 (176°-355°) 125.8 120.25 (356°-175°)
    TOWER 118.3 (Rwy 09-27, 03-21, 15-33) 119.7 (18L-R, 36R-L)
    GND CON 121.9 (121.65 Air Carrier Only)   CLNC DEL 125.2
  ® DEP CON 124 65 (176°-355°) 124.15 (356°-175°)
  ARSA ctc APP CON
  RADIO AIDS TO NAVIGATION: NOTAM FILE MEM.
    (H) VORTAC 117.5   MEM   Chan 122   35°03′45″N 89°58′53″W   at fld. 250/03E.
      VOR portion unusable 020°-120° beyond 20 NM below 5000′   170°-244° beyond 20 NM below
      4000′   245°-265° beyond 34 NM below 3000′.
    AULON NDB (MHW/LOM) 287   ME   35°03′42″N 090°04′18″W   089°4.2 NM to fld.
    ELVIS NDB (HW/LOM) 371   TS   34°57′12″N 89°58′25″W   356°4.7 NM to fld.
    ILS 109.5 I-MEM Rwy 09 LOM AULON NDB
    ILS 110.5 I-TSE Rwy 36R BC unusable. LOM ELVIS NDB
    ILS 108 3 I-SDU Rwy 18L BC unusable
    ILS/DME 108.9 I-OHN   Chan 26   Rwy 36L (CAT II) BC unusable. LOC unusable middle marker in bound.
    ILS 109.9 I-OOI Rwy 18R (BC unusable) ILS unusable middle marker inbound.
    ILS 108.7 I-JIM Rwy 27
    ASR

§ **NASHVILLE METROPOLITAN** (BNA)   5.2 SE   UTC–6(–5DT)   36°07′37″N 86°40′52″W   ST. LOUIS
  599   B   S4   FUEL 100LL, JET A   OX 2   LRA   ARFF Index C   H-4H, 4F, L-14H, 21D
  RWY 13-31: H8500X150 (ASPH-GRVD)   S-129, D-151, DT-229   HIRL   IAP
    RWY 13: REIL. SAVASI(V6L)—Upper GA 3.25° TCH 113.6′. Lower GA 2.75° TCH 43.5′. Trees.
    RWY 31: REIL. MALSR. Fence.
  RWY 02L-20R: H7702X150 (CONC-GRVD)   S-100, D-175, DT-360   HIRL, CL   0.6% up S
    RWY 02L: ALSF1. TDZ.   RWY 20R: ODALS. VASI(V4L)—GA 3.0° TCH 56′. Tree.
  RWY 02R-20L: H5186X150 (ASPH-CONC-GRVD)   S-60, D-84, DT-128   MIRL
    RWY 02R: SAVASI(S2L)—GA 3.0° TCH 38′. Thld dsplcd 881′. Road.
    RWY 20L: REIL. VASI(V4L)—GA 3.0° TCH 40′. Ground.
  AIRPORT REMARKS: Attended continuously. Fee charged to Coml users only. Acft conducting visual apch to Rwy 20R,
    20L, or 13 avoid Cornelia Fort Airpark (5 mi NW of Nashville) below 2000′ MSL. Rwy 02R-20L length of dsplcd thld
    not grvd. Flight Notification Service (ADCUS) available.
  WEATHER DATA SOURCES: LLWAS.
  COMMUNICATIONS: ATIS 120.0   UNICOM 122.95
    NASHVILLE FSS (BNA) on arpt 122.55 122.2 122.1R. LC 360-3619. TF 1–800–WX–BRIEF. NOTAM FILE BNA.
  ® APP CON 124.0 (019°-199°) 120.6 (200°-018°)
  ® DEP CON 124.0 118.4 (019°-199°) 120.6 119.35 (200°-018°)
    TOWER 118.6   GND CON 121.9   CLNC DEL 126.05
  ARSA ctc APP CON
  RADIO AIDS TO NAVIGATION: NOTAM FILE BNA.
    (H) VORTAC 114.1   BNA   Chan 88   36°07′10″N 86°40′57″W   at fld. 620/01W.
      VOR portion unusable 134°-173° below 17,500′   195°-260° within 20 NM below 7000′ and beyond 20 NM
      below 17,500′   260°-270° below 7000′   030°-052° beyond 17 NM below 4000′
    DOBBS NDB (HW/LOM) 304   BN   36°02′18″N 86°43′02″W   019°5.0 NM to fld.
    OPERY NDB (MHW/LOM) 344   VI   36°12′13″N 86°39′07″W   199°4.1 NM to fld.
    ILS/DME 109.9 I-BNA Chan 36 Rwy 02L LOM DOBBS NDB
    ILS 109.7 I-PNO Rwy 31
    ILS 111.3 I-VIY Rwy 20R LOM OPERY NDB
    ASR

Fig. 8-21. *Airport/Facility Director.* Legend and data for Huntsville, Memphis, and Nashville airports and facilities. A full explanation of the symbols is given in the Appendix of this book.

DIRECTORY LEGEND

FREQUENCY PAIRING PLAN AND MLS CHANNELING

The following is a list of paired VOR/ILS VHF frequencies with TACAN channels and MLS channels.

TACAN CHANNEL	VHF FREQUENCY	MLS CHANNEL	TACAN CHANNEL	VHF FREQUENCY	MLS CHANNEL	TACAN CHANNEL	VHF FREQUENCY	MLS CHANNEL
17X	108.00							
17Y	108.05	540	50Y	111.35	606	94X	114.70	
18X	108.10	500	51X	111.40		94Y	114.75	648
18Y	108.15	542	51Y	111.45	608	95X	114.80	
19X	108.20		52X	111.50	534	95Y	114.85	650
19Y	108.25	544	52Y	111.55	610	96X	114.90	
20X	108.30	502	53X	111.60		96Y	114.95	652
20Y	108.35	546	53Y	111.65	612	97X	115.00	
21X	108.40		54X	111.70	536	97Y	115.05	654
			54Y	111.75		98X	115.10	

TENNESSEE

SEWANEE

FRANKLIN CO (UOS) .9 E UTC-6(-5DT) 35°12'14"N 85°53'55"W ATLANTA L-14H
1950 B FUEL 100LL
RWY 06-24: H3300X50 (ASPH) S-20 URL
RWY 06: SAVASI(S2L)—GA 3.5°TCH 28'. Trees. RWY 24: VASI(V2L). Trees.
AIRPORT REMARKS: Attended 1500-0600‡‡. Sporadic crosswinds and turbulence. Deer on and in vicinity of rwy.
COMMUNICATIONS: CTAF/UNICOM 122.8
NASHVILLE FSS (BNA) TF 1-800-WX-BRIEF. NOTAM FILE BNA.
RADIO AIDS TO NAVIGATION: NOTAM FILE BNA.
SHELBYVILLE (L) VOR/DME 109.0 SYI Chan 27 35°33'43"N 86°26'21"W 130°34.1 NM to fld. 810/01W.
SEWANEE NDB (MHW) 275 UOS 35°12'15"N 85°53'45"W at fld. (VFR only).

HELIPORTS

ALABAMA

SEAPLANE BASES

FLORIDA

SPECIAL NOTICES

ST. PETERSBURG, FLORIDA

Pilots planning to overfly the St. Petersburg VOR (PIE) below 13,000 feet MSL should file via the Lakeland VOR (LAL) between 1100 and 2300 UTC.

GEORGIA

Atlanta Tower: Low altitude airway structure in proximity of The William B. Hartsfield Atlanta International Airport is aligned to provide bypass routes for traffic overflying Atlanta. To avoid heavy concentration of high performance and wide-bodied aircraft pilots should file for airways beyond 35 nautical miles from Atlanta VOR. Aircraft operating IFR below 15,000 MSL via ___ within 35 nautical mi___ _____ Atlanta VOR ma___ _____ ___ ____ _____ and/or rerouting be___ _____

FAA AND NWS
TELEPHONE NUMBERS

Flight Service Station (FSS) numbers provide direct contact with an FAA pilot weather briefer.

Pilots Automatic Telephone Weather Answering Service (PATWAS) provides a recorded summary of weather conditions over a limited area in the vicinity of the associated facility.

Transcribed Weather Broadcast telephone numbers (TEL-TWEB) provide access to the transcribed weather broadcast on selected navigational facilities.

National Weather Service (WS) numbers will connect you with a national weather service pilot briefer.

Interim Voice Response System (IVRS), available in some metropolitan areas as listed at the end of this section provides selected weather products via computer voice-generated system on touch-tone telephones.

Further information can be found in the Airman's Information Manual, Chapter 6.

PREFERRED IFR ROUTES

A system of preferred routes has been established to guide pilots in planning their route of flight, to minimize route changes during the operational phase of flight, and to aid in the efficient orderly management of the air traffic using federal airways. The preferred IFR routes which follow are designed to serve the needs of airspace users and to provide for a systematic flow of air traffic in the major terminal and en route flight environments. Cooperation by all pilots in filing preferred routes will result in fewer traffic delays and will better provide for efficient departure, en route and arrival air traffic service.

The following lists contain preferred IFR routes for the low altitude stratum and the high altitude stratum. The high altitude list is in two sections; the first section showing terminal to terminal routes and the second section showing single direction route segments. Also, on some high altitude routes low altitude airways are included as transition routes.

LOW ALTITUDE

Terminals	Route	Effective Times (UTC)
ATLANTA METRO AREA		
Chicago Midway	(60-170 incl) V97 NELLO V51W HCH V51 CGT	1200-0300
Chicago O'Hare	(60-170 incl) V97 NELLO V51W HCH V51 CGT V7 BEBEE	1200-0300
Cincinnati	(80-170 incl) V97 HYK V57 FLM	1200-0300
CHARLOTTE		
Cleveland	(60-170 incl) MOPED V37 PSK V59 BSV V40 RITZS	1200-0300

REGULATORY NOTICES

The following narratives summarize the FAR Part 93 Special Air Traffic Rules, Patterns, and/or Airport Traffic Areas in effect as prescribed in the rule. This information is advisory in nature and in no way relieves the pilot from compliance with the specific rules set forth in FAR Parts 91 and 93.

Special Airport Traffic Areas prescribed in Part 93 are depicted on Sectional Aeronautical Charts, World Aeronautical Charts, Enroute Low Altitude Charts, and where applicable, on VFR Terminal Area Charts.

CLARKSVILLE, TENNESSEE
SABRE U.S. ARMY HELIPORT
AIRPORT TRAFFIC AREA

Part 93, Subpart N, prescribes the Sabre U.S. Army Heliport airport traffic area located in the vicinity of Clarksville, Tennessee. It is effective during the hours that the Sabre Control Tower is operating. It includes that airspace extending from the surface up to but not including an altitude of 2,000 feet above the surface of the heliport and within a two-statute-mile radius of the heliport's geographical center.

VOR RECEIVER CHECK POINTS
AND
VOR TEST FACILITIES (VOT)

The use of VOR airborne and ground check points is explained in Airman's Information Manual. Basic Flight Information and ATC Procedures.

NOTE: Under columns headed "Type of Check Point" & "Type of VOR Facility" G stands for ground. A/ stands for airborne followed by figures (2300 or (1000-3000)indicating the altitudes above mean sea level at which the check should be conducted. Facilities are listed in alphabetical order, in the state where the check points or VOTs are located.

ALABAMA

VOR RECEIVER CHECK POINTS

Facility Name (Arpt Name)	Freq/Ident	Type Check Pt. Gnd. AB/ALT	Azimuth from Fac. Mag	Dist. from Fac. N.M.	Check Point Description
Brookley (Mobile Aerospace)	112.8/BFM	G	311	1.68	On runup area for rwy 14.
Monroeville (Monroe Co Arpt)	116.8/MVC	G	195	0.6	Runup area rwy 03.

PARACHUTE JUMPING AREAS

The following tabulation lists all reported parachute jumping sites in the area of coverage of this directory. Unless otherwise indicated, all activities are conducted during daylight hours and under VFR conditions. The busiest periods of activity are normally on weekends and holidays, but jumps can be expected at anytime during the week at the locations listed. Jumps within restricted airspace are not listed.

All times are local and altitudes MSL unless otherwise specified.

Refer to Federal Aviation Regulations, Part 105 for required procedures relating to parachute jumping.

Organizations desiring listing of their jumping activities in this publication should contact the nearest FAA facility (FSS, tower, or ARTCC).

Qualified parachute jumping sites will be depicted on sectional charts.

Note: (c) in this publication indicates that the parachute jump area is charted.

To qualify for charting, a jump area must meet the following criteria:

(1) Been in operation for at least 1 year.
(2) Operate year round (at least on weekends).
(3) Log 4,000 or more jumps each year.

In addition, jump sites can be nominated by FAA Regions if special circumstances require charting.

ALABAMA

LOCATION	DISTANCE AND RADIAL FROM NEAREST VOR/VORTAC	MAXIMUM ALTITUDE	REMARKS
Albertville, Albertville Muni Arpt	17 NM; 331° Gadsden	10,000	0900-SS.
Allen Army Heliport	11 NM; 253° Wiregrass	12,500	1 NM radius. SR-SS weekends and holidays.
(c) Bayou La Batre, Roy E. Ray Arpt	12 NM; 217° Brookley	12,500	Daily SR-SS
Bessemer, Old Bessemer Arpt	16 NM; 057° Brookwood	10,000	1030-SS weekends

---

AERONAUTICAL CHART BULLETIN

HOUSTON SECTIONAL
37th Edition, February 13, 1986

Add obst. 859' MSL (419' AGL) 31°31'21"N 93°24'11"W. Add obst. 269' MSL (230' AGL) 30°25'27"N 91°08'02"W. Add obst. 220'MSL (205'AGL) 30°00'30"N 94°04'26"W. Add obst. 636'MSL (216'AGL) 30°44'48"N 96°57'15"W. Add obst. 363'MSL (310'AGL) 29°26'40"N 95°21'29"W. Add obst. 700'MSL (675'AGL) 28°32'10"N 96°43'20"W. Add obst. 613'MSL (600'AGL) 28°23'50"N 96°35'59"W. Change Houston-Southwest Arpt. 29°30'20"N, 95°28'36"W UNICOM to 123.0

Military Training Routes

No Changes

TOWER ENROUTE CONTROL
(TEC)

Within the national airspace system it is possible for a pilot to fly IFR from one point to another without leaving approach control airspace. This is referred to as "tower enroute" which allows flight beneath the enroute structure. The tower enroute concept has been expanded (where practical) by reallocating airspace vertically/geographically to allow flight planning between city pairs while remaining within approach control airspace. Pilots are encouraged to solicit tower enroute information from FSS's and to use the route descriptions provided in this directory when filing flight plans. Other airways which appear to be more direct between two points may take the aircraft out of approach control airspace thereby resulting in additional delays or other complications. All published TEC routes are designed to avoid enroute airspace and the majority are within radar cover⌐

Additional routes and other changes will appear in forthcoming editions as necessary. The acronym "TEC" shou⌐
the remarks section of the flight plan. This will advise ATC that the pilot⌐

1. The gr⌐ ⌐o be used for navi⌐

show⌐ ⌐on⌐

TOWER ENROUTE CONTROL CITY PAIRS

Approach Control Area (Including Satellites)	Route	Highest Altitude	Destination
Albany	V97	5000	Atlanta
	V35 V56	5000	Augusta
	V159	5000	Birmingham
	DIRECT	5000	Cairns AAF
	V35 V56 V37 FML	5000	Charlotte

Numerous additional telephone numbers are listed under COMMUNICATIONS in the A/FD tabulation. If you wish to call an FSS, but do not have access to a directory listing, call the toll-free number, 1-800-555-1212.

FAST FILE FLIGHT PLAN SYSTEM

Some flight service stations have inaugurated this system for pilots who already have obtained a weather briefing and desire only to file a flight plan. Pilots may call the discrete telephone numbers listed and file flight plans in accordance with recorded taped instructions. IFR flight plans will be extracted and entered in the appropriate ARTCC computer. VFR flight plans will be retained at the FSS for activation by the pilot. This equipment is designed to automatically disconnect after 8 seconds of no transmission, so pilots are instructed to speak at a normal speech rate without lengthy pauses between flight plan elements. Pilots are urged to file flight plans into this system at least 30 minutes in advance of proposed departure.

★ PATWAS
■ TWEB
◆ Restricted Number for Aviation Weather Information
§§ Fast File (Flight Plan Filing Only)

Location and Identifier		Area Code	Telephone
ALABAMA			
Anniston ANB	FSS	(205)	831-2303
			1-800-762-2372
	FSS	(205)	254-1387
Birmingham BHM	FSS	(205)	595-2101 ★
	INWATS		1-800-292-6218

AIR ROUTE TRAFFIC CONTROL CENTERS

H-3-4, L-6-8-14-17-21

® **MEMPHIS CENTER - 121.5** (KZME)
Brinkley -126.85
Columbus -135.3 127.1 124.25
Fayetteville -132.55 126.1
Graham -124.275 125.85
Greenville -135.7 132.5 123.75
Greenwood -132.5
Harrison -126.85
Hot Springs -118.85
Huntsville -120.8
Ja⌐ ⌐ -132.1

GADOs AND FSDOs

GENERAL AVIATION DISTRICT OFFICES (GADO) AND FLIGHT STANDARDS DISTRICT OFFICES (FSDO)

The following is a list of GADOs and FSDOs in the area of coverage of this Directory. (FSDOs also perform the same functions as GADOs. All locations listed are GADOs unless specifically identified as FSDOs.) Address letters to Manager, General Aviation District Office or Manager, Flight Standards District Office—Federal Aviation Administration.

Flight Standards personnel in these offices are responsible for serving the aviation industry and the general public on all matters relating to the certification and operation of general aviation aircraft.

ALABAMA

Municipal Airport
6500 43rd Ave. North
Birmingham, Alabama 35206
Telephone: 205-254-1557

NORTH CAROLINA

Charlotte Office FSDO-66
Charlotte/Douglas Intl Airport
National/Weather Service Building
Charlotte, North Carolina 28208
Telephone: 704-392-3214

Fig 8-22. Sample of contents of the *Airport/Facility Directory*. Information may be deleted or added to the array shown here.

U.S. Department
of Transportation

**Federal Aviation
Administration**

NOTICES TO AIRMEN

Domestic/International

The Notice to Airmen is now on the FAA Home Page: www.faa.gov/NTAP

April 20, 20

Next Issue

May 18, 20

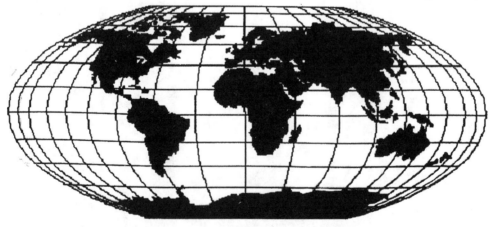

*Notices to Airmen included in this publication are **NOT** given during pilot briefings
unless specifically requested by the pilot.*

Air Traffic Publications (ATA-10)

Fig. 8-23. Printed NOTAMs.

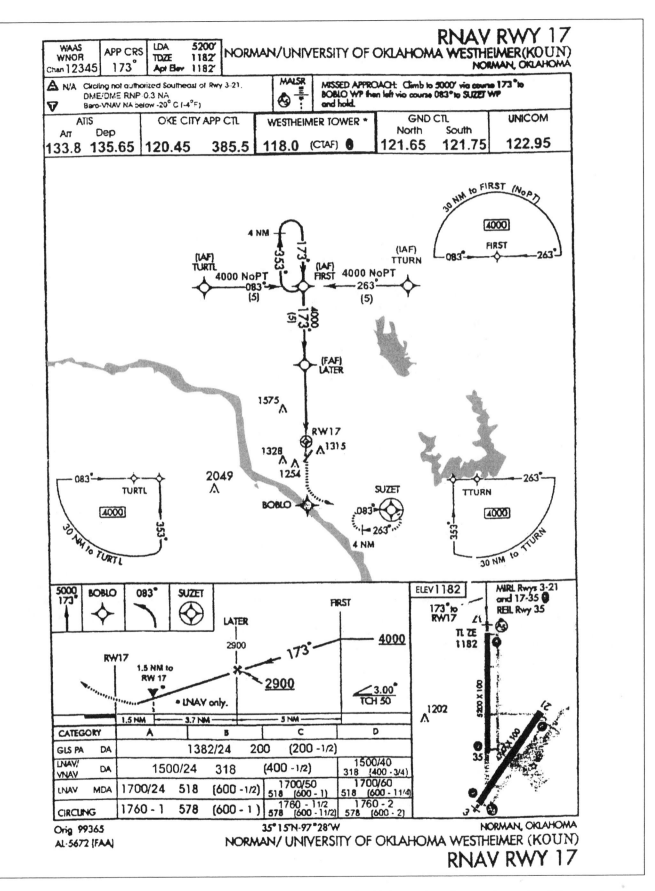

Fig. 8-24. Instrument Approach Chart for Norman/University of Oklahoma/Westheimer. Note the difference between the symbol for a "flyover" Waypoint (Suzet, with a circle) and a "flyby" Waypoint (Turtle, without a circle). Note that the Missed Approach Procedure is given at the top of the chart and by the symbols in the profile chart (not to be used for navigation). This illustration is from NOTAMs (ATA-10).

Part 1—Airway NOTAMs, Airports/Facilities and Procedural NOTAMs plus General FDC NOTAMs.

Part 2—FAR Part 95 Revision to Minimum En Route IFR Altitudes and Changeover Points.

Part 3—International Notices to Airmen.

Part 4—Graphic Notices. This art includes Notices to General Information, Special Military Operations and Major Sporting and/or Entertainment Events. Also in Part 1 are MOTAMs broken down by sections of the United States (NE, SE, E, S central, N central, NW, SW, and Alaska/Hawaii).

As a rated instrument pilot you should be familiar with the contents of this publication.

The Notices to Airmen included in the printed publication are NOT given during pilot briefings unless specifically requested by the pilot because the information is expected to remain in effect for an extended period as opposed to (for instance) your needing to know that your destination airport sent out a NOTAM an hour ago that all runways were closed due to snow and ice.

If you have a problem caused by not checking NOTAMs before a flight, you would be responsible (see FARs 91.3 and 91.103).

SUMMARY

Instrument charts and other information sources are constantly changing. This chapter has taken a general look at the types of information available, but you might find that some details or methods of presenting information may have changed before you read this. The point is to use this as an introduction to charts and other services. When you get the instrument rating, make sure that you are able to get the latest changes or corrections to the material you are *using*.

A heads-up for the reader as this printing is going to Press:

Decision Height (DH)— As indicated earlier in the chapter, this term will be gradually changed to decision altitude (DA) to agree with other nations' terminology.

Descent Profile—The published descent profile for RNAC will differ from the traditional depiction of an ILS glide slope (feather) through the use of a simple vertical track.

Approach Chart Title Changes—Through a transition period, approach charts involving GPS will be retitled. For example, for RNAV RWY 13, for multiple RNAV procedures that exist for the runway, subsequent RNAV procedures will be RNAV Z RWY 13 and RNAV Y RWY 13. (Use Zulu and Yankee when communicating.) So, you may see some charts with RNAV headings and others with GPS in the Approach Chart book during the transition.

Visual Descent Point—See Figure 5-62. A VDP will be published on most RNAV IAPs (area navigation approach procedures) and will pertain only to LNAV (lateral navigation) and a notation "LNAV" will be located in the profile view.

PLANNING THE NAVIGATION

9

Maybe later you'll be able to grab an en route chart and an approach procedures chart and do a real good job of flying IFR. But for now you'd better make sure that you've gone over the situation with a fine-tooth comb.

CHECKING THE ROUTE

Look at the en route chart. Check your proposed route, and it might not be a bad idea for your first few flights to mark along the route with a black or green pen. The VOR airways and radio data will be in blue on the map, so you'll want a contrasting color. While red would be great for daytime work, it would be hard to spot in red cockpit lighting at night. Take a few minutes to get a rough idea of distances and the VOR names and frequencies en route. What about the minimum en route altitudes (MEAs)? You can file for several different altitudes, but most pilots generally will file for the highest MEA (or the next 1000 ft higher) for the route unless there's a wide divergence in MEAs along the way. In planning for a trip from Memphis to Nashville, you would probably file for V16, the most direct route. Look at the reduced section of the L-14 low-altitude en route chart in the back of this book.

The chances are good that V16 would be what you'd get, but look at the en route chart for other possible routes you *could* be assigned.

One in-flight problem is getting a clearance for an alternate (strange) route and then being unable to find it on the map right away. If you have your main route well marked, you will at least know where it is as a starting point and can more easily find the alternate routes to either side. In congested areas there will be a maze of airways and possible alternates, so make it easy on yourself. Maybe you don't want to mark up your chart. But if you have subscribed to the service, you'll get a new one every 56 days anyway; and if you make the trip several times in that period, the route will already be marked. You'll find that after flying the same route a few times, you'll know every intersection along the way and won't be so astounded by the way the airline pilots seem to come back so quickly with clearances.

When you are planning a route into a new area of expected higher terrain, you should examine the sectional chart to get a general look at geographic and topographic points. It would be helpful to have some idea of possible obstruction problems if things don't go perfectly. You should carry a set of sectional charts of your flight route in case you have to do some flying by reference to the ground.

This doesn't exactly tie in with planning the navigation, but you should consider oxygen equipment. If you have your own airplane or are flying a company airplane all the time, why not have an oxygen bottle and masks available? Not only might you have to fly at higher than usual altitudes, but what if one of your passengers needs oxygen when you are on solid IFR and can't get down immediately?

FLIGHT LOG

A flight log will be of particular value during your training. Making such a log will ensure your having some advance knowledge of the route.

By the time you get to instrument training, it's likely that you'll have a good idea of cruising speeds (true airspeed, TAS) at expected cross-country altitudes for your airplane. Or, if you are the thorough type, you may check the power setting chart for TAS for the chosen altitudes for 65% (or 75%) power. Then you could feed in wind information for that altitude as it would apply.

When flying IFR and using radio aids, the wind side of the computer will be of less value than before, and you won't usually work out wind triangles. It's still an aid in figuring out your estimated groundspeed, however. You should be conscientious in planning, since you'll want to be within the 3-min allowance at your reporting points if not in radar contact with the Center. With radar contact, the Center will be keeping right up and will know your position better than you do.

Back to the wind problem: In dead reckoning, precomputing of the drift correction is necessary. Here it is not—you'll take care of that with the VOR left-right needle (course deviation indicator, to be more technical). You *are* interested in the component of wind acting along the route (for or against), and for a quick estimate you can use the following:

The wind at your altitude will be given in knots and *true* direction. Your course is *magnetic;* and in areas where large magnetic variation exists, a correction is necessary. If you are flying in an area where the variation is 5° or less either way, forget it. Consider the true direction as being magnetic in getting a quick estimate.

For wind directly on the tail, use full value (25 knots, etc.) to get groundspeed. Figure 9-1 shows the idea.

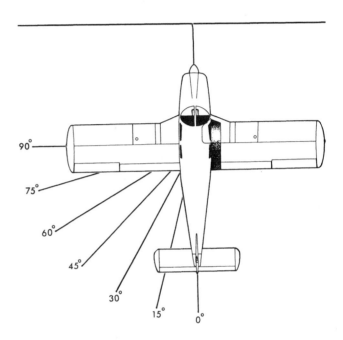

WIND ANGLE FROM NOSE OR TAIL

Fig. 9-1. Multipliers for head- or tailwind components at various angles to the course line: 0°—use full value (head or tail), 15°—use full value given, 30°—use 0.9 of value, 45°—use 0.7 of value, 60°—use 0.5 of value, 75°—use 0.3 of value, 90°—no value.

As an example, suppose your course is 065° magnetic, TAS is 150 knots, the wind is from 280° (true) at 30 knots at the altitude chosen. Assume that variation is small and can be ignored. If the wind was right on the tail, it would be from 245°. Here it is 35° off the (left) tail; the component of wind acting along the course (picking the nearest value) is 0.9 of 30, or 27 knots. Your groundspeed at that altitude will be 150 + 27 = 177 knots. To check the possible inaccuracies, reference to a trigonometric table would show that a wind at a 35° angle to the tail would have a component (along the course) of 0.81915 (the cosine of the angle) or about 82% of the wind value. This would mean a component of 24.5 knots or a groundspeed of 174.5 knots. On a 400-NM trip this would mean a difference of about 3 *min total time*. You could split the difference between 30° (0.7) and 45° (0.9) for 35° and get 0.8, which would make it even more accurate. Only minor errors would result on this or any trip with the normally expected distance between check points by using this method.

How much time do you allow if you are climbing en route to the next reporting point?

For fixed-gear airplanes add $^2/_3$ *min/1000 ft to be climbed. For single-engine, retractable-gear airplanes and light twins* add $^1/_2$ *min/1000ft.* As an example, suppose you are flying a single-engine, retractable-gear airplane and plan to fly at an altitude of 8000 ft (MSL). The airport elevation is 2000 ft, so you'll have to climb 6000 ft to get to that altitude. The first leg is 50 NM, and you compute that at *cruise speed* it would take 20 min. For your climb you would add 3 min (6 × ½ min) to get a total of 23 min ETE (estimated time en route).

For the same leg in a fixed-gear type, you might get an ETE at cruise of 23 min. Adding the $^2/_3$ min/1000 ft you'd get (6 × $^2/_3$ = 4), or 4 + 23 = 27 min for the leg, including climb. Expect these thumb rules to be accurate up to assigned altitudes of about 12,000 ft MSL.

On the flight log you can take into account the time required to fly from the fix serving the destination airport (VOR, etc.) to the destination airport *for your own purposes. However, when you file the flight plan, you'll include only the flying time from the takeoff to the en route navigation aid serving the destination airport and then to the final approach fix.*

As a part of your preflight planning and flight log work, look over the approach charts for the *destination airport,* *alternate airport,* and the *airport of departure.* Be sure to have these latter approach charts accessible during take-off—you might have problems and have to return to the airport of departure.

■ **Alternate Airport** In earlier times an alternate airport was required for *all* IFR flights; and your airplane had to carry enough fuel to *complete the flight* to the first intended point of landing, to fly from that point to an alternate airport, and to fly thereafter for 45 min at normal cruising speeds. In Chapter 8 the weather minimums for alternate airports as listed on approach charts are discussed.

(FAR 91.169 states that the alternate airport requirement considers weather reports and forecasts and weather conditions.)

You are allowed to omit the designation of an alternate airport on the IFR flight plan provided the first airport of intended landing has a standard instrument approach procedure and, for at least 1 hr before and for 1 hr after the estimated time of arrival, the weather reports or forecasts or any combination of them indicate that the ceiling will be at least 2000 ft above the airport elevation and the visibility will be at least 3 mi. (Remember 1, 2, 3.)

If no instrument approach procedure has been published and no special instrument approach procedure has been issued by the Administrator to the operator, for the alternate airport, the ceiling and visibility minimums are those allowing descent from the MEA, approach, and landing under basic VFR. See FAR 91.169 for details on all aircraft categories.

If an alternate airport is required, be sure to *plan the flight from the destination to the alternate.* It's disconcerting to get to the destination and discover that it's gone below minimums, and you are faced with flying a route to the alternate that you haven't really checked out. Later, with more experience, you'll be able to pick the figures right off the en route chart.

Look back at Figure 8-9 for a start on alternate facilities. Huntsville Airport will be the alternate for this trip, and you would look over the various approaches there.

ACTUALLY PLANNING THE TRIP

For this sample flight you will be using a Zephyr Six, a four-place single-engine, retractable-gear, high-performance airplane. Following are its specifications:

Engine—Lycoming IO-540, 260 hp
Gross weight—2900 lb
Basic empty weight—1744 lb
Total fuel—60 gal
Usable fuel—56 gal (6 lb/gal)
Baggage capacity—200 lb

You weigh 160 lb and have two passengers weighing 190 and 210 lb respectively. The baggage to be carried weighs 150 lb.

Since the unusable fuel (4 gal) and oil (23 lb) is already included in the basic empty weight of 1744 lb, you'll only add the weight of 56 gal of usable fuel. The arms given here are the same as those used in Chapter 3 for the first example of weight and balance and would be given on the weight and balance form of the airplane.

Item	Weight (lb)	Arm (in.)	Moment
Basic empty weight	1744		142,927
Fuel (56 gal)	336	90.0	30,240
Pilot	160	84.8	13,568
Passenger (front)	190	84.8	16,112
Passenger (rear)	210	118.5	24,885
Baggage1	150	142.0	21,300
Total	2790 lb		249,032 lb-in

Adding the 1266 lb-in. as required in Figure 3-22, the total moment is 250,298 lb-in.

You can see that you have 110 lb to spare in weight, but the CG should be checked by dividing the total moment by the total weight, getting an answer of 89.7 in. (rounded off) aft of the datum. A check of Figure 3-22, which is the weight and balance envelope for this airplane, shows that the CG is within the limits. The heavy passenger was placed in the rear seat to give the worst loading combination for this example.

Looking at the en route chart and planning to fly (for training purposes) to Nashville from Memphis via V159 (direct) to Holly Springs, V54 to Muscle Shoals, V7 to Graham, V16 to Nashville at 5000 ft, you can add up the mileage to get the total distance. In addition, Huntsville will be your alternate, and the distance from Nashville to Huntsville should also be considered. For this example the wind at 5000 ft (your planned altitude) to BNA is from 190 (true) at 25 knots. (Note that you would have a hefty headwind if you have to fly to Huntsville—see Fig. 9-2.)

The total distance from the Memphis Airport to Nashville VOR over the route planned is 237 NM. You'll have a basis for computing the time and fuel required. The figure of 237 NM was obtained by assuming that you will fly from Memphis Airport directly to Holly Springs VOR and then follow the Victor route. The chances of this being necessary are slim, but you could be asked to do it. Besides, it is a conservative approach to the problem.

You will have a tailwind component on all legs to BNA, but you should get a no-wind estimate to the destination and on to the alternate. From the Nashville Airport to the Huntsville Airport is 94 NM, for a total of 331 NM to be flown. Looking back to Figure 3-12, you'll note that at 5000 ft (density-altitude) the TAS at that altitude at 65% power is 148 knots. You plan on using 65% because it is much easier on the engine, with a cost of only a few knots in speed. Figure 3-13 indicates that this airplane uses 12.7 gal fuel/hr when properly leaned at 65%.

Using your computer, the no-wind time to make the trip of 2 hr and 14 min is found (if it is necessary to go to Huntsville). Allowing ⅔ min/1000 ft to climb from Memphis Airport (elevation 331 ft) to 5000 ft MSL would be another 2.5 min (call it 3). The no-wind time could be figured as 2 hr and 17 min. Again, referring to a computer with this knowledge, you'll find that the fuel required will be 29 gal. Add another 6 gal for taxiing, waiting, and extra fuel used in the climb and figure on about 35 gal required to fly from Memphis to Nashville to Huntsville. The requirement is to have a 45-min reserve at normal cruising speed after reaching the alternate. The fuel burned in 45 min, at 12.7 gal/hr, is 9.5 gal (call it 10). The fuel now required is 35 + 10 = 45 gal. Better also allow another 5 gal to assume you make an approach to Nashville, miss it, and have to climb back up to proceed to the alternate. This makes a total of 50 gal to cover all requirements, and you have 56 gal of usable fuel. *Remember that this is a quick initial look at the trip to check its feasibility. You will check the details as you further plan the trip.*

If there had been a headwind, the rough check should have been done using the expected headwind component for all legs, again a conservative approach. If the rough check shows that the trip can't be made in one hop as first supposed, or if it looks very close, the final, more accurate check and flight log will be completed before committing to the flight. (There will be no commitment, naturally, until the weather and NOTAMs are taken into account.)

Not indicated on this copy of the en route chart is that the magnetic variation is 2° East in the vicinity of Memphis and tapers off to about 0° East in the vicinity of Nashville. For simplicity it can be averaged as 1° East, which can be ignored for wind computations.

Figure 9-2 is the flight log made out for the flight from Memphis to Nashville and on to Huntsville via the route just discussed. In the early part of your training you might list every intersection, but for later actual flights the best idea is to use *all* VORs as check points (compulsory reporting points or not) and any intersections that are compulsory.

The symbols ▲ and △ aid in ascertaining from the flight log whether the particular fix is a compulsory reporting point. You may use your own shorthand; for instance, an X or an asterisk (*) can be used as a symbol for "intersection."

Working out the flight log beforehand is a good way to avoid the problem of misreading map distances in the air. Remember that the en route charts give the *total* distance between compulsory reporting points or VORs in a box (check it), and the other distances (between noncompulsory intersections, etc.) are in the open. It seems that distracted pilots sometimes add the series of distances between compulsory points and leave out maybe a 10- or 15-mi section somehow. Needless to say, this also affects the *minutes* of a new estimate. As a check after completing the flight log, you should add the minutes required to fly individual legs. They should add up very close to the *total time* required to fly the *total distance*. Probably you'll be a couple of minutes off because of rounding-off times on various legs, but at least you have a double check of distances and times.

Included in Figure 9-2 are position report and clearance forms for easier organization in flight. If you were not in radar contact and had to give position reports, you could write that information out before transmitting to save some stumbling. It would also serve as a permanent record if desired. The clearance box in Figure 9-2 contains the information in the order that it will be given to you. The example here might be the clearance you'd get before departing Memphis and states that "N3456J IS CLEARED TO THE NASHVILLE METRO AIRPORT WITH A HOLLY FOUR DEPARTURE." They might give you specific departure instructions here. The route is next: "VIA DIRECT HOLLY SPRINGS (OR RADAR VECTORS), V54, V7, V16" to Nashville, with altitude data as flown, such as "MAINTAIN 4000 UNTIL 10 MINUTES FROM MEMPHIS, THEN MAINTAIN 5000." Holding instructions, if any, would be then given ("EXPECT TO HOLD AT HOLLY SPRINGS, etc."), followed by any special instructions. The last item would be frequency and transponder code information: You are to contact Memphis departure control on 124.15 MHz and are assigned a discrete beacon code of 5512.

The estimated groundspeeds and times were worked out on three different types of computers. There were very minor variations in answers, so the average was used here.

Figure 9-3 is the standard instrument departure (DP) chart for Memphis showing the area facilities used for the various departures.

FLIGHT PLAN

Figure 9-4 is a sample instrument flight plan for the trip from Memphis to Nashville just planned.

N 3456J DATE – Jan 18 TIME OFF	WEATHER											WINDS ALOFT	

WEATHER

CURRENT: MEM SA 1950 M13 OVC 6F 129/58/53/1110/991
FCST: MEM 18Z 10 SCT C25 OVC 6H 0908 OCN C10 BKN 3F. 05Z-
CURRENT: BNA SA 1947 M23 BKN 250 OVC 10 165 57/50/0904/002
FCST: BNA 18Z C25 BKN 1208. 23Z C12 OVC 5F 1410. 08Z-
SPECIALS/NOTAMS

WINDS ALOFT

	BNA	MEM
3-	1518	1623
6-	1920	1929
9-	2222	2028
12-	2325	2725

FROM	IDENT FREQ	TO	IDENT FREQ	VIA	MC	DIST NM	EGS ETE	TIME OVER	ATE	GS	ETA NEXT	REMARKS
MEM AIRPORT	✓	HOLLY SPRINGS VOR	HLI 112.4	↗ DIRECT	123°	29	88/138 15					CLMB 100KTS 7MIN 88K G.S. — 19 MLES @138K=8MIN
HOLLY SPRINGS VOR	HLI 112.4	SULLY *	JKS 109.4	V54	089°	20	151 8					SULLY *-214R JKS MEA 3000
SULLY *	MSL 116.5	KERMI *	JKS 109.4	V54	092°	48	150 19					KERMI *-167R JKS MEA 3000
KERMI *	MSL 116.5	BRADS *	HAB 110.4	V54	092°	15	150 6					BRADS * 013R HAB MEA 3000
BRADS *	MSL 116.5	MUSCLE SHOALS VOR	MSL 116.5	V54	092°	16	150 6					MSL-NO VOICE ON VOR MEA 3000
MUSCLE SHOALS VOR	MSL 116.5	GILLE *	RQZ 112.2	V7	001°	15	172 5					GILLE* 281R RQZ RQZ-NO VOICE VOR MEA-2500
GILLE *	MSL 116.5	POLAN *	JKS 109.4	V7	000°	38	172 13					POLAN *-089R JKS MEA-3000
POLAN *	GHM 111.6	GRAHAM VOR	GHM 111.6	V7	359°	15	172 5					MEA 3000
GRAHAM VOR	GHM 111.6	TICTO *	SYI 109.0	V16	062°	16	162 6					TICTO *-305R SYI
TICTO *	BNA 114.1	NASHVILLE VOR AIRPORT	BNA 114.1	V16	067°	25	161 9					BNA APC 120.6 TWR 119.1
						237	1:32					TOTAL DISTANCE 237NM TOTAL TIME (EST.) 1:32
NASHVILLE VOR	BNA 114.1	SHELBYVILLE VOR	SYI 109.0	V362 ↗	161°	35	132 16					USE BNA WINDS 190°-20K MEA 3000
SYI VOR	SYI 109.0	ROCKET VOR	RQZ 112.2	V321	193°	47	128 22					RQZ – NO VOICE MEA 3000
ROCKET VOR	RQZ 112.2	HUNTSVILLE AIRPORT	I-HSV 109.3	↓ DIRECT	210°	12	129 6					HSV WX-
						94	0:44					HSV-APC-125.6 TWR-119.7

POSITION REPORTS

POS.	TIME	ALT.	TYPE	EST.	NEXT

N 3456J CLEARED — CLEARANCES

TO	BNA METRO
DEPT. OR SID	HOLLY FOUR
ROUTE	AS VECTORED, V54 V7, V16
ALTITUDE	5000
HOLDING	–
SPECIAL	–
FREQ / CODE	DPT. 124.15 / 5512

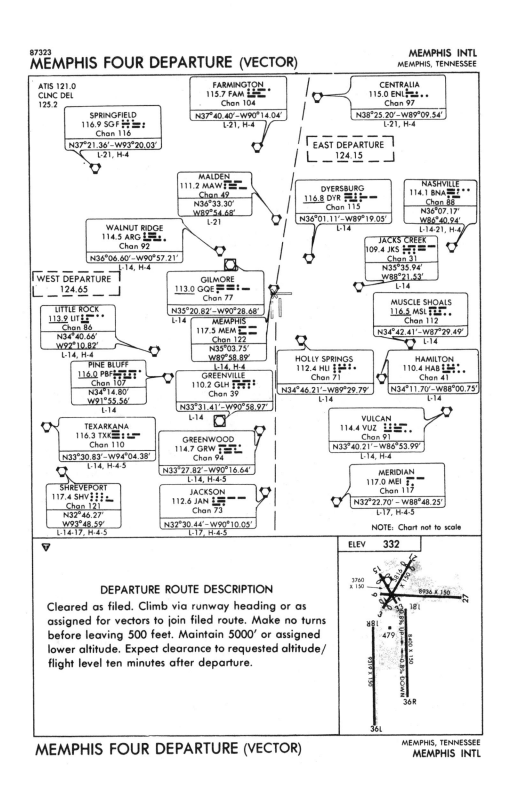

Fig. 9-3. The MEMPHIS FOUR DEPARTURE (vector) system.

◀ **Fig. 9-2.** (left) A flight log for an IFR flight from Memphis to Nashville and on to the alternate, Huntsville. Times have been rounded off to the minute. For the Memphis–Nashville portion of the trip, the wind will be assumed to be 190/25 at 5000 ft. For Nashville to Huntsville the wind is from 190° at 20 knots. You can put expected fuel consumption for various segments in the remarks section if you want to. Note: The pilot wrote the weather at the top of the log, listing the most important items first (clouds/ceilings and visibility)—the order used for weather reporting *before* METAR/TAF was instituted.

1. TYPE	2. AIRCRAFT IDENTIFICATION	3. AIRCRAFT TYPE/ SPECIAL EQUIPMENT	4. TRUE AIRSPEED	5. DEPARTURE POINT	6. DEPARTURE TIME		7. CRUISING ALTITUDE

U.S. DEPARTMENT OF TRANSPORTATION FEDERAL AVIATION ADMINISTRATION

FLIGHT PLAN

(FAA USE ONLY) ☐ PILOT BRIEFING ☐ VNR
☐ STOPOVER

TIME STARTED

SPECIALIST INITIALS

1. TYPE	2. AIRCRAFT IDENTIFICATION	3. AIRCRAFT TYPE/ SPECIAL EQUIPMENT	4. TRUE AIRSPEED	5. DEPARTURE POINT	6. DEPARTURE TIME		7. CRUISING ALTITUDE
VFR ☒ IFR ☐ DVFR	N3456J	ZA-6/A	148 KTS	MEMPHIS INTL. AP	PROPOSED (Z) 2040	ACTUAL (Z)	5000

8. ROUTE OF FLIGHT

DIRECT HLI, V54 MSL, V7 GRAHAM, V16 BNA

9. DESTINATION (Name of airport and city)	10. EST. TIME ENROUTE		11. REMARKS
	HOURS	MINUTES	
NASHVILLE METRO	1	32	

12. FUEL ON BOARD		13. ALTERNATE AIRPORT(S)	14. PILOT'S NAME, ADDRESS & TELEPHONE NUMBER & AIRCRAFT HOME BASE	15. NUMBER ABOARD
HOURS	MINUTES	HUNTSVILLE- MADISON CO. AL	STEWART G. DICKSON (615) 598-5318 NASHVILLE, TN, (NASHVILLE METRO)	3
4	25		17. DESTINATION CONTACT/TELEPHONE (OPTIONAL) JONES FLYING SERVICE	

16. COLOR OF AIRCRAFT	
WHITE AND BLUE	CIVIL AIRCRAFT PILOTS. FAR Part 91 requires you file an IFR flight plan to operate under instrument flight rules in controlled airspace. Failure to file could result in a civil penalty not to exceed $1,000 for each violation (Section 901 of the Federal Aviation Act of 1958, as amended). Filing of a VFR flight plan is recommended as a good operating practice. See also Part 99 for requirements concerning DVFR flight plans.

CLOSE VFR FLIGHT PLAN WITH_____ FSS ON ARRIVAL

Fig. 9-4. The flight plan as given to the Flight Service Station.

Taking the items on the flight plan one by one:

Type of flight plan—You'd check IFR, naturally.

Aircraft identification—The full identification (registration number of the airplane).

Aircraft type—If you know the "official" designation of your airplane, use it. For instance, "PA-23-250" is the designator for the *Piper Aztec,* rather than "Aztec." The FSS will have a list of official designators for various airplanes. If you don't know the model number, they will help you in this regard. Here you would put the information concerning DME or transponder or other equipment aboard. Shown as an example is the designator for a 4096-code transponder with altitude encoding ability and DME. For practice purposes, the flight in the following chapters will not be so equipped except at isolated situations as needed to make a point. (On paper you can throw equipment in or out, erase NOTAMs, or change the weather as desired, with little trouble or expense.)

True airspeed (knots)—If heretofore you've been shying away from knots, you'll soon find that for IFR work you'll have to *think* in knots. All distances on the en route charts, area charts, and approach charts (except visibility minimums) are in nautical miles. If you aren't

used to knots, don't make the mistake of talking in terms of "knots per hour." The term "knot" means 1 *NM/hr* and is a short way of saying it. Another error made by the knot neophytes is to speak of knots as a distance. They'll look at the chart and say, for instance, "I measure it to be 163 knots between A and B." What they should say is that it's 163 NM between A and B.

One other confusion that arises is that the new pilot wants to put groundspeed in that item. *Don't.* ATC wants to know your TAS, which will give them comparative speeds of airplanes operating in the same airspace. They will have the winds at your altitude and can come right back to you if you give a bum estimate to your next reporting point (such an estimate by *you* was based on your computation of groundspeed).

If your TAS varies more than 10 K or 5% during the flight, let ATC know about it if you are in a nonradar environment. It won't be necessary if you are under radar surveillance. *Don't* get mixed up and discover that your *groundspeed* has changed that amount and let ATC know about it—except as a revised estimate to a fix. In other words, they'll have access to wind info but can't read your mind if you decide to do something radical about indicated (and calibrated and true) airspeed.

Point of departure—If you are phoning in the flight plan or for some reason don't plan to fly from the particular airport where you are filing the flight plan in person, you'd better make this point clear.

Departure time—You'll put the proposed time of departure in Zulu time. Needless to say, you should know by now to add 5 hr to Eastern *Standard* Time, 6 hr to Central *Standard,* etc., to get Zulu time.

  The actual departure time will be recorded after you've departed. Remember, if at all possible, file the flight plan at least 30 min before the proposed time of departure.

Cruising altitude—This will be the requested level en route flight altitude. Normally file odd altitudes eastbound (0°–179° magnetic) and even altitudes when westbound (180°–359°). However, you may want to take advantage of being able to get a handy low altitude just above the MEA (minimum en route altitude) at an even altitude (say 4000 ft) when eastbound. You may ask for it but may not get it.

Route of flight—In this case, a complicated route was picked to show a point. When you have a number of segments, which may be the case on some long flights, it's best to name the fix at the end of each different airway to avoid possible errors.

Destination—You'll put the airport name and city here because some cities have more than one airport capable of handling IFR traffic.

Estimated time en route—This is based on the time required from takeoff to the final approach fix to be used for the approach to the destination airport. This is done in case of communications failure en route. If you lose communications, you'll be expected to continue the flight at the last assigned altitude or the MEA (whichever is higher) and route to the navaid serving the destination airport and thence to the facility or fix to be used for the approach. You will depart that facility to start an approach (ILS, VOR, etc.) at the time of arrival, based on the last estimate to that point, whether it is from the flight plan (you lost communications before reaching the first en route fix to set up estimates with ATC) or from later estimates given to ATC, based on known groundspeeds. This will be covered in more detail in Chapter 12.

Fuel on board—This is *usable fuel available* at takeoff. If you've been flying and haven't refueled, be sure to put the actual hours of fuel left at the cruising speed you used in item 4 in Figure 9-4. Make sure that you will have enough to get to the destination and to the alternate (if required) *plus* 45 min at normal cruise.

Remarks—You can make snide remarks such as "I hope that this time I get an altitude and route somewhat near that filed for" and other such statements guaranteed to tickle the ATC dragon. (More likely you'll use this space to list your passengers' names or other such serious information.)

Alternate airport—If an alternate is necessary, put it down here.

Name of pilot—You should be able to handle this with no trouble.

Address of pilot or *aircraft home base*—Usually it's best to list the aircraft home base if there's a difference.

Number of persons on board—Another obvious one.

Color of aircraft—Self-explanatory.

Destination contact/telephone—This is probably a good item to have filled out if you disappear en route somewhere or if someone needs to get in touch with you at the completion of the flight.

SUMMARY

  Good preflight planning can make the difference between a no-sweat situation and everything turning to worms. You'll work out your own shorthand for use on the flight log and clearance copying. A small clipboard can be modified to have an elastic band (with a snap fastener) for strapping around your leg or on the control wheel, or you may want to buy one of the custom-made clipboards you see in ads in aviation magazines.

  Figure 9-5 shows the probable order of your paperwork on the clipboard.

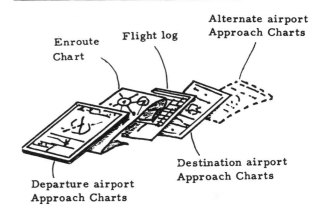

Fig. 9-5. Probable order of paperwork on the kneeboard.

  The flight planning ideas offered in this chapter may make the instrument flight seem very complicated; this is not the case at all in the vast majority of IFR trips. As the ATC system continues to improve, the headaches of "reporting points" will be completely phased out. It's unlikely that you will make *any* routine reports after the departure to the approach. However, since reporting points are still required on some flights (in certain areas), this book will try to cover different possibilities.

  Part of preflight planning is ensuring that if you should lose all radios you know the route to better (VFR) weather. Later in your training you will probably dispense with the flight log and will use the en route chart for that purpose.

4 THE INSTRUMENT FLIGHT

BEFORE THE TAKEOFF

10

It's important that you make a thorough preflight inspection anytime you fly, but for IFR work it's vital. For instance, you just get leveled off at your assigned altitude and are solidly on the gauges, when one of the passengers says, "Hey, there's a solid stream of gas pouring off the back of both wings." You were in a kind of a hurry to get off. You saw the line boy fueling, so were sure that the tanks were full and didn't bother to check that the caps were on properly or secured. Now you have two choices: (1) Continue on your way and hope to complete the trip before you lose all the fuel (that's asking for it) or (2) let ATC in on the act and get a clearance to the nearest airport that has an instrument letdown procedure. Well, in that case, by not using 15 sec of your valuable time, you've caused the reshuffling of IFR traffic clear back to What Cheer, Iowa. Assuming you make it safely, the least you've done is to have caused a lot of people a lot of trouble.

PREFLIGHT INSPECTION

Figure 10-1 is a preflight inspection for a light twin-engine airplane showing special IFR items to consider. (As far as checking the rest of the airplane is concerned, if you don't have a check system set up already, then it's too late to bring it up here.)

The following check is meant to bring up some ideas rather than give a specific system. There are too many airplane types and variations in antennas and other equipment for this to hit your situation exactly, but you should use the *POH* recommended preflight inspection and other procedures for *your* airplane as available.

1. As always, the first thing to do is to make sure *all the switches are OFF.*
2. Shown at (2) is a combination *navigation-communications* (broadband) *antenna.* Check it for security of attachment and general condition.
3. This is a *broadband communications antenna.* Check it for security and general condition. (Of course, *your* airplane may be using whip antennas and you should check them carefully.)
4. The *marker beacon antenna* may not be in the exact spot on the belly as shown in Figure 10-1 and may be the older type, but you should check it for security and possible dirt and oil on it. (The dirt and oil problem is usually worse on a single-engine airplane.)

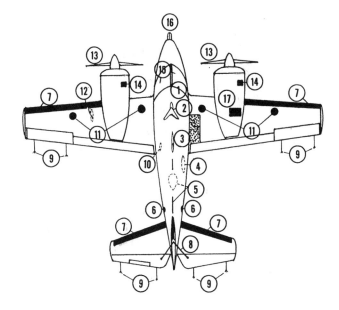

Fig. 10-1. A preflight inspection showing items of special interest for IFR operations.

5. Check the *automatic direction finder loop housing* and the *sensing antenna* for security and general condition.
6. If your airplane has the "separate pitot tube and static inlet" system, make sure that the *static vents* are clear. Some airplanes have these static vents nearer the tail cone, while others may have them farther forward than shown.
7. This number covers *deicer* boots. You would check the boots as you came to them in your clockwise (or counterclockwise) check. The statements made about the tail deicers will stand for the wing boots, hence the same reference numbers.

   Check for the condition of the rubber to ensure that there are no large cracks that could cause leaks. Check the attachment of the boots to the airframe.
8. Shown here on the top of the fin is a *whip* (V type) *VOR/LOC antenna.* If your plane has such an antenna, check it for security and general condition.
9. If your plane has *static wicks,* which are designed to gradually discharge static electricity buildups, check

them for security. Their job is to keep radio static down when the plane is flying through rain and other precipitation (or dust in extreme cases). You'll get the wing static wicks as you come to them.

10. The *DME antenna* is likely to be on the belly in the area of the spot indicated. Look it over. If you are not sure of the various types of antennas on your plane, you might review Chapter 5 or talk to some of the old hands around the airport. There may be some pretty exotic looking antennas. The *transponder antenna* will be quite similar (in the majority of types) to the small DME blade antenna and will be on the belly in or near the center section.

11. You should have *full tanks and secured fuel tank caps.* Unless weight and balance considerations for a particular passenger and baggage loading require otherwise, *always* have full tanks when going IFR. In a partially filled tank situation you'd better *know* exactly how much fuel the plane has and how much will be needed. Remember, you may have to hold or go to an alternate airport (or both).

12. The *pitot tube* is shown as being attached to the bottom of the left wing on this sample airplane. Check the pitot tube opening for obstructions. If this is a pitot-static combination, check the static vents for obstructions. Make sure the assembly is firmly attached, whether left or right wing or fuselage.

13. If the plane has *electric prop deicers,* check the slip ring and brush-block assemblies. If in doubt concerning their condition, have a mechanic check them.

    The propeller heating elements are wires or foil encased in an oil- and abrasion-resistant pad of rubber bonded to each propeller blade. Check these for general conditions, including bonding integrity and worn or torn rubber.

14. Make sure that the oil is at the proper level and the *oil cap is secure.*

15. A *clean windshield* is a lot of help when you break out on final. Check the windshield wiper blades if the airplane is so equipped.

16. Shown in the figure is the older type of *glide slope antenna.* Make sure that it is on securely. (Well, it certainly looks like a handle to be used to pull the airplane and may have been used for that.)

17. If the airplane uses a propeller *fluid anti-icing system,* check the fluid level and make sure the outlets aren't clogged and that the cap and flap are secure after you've done so.

During the check make sure that the fuel sumps and strainers are drained. Water in the sumps may freeze if the airplane is left out overnight in the winter, and the quick-drains may be "stuck" to where they cannot be moved. There *may* be just a drop or so of water frozen in the assembly, or there may be enough built-up ice in there to cut off part of the fuel flow. Everything is fine while you taxi, and maybe nothing shows up during the run-up; but when full

power is applied, the engine(s) is just not getting enough fuel to pull it off. This could happen just as you lifted off into the murk (and drained the carburetor float chamber). Even if you discover this problem during the run-up (or earlier), it means taxiing back to take care of it, with a resulting time loss. If the drains won't drain, find out why and thaw them as necessary. Don't, however, be like Archibald Zorp, instrument pilot, who expedited the thawing process with an acetylene torch. Not only was his airplane completely thawed all over, but several other airplanes and one-half the hangar received the benefit of his efforts. Archibald has yet to make the instrument flight he planned so carefully. (He is now busily growing back his eyebrows.)

Check the alternator(s) belt(s) if you can see into that area.

When you get into the cabin, make sure that your checklist includes moving the fuel selectors to verify the ease of switching tanks. It could cause trouble if you fly all fuel out of a tank (or tanks) and then discover, some miles from an airport, that the selector can't be moved to another tank.

STARTING

There is little to be added in regard to starting. You have the word on starting your particular airplane. Make sure all avionics are off to save the battery. Also, the sudden surge of power through the system on starting doesn't do radios *any good at all,* so leave them off. Use the *POH* procedure.

After the start, check the oil pressure(s). As you make the run-up check, be sure that you have the proper vacuum pressure. For full-fledged IFR work, it's best to have an engine-driven vacuum pump rather than venturi-driven instruments. With the pump you'll have gyro instruments operating *before* takeoff and can tell if one of the instruments is not up to snuff. With the venturi you could be pretty well committed during takeoff before discovering problems. In heavy icing conditions, the venturi(s), being exposed, could ice over, with a resulting loss of gyro instruments.

As noted earlier in Chapter 4 ("Instrument Takeoff") allow 5 min for the vacuum- or pressure-pump(s) to bring the gyros up to speed.

TAXIING

Before taxiing you should check ATIS (Automatic Terminal Information Service) for the latest weather and runway information.

Get your clearance on the clearance delivery frequency if available, or if not, alert ground control that you are on an IFR flight plan so that they'll have your clearance ready for you when you request it.

Here is a good time to check your VOR receivers with the VOT if available.

Now you can call for taxi instructions.

(Wait until the frequency is clear and then...)

You: "MEMPHIS GROUND (CONTROL) THIS IS ZEPHYR THREE FOUR FIVE SIX JULIET, JONES

FLYING SERVICE (RAMP) INFORMATION UNIFORM TAXI."

Memphis ground: "ZEPHYR FIVE SIX JULIET, MEMPHIS GROUND CONTROL, TAXI TO RUNWAY ONE SEVEN" (plus any necessary instructions for taxi). The clearance delivery frequency is listed just after the tower and ground control frequencies in the *Airport/Facility Directory,* as shown by Figure 8-22 for Memphis. It was mentioned in Chapter 6 that, at some places, you could get your clearance on this frequency before taxiing, and you would have looked it up beforehand. (Memphis has regular clearance delivery.)

PRETAKEOFF CHECK

You will, of course, check the controls, trim settings, manifold heat, magnetos, and prop controls as given in the *POH.*

If you have electric prop deicers, you should check them for operation (the prop deicer ammeter will show surges as the equipment works). You should cycle the wing and tail deicer boots if installed.

The turn and slip or turn coordinator should be checked as you taxi. The heading indicator and attitude gyro should be holding. (Set the heading indicator to the compass; set the attitude indicator as near to the actual attitude of the airplane as possible.) The vacuum pressure should be normal. In the twin both vacuum pumps should be working, as indicated by either the manual selector on the panel or the lack of red indicators on either of the vacuum gauges (whichever type of equipment you have). Check pitot heat (ammeter). Tap the altimeter to make sure it has settled down.

The radios will be of "great interest" and you should check all such equipment. (You should, however, keep the transponder on standby until starting the takeoff roll.) The avionics check should include all communications and navigation equipment. Sometimes you may have to wait for a clearance, so don't sit there with all radios on draining the battery. The use of alternators has alleviated this problem somewhat, but you still may have to run the engine(s) up to a high rpm.

While we're on the subject of radios, you'd better have a headset aboard in case the cabin speaker malfunctions. An extra microphone is a good idea too. Some pilots have a hand-held transceiver on board and available.

An added point: If it's night, you wouldn't want to sit at the warm-up area with taxi lights (and/or landing lights) and white cabin lights on. (White cabin lights raise havoc with night vision.) Some pilots also turn off the rotating beacon and/or strobes if they are sitting at the approach end of the runway. Not only does the beacon use electric power, but it could also distract landing pilots as they cross the threshold. *Leave the navigation (position) lights* on, unless you want a 767 or something in the cabin with you.

Speaking generally about pretakeoff checks, it would be very well for you to make up a new checklist for your particular airplane and include the special checks for IFR flight in the places where they would apply. (For instance, the vacuum

pressure check might fall logically right after the magneto check, etc.) Check the deicer boot operation (if you have them), as outlined in the Supplement to the *Pilot's Operating Handbook.* You might want to underline the special IFR checks to separate them from the usual VFR check items. If you are getting formal instrument training with a flight school, such a checklist may already be available. There are too many different airplane models to set up a pretakeoff check here, and you'll probably have plenty of VFR experience in the airplane before taking IFR training.

CLEARANCES

Your clearance will be issued in the following or*der,* but may differ slightly in details.

1. Aircraft identification (N 3456 Juliet).
2. Clearance limit ("CLEARED TO THE NASHVILLE AIRPORT").
3. Departure procedure or SID ("MEMPHIS FOUR DEPARTURE, COMON ONE SID, MAINTAIN 4000, EXPECT 5000 TEN MINUTES AFTER DEPARTURE").
4. Route of flight ("DIRECT HOLLY SPRINGS, VICTOR 54, VICTOR 7, VICTOR 16"). If a route given by a previous clearance is amended it may be given to you thus:
   (a) "CHANGE VICTOR 7 TO READ VICTOR XX" (for example) or (b) "VICTOR XX TO MUSCLE SHOALS, REST OF ROUTE UNCHANGED." Or they may issue the fun route.
5. Altitude data in the order flown ("MAINTAIN 4000 UNTIL 10 MINUTES FROM MEMPHIS, MAINTAIN 5000"). When a route or altitude in a previously issued clearance is amended, clearance delivery will restate all applicable altitude restrictions or state that altitude restrictions are canceled.
6. Holding instructions (if applicable). If a delay is anticipated en route and the holding pattern is not depicted, you'll be issued either a general or detailed holding procedure (see Chapter 12 for details on holding).
7. Any special information.
8. Frequency and beacon code information ("DEPARTURE CONTROL FREQUENCY 124.15, SQUAWK 5512").

You may get a "cleared as filed" clearance, which means that there were no complications or changes in the *route.* The *altitude* will always be stated by ATC, and you will confirm it. This does not include DPs.

If you are a refresher instrument pilot, you'll note that ATC facilities do not say, "ATC CLEARS N 3456 JULIET," anymore. They'll say, "N 3456 JULIET (IS) CLEARED (TO, FROM, FOR," etc.). However, FSSs or other sources *relaying* ATC information to you will prefix the clearance with "ATC CLEARS" (or "ADVISES," "REQUESTS," etc.).

If a clearance is one with which you can't comply, let them know and ask for a new one. (Expect a possible delay.)

A suggestion is to write down beforehand, widely spaced, the route and altitude you filed for, so that changes can be made without having to do a lot of writing of the symbols. Write the new route(s) and altitude above the old. Figure 10-2 shows this method for a different routing and altitude to Nashville. (You filed for V159 [direct] to HLI [Holly Springs] V54, V7, V16 and for 5000 ft, but ATC wants you to go another way.) After copying, mark out the original figures as shown in Figure 10-2 and check the en route chart.

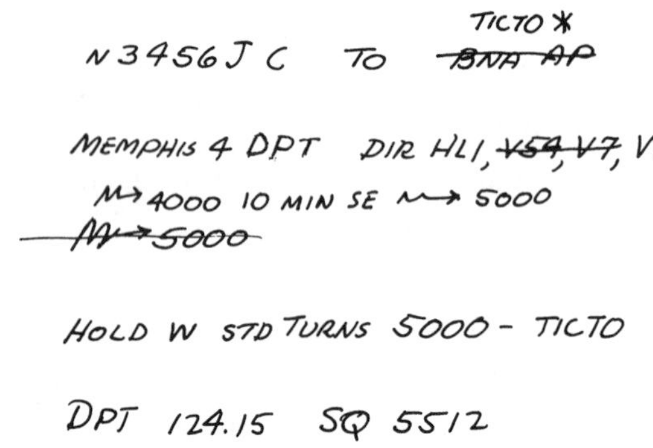

N3456JC   TO   TICTO *
                 ~~BNA AP~~

MEMPHIS 4 DPT   DIR HLI, ~~V54 V7~~, V16
    ↝ 4000 10 MIN SE ↝ 5000
    ~~↝ 5000~~

HOLD W STD TURNS 5000 - TICTO

DPT 124.15   SQ 5512

Fig. 10-2. Revising the expected clearance. Leave plenty of space between lines for inserting new routes and climb instructions.

But, going back to the example trip, we'll say that you're still going the V159, V54, V7, V16 route.

The clearance you'll get before departure *normally* will be to the airport of intended landing. Under some conditions at certain locations, a short-range clearance procedure is used; and you would be advised of the frequency with which to contact the Center for the long-range clearance.

When you've accepted a clearance, you are expected to follow it. Any clearance in which the time of execution by the pilot is optional will state, "At pilot's discretion."

If you get a clearance en route, for instance, "(YOUR NUMBER) CLIMB AND MAINTAIN SIX THOUSAND *IMMEDIATELY*;" you'd better clear your present altitude for 6000 *immediately,* if not sooner. ATC doesn't throw "immediately" around without a reason.

Amendments to the initial clearance may be given en route. You may have been cleared to the destination airport via a certain route before takeoff, but you may be given an amendment (or amendments) en route to avoid conflict with other traffic. It can include holding, change of altitude, and rerouting. Unless it will exercise an extreme hardship, don't argue but accept the clearance and comply. *Don't* tie up valuable time and frequencies by chatter unless you are going to be placed in a dangerous situation. The controllers

don't like to upset the status quo any more than you do unless it is absolutely necessary. If you have a beef, write or call the Center *after* the flight.

If you've been cleared to a fix short of the destination airport, it's the responsibility of ATC to give additional clearance at least 5 *min prior* to the time the flight arrives at the clearance limit. The new clearance may authorize flight beyond the limit or contain holding instructions. However, if for some reason you don't get the clearance by the time you're 3 min from the fix, you'll be expected to reduce speed so as to cross the limit initially at or below maximum holding speed (unless further clearance comes through while you're slowing). If no clearance has come through, you will establish a *standard* holding pattern—meaning that you would make right-hand turns and 1-min inbound legs—on the course on which you approach the fix, unless the pattern is charted otherwise. When you get clearance to another fix, you will acknowledge—giving time of departure—and will depart.

The ARTCC Sector controller may be watching your antics on radar, will know you're holding, and will try to get you on your way. So it won't do any good to mention casually over the radio, "Well, here I am, still holding at Zilch intersection, well, well." They'll get you going as soon as possible.

You *always* should write down your clearances; it will help in a read-back and can serve as a record if you should need it later.

Normally, when given an altitude, you'll be told to *maintain* that altitude. This means you must maintain that altitude until cleared by ATC for another. On short flights in uncongested areas, you may be given, "Cruise at such and such an altitude." *Cruise* means that you may ascend to or descend from cruising altitude and make an (approved) approach at the destination without further clearance from ATC. *This does not clear you to descend below minimum en route altitude (minimum obstruction clearance altitude, MOCA), if applicable, or other minimum altitudes unless in VFR conditions.* If you've been cleared to cruise at a certain altitude, start descent, and verbally report leaving it, you can't change your mind and go back up to it without a new clearance.

It's your responsibility to notify ATC immediately if your radio equipment cannot receive the type of signals required to comply with the clearance.

ATC will not issue a clearance specifying that a climb or descent on any portion of the flight be made under "VFR conditions" on any IFR flight, unless specifically requested by the pilot. You can sometimes save time at the departure if conditions are VFR by requesting this rather than waiting for the full treatment.

■ **A Last Note** Again, since there is a lot happening as you start the trip, it's doubly important that you have a checklist for preflight, starting, and pretakeoff checks so that nothing is overlooked.

11

TAKEOFF AND DEPARTURE

The pretakeoff check is complete, you've read the clearance back, and gotten "CLEARANCE CORRECT" from clearance delivery, so you'll switch to ground control frequency for taxi. Make sure all necessary radios (and lights, if applicable) are on when you're ready for takeoff. Have one VOR and/or ADF, as applicable, receiver on one of the approach facilities serving the airport of departure and have the local approach charts available just in case you have to make an unscheduled return. The other VOR receiver should be tuned to the first en route VOR.

It was said earlier and will be said again: If conditions are such that a full-fledged instrument takeoff is required, how do you plan to get back in if something goes wrong? If the bad conditions are local and other airports are available—and flyable—it might be feasible, but if the lousy weather is extensive, you'd better look closely before busting off.

You: "MEMPHIS TOWER, (ZEPHYR THREE FOUR) FIVE SIX JULIET READY FOR TAKEOFF ON (RUNWAY) ONE EIGHT RIGHT."
Memphis tower: "ZEPHYR FIVE SIX JULIET, MEMPHIS TOWER, RUNWAY ONE EIGHT RIGHT, CLEARED FOR TAKEOFF." (The tower may give headings to turn to after takeoff or other instructions; it depends on local and current conditions.)
You: "ZEPHYR FIVE SIX JULIET."

You would turn the transponder from standby ON to the assigned discrete code as late as possible before taking off.

After you've reached a point about ½ mi past the end of the runway, you will be switched to departure control; heavy chatter on the radio or the traffic situation could delay this slightly.

Memphis tower: "ZEPHYR FIVE SIX JULIET, CONTACT DEPARTURE CONTROL. OVER." (No frequency given; you had that earlier and should have written it down.) As soon as the tower tells you to make the switch, acknowledge and do so.
You: "ZEPHYR FIVE SIX JULIET, DEPARTURE CONTROL ONE TWO FOUR POINT ONE FIVE."

DEPARTURE CONTROL

You: "MEMPHIS DEPARTURE (CONTROL) THIS IS ZEPHYR THREE FOUR FIVE SIX JULIET." If your airplane has a working encoder altimeter, you would give an altimeter check. For instance say, "LEAVING 800 FEET," or whatever. Report to the nearest 100 ft. If your airplane has the 3/A mode (or no transponder), you could give departure control a general altitude check as noted shortly: "PASSING TWO THOUSAND. OVER."
Memphis departure control: "ZEPHYR FIVE SIX JULIET, MEMPHIS DEPARTURE RADAR CONTACT. TURN LEFT HEADING ONE FOUR ZERO. MAINTAIN FOUR THOUSAND (FEET)."
You: "ZEPHYR FIVE SIX JULIET, MAINTAIN FOUR THOUSAND, PASSING TWO (THOUSAND)."

The Memphis tower computer has passed your time off to the Center.

After reaching a safe altitude, you'll set climbing power, turn off the boost pumps, and do the other required cockpit chores as you finish the turn and continue to climb. Your tendency may be to get so engrossed in voice reports and the other jobs that the instrument scan is neglected, and you turn past the heading. (The bank sneaks over more steeply, and the climb may stop or turn into a descending turn for a few seconds.)

While you're getting things under control, it would be well to discuss the coordination between the tower (departure control) and Center. Unknown to you, the tower and Center have coordinated their actions and established a "letter of agreement" between the two facilities. Copies are on file at both places.

This letter and diagram outlined the jurisdiction of the two facilities, *but variations can be made from the so-called "rigid rules" at any time with coordination between the two.*

The tower has control of you at altitudes of up to 16,000 ft MSL and below and will notify the Center of your takeoff. It's likely that you'll be picked up on radar by Center shortly after crossing the airport boundary.

Unless coordination has been effected with the Center, departure control will retain departures from the airport to required altitudes (in this case 5000 ft MSL and below) until the aircraft is established in the departure area along the assigned route or (in the case of Memphis) until approximately 40 NM from the Memphis airport on the assigned route.

If the altitude conflict is cleared up while you are still in the area of the tower's (departure control) jurisdiction, you may be told by departure control to "delete the 4000 restriction" or be given clearance to climb to your assigned altitude. If you don't have DME, you may ask departure control to let you know. Normally, you will be handed off to Center before reaching the 25-NM (or other) limit.

Memphis departure control: "ZEPHYR FIVE SIX JULIET, CONTACT MEMPHIS CENTER (ON) ONE TWO FOUR POINT THREE FIVE (124.35 MHz)."

You: "ZEPHYR FIVE SIX JULIET, CENTER (ON) ONE TWO FOUR POINT THREE FIVE. OUT."

Write down the frequency.

You may also be given a time or point at which to contact the Center ("CONTACT CENTER AT HOLLY SPRINGS" or "CONTACT CENTER AT FIVE FOUR"—54 minutes past the hour).

You: "MEMPHIS CENTER, (THIS IS) ZEPHYR THREE FOUR FIVE SIX JULIET, FOUR THOUSAND. OVER."

Center: "ZEPHYR FIVE SIX JULIET, MEMPHIS CENTER, MAINTAIN FIVE THOUSAND. OVER."
Assume that once you are in radar contact you are remaining so, unless otherwise stated. More about this in Chapter 12.

You: "ZEPHYR FIVE SIX JULIET, CLEARED TO FIVE (THOUSAND). LEAVING FOUR (THOUSAND)."
You'll then leave 4000 immediately for 5000 or will start to climb as you acknowledge the clearance.

Looking back at Figure 6-6, the V159, V54, V7, V16 heavy line (or the planned route to Nashville), you can see that you are in Sector 8 and the VHF frequency is 124.35 MHz. The UHF frequency is 239.3 MHz, but this is probably of no interest to you at this stage. Your route is marked as a heavy line in Figures 6-3 and 6-4, and you can see that

you'll have several en route frequency changes to make before getting to Nashville. You'll pass through Sectors 8 (124.35), 14 (135.9), 13 (127.1, 120.8), and 42 (125.85) before being handed off to Nashville approach control. Your pertinent flight strips will have been passed to these Sectors, following the same idea as shown back in Figure 6-8.

Obviously, you're not going to carry a Sector chart of every Center and will change frequencies when, and as, requested.

You made a report upon leaving your last assigned altitude. This is required without a special request from ATC.

You are not required automatically to report reaching the new assigned altitude but may be asked by ATC to "report reaching five thousand." Or, you may have to report at interim altitudes on your way to the assigned altitude, such as "CLIMB AND MAINTAIN EIGHT THOUSAND, REPORT PASSING SIX AND SEVEN THOUSAND." There is traffic that might possibly cause problems at the interim altitudes and ATC wants to know when you've cleared them (no transponder).

When you are assigned a new altitude, climb (or descend) as rapidly as practicable to within 1000 ft of the assigned altitude and then climb (or descend) to the assigned altitude at a rate of no more than 500–1500 fpm. It would be best to limit your *"as rapidly as practicable"* to no *more than 1000 fpm* to *lessen chances of loss of control.* In climbing, this probably will be no problem; in descending, however, you might overdo the rate (Chapter 4).

And the most important thing of all to remember is this (it was said before): NEVER SACRIFICE CONTROL OF THE AIRPLANE TO MAKE VOICE TRANSMISSIONS. The person on the ground can't see that you might be having problems with turbulence, icing, and other such situations so may call at an "inopportune moment." Let the call wait until you have things under control.

EN ROUTE

12

Refer to the en route chart for your route to Nashville. After you reach the assigned altitude (5000 ft MSL), leave the power at climb setting to expedite reaching cruise speed as you level off. Then adjust power, lean the mixture(s), and switch tanks as required. Make sure the airplane is well trimmed. Keep your scan going.

POSITION REPORTS

The en route portion of the flight will bring up the subject of position reports, and they should be discussed here before you get too far from Memphis.

As far as en route, constant altitude flight is concerned, you'll make position reports as follows:

1. At a compulsory reporting point as shown on the en route chart. Holly Springs VOR is *not* a compulsory reporting point; Muscle Shoals and Graham VORs are, as shown by the black triangle (▲).
2. When requested by ATC, Center may just want a report over Holly Springs VOR or BRADS intersection (△). These are "on request" reporting points.

Remember, if you are radar identified and will be remaining under radar surveillance, you will discontinue position reports even over compulsory reporting points. If you are in radar contact, the controller, at the time radar service is lost or terminated, will say, "RADAR CONTACT LOST" or "RADAR SERVICE TERMINATED." This sometimes catches low-time instrument pilots napping. They've put the flight log away and only glance at the chart to get courses for following segments—now it's back to work. (One of the controller's biggest gripes is that the pilot does not get back to work with estimates.) That's why preflight planning is important.

As far as the exact *time* to give a position report (if required), you might note the following:

Over a VOR—The time reported should be the time at which the TO-FROM indicator makes its first complete reversal.
Over an ADF—The time reported should be the time when the needle makes a complete reversal.
Over a Z-marker or fan marker—The time should be noted when the signal begins (aural or light) and when it ends. The mean of the two times should be taken as the actual time over the fix.

If you are giving a position with respect to a bearing and distance from a reporting point, be as accurate as possible.

■ **Position Reporting Items** Position reports should include the following items:

1. Identification.
2. *Position*.
3. *Time*.
4. *Altitude or flight level* (include actual altitude or flight level when operating on a clearance specifying VFR ON TOP).
5. *Type* of flight plan (not required if IFR position reports are made directly to ARTCCs or approach control).
6. *ETA* and name of next reporting point.
7. *Name* only of the *next* succeeding reporting point along the route of flight.
8. Pertinent remarks.

The best way to remember the required items above is to use PTA-TEN (Parent-Teacher Association–TEN).

ADDITIONAL REPORTS

The following reports should be made to ATC or FSS facilities *without a specific ATC request:*

1. At all times:
   a. When vacating any previously assigned altitude or flight level for a newly assigned altitude or flight level.
   b. When an altitude change will be made when operating on a clearance specifying VFR ON TOP.
   c. When unable to climb/descend at a rate of at least 500 fpm.
   d. When an approach has been missed. (Request clearance for specific action; that is, to an alternate airport, another approach, etc.).
   e. When a change in the average true airspeed (at cruising altitude) is 5% or 10 knots (whichever is greater) from that filed in the flight plan.
   f. The time and altitude or flight level upon reaching a holding fix or point to which cleared.
   g. When leaving any assigned holding fix or point.
   h. Any loss in controlled airspace of VOR, TACAN, ADF, low-frequency navigation receiver capability, complete or partial loss of ILS receiver capability, or impairment of air/ground communications capability. Also include aircraft identification equipment affected, degree that the ability to operate under IFR in the ATC system is impaired, and the nature and extent of assistance desired from ATC.
   i. Any information relating to safety of flight. (This would include aircraft mechanical problems as well as turbulence or icing that would cause problems of performance and control.)
2. When not in radar contact:
   a. When leaving a final approach fix inbound on final approach (nonprecision approach) or when leaving the outer marker or the fix used in lieu of the outer marker inbound on final approach (precision approach).
   b. A corrected estimate at any time it becomes apparent that an estimate as previously submitted is in error in excess of 3 min.

If you encounter weather conditions that have not been forecast or *hazardous conditions that have been forecast,* you are to report this to ATC.

EN ROUTE

(Refer to the en route chart in the back of the book unless a specific figure number is given.)

You got off at 2040Z and are at SULLY Intersection at 2101Z, as confirmed by your VORs. (You were initially vectored directly to this point by Memphis departure control but are now on the Sector frequency and cut off a couple of minutes from the flight plan estimated time en route.)

Figure 12-1 is the flight log for the trip with the estimated and actual times of arrival at SULLY intersection.

Assume for example purposes that at this point radar contact is lost temporarily and ATC needs certain information for traffic separation ahead.

N 3456J

DATE – Jan 18

TIME OFF MEM 2040 Z

WEATHER

CURRENT
MEM SA 1950 M13 OVC 6F 129/58/53/1110/991

FCST
MEM 18Z 10 SCT C25 OVC 6H 0908 OCN C10 BKN 3F. 05Z –

CURRENT
BNA SA 1947 M23 BKN 250 OVC 10 165 57/50/0904/002

FCST
BNA 18Z C25 BKN 1208. 23Z C12 OVC 5F 1410. 08Z –

SPECIALS/NOTAMS

WINDS ALOFT

	BNA	MEM
3–	1518	1623
6–	1920	1929
9–	2222	2028
12–	2325	2725

FROM	IDENT FREQ	TO	IDENT FREQ	VIA	MC	DIST NM	EGS ETE	TIME OVER	ATE	GS	ETA NEXT	REMARKS
MEM AIRPORT	/	HOLLY SPRINGS VOR	HLI 112.4	↗ DIRECT	123°	29	88/138 15	–	–	–		CLIMB 100 KTS — 7 MIN 88 K G.S. 19 MILES @ 138K = 8 MIN
HOLLY SPRINGS VOR	HLI 112.4	SULLY *	JKS 109.4	V54	089°	20	151 8	2101	21	151	2120	SULLY * – 214R · JKS MEA 3000
SULLY *	MSL 116.5	KERMI *	JKS 109.4	V54	092°	48	150 19	2120	19	151	2126	KERMI * – 167R · JKS MEA 3000
KERMI *	MSL 116.5	BRADS *	HAB 110.4	V54	092°	15	150 6	2126	6	151	2132	BRADS * 013R HAB MEA 3000
BRADS *	MSL 116.5	MUSCLE SHOALS VOR	MSL 116.5	V54	092°	16	150 6	2131	5	155	2136	MSL – NO VOICE ON VOR MEA 3000
MUSCLE SHOALS VOR	MSL 116.5	GILLE *	RQZ 112.2	V7	001°	15	172 5	2136	5	175	2149	GILLE * 281R RQZ RQZ – NO VOICE VOR MEA – 2500
GILLE *	MSL 116.5	POLAN *	JKS 109.4	V7	000°	38	172 13	2149	13	172		POLAN * – 089R JKS MEA – 3000
POLAN *	GHM 111.6	GRAHAM VOR	GHM 111.6	V7	359°	15	172 5					MEA 3000
GRAHAM VOR	GHM 111.6	TICTO *	SYI 109.0	V16	062°	16	162 6					TICTO * – 305R SYI
TICTO *	BNA 114.1	NASHVILLE VOR AIRPORT	BNA 114.1	V16	067°	25	161 9					BNA APC 120.6 TWR 119.1
						237	1:32 ←					TOTAL DISTANCE 237 NM TOTAL TIME (EST.) 1:32
NASHVILLE VOR	BNA 114.1	SHELBYVILLE VOR	SYI 109.0	V362 ↗	161°	35	132 16					USE BNA WINDS 190° – 20K MEA 3000
SYI VOR	SYI 109.0	ROCKET VOR	RQZ 112.2	V321	193°	47	128 22					RQZ – NO VOICE MEA 3000
ROCKET VOR	RQZ 112.2	HUNTSVILLE AIRPORT	I-HSV 109.3	↘ DIRECT	210°	12	129 6					HSV WX –
						94	0:44 ←					HSV – APC – 125.6 TWR – 119.7

POSITION REPORTS							N 3456J CLEARED	CLEARANCES	
POS.	TIME	ALT.	TYPE	EST.	NEXT		TO	BNA METRO	POLAN *
							DEPT. OR SID	HOLLY FOUR	–
							ROUTE	AS VECTORED, V54 V7, V16	V54, V7
							ALTITUDE	5000	5000
							HOLDING	–	SOUTH STD
							SPECIAL	–	EFC 01
							FREQ	CODE	DPT. 124.15	5512	–	–

Fig. 12-1. Flight log. As soon as you reach each fix, a new ETA would be worked out for the next one, based on the latest groundspeed information. Note that you were vectored past Holly Springs and so don't have a time over there. Write down the takeoff time on the log.

Center: "ZEPHYR FIVE SIX JULIET, GIVE BRADS ESTIMATE AND REPORT PASSING THE TWO ZERO ZERO RADIAL OF JACK'S CREEK VOR."
You: "ZEPHYR FIVE SIX JULIET, BRADS ESTIMATE TWO SIX. OVER."
Center: "BRADS ESTIMATE TWO SIX, MEMPHIS ALTIMETER NINER NINER ONE. OUT."

Now, have you passed the 200 radial of Jack's Creek VOR? You tune in Jack's Creek (109.4 MHz) and *identify* it. You could check by one of the two ways discussed in Chapter 5: (1) setting the OBS TO the cross-bearing station inbound bearing (020) and "turning" the airplane to that heading in your mind or (2) setting 200 on the OBS (FROM) and noting whether the relative bearing of the station and needle match. (In this example they do—left and left—so you haven't passed it yet.)

It's best always to use one VOR receiver as the en route or course receiver and the other (if there are two) for any cross-bearing work. Usually the top (or No. 1 set) would be used for on-course indications and the lower set used for cross bearings (or set up whatever is the most convenient for you). If you don't have a routine established and are slightly off course, under pressure you could read the wrong VOR indication.

When the cross-bearing needle centers, you are on the 200 radial of Jack's Creek and would duly report this fact:

You: "MEMPHIS CENTER, ZEPHYR FIVE SIX JULIET CROSSING TWO ZERO ZERO RADIAL JACK'S CREEK AT ZERO SEVEN (seven minutes past the hour), FIVE THOUSAND. OVER."
Center: "ZEPHYR FIVE SIX JULIET. REPORT PASSING BRADS INTERSECTION. OUT." (Sometimes if you want a time check you would say as you crossed, "CROSSING TWO ZERO ZERO RADIAL *NOW;* AT ZERO SEVEN.") If you forgot to set the clock or set it wrong before taxi, Center might come back with: "FIVE SIX JULIET, TIME NOW ZERO NINE." If you had given them an estimate earlier based on your clock time, you'd better add 2 min to the earlier estimate so you'll be there at "Center time" (the correct time). The BRADS estimate would now be "two eight" instead of "two six" as given earlier. *Assume here, however, that your clock is correct.*

Speaking of time, one problem with pilots is the simple misreading of the clock when giving the actual time over a fix. The most troublesome times for this are between 20 and 29 min past the hour and 34–50 min past. Sometimes the pilot will read "28" instead of "23" or vice versa.

(Assume now that you are back in radar contact.)

At a point about KERMI intersection, you'll enter a new Sector (Fig. 6-6) and will hear:

Center: "ZEPHYR FIVE SIX JULIET, CONTACT CENTER ON ONE TWO SEVEN POINT ONE (127.1 MHz) NOW."
You: "ZEPHYR FIVE SIX JULIET, ONE TWO SEVEN POINT ONE."

You: "(on 127.1 MHz) MEMPHIS CENTER, ZEPHYR THREE FOUR FIVE SIX JULIET, FIVE THOUSAND. OVER."
Center: "ROGER, ZEPHYR FIVE SIX JULIET, I HAVE A CLEARANCE FOR YOU. OVER."
You: "ZEPHYR FIVE SIX JULIET, READY TO COPY. OVER."
Center: "ZEPHYR THREE FOUR FIVE SIX JULIET (IS) CLEARED OVER THE MUSCLE SHOALS VOR TO POLAN INTERSECTION VIA VICTOR FIVE FOUR, VICTOR SEVEN, MAINTAIN FIVE THOUSAND, EXPECT FURTHER CLEARANCE AT ZERO ONE. OVER."

You write down and read back the clearance as given, as you look for POLAN intersection on the map. You find it and make sure that there are no gaps in the clearance. POLAN intersection is now your clearance limit. If there are gaps, ask for a readback. And, of course as always, if you are unable to comply for some reason, let ATC know about it.

Assuming that the clearance is acceptable, you continue and pass over Muscle Shoals VOR at 1531 (2131Z), a minute ahead of your estimate.

When talking directly to the Center and *not* in radar contact, you would alert them to a pending position report as follows:

You: "MEMPHIS CENTER, ZEPHYR THREE FOUR FIVE SIX JULIET, MUSCLE SHOALS. OVER." (By naming a *fix* you alert the Center for the position report to follow.)
Center: "GO AHEAD, ZEPHYR FIVE SIX JULIET. OVER."

(You would then proceed with your position report; see Fig. 12-1.)

If you had lost contact with the Center before reaching MSL but after getting the clearance to POLAN and still had 122.1, 122.2, 122.4, or 123.6 MHz (or 121.5 MHz) left, as well as being able to receive on VOR, 122.2, 122.4, or 123.6 MHz, you would call Muscle Shoals (or *other facilities* as *necessary*) to pass the word to the Center about your MSL passage, since it is a compulsory reporting point; you aren't in voice contact with the Center and so you don't know whether you're back in radar contact or not. (See Appendix A for FSS frequencies.) You note that POLAN is your clearance limit, using the PTA-TEN method of reporting. (Note: MSL does *not* have voice on *VOR*.)

You should add remarks such as "moderate turbulence" or "light icing" at the end of the position report—it will help other pilots in the area. Such remarks as "what's going on down there" or "get me down from here" are not considered cricket and can lose you points as well as causing you to move back three fixes (or result in elimination from the game).

In a fast airplane a turn such as required at MSL, up V7, would mean that the airplane would move out of the airway route boundary or protected airspace if the turn was started at or after fix passage. It's legal to lead the turn enough to ensure staying within the boundaries. (If you lead too soon, you'll crash the boundary on the *inside* of the turn, and this isn't good either.) This is usually only a factor for planes with groundspeeds approaching 300 knots, so probably you'll not have any worries about this yet.

TOTAL LOSS OF COMMUNICATIONS (FAR 91.185)

Let's backtrack a little and look at the en route chart again. Before takeoff you were cleared via V54, V7, and V16 to Nashville. You got another clearance at 2119, approaching KERMI intersection, as shown on the chart. If you had a total communications loss before this clearance was confirmed by you, even after ATC had broadcast it (your radios went out the instant ATC finished delivering the clearance—you didn't get to acknowledge), the pretakeoff clearance still holds. You'd fly on to MSL, make a sharp left turn up V7 to GHM, and continue to the Nashville VOR (which is the en route navigation aid serving the destination airport).

You would depart the Nashville VOR and fly to the facility to be used for the approach (unless you plan to make a VOR approach). You would hold on the procedure-turn side of the approach course at the ETA for the route and altitude of the last clearance, which was the one received and acknowledged at the warm-up spot before takeoff.

As far as altitude requirements are concerned, you would fly the route segments at the last assigned altitude, the minimum en route altitude (MEA), or the altitude or flight level ATC has advised may be expected in a further clearance, *whichever is higher*. In this case, your last assigned altitude was 5000 ft, and the minimum altitudes are well below this. (The highest MEA will be 3500 ft, so you *would maintain the assigned 5000 ft.)* Figure 12-2 shows a hypothetical situation that could arise.

ATC will be expecting you to do as shown in Figure 12-2. If you decide "what the heck" and stay at 8000 for a couple more segments to save "all that stair-stepping down" you could find that you'd be in the airspace of other airplanes.

In the situation of the flight to Nashville, you would maintain 5000 ft until over the facility to be used for the approach. If you arrive *before* the time, based on an estimate along the route assigned, you would set up a holding pattern at 5000 ft on the procedure-turn side of the final approach course. When the estimated time has elapsed, you'd shuttle down in the holding pattern on the procedure-turn side of the leg to the initial approach altitude and commence your approach. If you arrive later than the ETA as worked out earlier for the latest clearance, you would shuttle down immediately and start your approach. All approaches for the destination airport will be held clear for 30 min past your ETA without question and may be held longer if the pilots of other aircraft awaiting approach (who've been cleared well out of the way) agree to it. ATC will be checking your progress by radar. You checked wind direction and velocity at the destination before leaving, but unless an extra strong

wind made it out of reason, you'd likely opt for an ILS front course approach. Listen to every possible available source of communication (VORs, LF/MF, etc.); ATC may give you further word or clear you for an earlier approach.

If you lost communications after receiving the airborne clearance to POLAN intersection, you would proceed as cleared and set up a holding pattern, if necessary, to ensure arriving at the facility to be used for the approach at the destination airport either at the time (1) given as the ETA on the flight plan or (2) as amended with, and by, ATC. The second situation is the more likely. Only if you were assigned the same route and altitude and hit every fix as predicted would (1) be valid.

If you are flying in the clouds when the communications loss occurs and you have a transponder, squawk 7600. This will alert ATC to your situation—see Chapter 5.

If you are in VFR conditions when the communications failure occurs or fly into VFR after the failure, remain in VFR conditions and land as soon as practicable. This doesn't mean "land as soon as possible" (the pastures down there might be a little soft or short—and this might be the same situation at the closest airports). If the destination airport is within a few minutes, then go on to it (you'd have to get light signals to land). Get to a phone and let the nearest ATC facility know what happened.

Using common sense and the knowledge that nearly all (if not all) airplanes flying IFR have two communications transceivers plus two navigation receivers, the chances of not being able to receive *any* instructions are slim indeed. The Center will pass the word to all FSSs to call you on navaid frequencies. One possibility is that the Center can call you on the normal frequencies (you can receive but not transmit) and tell you to acknowledge instructions and clearances by having you "ident" or squawk other codes on the transponder. Or, if you aren't transponder equipped, they may ask you to make turns to acknowledge instructions.

If you have lost all communications, the controllers will normally expect you to make a transition to the approach fix from the VOR (or applicable en route navaid). As said earlier, however, they will protect *all* approaches during the 30-min grace period.

Practically speaking, to lose both sets of communications and nothing else is indeed a remote possibility, but it could happen. Again, a hand-held transceiver would be a good backup.

HOLDING PATTERN

If it becomes necessary for you to hold at POLAN intersection, either because of waiting for an ATC clearance or the emergency situation of having to "kill time," you would set up a particular pattern as shown in Figure 12-3.

The standard holding pattern consists of right-hand turns with a 1-min inbound leg (below 14,000 ft MSL). Each pattern will take exactly 4 min to complete in a no-wind condition. (Each of the two 180°—standard-rate—turns will require 1 min and the two legs are 1 min each.) ATC may issue holding instructions.

TWO-WAY RADIO COMMUNICATIONS FAILURE

a. It is virtually impossible to provide regulations and procedures applicable to all possible situations associated with two-way radio communications failure. During two-way radio communications failure, when confronted by a situation not covered in the regulation, pilots are expected to exercise good judgment in whatever action they elect to take. Should the situation so dictate, they should not be reluctant to use the emergency action contained in FAR—91.3(b).

b. Whether two-way communications failure constitutes an emergency depends on the circumstances, and in any event, it is a determination made by the pilot. FAR—91.3(b) authorizes a pilot to deviate from any rule in Subparts A and B to the extent required to meet an emergency.

c. In the event of two-way radio communications failure, ATC service will be provided on the basis that the pilot is operating in accordance with FAR—91.185. A pilot experiencing two-way communications failure should (unless emergency authority is exercised) comply with FAR-91.185 quoted below. Capitalization and examples added for emphasis.

1. "91.185 IFR operations; two-way radio communications failure."

(1) General. Unless otherwise authorized by ATC, each pilot who has two-way radio communications failure when operating under IFR shall comply with the rules of this section.

(2) VFR conditions. If the failure occurs in VFR conditions, or if VFR conditions are encountered after the failure, each pilot shall continue the flight under VFR and land as soon as practicable.

NOTE.—This procedure also applies when two-way radio failure occurs while operating in Positive Control Airspace (PCA). The primary objective of this provision in FAR—91.185 is to preclude extended IFR operation in the ATC system in VFR weather conditions. Pilots should recognize that operation under these conditions may unnecessarily as well as adversely affect other users of the airspace, since ATC may be required to reroute or delay other users in order to protect the failure aircraft. However, it is not intended that the requirement to "land as soon as practicable" be construed to mean "as soon as possible." The pilot retains his prerogative of exercising his best judgment and is not required to land at an unauthorized airport, at an airport unsuitable for the type of aircraft flown, or to land only minutes short of his destination.

(3) IFR conditions. If the failure occurs in IFR conditions, or if paragraph (2) of this section cannot be complied with, each pilot shall continue the flight according to the following:

(a) Route.

1. By the route assigned in the last ATC clearance received;

2. If being radar vectored, by the direct route from the point of radio failure to the fix, route, or airway specified in the vector clearance;

3. In the absence of an assigned route, by the route that ATC has advised may be expected in a further clearance; or

4. In the absence of an assigned route or a route that ATC has advised may be expected in a further clearance by the route filed in the flight plan.

(b) Altitude. At the HIGHEST of the following altitudes or flight levels FOR THE ROUTE SEGMENT BEING FLOWN:

1. The altitude or flight level assigned in the last ATC clearance received;

2. The minimum altitude (converted, if appropriate, to minimum flight level as prescribed in FAR 91.121.(c» for IFR operations; or

3. The altitude or flight level ATC has advised may be expected in a further clearance.

NOTE.—The intent of the rule is that a pilot who has experienced two-way radio failure should, during any segment of his route, fly at the appropriate altitude specified in the rule for that particular segment. The appropriate altitude is whichever of the three is highest in each given phase of flight: (1) the altitude or flight level last assigned; (2) the MEA or; (3) the altitude or flight level the pilot has been advised to expect in a further clearance.

EXAMPLE:

A pilot with two-way radio failure had an assigned altitude of 7,000 feet, and while en route comes to a route segment for which the MEA was 9,000 feet. He would climb to 9,000 feet at the time or place where it became necessary to comply with the 9,000 feet MEA. (See FAR—91.177b.) If later, while still proceeding to his destination, the MEA dropped from 9,000 feet to 5,000 feet, he would descend to *7,000 feet* (the last assigned altitude), because that altitude is *higher* than the MEA.

EXAMPLE:

The MEA between **A** and **B**—5,000 feet. The MEA between **B** and **C**—5,000 feet. The MEA between **C** and **D**—11,000 feet. The MEA between **D** and **E**—7,000 feet. A pilot had been cleared via **A, B, C, D,** to **E**. While flying between **A** and **B** his assigned altitude was 6,000 feet and he was told to expect a clearance to 8,000 feet at **B**. Prior to receiving the higher altitude assignment, he experienced two-way failure. The pilot would maintain 6,000 to **B**, then climb to 8,000 feet (the altitude he was advised to expect). He would maintain 8,000 feet, then climb to 11,000 at **C**, or prior to **C** if necessary to comply with an MCA at **C** (FAR—91.177b). Upon reaching **D**, the pilot would descend to *8,000 feet* (even though the MEA was 7,000 feet), as 8,000 was the highest of the altitude situations stated in the rule (FAR—91.185).

(c) Leave clearance limit.

1. When the clearance limit is a fix from which an approach begins, commence descent or descent and approach as close as possible to the expect further clearance time if one has been received, or if one has not been received, as close as possible to the estimated time of arrival as calculated from the filed or amended (with ATC) estimated time en route.

2. If the clearance limit is not a fix from which an approach begins, leave the clearance limit at the expect further clearance time if one has been received, or if none has been received, upon arrival over the clearance limit, and proceed to a fix from which an approach begins and commence descent or descend and approach as close as possible to the estimated time of arrival as calculated from the filed or amended (with ATC) estimated time en route.

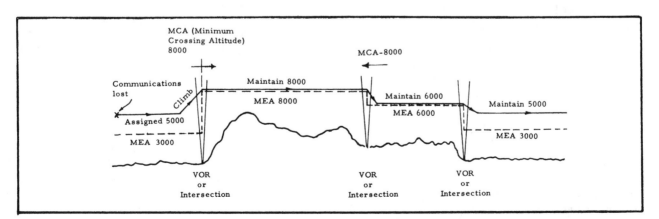

Fig. 12-2. Loss of communications procedures *(Aeronautical Information Manual)*. If in VFR conditions, maintain VFR and land as soon as practicable. This illustration shows an additional example of a loss of communications situation.

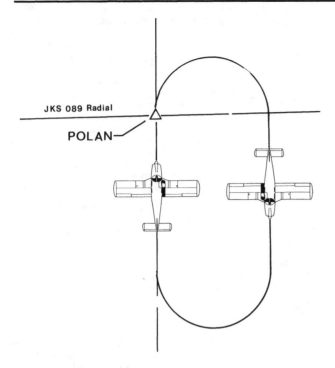

Fig. 12-3. Holding at POLAN intersection.

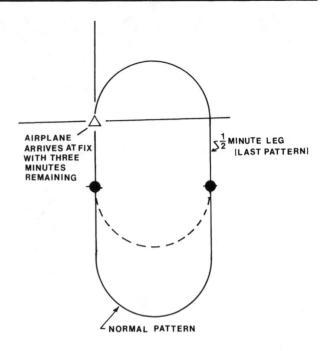

Fig. 12-4. The legs of the last pattern are shortened in order to hit the fix at the expected further clearance time.

Holding is a pretty simple matter in the situation of holding at an en route fix such as the POLAN intersection. You'd start slowing up to the holding airspeed within 3 min of the estimated initial time over the holding fix. It then becomes a matter of getting definite indication of a station (fix) passage and commencing a 180° right (or left, if so instructed) standard-rate turn. As soon as you entered holding, which would be at the initial fix passage, you would normally report to ATC, giving the time and altitude/flight level upon reaching the holding fix. Unless ATC says otherwise, when you arrive at a clearance limit such as POLAN, hold in a standard right pattern on the course on which you approached the fix until further clearance is received. You'll also be expected to hold at your last assigned altitude.

You: "ZEPHYR FIVE SIX JULIET. COMMENCED HOLDING AT FOUR NINE, FIVE THOUSAND. OVER."

Center: (Acknowledges.) "EXPECT FURTHER CLEARANCE AT ZERO ONE. OUT."

The "expected further clearance" time is given, so that you'll have something to work with if communications are lost *while you are in the holding pattern.* When the expected further clearance time approaches and you have lost communications, be prepared to depart the fix at that time. The 4-min no-wind pattern doesn't always work out evenly with this expected further clearance time, so you will modify your holding pattern to be at the fix at that time. For instance, you arrive over the fix in one of your patterns 3 min before the expected further clearance time. You don't have time to make a complete pattern and be back at the fix at the "go" time. Figure 12-4 shows the way to do it.

Note that it will require 2 min to make the two 180° turns, leaving 1 min to be divided between the two legs, as shown in Figure 12-4.

The previous discussion was based on no-wind conditions, an unlikely situation. ATC requires that the inbound leg be 1 min at altitudes below 14,000 MSL (1½ min above that altitude), and your *initial* outbound leg should be 1 min to check what's up. Suppose you enter holding, fly outbound for 1 min, and find you reach the fix 45 sec after rolling out inbound. (The inbound leg is measured from roll-out from the outer 180° turn into the fix and should be timed accordingly.) Okay, you arrived 15 sec early, so next time make that outbound leg 15 sec longer, or for 1 min and 15 sec (you have a headwind outbound and a tailwind inbound). The purists will argue that this is not the case; you'll have to fly outbound slightly longer than 15 sec in order to add the 15 sec to the inbound leg. This is true and can be worked out on a computer (since you have nothing else to do but fly the airplane on instruments, keep up with the clock, talk to ATC, etc.). You will get settled down at about the second pattern and can add what is necessary to get the required 1-min inbound leg. The same theory applies to a reversed wind situation. (The wind may vary during your holding period, also.)

Practically speaking, although it is very easy to work everything out nicely while sitting at a desk, it becomes a different matter in the airplane. As veteran instrument pilots often put it, "The holding pattern is a situation where you are holding somewhere in the general vicinity of a fix—you think."

The crosswind correction for the holding pattern as recommended by the FAA is to hold twice the wind correction angle outbound as was used to stay on the inbound course. This allows both turns to be standard rate but the inbound and outbound legs will not be parallel (which is okay).

The crosswind and tailwind components could give you some trouble at POLAN. Assuming a wind at your altitude of 190° true at 25 knots, you would be busy indeed. The crosswind angle would be about 11° with a crosswind component of about 5 knots, not too much of a problem. The tail- and headwind components will be over 24 knots (call them 25 knots) so that the inbound and outbound legs would have a *50-knot groundspeed differential.* If you were holding at 100 knots, the groundspeed inbound to POLAN would be 125 knots, outbound 75 knots; a quick and dirty estimate would be an outbound leg of (125 + 75) × 60 sec, or 100 sec to get an inbound leg of 60 sec. As indicated earlier, the outbound leg would have to be slightly longer than 1 min and 40 sec to get the 1-min inbound leg. In this case you'd have about 12 min, or three patterns, to work it out.

The straight-in or direct entry is the most usual case, but you may have variations on the theme. Holding-pattern entries can be quite confusing, and it's best when given holding instructions to actually sketch the pattern on the chart as shown by Figure 12-5.

Figure 12-6 indicates one way to enter the pattern. When the fix is passed, turn to a heading 30° (or less) to the holding side of the pattern as shown (105° bearing). Set your OBS to the outbound bearing 105°. Setting the OBS for the outbound bearing this first time is a good idea for orientation. Fly the outbound leg for 1 min. Start a standard-rate turn and reset the OBS for the *inbound* bearing of 315°. It is suggested that you leave the OBS on this setting for the rest of the holding pattern now that you are established.

One other simple method of entry in this case would be to turn parallel to the outbound leg after passing the fix and hold this for 1 min, then turn right to intercept the course. Your instructor may have some suggestions on this.

The numbered items in Figure 12-6 give left-right needle indications and headings at the points mentioned.

Your job will be to visualize the airplane's relationship to the holding pattern. If you don't "see" where you are, the problem of entry is very difficult.

After the end of 1 min, start a standard-rate turn to the right. When you get to point 2, which is 45° from the inbound heading, the moment of truth will arrive. Do you speed up the turn? (The needle is centering now.) Or do you roll out at that heading and fly straight until the needle gets nearly centered? It's a good move, if the needle isn't moving toward the center position as you think it should, to stop at that heading and hold it until the needle is nudging toward the center at what you have found (through practice) to be the proper rate. At this 45° entry angle on a *localizer,* if the needle is moving toward the center at all, you should keep turning because the localizer is *four* times as sensitive as the VOR as far as your receiver is concerned.

The actions you have to take in turning on that first inbound leg can tell you a lot about corrections to be required on the legs.

The FAA recommends a standard entry for holding patterns as shown in Figure 12-7.

This method has not had wide acceptance because of the problem of computing 70° from an odd heading (313°, for instance). It's really a matter of common sense on your holding pattern entries. There is a "buffer zone" around the racetrack pattern, but you would want to ensure that your entry did not cause you to fly outside the allowable area.

Holding at a VOR intersection is the toughest problem. Always use the same VOR indicator for on-course indications (usually the No. 1 set) and the other for cross-bearing information.

If you have only one VOR receiver, you'll be pretty busy switching back and forth. Holding at an LF/MF intersection in precipitation static with only one coffee grinder receiver is an experience old-time instrument pilots turn pale remembering—so maybe *one* VOR receiver isn't so bad after all.

■ **Distance Measuring Equipment (DME) Holding Pattern** The DME has simplified intersection holding to the point where it's as easy (or easier) than holding at a VOR. For instance, you are instructed to hold at an intersection that is 10 NM out from a VORTAC. You've been told by ATC to use an outbound leg length of 5 mi. You are holding *away* from the VORTAC, so your pattern and instrument indications will be as shown in Figure 12-8.

An ATC clearance requiring an aircraft to hold at a fix where the pattern is not charted will include the following information:

1. Direction of holding from the fix in terms of the eight cardinal compass points (that is, N, NE, E, SE, etc.).
2. Holding fix (the fix may be omitted if included at the beginning of the transmission as the clearance limit).
3. Radial, course, bearing, airway, or route on which the aircraft is to hold.
4. Leg length in miles if DME or RNAV is to be used (leg length will be specified in minutes on pilot request or if the controller considers it necessary).
5. Direction of turn if left turns are to be made, when the pilot requests it or the controller considers it necessary.
6. Time to expect further clearance and any pertinent additional delay information.

■ **Depiction of Holding Patterns on Charts** Holding patterns (standard or nonstandard) at fixes most consistently used to serve a terminal area/airport by either an Air Route Traffic Control Center or a terminal facility will be charted.

The holding patterns will be charted on either or both U.S. government en route high-/low-altitude and appropriate area charts. A particular pattern may be shown on both the

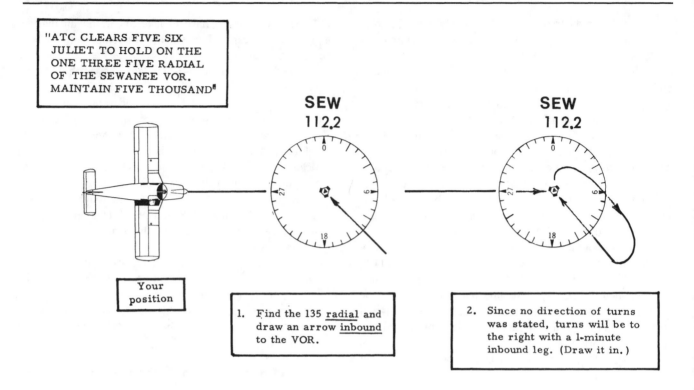

"ATC CLEARS FIVE SIX
JULIET TO HOLD ON THE
ONE THREE FIVE RADIAL
OF THE SEWANEE VOR.
MAINTAIN FIVE THOUSAND"

Your position

1. Find the 135 radial and draw an arrow inbound to the VOR.

2. Since no direction of turns was stated, turns will be to the right with a 1-minute inbound leg. (Draw it in.)

Fig. 12-5. Sketch the holding pattern; it makes the entry easier to accomplish.

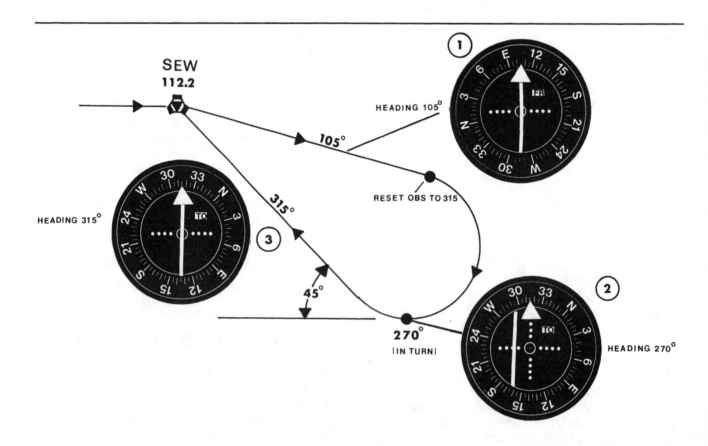

Fig. 12-6. Entering the holding pattern of Figure 12-5.

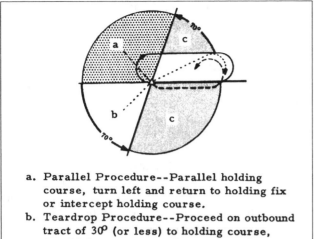

a. **Parallel Procedure**—Parallel holding course, turn left and return to holding fix or intercept holding course.
b. **Teardrop Procedure**—Proceed on outbound tract of 30° (or less) to holding course, turn right to intercept holding course.
c. **Direct Entry Procedure**—Turn right and fly the pattern.

Fig. 12-7. Standard entry for the holding pattern.

en route and area charts if the fix is consistently used for holding en route and terminal traffic.

If aircraft are generally held at particular en route fixes by ARTCC, the patterns are charted.

Only one holding pattern will be shown at a fix on an individual chart, and the patterns will not be labeled with altitude information or letter coding for any special purposes.

If you're required to hold at a fix where a pattern is charted, ATC will *not* issue holding instructions. You'll be expected to hold in the pattern shown unless otherwise advised by ATC.

If you're required to hold at a fix where the pattern is not charted, you will be given holding instructions by ATC at least 5 min before you are estimated to reach the clearance limit.

If you don't receive a clearance beyond the fix before arrival over it and the holding pattern is charted, maintain the assigned altitude and use the depicted holding pattern. If this happens at a fix *without* a charted holding pattern, use a standard right-hand pattern on the course on which you approached the fix.

If you are in doubt about holding, get instructions from ATC. Remember, below 14,000 ft MSL the inbound legs are 1 min.

■ Points on Holding

1. When holding at a VOR, you should begin the turn to the outbound leg at the time of the first complete reversal of the TO-FROM indicator.
2. The direction to hold with relation to the holding fix will be specified as one of the eight general points of the compass. Your instructions to hold at POLAN intersection could be: "HOLD SOUTH OF POLAN INTERSECTION ON VICTOR SEVEN" (or nautical miles will be given if DME is to be used). In some situations the argument could arise whether the holding pattern is closer, for instance, to "South" or "Southeast" (here it's obviously closer to South), so the airway is inserted. You'll hold on the airway, but on the southern side of the fix rather than on the northern side. Holding on an en route VOR could possibly entail *not* holding on the inbound airway, as covered in Figure 12-5. For holding at an intersection en route, there's little choice except whether you're to hold on "this side" or "the other side," and normally it will be on "this side."

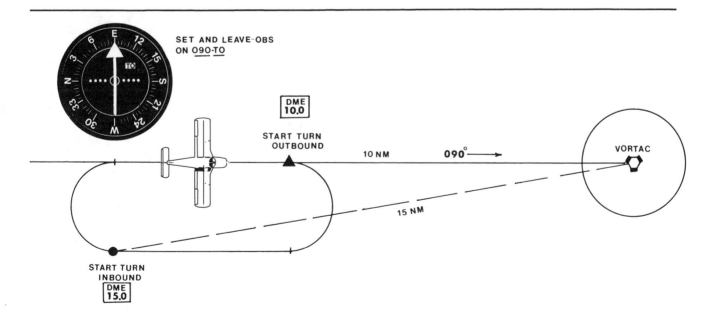

Fig. 12-8. DME holding.

■ **Holding Speed** The maximum holding speed for aircraft is 200 knots indicated airspeed (KIAS) from the minimum holding altitude (MHA) to 6000 ft MSL; for planes at 6001 ft to 14,000 ft MSL, it's 230 knots, and 265 knots above 14,000 ft MSL (all speeds IAS). (Check the *AIM* for the latest numbers.)

Holding patterns from 6001 ft to 14,000 ft may be restricted to a max airspeed of 210 knots, or 175 knots if an icon is depicted. Check the holding pattern on the chart for an icon for these nonstandard conditions.

At what speed should you hold? In theory, you should think in terms of the speed at which the minimum fuel is required as shown in Figure 12-9.

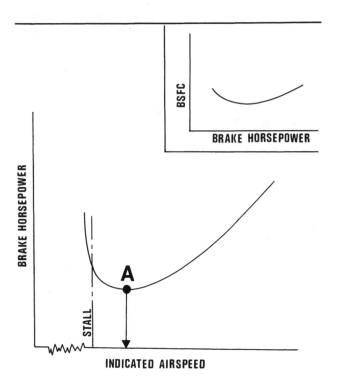

Fig. 12-9. Minimum power required to fly the airplane at a certain weight and altitude.

Point A shows the IAS at which the minimum brake horsepower is required. If the brake horsepower-specific fuel consumption is constant (which it isn't, as shown by the insert), then point A would be the airspeed for holding (and this would vary slightly with weight). Brake-specific fuel consumption (BSFC) is the *pounds of fuel per hour being used by each brake horsepower (BHP)*. You'll find that for most general aviation carburetor-equipped engines, it works out to about 0.45 lb/BHP per hour, leaned in the area of cruising power. For fuel-injected engines, the BSFC is about 0.43. The Lycoming IO-540 engine is rated at 260 BHP. The information on this engine in Figure 3-13 indicated that, at 75% power, the fuel consumption is 14.1 gal/hr.

Converting the pounds per horsepower per hour to gallons per hour: To convert to gallons per hour, divide the pounds (0.43) by 6 (the weight per gallon), getting a multiple of 0.072.

To find the gallons per hour consumption, the *actual* horsepower being used at 75% (195 BHP) is multiplied by 0.072.

0.072 × 195 = 14.04, slightly less than the book figure (Fig. 3-13) of 14.1, but at least close for an estimate.

All right, this is very interesting, you say—but what do you use for a holding speed? Because you don't have power curves or BSFC charts (and would be busy enough flying the airplane without setting up a research project), thumb rules may be substituted. Know the calibrated airspeed at stall for your airplane at the flaps-up power-off condition at the maximum certificated weight. The following thumb rules are based on that value.

For single-engine airplanes with fixed gear, multiply that figure (using 60 knots as an example) by 1.2 (1.2 × 60 = 72 knots).

For retractable-gear singles and twins, use a factor of 1.3 (1.3 × 60 = 78 knots). These factors apply whether the speeds are given in knots, miles per hour, kilometers per hour, or feet per second.

The holding speed has been discussed in terms of theory. But what about a practical situation? Turbulence may make it advisable to use a higher airspeed than given by the thumb rule. A speed of 20% (or 30%) above the stall doesn't give you much to play with in turbulent air, and control could be questionable, particularly in a situation where the airplane was loaded in a rearward CG condition. Add a few knots for better control, but don't exceed a speed of 1.6 times the stall speed—you might overstress the airplane if a strong vertical gust is encountered. (Remember, these rules are based on *calibrated* airspeeds.)

The airplane type you'll be flying will probably have a recommended holding speed of somewhere between 70 and 115 knots, so you'll have no problem of exceeding the maximum allowable speed.

To set up holding, you'll slow the airplane to the recommended speed by throttling back and maintaining altitude. You have no idea how long holding will be required, even though you've been given an "expect further clearance" time. Normally, this will be the time you *will* be cleared, but ATC has extended it on occasion and you'll want to economize. Pull the rpm back (if a controllable pitch prop is being used) to the lowest value you can get without the prop "hunting." Use whatever manifold pressure is necessary to maintain altitude at the chosen airspeed. Check on further leaning, but don't damage the engine. Obviously, the airplane should be as clean as possible—flaps up and gear up (if possible). You'll maintain a constant altitude in the pattern unless instructed by ATC to change altitudes—this technique was covered in Chapter 4. Remember, too, thumb rules are just that, and are for ballpark figures only. There's no substitute for information from the manufacturer or from pilots with experience in your airplane type and model.

DEPARTING POLAN

At 2201Z you receive the following clearance:

Center: "ZEPHYR FIVE SIX JULIET IS CLEARED TO THE TICTO INTERSECTION VIA VICTOR SEVEN, VICTOR SIXTEEN, DESCEND TO AND MAINTAIN FOUR THOUSAND. CONTACT NASHVILLE APPROACH CONTROL ONE TWO ZERO POINT SIX APPROACHING TICTO. OVER."

You: (Read back clearance and add): "LEAVING FIVE FOR FOUR THOUSAND AT ZERO ONE." (You leave 5000 at once.)

You've been tuned into Graham VOR and pass it at 2206Z. (Resume cruise speed immediately upon leaving POLAN.)

You: "GRAHAM AT ZERO SIX, FOUR THOUSAND, NASHVILLE TWO ONE." (Center acknowledges.)

It's 16 mi to TICTO, and if you haven't already done so, you'd take a last-minute glance over the approach charts for the type of approach planned. Your first choice (and that of Nashville approach control) would be the ILS.

Tune in the Nashville ATIS in the Graham area and get the latest information and use the code when initially contacting approach control, or they will have to give you all the information.

At this point you'd probably tune the No. 2 VOR receiver to Nashville (114.1 MHz) and have the DME tuned in also. The No. 1 receiver has the glide slope here, so this would be set on the frequency of the chosen ILS. The glide slope power switch should be turned on if necessary for your airplane.

The ADF should be tuned to the LOM. (You probably won't pick it up clearly until well past TICTO.)

The marker beacon receiver should be ON. (Press to test the lights.)

The Center handoff to approach control will be by computer. When Center equipment indicates that you've been accepted by approach control, the Center will give you the frequency change to approach control. In most cases (automatic radar terminal system) you'll stay on the discrete transponder code you used throughout the flight.

As you approach TICTO, you'll call Nashville approach control on 120.6 MHz.

You: "NASHVILLE APPROACH (CONTROL), ZEPHYR FIVE SIX JULIET, TICTO AT ONE TWO, FOUR THOUSAND, INFORMATION DELTA. OVER."

Approach Control: "ZEPHYR FIVE SIX JULIET."

Approach control may give turn or descent clearance like the following:

Approach Control: "ZEPHYR FIVE SIX JULIET, NASHVILLE APPROACH CONTROL, TURN RIGHT, HEADING ZERO EIGHT ZERO FOR VECTOR TO ILS RUNWAY TWO LEFT FINAL APPROACH COURSE" (for example).

You: (Acknowledge.)

Controller instructions are (ATC Manual 7110.65):

Issue approach information by including the following, except omit information currently contained in the ATIS broadcast if the pilot states the appropriate ATIS code or says he or she has received it from the Center or another source:

1. Approach clearance or type of approach to be expected if two or more approaches are published and the clearance limit does not indicate which will be used.
2. Runway in use if different from that to which the instrument approach is made.
3. Surface wind.
4. Ceiling and visibility if the ceiling at the airport of intended landing is reported below 1000 ft or below the highest circling minimum, whichever is greater, or the visibility is less than 3 mi.
5. Altimeter setting at the airport of intended landing.
6. Issue any known changes classified as special weather observations as soon as the volume of traffic, controller workload, and communications frequency congestion permit. Special weather observations need not be issued after they are included in the ATIS broadcast and the pilot states the appropriate ATIS code.
7. Advise pilots when the ILS/MLS on the runway in use is not operational if that ILS/MLS is on the same frequency as an operational ILS/MLS serving another runway.

Check for possible updates or changes in details of these 7 items.

Complete your landing checklist except for gear, flaps, and prop. Note if pitot heat or deicing (airframe and propeller) is necessary.

You now should be very glad that you took the time to study the approach charts thoroughly before the flight.

INSTRUMENT APPROACH AND LANDING

13-

The approach (and landing), particularly when the weather is at minimums, requires complete attention to the work at hand and is the part of the flight where precision is most required. Unfortunately, after a tough en route session, it is also the point where the pilot is most likely to be suffering from fatigue and get-on-the-ground fever. Sneaking down below minimums to "see if you can break out" can result in your carrying added weight in the form of television towers, smokestacks, or transmission or telephone lines. Sure, it's a pain in the neck to have to make a missed approach and fly to an alternate (you have no clean clothes, or maybe there's a big neighborhood shindig tonight). The controllers will want your intentions as to an alternate, etc.

This chapter covers some procedures for the most common approaches in instrument flight. The approach and missed approach is covered for ILS, VOR, and NDB plus a general look at airport surveillance radar and other approaches at Nashville.

Figure 13-1 is the Nashville Metropolitan Airport layout as published in the National Aeronautical Charting Office *Approach Chart Procedures*. It's a good idea to review the layout to check on obstacles near the runway (if any) and to see the taxiways and runways so you won't be totally confused, especially when you are making an approach and landing after dark. (There's nothing like trying to navigate while taxiing through what appears to be a sea of blue taxi lights at that strange field.) Of course, the lights, signs, and ground control will be the best aids, but a scan of the layout can sure help.

Okay, what kind of vectoring might you get upon arrival in the Nashville area? You aren't expected to know the possible routes that approach control will vector you on, but the controlling factor for your vector path is the *runway* being used, not the particular type of approach. You'll get the same vectoring for an approach to a particular runway for ILS, NDB, or VOR and other approaches. Busy conditions may result in a vector pattern that may seem to be sending you on to the alternate.

RUNWAYS 2L AND 2R

In most cases approach control will expect you to make an ILS approach for the runway in use, so if you have something else in mind you'd better mention it on an initial contact with them.

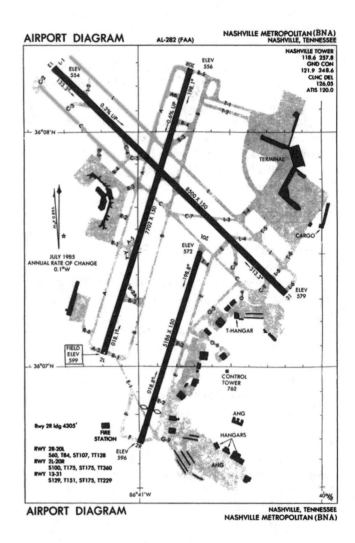

Fig. 13-1. The airport diagram for Nashville. All of the approach charts used in this chapter are NACO charts. These approaches, which are used as examples of the type, may be long out of date or nonexistent by the time you read this.

Under quiet traffic conditions you will be vectored directly toward FIDDS intersection (see the en route chart or the Runway 2L approach charts). At busy times you may be vectored to the approach fixes on a different path.

232

■ **ILS Approach** Figure 13-2 is the approach chart for the ILS Runway 2L approach to Nashville. (*To repeat: For Pete's sake don't use any of the en route charts or approach plates in this book for navigation.*) You'll be vectored so as to intercept the final course at no more than 30° (track) and far enough from the outer marker so that you won't be rushed. Your airplane is in category A for the approach minimums as shown on the approach chart.

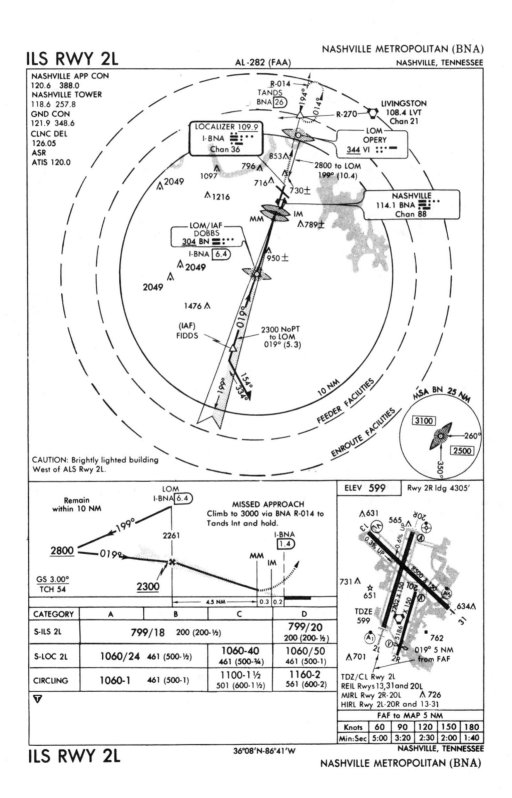

Fig. 13-2. ILS approach chart for BNA.

Be sure that you are ready to *take over and complete the approach at any time.* Sometimes pilots are caught short when approach control tells them to "take over and complete the approach."

Set the OBS to 019 on the No. 1 VOR/ILS receiver as a *reminder* of the base course on the ILS. (Remember, the OBS setting is not a factor when using the localizer frequencies.) For a missed approach, the OBS will have to be reset to 014, but more about this later.

Radar can descend you to the interception altitude at a safe point and thereby dispense with the problem of flying to the outer marker and shuttling down or making a procedure turn.

Approach control: "ZEPHYR FIVE SIX JULIET, FIVE MILES SOUTHWEST OF THE OUTER MARKER, TURN LEFT HEADING ZERO FOUR FIVE, MAINTAIN TWO THOUSAND FIVE HUNDRED OR ABOVE UNTIL ESTABLISHED ON THE LOCALIZER. CLEARED FOR AN ILS TWO LEFT APPROACH, CONTACT THE TOWER, ONE ONE EIGHT POINT SIX BEFORE CROSSING THE OUTER MARKER. OVER."
You: "ZEPHYR FIVE SIX JULIET."

You would start your descent to 2300 ft as you intercept the localizer south of the outer marker (OM) so as to cross the OM at that altitude.

Notice in Figure 13-2 that you are expected to stay above 2800 ft until out of the procedure turn, and the minimum safe altitude for the route from TICTO is 3100 ft. When you are being radar vectored in the approach control area, minimum vector altitudes (MVA) will apply. Each radar approach control has an MVA chart or charts showing the various sectors and minimum altitudes for each. Each sector boundary is at least 3 mi from the obstruction determining the MVA. Figure 13-3 shows a typical MVA chart.

You are approaching point 1 on the approach in Figure 13-4.

Radar will descend you as necessary after obstructions are passed.

Remember that the localizer is four times as sensitive as a VOR, so as soon as the needle starts moving from the peg, you'd better think of turning the airplane. The rate of turn naturally will depend on the interception angle. If you are intercepting it at a 10° angle, there would be no urgency in turning; a 90° interception could mean a fairly steep turn would be required to keep from overshooting the center line. (And rather than taking a chance on losing control of the airplane, you'd better work it so that such an angle is not necessary.) If you are being vectored by radar to the final approach course, the maximum (track) angle of intercept is 30°.

You are to call the tower now, according to your instructions from approach control earlier, as you intercept the localizer. Approach control could have coordinated with the tower and had you contact them when you first intercepted the localizer—it's up them. The tower at Nashville will be watching your airplane on their "bright display," a reproduction of

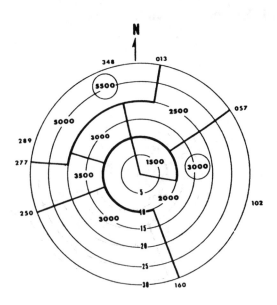

Fig. 13-3. A typical minimum vector altitude chart.

the radar screen. In a nonradar situation you'd call while passing the final approach fix (the outer marker).

You: "NASHVILLE TOWER, ZEPHYR FIVE SIX JULIET, YOUR FREQUENCY. OVER."
Nashville tower: "ZEPHYR FIVE SIX JULIET, CLEARED TO LAND RUNWAY TWO LEFT, WIND THREE FOUR ZERO DEGREES, ONE FIVE (³⁴⁰/₁₅ knots). OVER."
You: (Acknowledge.) If there is a possibility of traffic conflict, you may not get a landing clearance at this time. In conditions above VFR minimums (1000 ft ceiling and 3 mi visibility), there may be VFR traffic under the overcast that will have to be coordinated. (You are up at 2300 ft MSL and are on instruments.) With the ceiling of 300 ft and 1 mi visibility given here as an example, there would only be IFR traffic to coordinate (which will have been done), and landing clearance can often be given some distance out.

Figure 13-5 shows the instrument indications when the airplane has intercepted the localizer and is about ¼ mi south of the outer marker at point 2 in Figure 13-5. Note that the glide slope needle is beginning to show signs of life.

The outer marker is reached and the glide slope indicator centers. This is not always the case. The layout of a particular approach could require intercepting the glide slope before reaching the outer marker, but normally the systems are designed for glide slope interception at the outer marker. You put the gear down and confirm that it's down. Or if you preferred to have the gear already down and change power for the descent, that's fine—and you may want to do both. But as covered in Chapter 4, know what power is required for an approximate descent of 500 fpm with the gear down. The required rate of descent to stay on the glide slope varies

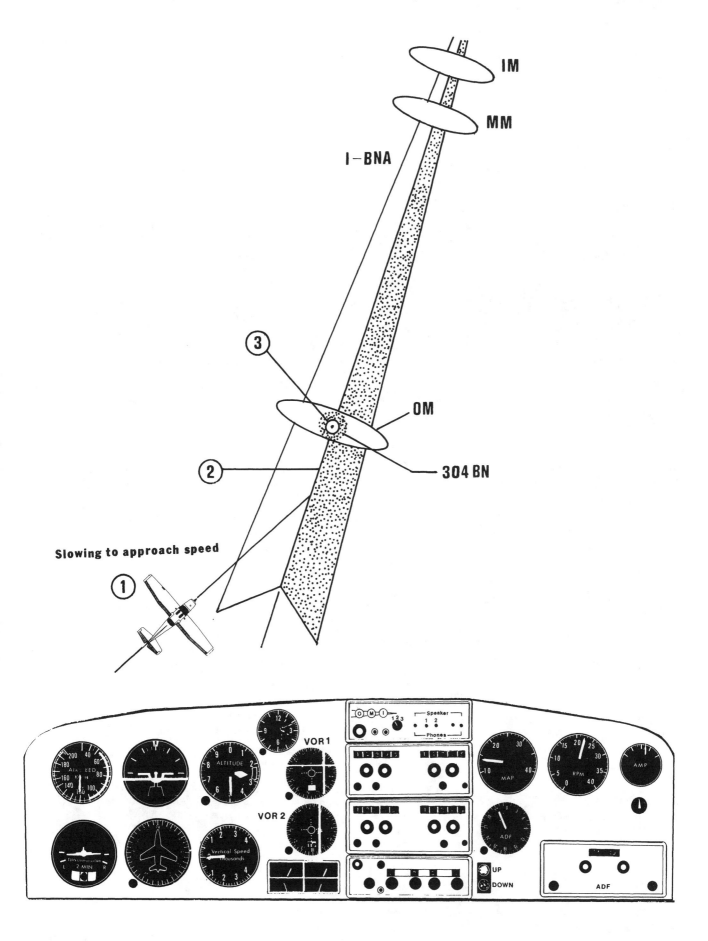

Fig. 13-4. Approaching the localizer. The instrument indications when the plane is at point 1. (The magnetic compass won't be shown in the "composite" cockpit illustrations following in this chapter.) VOR 2 is set on the BNA VOR for use if a missed approach is necessary.

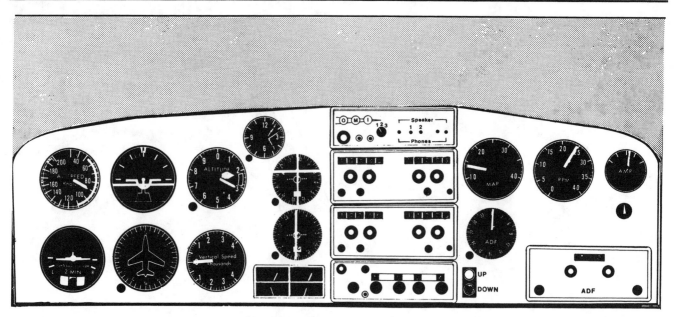

Fig. 13-5. The instrument indications at point 2 in the approach. (On the localizer and approaching the LOM.) On actual instruments the airplane will intercept the glide slope about 1 mi from the outer marker and start its descent. If the glide slope (ground or air equipment) is inoperative, you would maintain an altitude of 2300 ft to the outer marker.

with airspeed (or more properly, groundspeed). The rates of descent are based on no-wind conditions, and a head- or tailwind component would mean corrections in sink rate. The wind, as given, would result in a headwind component of about 10 knots, making your groundspeed about 80 knots.

Figure 13-6 shows all kinds of things happening as the plane reaches the outer marker (and locator) (point 3 in Fig. 13-4).

The surface wind at Nashville indicated that you might expect both a crosswind and headwind component on the approach. Figure 13-7 shows that the airplane is low and to

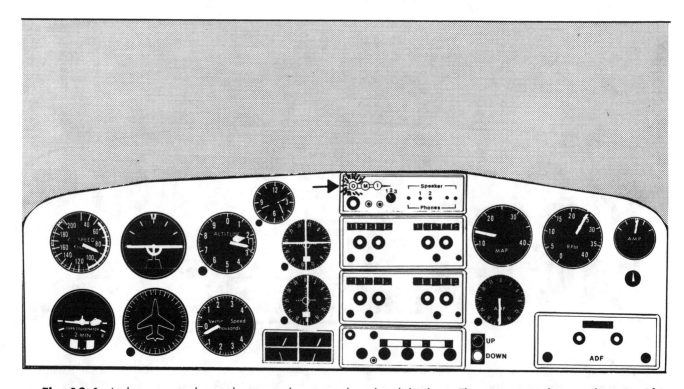

Fig. 13-6. At the outer marker and compass locator and on the glide slope. The gear is put down at this point (if not already down).

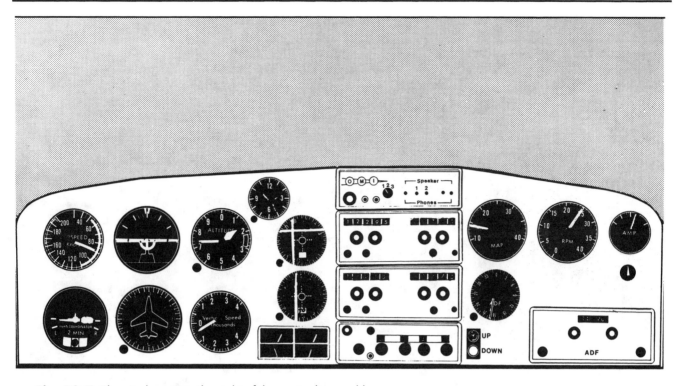

Fig. 13-7. The airplane is to the right of the center line and low.

the right of course. The ILS head shows that the airplane is to fly up and to the left. The heading indicator indicates that the heading is reasonable (disregarding such things as precession, which will not be a factor in this illustration). The altimeter shows 1750 ft MSL at this point.

A common problem of new instrument pilots is that of "flying" the localizer needle rather than picturing the position of the airplane relative to the system and using the heading indicator for corrections as should be done. "Making a turn" using the needle and guessing can result in overshooting back and forth across the center line *and* the likelihood of a dangerous condition or, at least, a missed approach.

Okay, you're off to the right and will turn left and hold the new heading until the needle is at the center position. Turn to *the selected heading and fly it.* Precise directional control is required. For most cases a 10° cut should be considered about the maximum. In this case a heading of 010° would be used because it can be easily read, even if it is 1° less than the "maximum" cut. In extreme cases of crosswinds, you may have to make corrections greater than 10°.

In close (approaching the middle marker), 5° corrections could be considered pretty much the outside limit once the drift correction heading is established. In other words, you know the proper heading for drift correction but have been careless and let the heading slip off.

What about altitude corrections? You are low at the position shown in Figure 13-8. By ramming open the throttle, you could gain altitude in short order (and probably fly on through the glide slope). Back in Chapter 4 in the section on descents, it was mentioned that throttle jockeying can ruin an approach. If you are below the glide slope, you don't want to *gain* altitude. Level flight probably would be the

most radical correction. Normally, you would just decrease the rate of descent—the amount of correction depending on the error, of course. (If you get so low that the glide slope needle is pegged at the top, you'd better add full power, clean up, and *climb for another shot at it.*)

You might have the right combination of power and airspeed for a nonturbulent condition, but an up- or downdraft could result in a glide slope needle deviation. On a hot bumpy day, correcting with throttle would be a chore. For very *minor* corrections use the elevators to ease back onto the glide slope; then a power change is unnecessary. Depending on the airplane and airspeed, you might set a limit of ±5 knots to be used for minor deviations from the glide slope. In other words, if you have to vary the airspeed more than, for instance, 5 knots to hold the glide slope, then you'd better do something with the power. Try *not to make radical power changes;* 1 in. of manifold pressure for the constant speed prop or 100-rpm change for a fixed-pitch prop should be sufficient for minor variations, and you may take off part of this after the glide slope is "wired" again.

Concerning the idea of using elevators to correct back to the glide slope: This will work if the airplane is operating on the "front side" of the power curve. In discussing the power in Chapter 4, it was noted that the rate of descent was proportional to the deficit power existing at a particular airspeed. In Chapter 12 it was noted that the point of minimum power required was found at 1.2 times the flaps-up, power-off stall speed for fixed-gear (but otherwise clean) airplanes and 1.3 for retractables, both singles and twins (calibrated airspeed).

Figure 13-8 shows the instruments just as the airplane crosses the middle marker. You'll reach the minimum (799 MSL) right after passing the middle marker.

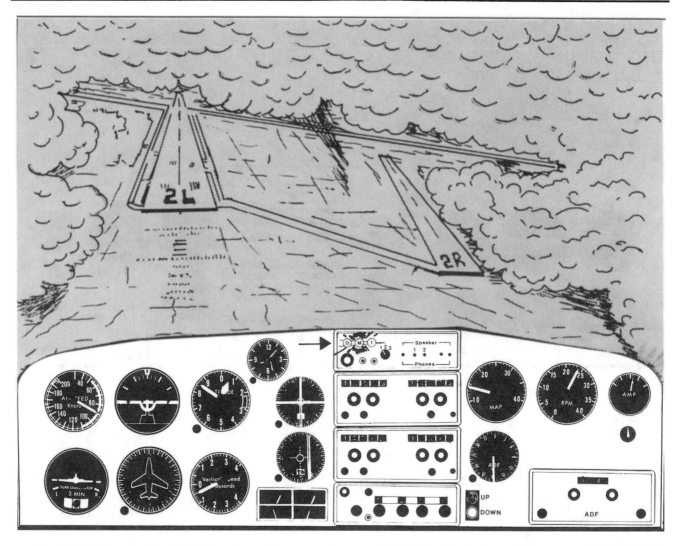

Fig. 13-8. Crossing the middle marker and compass locator at Nashville. The airplane broke out at 900 ft MSL. The airplane has just been turned to the runway heading for a wing-down approach. Flaps may be lowered now as required. The weather shown here is much worse than the actual reports for BNA at 2100Z and 2200Z (Fig. 7-27), but it makes for a better effect.

Don't be surprised if, on the final approach, varying winds are encountered. The surface wind may be reported as right down the runway, but you have quite a correction plugged in to hold the localizer needle centered during most of the approach. There may be a drop in wind velocity during the approach as you lose altitude, and you must adjust for it.

One problem (and it can be a hairy one for single-pilot planes) is that of flying half instruments, half VFR on the latter stages of the approach. Often there will be a low broken layer in the last part of the approach. Occasional glimpses of the ground are enticing enough to draw your eyes away from the instruments—just as you fly into the clouds again. It will take a second or two to get reoriented with the instruments, and at low altitudes this can be fatal. Of course, you have to look out, otherwise you'd make a missed approach when it was not necessary. On an actual instrument approach you'll be able to see out the windshield from the corners of your eyes, and any spectacular change of visibility will be readily

apparent. With hood work or dual-pilot actual instruments your safety pilot (or copilot) will be watching for the ground. It's best to complete the approach down to DH or MDA *on the gauges* if there is any doubt.

You might try some practice approaches at 1.3 times the landing flaps (bottom of the white arc) stall speed with the landing flaps extended and see how it grabs you. Remember that you won't want to make the approaches at too slow an airspeed because of the delaying of traffic. There's also the problem of control in turbulence at too low a speed.

Once you've broken out, double check the gear and other check list items and complete your landing. From here on it's just like a VFR approach and landing. You'll be told to contact ground control after turning off and will taxi into the point of destination.

You don't have to cancel your instrument flight plan if you complete an approach and land—it's done automatically. However, if you start the approach and decide it can be done VFR, you would cancel it with approach control if this was your wish. A lot of times, even though you've broken out VFR, you'll want to continue IFR for practice purposes. Don't be too hasty in canceling your IFR flight plan. Sometimes things could deteriorate before you complete the approach.

You can always ask for a visual approach if conditions allow it, rather than canceling IFR.

ILS approaches may have DME distances given. The *AIM* notes that:

1. When installed with the ILS and specified in the approach procedure, DME may be used:
   a. In lieu of the outer marker (OM).
   b. As a back course (BC) final approach fix (FAF).
   c. To establish other fixes on the localizer course.
2. In some cases DME from a separate facility may be used within terminal instrument procedures (TERPS) limitations:
   a. To provide ARC initial approach segments.
   b. As a FAF for BC approaches.
   c. As a substitute for the OM.

A couple of added notes:

1. BC approaches are gradually being phased out as indicated in Chapter 8, so maybe you won't get to make one.
2. As far as inoperative ILS components are concerned, if the localizer has failed, an ILS approach is not authorized. If the glide slope has failed, the ILS reverts to a nonprecision localizer approach. (Makes sense.)

MISSED APPROACH. Check Figure 13-2 for the missed approach procedure. If you got to the minimum altitude and did not have the runway in sight, you'd apply climb power, clean up the airplane, and climb to 3000 ft MSL outbound on the Nashville R-014 to TANDS intersection and hold.

This is one of the required reports as mentioned in Chapter 12. *You'll* have to make up *your* mind what the next move is to be. If the field has obviously gone below minimums, there's no use (and it is a waste of time and fuel) in trying another approach. It will depend on the situation; perhaps scud or rain showers moved across the field and momentarily caused the problem. You might check on the weather before going to the alternate.

Obviously, if the weather is below minimums for an ILS (with glide slope operative), you wouldn't be able to complete a VOR or ADF approach with their higher minimums.

If you're moving on to the alternate, you'll get a clearance and follow it. You'd notify the tower of your missed approach and would be switched to departure control at Nashville.

Figure 13-9 is the approach chart of ILS Runway 2 left for *Category II approaches.* The difference is in the runway visual range and aircraft equipment, including a radio altimeter (see the notations RA 158 and RA 104 on the profile part of the approach in Fig. 13-9). Category II, IIIa, IIIb, and IIIc approaches are a little in the future for you and won't be covered here.

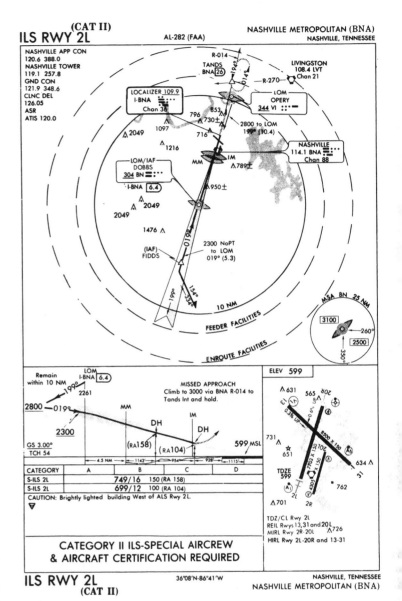

Fig. 13-9. ILS RWY 2L (CAT II) approach chart.

Note that there is touchdown zone center-line lighting for Runway 2 left and that this is mentioned in all the Nashville approach charts (TDZ/CL RWY 2L) on the airport diagram. Lighting information for all runways is included on each approach plate.

■ Nondirectional Beacon (NDB) RWY 2L Approach

The NDB approaches for runways 2L *and* 2R are covered here. As indicated earlier, the runway to be used dictates the vector path.

Figure 13-10 is the approach chart for NDB Runway 2 left.

The radar vector will likely be to FIDDS intersection and then, once established on the final approach course, descent would be made so as to cross the LOM (FAF) at no lower than 2300 MSL. Note that the profile headings and

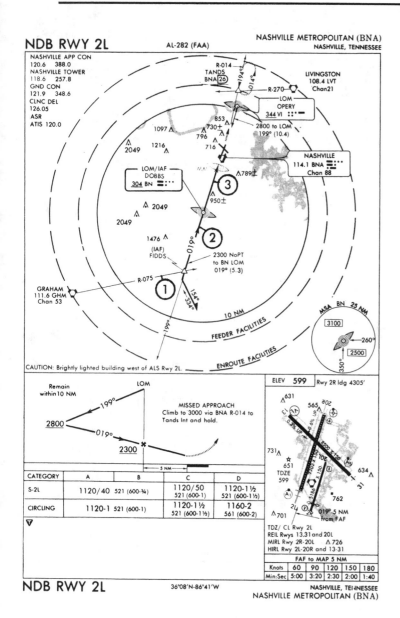

Fig. 13-10. NDB RWY 2L approach chart. The circled numbers (1, 2, 3) have been added by the writer.

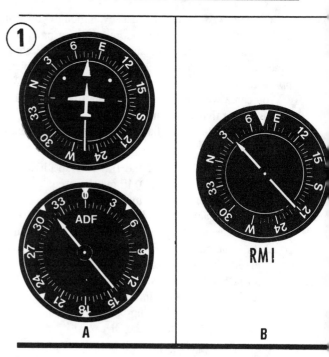

Fig. 13-11. Indications of (A) the heading indicator and fixed-face ADF and (B) a radio magnetic indicator (RMI) at point 1 of Figure 13-10 (NDB RWY 2L).

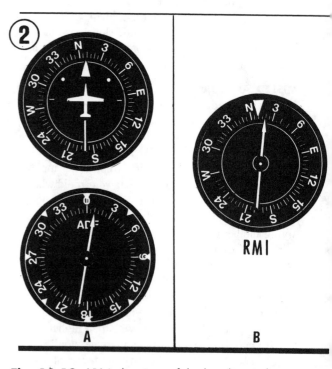

Fig. 13-12. (A) Indications of the heading indicator and ADF and (B) an RMI at point 2 of Figure 13-11. A wind correction of 10° left is used here.

altitudes are like those of the ILS RWY 2L just discussed (at least until the FAF at Dobbs LOM).

Figures 13-11, 13-12, and 13-13 show the indications of both an ADF/heading indicator combination and radio magnetic indications at the points (1), (2), and (3) of the NDB RWY 2L approach. A left crosswind on the final approach course will require a 10° correction. Assume for example purposes that the airplane is flying the R-075 from Graham VOR.

MISSED APPROACH. Note that the missed approach for NDB RWY 2L (Fig. 13-10) requires climbing to 3000 ft on the Nashville R-014 to TANDS intersection and hold. This means that, having *studied the missed approach procedure beforehand,* you will have set the No. 1 VOR on BNA

(OBS-014) and the No. 2 VOR to Livingston (LVT) R-270. Maybe you would tend to want to set the No. 1 VOR to BNA R-019 at TO, even though there is *no* VOR RWY 2L or 2R approach. However, this could lead to confusion during the

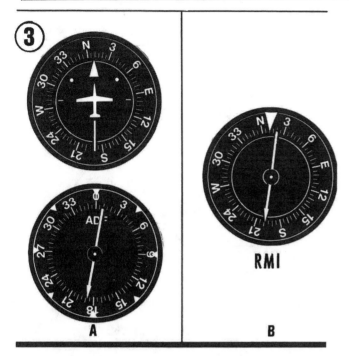

Fig. 13-13. (A) Indications of the heading indicator and ADF and **(B)** an RMI at point 3 of the NDB RWY 2L approach. The 10° left wind correction is still required at this point.

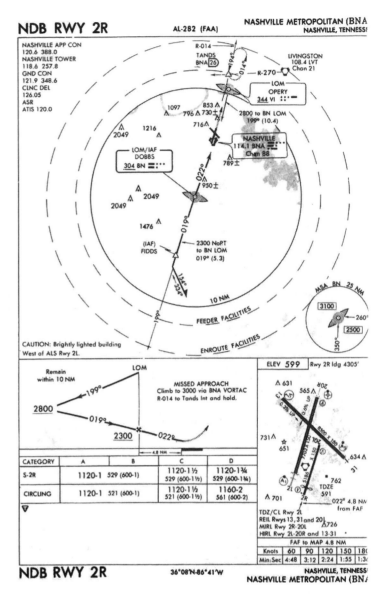

Fig. 13-14. NDB RWY 2R approach chart.

excitement of the missed approach, and you would track outbound from the VOR on the incorrect R-019 and not be holding at TANDS intersection.

Looking at Figure 13-10, you can see that the holding pattern is nonstandard (left turns), and a teardrop entry would be the choice.

■ **NDB RWY 2R** Looking at the approach chart in Figure 13-14, you will note a few differences from the NDB RWY 2L:

1. After passing the LOM, the final course is changed 3° right from 019° to 022°.
2. The visibility minimums for the straight-in approach are slightly higher for this approach; the circling minimums are the same as for NDB RWY 2L.
3. The time from the FAF to the missed approach point is a few seconds less because the distance from the LOM is 0.2 NM less for this approach.
4. The information for the radial (R-075) from Graham VOR has been deleted.

The missed approach procedure is the same for both RWY 2 NDB approaches.

RWY 31 APPROACHES

Usually for an ILS approach, you'll be turned in slightly sooner than for the VOR approach.

■ **ILS RWY 31** Figure 13-15 is the ILS Runway 31 approach for BNA. The minimum safe altitude for the RWY

31 approach is noted as 3100 ft for all quadrants. (Look back at the approaches for 2L and 2R.)

Note the caution on the approach chart: "The Smyrna Airport outer marker and middle marker may be received prior to AYERS intersection/outer marker." This has been a problem over the years, and several airline pilots (plus many other pilots) have found themselves on a low approach to Smyrna airport and lame excuses like, "Uh, we were just taking a closer look at the former Army Air Force field while we were, uh, passing by," hasn't fooled the Nashville approach control folks for a second. You can see the "ghostly" outlines of the Smyrna markers on the final approach course on the plate.

AYERS intersection is named after the late James Ayers, ATC specialist at the Nashville tower, who was of great help in the first edition of this book.

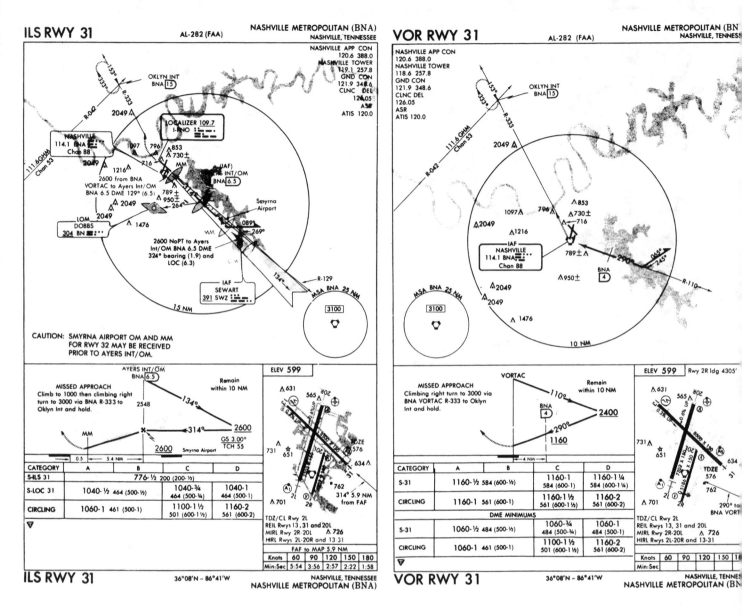

Fig. 13-15. ILS RWY 31 approach chart.

Fig. 13-16. VOR RWY 31 approach to Nashville.

MISSED APPROACH. Climb to 1000 ft and make a climbing right turn to 3000 ft via BNA R-333 to OKLYN intersection to set up a standard holding pattern as depicted. Note that OKLYN is formed either by the R-042 from Graham VOR or the 15-NM DME point from Nashville VORTAC. If you have DME equipment, this would be the easiest and most accurate method of establishing the intersection.

■ **VOR RWY 31** Figure 13-16 is the VOR Runway 31 approach and, as indicated, DME equipment aboard the airplane lowers the minimums for both straight-in and circling for categories A and B.

MISSED APPROACH (In More Detail). The missed approach procedure (the VOR RWY 31 approach) is slightly different from that of ILS RWY 31 in that here the climbing right

turn is started slightly sooner (you are higher), but the holding at OKLYN intersection is the same.

Okay, stop a minute and look in more detail at what happens when you make a missed approach, and the ones for the RWY 31 approaches could also make a good general example.

You've decided that, for some reason, you'll have to make a missed approach (maybe weather, or maybe things have gotten a little out of hand with the approach itself). *Fly the airplane first, last, and always.*

Do the necessary go-around procedures (full power, gear-up, etc., as the *POH* recommends—and which you've memorized).

After the airplane is under control and climbing, tell the tower you are executing a missed approach. Before you get a mile off the upwind end of the runway, the tower will tell you to contact departure control (or approach control in some cases; it depends on which is busier), giving you the frequency to be used.

After contacting departure control (who will have been told that you're executing a missed approach), let them know of your plans. If you want another approach, you'll be vectored back to set up again.

If you want to proceed to the alternate, let departure control know the destination (as an example, assume here that Chattanooga is the chosen alternate instead of the earlier choice of Huntsville) and V5 is the route at 5000 ft. Departure control will contact Memphis Center for a clearance but meanwhile will be vectoring you to join the airway at a prechosen point at 5000 ft.

In most cases you'll get a clearance with little delay and will be vectored onto the airway and be switched over to the Center as you leave the departure control jurisdiction. If there is a delay in the clearance from Center, departure control will hold you at (in this case) GUMOL intersection 22 NM southeast of the VOR (check the en route chart in the back of this book).

You'll be given an expected further clearance time, which may be updated as necessary because of added delay of the delivery of the clearance. *Nashville departure control cannot clear you out of their area of control* into the Center area without the clearance.

Without specific holding instructions you'd hold in standard right-hand turns northwest of GUMOL at 5000 ft.

(You know you're in deep trouble if you ask departure control for an estimate of when you can expect further clearance and they ask if you have a calendar handy.)

Your Center clearance, when it comes, could still give you an interim clearance limit well on the way to, but short of, the Chattanooga airport, to be followed at the proper time by further clearance; but that's not the situation to be covered here.

Speaking generally, if you decide to make an early missed approach, fly the instrument approach as specified on the approach chart to the missed approach point *at* or *above* the minimum descent altitude (or decision height) before turning; the obstacle clearance is predicated on this. If you turn early, it's possible that you wouldn't have proper obstruction clearance in some cases.

Again, know the steps of the missed approach. This is no time to be fumbling around. One check pilot used to say "execute a missed approach" then would cover the missed approach procedure. Woe betide the trainee who hadn't already memorized it. Too often a pilot is psychologically set to land and finish the flight (that attractive member of the opposite sex is down there waiting with the champagne), and the requirement for a missed approach catches him or her short. When IFR, clearance to make an approach automatically clears you to make a missed approach as you deem necessary.

When going to an alternate, remember WARP (*W*eather, *A*ltitude, *R*efile, and *P*rocedures) and DRAFT (*D*estination, *R*oute, *A*ltitude, *F*uel, and *T*ime). But remember most of all

(again) that *you are to fly the airplane; voice procedures can wait.*

Incidentally, the chances are that you would not fly to OKLYN and hold as shown on the RWY 31 approach charts (or any other holding points for the missed approach) but instead would be vectored by departure control to a "quiet" area (to the east in this example) and *then* vectored to a holding or en route point within the departure control's jurisdiction. However, if you lost communications before or as you started the missed approach procedure, you would be expected to proceed to OKLYN as shown on the approach chart.

Assuming, as an example, that communications were lost earlier and you missed the approach because of deteriorating weather, the decision must be made to try again or go the alternate. You would set the transponder to 7600. You should understand that your aircraft may not be in an area of radar coverage.

Again, the chance of *losing both* communications transceivers *and keeping* the navigation receivers and transponder is rare indeed. If you are in a radar environment, ATC will keep other traffic out of your way while you decide whether to make another approach or go on to the alternate. With the loss of all COMM/NAV your primary target (just a return, no transponder enhancement) will usually show up enough to allow ATC to keep up with your movements.

Whether you will make another shot at the approach will, of course, depend on the equipment left available to you, the fuel remaining, and your estimate of the weather trend. If during your preflight preparation you had checked for areas of better weather relative to the departure point, route, and destination and have now lost COMM/NAV capability, you might set up the proper VFR altitude for your magnetic course and fly in that direction. After getting clear of clouds or to where you can see the ground, you'd land at the nearest available airport (not that you'd necessarily know *what* airport is down there until you've landed) and call the nearest ATC facility.

There are enough possibilities and variations on missed approaches with equipment problems that there's no way they could be all covered. The main thing is to maintain aircraft control and be rigid in your planning. Okay, now back to "routine" approaches.

APPROACHES TO RWYS 20L AND 20R

■ **ILS RWY 20R** Figure 13-17 is the approach chart for the ILS Runway 20 right at BNA. Note that there are straight-in localizer-only and straight-in and circling minimums for the use of the "normal" ILS components, plus DME and radar minimums for the straight-in localizer and circling.

Looking at the profile view, you can see *1120* is the minimum for the localizer-only approach at the particular DME or radar points shown. Note also that the minimum safe altitude (MSA) circle is centered around OPERY LOM (344 VI) *not* the VOR. Check this for the other approaches discussed earlier.

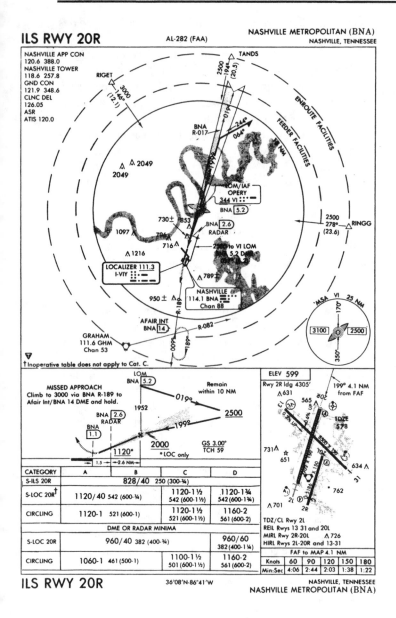

Fig. 13-17. ILS RWY 20R approach.

MISSED APPROACH. Climb to 3000 via BNA R-189 to AFAIR intersection/BNA 14 mi DME and hold in a standard pattern. Make all voice reports as required.

Figure 13-18 shows the approach charts for VOR/DME and NDB for Runway 20 right.

Note that the center of the MSA circles are the VOR and OPERY LOM, respectively. For *straight-in* approaches the VOR/DME has noticeably lower ceiling minimums for all categories, but the NDB/DME minimums (circling) are the same as for the VOR/DME, which makes sense, since once you come in contact, the problems are essentially the same in completing the landing.

■ **VOR/DME RWY 20L** Figure 13-19 is the VOR/DME approach for Runway 20 *left,* the "short" runway at BNA. (This runway is on the general aviation side of the airport.)

Notice that the initial approach fix is VIKEN, a 5-NM DME fix from the Nashville VORTAC.

The information on the approach chart is straightforward and clear.

RUNWAY 13

Figure 13-20 is the approach chart for (at present) the only approach for Runway 13. The missed approach procedure for this approach uses AFAIR intersection also.

RADAR-CONTROLLED APPROACH

Airport surveillance radar (ASR) scans through 360° and have a relatively short range designed to provide coverage in the vicinity of an airport for handling terminal air traffic. The ASR can also be used as an instrument approach aid.

Figure 13-21 shows the ASR approach minimums for BNA. Nashville doesn't have a PAR (precision approach radar, to be discussed shortly), which would have lower minimums than shown in Figure 13-21 and would include height above touchdown and decision height values.

The surveillance approach at Nashville is good for the longer runways. Runway 2L has the lowest minimums for all categories. Circling approaches, as usual, have higher MDA and visibility minimums.

You may receive a radar approach upon request, but this does *not* waive any of the prescribed weather for the airport. It's up to *you* to determine if you can legally make an approach and landing under the existing weather minimums.

You won't be given ATIS information if you state the proper ATIS code.

In any radar approach, you'll be told the type of approach and to what runway. If the approach is to be made to a secondary airport, the name will be given so that the problem in Figure 13-22 won't happen.

■ **Surveillance Approach** The controller will give you recommended altitudes on final if you request them. These altitudes will be given each mile on final, since there is no altitude or glide slope readout for ASR equipment. You'll correct as necessary to get back on the "glide slope." The *approximate* rate of descent for a 3° approach slope can be calculated by taking the expected groundspeed, dividing it by half, and adding a zero. For instance, for a groundspeed of 90 knots, the answer is 90 ÷ 2 = 45; 45 + 0 = 450 fpm.

As the wind changes, you may have to adjust power to get the right rate of descent. The same thing would apply as on the front course ILS; the manifold pressure will have to be reduced so that, as it increases during the descent, the rate of descent won't be slowed or stopped.

You'll be given heading information as necessary to correct the final course. ("HEADING 020°, ON COURSE," or "SLIGHTLY/WELL LEFT/RIGHT OF COURSE," etc.) You'll soon establish a proper correction angle under "normal" conditions.

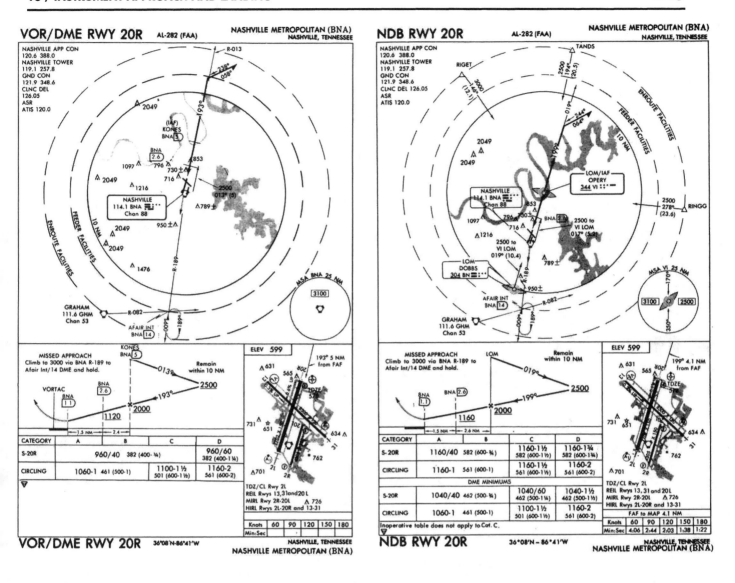

Fig. 13-18. VOR/DME and NDB approach charts for Runway 20R.

On a nonhooded practice approach, you'll be using body English to help the controller get you lined up.

The controller will discontinue the ASR approach for the following three reasons:

1. If you, the pilot, request it.
2. If in the controller's opinion continuation of a safe approach to the missed approach point (MAP) is questionable.
3. The aircraft is over the MAP.

Let the controller know when the approach or runway lights are in sight. (At the MAP the controller will advise you that if the lights are not in sight you are to execute a missed approach.)

ASR—SOME ADDED NOTES. Acknowledge altitude and heading instructions until on final. You may want to hold the gear extension (if applicable) until ready to start descending. The controller will issue advance notice of where the descent will begin and issue a straight-in MDA before

descent clearance. ("PREPARE TO DESCEND IN ONE MILE. MINIMUM DESCENT ALTITUDE NINE HUNDRED AND EIGHTY FEET.")

If the ASR approach will terminate in a circle-to-land maneuver, you'll be expected to know your airplane's category (A, B, C, D) and to have checked out the circling minimums as applicable to your approach situation. It's up to you in *any* circling maneuver to keep the airport in sight.

■ **Precision Approach** The PAR has lower minimums than the ASR because elevation information is available to the controller.

The initial part of the approach pattern for the PAR will be close to that of the ASR approach.

As you approach the glide path, the controller will give you between 10 and 30 sec notice. This may be the point where you want to extend the landing gear (if it was not extended earlier). When you get to the glide path, the controller will say: "BEGIN DESCENT" (which makes good sense).

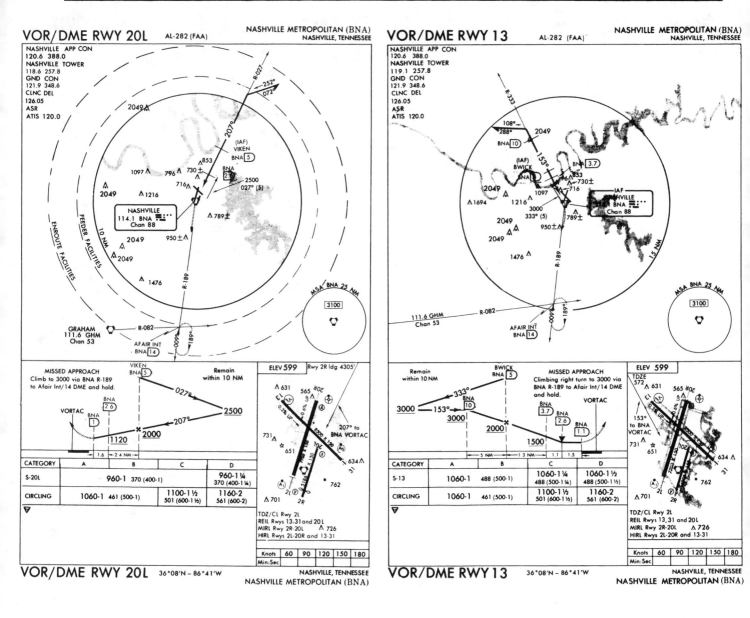

Fig. 13-19. VOR/DME approach chart for Runway 20L, or the "short" runway at Nashville.

Fig. 13-20. VOR/DME approach to Runway 13. Notice in the profile view that there are plenty of references (DME) on final approach, but the minimums are still relatively high.

Once you start the descent, the controller will issue course and glide slope guidance and tell you of any deviations from either. If no transmissions are heard for a 5-sec interval, be prepared for a missed approach because of lost communications. Usually, the final controller will be talking at such a rate that you couldn't get a word in edgewise if you wanted to.

You'll be given weather information and other information vital to operations ("YOU ARE OVER THE APPROACH LIGHTS" or "YOU ARE OVER THE LANDING THRESHOLD," etc.).

You will also be given the distance from touchdown at least each mile on final approach and notified when the aircraft is at decision height.

You'll also be told who to contact after landing, but controllers are specifically warned not to do so during transition and touchdown.

The PAR may be used for approach monitoring on the localizer frequency if its final approach course coincides with the NAVAID final approach fix to the runway and other requirements are met. (See *ATC Procedures Manual* 7110.65 for further details on any of the controller's requirements for approaches as given in this chapter.)

There are comparatively few PAR approaches and PAR-monitored approaches left at civilian airports, but the subject was mentioned in case you get a chance to use the facilities.

■ **No-Gyro Approach** As an emergency standby, you may practice what is termed as "no-gyro approach." This is not a completely accurate title because it is assumed that the

NASHVILLE METRO TN   Amdt. 20, DEC 20, 19   ELEV **599**
RADAR—120.6 388.0

	RWY	GS/TCH/RPI	CAT	DH/ MDA-VIS	HAT/ HAA	CEIL-VIS	CAT	DH/ MDA-VIS	HAT/ HAA	CEIL-VIS
ASR	2L		ABC	980/40	381	(400—¾)	D	980/50	381	(400—1)
	20R		ABCD	980/60	402	(400—1¼)				
	31		ABC	1040—¾	464	(500—¾)	D	1040—1	464	(500—1)
	13		ABC	1060—1¼	488	(500—1¼)	D	1060—1½	488	(500—1½)
CIRCLING			AB	1060—1	461	(500—1)	C	1100—1½	501	(600—1½)
			D	1160—2	561	(600—2)				

Category D S—2L visibility increased to RVR 6000 for inoperative ALS.
Inoperative table does not apply to S—20R.

▼

SE-1

CIVIL RADAR INSTRUMENT APPROACH MINIMUMS

Fig. 13-21. Airport surveillance radar minimums at Nashville. There's a note that for Category D straight-in approaches, the runway visibility range is increased to 6000 ft if the approach lighting system is inoperative. The inoperative equipment table does not apply to the straight-in approach for Runway 20R.

attitude gyro and heading indicator are inoperative, with the turn and slip or turn coordinator remaining. (The needle or small airplane is gyro operated, so it's not really a "no-gyro approach.")

Because it is assumed that you have no *accurate* means of turning to headings (the magnetic compass will not be precise enough), the controller will say, "TURN LEFT ...STOP TURN." You will be expected to use standard-rate turns by reference to the turn and slip for the pattern except after turning final where half standard-rate turns will be expected.

It will keep you busy, and it would be good training to practice one or more of these approaches if possible.

MINIMUM SAFE ALTITUDE WARNING (MSAW)

To assist air traffic controllers in detecting aircraft that are within or are approaching unsafe proximity to terrain/obstacles, the FAA has furnished automated radar terminal system with a computer function called minimum safe altitude warning. The function generates an alert when a participating aircraft is or is predicted to be below a predetermined minimum safe altitude. Aircraft on an IFR flight plan that are equipped with an operating altitude encoding transponder (Mode C) automatically participate in the MSAW program. That is, no specific request is necessary. Pilots on VFR (or no flight plans) may, provided they are equipped with an operating altitude encoding transponder, participate by asking the air traffic controller. The controller will evaluate any observed alerts and, when appropriate, issue a radar safety advisory.

FARs place responsibility for safe altitude management on the pilot. MSAW provides the controller with information that, when judged to be significant, can be relayed to assist the pilot with that responsibility. Participation in the MSAW program does not relieve you, as the pilot, of responsibility for safe altitude management.

If an aircraft is or is predicted to be below a minimum safe altitude, the computer alerts the controller. The controller will evaluate the situation and, if appropriate, issue a radar safety advisory: i.e.. "LOW ALTITUDE ALERT. CHECK YOUR ALTITUDE IMMEDIATELY."

It is the pilot's responsibility to evaluate the situation and determine what action may be necessary when an advisory is received. The pilot is expected to inform ATC immediately if any action should be taken after receiving a radar safety advisory.

Fig. 13-22. A precise instrument approach is a fitting end to a well-planned and well-executed instrument flight.

GENERAL NOTES ON APPROACHES

You should have done as many types of approaches as possible during the training process. The radar controllers are always glad to allow you to practice ASR and PAR approaches if traffic permits, since they want the practice also. Sometimes you'll be asked to comment on the approach, and you should give your honest opinion; it helps them and will help you also in analyzing possible future problems of your own.

Here are a few points you should keep in mind concerning approaches:

1. The missed approach procedure might be required anywhere during the approach; even while making the procedure turn, it might be necessary to call it off. Don't be ashamed to start all over again if things start going to pot. Too many pilots try to salvage an approach that should be stopped in favor of a new try; but no, they fight it all the way down and make a deep impression—on some fixed object.

    It's a good idea in that case to let the tower (or approach control, as applicable) know that the rea-

son you want to make the approach again is because you "didn't like the way that one was going," or some other such subtle clue, so that the pilots following won't think the weather was the cause.

2. Forget the part of the trip that's behind you and concentrate on the approach. For some reason this is the time when passengers suddenly remember a lot of questions. Don't allow any outside distractions to interfere.

3. There have been a number of instances of aircraft striking the ground on approach when visual cues were lost during low-visibility landing. Pilots have been known to continue the descent below decision height or minimum descent altitude after flying into a thin layer of fog (or snow or rain). So...if you lose the runway at that point, you'd better add full power and execute a missed approach, or you could break your airplane.

4. The approach is not complete until the airplane is locked in the hangar or tied down. *Don't* feel that you have it made as soon as you break out and have the field in sight. There's still some work for you to do.

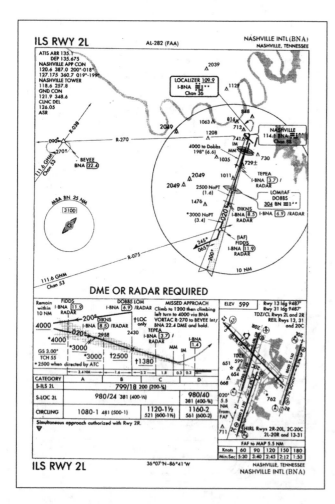

Fig. 13-23. A more complex ILS RWY 2L after the fourth runway was added at Nashville. Compare this to Figure 13-2.

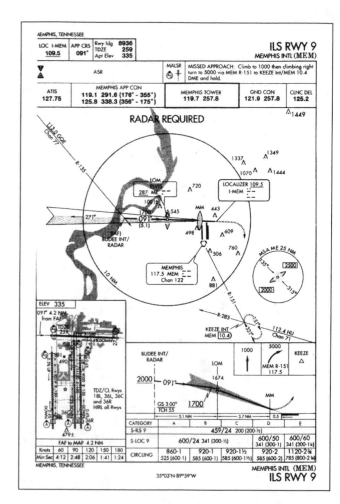

Fig. 13-24. An up-to-date presentation of the ILS RWY 9 approach for Memphis. (As the old charts are up-dated, the new charts will use this new format.)

A SPECIAL NOTE TO THE READER

During the process of completing an earlier edition of this book, Nashville Airport opened a fourth runway with (I concluded) more complex approaches and vectors than were suitable for an introductory text. The earlier BNA approach charts (still used here) are better examples of the various approaches than the new ones, at least for the person just starting on the instrument rating. I wanted to continue using the Memphis to Nashville instrument trip because the en route portion is simple, easily discussed, and relatively close-by, so I could have my questions answered by phone or by visits to the various facilities.

Since the material in this book is not to be used for navigation purposes anyway, I have used the older approach charts for Nashville with the latest changes in symbols added on.

Compare Figure 13-23, a later ILS RWY 2L approach chart, with Figure 13-2 to get an idea why the simpler example is best for the introduction of this information. As you gain experience, you'll be using more complex approaches.

Figure 13-24 is an ILS RWY 9 approach chart at Memphis. This new format will be used as each chart is replaced. (Also see Figures 5-23, 5-25, 5-51 and 5-61.)

INSTRUMENT RATING KNOWLEDGE TEST 14-

The knowledge test for the instrument rating is considered to be one of the toughest you'll take during your flying career (if not *the* toughest). The information you need to know requires a lot of memory work concerning FARs, chart symbols, approach minimum requirements, and much more. If you take the knowledge test before starting work on the flying part of the rating or very early during your instruction, some of the questions won't make sense because you haven't used the ATC system to that extent. So it's suggested that the knowledge test be taken somewhere near the point of your long IFR cross-country.

INSTRUMENT RATING KNOWLEDGE TEST GUIDE

INTRODUCTION

The FAA has hundreds of computer testing centers available nationwide. These testing centers offer the full range of airman knowledge tests including military competence, instrument rating, and foreign pilot—and pilot examiner predesignated tests.

The FAA has developed a bank of questions covering the specific subject matter areas pertaining to Instrument rating:

Instrument Rating—Airplane
Instrument Rating—Helicopter
Instrument Rating—Foreign Pilot

Knowledge tests for these ratings consist of a selection of questions in the areas that pertain to the FAR requirements,

attitude instrument flying, flight planning, meteorology, the pilot's responsibility when operating under instrument flight rules (IFR), and IFR operations pertinent to preflight, departure, en route, and arrival. The instrument rating—foreign pilot test includes questions that pertain to instrument flight rules and related procedures. These tests can be administered by any authorized computer testing center.

ELIGIBILITY REQUIREMENTS (PARAPHRASED—SEE 14 CFR 61.65)

The general prerequisites for an instrument rating require that the applicant have a combination of experience, knowledge, and skill. For specific information pertaining to certification, an applicant should carefully review the appropriate sections of FAR Part 61 for instrument rating requirements.

Additionally, to be eligible for an instrument rating, applicants must:

1. Hold at least a current private pilot certificate with an aircraft rating appropriate to the instrument rating sought.
2. Be able to read, speak, write, and understand the English language. If an applicant is unable to meet these requirements due to a medical condition, operating limitations may be placed on his or her certificate.
3. Show satisfactory completion of ground instruction or a home study course (logged) required by FAR Part 61 for the certificate or rating sought.

4. Present as personal identification an airman certificate, driver's license, or birth certificate showing that they meet the age requirements prescribed for the certificate sought no later than 2 years from the date of application for the test.

KNOWLEDGE AREAS ON THE TESTS

An applicant for the knowledge test for an instrument rating must have received ground instruction or have logged home study in at least the following areas:

1. The FARs that apply to flight under IFR conditions, the *Aeronautical Information Manual (AIM),* and the IFR air traffic system and procedures.

2. Dead reckoning appropriate to IFR navigation; IFR navigation by radio aids using the VOR, ADF, and ILS systems; and the use of IFR charts and instrument approach procedures.

3. The procurement and use of aviation weather reports and forecasts, and the elements of forecasting weather trends on the basis of that information and personal observation of weather conditions.

4. The safe and efficient operation of aircraft, as appropriate, under instrument weather conditions.

DESCRIPTION OF THE TESTS

All test questions are the objective, multiple-choice type, with three choices of answers. Each question can be answered by the selection of a single response. Each test question is independent of other questions, that is, a correct response to one does not depend upon or influence the correct response to another.

A significant number of the questions are "category specific" and appear ONLY on the airplane test, the helicopter test, or the airship test. The 20-question "added rating" tests are composed mostly of these "category-specific" questions. A 20-question "added rating" test is administered to an applicant who already holds an instrument rating in one category (airplane or helicopter) and wishes to meet the knowledge requirements for the other category. The "category-specific" questions pertain to such knowledge areas as recency of experience and weather minimums.

Tests developed from the instrument rating knowledge bank of questions:

Instrument Rating—Airplane
Instrument Rating—Rotorcraft/Helicopter
Instrument Rating—Airplane (Added Rating)
Instrument Rating—Rotorcraft/Helicopter (Added Rating)
Instrument Rating—Foreign Pilot
Instrument Flight Instructor—Airplane
Instrument Flight Instructor—Rotorcraft/Helicopter
Instrument Flight Instructor—Airplane (Added Rating)
Instrument Flight Instructor—Rotorcraft/Helicopter (Added Rating)
Ground Instructor—Instrument

Ground instructor—applicants for the instrument rating should be prepared to answer any question that appears in the instrument question bank because they are expected to teach all instrument ratings.

The instrument rating—airplane and helicopter tests have 60 questions each, and 2.5 hours is allowed for taking each test.

The instrument flight instructor—tests for airplane and helicopter, ground instructor—instrument, and the instrument rating—foreign pilot have 50 questions each, and 2.5 hours is allowed for taking each test.

All added rating tests have 20 questions each, and 1.0 hour is allowed for taking each test.

A score of 70 percent must be attained to successfully pass each test.

Communication between individuals through the use of words is a complicated process. In addition to being an exercise in the application and use of aeronautical knowledge, a test is also an exercise in communication since it involves the use of the written language. Since the tests involve written rather than spoken words, communication between the test writer and the person being tested may become a difficult matter if care is not exercised by both parties. Consequently, considerable effort is expended to write each question in a clear, precise manner. Make sure you carefully read the instructions given with each test, as well as the statements in each test item.

When taking a test, keep the following points in mind:

1. Answer each question in accordance with the latest regulations and procedures.

2. Read each question carefully before looking at the possible answers. You should clearly understand the problem before attempting to solve it.

3. After formulating an answer, determine which choice most nearly corresponds with that answer. The answer chosen should completely resolve the problem.

4. From the answers given, it may appear that there is more than one possible answer. However, there is *only one* answer that is correct and complete. The other answers are either incomplete or are derived from popular misconceptions.

5. If a certain question is difficult for you, it is best to mark it for RECALL and proceed to the other questions. After you answer the less difficult questions, return to those that you marked for recall and answer them. The recall marking procedure will be explained to you prior to starting the test. Although the computer should alert you to unanswered questions, make sure every question has an answer recorded. This procedure will enable you to use the available time to the maximum advantage.

6. When solving a calculation problem, select the answer nearest to your solution. The problem has been checked with various types of calculators; therefore, if you have solved it correctly, your answer will be closer to the correct answer than any of the other choices.

TAKING A KNOWLEDGE TEST BY COMPUTER

You should determine what authorization requirements are necessary before contacting or going to the computer testing center. Testing center personnel cannot begin the test until you provide them with the proper authorization, if one is required. A limited number of tests require no authorization. However, you should always check with your instructor or local Flight Standards District Office if you are not sure what kind of authorization you need to bring to the testing facility.

The next step is the actual registration process. Most computer testing centers require that all applicants contact a central 1-800 phone number. At this time you should select a testing site of your choice, schedule a test date, and make financial arrangements for test payment. You may register for tests several weeks in advance of the proposed testing date. You may also cancel your appointment up to 2 business days before test time, without financial penalty. After that time, you may be subject to a cancellation fee as determined by the testing center.

You are now ready to take the test. Remember, you always have an opportunity to take a sample test before the actual test begins. Your actual test is under a time limit, but if you know your material, there should be sufficient time to complete and review your test.

Within moments of completing the test, you will receive an airman test report, which contains your score. It will list those subject matter areas where questions were answered incorrectly. *The total number of subject matter knowledge codes shown on the test report is not necessarily an indication of the total number of questions answered incorrectly.* You can study these knowledge areas to improve your understanding of the subject matter.

Your instructor is required to review with you each of the knowledge areas listed on your airman test report and complete an endorsement that remedial study was conducted in these deficient areas. The examiner may also quiz you on these areas of deficiency during the practical test.

The airman test report, which must show the computer testing company's embossed seal, is an important document. DO NOT LOSE THE AIRMAN TEST REPORT, because you will need to present it to the examiner prior to taking the practical test. Loss of this report means that you will have to request a duplicate copy from the FAA in Oklahoma City. This will be costly and time consuming.

CHEATING OR OTHER UNAUTHORIZED CONDUCT

Computer testing centers follow rigid testing procedures established by the FAA. This includes test security. When entering the test area, you are permitted to take only scratch paper furnished by the test administrator and an authorized aviation computer, plotter, etc., approved for use in accordance with the FAA. The FAA has directed testing centers to stop a test any time a test administrator suspects a cheating incident has occurred. An FAA investigation will then follow. If the investigation determines that cheating or other unauthorized conduct has occurred, any airman certificate that you hold may be revoked, and you may not be allowed to take a test for 1 year.

RETESTING PROCEDURES

If the score on the airman test report is 70 percent or above, it is valid for 24 calendar months. You may elect to retake the test, in anticipation of a better score, after 30 days from the date of the last test. Prior to retesting, you must give your current airman test report to the test proctor. (The original test report will be destroyed by the test proctor after administering the retest.) The latest test taken will reflect the official score.

A person who fails a knowledge test may apply (no 30-day waiting period) for retesting providing that person presents the failed test report and an endorsement from an authorized instructor certifying that additional instruction has been given and that the instructor finds the person competent to pass the test.

INSTRUMENT RATING PRACTICAL TEST

This chapter will cover the basics of the practical (flight) test, paraphrased and in general, with discussions on the various maneuvers with some additions and other requirements, but you should have on hand a copy of the latest practical test book. Some suggestions for review will be inserted by this writer at various points: references in this book, and others, are added.

Before taking the test, you and your instructor should review the areas of weakness as shown by the Subject Matter Knowledge on the grade slip for the knowledge test.

THE TEST BOOK

The instrument rating practical test standards are designed to evaluate competency in both knowledge and skill.

The FAA requires that all practical tests be conducted in accordance with the appropriate practical test standards and the policies set forth in the Introduction. Instrument rating applicants shall be evaluated in all Tasks included in the Areas of Operation of the appropriate practical test standard (unless instructed or noted otherwise).

The Tasks apply to airplanes, helicopters, powered lifts, and airships. In certain instances, Notes describe differences in the performance of a Task by an "airplane" applicant, "helicopter" applicant, or "powered lift" applicant. When using the practical test standards book, the examiner must evaluate your knowledge and skill in sufficient depth to determine that the standards of performance listed for all Tasks are met.

All Tasks in these practical test standards are required for the issuance of an instrument rating in airplanes, helicopters, and powered lifts. However, when a particular element is not appropriate to the aircraft, its equipment, or operational capability, that element may be omitted. Examples of these element exceptions would be high altitude weather phenomena for helicopters, integrated flight systems for aircraft not so equipped, or other situations where the aircraft or operation is not compatible with the requirement of the element.

Examiners shall place special emphasis upon areas of aircraft operation that are most critical to flight safety. Among these are precise aircraft control and sound judgment in Aeronautical Decision Making (ADM). Although these areas may or may not be shown under each Task, they are essential to flight safety and shall receive careful evaluation throughout the practical test. If these areas are shown in the Objective, additional emphasis shall be placed on them.

The examiner shall place special emphasis upon areas of aircraft operations considered critical to flight safety. Among these are:

1. Positive aircraft control;
2. Positive exchange of the flight controls procedure (who is flying the aircraft);
3. Stall/spin awareness;
4. Collision avoidance;
5. Wake turbulence avoidance;
6. LAHSO (Land and Hold Short Operation);
7. Runway incursion avoidance;
8. CFIT (Controlled Flight Into Terrain);
9. ADM (Aeronautical Decision Making) and risk management;
10. Other area deemed appropriate to any phase of the practical test.

Although these areas may not be specifically addressed under each TASK, they are essential to flight safety and will be evaluated during the practical test.

A couple of points: The examiner will put special emphasis on areas of aircraft operation that can be most critical to flight safety, such as positive aircraft control and sound judgment in decision making. He or she will emphasize division of attention, control touch, two-way radio communications, and other areas that may be covered in future revisions of the test book. (If you spin out of a holding pattern, you could be in a little trouble.)

TEST PREREQUISITES

You, as an applicant, better make sure of the following:

1. Hold at least a current private pilot certificate with an aircraft rating appropriate to the instrument rating sought.
2. Pass the appropriate instrument rating knowledge test since *the beginning of the 24th month before the month in which the practical test is taken.* (This has always been a forehead wrinkler for this writer.)

3. Have gotten the applicable instruction and aeronautical experience prescribed for the instrument rating sought.

4. Hold at least a third-class medical certificate issued since the beginning of the 24th month before the month in which the practical test is taken.

5. Be able to read, speak, write, and understand the English language.

6. Obtain a written statement from an appropriately certificated flight instructor certifying that you have been given flight instruction in preparation for the practical test within 60 days preceding the date of application. The statement shall also indicate that the instructor finds the applicant competent to pass the practical test and has satisfactory knowledge of the subject area(s) in which a deficiency was indicated by the airman knowledge test report.

The FAA is emphasizing attitude instrument flying *and* the ability to fly partial-panel. There have been a number of accidents when vacuum/pressure systems have failed and the pilot was unable to fly the partial-panel (or emergency panel) instruments. You'll be checked on your ability to fly the airplane in various regimes and to make partial-panel nonprecision approaches without the attitude indicator or heading indicator.

You'll be expected to demonstrate competency in either the PRIMARY and SUPPORTING or the CONTROL and PERFORMANCE concept of instrument flying.

For a few years the FAA de-emphasized partial-panel skills on the practical tests. However, losses of vacuum/pressure systems that control the attitude and heading indicator in light aircraft (and accidents) resulted in requiring partial-panel training and skills for the pilot applying for the instrument rating. Certain maneuvers on the practical test area are required to be done partial-panel (see the section Flight by Reference to Instruments).

This chapter is aimed at the *airplane* practical test, so Tasks that are for helicopters are omitted here.

AIRCRAFT AND EQUIPMENT REQUIREMENTS

You'd better provide an appropriate and airworthy aircraft for the practical test. Its operating limitations must not prohibit the Tasks required on the practical test. Flight instruments are those required for controlling the aircraft without outside references. The required radio equipment is that necessary for communications with ATC and for the performance of VOR, NDB, GPS, LDC, LDA, SDF, and ILS (glide slope, localizer, and market beacon) approaches.

USE OF A FLIGHT SIMULATOR OR FLIGHT TRAINING DEVICE

An airman applicant for instrument rating certification is authorized to use an FAA-qualified and -approved flight simulator or flight training device to complete certain flight Task requirements listed in this practical test standard.

When flight Tasks are accomplished in an aircraft, certain Task elements may be accomplished through "simulated" actions in the interest of safety and practicality, but when accomplished in a flight simulator or flight training device, these same actions would not be "simulated." For example, when in an aircraft, a simulated engine fire may be addressed by retarding the throttle to idle, simulating the shutdown of the engine, simulating the discharge of the fire suppression agent, if applicable, and simulating the disconnect of associated electrical, hydraulic, and pneumatics systems, etc. However, when the same emergency condition is addressed in a flight simulator or flight training device, all Task elements must be accomplished as would be expected under actual circumstances.

Similarly, safety of flight precautions taken in the aircraft for the accomplishment of a specific maneuver or procedure (such as limiting altitude in an approach to stall or setting maximum airspeed for an engine failure expected to result in a rejected takeoff) need not be taken when a flight simulator or flight training device is used.

It is important to understand that whether accomplished in an aircraft, flight simulator, or flight training device, all Tasks and elements for each maneuver or procedure shall have the same performance standards applied equally for determination of overall satisfactory performance.

You must demonstrate all of the instrument approach procedures required by 14 CFR Part 61. At least one instrument approach procedure must be demonstrated in an airplane, helicopter, or powered lift, as appropriate. At least one precision and one nonprecision approach not selected for actual flight demonstration may be performed in flight simulators or flight training devices that meet the requirements of the practical test standard.

SATISFACTORY PERFORMANCE

Satisfactory performance to meet the requirements for certification is based on your ability to safely

1. Perform the approved Areas of Operation for the certificate or rating sought within the approved standards.

2. Demonstrate mastery of the aircraft with the successful outcome of each Task performed never seriously in doubt.

3. Demonstrate satisfactory proficiency and competency with the approved standards.

4. Demonstrate sound judgment and ADM.

5. Demonstrate single-pilot competence if the aircraft is type certificated for single-pilot operations.

UNSATISFACTORY PERFORMANCE

If, in the judgment of the examiner, you do not meet the standards of performance of any Task performed, the associated Area of Operation is failed and, therefore, the practical test is failed. The examiner or you may discontinue the test at any time after the failure of an Area of Operation that makes you ineligible for the certificate or rating sought. The test will be continued only with your consent. Whether the test is continued or discontinued, you are entitled to credit for only those Areas of Operation satisfactorily performed. However, during the retest and at the discretion of the examiner, any Task may be reevaluated including those previously passed.

Typical areas of unsatisfactory performance and grounds for disqualification are

1. Any action or lack of action by you that requires corrective intervention by the examiner to maintain safe flight.
2. Failure to use proper and effective visual scanning techniques, when applicable, to clear the area before and while performing maneuvers.
3. Consistently exceeding tolerances stated in the Objectives.
4. Failure to take prompt corrective action when tolerances are exceeded.

■ **Letter of Discontinuance** When a practical test is discontinued for reasons other than unsatisfactory performance (i.e., equipment failure, weather, illness), FAA Form 8710.1, Airman Certificate and/or Rating Application, and, if applicable, AC Form 8080-2, Airman Knowledge Test Report, shall be returned to you. The examiner at that time should prepare, sign, and issue a Letter of Discontinuance to you. The Letter of Discontinuance shall identify the Areas of Operation of the practical test that were successfully completed. You shall be advised that the Letter of Discontinuance shall be presented to the examiner when the practical test is resumed, and be made part of the certification file.

■ **Crew Resource Management (CRM)** CRM refers to the effective use of all available resources: human resources, hardware, and information. Human resources includes all other groups routinely working with the cockpit crew (or pilot) who are involved in decisions that are required to operate a flight safely. These groups include, but are not limited to, dispatchers, cabin crewmembers, maintenance personnel, and air traffic controllers. CRM is not a single Task; it is a set of skill competencies that must be evident in all Tasks in this practical test standard as applied to either a single-pilot or crew operation. Examiners are required to exercise proper CRM compentencies in conducting tests and expect the same from you.

■ **Applicant's Use of Checklists** Throughout the practical test, you will be evaluated on the use of an appropriate checklist. Proper use is dependent on the specific Task being evaluated. The situation may be such that the use of the checklist, while accomplishing elements of an Objective, would be either unsafe or unfeasible, especially in a single-pilot operation. In this case, the method might demand the need to review the checklist after the elements have been met. In any case, use of a checklist must consider proper scanning vigilance and division of attention at all times.

■ **Distractions During Practical Tests** Numerous studies indicate that many accidents have occurred when the pilot has been distracted during critical phases of flight. To evaluate your ability to utilize proper control technique while dividing attention both inside and outside the cockpit, the examiner shall cause a realistic distraction during the flight portion of the practical test to evaluate your ability to divide attention while maintaining safe flight.

■ **Positive Exchange of Flight Controls** During flight, there must be a clear understanding between pilots as to who has control of the aircraft. Prior to flight, a briefing should be conducted that includes the procedure for the exchange of the flight controls. A positive three-step process in the exchange between pilots is a proven procedure and one that is strongly recommended:

1. When one pilot wishes to give the other pilot control of the aircraft, he or she will say, "You have the flight controls."
2. The other pilot acknowledges immediately by saying, "I have the flight controls."
3. The first pilot again says, "You have the flight controls."

When control is returned to the first pilot, the same procedure is followed. Visually verify that the exchange has occurred. (Writer's note: For Pete's sake, don't crawl out of the wreckage saying, "I thought YOU were flying it!")

PREFLIGHT PREPARATION

■ **Weather Information**
References: 14 CFR Part 61; Aviation Weather AC 00-6, Aviation Weather Services AC 00-45; Chapter 7 in this book; *AIM.*
Objective: You'll be checked on your ability to

1. Exhibit adequate knowledge of aviation weather information by obtaining, reading, and analyzing the applicable items such as
   a. Weather reports and forecasts.
   b. Pilot and radar reports.
   c. Surface analysis charts.
   d. Radar summary charts.
   e. Significant weather prognostics.
   f. Winds and temperatures aloft.
   g. Freezing level charts.
   h. Stability charts.
   i. Severe weather outlook charts.
   j. SIGMETs and AIRMETs.
   k. ATIS reports.
2. Correctly analyze the assembled weather information pertaining to the proposed route of flight and designation airport. You'll also have to determine whether an alternate airport is required, and if so, whether the selected alternate airport meets the regulatory requirements.

As noted in Chapter 7 in this book, the various charts will give you an overall look at the weather, and the printed forecasts (area and terminal) will be more local in scope.

Check the earlier forecasts against the earlier weather reports; were the forecasts optimistic or pessimistic? This may give you some idea of how to believe the most recent forecasts. It's a good idea to check the weather to the west of your route and the destination. Since weather in the United States moves generally from west to east, weather west of your area of interest could be at the route or destination in a few hours.

Note: Where current weather reports, forecasts, or other pertinent information are not available, this information will be simulated by the examiner in a way that will measure your competence.

■ Cross-Country Flight Planning

References: 14 CFR Parts 61 and 91; *Instrument Flying Handbook; AIM;* Chapters 3, 6, 8, and 9 in this book.

Objective: You'll be expected to

1. Exhibit adequate knowledge of the elements by presenting and explaining a preplanned cross-country flight, as previously assigned by the examiner (preplanning at examiner's discretion). You'll plan it using real time and weather, conforming to the regulatory requirements for instrument flight rules within the airspace in which the flight will be conducted.

2. Have and show adequate knowledge of the aircraft's performance capabilities by calculating the estimated time en route and total fuel requirement based upon such factors as
   a. Power settings.
   b. Operating altitude or flight level.
   c. Wind.
   d. Fuel reserve requirements.

3. Select and correctly interpret the current and applicable en route charts, DPs (instrument departure procedures), STAR (standard terminal arrival), and standard instrument approach procedure charts. (Review Chapter 8 in this book and *AIM* in particular for this.)

4. Obtain and correctly interpret applicable NOTAM information.

5. Determine that the calculated performance is within the aircraft's capability and operating limitations.

6. Complete and file a flight plan in a manner that accurately reflects the conditions of the proposed flight (this does not have to be filed with ATC).

7. Demonstrate adequate knowledge of the global positioning system (GPS) and receiver autonomous integrity monitoring (RAIM) capability, when the aircraft is so equipped.

PREFLIGHT PROCEDURES

■ Aircraft Systems Related to IFR Operations

References: 14 CFR Parts 61 and 91; *Instrument Flying Handbook;* Chapters 2 and 7 in this book.

Objective: The examiner will determine that you have adequate knowledge of the aircraft's anti-icing/deicing system(s) and their operating methods to include

1. Airframe.
2. Propeller
3. Intake.
4. Fuel system.
5. Pitot-static.

■ Aircraft Flight Instruments and Navigation Equipment

References: 14 CFR Parts 61 and 91; *Instrument Flying Handbook;* Chapters 2 and 5 in this book.

Objective: To determine that you

1. Exhibit adequate knowledge of the applicable aircraft flight instrument system(s) and their operating characteristics to include
   a. Pitot-static.
   b. Altimeter.
   c. Airspeed indicator.
   d. Vertical speed indicator.
   e. Attitude indicator.
   f. Horizontal situation indicator.
   g. Magnetic compass.
   h. Turn-and-slip indicator/turn coordinator.
   i. Heading indicator.
   j. Electrical systems.
   k. Vacuum systems.

2. Exhibit adequate knowledge of the applicable aircraft navigation system(s) and their operating methods to include
   a. VHF omnirange (VOR).
   b. Distance measuring equipment (DME).
   c. Instrument landing system (ILS).
   d. Marker beacon receiver/indicators.
   e. Transponder/altitude encoding.
   f. Automatic direction finder (ADF).
   g. Global positioning system (GPS).
   h. Flight Management System (FMS).

■ Instrument Cockpit Check

References: 14 CFR Parts 61 and 91; *Instrument Flying Handbook;* Chapters 2, 5, and 10 in this book.

Objective: Here is where it will be checked if you

1. Exhibit adequate knowledge of the preflight instrument, avionics, and navigation equipment cockpit checklist by explaining the reasons for the check and how to detect possible defects.

2. Are able to perform the preflight instrument, avionics, and navigation equipment cockpit check by following the checklist appropriate to the aircraft flown.

3. Determine that the aircraft is in condition for safe instrument flight including
   a. Communications equipment.
   b. Navigation equipment, as appropriate to the aircraft flown:

c. Magnetic compass.

d. Heading indicator.

e. Attitude indicator.

f. Altimeter.

g. Turn-and-slip indicator/turn coordinator.

h. Vertical speed indicator.

i. Airspeed indicator.

j. Clock.

k. Power source for gyro instruments.

l. Pitot heat.

m. Electronic flight instrument display.

n. Traffic awareness/warning/avoidance system.

o. Terrain awareness/warning/avoidance system.

p. FMS (Flight Management System).

q. Auto pilot.

4. Note any discrepancies and determine whether the aircraft is safe for instrument flight or requires maintenance. *(A rule of thumb is that the attitude indicator and heading indicator should have been running at least 5 min before takeoff to ensure that the gyros are up to speed.)*

AIR TRAFFIC CONTROL CLEARANCES AND PROCEDURES

Note: The ATC clearance may be an actual or simulated ATC clearance based upon the flight plan.

■ Air Traffic Control Clearances

References: 14 CFR Parts 61 and 91; *Instrument Flying Handbook; AIM;* Chapters 6, 9, 10, 12, and 13 in this book.

Objective: You'll be expected to

1. Exhibit adequate knowledge of the elements of ATC clearances and pilot/controller responsibilities to include tower en route control and clearance void times.

2. Copy correctly, in a timely manner, the ATC clearance as issued.

3. Determine that it is possible to comply with ATC clearance.

4. Interpret correctly the ATC clearance received and, when necessary, request clarification, verification, or change.

5. Read back correctly, in a timely manner, the ATC clearance in the sequence received.

6. Use standard phraseology when reading back clearance.

7. Set the appropriate communication and navigation frequencies and transponder codes in compliance with the ATC clearance.

■ Compliance with Departure, En Route, and Arrival Procedures and Clearances

References: 14 CFR Parts 61 and 91; *Instrument Flying Handbook;* DPs; en route low altitude chart; STARs; Chapters 6, 9, 10, 11, 12, and 13 in this book.

Objective: Make sure that you understand how and are able to

1. Show adequate knowledge of DPs, en route low altitude charts, STARs, and related pilot/controller responsibilities. (Includes tower en route central and clearance void times.)

2. Use the current and appropriate navigation publications for the proposed flight. *(Double check this. Too many times people arrive for the flight test with outdated publications.)*

3. Select and use the appropriate communications frequencies; select and *identify* the navigation aids associated with the proposed flight. *Another problem found on flight tests (and in real life too) is that pilots assume that the frequency used last week or month is still good or that the facility is not down for repairs. Of course, if you'd check the NOTAMs....*

4. Perform the appropriate aircraft checklist items relative to a particular phase of a flight. *It's hoped that you've been using a proper checklist throughout your training and don't start using one just for the test.*

5. Establish two-way communications with the proper controlling agency and use the proper phraseology.

6. Comply, in a timely manner, with all ATC instructions and airspace restrictions.

7. Exhibit adequate knowledge of two-way radio communications failure procedures. *If you haven't heard talking for a few minutes, get a "time check" or "altimeter setting" to make sure you still have communications. If there's no answer after a reasonable time, execute the lost communications procedures you've learned.*

8. Intercept, in a timely manner, all courses, radials, and bearings appropriate to the procedure, route, or clearance.

9. Maintain the applicable airspeed within ±10 knots, headings within ±10°, altitude within ±100 ft, and track a course, radial, or bearing within a $3/4$ scale deflection of the CDI.

■ Holding Procedures

References: 14 CFR Parts 61 and 91; *Instrument Flying Handbook; AIM;* Chapter 12 in this book.

Note: Any reference to DME will be disregarded if the aircraft is not so equipped.

Objective: To determine that you

1. Exhibit adequate knowledge of elements relating to holding procedures.

2. Change to the holding airspeed appropriate for the altitude or aircraft when 3 min or less from, but prior to arriving at, the holding fix.

3. Explain and use an entry procedure that ensures that the aircraft remains within the holding pattern airspace for a standard, nonstandard, published, or nonpublished holding pattern.

4. Recognize arrival at the holding fix and initiate prompt entry into the holding pattern.

5. Comply with ATC reporting requirements.

6. Use the proper timing criteria, where applicable, as required by altitude or ATC instructions.

7. Comply with pattern leg lengths when a DME distance is specified.

8. Use proper wind correction procedures to maintain the desired pattern and to arrive over the fix as close as possible to a specified time.

9. Maintain the airspeed within 10 knots, altitude within ±100 ft, headings within ±10°, and track a selected course, radial, or bearing within $^3/_4$ scale deflection of the CDI.

FLIGHT BY REFERENCE TO INSTRUMENTS

Basic Instrument Flight Maneuvers

The examiner wants to determiine that you can perform basic flight maneuvers. You'll be expected to:

1. Exhibit adequate knowledge of the elements related to attitude instrument flying during straight and level, climbs, turns, and descents while conducting various instrument flight procedures.

2. You'll maintain altitude within ±100 feet during level flight, headings within ±10°, airspeed within ±10 knots and bank angles within ±5° during turns.

3. You'll use proper instrument cross-check and interpretation and apply the appropriate pitch, bank power and trim corrections when applicable.

The following detailed exercises are NOT specifically included in the current PTS but are included by the writer from earlier Practical Test Standards and as an aid to prepare for basic flight maneuvers as currently required.

■ Straight and Level Flight (Full- *or* Partial-Panel)

References: 14 CFR Part 61; *Instrument Flying Handbook;* Chapter 4 in this book.
Objective: To determine that you are able to

1. Exhibit adequate knowledge of the factors relating to attitude instrument flying during straight and level flight.

2. Maintain straight and level flight in the aircraft configuration specified by the examiner.

3. Maintain the heading within 10°, altitude within 100 ft, and airspeed within 10 knots.

4. Use proper instrument cross-check and interpretation and apply the appropriate pitch, bank, power, and trim corrections.

If there's one most common error in flying without the attitude and heading indicators (partial-panel), it's that of poor heading control. Even a small deflection of the needle (or small airplane in the turn coordinator) for a few seconds can get the airplane off heading more than you realize. If you're like most pilots at this stage, your altitude control will be better than your heading control.

■ Change of Airspeed (Full- *or* Partial-Panel)

References: 14 CFR Part 61; *Instrument Flying Handbook;* Chapter 4 in this book.
Objective: To make sure that you are able to

1. Exhibit adequate knowledge of the elements relating to attitude instrument flying during change of airspeeds in straight and level flight and in turns.

2. Establish a proper power setting when changing airspeed.

3. Maintain the heading within 10°, angle of bank within ±5° when turning, altitude within 100 ft, and airspeed within 10 knots.

4. Use proper instrument cross-check and interpretation and apply the appropriate pitch, bank, power, and trim corrections.

If you've been having problems with heading control (partial-panel) in straight and level flight, changing airspeeds with the required power changes needed to maintain a constant altitude will complicate the situation. This is a tough exercise because the tendency is to spend too much time looking at the altimeter and/or power instruments. Keep that scan going.

■ Constant-Airspeed Climbs and Descents (Full- *or* Partial-Panel)

References: 14 CFR Part 61; *Instrument Flying Handbook;* Chapter 4 in this book.
Objective: To determine that you are able to

1. Exhibit adequate knowledge of the factors relating to attitude instrument flying during constant-airspeed climbs and descents.

2. Demonstrate climbs and descents at a constant airspeed between specific altitudes in straight or turning flight, as specified by the examiner.

3. Enter constant-airspeed climbs and descents from a specified altitude, airspeed, and heading.

4. Establish the appropriate change of pitch and power to establish the desired climb and descent performance.

5. Maintain the desired airspeed within 10 knots, heading within 10°, or, if in a turning maneuver, within 5° of the desired bank angle.

6. Perform the level-off within 100 ft of the desired altitude.

7. Use proper instrument cross-check and interpretation and apply the appropriate pitch, bank, power, and trim corrections.

The airspeed indicator will be the major reference for pitch control in these climbs and descents. In smooth air you should be able to hold within 1 knot of the chosen climb or descent airspeed (disregarding checkitis). Remember that if the airspeed is off the mark, don't try to get back to it all at once; the tendency is to over control with the airspeed going out of the practical test limits. And while the airspeed chase is going on, the heading is neglected, with "torque" (in the climb) giving a smooth 90° turn, or more before you catch it.

■ Rate Climbs and Descents (Full- *or* Partial-Panel)

References: 14 CFR Part 61; *Instrument Flying Handbook;* Chapter 4 in this book.

Objective: To determine that you are able to

1. Exhibit adequate knowledge of the factors relating to attitude instrument flying during rate climbs and descents.
2. Demonstrate climbs and descents at a constant rate between specified altitudes in straight or turning flight, as directed by the examiner.
3. Enter rate climbs and descents from a specified altitude, airspeed, and heading.
4. Establish the appropriate change of pitch, bank, and power to establish the desired rate of climb or descent.
5. Maintain the desired rate of climb and descent within 100 fpm, airspeed within 10 knots, heading within 10°, or, if in a turning maneuver, within 5° of the desired bank angle.
6. Perform the level-off within 100 ft of the desired altitude.
7. Use proper instrument cross-check and interpretation and apply the appropriate pitch, bank, power, and trim corrections.

Don't get the idea that if the climb or descent rate is off your only correction is to fly the airplane with the elevators. Remember that the rates of climb and descent are controlled by the excess or deficit thrust horsepower respectively, if you don't have the proper power setting or don't reset it as necessary, you may be trying to, for instance, climb by your own bootstraps and the airspeed gets out of the limits allowed in flight test. Pull to climb; pull a little more to go down.

■ Timed Turns to Magnetic Compass Headings (Full- *or* Partial-Panel)

References: 14 CFR Part 61; *Instrument Flying Handbook*; Chapter 4 in this book.
Note: If the aircraft has a turn-and-slip indicator, the phrase "miniature aircraft of the turn coordinator" applies to the turn needle.
Objective: To determine that you are able to

1. Exhibit adequate knowledge of procedures relating to calibrating the miniature aircraft of the turn coordinator, the operating characteristics and errors of the magnetic compass, and the performance of timed turns to specified compass headings.
2. Establish indicated standard-rate turns, both right and left.
3. Apply the clock correctly to the calibration procedure.
4. Change the miniature aircraft position, as necessary, to produce a standard-rate turn.
5. Make timed turns to specified compass headings.
6. Maintain the altitude within 100 ft, airspeed within 10 knots, bank angle 5° of a standard- or half-standard-rate turn, and roll-out on specified headings within 10°.

■ Steep Turns (All Flight Instruments)

References: 14 CFR Part 61; *Instrument Flying Handbook*; Chapter 4 in this book.
Objective: To determine that you are able to

1. Exhibit adequate knowledge of the factors relating to attitude instrument flying during steep turns.
2. Enter a turn using a bank of approximately 45°.
3. Maintain the desired angle of bank for either 180° or 360° of turn, both left and right.
4. Maintain altitude within 100 ft, airspeed within 10 knots, within 5° of the desired bank angle, and roll-out within 10° of the specified heading.
5. Use proper instrument cross-check and interpretation and apply the appropriate pitch, bank, power, and trim corrections.

One common error is that, even though you have been doing 45° banked turns very well visually, there is a definite tendency, when hooded, to get behind the airplane with too little back pressure being applied too late and an ensuing rapid loss of altitude. Also, under the hood, it seems that the tendency is to get so involved in the 45° banked turn that you suddenly realize that the airplane is well past the roll-out heading. A turn of 180° can go by quickly in a 45° bank.

■ Recovery from Unusual Flight Attitudes (Attitude Indicator Inoperative)

References: 14 CFR Part 61; *Instrument Flying Handbook*; Chapter 4 in this book.
Note: Any intervention by the examiner to prevent the aircraft from exceeding any operating limitations or entering an unsafe flight condition is disqualifying.
Objective: To determine that you are able to

1. Exhibit adequate knowledge of the factors relating to attitude instrument flying during recovery from unusual flight attitudes (both nose-high and nose-low).
2. Use proper instrument cross-check and interpretation and apply the appropriate pitch, bank, and power corrections in the correct sequence to return the aircraft to a stabilized level flight attitude.

A couple of notes: Review this area of flying carefully in Chapter 4 of this book. A problem in the recovery from a nose-low unusual attitude is that the (usually) excessive airspeed will tend to bring the nose up radically as the wings are leveled, and you may have to come in smoothly with strong forward pressure to stop the excessive pitch-up.

A common error in the nose-high, or approach to, stall recovery is that the nose, after being lowered, is brought back up to the level flight attitude too soon and a secondary stall occurs.

NAVIGATION SYSTEMS

Note: Be sure that you are fully current on the navigation systems as required in this Area of Operation.

■ Intercepting and Tracking Navigational Systems and DME Arcs

References: 14 CFR Parts 61 and 91; *AIM; Instrument Flying Handbook;* Chapter 5 in this book.

Note: Any reference to DME ARCs, ADF, or GPS shall be disregarded if the aircraft is not equipped with these specified navigational systems.

Objective: To determine that the applicant

1. Exhibits adequate knowledge of the elements related to intercepting and tracking navigational systems and DME arcs.
2. Tunes and correctly identifies the navigational facility.
3. Sets and correctly orients the radial to be intercepted into the course selector or correctly identifies the radial on the radio magnetic indicator (RMI).
4. Intercepts the specified radial at a predetermined angle, inbound or outbound from a navigational facility.
5. Maintains the airspeed within 10 knots, altitude within 100 feet, and selected headings within 5°.
6. Applies proper correction to maintain a radial, allowing no more than three-quarter-scale deflection of the CDI or within 10° in case of an RMI.
7. Determines the aircraft position relative to the navigational facility or from a waypoint in the case of GPS.
8. Intercepts a DME arc and maintains that arc within 1 NM.
9. Recognizes navigational receiver or facility failure and, when required, reports the failure to ATC.

INSTRUMENT APPROACH PROCEDURES

■ Nonprecision Approach (NPA)

References: 14 CFR Parts 61 and 91; *Instrument Flying Handbook;* IAP; *AIM;* Chapters 5 and 13 in this book.

Note: You must accomplish at least two nonprecision approaches (one of which must include a procedure turn or, in the case of an RNAV approach, a Terminal Arrival Area (TAA) procedure) in simulated or actual weather conditions. At least one nonprecision approach must be flown without the use of autopilot and without the assistance of radar vectors. (The yaw damper and flight director are not considered parts of the autopilot for purpose of this part). The examiner will select nonprecision approaches that are representative of the type that the applicant is likely to use. The choices must utilize two different types of navigational aids. Some examples of navigational aids for the purposes of this part are: NDB, VOR, LOC, LDA, GPS, or RNAV.

Objective: To determine that you

1. Exhibit adequate knowledge of the elements related to an instrument approach procedure.
2. Select and comply with the appropriate instrument approach procedure to be performed.
3. Establish two-way communications with ATC, as appropriate to the phase of flight or approach segment, and use proper radio communication phraseology and technique.

4. Select, tune, identify, and confirm the operational status of navigation equipment to be used for the approach procedure.
5. Comply with all clearances issued by ATC or the examiner.
6. Recognize if any flight instrumentation is inaccurate or inoperative, and take appropriate action.
7. Advise ATC or examiner anytime the aircraft is unable to comply with a clearance.
8. Establish the appropriate aircraft configuration and airspeed considering turbulence and wind shear, and complete the aircraft checklist items appropriate to the phase of the flight.
9. Maintain, prior to beginning the final approach segment, altitude within 100 feet, heading within 10°, and allow less than a full-scale deflection of the CDI or within 10° in the case of an RMI, and maintain airspeed within 10 knots.
10. Apply the necessary adjustments to the published MDA and visibility criteria for the aircraft approach category when required, such as
    a. NOTAMs.
    b. Inoperative aircraft and ground navigation equipment.
    c. Inoperative visual aids associated with the landing environment.
    d. National Weather Service (NWS) reporting factors and criteria.
11. Establish a rate of descent and track that will ensure arrival at the MDA prior to reaching the MAP with the aircraft continuously in a position from which descent to a landing on the intended runway can be made at a normal rate using normal maneuvers.
12. Allow, while on the final approach segment, no more than a three-quarter-scale deflection of the CDI or within ±10° in case of an RMI, and maintain airspeed within ±10 knots.
13. Maintain the MDA, when reached, within +100 ft, –0 ft of the MAP.
14. Execute the missed approach procedure when the required visual references for the intended runway are not distinctly visible and identifiable at the MAP.
15. Execute a normal landing from a straight-in or circling approach when instructed by the examiner.

■ Precision Approach (PA)

References: 14 CFR Parts 61 and 91; *Instrument Flying Handbook;* IAP; *AIM,* Chapters 5 and 13 in this book.

Note: A precision approach, utilizing aircraft NAVAID for centerline and vertical guidance, must be accom simulated or actual instrument conditions to DA/DH.

Objective: To determine that you

1. Exhibit adequate knowledge of the precision instrument approach procedures.

2. Accomplish the appropriate precision instrument appproaches as selected by the examiner.

3. Establish two-way communications with ATC using the proper communications phraseology and techniques as required for the phase of flight or approach segment.

4. Comply, in a timely manner, with all clearances instructions, and procedures.

5. Advise ATC anytime that you are unable to comply with a clearance.

6. Establish the appropriate airplane configuration and airspeed/v-speed considering urbulence, wind shear, microburst conditions, or other meteorological and operating conditions.

7. Complete the aircraft checklist items appropriate to the phase of flight or approach segment, including engine out approach and landing checklists, if appropriate.

8. Prior to beginning the final approach segment, maintain the desired altitude ±100 feet, the desired airspeed within ±10 knots, the desired heading within ±10°; and accurately track radials, coures and bearings.

9. Select, tune, identify, and monitor the operational status of ground and airplane navigation equipment used for the approach.

10. Apply the necessary adjustments to the published DA/DH and visibility criteria for the airplane approach category as required, such as—
    a. NOTAMs.
    b. Inoperative airplane and ground navigation equipment.
    c. Inoperative visual aids associated with the landing environment.
    d. NWS reporting factors and criteria.

11. Establish a predetermined rate of descent at the point where the electronic glide slope begins, which approximates that required for the aircraft to follow the glide slope.

12. Maintain a stabilized final approach, from the Final Approach Fix to DA/DH allowing no more than three-quarter scale deflection of either the glide slope or localizer indications and maintain the desired airspeed within ±10 knots.

13. A missed approach or transition to a landing shall be initiated at Decision Height.

14. Initiate immediately the missed approach when at the DA/DH, and the required visual references for the runway are not unmistakably visible and identifiable.

15. Transition to a normal landing approach (missed approach for seaplanes) only when the aircraft is in a position from which a descent to a landing on the runway can be made at a normal rate of descent using normal maneuvering.

16. Maintain localizer and glide slope within three-quarter-scale deflection of the indicators during the visual descent from DA/DH to a point over the runway where glide slope must be abandoned to accomplish a normal landing.

■ Missed Approach

References: 14 CFR Parts 61 and 91: *Instrument Flying Handbook;* standard instrument approach procedure chart; *AIM;* Chapters 8 and 13 in this book.

Objective: To determine that you are able to

1. Exhibit adequate knowledge of the elements related to missed approach procedures associated with standard instrument approaches.

2. Initiate the missed approach promptly by applying power, establishing a climb attitude, and reducing drag in accordance with the aircraft manufacturer's recommendations.

3. Report to ATC when beginning the missed approach procedure.

4. Comply with the published or alternate missed approach procedure.

5. Advise ATC or the examiner any time the aircraft is unable to comply with a clearance, restriction, or climb gradient.

6. Follow the recommended checklist items appropriate to the go-around procedure.

7. Request, if appropriate, ATC clearance to the alternate airport, clearance limit, or as directed by the examiner.

8. Maintain the recommended airspeed within ±10 knots; heading, course, or bearing within ±10°; and altitude(s) within +100 ft during the missed approach procedure.

■ Circling Approach

References: 14 CFR Parts 61 and 91; *Instrument Flying Handbook;* standard instrument approach procedure chart; *AIM;* Chapters 8 and 13 in this book.

Objective: To determine that you are able to

1. Exhibit adequate knowledge of the elements of a circling approach procedure.

2. Select and comply with the appropriate circling procedure considering turbulence, wind shear, and considering the maneuvering capabilities of the aircraft.

3. Confirm the direction of traffic and adhere to all restrictions and instructions issued by ATC and the examiner.

4. Avoid exceeding the visibility criteria or descending below the appropriate circling altitude until in a position from which a descent to a normal landing can be made.

5. Maneuver the aircraft after reaching the authorized MDA and maintain that altitude between +100 feet, −0 feet and a flight path that permits a normal landing on a runway. The runway selected must be such that it requires at least a 90° change of direction, from the final approach course, to align the aircraft for landing.

■ Landing from a Straight-In or Circling Approach

References: 14 CFR Parts 61 and 91; IAP; *Instrument Flying Handbook; AIM;* Chapters 5, 8, and 13 in this book.

Objective: To determine that you are able to

1. Exhibit adequate knowledge of the pilot's responsibilities, and the environmental, operational, and meteorological factors that affect a landing from a straight-in or circling approach.
2. Make transition at the DA/DH, MDA, or visual descent point to a visual flight condition, allowing for safe visual maneuvering and a normal landing.
3. Adhere to all ATC (or examiner) advisories such as: NOTAMs, wind shear, wake turbulence, runway surface, braking conditions, and other operational considerations.
4. Complete appropriate checklist items for the prelanding and landing phase.
5. Maintain positive aircraft control throughout the complete landing maneuver.

EMERGENCY OPERATIONS

Note to reader: The order of the introduction of the Tasks of EMERGENCY OPERATIONS has been changed by this writer to initially emphasize the items most important to *both* single- and multiengine instrument rating applicants.

■ Loss of Communications

Objective: You'll be expected to

1. Recognize the loss of communication.
2. Continue to the destination according to the flight plan.
3. Know when to deviate from the flight plan.
4. Know the timing for beginning an approach at the destination.

■ Approach with Loss of Primary Flight Instrument Indicators

Note: This Task may be considered satisfactory if you have successfully completed a nonprecision approach without using the attitude and heading indicators (in the appropriate class aircraft).

Objective: You'll be expected to

1. Exhibit adequate knowledge of the elements that relate to recognizing if the attitude indicator and/or heading indicator is inaccurate or inoperative and advise ATC or the examiner.
2. Advise ATC or the examiner anytime the aircraft is unable to comply with a clearance.
3. Demonstrate a nonprecision instrument approach without gyro attitude and heading indicators, using the objectives of a nonprecision approach.

■ Instrument Flight in a Multiengine Airplane

In addition to getting the usual airspeeds and power settings for engine performance at different phases of flight (holding, rate climbs, descents, etc.), you'll also have to have the right numbers for flying the airplane with an engine out.

For instance, you would need to know the numbers for best angle and rate of climb, maintaining altitude, or making a 500-fpm descent, clean and/or with the gear down.

One thing that multiengine pilots don't like to think about is a missed approach on one engine in solid IFR conditions. (They don't like to think of a for-real go-around on one in *VFR* conditions either.)

With an engine out, heading will again be a major problem; you'll have to directionally trim for the various regimes of flight: (1) straight and level, (2) the approach with *some* power and the break-out, and (3) landing with the throttle at idle. The heading will slide off rapidly at the initial power loss and will continually be a factor throughout the approach.

Altitude will also be a problem, particularly if the airplane is heavy and the density-altitude is high. *If you are IFR and lose an engine, a definite emergency exists;* and after you have the airplane under control, let ATC know that you must have priority (unless somebody else has *both* engines gone or has a fire).

The point is, with an engine out you'll want to make the runway the first time and should get plenty of dual instruction and drill for this.

In addition to the usual FAA book references, a couple have been added to each of the following Tasks for your information (see the Bibliography).

■ One Engine Inoperative During Straight and Level Flight and Turns (Multiengine)

References: 14 CFR Part 61; *Advanced Pilot's Flight Manual (APFM),* Chapter 15; *Flight Instructor's Manual (FIM),* Chapter 18.

Objective: Here it will be ascertained that you

1. Have and show adequate knowledge of the procedures used if engine failure occurs during straight and level flight and turns while on instruments.
2. Recognize engine failure simulated by the examiner during straight and level flight and turns.
3. Set all engine controls, reduce drag, and identify and verify the inoperative engine.
4. Establish the best engine-inoperative airspeed and trim the aircraft.
5. Verify the accomplishment of prescribed checklist procedures for securing the inoperative engine.
6. Establish and maintain the recommended flight attitude, as necessary, for best performance during straight and level and turning flight.
7. Attempt to determine the reason for the engine failure.
8. Monitor all engine control functions and make necessary adjustments.
9. Maintain the specified altitude within ±100 ft, if within the aircraft's capability, airspeed within ±10 knots, and the desired heading within ±10°.
10. Assess the aircraft's performance capability and decide an appropriate action to ensure a safe landing.
11. Avoid loss of aircraft control or attempted flight contrary to the engine-inoperative operating limitations of the aircraft.

■ Instrument Approach—One Engine Inoperative (Multiengine)

References: 14 CFR Part 61; *Instrument Flying Handbook;*
    APFM, Chapter 15; *FIM,* Chapter 18.

Objective: To make sure you are able to

1. Exhibit adequate knowledge by explaining the procedures used during an instrument approach in a multiengine aircraft with one engine inoperative.

2. Recognize promptly engine failure simulated by the examiner.

3. Set all engine controls, reduce drag, and identify and verify the inoperative engine.

4. Establish the best engine-inoperative airspeed and trim the aircraft.

5. Verify the accomplishment of prescribed checklist procedures for securing the inoperative engine.

6. Establish and maintain the recommended flight attitude and configuration for the best performance for all maneuvering necessary for the instrument approach procedures.

7. Attempt to determine the reason for the engine failure.

8. Monitor all engine control functions and make necessary adjustments.

9. Request and receive an actual or a simulated ATC clearance for an instrument approach.

10. Follow the actual or a simulated ATC clearance for an instrument approach.

11. Establish a rate of descent that will ensure arrival at the minimum descent altitude (MDA/DH) prior to reaching the missed approach point (MAP), with the aircraft continuously in a position from which descent to a landing on the intended runway can be made straight in or circling.

12. Maintain, where applicable, the specified altitude within 100 ft (if within the aircraft's capability), the airspeed within 10 knots, and heading within 10°.

13. Set the navigation and communication equipment used during the approach and use the proper communications technique.

14. Avoid loss of aircraft control or attempted flight contrary to the engine-inoperative operating limitations of the aircraft.

15. Comply with the published criteria for the aircraft approach category when circling.

16. Allow, while on the final approach segment, no more than three-quarter-scale deflection of either the localizer or glide slope or GPS indications, or within ± 10° or ¾ scale deflection of the nonprecision final approach course.

17. Complete a safe landing (most important item of all).

POSTFLIGHT PROCEDURES

■ Task—Checking Instruments and Equipment

References: 14 CFR Part 91; *Instrument Flying Handbook;*
    Chapters 2, 4, and 5 in this book.

Objective: To make sure you

1. Exhibit knowledge of elements relating to instrument and navigation equipment for proper operation.

2. Note all flight equipment for proper operation.

3. Note all equipment and/or aircraft malfunctions and make appropriate documentation of improper operation or failure of such equipment.

Practical test book is based on these references:

14 CFR Part 61: Certification: Pilots and Flight Instructors
14 CFR Part 91: General Operating and Flight Rules
AC 00-6: Aviation Weather
AC 00-45: Aviation Weather Services
FAA-H-8083-3A: Airplane Flying Handbook
FAA-H-8083-15: Instrument Flying Handbook
FAA-H-8083-21: Rotorcraft Flying Handbook
FAA-H-8083-25: Pilot's Handbook of Aeronautical Knowledge
AC 61-84: Role of Preflight Preparation
AC 90-48: Pilot's Role in Collision Avoidance
AC 120-51: Crew Resource Management Training (CRMT)
AIM: Aeronautical Information Manual
DPs: Standard Instrument Departures
STARs: Standard Terminal Arrivals
A/FD: Airport/Facility Directory
FDC NOTAM: National Flight Data Center Notice to Airmen
IAP: Instrument Approach Procedures
Pertinent Pilot Operating Handbooks and FAA-approved
    flight manuals
En Route Low-Altitude Chart(s)

This version of the practical test is to give you an overall look at the basic requirements current at this writing. You should get the latest FAA issuance when you work on the practical test, so you aren't caught short if maneuvers or limits have changed.

...AND BEYOND THE TESTS

Keep up your proficiency—After you get the instrument rating, try not to be too lordly with the noninstrument-rated pilots at the airport. Of course, you may be expected to do a little snowing, but hold it down to a dull roar. Remember that those VFR types have been sitting on the ground for a long time now, watching pilots like you take off into weather that has kept them haunting the Weather Service Office at Podunk Greater International Airport and other such well-known places. They squeaked in by the skin of their teeth (the airport went well below VFR minimums shortly after they got in and has been that way for days). The bitter part about it is that the tops are running only 3000 or 4000 ft. It's CAVU (Ceiling and Visibility Unlimited) above, and the weather at their destination is very fine VFR—and there they sit. You think about that as you complete the filing of your IFR flight plan and move toward your airplane. The VFR pilots in the FSS watch you, and you have a pretty good idea of what they're thinking ("She's filing IFR and is going..." or, "He doesn't look like he's got any more on the ball than I do.")

Since this sounds suspiciously like paragraph one of Chapter 1 of this book, it looks as if this is where we came in.

5 SYLLABUS

INSTRUMENT FLIGHT MANUAL SYLLABUS

A FLIGHT INSTRUCTOR'S CHECKLIST AND PILOT'S GUIDE TO THE INSTRUMENT RATING

CONTENTS

HOURLY BREAKDOWN—GROUND AND FLIGHT INSTRUCTION, 267

BOOKS AND EQUIPMENT, 268

INTRODUCTION, 268

STAGE 1 AIRPLANE PERFORMANCE AND BASIC INSTRUMENT FLYING, 269

UNIT 1   Instrument Rating Requirements and Outline of the Course, 269

UNIT 2   Introduction to the Flight Instruments—The Four Fundamentals, 269

UNIT 3   The Pitch Instruments, 271

UNIT 4   The Bank Instruments, 272

UNIT 5   The Four Fundamentals, 274

UNIT 6   Exercises Using the Four Fundamentals, 274

UNIT 7   Six Basic Maneuvers, 275

UNIT 8   Introduction to Partial-panel and a Review of Full-panel Instrument Flying, 276

UNIT 9   Partial-panel Exercises, 278

UNIT 10   The Six Basic Maneuvers, Partial-panel, 279

UNIT 11   Full-panel Exercises, 280

UNIT 12   Recoveries from Unusual Attitudes, Full- and Partial-panel, 281

UNIT 13   Stage Check, 282

STAGE 2 NAVIGATION AND COMMUNICATION, 283

UNIT 1   Navigational Aids and Instruments, 283

UNIT 2   Communications and ATC, 284

STAGE 3 PLANNING THE INSTRUMENT FLIGHT, 285

UNIT 1   Weather Systems and Weather Planning, 285

UNIT 2   Charts and Other Printed Aids, 287

UNIT 3   Planning the Navigation, 288

STAGE 4 THE INSTRUMENT FLIGHT, 289

UNIT 1   Before the Takeoff, 289

UNIT 2   Takeoff and Departure, 289

UNIT 3   En Route, 290

UNIT 4   The Instrument Approach and Landing, 291

UNIT 5   IFR Cross-country, 291

UNIT 6   IFR Cross-country, 291

UNIT 7   Basic Instrument Flying, 292

UNIT 8   Long IFR Cross-country, 293

STAGE 5 THE KNOWLEDGE TEST, 293

STAGE 6 THE PRACTICAL TEST, 294

UNIT 1   IFR Cross-country, 294

UNIT 2   Basic Instrument Flying, 295

UNIT 3   IFR Cross-country and Approaches, 295

UNIT 4   General Review and Extra Practice Flights, 295

UNIT 5   Final School Practical Check, 296

UNIT 6   FAA Practical Test, 296

HOURLY BREAKDOWN—GROUND AND FLIGHT INSTRUCTION

■ Stage 1—Airplane Performance and Basic Instrument Flying

	Ground	Flight
UNIT 1	1.0	0.0
UNIT 2	2.0	1.5
UNIT 3	1.5	1.0
UNIT 4	1.5	1.0
UNIT 5	1.0	1.5
UNIT 6	1.0	1.0
UNIT 7	1.0	1.5
UNIT 8	1.0	1.5
UNIT 9	1.0	1.0
UNIT 10	1.0	1.5
UNIT 11	1.0	2.0
UNIT 12	1.0	1.0
UNIT 13	1.0	1.5
	15.0	16.0

■ Stage 2—Navigation and Communications

	Ground	Flight
UNIT 1	3.0	0.0
UNIT 2	2.0	0.0
	5.0	0.0

■ Stage 3—Planning the Instrument Flight

	Ground	Flight
UNIT 1	6.0	0.0
UNIT 2	4.0	0.0
UNIT 3	1.0	2.0
	11.0	2.0

■ Stage 4—The Instrument Flight

	Ground	Flight
UNIT 1	2.0	0.0
UNIT 2	0.5	1.5
UNIT 3	2.0	0.0
UNIT 4	1.0	2.0
UNIT 5	1.0	2.0
UNIT 6	1.0	2.0
UNIT 7	1.0	1.5
UNIT 8	1.5	4.0
	10.0	13.0

■ Stage 5—The Knowledge Test

	Ground	Flight
Review	4.0	0.0
Practice Test (allow)	2.0	0.0
	6.0	0.0

■ Stage 6—The Practical Test

	Ground	Flight
UNIT 1	1.0	2.0
UNIT 2	1.0	2.0
UNIT 3	1.0	2.0
UNIT 4	2.0	2.0
UNIT 5	1.0	2.0
UNIT 6	3.0	3.0
	9.0	13.0

Total Hours	56 Ground	44 Flight

BOOKS AND EQUIPMENT

This syllabus is based on the use of the following books and equipment. They should be available for study and use by the instrument trainee and flight instructor during this course.

- *The Instrument Flight Manual (IFM)* (This Edition, of course).
- *The Flight Instructor's Manual (FIM).* For the flight instructors to cross-reference with this book.
- *Pilot's Operating Handbook (POH)* for the airplane being used. (Makes sense.)
- Flight computer (E6-B or electronic type).
- FAR/AIM(ASA 7005 132nd Place SE) Newcastle, WA 98059-3153.
- *Aviation Weather (AW)* AC 00-6 (or latest issuance).
- *Aviation Weather Services* (AWS) AC 00-45 (or latest issuance).
- Current en Route IFR Charts for the area of training.
- Current Approach Charts for the area of training plus other sample charts as directed by the instrument flight instructor.
- *Airport/Facility Directory (A/FD)* for the U.S. states of training.
- *Pilot logbook.*
- *Practical Test Standards* (latest) for the instrument rating (ASEL).

INTRODUCTION

This syllabus is written and included in this book to help the instrument instructor and the pilot, working on the instrument rating (ASEL) and is intended to serve as a checklist and guide from the first instrument lesson through the practical test for both parties. It is written to follow the order of this book, so here are the various instrument approaches are briefed in Units 3 and 4 of Stage 4 in preparation for the cross-country flights in Units 5 and 6. The instructor may be flying from, or near, airports that have the approaches covered in Stage 4. These approaches may be practiced *before* the cross-country phase is entered, but the instrument basics should be nearly completed *before* starting approaches. Sometimes the basics are left behind because of the temptation to "get on with it," only to show up as problems during the latter part of the cross-country and approach phases.

The ground and flight requirements for CFR 14 Part 61.65 and CFR 14 Part 141 Appendix C are met.

The syllabus is broken into Units rather than flights or specific ground instruction times, though time estimates are given. The times are just that, *estimates,* and may be changed by local conditions or requirements by the school or instructor for a particular trainee. In some cases the instructor may skip to a following Unit because of weather or other factors. At the end of each Unit the Assigned Reading is for preparation for the next Unit.

The use of flight simulators or flight training devices are covered in Parts 61.65, 141 Appendix C (4)(b1-4) and will depend on the flight school's operating approval.

I would appreciate comments and suggestions to make this syllabus more useful to the instructor *and* trainee.

William K. Kershner ATPC 442723 CFII
P.O. Box 3266
Sewanee, TN 37375

AIRPLANE PERFORMANCE AND BASIC INSTRUMENT FLYING

The biggest mistake made in instrument training is to move on too quickly to cross-country and approaches in the instrument syllabus, to the detriment of the trainee's progress. A too-early transition away from the basic instrument instruction will result in problems with the ATC flight portion of the training requiring a return to basics. The basics will be applied the rest of an instrument flying career in en route and approach work, and *should be covered thoroughly before moving on.*

UNIT 1—INSTRUMENT RATING REQUIREMENTS AND OUTLINE OF THE COURSE

■ **Ground Instruction—1.0 Hour.** Review of FAR 61.65. Briefly note the following as areas to be covered in the course.

____ Instrument rating requirements. (See Chapter 1 of this book.)
____ Ground training; aeronautical knowledge.
Aeronautical Information Manual.
  ____ ATC system and IFR operations.
  ____ IFR navigation and approaches.
  ____ Use of IFR en route and instrument approach procedure charts.
  ____ Weather reports and forecasts.
  ____ Safe and efficient operation of the aircraft under IFR rules.
  ____ Recognition of critical situations and windshear avoidance.
  ____ Aeronautical decision and judgment.
  ____ Crew resource management.
____ Flight proficiency.
  ____ Preflight preparation (flight planning).
  ____ Preflight procedures. Checking the weather and NOTAMs.
  ____ Preflight check.
  ____ Air traffic control clearances and procedures.
  ____ Flight by reference to instruments.
  ____ Navigation systems.
  ____ Instrument approach procedures.
  ____ Emergency operation.
  ____ Postflight procedures.
____ Aeronautical experience (minimums).
  ____ 50 hours of cross-country, 10 hours in airplanes.

____ 40 hours of actual or simulated instrument time.
  ____ 15 hours of instrument flight training by a CFII.
  ____ 3 hours of instrument instruction within 60 days in preparation for the practical test.
____ Cross-country flight of 250 NM along airways or ATC-directed routing.
  ____ Instrument approach at each airport.
  ____ Three different kinds of approaches with the use of navigation systems.
____ Use of approved flight simulators or approved flight training devices.
  ____ 30 hours may be used (FAR Part 142).
  ____ 20 hours may be used if not FAR Part 142.
____ Discussion of the instrument and COMM/NAV equipment available in the training airplane(s) and/or flight simulator/flight training device to be used in the course.
____ Papers required to be on board (A ROW).
____ Discussion of the trainee's and instructor's schedules for the course.

ASSIGNED READING.

Trainee: *IFM* Chapters 1, 2, and 4
Instructor: *FIM* Chapter 24

Comments _____

_____

_____

Instructor _____

Date _____ Ground Instruction _____

Trainee Initials _____

UNIT 2—INTRODUCTION TO THE FLIGHT INSTRUMENTS—THE FOUR FUNDAMENTALS

■ **Ground Instruction—2.0 Hours.** This will be an introduction to the flight instruments so that basic instrument flight instruction may start. More details on the operations and errors of these instruments in later briefings and flights. This period may be broken up into 2 sessions or more time may be used for ground instruction.

____ Basic T instrument arrangement.

____ Pitch instruments.

    ____ Attitude indicator.

    ____ Altimeter.

    ____ Airspeed.

    ____ Vertical speed indicator.

____ Bank instruments.

    ____ Attitude indicator. Used for both pitch and bank indications; so it is the center of the Basic T scan.

    ____ Heading indicator. Old and new types.

    ____ Turn and slip. Usually electric but may be vacuum. Measures yaw only. Operates on the principle of precession.

    ____ Turn coordinator. Usually electric-driven. Measures both roll and yaw; also, operates on principle of precession.

    ____ Standard-rate turn.

    ____ Magnetic compass. A short review of the compass as a heading instrument.

____ The instrument scan.

    ____ Cross-check. The flight instruments must be checked continuously. (The attitude indicator should be included in every sweep of the other instruments.)

    ____ Interpretation. Watch for *trends*; confirm with other instruments.

    ____ Control. Control the airplane through instrument indications and/or trends.

    ____ Use a slower scan in initial training and include all flight instruments.

    ____ Engine instruments should be checked routinely (not every scan but every couple of minutes).

____ Working speeds of the airplane. The instructor should have these figured out in advance of the ground school session for the particular trainer being used. Use the procedure as indicated in *FIM* Figures 24-1 and 24-2 and accompanying description.

    ____ Approach speed. This is the most important working speed. Gear down, flaps or partial flaps optional depending on the airplane. Probably no flaps used on the approach, but the speed should be chosen so that flaps may be extended after breaking out on final.

        ____ Power setting (rpm, or manifold pressure and rpm as applicable) for a 500-fpm descent at the chosen configuration (clean or dirty).

    ____ Holding. Clean configuration (no flaps, gear up if possible).

        ____ Should be close to the approach airspeed, if not the same.

        ____ Power setting. May vary slightly with weight and altitude.

        ____ Max endurance is found at lowest altitude for reciprocating engines. (ATC will control altitude, however.)

    ____ Max rate of climb speed. Vary (slightly) to match holding and/or approach speed.

____ Control and performance instruments.

    ____ Control instruments control the airplane's performance.

        ____ Attitude indicator.

        ____ Manifold pressure and tachometer or tachometer alone (fixed-pitch props).

    ____ Performance instruments. These indicate the actions of the airplane in straight and level, climbs, descents, and turns (the Four Fundamentals).

        ____ Airspeed. Controlled by elevator or stabilator.

        ____ Altimeter. Controlled by power; a trend indicator.

        ____ Heading indicator. Coordinated turns—always.

        ____ Turn Coordinator or turn and slip. Coordinated turns.

        ____ Vertical speed indicator. A trend instrument.

Note each of the control and performance instruments *briefly*; more detail will be given in later ground and flight instruction.

____ Primary and supporting instruments.

    ____ Primary—describe. The instrument that is primary at the initiation of a maneuver may be *supporting* as the maneuver progresses.

    ____ Supporting—describe. The supporting instrument may return to primary as a maneuver is completed.

This syllabus (and the references) *does not* subscribe to the primary and supporting concept, considering it to be confusing for many trainees.

■ Flight Instruction—1.5 Hours

____ Preflight check. Point out additional checks for IFR work but no detail.

____ Normal pretakeoff check and climb. Suction gage and ammeter(s) are more important now.

____ The Four Fundamentals and the instrument indications. (Not hooded and using full-panel.) Set up the working airspeeds and power settings.

    ____ Straight and level.

        ____ Set up the scan.

        ____ Corrections for altitude excursions.

        ____ Corrections for heading excursions.

    ____ Climb.

        ____ Correction for "torque"; a bigger problem on instruments.

        ____ Airspeed control.

    ____ Descents.

        ____ Set up the proper airspeed and power setting (clean) for a 500-fpm descent.

        ____ Power required for descents at 500 fpm (with gear down, as applicable).

    ____ Holding (always in cleanest configuration).

        ____ Set up airspeed for holding if different from approach or climb speeds.

_____ Turns.

    _____ Standard-rate turn practice.

_____ Return to airport.

    _____ Trainee is vectored back to the airport by instructor, using instruments but not hooded.

    _____ Prelanding checklist.

    _____ Check brake pedal pressure.

_____ Normal pattern and landing.

_____ Postflight instruction.

    _____ Evaluation.

    _____ Review.

ASSIGNED READING.

Trainee: _IFM_ Chapters 3 and 4
Instructor: _FIM_ Chapter 24

Comments _____

_____

_____

Instructor _____

Date ____ Ground Instruction _____ Flight Time _____

Aircraft type/model _____ N number _____

Trainee Initials _____

UNIT 3—THE PITCH INSTRUMENTS

■ **Ground Instruction—1.5 Hours.** This ground session is a more detailed look at the pitch instruments than in Unit 2 and is the first Unit in which the hood is used. The instruction is a briefing for the introduction in flight of the various instruments, one-by-one. It is very important that the trainee have an excellent foundation of the instruments before moving on to navigation. A few instrument instructors fail to understand this and find that retrograde training must occur, which is bad for the learning process and morale.

_____ Attitude Indicator (A/I).

    _____ Indications on the face for various pitch attitudes (for the particular training airplane).

    _____ The attitude indicator is just that, does not show performance.

    _____ Various attitude/power combinations will be used during this flight to show the trainee the technique in how to use the A/I to change or maintain a chosen attitude.

_____ Altimeter (ALT).

    _____ Altimeter as a performance instrument for constant altitude control.

    _____ Altimeter as a trend instrument.

    _____ The altimeter is the most important pitch instrument for IFR flying.

    _____ At cruise, altitude may be corrected by pitch control.

_____ Airspeed Indicator (ASI).

    _____ Best performance instrument for proper climb schedule.

    _____ If the airspeed is off for a given condition (climb, descent, approach) _do not_ try to get the required value immediately. Make a slight correction then check the airspeed response.

    _____ Trim is _very important_ in instrument flying for long-term airspeed control.

_____ Vertical Speed Indicator (VSI). A trend and vertical rate instrument.

    _____ Discuss briefly the principle of operation.

        _____ Resulting 6- to 9-second lag.

_____ Discuss the pitch instrument exercises to be done on this flight.

Of approximately 15 minutes of flight on each instrument, 10 minutes will be hooded.

■ **Flight Instruction—1.0 Hour** (including preflight check).

_____ Preflight check. Point out in more detail the antennas and other added instrument flight equipment. Heated pitot/static tube, location of the static port(s).

    _____ Point out the communications antenna; note that the antenna on top may be blanketed when directly overhead the station transmitting and the bottom antenna may not be useful when sitting (for instance) directly under the tower's communications antenna.

_____ Start. Assure that all avionics equipment is OFF to avoid damage during start. (A master radio switch is useful.) Use the prestart and start checklist.

    _____ Emphasize that a checklist is even more important in IFR work because the pilot will be in IMC and committed to the system.

    _____ Cold or hot start procedures as needed.

_____ Depending on the locale and the trainee's previous experience, ATIS, clearance delivery, and ground control may be monitored or simulated. For some trainees, the instructor should handle all communications initially.

_____ Taxi. Turn indicator operates properly. Some may have an OFF-ON switch.

_____ Pretakeoff check. Use checklist.

    _____ Items for VFR flight.

    _____ Items for IFR flight. Instructor points out the added importance of setting the heading indicator correctly to magnetic compass (_IFM_ Figure 2-21).

_____ Normal takeoff and climb to the practice area and smooth air.

    _____ Pitch instrument indications during the climb. (Refer to the heading and bank instruments as necessary to maintain a proper course.)

_____ Attitude indicator (A/I) set to zero pitch at cruise. (Visual, then hooded.)

    _____ Maintain level flight (wings level).

    _____ Make minor changes up and down, using pitch lines and bar widths, as applicable and note effects on other instruments.

_____ Return to normal cruise maintaining a level pitch attitude. (Make turns as necessary to stay in the practice area.)

_____ Altimeter (ALT). Normal cruise.

_____ Maintain level flight with altimeter as major reference-visual, then hooded.

_____ Ease the nose up and down for minor altitude variations; check with attitude indicator.

_____ Altimeter reactions to rate of pitch change.

_____ Hold constant altitude using the altimeter _and_ attitude indicator.

_____ Lose or gain 200 feet of altitude by no more than one bar width or a selected marker pitch change.

_____ Return to original altitude using the same technique.

_____ Altitude changes by cross-checking altimeter _and_ attitude indicator. (_FIM_ Figure 24-7.)

_____ Level flight altitude held to within ±20-foot deviations.

_____ Airspeed indicator (ASI). This may be the first time some trainees have noticed the actions of the airspeed during _very minor_ pitch changes in straight and level flight.

_____ Straight and level cruise flight (visual, then hooded).

_____ Minor changes in pitch. Note slow change in airspeed.

_____ Large changes in pitch. Note reaction of airspeed.

_____ Straight and level with the ASI as the primary reference for pitch.

_____ Fly straight and level at cruise, using cross-check of airspeed, altimeter, and attitude indicator.

_____ Trim as an aid to pitch control.

Break

_____ Vertical speed indicator (VSI) and instantaneous VSI (or IVSI).

_____ At cruise (smooth air) maintain a constant zero indication (visual, then hooded).

_____ Make predetermined pitch changes with the attitude indicator and note the response of the VSI.

_____ Set up 500-fpm climbs and descents using the VSI.

_____ Make altitude deviations from level flight at 200 fpm and 100 fpm, with the VSI being the primary reference but cross-check with A/I, ALT, and ASI.

_____ Cross-check A/I, ALT, ASI, and VSI in straight and level, climb, and descent exercises (hooded).

_____ Return to airport (visual).

_____ Postflight discussion. Instructor reviews:

_____ Preflight check.

_____ Start.

_____ Taxi.

_____ Pretakeoff check.

_____ Takeoff.

_____ Climb.

_____ Pitch control.

_____ Altitude control.

_____ Cross-check.

_____ Interpretation.

_____ Control.

_____ Smoothness.

ASSIGNED READING.

Trainee: _IFM_ Chapters 3 and 4
Instructor: _FIM_ Chapters 24–25

Comments _____

_____

_____

Instructor _____

Date _____ Ground Instruction _____ Flight Time _____

Aircraft type/model _____ N number _____

Trainee Initials _____

UNIT 4—THE BANK INSTRUMENTS

The purpose of this Unit is to introduce the bank instruments and to establish the basics of the operation and reaction of these flight instruments. An approved flight simulator or flight training device may be used for this Unit.

■ Ground Instruction—1.5 Hours

_____ Review the instrument scan.

_____ Review briefly the pitch instrument flight before moving on to the bank instruments.

_____ Standard-rate turn.

_____ 3° per second.

_____ Rule of thumb for the bank required for a standard-rate turn: (Airspeed in knots, divided by 10 and then add one-half of that result.) At 100 knots: 100/10 = 10 + ½ of 10 = 15°.

_____ The standard-rate turn is used to avoid too-steep banks and the resulting inadvertent spirals.

_____ Attitude indicator.

_____ This instrument directly indicates pitch _and_ bank and is the center of the instrument scan.

_____ The attitude indicator may be used to set up a standard-rate turn using the rule of thumb just discussed.

_____ The attitude indicator reacts to airplane acceleration by showing a more nose-up indication. This could be critical on a very low visibility or instrument takeoff because the pilot could lower the nose to the "correct" attitude and hit obstacles.

_____ Except for practice exercises, when *correcting* to headings, the pilot should use the degrees of bank equal to the degrees to be turned, *up to the bank required for a standard-rate turn.*

_____ Heading indicator.

    _____ Gives an indirect indication of bank. (Assume a balanced turn.) A high rate of heading change means a steep bank, and (obviously) a slow rate of heading change means a shallow bank.

    _____ Repeat: *Correcting* to heading, the pilot should use the degrees of bank equal to the degrees to be turned, *up to the bank required for a standard rate turn.* Do not exceed the standard-rate turn in normal (actual) instrument flying.

_____ Turn indicator. Turn and slip (T/S) or turn coordinator (T/C).

    _____ Needle or small airplane indirectly indicates the bank attitude of the airplane. When the airplane is banked (ball centered), it is turning, the rate of turn being proportional to the angle of bank.

    _____ Turn coordinator also indicates roll for roll-in and roll-out of turn.

    _____ Turn and slip (needle) only indicates rate of *yaw* or nose movement.

    _____ The advantage of these instruments is that they will not tumble, and they normally have a source of power (electric) different from that of the attitude indicator or heading indicator.

_____ Introduction of a simple clearance.

■ **Flight Instruction—1.0 Hour.** Plan to spend no more than 15 minutes (10 minutes hooded) on each of the three bank instruments. If the trainee is not too fatigued, a short period of practice using full-panel is suggested.

_____ Preflight check. Review any unclear areas of the preflight check including pointing out various antennas but not in detail. Use a checklist.

_____ Starting. Avionics must be OFF. Use a prestarting and starting checklist.

_____ Taxi. Check operations of the turn indicator.

_____ Pretakeoff check. Use a checklist. Five minutes from start to takeoff is a minimum time for gyro spin-up.

_____ Takeoff. Trainee makes visual takeoff and then may make hooded climb with the instructor keeping a sharp lookout.

_____ Trainee makes 90° climbing turns (hooded) to reach practice area and altitude.

_____ Trainee practice. Plan on 15 minutes per instrument (10 minutes of this time, hooded).

    _____ Attitude indicator (A/I).

        _____ 5° constant bank for 90°. Fly straight and level for a few seconds, then reverse the turn.

        _____ Practice constant banks of 10°, 15°, 20°, 25°, and 30°, then reverse directions. Banks should be maintained within ±5°.

    _____ Instructor places the attitude indicator in various banks (shallow and medium, left and right) to assure the trainee's understanding and correct reading of the instrument.

    _____ Practice pitch and bank control using the attitude indicator.

_____ Heading indicator. The attitude indicator will be used as an aid to the H/I.

    _____ Straight flight.

    _____ 180° turns—10° banks, then 20° banks. Note difference in rates.

    _____ Straight and level flight, all flight instruments except turn indicator.

    _____ Practice 90°, 180°, and 360° turns (15° banks) using all flight instruments except turn indicator.

_____ Turn indicator. (All turns ball-centered!)

    _____ (1) Straight and level at cruise. Check heading with centered turn indication and ball.

    _____ (2) Cover attitude and heading indicators and have trainee fly straight and level for 2 minutes (smooth air). Uncover and check heading.

    _____ (3) Reverse course and repeat.

    _____ Repeat (2) and (3) until the heading is within ±5° (smooth air).

_____ Use all instruments for straight and level and selected turn sequences done earlier.

_____ Return to airport.

    _____ Trainee may be "vectored" back to the vicinity of the airport hooded if fatigue is not a factor. Then visual pattern entry.

    _____ Checklist (visual).

    _____ *(Check brake pedal pressure before every landing.)*

    _____ Traffic pattern entry.

    _____ Landing.

    _____ Taxi.

    _____ Shutdown and securing of airplane.

    _____ Fueling.

_____ Postflight discussion. The instructor will evaluate and discuss the following as applicable:

    _____ Heading control.

        _____ Attitude indicator only.

        _____ Heading indicator only.

        _____ Turn indicator only.

        _____ All instruments.

    _____ Altitude control.

        _____ Attitude indicator only.

        _____ Altimeter indicator only.

        _____ Airspeed indicator only.

        _____ Vertical speed indicator.

        _____ All instruments.

ASSIGNED READING.

Trainee: *IFM* Chapter 4
Instructor: *FIM* Chapters 24–28

Comments _____

_____

_____

Instructor _____

Date ____ Ground Instruction _____ Flight Time _____

Aircraft type/model _____ N number _____

Trainee Initials _____

UNIT 5—THE FOUR FUNDAMENTALS

This Unit is used to tie together the use of the pitch and bank instruments and to introduce the Four Fundamentals (straight and level, climbs, descents, and turns). Full-panel.

■ Ground Instruction—1.0 Hour

____ Review the earlier flights and resolve questions as necessary.
____ Review the working airspeeds of the airplane.
____ Four Fundamentals.
    ____ Straight and level at 65% (cruise) power.
        ____ Power and expected IAS range.
        ____ Airspeed for holding.
    ____ Climb.
        ____ Airspeed and power for best rate of climb.
        ____ Power for climbs at 500-fpm.
        ____ Constant-rate climbs.
        ____ Constant-airspeed climbs (most desired).
        ____ Torque corrections and rudder trim for extended climbs.
    ____ Descent.
        ____ Airspeed and power setting for a 500-fpm clean descent.
        ____ Airspeed and power setting for a 500-fpm descent for an instrument approach configuration.
    ____ Vertical exercises (also called vertical S-1 [*FIM* Figure 24–17 and *IFM* Figure 4-17]).
        ____ Climb at holding or climb speed (as selected) for 2 minutes at 500 fpm.
        ____ Two minutes level at that speed.
        ____ Two-minute descent at that speed at 500 fpm.
    ____ Turns. Use all instruments.
        ____ Standard-rate turns, 90°, 180°, and 360°, each interspersed with 1-minute straight and level at cruise speed.
        ____ Calibrating the turn indicator (needle or turn coordinator).
____ Return to airport.
    ____ Instructor may discuss vectoring of the trainee back to the airport (hooded) for a visual pattern approach and entry.

■ Flight—1.5 Hours (Full-panel)

____ Preflight check. (Instructor will supervise and review earlier checks.)
____ Starting.
____ Taxi.
____ Pretakeoff check.
____ Takeoff. Visual, with hooded climb-out at a safe altitude.
____ Climbs, 90° turns at standard rate.
    ____ Torque correction.
____ Level off and 2 minutes straight and level, reverse course and repeat.
____ Level at holding speed for 2 minutes. (Hooded, full-panel.)
    ____ Transition from cruise to holding speed ±100-foot altitude deviation.
    ____ Straight and level, ±100 feet, 10 knots. (Deviation allowance will be tightened up later.)
____ Vertical S. (Hooded, full-panel.)
    ____ Climb at 500 fpm for 2 minutes at chosen climb (or holding pattern airspeed as required).
    ____ Level for 2 minutes at holding airspeed.
    ____ Descent for 2 minutes at 500 fpm at holding airspeed.
    ____ Level for 2 minutes at holding airspeed. Repeat the exercises as required or time allows.
    ____ 180° turn at the end of each 2-minute straightaway.
____ Return to airport.
    ____ Instructor vectors hooded trainee to vicinity of airport, then a visual pattern entry and landing after use of checklist.
____ Shutdown and postflight check.

ASSIGNED READING.

Trainee: *IFM* Chapter 4
Instructor: *FIM* Chapter 24

Comments _____

_____

_____

Instructor _____

Date ____ Ground Instruction _____ Flight Time _____

Aircraft type/model _____ N number _____

Trainee Initials _____

UNIT 6—EXERCISES USING THE FOUR FUNDAMENTALS

This Unit will review Unit 5 and introduce new exercises to use to pin down possible full-panel scan problems and to assure a solid background in flying the Four Fundamentals.

■ Ground Instruction—1.0 Hour

____ The instrument scan. Review any possible problems from the last Unit.

____ Four Fundamentals: airspeeds, pitch attitudes, and banks for each, as applicable.

    ____ Straight and level. Start at cruise (65%) and at a *constant altitude*; make transitions by reducing airspeed in 10-knot intervals until an airspeed of 1.2 V_{SI} is reached. Reverse procedure in 10-knot intervals (180° turns can be made [hooded] to stay in the practice area).

____ Vertical S-2. (*FIM Figure 24–18.*)

____ Introduction to the holding pattern (*not* using a reference such as a VOR or making wind corrections). Two-minute legs.

____ *Introduction of the clock to the scan.*

■ Flight—1.0 Hour

____ Preflight, start, pretakeoff check, and visual takeoff made by the trainee.

____ Hooded climb to the practice area. The instructor may require a series of 90° climbing turns.

____ Level at the practice altitude:

    ____ Straight and level for 2 minutes.

    ____ Climb at 500 fpm for 2 minutes.

    ____ Straight and level for 2 minutes.

    ____ 180° turn (left) at standard rate.

    ____ Straight and level for 2 minutes.

    ____ 180° turn (right) at standard rate.

    ____ 2-minute straight descent, repeat as time allows.

____ Holding (full-panel, hooded).

    ____ Establish holding airspeed.

    ____ 2-minute legs "in the clear."

    ____ Hold left and right turns.

    ____ Introduce descending in a holding pattern.

____ Return to airport (hooded).

    ____ Checklist.

    ____ Instructor vectors airplane into downwind leg, base, and final (traffic permitting). Trainee removes hood on final and lands airplane.

____ Postflight checklist.

ASSIGNED READING:

Trainee: *IFM* Chapter 4
Instructor: *FIM* Chapter 24

Comments _____

_____

_____

Instructor _____

Date ____ Ground Instruction _____ Flight Time _____

Aircraft type/model _____ N number _____

Trainee Initials _____

UNIT 7—SIX BASIC MANEUVERS

This Unit allows the trainee to use the Four Fundamentals in a practical manner for "realistic" situations. This concept was covered in Chapter 15 of *The Student Pilot's Flight Manual* and was intended as a practical approach for the low-time pilot to get out of a hazardous IMC condition.

■ Ground Instruction—1.0 Hour

____ Review Unit 5 briefly for questions and discussions of unclear areas.

____ The Six Basic Maneuvers covered in the order that they might occur in an actual situation. These will be done full-panel and hooded.

    ____ Recovery from an approach to a power-on spiral.

        ____ This is the most common loss of control.

        ____ Reduce power.

        ____ Level the wings using the attitude indicator.

        ____ Back pressure as needed to bring the nose up to level. (Don't overshoot! Nose may *rise* as wings are leveled, so attention must be paid to pitch attitude to avoid a nose-high attitude.)

    ____ Recovery from an approach to a turning, power-on stall.

        ____ Primary need is to reduce the angle of attack, then level wings.

        ____ Add power, if not already used, to decrease altitude loss.

        ____ Lower the nose *below* level flight position (on attitude indicator) to assure no secondary stall.

    ____ Descending turn to a predetermined altitude/heading.

    ____ Climbing turn to a predetermined altitude/heading.

        ____ The problem is complete when *both* the predetermined *altitude and heading* have been attained. If the altitude is reached first; the airplane is leveled off and the turn continued. In others, the turn is complete, but straight climb/descent is required to attain the altitude.

    ____ 180° constant-altitude turn. This may be needed to reverse course but an ATC clearance should be obtained if done in real life. It is more of a maneuver for a non-instrument rated pilot who encounters unexpected IMC conditions.

    ____ Straight and level. This is needed to get back to VMC conditions after the recovery has been completed.

____ Instrument takeoff (ITO). Depending on the trainee's previous progress, the ITO may be introduced at this time.

    ____ Primarily a training maneuver.

    ____ Hazardous because of using ITO when below *approach* minimums.

    ____ Ensure sufficient time after engine start so that gyros are up to proper rpm.

    ____ ITO procedure (*IFM* Fig. 4-42; *FIM* Fig. 24-15.)

——— Set attitude indicator (A/I) for the proper ground attitude of the airplane.

——— Line up on runway and set heading indicator.

——— Taxi forward to straighten nose or tail-wheel.

——— Apply full power (smoothly!).

——— Use heading indicator (H/I) to maintain a straight path on the runway.

——— Instructor gives *commands for correction* ("right," "left") on practice ITOs.

——— At the prechosen airspeed, the airplane is rotated to a marker or value on the attitude indicator.

——— After lift-off maintain the proper pitch indication on the A/I as the other instruments are scanned. (Warn again of the A/I and the acceleration factor on takeoff.)

——— When the altimeter indicates altitude increase, relax the back pressure to avoid a too-high nose position as the airplane leaves ground effect.

——— Retract the landing gear (if applicable) at a safe (at least 100 feet) altitude.

——— Maintain the proper climb airspeed.

——— Review holding.

■ **Flight—1.5 Hours**

——— Preflight check, starting, pretakeoff check.

——— Instructor gives a simple clearance with departure instructions.

——— Climb (hooded) to practice area and altitude, using 90° standard-rate turns. (Initial turn 45° from chosen course, then 90° turns left and right.)

——— The Six Basic Maneuvers (full-panel, hooded).

——— Recovery from an approach to a power-on spiral.

——— Climbing turn to a predetermined altitude and heading.

——— Recovery from an approach to a turning power-on stall.

——— Descent to a predetermined altitude and heading.

——— 180° constant-altitude turn.

——— Straight and level flight.

——— Holding practice, 2-minute, then 1-minute legs (hooded). A clock is added to the scan.

——— Return to airport (hooded). Instructor may act as approach control and ASR operator at an airport without a control tower.

——— Checklist (use checklist and check brake pedals' pressure).

——— Visual final for landing (naturally).

——— Postflight checklist.

——— Postflight debriefing.

ASSIGNED READING

> Trainee: *IFM* Chapter 4
> Instructor: *FIM* Chapter 24

Comments _____

_____

_____

Instructor_____

Date_____ Ground Instruction_____ Flight Time _____

Aircraft type/model_____ N number _____

Trainee Initials_____

UNIT 8—INTRODUCTION TO PARTIAL-PANEL AND A REVIEW OF FULL-PANEL INSTRUMENT FLYING

■ **Ground Instruction—1 Hour.** This Unit will introduce partial-panel flying for the Four Fundamentals. Partial-panel (P/P) recoveries from unusual attitudes will not be covered in this Unit. Instruments not in use for a particular exercise should be covered.

——— Straight and level flight without the attitude indicator and heading indicator and other combinations.

——— Attitude and heading indicators should be covered if inoperative or undependable in actual IMC conditions.

——— New scan.

——— The vertical speed indicator as a trend instrument.

——— Corrections for suspected excursions of heading.

——— Discuss instrument combinations for practice (*IFM* Figure 4-25).

——— Climbs.

——— Torque is a particular problem in climbs on partial-panel.

——— Climb entry.

——— Steps: (1) Climb attitude (airspeed). (2) Climb power. (3) Torque correction. (4) Trim.

——— Establish climb.

——— Climbing turn.

——— Leveling from the climb.

——— Steps: (1) Ease over to stop altimeter. (2) Ease off the torque correction. (3) Reduce power at cruise. (4) Trim.

——— Constant-altitude turns.

——— Airspeed decrease of 3% to maintain a constant altitude in a partial-panel standard-rate level turn (*IFM* Figure 4-26 C).

——— Tendency to gain altitude on roll-out.

——— Brief review of possible instrument combinations for the turn.

——— Descents.

——— Review power required for descents at 500 fpm.

_____ Clean.

_____ Approach configuration.

_____ Lead level-off by 10% of the rate of descent.

_____ Descending turns at 500 fpm (clean).

_____ Combinations of instruments (*IFM* Figure 4-27).

_____ Return to airport.

_____ Normal pattern procedures.

_____ Special pattern procedures.

■ Flight—1.5 Hours

_____ Preflight check, start, taxi, and pretakeoff check.

_____ Instrument takeoff—full-panel (optional).

_____ Climb and climbing turns to the practice area hooded (full-panel).

_____ Level off and set power hooded (full-panel).

_____ Partial-panel. Turn indicator, altimeter, airspeed, and vertical speed indicator. Add clock to scan.

_____ Straight and level flight at cruise for 4 minutes.

_____ Reverse course (P/P). Straight and level for 4 minutes.

_____ Climb straight ahead at airspeed for best rate of climb.

_____ Straight and level for 2 minutes. (Make turns as necessary to stay within the practice area.)

_____ Descent, clean for 2 minutes at 500 fpm.

_____ Straight and level for 2 minutes.

_____ 180° and 360° turns at standard rate.

_____ Combinations of flight instruments (hooded). Some or all of these may be done at the instructor's discretion and based on the trainee's progress.

_____ Straight and level (*IFM* Figure 4-25) using only the following:

_____ Airspeed, attitude indicator, altimeter.

_____ Heading indicator, altimeter.

_____ Turn indicator, attitude indicator, altimeter.

_____ Airspeed, turn indicator.

_____ Heading indicator, vertical speed indicator.

_____ Airspeed indicator, heading indicator.

_____ Climbs (*IFM* Figure 4-28).

_____ Full-panel, then:

_____ Attitude indicator covered for 500-fpm climb (2 minutes).

_____ Turn indicator, heading indicator, altimeter, vertical speed. Climb to a predetermined altitude and heading using only these instruments.

_____ Full-panel climb to a predetermined altitude and heading.

_____ Descents (*IFM* Figure 4-27). Power instruments will be part of the scan.

_____ Straight descent without attitude indicator at 500 fpm, clean.

_____ Timed *straight* descent without attitude or heading indicators. Lead level-off altitude by 10% of the rate of descent.

_____ Timed straight descent (500 fpm for 2 minutes) using power instruments, attitude indicator, and vertical speed. Level off after 2 minutes and uncover altimeter.

_____ A timed descending turn to a predetermined altitude and heading (heading indicator and altimeter covered). Uncover to check results.

_____ Constant-altitude, standard-rate turns (*IFM* Figure 4-26). Practice the following combinations in addition to the standard partial-panel (turn indicator, airspeed, altimeter, and vertical speed).

_____ Attitude indicator and altimeter. After starting at a particular heading, a timed standard-rate turn is made to a prechosen heading. The heading indicator is then uncovered to check results.

_____ Turn indicator and altimeter. After the timed turn is completed, uncover the heading indicator to check results. Bank required for a standard rate turn is airspeed (knots) divided by 10 plus one-half of the result. For instance, 130 knots/10 = 13 + 6 $\frac{1}{2}$° = 19 $\frac{1}{2}$° (call it 20°).

_____ Standard-rate turns, airspeed, and heading indicator. Let airspeed settle at cruise, then decrease airspeed 3% to maintain altitude in a standard-rate turn. Altimeter is uncovered and checked for results after the roll-out at a prechosen heading.

_____ Hooded return to vicinity of the airport if the trainee is not too fatigued.

_____ Normal (visual) pattern and landing.

_____ Postflight check.

Note: This Unit may be broken into two flights or more as the instructor feels necessary.

ASSIGNED READING:

Trainee: *IFM* Chapter 4, Partial-Panel
Instructor: *FIM* Chapter 24

Comments_____

_____

_____

Instructor_____

Date _____ Ground Instruction _____ Flight Time _____

Aircraft type/model _____ N number _____

Trainee Initials _____

UNIT 9—PARTIAL-PANEL EXERCISES

This Unit is for further practice flying with concentration on the turn and slip or turn coordinator, airspeed, altimeter, and vertical speed instruments (attitude indicator and heading indicator covered).

■ Ground Instruction—1.0 Hour

____ Review Unit 8 as needed (questions and answers).

____ The Four Fundamentals and combinations using only the partial-panel instruments.

    ____ Straight and level. If the needle or small airplane is deflected, stop it and turn in the opposite direction for an equal amount of time. The heading indicator is uncovered after a selected period of time to check heading accuracy. Trim is very important.

    ____ Calibrating procedure for the turn and slip or turn coordinator.

    ____ Standard-rate left and right turn practice; the tendency is to overbank.

    ____ Standard-rate level timed turns to a predetermined heading. Using altimeter, vertical speed indicator, and the concept of reducing the airspeed by 3% to maintain a constant altitude in the standard-rate turn. Uncover the heading indicator to check accuracy of the turn.

    ____ Straight climbs. The trainee will tend to chase the climb airspeed. Emphasis should be put on *easing* the nose up or down to regain the proper airspeed. Use slight forward or back pressure as needed, then wait and see. Trim. Uncover the heading indicator after a selected period of time to check accuracy of heading.

    ____ Climbing turns.

        ____ Climbing turns in each direction without a prechosen heading. Practice the technique of holding a constant airspeed and rate of turn. These may be interspersed with straight and level flight, descents, and descending turns (to be covered later in the briefing).

        ____ Climbing turns to a preselected heading.

        ____ Climbing turns to a preselected heading and altitude if time and the trainee's progress permit.

        ____ Straight descents. Review the airspeed power settings for 500-fpm straight descents in the clean configuration. These should be used alternately with straight climbs to keep the altitude within limits.

        ____ Straight descents in approach configuration at 500 fpm.

        ____ Descending turns to a predetermined altitude. There is a tendency to enter a spiral.

        ____ Descending turns to a predetermined altitude and heading.

■ Flight Instruction—1.0 Hour.

The brief exercises should be covered but only enough to assure that the trainee has an introductory understanding of the requirements of the Four Fundamentals using *partial-panel*. Additional practice sessions will be included in STAGE 1 or as a break and review in STAGE 2 (Navigation and Communications).

____ Visual takeoff and initial climb.

____ Hooded climb after a safe altitude is reached (full-panel).

____ Level off and cover attitude indicator.

____ Calibration of the turn and slip or turn coordinator (not hooded). Then cover heading indicator.

____ The Four Fundamentals and combinations (hooded).

    ____ Straight and level flight.

    ____ Constant-altitude, timed turns to a preselected heading.

    ____ Visual break.

    ____ Straight climbs.

    ____ Climbing turns to a preselected altitude.

    ____ Straight and level.

    ____ Visual break.

    ____ Descents to a preselected altitude.

    ____ Descents to a preselected altitude and heading.

    ____ Straight and level.

    ____ Visual break.

    ____ Climbing turns to a preselected altitude and heading.

    ____ Repeat the exercises as necessary.

____ Return to airport.

    ____ Instructor vectors the hooded trainee using *all* flight instruments.

    ____ Visual traffic pattern entry, pattern, and landing.

    ____ Postlanding and postshutdown procedures (checklist).

____ Postflight instruction.

    ____ Evaluation.

    ____ Review.

ASSIGNED READING:

Trainee: *IFM* Chapter 4, Recoveries from Unusual Attitudes

Instructor: *IFM* Chapter 4; *FIM* Chapter 24

Comments _____

_____

_____

Instructor _____

Date ____ Ground Instruction _____ Flight Time _____

Aircraft type/model _____ N number _____

Trainee Initials _____

UNIT 10—THE SIX BASIC MANEUVERS, PARTIAL-PANEL

This Unit is a follow-up to Unit 7, but the Six Basic Maneuvers will be done partial-panel as much as practicable.

■ Ground Instruction—1.0 Hour

____ Six Basic Maneuvers are covered in ground school in the order of their simplicity.

____ Straight and level.

    ____ Fly for at least 2 minutes (hooded) monitoring the turn indicator, altimeter, A/S, and vertical speed.

    ____ Uncover heading indicator to confirm heading. Make turns as necessary to stay in the practice area or to avoid controlled airspace as necessary and re-cover heading indicator.

    ____ Repeat the exercise as necessary.

____ 180° standard-rate, timed turns.

    ____ This exercise is to reverse course to avoid weather hazards or other IFR requirements.

    ____ Set up on a cardinal heading, then cover the heading indicator.

    ____ Timing may be done by starting the turn and counting "One thousand and one, one thousand and two, etc." for each 3° of turn, if a time piece is not available. (The clock with a sweep second hand was introduced back in Unit 6.)

____ Recovery from the start of a power-on spiral.

    ____ The spiral may be well started before the pilot is aware of it.

    ____ Most airplanes are designed to be slightly spirally unstable and will slowly and subtly enter a spiral if neglected, particularly in turbulence.

    ____ It is usually the result of distractions such as arranging or picking up dropped charts or approach plates.

    ____ Voice reports may be another distraction. Aviate, Navigate, Communicate.

    ____ Fly the airplane *first*. If charts or approach charts are dropped, check instruments, then pick up charts. Check instruments, then turn to general area of required charts. Check instruments, then return to the required chart area or approach chart. Do not neglect flying the airplane for more than 5 to 7 seconds at any time during distractions.

    ____ Steps in recovery.

        ____ Recognize the situation by the turn indicator, high and/or increasing airspeed, loss of altitude, and high rate of descent.

    ____ Reduce power.

    ____ Center the turn indicator with coordinated controls to level the wings.

    ____ As the wings are leveled, the nose will start to rise. (The pitch-up tendency depends directly on the airspeed.)

    ____ Check airspeed. When it hesitates or decreases, apply forward pressure. The pitch attitude is approximately level.

    ____ Check the altimeter and "fly" the closest 100-foot hand.

    ____ Keep the wings level with the turn coordinator.

    ____ As the airspeed approaches cruise, add power to cruise.

    ____ Perform climb-and-turn to a prechosen altitude and heading.

____ Climbing turn to a predetermined altitude and heading.

    ____ Starting from cruise, initiate a straight climb.

    ____ Then set up a standard-rate turn to the preselected heading.

    ____ If altitude is reached first, level off but continue the timed turn.

    ____ If estimated (timed) heading is reached first, roll-out and continue climb with close attention to keeping the turn indicator centered.

    ____ The exercise is complete when both the predetermined altitude and heading are reached.

____ Approach to a climbing stall (cruise power).

    ____ From level flight, instructor will ease the nose up to the stall attitude.

    ____ Trainee lowers the nose with forward pressure until the airspeed changes (hesitates or increases).

    ____ Full power is added as the nose is lowered.

    ____ Center the turn indicator. It's important that the *ball* be kept centered, particularly if the stall has broken; use rudder to center the ball.

    ____ When the altimeter hesitates, allow another 100 feet of descent to ensure staying out of a secondary stall.

    ____ Maintain that altitude.

    ____ Keep turn indicator centered as cruise airspeed is approached.

    ____ Reduce power to cruise setting.

____ Descending turn to a predetermined altitude and heading.

_____ From cruise flight, reduce power to descent value while slowing up to airspeed for descent.

_____ Descend and turn using turn indicator, airspeed, altimeter, and vertical speed.

_____ An uncontrolled spiral may result if attention wanders.

_____ When the predetermined altitude or heading is attained, stop that factor and continue to complete the other requirement. The exercise is complete when both are attained.

■ Flight Instruction—1.5 Hours

_____ Preflight check, pretakeoff check, takeoff (visual), and climb (full-panel, hooded) when out of the traffic pattern to the practice area under instructor's directions.

_____ Calibrate turn indicator, left and right 360° turn.

_____ Partial- or emergency-panel exercises (the Basic Six Maneuvers, hooded). Use airspeed, altimeter, turn indicator, and vertical speed for the following exercises.

_____ Straight and level flying on a predetermined heading (then cover the heading indicator). Check heading after a prespecified time.

_____ 180° level turns in each direction from a cardinal heading with 2- to 4-minute straight and level flying in between. Uncover heading indicator to check for accuracy.

_____ 180° turn, plus 2 to 4 minutes of straight and level. Uncover heading indicator.

Break: Trainee removes hood for 5 minutes of rest.

_____ Recovery from the start of a power-on spiral. Practice in both directions.

_____ Review briefly steps in recovery as covered in the ground instruction.

_____ Climbing turns to a predetermined altitude and heading.

_____ These criteria may be established _before_ the start of the power-on spiral or after the recovery.

Break: Five minutes of unhooded flight for a rest period.

_____ Recovery from the approach to a climbing stall. Briefly review stops, as covered in ground instruction.

_____ Descending turn(s) to a predetermined altitude and heading.

_____ Return to the airport visually. Make a normal pattern entry and landing.

_____ Postshutdown checklist and securing of airplane.

_____ Postflight instruction.

_____ Evaluation.

_____ Review.

ASSIGNED READING:

Trainee: _IFM_ Chapter 4 and Chapter 5, Review of the VOR

Instructor: _IFM_ Chapter 4; _FIM_ Chapter 24

Comments_____

_____

_____

Instructor_____

Date _____ Ground Instruction _____ Flight Time _____

Aircraft type/model _____ N number _____

Trainee Initials _____

UNIT 11—FULL-PANEL EXERCISES

This Unit repeats the use of full-panel so that the trainee will not get "fixed" on a partial-panel scan. Partial-panel (hooded) will be practiced during flights later in the syllabus.

If a VOR is available nearby (and the airplane is so equipped), introduction to holding at a fix should be introduced in this Unit. More-complex exercises should be done during this Unit as the trainee's skill increases. Otherwise, the instructor may choose to repeat one or more of the Units as necessary. This Unit will assume that repetition is not necessary and the trainee is ready to move on.

■ Ground Instruction—1.0 Hour

_____ Review earlier exercises, such as the Vertical S-1 and S-2.

_____ Introduction and/or brief review of the VOR.

_____ Holding patterns and entries at a constant altitude using the VOR (2-minute legs initially then 1-minute legs).

_____ Introduction of the Charlie pattern (_IFM_ Figure 4-22 and _FIM_ Figure 24-28). (The instructor may carry a diagram on the flight as a memory jogger but still should keep an eye out as safety pilot.)

_____ PAR (Precision Approach Radar) approach procedures.

_____ Review the instrument takeoff. Again, emphasize the hazards of taking off when conditions are so low that a return to the airport in an emergency would be impossible.

■ Flight—2.0 Hours

_____ Preflight check, pretakeoff check.

_____ Instrument takeoff (optional).

_____ Hooded climb to the practice area under the instructor's directions.

_____ Holding at a VOR. Introduction of headwind or tailwind on leg (_IFM_ Figure 4-24).

_____ Vertical S-1 and S-2.

Break: Trainee removes hood and takes a 5-minute break.

_____ Charlie pattern (_IFM_ Figure 4-22).

Break: Five minutes.

____ "Radar" vector by instructor to traffic pattern (full-panel, hooded).

____ Prelanding checklist complete, check brake pedal pressures.

____ PAR approach (traffic permitting) by instructor to "minimums." (Later, the instructor may keep the trainee under the hood, giving verbal instructions until touchdown on the runway, though this is more of a confidence-building exercise than for practical application.)

____ Postlanding, postflight checklist, and securing of the airplane.

____ Postflight instruction.

____ Evaluation.

____ Review.

ASSIGNED READING:

Trainee: *IFM* Chapter 4, Recoveries from Unusual Attitudes

Instructor: *FIM* Chapter 24, Unusual Attitudes and Situations

Comments _____

_____

_____

Instructor _____

Date ____ Ground Instruction _____ Flight Time _____

Aircraft type/model _____ N number _____

Trainee Initials _____

UNIT 12—RECOVERIES FROM UNUSUAL ATTITUDES, FULL- AND PARTIAL-PANEL

This is a repeat of Units 9 and 11 with the introduction to hooded or IMC spin recoveries. The training airplane may be restricted from spinning, but the subject should be covered in ground instruction.

■ Ground Instruction—1.0 Hour

____ Review earlier Units as necessary. (Instructor answers questions on maneuvers or procedures discussed or practiced earlier, including the Charlie pattern.)

____ Recoveries from unusual attitudes.

____ Spirals and approaches to stalls.

____ Full-panel.

____ Partial-panel.

____ Spin recoveries.

____ *Pilot's Operating Handbook* has precedent over the following procedures.

____ Attitude and heading indicators in most training aircraft are normally not available for spin recoveries (tumbled).

____ Indications of a spin (partial-panel) are:

____ Airspeed very low.

____ Turn indicator pegged in the direction of the rotation. Ball to left in instrument on pilot's side, right on right side of the panel.

____ Altimeter shows a high rate of descent.

____ Vertical speed indicator is pegged since the airplane may be descending at 7000 fpm or more.

____ Recovery procedure.

____ Power off.

____ Ailerons neutral.

____ Full rudder opposite to needle or small airplane in the turn indicator.

____ Ignore the ball position.

____ When the rudder hits the stop, apply brisk forward motion to the wheel or stick.

____ Airspeed starts to increase: neutralize the rudder and start the pull-out.

____ Airspeed hesitates: apply sufficient forward pressure to "stop" the altimeter at the nearest 100-foot indication.

____ Monitor the turn indicator to maintain straight flight.

____ As the airspeed approaches cruise, apply cruise power.

____ Climb and turn to a predetermined altitude and heading, using all instruments available.

____ Spiral recoveries.

____ Full-panel.

____ Partial-panel.

____ Approach to stall recoveries.

____ Full-panel.

____ Partial-panel.

____ Return to airport (visual) and land.

■ Flight Instruction—1.0 Hour

____ Preflight and pretakeoff checks. Checklist.

____ Instrument takeoff (optional).

____ Climb to practice area (hooded), initially full-panel then partial-panel.

____ Recoveries from unusual attitudes.

____ Approach to a climbing stall.

____ Full-panel.

____ Partial-panel.

____ Start of a power-on spiral.

____ Full-panel.

____ Partial-panel.

____ Spin recovery if airplane and airspace permit.

____ Suggest a break period of VFR flying.

____ Charlie pattern, if time permits.

____ Return to the airport. (Use checklist, check brake pedal pressure.)

_____ Instructor may choose to vector the trainee to the pattern for an ASR or PAR approach (hooded) or have the trainee return and land visually, depending on fatigue.

_____ Postlanding and shutdown procedures (checklist).

_____ Postflight instruction.

    _____ Evaluation.

    _____ Review.

ASSIGNED READING:

    Trainee: Review _IFM_ Chapter 4

    Instructor: _FIM_ Chapter 24

Comments _____

_____

_____

Instructor _____

Date _____ Ground Instruction _____ Flight Time _____

Aircraft type/model _____ N number _____

Trainee Initials _____

UNIT 13—STAGE CHECK

This will be a STAGE check to confirm that the trainee is competent and ready to move on to STAGE 2, the navigation and communications part of the training. The chief pilot or another flight instructor may conduct the check and mark grades 1 (excellent), 2 (good), 3 (average), 4 (below average), or 5 (failure) on this sheet.

■ **Ground—1.0 Hour.** The check pilot may review or ask questions on the following subjects of STAGE 1.

_____ Pitch instruments.

_____ Bank instruments.

_____ Scan.

_____ Working speeds of the airplane being used.

_____ Control and performance instruments.

_____ Primary and supporting instruments.

_____ The Four Fundamentals.

_____ Six Basic Maneuvers.

_____ Partial-panel instruments.

_____ Instrument takeoff (optional discussion).

■ **Flight—1.5 Hours**

_____ Preflight check.

_____ Starting.

_____ Taxi.

_____ Instrument takeoff (hooded optional).

_____ Climb (hooded) to practice area.

_____ Four Fundamentals (full-panel).

    _____ Straight and level.

    _____ Climbs.

    _____ Descents.

    _____ 180° and 360° standard-rate turns.

_____ Recoveries from unusual attitudes (partial-panel).

    _____ Approach to a climbing stall.

    _____ Recovery from the start of a power-on spiral.

_____ Vectors back to the airport (hooded, full-panel).

_____ Visual pattern entry, pattern, and landing.

_____ Postlanding procedures.

_____ Postshutdown and securing of the aircraft.

    _____ Evaluation.

    _____ Critique.

    _____ Review.

        _____ Headwork.

        _____ Air discipline.

        _____ Attitude toward flying.

ASSIGNED READING:

    Trainee: _IFM_ Chapter 5, VOR

    Instructor: _IFM_ Chapter 5, VOR; _FIM_ Chapter 25, VOR AIRWORK

Comments _____

_____

_____

Instructor _____

_____ Recommendation for STAGE 2.

_____ Recommendation for extra time and recheck.

Check pilot _____

Date _____ Ground Instruction _____ Flight Time _____

Aircraft type/model _____ N number _____

Trainee Initials _____

NAVIGATION AND COMMUNICATION

UNIT 1—NAVIGATIONAL AIDS AND INSTRUMENTS

There will be no flying in this Unit, which should be broken into two or three sessions.

■ Ground Instruction—3.0 Hours

____ VHF Omni Range.
  ____ Advantages and disadvantages (line of sight, etc.).
  ____ Frequency range (108.00–117.95 MHz).
  ____ VOR identification.
  ____ Accuracy.
  ____ Roughness.
  ____ VOR receiver check (FAR 91.171).
    ____ VOT (VOR Test facility).
    ____ Airborne receiver checks.
    ____ VOR receiver antennas.
  ____ Always identify the station.
  ____ Discuss the VOR receivers in the particular airplane being used for training.
  ____ VOR exercises.
    ____ Tracking TO and FROM the station.
    ____ Holding.
    ____ Double the angle off the bow (*IFM* Figure 5-14).
    ____ Time to the station.
    ____ Tracking around the station (*IFM* Figure 5-23).
    ____ Station passage indications (*AIM*).
    ____ VOR intersections using one or two receivers.
      ____ "Turning" the airplane (*IFM* Figures 5-7 and 5-11).
      ____ Set up FROM on the cross bearing VOR (*IFM* Figure 5-12).
____ HSI (Horizontal Situation Indicator) and the VOR (*IFM* Figure 5-15).
____ Non-Direction Beacon (NDB). Using the Automatic Direction Finder (ADF).
  ____ Advantages and disadvantages.
  ____ Homing and tracking.
  ____ Relative bearings plus heading equals course TO or FROM the station.

____ As navigation and approach aids, these are being replaced.
____ Three-letter identifiers (IDs) are Low and Medium Frequency (LF/MF) facilities.
____ Compass locators (ILS component). Refer to *IFM* Figure 5-26.
  ____ Frequencies, 190–535 kHz for NDBs.
  ____ Transmitters less than 25 watts, with a range of up to 15 miles.
  ____ Two-letter IDs. Outer Marker Locator (LOM) transmits first 2 letters of the 3-letter localizer identifier, middle marker transmits last 2, such as "BN" (outer locator) and " NA" (middle locator) for BNA (Nashville).
____ Timing to the station.
____ Tracking around the station.
____ Radio Magnetic Indicator (RMI).

Suggested Break Point

____ ILS (Instrument Landing System). See *IFM* Figure 5-42.
  ____ Localizer, theory of operation.
    ____ Frequency range: 108.1 to 111.95 MHz.
    ____ Tracking inbound and outbound on the front course.
    ____ Using the back course inbound.
    ____ ILS/DME arc.
  ____ Glide slope.
    ____ Different frequency but "paired" to localizer (*IFM* Figure 5-46).
      ____ Glide slope antennas.
      ____ Marker Beacon.
        ____ Marker beacon antennas.
      ____ ILS glide slope distortion and false courses.
      ____ Rate of descent table (*U.S. Terminal Procedures*).
  ____ Simplified Directional Facility (SDF).
  ____ Transponder.
    ____ FAR 91.215.
    ____ Modes A and C.
    ____ Flight plan designators /B, /U, etc.
    ____ Theory of operation (an airborne radar transceiver).

____ Codes: VFR and emergency codes.

____ Identification (IDENT) feature.

____ LORAN C.

____ Theory of operation.

____ Losing popularity with the advent of GPS.

____ Radar altimeter (*IFM* Figure 5-55).

____ Use over flat terrain.

____ Errors over mountainous terrain.

____ Global positioning system (GPS).

____ Satellites operated by the Department of Defense.

____ At least three satellites needed with timing corrections from a fourth.

____ Discuss equipment for the training aircraft (if available).

____ Visual descent point (VDP).

____ Nonprecision approach aid.

____ Examination and discussion of the navigation antennas on the airplane being used for the instrument course, plus looking at other airplanes on the flight line with different types of antennas.

____ Postflight instruction.

____ Evaluation.

____ Review.

ASSIGNED READING:

Trainee and Instructor: *IFM* Chapter 6

Comments _____

_____

_____

_____

Instructor_____

Date____ Ground Instruction_____ Flight Time _____

Aircraft type/model_____ N number _____

Trainee Initials_____

UNIT 2—COMMUNICATIONS AND ATC

This will be a ground session as was Unit 1 and may be broken into two or three sessions. If the trainee is unfamiliar with Flight Service Stations, towers, approach controls, or Air Route Traffic Control Centers, it is suggested that a visit be arranged on one or more of the instrument cross-countries. The variation of facility availability in various areas precludes a set schedule. The instructor can arrange tours or visits as training schedules allow. Reference for this session is the *AIM* and *Airport/Facilities Directory*.

■ **Ground Instruction—2.0 Hours.** (AIM Chapter 4.)

____ Flight Service Stations (FSS or AFSS).

____ Provide pilot briefings, en route communications VFR search and rescue, Flight Watch,

relay ATC clearances, originate NOTAMs, monitor NAVAIDs, broadcast available weather and National Airspace System information, and receive and process IFR flight plans.

____ Airports without an operating tower.

____ Common Traffic Advisory Frequency (CTAF).

____ " The Tower" (local control).

____ Automatic Terminal Information Service (ATIS).

____ Listen first, before taxi (ground control) or clearance delivery.

____ Clearance Delivery.

____ Primarily a frequency used for IFR clearances before taxi; it may also be used for clearance for VFR departures at busier airports.

____ Ground Control.

____ Regulates traffic moving on the taxiways and on those runways not being used for takeoffs and landings.

____ Clearance to taxi *to* a runway. The absence of holding instructions authorizes the aircraft to "cross" all runways that the taxi route intersects except the assigned takeoff runway. (This may change with time because of runway incursion incidents.)

____ Pilot is still responsible for unexpected taxi traffic or obstacles.

____ Stay on the ground control frequency until ready to switch to the tower.

____ When *landing,* don't switch to ground control until tower says so.

____ Local Control.

____ Traffic patterns (visual).

____ Be sure that the N number being used for takeoff or landing clearances is *yours*.

____ Departure Control.

____ Frequency given during clearance delivery. Write it down.

____ May repeat altitude or heading restrictions or instructions, if necessary.

____ Approach Control.

____ Listen to ATIS before contacting approach control.

____ VFR. Contact about 20 miles out.

____ IFR. When directed by Center.

____ Air Route Traffic Control Center (ARTCC).

____ Centers in the United States are primarily for en route flight.

____ Center sectors.

____ Remote communications air/ground sites in the sectors (RCAG).

____ Controllers work each assigned sector on its discrete frequency.

____ *Airport/Facilities Directory* has sector frequencies with remote communications—air to ground (RCAF) locations and frequencies.

____ Instrument departures (DPs).

____ Radar handoffs. The steps from tower to departure control to Center.

____ Radar handoffs—Center to approach control to tower.

____ Instrument arrivals (Holly 4 arrival at Memphis as an example).

____ Loss of Radar contact with the Center.

____ Procedures for working with an FSS.

____ Position reports.

____ Letters of agreement between towers and Centers. Areas of control.

____ Tower en route control.

____ Center's handling and routing of the IFR flight plans.

____ Communications techniques.

____ Aviate, Navigate, Communicate.

____ *Listen* before communicating and *think* before keying the mike.

____ Be alert to a lack of sounds in the receiver(s). (Check volume, recheck frequency, microphone stuck?)

____ Evaluation.

____ Review.

ASSIGNED READING

Trainee: *IFM* Chapter 7
Instructor: *FIM* Chapter 25

Comments_____

_____

_____

Instructor_____

Date ____ Ground Instruction _____ Flight Time _____

Aircraft type/model _____ N number _____

Trainee Initials _____

STAGE

3

PLANNING THE INSTRUMENT FLIGHT

UNIT 1—WEATHER SYSTEMS AND WEATHER PLANNING

This Unit will consist of ground instruction on basic meteorology and weather services available. Particular attention will be paid to the hazards of flight and how to recognize them both on the ground and in flight. These subjects should be covered in three *or more* ground school sessions and may be interspersed between the following flight Units.

■ Ground Instruction—6.0 Hours

____ Basic meteorology, *Aviation Weather* AC 00–6.

____ Heat and circulation.

____ Coriolis effect in Northern and Southern hemispheres.

____ Moisture: temperature and dewpoint effects on the atmosphere's ability to produce or hold moisture.

____ Relative humidity.

____ Lapse rates: normal, dry, and wet.

____ Pressure areas. Circulation about highs and lows.

____ Weather effects.

____ Isobars, lines of equal pressure.

____ Ridges and troughs.

____ Clouds, families.

____ Low clouds—surface to 6500 feet in middle latitudes.

____ Middle clouds—bases 6500 to 23,000 feet.

____ High clouds—bases to 16,500 to 45,000 feet.

____ Clouds with extensive vertical development. Cumulus and cumulonimbus (CB). In extreme cases CBs may go to 60,000 to 70,000 feet.

____ Nimbo or nimbus in name means precipitation.

____ How clouds are formed.

____ Clouds, cumulus and stratus forms.

____ Fog: Advection, radiation, upslope, precipitation, and ice fog.

____ Precipitation: Rain, hail, sleet (ice pellets), and snow.

____ Fronts: Warm, cold occluded, and stationary; the weather (and precipitation) expected with each.

 ____ Cold front: Type of clouds and weather turbulence, area covered, and precipitation. Cross-section of the front. Moves faster than warm front.

  ____ Squall lines.

 ____ Warm front: Expected clouds and weather, extent of area covered. Freezing rain in winter may occur. Cross-section.

  ____ Slow moving.

 ____ Occluded front: May contain weather of both warm and cold fronts.

  ____ Warm front occlusion.

   ____ Associated weather.

  ____ Cold front occlusion.

   ____ Associated weather.

  ____ Stationary front.

  ____ Frontogenesis and frontolysis.

Suggested break point

____ Hazards to flight.

 ____ Thunderstorms.

  ____ How thunderstorms are formed. The three requirements are instability, lifting force, and moisture.

  ____ Cumulus clouds. Mature stage, updrafts, downdrafts, and precipitation. Mature stage is the most hazardous.

  ____ Dissipating stage, the anvil head. *Do not fly under the anvil head; stay at least 10 miles away* (VFR).

  ____ Turbulence.

  ____ Maneuvering and gust envelopes.

   ____ 15 and 30 fps instantaneous vertical gust effects.

   ____ Maneuvering speeds(s).

   ____ Gust penetration speeds.

  ____ Clear air turbulence.

  ____ Autopilot OFF in turbulence.

   ____ *Altitude Hold* could cause over-stress.

  ____ Hail. How it is formed.

  ____ Icing.

   ____ Carburetor ice.

    ____ Symptom of icing for fixed-pitch and constant-speed propellers.

    ____ Full or partial carb heat?

    ____ Alternate air.

   ____ Structural icing.

    ____ Rime ice characteristics.

     ____ Clear ice characteristics.

     ____ Ice accretion rates (factors involved).

____ Deicing and anti-icing systems (when to use).

 ____ Reporting structural icing in a PIREPs (see *AIM*).

  ____ Trace, light, moderate, and severe.

 ____ Deicing the tied-down airplane.

 ____ Ice effects on performance and stability.

____ Frost.

 ____ The effects of frost on takeoff. (It's not the weight!)

 ____ Frost is most likely in the morning after a clear, cold night.

____ Freezing rain. When it may occur (warm air above).

____ Lightning.

____ Hazards on approach and landing.

 ____ Microbursts. How they occur.

 ____ Windshear (loss of airspeed).

  ____ Low-level wind shear alert systems (LLWAS).

 ____ Fog: A 4°F temperature and dewpoint spread could indicate that fog formation may start.

  ____ Types of fog and how they may form.

   ____ Advection.

   ____ Ground.

   ____ Ice.

   ____ Precipitation induced.

   ____ Radiation.

   ____ Sea.

   ____ Steam.

   ____ Upslope.

  ____ Major hazards of fog.

____ Hydroplaning.

 ____ Types and causes of hydroplaning.

 ____ Hydroplaning, minimum speed — $8.6 \times \sqrt{\text{tire pressure, psi}}$.

Suggested break point

____ *Weather Services*—AC 00–45.

____ Weather charts.

 ____ Times issued.

 ____ Symbols.

 ____ Weather depiction chart.

  ____ Symbols.

 ____ Radar summary chart.

  ____ Symbols.

____ Weather prognostic chart.
____ Low-level charts to 24,000 feet.

Suggested break point

____ Hourly reports. Review a typical hourly report.
____ METAR (meteorological report, aviation routine).
____ TAF (Terminal Aerodrome Forecast).
____ Compare earlier METARs with earlier TAFs. (Accuracy of forecasts.)
____ Area forecasts.
____ Inflight advisories.
____ EFAS (Enroute Flight Advisory Service).
____ SIGMETs (Significant Meteorological Information).
____ AIRMETs (Meteorological phenomena that are potentially hazardous to aircraft).
____ Convective SIGMETs.
____ TWEBs (Transcribed Weather Broadcasts).
____ ASOS (Automated Surface Observation System) and AWOS.
____ PIREPs (Pilot Reports).
____ Wind information.
____ Winds aloft forecasts.
____ Winds and temperature aloft charts.
____ Other services.
____ TIBS (Telephone Information Briefing Service).
____ HIWAS (Hazardous Inflight Weather Advisory Service).
____ Flight watch, 122.0 MHz.
____ Evaluation.
____ Critique.
____ Review.

ASSIGNED READING:

Trainee and Instructor: *IFM* Chapter 7

Comments _____

_____

_____

Instructor _____

Date ____ Ground Instruction _____ Flight Time _____

Aircraft type/model _____ N number _____

Trainee Initials _____

UNIT 2—CHARTS AND OTHER PRINTED AIDS

This Unit is ground school only and will cover the various requirements and charts to be used in instrument flying.

■ **Ground Instruction—4.0 Hours.** The instructor will sign off when all items have been covered (suggested 3 to 4 sessions).

____ Instrument flight rules.
____ 14 CFR Part 91.175. Takeoff and Landing under IFR: General.
____ En Route charts.
____ NACO chart symbols.
____ Jeppesen chart symbols.
____ Discuss the advantages and disadvantages of each type.
____ Area charts.
____ Instrument approach procedure charts.
____ U.S. coverage approach charts.
____ Definitions (HAA, HAT, DH/DA, MDA, no PT).
____ IFR landing minimums.
____ Planview.
____ Chart pages are oriented to True North but bearings and courses are magnetic.
____ Information in the solid 10-NM inner ring is to scale. Base information is only shown within the 10-NM ring.
____ Radio (navigation) aid for final part of the approaches is positioned in the center of the inner ring.
____ Middle ring, "feeder facilities" not in all charts.
____ Outer ring, en route facilities.
____ Minimum safe altitudes are shown with inbound bearings.
____ Profile view.
____ Legend.
____ Airport diagram.
____ Minimums data.
____ Alternate requirements.
____ Takeoff requirements.
____ Inoperative components.
____ Lighting.
____ Runway markings.

Suggested break point

____ Sample approach charts.
____ VOR and VOR/DME.
____ NDB.
____ GPS.
____ ILS.
____ RADAR (ASR and PAR [Precision Approach Radar] approaches).
____ Instrument departure (DP) procedures.
____ Standard terminal arrival routes (STARs).
____ *Aeronautical Information Manual*
____ Nav aids and procedures.
____ Emergency procedures.
____ Safety of flight.
____ Medical facts for pilots.

Suggested break point

_____ *Airport/Facility Directory (A/FD).*
    _____ Published every 56 days.
    _____ Seven areas/publications available for the continental United States and Puerto Rico/Virgin Islands.
    _____ Table of contents. Review each item briefly using the publication.
        _____ General information.
        _____ Abbreviations.
        _____ Legend, *A/FD.*
        _____ Pick various airports as examples.
        _____ Seaplane landing areas. (Probably not a factor for the instrument pilot.)
        _____ Notices.
        _____ Land and hold short operations.
        _____ FAA and National Weather Service telephone numbers.
        _____ Air Route Traffic Control Centers/FSS communications frequencies.
        _____ FSDO addresses/telephone numbers.
        _____ Preferred IFR routes/VFR waypoints/NAR routes.
        _____ VOR receiver check.
        _____ Parachute jumping areas. Not likely a factor for IFR pilots on airways, *but* with more direct routing being approved, these areas could, in VFR conditions, be a problem; the pilot is responsible for avoidance.
        _____ Aeronautics chart bulletin changes to sectional charts, terminal area, and helicopter route charts.
        _____ Tower en route control (TEC).
        _____ National Weather Service (NWS) upper air observing stations.
        _____ En Route Flight Advisory Service (EFAS).
_____ Notices to Airmen (NOTAMs).
    _____ NOTAM Ds.
    _____ NOTAM Ls.
    _____ Flight Data Center.

ASSIGNED READING:

Trainee and Instructor: *IFM* Chapters 8 and 9

Comments _____

_____

_____

Instructor_____

Date_____ Ground Instruction_____ Flight Time _____

Trainee Initials_____

UNIT 3—PLANNING THE NAVIGATION

The instructor will work with the trainee in setting up a triangular IFR cross-country with approaches at two other airports or two different approach-types at one airport. This is considered the first preplanned flight and should be reasonably simple. The following dual flights should be progressively more complex.

▪ Ground Instruction—1.0 Hour. Flight—2.0 Hours.

_____ Checking the weather, current and forecast (use all available information).
_____ Checking the route.
    _____ Marking the chart.
_____ Choosing an altitude.
    _____ Winds.
    _____ MEAs (Minimum Enroute Altitudes).
    _____ MOCAs (Minimum Obstruction Clearance Altitudes).
_____ Flight Log.
    _____ Cruising TAS.
    _____ Check points.
    _____ Estimating wind effects (multiplier, *IFM* Figure 9-1).
    _____ Climb effects.
        _____ Fixed gear airplane add $^2/_3$ minute/1000 feet to be climbed for time en route.
        _____ Retractable gear airplane add $^1/_2$ minute/1000 feet to be climbed.
    _____ Alternate airport.
        _____ Requirements (FAR 91.169).
    _____ Weight and balance computations.
        _____ Fuel available, gallons (pounds) and moment(s).
        _____ Fuel required for the trip.
        _____ Weights and moments of passengers and baggage.
    _____ Flight plan, factors to be considered.
    _____ NOTAMs.

ASSIGNED READING:

Trainee and Instructor: *IFM* Chapter 10

Comments

_____

_____

Instructor_____

Date_____ Ground Instruction_____ Flight Time _____

Aircraft type/model_____ N number _____

Trainee Initials_____

THE INSTRUMENT FLIGHT

UNIT 1—BEFORE THE TAKEOFF

■ Ground Instruction—2.0 Hours

____ Preflight inspection (in addition to "normal" VFR check).

    ____ Review com/nav antennas and their positions on the airplane in use.

    ____ Prop deicers or anti-icing fluid.

    ____ Fuel quick-drains may be frozen in winter if water was present earlier.

    ____ Deicing the airplane in a heated hangar—hazards.

____ Starting.

    ____ *All* avionics OFF before starting.

    ____ Nav lights ON before engaging starter(s) at night.

    ____ Five minutes required after starting for gyros to spool up.

    ____ Cold weather starting.

    ____ Hot engine starting.

    ____ Use of auxiliary power units for starting.

____ Taxiing.

    ____ Automatic Terminal Information Service (ATIS).

    ____ Clearance delivery before taxiing.

    ____ VOT (VOR Test facility).

    ____ Ground Control.

    ____ Check turn indicator while taxiing.

____ Pretakeoff check. Special IFR items.

    ____ Deicers and anti-icers check.

    ____ Avionics check.

    ____ At night keep white cabin lights off. Use red flashlight.

    ____ Ammeter shows proper indication.

    ____ Vacuum pump(s) operating normally.

    ____ Make up a special IFR checklist if not already available for your airplane.

____ Clearances.

    ____ Order of items on the clearance. ATC Clears:

        ____ Aircraft ID.

        ____ Clearance limit.

        ____ Departure procedure or DP.

        ____ Route of flight. (May have been changed by ATC since filed.)

        ____ Altitude data in the order to be flown.

        ____ Cruise clearances.

        ____ Holding instructions (if applicable).

        ____ Special information.

        ____ Frequencies and beacon code information.

        ____ Clearance amendments may be given en route.

        ____ Clearance shorthand suggestions.

        ____ Clearance readback.

____ Inflight problems and emergencies.

    ____ Loss of nav equipment (unable to comply).

    ____ Loss of communications (repeat briefing).

    ____ Loss of vacuum/pressure system.

        ____ Instruments affected.

        ____ Cover the "bad" instruments.

    ____ Severe structural icing.

    ____ Engine problems.

        ____ Carb or intake icing.

        ____ Loss of an engine (multiengine).

        ____ Rough-running engine (single engine).

        ____ Carb or intake icing.

ASSIGNED READING:

    Trainee: *IFM* Chapter 11
    Instructor: *FIM* Chapter 25

Comments _____

_____

_____

Instructor _____

Date ____ Ground Instruction _____ Flight Time _____

Aircraft type/model _____ N number _____

Trainee Initials _____

UNIT 2—TAKEOFF AND DEPARTURE

■ Ground Instruction—0.5 Hour. Flight—1.5 Hours.

Special attention is paid as to whether the departure should be made. All avionics and other airplane systems must be fully working. Once the departure is made (actual IMC), the pilot and airplane are committed to the ATC system.

____ Departure control.
  ____ May be restricted in altitude while in the DP jurisdiction.
____ Safe altitude. Set power and other cockpit chores. Fly the airplane *first*, then communicate as necessary.

ASSIGNED READING:

Trainee: *IFM* Chapter 12
Instructor: *FIM* Chapter 25

Comments _____

_____

_____

Navaids used _____

Instructor _____

Date ____ Ground Instruction _____ Flight Time _____

Aircraft type/model _____ N number _____

Trainee Initials _____

UNIT 3—EN ROUTE

■ Ground Instruction—1.0 Hour

____ En Route.
  ____ Review of sectors.
  ____ Loss of radar contact.
  ____ Total loss of communications.
    ____ Altitudes to be flown.
    ____ Route to be flown (usually the last assigned route/ATC clearance or in original flight plan).
      ____ Radar vectors. Go directly to fix, route, or airway specified in the vector clearance.
  ____ Position reports.
    ____ When position reports are required.
    ____ Position report items. Identification of A/C, then PTA-TEN (Position, Time, Altitude-Type flight plan, Estimate to next fix, Next fix after that).
____ Other voice reports. (Should be made to ATC or FSS facilities without a specific ATC request *at all times*.)
  ____ Vacating a previously assigned altitude for a new assigned altitude or flight level.
  ____ When an altitude change will be made when operating on a clearance specifying VFR-ON-TOP.
  ____ When unable to climb/descend at a rate of at least 500 fpm.

____ When an approach has been missed. (Request clearance for specific action; i.e., to an alternate airport, another approach, etc.)
____ When a change in the average true airspeed (at cruising altitude) varies by 5% or 10 knots from that filed.
____ The time and altitude or flight level upon reaching a holding fix or point to which you are cleared.
____ When leaving any assigned holding fix or point.
____ Any loss, in controlled airspace of VOR, of ADF capability, or complete or partial loss of ILS capability, or impairment of air/ground communications capabilities.
____ Any information relating to safety of flight.
____ When not in radar contact:
  ____ When leaving final approach inbound on final approach (nonprecision approach) or when leaving the outer marker or fix used in lieu of the outer marker inbound on final approach (precision approach).
  ____ Corrected estimate (3 minutes or more off).
  ____ Hazardous or unforecast conditions.
____ Holding patterns.
  ____ Standard and nonstandard.
  ____ Clearance limits and holding.
  ____ Expected further clearance time and when to depart the en route holding pattern.
  ____ Holding pattern entries: parallel, teardrop, and direct entry.
  ____ VOR and VOR/DME holding patterns.
  ____ Holding airspeeds at various altitudes.
  ____ Minimum-power-required point on the horsepower-required chart.
____ Holding in turbulence.

ASSIGNED READING:

Trainee: *IFM* Chapter 13
Instructor: *FIM* Chapter 25

Comments _____

_____

_____

Navaids used _____

Instructor _____

Date ____ Ground Instruction _____ Flight Time _____

Aircraft type/model _____ N number _____

Trainee Initials _____

UNIT 4—THE INSTRUMENT APPROACH AND LANDING

■ GROUND INSTRUCTION—1.0 Hour

____ Know the approaches available at the destination and alternate airports.

____ ILS approaches.

     ____ Front course minimums.

     ____ Back course minimums.

     ____ Localizer-only minimums.

     ____ Other missing component minimums.

     ____ ILS/DME arcs.

     ____ Missed approach procedures for each.

         ____ Cockpit resource management.

         ____ Make a new approach or move on to the alternate: a judgment call.

____ VOR approach.

     ____ Minimums and missed approach.

____ VOR/DME approaches.

     ____ Minimums and missed approach.

____ RNAV/GPS approaches.

     ____ Minimums and missed approach.

____ Radar-controlled approaches.

     ____ Airport surveillance radar (ASR).

     ____ Precision approach radar (has lower minimums).

     ____ No gyro approach.

____ Minimum safe altitude warning (MSAW).

     ____ Going to the alternate.

         ____ WARP—Weather, Altitude, Refile, and Procedures.

         ____ DRAFT—Destination, Route, Altitude, Fuel, and Time.

         ____ Fly the airplane. Voice procedures can wait.

         ____ These suggestions apply to any missed approach requiring an alternate.

ASSIGNED READING:

     Trainee: *IFM* Chapters 11, 12, and 13
     Instructor: *FIM* Chapter 25

Comments_____

_____

_____

Navaids used_____

Instructor_____

Date ____ Ground Instruction _____ Flight Time _____

Aircraft type/model _____ N number _____

Trainee Initials _____

UNIT 5—IFR CROSS-COUNTRY

■ Ground Instruction—1.0 Hour. Flight—2.0 Hours. The trainee will plan a 2-hour cross-country IFR

flight with different types of approaches to be repeated as training and traffic permit.

As noted in the Syllabus Introduction, the trainee may be flying from an airport or have airports nearby so that an early start on the various approaches may be available and practiced before getting into Stage 4 here. This would work well, but the basic instrument flying requirements should not be neglected to do this. Some instructors get bored with the basic maneuvers and are too eager to move on to "real" instrument flying. This can result in a problem for trainees.

This local availability of approaches should be considered in this Unit and the cross-country Units to follow. Note that Unit 7 has a review of basic instrument flying to make sure that the trainee hasn't forgotten basic instrument flying, and it provides a needed break.

ASSIGNED READING:

     Trainee: *IFM* Chapter 12
     Instructor: *FIM* Chapter 25

Comments_____

_____

_____

Airports/Approaches (ILS, VOR, etc.) _____

Instructor_____

Date ____ Ground Instruction _____ Flight Time _____

Aircraft type/model _____ N number _____

Trainee Initials _____

UNIT 6—IFR CROSS-COUNTRY

■ Ground Instruction—1.0 Hour. Flight—2.0 Hours. The trainee will plan a 2-hour cross-country IFR flight to airports other than those flown to in Unit 5. Different approaches, including ILS, VOR, or NDB will be completed. Holding with VOR receiver or ADF will be practiced at one of the new facilities.

ASSIGNED READING:

     Trainee: *IFM* Chapter 4
     nstructor: *FIM* Chapter 24

Comments_____

_____

_____

Airports/Approaches (ILS, VOR, etc.) _____

Instructor_____

Date ____ Ground Instruction _____ Flight Time _____

Aircraft type/model _____ N number _____

Trainee Initials _____

UNIT 7—BASIC INSTRUMENT FLYING

This Unit will be a review of basic instrument flying including recoveries from unusual attitudes (hooded, full-panel, and partial-panel).

■ **Ground Instruction—1.0 Hour. Flight—1.5 Hours**

_____ Review of the Four Fundamentals.

    _____ Straight and level.

    _____ Climbs.

    _____ Descents.

    _____ Turns.

_____ Basic maneuvers, full-panel (heading ±10°, altitude ±100 feet, airspeed ±10 knots).

    _____ Straight and level.

    _____ 180° turns (±10° of recovery headings, ±100 feet).

    _____ Climbing turns to a predetermined altitude and heading (±10°, ±100 feet—final altitude, ±10 knots).

    _____ Descending turns to a predetermined altitude and heading (±10°, ±100 feet—final altitude, ±10 knots).

_____ Recovery from unusual attitudes.

    _____ Power-on spiral.

    _____ Approach to a climbing stall.

    _____ Spin recoveries (by instruments).

_____ The instrument takeoff.

    _____ When is it necessary, if at all.

    _____ Setting of attitude indicator and heading indicator after runway line-up.

    _____ Smooth opening of throttle(s).

    _____ Maintain exact heading.

    _____ Rotate to proper attitude at _____ knots.

    _____ Maintain climb attitude.

    _____ Attitude indicator may read high because of acceleration, causing the pilot to adjust to a too-low attitude right after takeoff.

    _____ Gear up at 100 feet AGL or above.

    _____ Contact departure control when the airplane is in a controlled climb.

    _____ Discuss concept of clearance void time when not at a controlled field.

■ **Flight Instruction—1.5 Hours. Use checklist.**

_____ Preflight inspection.

_____ Starting and taxiing.

    _____ Check turn indicator while taxiing.

_____ Run-up and pretakeoff check.

    _____ Pay special attention to amps and suction instruments in addition to other instruments and systems.

_____ Communications procedures.

_____ Instrument takeoff (ITO, hooded).

    _____ Line-up.

    _____ Directional control.

    _____ Rotation to proper pitch at the correct airspeed.

_____ Climbing to prechosen altitude and heading.

    _____ Leveling procedures.

_____ Four Fundamentals.

    _____ Straight and level.

    _____ Climbs.

    _____ Descents.

    _____ Turns.

_____ Basic (normal) maneuvers (hooded, full-panel).

    _____ Straight and level (heading ±10°, altitude ±100 feet, airspeed ±10 knots).

    _____ 180° level turns (±10° of recovery headings, ±100 feet).

    _____ Climbing turns to a predetermined altitude and heading (±10° on roll-out, 10 knots, and within 100 feet of final altitude).

    _____ Descending turns to a predetermined altitude and heading (±10° on roll-out, ±100 feet, ±10 knots).

_____ Recovery from unusual attitudes (hooded, full-panel).

    _____ Power-on spiral.

    _____ Approach to a climbing stall.

    _____ Spins (optional, using partial-panel instruments).

_____ Return to airport (hooded, full-panel—if conditions permit).

    _____ Checklist use.

    _____ Instructor acts as "approach control radar."

    _____ Heading (±10°, altitudes ±100 feet, airspeeds ±10 knots).

    _____ Landing (visual).

    _____ Postlanding procedures.

        _____ Taxi.

        _____ Shutdown.

        _____ Postflight inspection.

ASSIGNED READING:

> Trainee: *IFM* Chapters 11, 12, and 13
> Instructor: *FIM* Chapter 25

Comments _____

_____

_____

Instructor _____

Date ____ Ground Instruction _____ Flight Time _____

Aircraft type/model _____ N number _____

Trainee Initials _____

UNIT 8—LONG IFR CROSS-COUNTRY

This will be the trip as required by FAR 61.65 and will be a flight performed under IFR, consisting of a distance of at least 250 NM along airways or ATC-directed routing with one segment of the flight consisting of at least a straight-line distance of 100 NM between airports.

It is suggested that a triangular IFR cross-country be made to three airports with a different type of approach made at each.

■ Ground Instruction—1.5 Hours. Flight—4.0 Hours

Comments _____

_____

_____

Airports _____

Approaches (types) _____

Instructor _____

Date ____ Ground Instruction _____ Flight Time _____

Aircraft type/model _____ N number _____

Trainee Initials _____

STAGE 5

THE KNOWLEDGE TEST

Before taking the Knowledge Test, a review of the following is in order. There is no suggested time for each subject. Use the following items as a checklist to ensure that no area of the Knowledge Test and subsequent experience as an instrument-rated pilot is neglected. The suggested 4.0 hours of review should be broken into two or *more* sessions at the discretion of the trainee and/or instructor.

■ Ground Instruction—4 Hours (in at least 2 sessions).

____ ATO, general.
____ Flight rules—general.
____ Instrument flight rules.
____ Equipment, instrument, and certification.
____ Maintenance, preventive.
____ Maintenance and alterations.
____ FAR, general.
____ Emergency flight by reference to instruments.
____ Training considerations.
____ Instrument flying: Coping with illusions in flight.
____ Basic flight instruments.
____ Attitude instrument flying—airplanes.
____ Electric aids to instrument flying.
____ Using the navigation instruments.
____ Radio communications, facilities, and equipment.
____ The Federal Airways System and controlled airspace.
____ Air traffic control.
____ ATC operations and procedures.
____ Flight planning.

_____ The earth's atmosphere.
_____ Temperature.
_____ Atmospheric pressure and altimetry.
_____ Wind.
_____ Moisture, cloud formation, and precipitation.
_____ Stable and unstable air.
_____ Clouds.
_____ Air masses and fronts.
_____ Turbulence.
_____ Icing.
_____ Thunderstorms.
_____ Common IFR producers.
_____ High altitude weather.
_____ Glossary of weather terms.
_____ The Aviation Weather Service Program.
_____ Surface aviation weather reports.
_____ Pilot and radar reports and satellite pictures.
_____ Aviation weather forecasts.
_____ Surface Analysis Chart.
_____ Weather Depiction Chart.
_____ Radar Summary Chart.
_____ Significant Weather Prognostics.
_____ Winds and temperatures aloft.
_____ Composite Moisture Stability Chart.
_____ Severe Weather Outlook Chart.
_____ Constant Pressure charts.
_____ Tropopause Data Chart.
_____ Air navigation radio aids.
_____ Radar services and procedures.
_____ Airport light aids.
_____ Air navigation and obstruction lighting.
_____ Airport marking aids and signs.
_____ Airspace, general.

_____ Service available to pilots.
_____ Radio communications phraseology and techniques.
_____ ATC clearance/separations.
_____ Preflight.
_____ Departure procedures.
_____ En route procedures.
_____ Arrival procedures.
_____ Pilot/controller roles and responsibilities.
_____ Emergency procedures, general.
_____ Distress and urgency procedures
_____ Two-way radio communications failure.
_____ Wake turbulence.
_____ Potential flight hazards.
_____ Fitness for flight.
_____ Types of charts available.
_____ _Airport/Facility Directory._
_____ En Route Low-Altitude charts.
_____ En Route High-Altitude charts.
_____ Terminal charts.
_____ Instrument Departure (DP) Chart.
_____ Standard Terminal Arrival (STAR) Chart.
_____ Instrument approach procedures (IAP).

Authorization to take the Aeronautical Knowledge Test, reference, FAR 61.35 (a)(1) and 61.65 (a) and (b).

I certify that Mr./Ms._____ has received the required training of 61.65(b). I have determined that he/she is prepared for the Instrument (ASEL) Knowledge test.

Date _____

Signed_____ Number _____ Exp_____

STAGE **6**

THE PRACTICAL TEST

This Stage includes more IFR cross-country and a review of basic instruments including partial-panel work. Review Chapter 15 of this book for an outline of the Practical Test requirements.

UNIT 1—IFR CROSS-COUNTRY

The trainee will plan a 2-hour cross-country to a different airport(s) than used for destinations before, if possible.

If not feasible, an attempt should be made to execute different types of approaches than used in earlier trips. File IFR.

■ **Ground Instruction—1.0 Hour. Flight—2.0 Hours**

Comments _____

_____

_____

Airports/Approaches _____

(Example of Airports/Approaches: BNA-ILS, VOR; HSV-ILS, GPS, etc.)

Instructor _____

Date ____ Ground Instruction _____ Flight Time _____

Aircraft type/model _____ N number _____

Trainee Initials _____

UNIT 2—BASIC INSTRUMENT FLYING

This flight (airplane or flight training device) will consist of a review of basic instrument flying, including a short period of partial-panel work.

■ **Ground Instruction—1.0 Hour. Flight—2.0 Hours**

____ Review of basic instrument flying. All maneuvers hooded and full-panel unless noted otherwise.
____ Briefing for the flight.
    ____ ITO (full-panel, hooded).
    ____ Climb to practice area (partial-panel).
    ____ Holding using one VOR or NDB (partial-panel).
    ____ Vertical S-1 and/or S-2. (*IFM* Figure 4-17 and *FIM* Figures 24-17 and 24-18.)
    ____ Steep turns (45° bank, 180° turn, full-panel).
    ____ Charlie pattern (optional). (*IFM* Figure 4-22 and *FIM* Figure 24-28.)
    ____ Recoveries from unusual attitudes (partial-panel).
        ____ Power-on spiral.
        ____ Approach to a climbing stall.
        ____ Discussion only of spin recoveries (partial-panel) *IFM* Figures 4-36–4-41.
____ Return to airport (visually).

■ **Flight Instruction—2.0 Hours**

____ ITO (full-panel, hooded).
____ Climb to practice area (partial-panel).
____ Holding at VOR (or NDB or commercial broadcast station) if ADF equipment is available in the aircraft.
____ Vertical S-1 and/or S-2 (partial-panel).
____ Steep turns (45° banks, 720° turns both ways, full-panel).
    ____ Charlie pattern (optional). May take up time that could be used on other maneuvers.

____ Recoveries from unusual attitudes.
    ____ Approach to a climbing stall.
    ____ Power-on spiral.
____ Visual return to airport.
    ____ Communications.
    ____ Landing.
    ____ Postlanding procedures.
    ____ Post shutdown procedures.

Comments _____

_____

_____

Airports/ Approaches _____

Instructor _____

Date ____ Ground Instruction _____ Flight Time _____

Aircraft type/model _____ N number _____

Trainee Initials _____

UNIT 3—IFR CROSS-COUNTRY AND APPROACHES

The trainee and instructor will fly to the nearest airport/facility to shoot two of three types of approaches.

■ **Ground Instruction—1.0 Hour. Flight—2.0 Hours.**

A review of approaches made thus far in the course and a briefing for this flight.

Comments _____

_____

_____

Airports/ Approaches _____

Instructor _____

Date ____ Ground Instruction _____ Flight Time _____

Aircraft type/model _____ N number _____

Trainee Initials _____

UNIT 4—GENERAL REVIEW AND EXTRA PRACTICE FLIGHTS AS REQUIRED

This Unit(s) will be used at the discretion of the instructor and trainee to complete the flight hour requirements (to 40 hours) of FAR 61.65 and at least 3 hours of instrument training in preparation for the practical test within the last 60 days before the practical test.

The instructor will cover the requirements for the instrument rating and review the Knowledge Test and flying elements of the Practical Test Standards.

Comments _____

_____

_____

Airports/ Approaches _____

Instructor _____

Date _____ Ground Instruction _____ Flight Time _____

Aircraft type/model _____ N number _____

Trainee Initials _____

UNIT 5—FINAL SCHOOL PRACTICAL CHECK

A final check by the chief pilot or another instructor/check pilot before recommending the trainee for the FAA Practical Test.

■ Ground Instruction—1.0 Hour. Flight—2.0 Hours

_____ Extra time and school recheck required.
_____ Passed, ready for FAA Practical Test.

Reference Paragraphs 61.65 (a)(6).

I certify that Mr./Ms. _____ has received the required training for 61.65(c) and (d). I have determined that he/she is prepared for the Practical Test (ASEL).

Date _____

Signed _____ Number _____ Exp _____

UNIT 6—FAA PRACTICAL TEST

■ **Checklist.** Allow 3.0 hours ground and 3.0 hours flight for the Practical Test.

_____ Student pilot certificate current, plus medical certificate, if required.
_____ Logbook. All endorsements correct, including stage checks and recommendations for Knowledge and Practical Test.
_____ Charts (en route and approach), *Airport/Facility Directory,* plus computers.
_____ Airplane papers and logbooks in order.
_____ Examiner's fee.
_____ Graduation certificate, if applicable.
_____ Application for Practical Test correctly filled out and signed.

Date _____

PASSED _____ Temporary certificate issued _____

FAA Inspector or Examiner _____

FAILED_____ Recheck required.

Notes and Comments _____

_____

_____

_____

Student Initials _____

APPENDIX:
AIRPORT/FACILITY
DIRECTORY LEGEND

DIRECTORY LEGEND

LEGEND

This Directory is an alphabetical listing of data on record with the FAA on all airports that are open to the public, associated terminal control facilities, air route traffic control centers and radio aids to navigation within the conterminous United States, Puerto Rico and the Virgin Islands. Airports are listed alphabetically by associated city name and cross referenced by airport name. Facilities associated with an airport, but with a different name, are listed individually under their own name, as well as under the airport with which they are associated.

The listing of an airport in this directory merely indicates the airport operator's willingness to accommodate transient aircraft, and does not represent that the facility conforms with any Federal or local standards, or that it has been approved for use on the part of the general public.

The information on obstructions is taken from reports submitted to the FAA. It has not been verified in all cases. Pilots are cautioned that objects not indicated in this tabulation (or on charts) may exist which can create a hazard to flight operation.

Detailed specifics concerning services and facilities tabulated within this Directory are contained in Airman's Information Manual, Basic Flight Information and ATC Procedures.

The legend items that follow explain in detail the contents of this Directory and are keyed to the circled numbers on the sample on the preceding page.

① CITY/AIRPORT NAME

Airports and facilities in this directory are listed alphabetically by associated city and state. Where the city name is different from the airport name the city name will appear on the line above the airport name. Airports with the same associated city name will be listed alphabetically by airport name and will be separated by a dashed rule line. All others will be separated by a solid rule line.

② NOTAM SERVICE

§—NOTAM "D" (Distance teletype dissemination) and NOTAM "L" (local dissemination) service is provided for airport. Absence of annotation § indicates NOTAM "L" (local dissemination) only is provided for airport. Airport NOTAM file identifier will be shown as "NOTAM FILE IAD" for all public-use airports. See AIM, Basic Flight Information and ATC Procedures for detailed descriptions of NOTAM.

③ LOCATION IDENTIFIER

A three or four character code assigned to airports. These identifiers are used by ATC in lieu of the airport name in flight plans, flight strips and other written records and computer operations.

④ AIRPORT LOCATION

Airport location is expressed as distance and direction from the center of the associated city in nautical miles and cardinal points, i.e., 4 NE.

⑤ TIME CONVERSION

Hours of operation of all facilities are expressed in Coordinated Universal Time (UTC) and shown as "Z" time. The directory indicates the number of hours to be subtracted from UTC to obtain local standard time and local daylight saving time UTC–5(–4DT). The symbol ‡ indicates that during periods of Daylight Saving Time effective hours will be one hour earlier than shown. In those areas where daylight saving time is not observed the (–4DT) and ‡ will not be shown. All states observe daylight savings time except Arizona and that portion of Indiana in the Eastern Time Zone and Puerto Rico and the Virgin Islands.

⑥ GEOGRAPHIC POSITION OF AIRPORT

⑦ CHARTS

The Sectional Chart and Low and High Altitude Enroute Chart and panel on which the airport or facility is located. Helicopter Chart locations will be indicated as, i.e., COPTER.

⑧ INSTRUMENT APPROACH PROCEDURES

IAP indicates an airport for which a prescribed (Public Use) FAA Instrument Approach Procedure has been published.

⑨ ELEVATION

Elevation is given in feet above mean sea level and is the highest point on the landing surface. When elevation is below sea level it will be indicated as (00). When elevation is sea level it will precede the figure.

⑩ ROTATING LIGHT BEACON

B indicates rotating beacon is available. Rotating beacons operate dusk to dawn unless otherwise indicated in AIRPORT REMARKS.

⑪ SERVICING

S1: Minor airframe repairs.
S2: Minor airframe and minor powerplant repairs.
S3: Major airframe and minor powerplant repairs.
S4: Major airframe and major powerplant repairs.

DIRECTORY LEGEND SAMPLE

① ② ③ ④ ⑤ ⑥ ⑦

CITY NAME

| § | AIRPORT NAME | (ORL) | 4 E | UTC–5(–4DT) | 28°32′43″N 81°20′10″W | | JACKSONVILLE | COPTER |
| 200 | B | S4 | FUEL 100, JET A | OX 1, 2, 3 | | AOE | ARFF Index A | Not insp. | H-4G, L-19C |

⑨ ⑩ ⑪ ⑫ ⑬ ⑭ ⑮ ⑯ ⑰ ⑧ IAP

⑱ RWY 07-25: H6000X150 (ASPH-PFC) S-90, D-160, DT-300 HIRL
　RWY 07: ALSF1. Trees.　RWY 25: REIL. Rgt tfc.
　RWY 13-31: H4620X100 (ASPH) HIRL
　RWY 13: SAVASI(S2L)—GA 3.3° TCH 89′. Pole.　RWY 31: PAPI(P2L)—GA 3.1° TCH 36′. Tree. Rgt tfc.

⑲ AIRPORT REMARKS: Special Air Traffic Rules—Part 93, see Regulatory Notices. Attended 1200-0300Z‡. Parachute Jumping. CAUTION cattle and deer on arpt. Acft 100,000 lbs or over ctc Director of Aviation for approval 305-894-9831. Fee for all airline charters, travel clubs and certain revenue producing acft. Flight Notification Service (ADCUS) available. Control Zone effective 1500-0700Z‡.

⑳ WEATHER DATA SOURCES: AWOS-1 120.3 (202) 426-8000. LLWAS.
㉑ COMMUNICATIONS: ATIS 127.25　UNICOM 122.95
Ⓡ NAME FSS (ORL) on arpt. 123.65 122.65 122.2. LD 305-894-0861. NOTAM FILE ORL.
Ⓡ NAME APP/DEP CON 128.35 (1200-0400Z‡)
　TOWER 118.7　GND CON 121.7　CLNC DEL 125.55　PRE TAXI CLNC 125.5
　TCA GROUP II: See VFR Terminal Area Chart.

㉒ RADIO AIDS TO NAVIGATION: NOTAM FILE MCO. VHF/DF ctc FSS.
　(H) ABVORTAC 112.2 ■ MCO Chan 59　28°32′33″N 81°20′07″W　at fld.　1110/8E.
　　TWEB avbl 1300-0100Z‡. VOR unusable 050°-060° beyond 15 NM below5000′.
　HERNY NDB (LOM) 221　OR　28°30′24″N 81°26′03″W　067° 5.4 NM to fld.
　ILS 109.9 I-ORL Rwy 07. LOM HERNY NDB.
　ASR/PAR

㉓ COMM/NAVAID REMARKS: Emerg frequency 121.5 not available at tower.

| | AIRPORT NAME | (X30) | 7 W | UTC–5(–4DT) | 28°31′50″N 81°32′26″W | | JACKSONVILLE |
| 130 | S4 | FUEL 100 | OX 2 | | LRA | | | |

RWY 18-36: 2430X150 (TURF)　RWY LGTS (NSTD)
　RWY 18: Thld dsplcd 215′. Trees.　RWY 36: Thld dsplcd 270′. Road.
AIRPORT REMARKS: Attended dawn-0300Z‡. Rwy lgts west side only.
COMMUNICATIONS: CTAF/UNICOM 122.8
　NAME FSS (ORL) LC 894-0861. NOTAM FILE ORL.
　NAME RCO 122.4 122.1R 112.2T (NAME FSS)

| § D | AIRPORT NAME | (MCO) | 6.1 SE | UTC–5(–4DT) | 28°25′53″N 81°19′29″W | | JACKSONVILLE |
| 96 | B | FUEL 100, JET A, MOGAS | LRA | | | | H-4G, L-19C |

RWY 18-36L: H12004X300 (CONC-GRVD)　RWY 18R: ALSF1.　RWY 36L: ALSF1.　IAP
RWY 18R: ALSF1. REIL. Rgt tfc.　RWY 36R: S-100, D-200, DT-400　HIRL
RWY 18L-36R: H12004X200 (ASPH)　S-165, D-200, DT-400　HIRL
RWY 18L: LDIN. ALSF1. TDZ. REIL. VASI(V4L)—GA 3.5° TCH 36′. Thld dsplcd 300′. Trees. Rgt tfc.
RWY 36R: LDIN. ALSF1. TDZ. REIL. ACTIVATE HIRL Rwy 18L-36R—CTAF.
COMMUNICATIONS: CTAF 124.3　ATIS 127.75　UNICOM 122.8
　NAME FSS (MCO) LC 894-0869. NOTAM FILE MCO.
Ⓡ APP CON 124.8 (337°-179°)　120.1 (180°-336°)　DEP CON 120.15
　TOWER 124.3 NFCT (1200-0400Z‡)　GND CON 121.85　CLNC DEL 134.7
　ARSA ctc APP CON
RADIO AIDS TO NAVIGATION: NOTAM FILE MCO.
　NAME (H) VORTAC 112.2　MCO Chan 59　28°32′33″N 81°20′07″W　173° 5.7 NM to fld. 1110/8E.
　MLS Chan 514 Rwy 36R

E AIRPORT NAME　(See PLYMOUTH)

All Bearings and Radials are Magnetic unless otherwise specified.
All mileages are nautical unless otherwise noted.
All times are UTC except as noted.

DIRECTORY LEGEND

DIRECTORY LEGEND

⑫ FUEL

CODE	FUEL	CODE	FUEL
80	Grade 80 gasoline (Red)	B	Jet B—Wide-cut turbine fuel, freeze point–50° C.
100	Grade 100 gasoline (Green)		
100LL	Grade 100LL gasoline (low lead) (Blue)	B+	Jet B—Wide-cut turbine fuel with icing inhibitor, freeze point–50° C.
115	Grade 115 gasoline		
A	Jet A—Kerosene freeze point–40° C.		
A1	Jet A-1—Kerosene, freeze point–50° C.		
A1+	Jet A-1—Kerosene with icing inhibitor, freeze point–50° C.		
MOGAS	Automobile gasoline which is to be used as aircraft fuel.		

NOTE: Automobile Gasoline. Certain automobile gasoline may be used in specific aircraft engines if a FAA supplemental type certificate has been obtained. Automobile gasoline which is to be used in aircraft engines will be identified as "MOGAS", however, the grade/type and other octane rating will not be published.

Data shown on fuel availability represents the most recent inforntion the publisher has been able to acquire. Because of a variety of factors, the fuel listed may not always be obtainable by transient civil pilots. Confirmation of availability of fuel should be made directly with fuel dispensers at locations where refueling is planned.

⑬ OXYGEN
OX 1 High Pressure
OX 2 Low Pressure
OX 3 High Pressure—Replacement Bottles
OX 4 Low Pressure—Replacement Bottles

⑭ TRAFFIC PATTERN ALTITUDE
Traffic Pattern Altitude (TPA)—The first figure shown is TPA above mean sea level. The second figure in parentheses is TPA above airport elevation.

⑮ AIRPORT OF ENTRY AND LANDING RIGHTS AIRPORTS
AOE—Airport of Entry—A customs Airport of Entry where permission from U.S. Customs is not required, however, at least one hour advance notice of arrival must be furnished.

LRA—Landing Rights Airport—Application for permission to land must be submitted in advance to U.S. Customs. At least one hour advance notice of arrival must be furnished.

NOTE: Advance notice of arrival at both an AOE and LRA airport may be included in the flight plan when filed in Canada or Mexico, where Flight Notification Service (ADCUS) is available the airport remark will indicate this service. This notice will also be treated as an application for permission to land in the case of an LRA. Although advance notice of arrival may be relayed to Customs through Mexico, Canadian, and U.S. Communications facilities by flight plan, the aircraft operator is solely responsible for insuring that U.S. Customs receives the notification. (See Customs, Immigration and Naturalization, Public Health and Agriculture Department requirements in the International Flight Information Manual for further details.)

⑯ CERTIFICATED AIRPORT (FAR 139)
Airports serving Department of Transportation certified carriers and certified under FAR, Part 139, are indicated by the ARFF index; i.e., ARFF Index A, which relates to the availability of crash, fire, rescue equipment.

FAR–PART 139 CERTIFICATED AIRPORTS
INDICES AND AIRCRAFT RESCUE AND FIRE FIGHTING EQUIPMENT REQUIREMENTS

Airport Index	Required No. Vehicles	Aircraft Length	Scheduled Departures	Agent + Water for Foam
A	1	<90'	≥1	500#DC or HALON 1211 or 450#DC + 100 gal H2O
B	1 or 2	≥90', <126'	≥5	Index A + 1500 gal H2O
		≥126', <159'	<5	
C	2 or 3	≥126', <159'	≥5	Index A + 3000 gal H2O
		≥159', <200'	<5	
D	3	≥159', <200'	≥5	Index A + 4000 gal H2O
		>200'	<5	
E	3	≥200'	≥5	Index A + 6000 gal H2O

> Greater Than; < Less Than; ≥ Equal or Greater Than; ≤ Equal or Less Than; H2O–Water; DC–Dry Chemical.

NOTE: The listing of ARFF index does not necessarily assure coverage for non-air carrier operations or at other than prescribed times for air carrier. ARFF Index Ltd.—indicates ARFF coverage may or may not be available, for information contact airport manager prior to flight.

⑰ FAA INSPECTION
All airports not inspected by FAA will be identified by the note: Not insp. This indicates that the airport information has been provided by the owner or operator of the field.

⑱ RUNWAY DATA
Runway information is shown on two lines. That information common to the entire runway is shown on the first line while information concerning the runway ends are shown on the second or following line. Lengthy information will be placed in the Airport Remarks.

Runway direction, surface, length, width, weight bearing capacity, lighting, gradient and appropriate remarks are shown for each runway. Direction, length, width, lighting and remarks are shown for sealanes. The full dimensions of helipads are shown; i.e., 50X150.

RUNWAY SURFACE AND LENGTH
Runway lengths prefixed by the letter "H" indicate that the runways are hard surfaced (concrete, asphalt). If the runway length is not prefixed, the surface is sod, clay, etc. The runway surface composition is indicated in parentheses after runway length as follows:

(AFSC)—Aggregate friction seal coat	(GRVD)—Grooved	(TURF)—Turf
(ASPH)—Asphalt	(GRVL)—Gravel, or cinders	(TRTD)—Treated
(CONC)—Concrete	(PFC)—Porous friction courses	(WC)—Wire combed
(DIRT)—Dirt	(RFSC)—Rubberized friction seal coat	

RUNWAY WEIGHT BEARING CAPACITY
Runway strength data shown in this publication is derived from available information and is a realistic estimate of capability at an average level of activity. It is not intended as a maximum allowable weight or as an operating limitation. Many airport pavements are capable of supporting limited operations with gross weights of 25-50% in excess of the published figures. Permissible operating weights, insofar as runway strengths are concerned, are a matter of agreement between the owner and user. When desiring to operate into any airport at weights in excess of those published in the publication, users should contact the airport management for permission. Add 000 to figure following S, D, DT, DDT and MAX for gross weight capacity:

S—Runway weight bearing capacity for aircraft with single- wheel type landing gear, (DC-3), etc.

D—Runway weight bearing capacity for aircraft with dual-wheel type landing gear, (DC-6), etc.

DT—Runway weight bearing capacity for aircraft with dual-tandem type landing gear, (707), etc.

DDT—Runway weight bearing capacity for aircraft with double dual- tandem type landing gear, (747), etc.

Quadricycle and dual-tandem are considered virtually equal for runway weight bearing consideration, as are single-tandem and dual-wheel.

Omission of weight bearing capacity indicates information unknown.

RUNWAY LIGHTING
Lights are in operation sunset to sunrise. Lighting available by prior arrangement only or operating part of the night only and/or pilot controlled and with specific operating hours are indicated under airport remarks. Since obstructions are usually lighted, obstruction lighting is not included in this code. Unlighted obstructions on or surrounding an airport will be noted in airport remarks. Runway lights nonstandard (NSTD) are systems for which the light fixtures are not FAA approved L-800 series: color, intensity, or spacing does not meet FAA standards. Nonstandard runway lights, VASI, or any other system not listed below will be shown in airport remarks.

Temporary, emergency or limited runway edge lighting such as flares, smudge pots, lanterns or portable runway lights will also be shown in airport remarks.

Types of lighting are shown with the runway or runway end they serve.

NSTD—Light system fails to meet FAA standards.	SALS—Short Approach Lighting System.	
LIRL—Low Intensity Runway Lights	SALSF—Short Approach Lighting System with Sequenced Flashing Lights.	
MIRL—Medium Intensity Runway Lights		
HIRL—High Intensity Runway Lights	SSALS—Simplified Short Approach Lighting System.	
REIL—Runway End Identifier Lights	SSALF—Simplified Short Approach Lighting System with Sequenced Flashing Lights.	
CL—Centerline Lights		
TDZ—Touchdown Zone Lights	SSALR—Simplified Short Approach Lighting System with Runway Alignment Indicator Lights.	
ODALS—Omni Directional Approach Lighting System.		
AF OVRN—Air Force Overrun 1000' Standard Approach Lighting System.	ALSAF—High Intensity Approach Lighting System with Sequenced Flashing Lights	
LDIN—Lead-In Lighting System.		
MALS—Medium Intensity Approach Lighting System.	ALSF1—High Intensity Approach Lighting System with Sequenced Flashing Lights, Category I, Configuration.	
MALSF—Medium Intensity Approach Lighting System with Sequenced Flashing Lights.	ALSF2—High Intensity Approach Lighting System with Sequenced Flashing Lights, Category II, Configuration.	
MALSR—Medium Intensity Approach Lighting System with Runway Alignment Indicator Lights.	VASI—Visual Approach Slope Indicator Lights.	

NOTE: Civil ALSF-2 may be operated as SSALR during favorable weather conditions.

DIRECTORY LEGEND

VISUAL GLIDESLOPE INDICATORS

VASI—Visual Approach Slope Indicator
SAVASI—Simplified Abbreviated Visual Approach Slope Indicator
PAPI—Precision Approach Path Indicator

P2R	2-identical light units placed on right side of runway
P2L	2-identical light units placed on left side of runway
P4R	4-identical light units placed on right side of runway
P4L	4-identical light units placed on left side of runway
S2L	2-box SAVASI on left side of runway
S2R	2-box SAVASI on right side of runway
V2R	2-box VASI on right side of runway
V2L	2-box VASI on left side of runway
V4R	4-box VASI on right side of runway
V4L	4-box VASI on left side of runway
V6R	6-box VASI on right side of runway
V6L	6-box VASI on left side of runway
V12	12-box VASI on both sides of runway
V16	16-box VASI on both sides of runway
*NSTD	Nonstandard VASI, VAPI, or any other system not listed above

PAPI/VASI approach slope angle and threshold crossing height will be shown when available; i.e., GA 3.5° TCH 37'.

PILOT CONTROL OF AIRPORT LIGHTING

Key Mike	Function
7 times within 5 seconds	Highest intensity available
5 times within 5 seconds	Medium or lower intensity (Lower REIL or REIL-Off)
3 times within 5 seconds	Lowest intensity available (Lower REIL or REIL-Off)

Available systems will be indicated in the Airport Remarks, as follows:

ACTIVATE MALSR Rwy 7, HIRL Rwy 7-25-122.8.
or
ACTIVATE MIRL Rwy 18-36-122.8.
or
ACTIVATE VASI and REIL, Rwy 7-122.8.

Where the airport is not served by an instrument approach procedure and/or has an independent type system of different specification installed by the airport sponsor, descriptions of the type lights, method of control, and operating frequency will be explained in clear text. See AIM, "Basic Flight Information and ATC Procedures," for detailed description of pilot control of airport lighting.

RUNWAY GRADIENT

Runway gradient will be shown only when it is 0.3 percent or more. When available the direction of slope upward will be indicated, i.e., 0.5% up NW.

RUNWAY END DATA

Lighting systems such as VASI, MALSR, REIL; obstructions; displaced thresholds will be shown on the specific runway end. "Rgt tfc"—Right traffic indicates right turns should be made on landing and takeoff for specified runway end.

⑲ AIRPORT REMARKS

Landing Fee indicates landing charges for private or non-revenue producing aircraft, in addition, fees may be charged for planes that remain over a couple of hours and buy no services, or at major airline terminals for all aircraft.

Remarks—Data is confined to operational items affecting the status and usability of the airport.
Parachute Jumping.—See "PARACHUTE" tabulation for details.

⑳ WEATHER DATA SOURCES

AWOS—Automated Weather Observing System
AWOS-1—reports altimeter setting, wind data and usually temperature, dewpoint and density altitude.
AWOS-2—reports the same as AWOS-1 plus visibility.
AWOS-3—reports the same as AWOS-1 plus visibility and cloud/ceiling data.
See AIM, Basic Flight Information and ATC Procedures for detailed description of AWOS.

SAWRS—Identifies airports that have a Supplemental Aviation Weather Reporting Station available to pilots for current weather information.
LAWRS—Limited Aviation Weather Reporting Station where observers report cloud height, weather, obstructions to vision, temperature and dewpoint (in most cases), surface wind, altimeter and pertinent remarks.
LLWAS—indicates a Low Level Wind Shear Alert System consisting of a center field and several field perimeter anemometers.
HIWAS—See RADIO AIDS TO NAVIGATION

DIRECTORY LEGEND

㉑ COMMUNICATIONS

Communications will be listed in sequence in the order shown below:

Common Traffic Advisory Frequency (CTAF), Automatic Terminal Information Service (ATIS) and Aeronautical Advisory Stations (UNICOM) along with their frequency is shown, where available, on the line following the heading "COMMUNICATIONS." When the CTAF and UNICOM is the same frequency, the frequency will be shown as CTAF/UNICOM freq.

Flight Service Station (FSS) information. The associated FSS will be shown followed by the identifier and information concerning availability of telephone service, e.g., Direct Line (DL), Local Call (LC-384-2341), Toll free call, dial (TF 800-852-7036 or TF 1-800-227-7160), Long Distance (LD 202-426-8800 or LD 1-202-555-1212) etc. The airport NOTAM file identifier will be shown as "NOTAM FILE IAD." Where the FSS is located on the field it will be indicated as "on arpt" following the identifier. Frequencies available will follow. The FSS telephone number will follow along with any significant operational information. FSS's whose name is not the same as the airport on which located will also be listed in the normal alphabetical name listing for the state in which located. Remote Communications Outlet (RCO) providing service to the airport followed by the frequency and name of the Controlling FSS.

FSS's provide information on airport conditions, radio aids and other facilities, and process flight plans. Airport Advisory Service is provided on the CTAF by FSS's located at non-tower airports or airports where the tower is not in operation.
(See AIM, Par. 157/158 Traffic Advisory Practices at airports where a tower is not in operation or AC 90 - 42C.)
Aviation weather briefing service is provided by FSS specialists. Flight and weather briefing services are also available by calling the telephone numbers listed.

Remote Communications Outlet (RCO)—An unmanned air/ground communications facility, remotely controlled and providing UHF or VHF communications capability to extend the service range of an FSS.

Civil Communications Frequencies—Civil communications frequencies used in the FSS air/ground system are now operated simplex on 122.0, 122.2, 122.3, 122.4, 122.6, 123.6; emergency 121.5; plus receive-only on 122.05, 122.1, 122.15, and 123.6.

a. 122.0 is assigned as the Enroute Flight Advisory Service channel at selected FSS's.
b. 122.2 is assigned to all FSS's as a common enroute simplex service.
c. 123.6 is assigned as the airport advisory channel at non-tower FSS locations, however, it is still in commission at some FSS's collocated with towers to provide part time Airport Advisory Service.
d. 122.1 is the primary receive-only frequency at VOR's. 122.05, 122.15 and 123.6 are assigned at selected VOR's meeting certain criteria.
e. Some FSS's are assigned 50 kHz channels for simplex operation in the 122-123 MHz band (e.g. 122.35). Pilots using the FSS A/G system should refer to this directory or appropriate charts to determine frequencies available at the FSS or remoted facility through which they wish to communicate.

Part time FSS hours of operation are shown in remarks under facility name.

Emergency frequency 121.5 is available at all Flight Service Stations, Towers, Approach Control and RADAR facilities, unless indicated as not available.

Frequencies published followed by the letter "T" or "R", indicate that the facility will only transmit or receive respectively on that frequency. All radio aids to navigation frequencies are transmit only.

TERMINAL SERVICES

CTAF—A program designed to get all vehicles and aircraft at uncontrolled airports on a common frequency.
ATIS—A continuous broadcast of recorded non-control information in selected areas of high activity.
UNICOM—A non-government air/ground radio communications facility utilized to provide general airport advisory service.
APP CON—Approach Control. The symbol ® indicates radar approach control.
TOWER—Control tower
GND CON—Ground Control
DEP CON—Departure Control. The symbol ® indicates radar departure control.
CLNC DEL—Clearance Delivery.
PRE TAXI CLNC—Pre taxi clearance
VFR ADVSY SVC—VFR Advisory Service. Service provided by Non-Radar Approach Control.
Advisory Service for VFR aircraft (upon a workload basis) ctc APP CON.
STAGE II SVC—Radar Advisory and Sequencing Service for VFR aircraft
STAGE III SVC—Radar Sequencing and Separation Service for participating VFR Aircraft within a Terminal Radar Service Area (TRSA)
ARSA—Airport Radar Service Area
TCA—Radar Sequencing and Separation Service for all aircraft in a Terminal Control Area (TCA)
TOWER, APP CON and DEP CON RADIO CALL will be the same as the airport name unless indicated otherwise.

8
㉒ RADIO AIDS TO NAVIGATION

The Airport Facility Directory lists by facility name all Radio Aids to Navigation, except Military TACANS, that appear on National Ocean Service Visual or IFR Aeronautical Charts and those upon which the FAA has approved an Instrument Approach Procedure.

All VOR, VORTAC ILS and MLS equipment in the National Airspace System has an automatic monitoring and shutdown feature in the event of malfunction. Unmonitored, as used in this publication for any navigational aid, means that FSS or tower personnel cannot observe the malfunction or shutdown signal. The NAVAID NOTAM file identifier will be shown as "NOTAM FILE IAD" and will be listed on the Radio Aids to Navigation line. When two or more NAVAIDS are listed and the NOTAM file identifier is different than shown on the Radio Aids to Navigation line, then it will be shown with the NAVAID listing. Hazardous Inflight Weather Advisory Service (HIWAS) will be shown where this service is broadcast over selected VOR's.

NAVAID information is tabulated as indicated in the following sample:

TWEB   TACAN/DME Channel   Geographical Position   Site Elevation

NAME (L) ABVORTAC 117.55 ■ ABE   Chan 122(Y)   40°43'36"N 75°27'18"W   180°   4.1 NM to fld.   1110/8E.   **HIWAS.**

Class   Frequency   Identifier   Bearing and distance facility to airport   Magnetic Variation   Hazardous Inflight Weather Advisory Service

VOR unusable 020°-060° beyond 26 NM below 3500'

Restriction within the normal altitude/range of the navigational aid (See primary alphabetical listing for restrictions on VORTAC and VOR/DME).

Note: Those DME channel numbers with a (Y) suffix require TACAN to be placed in the "Y" mode to receive distance information.

HIWAS—Hazardous Inflight Weather Advisory Service is a continuous broadcast of inflight weather advisories including summarized SIGMETs, convective SIGMETs, AIRMETs and urgent PIREPs. HIWAS is presently broadcast over selected VOR's and will be implemented throughout the conterminous U.S.

ASR/PAR—Indicates that Surveillance (ASR) or Precision (PAR) radar instrument approach minimums are published in U.S. Government Instrument Approach Procedures.

RADIO CLASS DESIGNATIONS

Identification of VOR/VORTAC/TACAN Stations by Class (Operational Limitations):

Normal Usable Altitudes and Radius Distances

Class	Altitudes	Distance (miles)
(T)	12,000' and below	25
(L)	Below 18,000'	40
(H)	Below 18,000'	40
(H)	Between 14,500' and 17,999'	100
(H)	18,000' FL 450	130
(H)	Above FL 450	100

(H) = High   (L) = Low   (T) = Terminal

NOTE: An (H) facility is capable of providing (L) and (T) service volume and an (L) facility additionally provides (T) service volume.

The term VOR is, operationally, a general term covering the VHF omnidirectional bearing type of facility without regard to the fact that the power, the frequency protected service volume, the equipment configuration, and operational requirements may vary between facilities at different locations.

AB — Automatic Weather Broadcast (also shown with ■ following frequency.)
DF — Direction Finding Service.
DME — UHF standard (TACAN compatible) distance measuring equipment.
DME(Y) — UHF standard (TACAN compatible) distance measuring equipment that require TACAN to be placed in the "Y" mode to receive DME.
H — Non-directional radio beacon (homing), power 50 watts to less than 2,000 watts (50 NM at all altitudes).
HH — Non-directional radio beacon (homing), power 2,000 watts or more (75 NM at all altitudes).
H-SAB — Non-directional radio beacons providing automatic transcribed weather service.
ILS — Instrument Landing System (voice, where available, on localizer channel).
ISMLS — Interim Standard Microwave Landing System.
LDA — Localizer Directional Aid.

DIRECTORY LEGEND

LMM — Compass locator station when installed at middle marker site (15 NM at all altitudes).
LOM — Compass locator station when installed at outer marker site (15 NM at all altitudes).
MH — Non-directional radio beacon (homing) power less than 50 watts (25 NM at all altitudes).
MLS — Microwave Landing System
S — Simultaneous range homing signal and/or voice.
SABH — Non-directional radio beacon not authorized for IFR or ATC. Provides automatic weather broadcasts.
SDF — Simplified Direction Facility.
TACAN — UHF navigational facility-omnidirectional course and distance information.
VOR — VHF navigational facility-omnidirectional course only.
VOR/DME — Collocated VOR navigational facility and UHF standard distance measuring equipment.
VORTAC — Collocated VOR and TACAN navigational facilities.
W — Without voice on radio facility frequency.
Z — VHF station location marker at a LF radio facility.

Bibliography and Suggested Reading for Further Study

Airport/Facility Directory. FAA, Washington, D.C., 2004.

Aeronautical Information Manual. Washington, D.C.: USGPO.

Air Traffic Manual. 7110.65. FAA, Washington, D.C., 1989.

Aviation Weather. AC 00-6. FAA Flight Standards Service and National Weather Service, Washington, D.C., 1975.

Aviation Weather Services. AC 00-45. FAA and National Weather Service, Washington, D.C., 1995.

Dogan, Peter. *The Instrument Flight Training Manual.* Professional Instrument Courses, Deep River, Conn., 1999.

Instrument Flying. Department of the Air Force, AF Manual 51-37, Washington, D.C., 1960.

Instrument Flying Handbook. FAA-8083-15. FAA, Washington, D.C., 2001.

Kershner, W. K. *The Advanced Pilot's Flight Manual,* 7th ed. Ames: Iowa State University Press, 2003.

Kershner, W. K. *The Flight Instructor's Manual,* 4th ed., Ames: Iowa State University Press. 2002.

Kershner, W. K. *The Student Pilot's Flight Manual.* 9th ed. Ames: Iowa State University Press, 2001.

Liston. Joseph. *Power Plants for Aircraft.* New York: McGraw-Hill, 1953.

Perkins, C. D., and Hage, R. D. *Airplane Performance, Stability and Control.* New York: Wiley, 1949.

Practical Test Standards, Instrument Rating. FAA-S-8081-4D Flight Standards Service. Washingtion, D.C., 2004.

Two very good instrument reference books for you to add to your library are *Weather Flying* by Robert N. Buck and *Instrument Flying* by Richard L. Taylor (both published by The Macmillan Company—the address can be found on the Internet). These two books give a practical look at actual coping with weather and ATC.

Pilot's Operating Handbooks, products referred to, information received from companies, or sources of information in aviation products are given below:

Aeronetics, Elk Grove Village, Ill. Flight instruments. Aircraft Radio Corporation (ARC), Boonton, NJ. Communications equipment.

Bendix/King Radio Corp., Olathe, KS. Avionics.

B. F. Goodrich Co., Uniontown, OH. Deicing and anti-icing equipment.

Castleberry Instruments and Avionics, Inc., Austin, TX. Flight and engine instruments.

Cessna Aircraft Co., Wichita, KS. *Pilot's Operating Handbooks.*

Collins Radio Company, Cedar Rapids, IA. Communications equipment.

Continental Development Corp., Ridgefield, CT. Instantaneous vertical speed indicator (IVSI).

Dayton-Granger, Inc., Fort Lauderdale, FL. Antennas. Foster Airdata Systems Inc., 7020 Huntley Road.

Columbus, OH 43229.

Garmin G1000 Cockpit Reference Guide for Cessna Nav III. Garmin International, Inc. 1200 East 151st Street, Olathe KS 66062, U.S.A.

Motorola Aviation Electronics, Culver City, CA. Avionics.

National Aeronautical Corp. (NARCO), Fort Washington, PA. Avionics.

Piper Aircraft Corp., Vero Beach, FL.

Safetech, Inc., Six Terry Drive, Newtown, PA. 18940. E-6B computer model: FDF-57-B.

Sigma-Tek, Augusta, KS. Flight instruments.

Textron Lycoming Williamsport, PA. Detail engine specifications.

INDEX

Absolute altitude, 9
Adiabatic lapse rate, 148–49
Advisory station, 126
Aeronautical Information Manual (AIM), 81, 96, 120
  on communications loss, 225
  on icing conditions, 156
  on navigation aids, 194–95, 197–98
Air
  density, 7, 32
  pressure, 24
  velocity, 7
Aircraft
  identification, 210
  operation, 4
  type, 210
Aircraft radio station license, 29
Airfoil-flap combination and coefficient of lift (C_L), 32
Airman test report, 251
AIRMETs, 171
Air-operated attitude indicator, 19
Airplane
  effect of drag, 33–34
  effect of life, 31–33
  effect of thrust, 30–31
  effect of weight, 29–30
  inspection, 29
  loading arrangements, 42, 44
  papers, 28–29
  stability, 37–38
Airplane Flight Manual, 9, 28–29
Airplane instrument rating requirements, 4–5
Airplane surveillance radar (ASR), 189, 244–45
Airplane systems, 25–28

anti-icing, 27–28, 155–56
deicing, 27–28, 155–56
electrical, 25–27
Airport
  alternate, 206, 211
  diagram, 181, 183, 185
  layout, 232
  operations, 195
Airport/Facility Directory (A/FD), 95–96, 128, 132, 198–201
Air pressure gauge, 7
Air route traffic control center (ARTCC), 126, 130–34
Air scoop icing, 154
Airspace, 194
Airspeed, 47
  in blocked static system, 13
  calculating, 7–8, 10
  calibration table, 13–14
  change, 257
  in a climb, 51–53, 257
  in a climbing stall, 71
  correction during instrument takeoff, 77–78
  during descent, 55–56, 59, 257
  equivalent, 8
  and exhaust gases, 37
  and horsepower, 35–36
  indicator, 6–9, 47–48, 50, 66
  instrument, 46
  and parasite drag, 34
  for penetrating thunderstorms, 150–52
  and rate turn, 48–49
  in a spin, 74, 76
  in straight and level flying, 63, 67
  system error, 8

true, 210
  in a turn, 61, 63, 67–68
Air traffic control, 195
  clearances, 195, 256
  procedures, 4
Air traffic controllers, 85, 129
  roles and responsibilities, 195
  and use of transponder, 116–17
Air traffic control radar beacon system (ATCRBS), 116, 120
Airworthiness, certificate of, 28–29
Alcohol drinking, affecting flying, 81
All-directional radio signal, 86
Alternator, 7
Altimeter, 6, 9–11, 47–48
  adjustable for barometric pressure, 6
  in blocked static system, 13
  in a climb, 54, 66, 69
  in a climbing stall, 71–73
  correction table, 13–14
  during descent, 59, 66
  encoding, 11
  errors in, 10–11
  radar, 11
  setting procedures, 198
  in a spin, 74, 76, 78
  in straight and level flying, 63, 67
  in a turn, 63, 65, 67–68
Altitude
  absolute, 9
  change in, 46, 130, 218
  control problems, 64–65
  conversion chart, 10
  density, 9
  indicated, 9–10
  management of, 247
  and maximum glide distance, 55

Altitude (*continued*)
  minimum safe warning, 181, 184
  pressure, 9–10
  true, 9
Altocumulus clouds in cold front, 146
Ammeter, 6, 26–27
Aneroid barometer, 9, 24
Angle
  of attack, 31–33
  of bank, 60
  of deflection, 109
  of interception, 109–10
Antenna(s), 99, 101
  ADF/MDF, 111, 113
  broadband communications, 215
  checking, 215–16
  communications, 99
  and deicing, 155
  DME, 216
  glide slope, 114, 118
  marker beacon, 115, 118
  NOR, 99
  in radar approaches, 192
  SDF, 119
Anti-icing equipment, 27–28
Anti-icing systems, 155–56
Approach
  charts, 206, 233, 239
  definitions, 179
  final, 169–71
  ILS, 96, 112–16, 178
  instrument, 4, 176, 203, 259–60
  lighting systems, 176, 178, 187, 190
  missed, 122, 125, 178, 189, 239–44,
    260
  no-gyro, 246–47
  nondirectional, 239–41
  precision, 179, 245–46
  procedure chart, 178–83, 187, 189,
    192–94
  radar, 244–46
  radar controlled, 189, 241–46
  simplified directional facility (SDF),
    115–16
  surveillance, 244–45
  vectors, 232–44
  visual descent point (VDP), 125–26,
    204
  VOR, 187, 189, 193
Arc, DME, 100, 102–3, 258
Arrival gates, 136
Arrival procedures, 195, 256
ARTS III radar scope, 134, 138
Asymmetric disk loading or P factor,
  31
"ATP: Airline Transport Pilot" book,
  160

Attitude
  loss, 261
  recoveries, 66–72, 258
Attitude gyro, 46, 66
Attitude indicator, 6, 16, 18–20,
    47–50
  in a climb, 50, 69
  in a climbing stall, 72–73
  in a descent, 58, 68
  in a power-on spiral, 70–71
  in a spin, 74–75
  in straight and level flying, 63, 67
  tumbling, 66, 69
  in a turn, 65, 67
Automated flight service station
    (AFSS), 126, 174
Automatic direction finder (ADF),
    101, 103, 106–12
  loop housing, 215
Automatic direction finder/manual
    direction finder (ADF/MDF)
    antenna, 111, 113
Automatic Terminal Information
    Service (ATIS), 127–30
Autopilot, 37
Autorotation, 74

Back course approach, 113, 115
Baggage compartment and center of
    gravity, 43
Balance, airplane, 37–38
Bank control, 49
Banking and northerly turning errors,
    15
Bank instruments, 49
Barometric pressure, 9
  decrease, 146
Basic empty weight, 41–42, 44
Basic design of terminal arrival area,
    122–23
Battery, 25–26
  discharge rate, 26–27
Battery-alternator system, 25–27
Battery-generator system, 25–26
Beacon
  marker, 112, 115, 118
  nondirectional (NDB), 100–1, 105
  timing to station, 109
Bearing, relative, 103, 106–8, 110
Beat frequency oscillator (BFO), 107
Bird hazards, 198
Blind encoders, 117, 120
Boots, deicer, 155, 215, 217
Brake horsepower (BHP), 35–36, 61
Brake-specific fuel consumption
    (BSFC), 230

Braking, 158–59
Broadband communications antenna,
    215
Broadcast stations, 101

Caging knob, gyro, 19
Caging of attitude indicator, 19
Calibrated airspeed (CAS), 7–9
Carburetor air temperature gauge, 154
Carburetor icing, 154
Center control, 219–20
Center of gravity, 43–45, 206
  in flight, 42–43
  and longitudinal stability, 40
Centrifugal tachometer, 23
Certificate of registration, 28–29
Chart, 176–204
  airspeed calibration, 13–14
  approach, 187–92
  area, 176
  DP, 132, 135, 192, 195–96
  en route, 126–27, 175–77, 204–8
  holding patterns on, 227, 229
  instrument approach procedure
    (IAP), 178–94, 204
  performance, 36
  radar summary, 161–62
  STAR, 192, 194, 196
  surface analysis, 160–61
  symbols, 166
  weather, 160–62
Checklist, use of, 254
Circling, 189, 260
Circuit breakers, 26
Clearance, 207, 216–18
  delivery, 129
  take off, 219
Clearance delivery frequency,
    216–17
Clear ice, 154
Climb
  and checking instruments, 47
  maneuvers, 50–54, 66, 69
  rate, 50–53
  recovering from stall, 71–73
  turns, 61
Clock, 7, 25
  misreading, 223
Clouds, 146, 148–49
Coefficient of lift (C_L), 31–32, 55
  and induced drag, 34
Col, 145
Cold front, 145–147
  fast-moving, 146
Cold-front occlusion, 147
COMM frequency selector knobs, 87

COMM frequency transfer button, 86–87
Communications
  control of air traffic and, 126–41
  loss, 224–25, 260–61
  techniques, 140–41
Compass
  calibration of, 16
  card, 96
  course, 16, 106
  gyro, 16–17
  heading, 107
  locators, 101, 105, 112
  magnetic float, 14–16
  remote indicating, 16
  slaved, 16–17
  warning flag, 96
Computer testing centers, 251
Constants: pressure, temperature, density, 37
Control instruments, 5, 47
Controlled airspace, 194
Coriolis effect, 145
Course deviation indicator (CDI), 86–87
Course select knob, 96
Crew resource management (CRM), 4, 254
Cross-bearings, VOR, 91–92
Crosswind component, 227
Cruise, 211
  and checking instruments, 47
Cumulonimbus clouds, 148
  in cold front, 146
Cumulus clouds, 148–49
Curve, 34–36
Cylinder head, 24–25
Cylinder head temperature gauge, 24–25

Datum, 41
Decision altitude (DA), 204
Decision height (DH), 120, 176, 178–79, 181, 204
  for descent, 56
Defroster for windshield, 156
Deicing equipment, 27–28
Deicing systems, 155–156
Density constant, 37
Departure, 128
  clearance, 256
  control, 130, 136, 219–20
  procedures, 195
  routes, 136
  time, 211
Departure procedure (DP), instru-

ment, 132, 135, 192
Descent, 54–60, 257–58
  maneuvers, 66, 68
  and modified basic design of terminal arrival area, 123–24
Deviation bar, 96, 98
Deviation scale, 96
Diaphragm in vertical speed indicator (VSI), 11, 13
Direction finder, automatic, 101, 103, 106–12
Direct pressure gauge, 24
Direct user access terminal (DUAT) system, 175
Distance measuring equipment (DME), 7, 99–102, 104, 227
  antenna, 216
Distortion, ILS course, 115
Distractions during practical testing, 254
Double the angle off the bow method, 94, 109–10
DP charts, 132, 135, 192, 195–96
Drag, 33–34
  and horsepower, 35
Drift problem, 107–10

Electrical system, 6, 25–27
Elevators
  and climb rate, 51
  during descent, 237
  and ground effect, 43
Emergency
  operations, 4, 28, 195, 198, 260–62
  panel, 53–54
Empty weight, 41–42, 44
Empty weight center of gravity, 41–42
Encoding altimeter, 11, 116, 120
Engine
  canting, 31
  cooling, 24
  critical, 31–32
  failure during flying, 261–62
  instruments, 17, 23–25
  rpm, 23
  unsupercharged, 36–37
En route facilities, 179–80
En route flight, 195, 220–31, 256
  charts, 176–77, 204–5
  reports, 220–21
En route flight advisory service (EFAS), 126–27, 175
Equal and opposite reaction, 31
Equation of state, 37
Equilibrium of forces, 38–39

Equivalent airspeed (EAS), 8
Errors
  acceleration, 5
  altimeter, 10–11
  turning, 15
Estimated time en route, 211
Exhaust gases and airspeed, 37
Exhaust gas temperature gauge, 25

Fast-moving cold front, 146
Fatigue affecting flying, 81
Feeder facilities, 179
Final approach (FA), 169–71
Final approach fix (FAF), 122, 125
Fin and slipstream effect, 30–31
Fixed-face ADF indicator, 106–8
Flap operating range on airspeed indicator, 8–9
Flaps and coefficient of lift (C_L), 32
Flight
  cross-country, 4, 255
  experience, 4
  hazards, 149–60, 198
  instruments, 255
    gyro, 16–23
    required, 6
    vacuum-driven, 17–18
  log, 29, 205–8, 222
  manual, 28–29
  plan, 85, 117–18, 132, 207, 210–11
  rules, 176–78
  safety, 198
  visibility and landing, 176, 178
Flight controls exchange, 254
Flight service station (FSS), 126–27, 133, 174–75
Flight simulators, 4–5, 253
Flight training device, 4–5, 253
Float and arm, 25
Float compass, 14–16
Flotation gear, 6
Fluid anti-icing systems, 28, 155, 216
Flying
  grounded from, 3
  straight and level, 49–50
Forces, 34–37
  four, 29–34
Forecasts
  area, 169–71
  temperature, 173–74
  terminal, 162, 165, 167–69
  wind, 173–74
Forward center of gravity limit, 43
Free-air thermometer, 9, 22–23

Freezing rain, 147
Frequency range of VOR, 85–86
Frequency selector, 86
Frontal systems, 145–48
  depicted on weather charts, 160
Frost on windshield, 156
Fuel, 211
  gauge, 6, 25
  selectors, 216
  sumps, 216
  supply calculation, 206–7
  tank, 216
Full-flaps speed, 57
Fuselage moment, 40
Fuses, 6, 26

Galvanometer, 25
Gauge
  carburetor air temperature, 154
  cylinder head temperature, 24–25
  direct pressure, 24
  exhaust gas temperature, 25
  fuel, 6, 25
  manifold pressure, 6, 23–24, 47
  oil pressure, 6, 24
  oil temperature, 6, 24
  outside air temperature, 9, 22–23
Generators, 7, 26
G forces, 33
Glide, 55–59, 96, 234, 236–37
  slope/path, 113–14
Glide slope antennas, 114, 118
Glide slope deviation scale, 96
Glide slope transmitter, 112–16
Global positioning system (GPS),
    120–26
Gravity, 29–30
  sensation, 79
Ground control, 129–30, 192
Ground-controlled approach (GCA),
    192
Ground effect
  and elevator effectiveness, 43
  during instrument takeoff, 77
Groundspeed, 210
  calculation, 205
  and descent, 56
Gust envelopes, 150–52
Gusts, 150–52
Gyro compass, 16–17
Gyro flight instruments,
    16–23
Gyrohorizon, 6–7, 18–20
Gyroscopic bank and pitch indicator.
    See Attitude indicator
Gyroscopic direction indicator, 7
Gyroscopic rate of turn indicator, 6

Hail, 148
Hazardous in-flight weather advisory
    service (HIWAS), 175
Hazards
  approach and landing, 156–60
  bird, 198
  weather, 149–60
Heading control problems, 65
Heading indicator (HI), 7, 16, 20–21,
    47, 49, 63, 67
  in a climb, 54, 66, 69
  correcting drift problem, 110–11
  in a descent, 68
  during instrument takeoff, 77, 80
  in a landing, 240–41
  in a spin, 74–75
  tumbling, 66, 69
Heading, affect on radio transmission,
    87–88
Heading select bug, 96, 98
Heading select knob, 96
Heading slip, 46
Heat to deice, 155
Height above airport (HAA), 179
Height above touchdown (HAT), 179
High clouds, 148
High frequency (HF), 85
High-level significant weather prog-
    nostics, 162
High-pressure areas, 145
Holding pattern, 63, 218, 224, 226–30
Holding procedures, 256–57
Holding speed, 230
Horizon and attitude indicator, 18
Horizontal situation indicator (HSI),
    21, 47, 96–99
Horsepower (hp)
  definition of, 34
  in a descent, 57–59
Hydroplaning, 159–60
Hyperventilation, 79

Ice, holding power of, 155
Icing, 154–56
  and outside air temperature (OAT)
    gauge, 22–23
  of pitot tube, 12
  *"Icing for Regional & Corporate
    Pilots"* video, 155
  "In-Flight Icing" book, 155
Indicated airspeed (IAS), 8–9
Indicated altitude, 9–10
Induced drag, 34
Initial approach fix (IAF), 122,
    124–25
Initial approach way point (IAWP),
    125

Inner ear, 79
Inoperative components, 187, 189
Inspection
  preflight, 215–16
  progressive, 29
Instantaneous vertical speed indicator
    (IVSI), 11–12
Instrument approach procedure (IAP),
    4, 176, 203, 259–60
Instrument approach procedure (IAP)
  charts, 178–83, 187, 189,
    192–94
  title changes, 204
Instrument check, 255–56, 262
Instrument departure procedure (DP),
    132, 135, 192
  charts, 195
Instrument flight rules (IFR), 4, 6–7
  takeoffs and approaches, 176, 178
Instrument flying, 45–81
Instrument landing system (ILS), 96,
    112–16, 178
  approach, 116, 233–39
  course distortion, 115
Instrument rating
  advantages of, 3–4
  informal program for, 5
  requirements for, 4–5
Instrument rating knowledge test, 4,
    249–51
Instrument rating practical test,
    252–62
Instrument(s)
  approach procedure (IAP) charts
    and definitions, 178–94
  arrangement of, 5, 46–48
  bank, 49
  control, 5, 47
  electrically driven, 18
  engine, 23–25
  flight and engine, 6–29, 46–52
  gyro flight, 16–18
  indicators in approach, 66
  instrument flight, 6
  landing system (ILS), 31, 75–79,
    112–16
  magnetic indicators, 14–16
  navigation, 6, 85–126
  performing, 47
  pitch, 48–9
  pitot-static, 7–14
  primary and secondary, 47
  required, 4–7
  scan, 46–48
  spin indicators, 74–75
  takeoff (ITO), 75–80
  turn and slip, 53–54, 59
  vacuum-driven, 17–18

Interference drag, 33
Intermediate fix (IF), 122, 124–25
International flights weather prognostics, 162
Isobars, 145

Landing, 260
  minimums, 179
  rules, 176, 178
Landing gear position indicator, 6
Landing hazards, 156–60
Landing light, electric, 6
Lapse rates, 148–49
Lead radials, 100, 117
Letter of discontinuance, 254
LF/MF navigation aids, 100–12
Licensed empty weight, 42
Lift, 31–33
Lift-to-drag ratio, 55
Lift-weight moment, 40
Lighting, 187, 190
  special approach, 112
  systems, 6, 194
  during thunderstorm, 152–53
Limited combined envelope, 151–52
Loading arrangements of airplane, 42, 44
Loadmeter, 27
Local controller, 129–30
Localizer, 112–13, 234–37
Logbooks, 29, 205–8, 222
Longitudinal stability, 38–41
Loop principle in radio signal reception, 103, 106
"Low-Altitude Approach Procedures" book, 179
Low-altitude center area, 132–33
Low-level wind shear alert systems (LLWAS), 158
Low-pressure areas, 145

Magnetic bearing, 86
Magnetic compass
  in a climb, 53
  float, 14–16
  and heading indicator, 20
  headings, 258
  slaved gyro, 16–17
  in a turn, 62
Magnetic direction indicator, 6
Magnetic indicators, 14–16
Magnetic North Pole, 14–16
Magnetic tachometer, 23
Maneuvering speed in a thunderstorm, 151–52
Maneuvers, 59–60

climb and descent, 59–60, 68–69
four fundamentals, 63–66
gust envelopes, 150–52
straight and level, 63–65, 67
turn, 65–67
Manifold pressure, 36–37
  in a climb, 52–53
  during descent, 56
  gauge, 6, 23–24, 47
  loss during carburetor icing, 154
Marker beacon, 112, 115, 118
Marker beacon antenna, 115, 118, 215
Maximum distance glide, 54–55
  ratio, 55
Medical facts, 198
Medical Handbook for Pilots, 81
Medium frequency (MF), 85
Memphis Air Route Traffic Control Center Area, 131–33
Metal-to-metal latching device, 6
Meteorological Aviation Report (METAR), 162–67
Microbursts, 156–58
Microphone, 141
Middle clouds, 148
Middle fan marker (LMM), 101
Middle marker (MM), 48, 115, 237–38
Minimum descent altitude (MDA), 176, 178–79, 181
Minimum en route altitudes (MEAs), 204
Minimum safe altitudes (MSAs), 181, 184
Minimum safe altitude warning (MSAW), 247
Minimums data, 181, 186–87
Minimum vector altitude chart, 234
Missed approach, 239–44, 260
  holding way point (MAHWP), 125
  point (MAP), 122
  procedures, 178, 189
  way point (MAWP), 125
Mixture density, 37
Moments: lift-weight, thrust, wing, 39–40

Nashville Metropolitan Airport layout, 232
NAV frequency transfer button, 87
Navigation
  aids, 194–95
  checking route, 204–5
  flight plan, 29, 205–8, 222
  instruments, 6, 85–126
  lights, 217
  planning, 204–11
  procedures, 198

systems, 258–59
Navigation-communications antenna, 215
NAV warning flag, 96
Needle lead for a turn, 94
Never exceed speed (V_{NE}), 8
No-gyro approach, 246–47
Non-control information, 127
Nondirectional beacon (NDB), 100–1, 105
  approach, 239–41
Nonprecision approach procedure, 179, 259
Nonvisual balance sensations, 79
No procedure turn required (NoPT), 179
Northerly turning error, 15
Nose-down moment, 40
Nose-up moment, 40
  during descent, 58–59
Nosewheel in instrument take off, 78–80
Notices to Airmen (NOTAMs), 198, 202, 204

Occluded front, 147
Oil
  pressure check, 216
  pressure gauge, 6, 24
  temperature gauge, 6, 24
Omni bearing selector (OBS), 86–88, 91–92, 94, 115
Outbound bearings, 91–92
Outer compass locator, 101
Outer marker (OM), 115, 118
  during descent, 236
Outside air temperature (OAT) gauge, 9, 22–23
Oxygen equipment, 205

Palmyra VOR (PAL), 88, 92
Papers, airplane, 28–29
Paralleling relay, 26
Parasite drag, 33–34
Partial-panel climb, 53–54
Performance chart, 36
P factor, 31
Pilot
  characteristics, 79–81
  estimates and position reporting, 132
  identification, 211
  medical facts, 28–29
  reports (PIREPS), 156, 158, 173
  roles and responsibilities, 195
Pilot reports (PIREPs), 156, 158, 173

Pilot's Operating Handbook (POH), 9, 25, 28–29
  airplane loading arrangements, 42
  electric prop deicers, 27
  pneumatic deicing systems, 28
Pitch
  change, 48
  instruments, 48–49
  stability, 38–41
Pitot heat, 156, 217
Pitot-static instruments, 7–14
Pitot tube, 7, 216
  blocking, 12
  icing of, 156
Placards, 28
Planning
  instrument flight, 143–211
  navigation, 204–11
  trip, 206–7
  weather systems and, 145–78
Planview portion of approach chart, 179–81, 183
Pneumatic deicing systems, 28
Pointing-to-the-thunderstorm tendency, 103
Point of departure, 211
POLAN intersection, 223, 226
  departing, 231
Position lights, 6
Position reports, 207, 220–21
Postflight procedures, 4, 262
Power
  during a climb, 51–53
  control problems, 65
  curve, 34–37
  definition of, 34
  during descent, 59
  setting table, 36–37
  during a turn, 60–61
Power-off condition, 54
Power-on spiral, 66, 69–71
Practice maneuvers, 59–60
  four fundamental, 63–66
Precession, 21, 22
  principle, 16–17
  and raising the tail, 31
Precipitation static, 152
Precision approach radar (PAR), 189, 245–46
Precision instrument approach, 259–60
Preflight procedures, 4, 28, 195, 254–56
Pressure
  air, 24
  altitude, 9–10
  areas, 145–46

barometric, 9, 146
  changes, 7, 10–12
  constant, 37
  dynamic, 7–8, 32
  manifold, 23–24
  oil, 24
  static, 7
Pretakeoff check, 217
Primary instruments, 47
Procedure turns, 124–25
  during landing, 178
Profile view portion of approach chart, 181, 183
Prop deicer, 27–28, 216–17
Propeller
  heating elements, 216
  and horsepower, 35
  icing, 155
  and thrust, 30–31
PTA-TEN procedure, 133–34, 221
Pyrotechnic signaling device, 6

Radar, 118, 120, 134
  airport surveillance, 189, 244–48
  altimeter, 11, 118, 120–21
  approach, 189, 192, 194
  echo areas, 161
  precision approach, 189, 245–46
  safety advisory, 247
  scope symbols, 134, 136–40
  summary chart, 161–62
  use in takeoffs and landings, 178
  weather report, 167
Radials, 87–91
Radio, 195, 217
  aids, 194
  altimeter, 118, 120–21
  failure, 224
  frequencies in low-attitude center areas, 132–33
  frequency bands, 85
  navigation, 47, 85
  two-way system, 6
Radio magnetic indicator (RMI), 110–12
  in landing, 240–41
Rate climb, 257–58
Rate of climb, 11–13, 66, 78
Rate of descent, 54–55, 244
Rate of sink, 54, 59, 66
Rate turn, 65
  and airspeed, 48–49
Rear center of gravity limit, 43
Receiver autonomous integrity monitoring (RAIM) function, 121, 125

Reception area in radio signals, 103, 106
Recoveries
  from spin, 72, 74–78
  from stall, 71–72
  from unusual attitudes, 66–72
Registration certificate, 28–29
Remote communications air/ground (RCAG) sites, 132–34
Remote indicating compass, 16
Reports, 173, 220–21
Retesting, 251
Reverted rubber hydroplaning, 159–60
Ridges, 145
Rigging procedures, 31
Rigidity in space principle, 16–18, 20
Rime ice, 154
RMI/VOR receiver, 95
Roll guidance bars, 187
Rolling out on a heading, 60
Rolling pull-out, 69–71
Rough leveling, 70
Route checking, 204–5
Rudder, 69
  in a spin, 74, 77
  trim, 31
Runway
  active, 129
  crossings, 129
  hydroplaning, 159–60
  markings, 191
  navigating, 129
  sectors, 131–33
  vector, 232
Runway braking reports, 128
Runway visual range (RVR), 181
  and ground visibility, 178

Safety belt, 6
Safety reports, 198
Scope symbols, 134–38
SDF antenna, 119
Sectional charts, 205
Selected course pointer, 96, 98
Sensing antenna, 215
Shaft horsepower, 34
Shoulder harness, 6
SIGMETS, 171–72
Simplified directional facility (SDF), 115–16
Skid condition, 21
Skin friction drag, 33
Slant range, 99–100
Slaved compass, 16–17

Slip condition, 21
Slip indicator, 20–21
Slip-skid indicator, 6
Slipstream effect, 30–32
Slope of a front, 146–47
Slow-moving cold front, 146
Slug, 32
  definition of, 7
Slush on landing gear, 159
Spatial disorientation (vertigo), 5,
      79–80
Special-use airspace, 194
Spin
  back pressure, 74, 77–78
  brisk forward pressure, 74
  recovery, 72, 74–78
Spiral, power-on, 66, 69–71
Squall lines, 147
Stabilator and icing, 155–56
Stability, 37–38
  dynamic, 38
  longitudinal, 38–41
  pitch, 38–41
  static, 38
  weight and balance, 41–42
Stall
  recovery, 71–72
  speed, 8
  in a thunderstorm, 150–51
Standard Instrument Approach
      Procedure (SIAP), 122–25
Standard-rate return, 21
Standard rate turn, 19, 60, 65–66
Standard terminal arrival routes
      (STARs), 192, 194, 196
Static pressure, 7, 9, 12–13
  during instrument takeoff, 77
Static system, 13
Static vents, 12, 215–16
  icing of, 156
Static wicks, 215–16
Stationary front, 147–48
Steady-state climb, 33
Straight and level flying, 49–50, 257
  practicing, 63–65, 67
Straight climb, 53–54
Stratus-type clouds, 147–48
Structural icing, 154–55
Sucker holes, 159
Suction gauge, 6
Supporting instruments, 47
Surface analysis chart, 160–61
Surface weather map, 160–61
Surveillance approach, 244–45
Surveillance radar, 189, 244–45
Symbols
  prognostics charts, 163–64

scope, 134–38
weather, 146, 163–64
System of moments in equilibrium,
      38–39

Tachometer, 6, 23, 47
Tactical Air Navigation (TACAN),
      99–100
Tail
  and icing, 155
  raising effecting thrust, 31
Tail-down moment, 40
"Tailplane Icing" video, 155
Tailwheel type, instrument takeoff,
      76–78
Tailwind component, 227
Takeoff, 219
  clearance, 217–18
  departure and, 219–20
  instrument, 176, 178
  minimums, 178
  requirements, 187–88
  rules, 176–78
  tailwheel type, 77–78
  tricycle gear, 78–79
Taxiing, 216–17
Telephone Information Briefing
      Service (TIBS), 174
Temperature
  aloft, 164
  constant, 37
  errors, 10
  forecast, 173–74
  gauge, 6, 24–25
  manifold pressure, 37
  oil, 24
  outside air, 23
  ram recovery and, 23
Terminal Arrival Area (TAA),
      122–25
Terminal Aviation Forecasts (TAFs),
      162, 165, 167–69
Terminal procedures (TP), 178–87
Test
  knowledge, 249–51
  practical, 4, 252–62
Thermocouple, 24
Third attitude instrument system, 6
Throttle
  in descent, 57
  in a spin, 74
Thrust, 30–31, 40
  horsepower, 35, 50–51, 61
Thunderstorms, 149–53
Timed descent, 68
Timed turns, 60, 61, 258

Time-to-station work, 91–96
Tire pressure affecting hydroplaning,
      159
Tobacco smoke affecting gyro instru-
      ments, 17–18
TO-FROM indicator, 86–88, 91–92,
      95–96, 98, 108
Torque, 30–31
  in a straight climb, 53–54
Tower, 127–30
  en route control (TEC), 138, 140
Tracking, 92–94, 103
Transcribed weather broadcast
      (TWEB), 175
Transitions in flying, 49–50, 63–65
Transmitter
  ground, 101, 105
  of remote indicating compass, 16
Transponder, 116–18, 120
Transponder antenna, 216
Tricycle-gear airplane and instrument
      takeoff, 76, 78–79
Trimming the airplane, 50, 64–65
Troughs, 145
True airspeed (TAS), 8, 210
  and unsupercharged engine, 36–37
True altitude, 9
Tumbling
  of attitude indicator, 19
  of heading indicator, 20
Turbulence, 79, 149–53, 198
  penetration airspeeds, 150–51
  in weather prognostic charts, 162
Turn, 60–63
  error, 15
  radius, 63
  steep, 258
Turn and slip, 67
  indicator, 16, 20–22, 49
Turn and slip or turn coordinator, 53,
      59, 217
Turn coordinator, 22, 46, 49, 59, 67
  in a climb, 53
Turn indicator, 61–63, 66–68
  in climbing stall, 71–72
  in a spin, 74, 77–78

Ultrahigh frequency (UHF), 85
Uncontrolled airspace, 194
Unicom, 126
Unsupercharged engine and power
      setting, 36–37

Vacuum-driven attitude indicator, 19
Vacuum-driven instruments, 17–18

Vacuum pressure, 216–17
Vacuum pump, 17–18, 22
Vectors, runway, 232
Velocity
  curve and rate of sink, 54
  and horsepower, 35
Vents, static, 12
Venturi system, 17, 22, 216
Vertical gusts, 150–52
Vertical speed indicator (VSI), 11–12,
    46–48, 52, 66–68
  in blocked static system, 13–14
  in a climbing stall, 71
  in a descent, 68
  in a spin, 74–76
Vertigo (spatial disorientation), 5,
    79–80
Very high frequency (VHF), 85
VHF omnirange. *See* VOR
Victor airways, 85, 94
Visual approach slope indicator,
    125
Visual descent point (VDP),
    125–26, 204
VOR, 85–99, 102
  antennas, 99
  approach, 192, 198
  for cross bearings, 88–91
  equipment check, 94–95

heads, 112
identification, 96
receiver, 86–88, 95, 223, 227
in RMI, 111–12
theory, 86–88
time to station, 109–12
and time-to-station work, 91–96
VOR-A approach, 187, 189, 193
VOR/DME-B approach, 189, 193
VOR/LOC antenna, 99
VORTAC, 99–100
VOR test facility (VOT), 95

Warm front, 147
Weather, 254–55
  advisories, 171–73
  charts, 160–62
  clouds, 148–49
  forecasting, 4, 167–75
  hazards, 149–60
  hourly reports (METARs), 162–67
  information sources, 174–75
  map symbols, 146, 163–64
  and planning, 145–75
  pressure areas, 145
  radar, 149
  reports, 162–67
  services, 160–67

systems and planning, 145–75
Weight, airplane, 206
Weight and balance, 41–45
  envelope, 42–45
Weight force, 29–30
Whip VOR/LOC antenna, 215
Wind
  affecting time-to-station estimate, 94
  affect on speed, 205
  forecast, 162
  shear, 156, 158
  and temperatures aloft weather
    charts, 162, 164
Windshield, 216
  and frost, 156
  icing, 156
Wing
  area, 32–33
  leveling, 16
  moment, 40
Wing-tip vortices (drag force), 34
Work, 34
Working thrust, 30

Yaw
  during spiral turn-out, 70
  tendency, 30–31
  type vent system, 12